# Germany

# Germany

## A Phaidon Cultural Guide

With over 750 colour illustrations
and 12 pages of maps

Phaidon

Compiled by Redaktionsbüro Harenberg, Schwerte, West Germany

Phaidon Press Limited, Musterlin House, Jordan Hill Road, Oxford OX2 8DP

First published in English 1985
Second impression 1986
Third impression 1990

Originally published as *Knaurs Kulturführer in Farbe: Deutschland*
© Droemersche Verlagsanstalt Th. Knaur Nachf. Munich 1976
Translation © Phaidon Press Limited 1985

A CIP catalogue record for this book is available from the British Library

ISBN 0 7148 2354 6

Translated and edited by Babel Translations, London
Typeset by Electronic Village Limited, Richmond, Surrey
Printed in Spain by H. Fournier, S.A.-Vitoria

Cover illustration: The hall of mirrors in the Schloss Herrenchiemsee, Bavaria
(photo: Toni Schneiders, Lindau)

# Preface

*The Phaidon Cultural Guide to Germany* aims to make the user more familiar with the treasures of German art and culture. Unlike traditional art guides, it gives the same importance to the illustrations as to the text: more than 750 of the churches, castles, palaces, theatres, museums and works of art described here are also shown in colour. This enables readers to form in advance an accurate impression of the places and objects of interest they would like to see during a visit to the country.

As with the other guides in this series the text is arranged in alphabetical order of place names. This gives the book the clarity of a work of reference and avoids the need for lengthy searching. The link between places which are geographically close, but which are separated by the alphabet, is provided by the maps on pages 412–23. This section shows all the places mentioned which are within a short distance from any given destination and which, therefore, it might be possible to include in a tour.

The heading to each entry gives the town and its post-code in bold type and, below, a reference to the map section, giving page number and grid reference. (Since each map covers two pages and the system of grid squares runs across both pages, only even-numbered page numbers are given.)

Within each entry the sights generally appear in the following order: sacred buildings, secular buildings, particularly significant objects of interest, museums, theatres, less significant objects of interest (under the heading **Also worth seeing**) and places of interest in the immediate vicinity (**Environs**). Larger cities are provided with a brief introductory text, which summarizes the city's cultural development and its importance. These introductions refer also to well-known people who were born in the city or who lived there. The individual sights are printed in bold type, followed by the street name and number where they are to be found.

The appendices consist of a glossary of technical terms and an index of the most important artists whose works are discussed.

The publishers would be grateful for notification of any errors or omissions.

## Aachen 5100

Nordrhein-Westfalen        p.416□A 12

**Cathedral** (Münsterplatz): The Cathedral Square is the original heart of the imperial city of Aachen (Lat. Aquae Granni: Springs of Grannus, the Celtic god of healing); the hot springs later became the *thermae* or public baths of the Roman Legions. Pepin the Short (714–68), the father of Charlemagne, developed the site as his court, with the Aula or Great Hall, imperial bath and chapels. Thirty German kings and emperors, from 946 (Otto I) to 1531 (Ferdinand I), were enthroned in the cathedral built by his son Charlemagne; later Frankfurt became the coronation city. Charlemagne and Otto III are buried in Aachen Cathedral.

*Building history*: From 786 to *c.*800 Charlemagne built the Palatine Chapel on the site of Pepin's older structure. In the 14&18C the W. front was greatly altered

*Aachen, panorama, with Elisenbrunnen and cathedral (left)*

by the erection of a tower with pinnacles. In 1355–1414 a choir was added to the E. of the Palatine Chapel. Six two-storeyed chapels, dating from the 15–18C, are set around the building. The original tent-shaped roof of the Octagon was replaced by a dome. War damage has been repaired since 1945. Today it is the cathedral church of the Aachen Diocese, newly established in 1930.

*The building:* The design of the two-storeyed Octagon, the core of the present cathedral, was derived from Byzantine sources; it is enclosed by a sixteen-sided outer structure. San Vitale, the court church of the Emperor Justinian I, and the two-storeyed tomb of the Ostrogoth King Theodoric (both in Ravenna), served as

**Aachen, cathedral 1** Proserpina sarcophagus, 200 **2** 'Wölfin[', (female wolf), Roman, *c.* 200 **3** Main altar, *c.* 800 with Pala d'Oro antependium, *c.* 1000-20 **4** Bronze door, *c.* 800, at the baroque portal of the main entrance **5** Pine cone, *c.* 900-1000 **6** Throne of Charlemagne, late 8C **7** Tombstone slab of Otto III **8** Ambo, donated by Henry II in *c.* 1014 **9** Chandelier, 1160-70, donated by Frederick I **10** Karlsschrein, 1200-15 **11** Stone figure of Charlemagne, *c.* 1414-30 **12** Double Madonna, front side by Jan Bieldesnider, 1524 **13** Singers' desk, 15C **14** Matthiaskapelle **15** Annakapelle **16** Hubertus- und Karlskapelle **17** Nikolaus- und Michaelskapelle **18** Ungarnkapelle (Hungary chapel)

models. Charlemagne wished the cathedral to show that he saw himself as the successor of the Roman Emperors, and so had antique columns brought from Ravenna and Rome for the arches of the double galleries. The 103 ft. high dome, for a long time the loftiest N. of the Alps, is surrounded by a two-storeyed gallery. The arrangement of the Octagon is governed by a system of mystical-theological mathematics. The central part of the chapel was opened to the E. by the addition of the Gothic choir (1355–1414). This enlargement of the old Palatine Chapel was necessary for the coronations of kings and emperors and as a result of the ever-growing influx of pilgrims to the tomb of Charlemagne, beatified in 1165.

*Interior and furnishings:* The arches of the galleries and the Octagon, copied from models in Ravenna models, are vaulted with parti-coloured stone slabs. The openings in the upper storey are protected by bronze railings, formerly gilded, from Carolingian workshops. There, too, stands Charlemagne's *imperial throne*; like King Solomon's throne it is approached by six steps. The upper walls of the Octagon and the vaulting are covered with mosaics. The *roof mosaics* were, however, severely

*Palatine chapel with chandelier* ▷

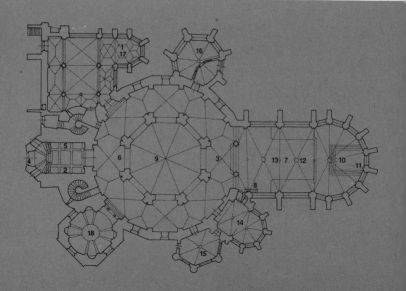

*Shrine of Charlemagne (1200–15) in the centre of the cathedral choir*

damaged when the Emperor Barbarossa caused the great *circular chandelier* (diameter 13ft. 9 ins.) to be hung there. This chandelier hangs from a 88 ft. 6 ins. iron chain, and with its sixteen turrets and broad rim it symbolizes Holy Jerusalem (inscription). In the choir the antependium of the *high altar* depicts Christ, scenes of the Passion and the symbols of the four Evangelists on 17 gold-chased reliefs commissioned in 1020 by the Emperor Henry II. In the centre of the choir is the silver-chased *Shrine of Charlemagne* (1200–15) commissioned by the Emperor Frederick II. The Emperor himself, at his coronation as King of Germany in Aachen, placed the bones of Charlemagne in the new sarcophagus. In the arches of the shrine are effigies of the eight successors of Charlemagne and on the top are scenes from the life of the Emperor. The 2C Roman sarcophagus in which Charlemagne was first interred is now in the *Chapel of St.Michael* in the cathedral. An *ambo* endowed in 1014 by the Emperor Henry and which used to be in the middle of the Octagon was removed to become part of the furnishings of the new choir and placed above the door of the sacristy as a pulpit. Its gilded copper surfaces are decorated

*Six steps lead to the throne of Charlemagne (late- 8C)*

*Gilded ambo* ▷

*Lothar Cross, Cathedral Treasury*

*Cameo of Augustus from the Lothar Cross*

with Alexandrian reliefs of antique ivory, oriental chessmen and Muslim ornaments from the Emperor's own treasure. (On holidays and for guided visits the protective wooden screen is opened.) In the *choir*, on the columns between the windows, are figures of Charlemagne (holding a model of the Palatine Chapel), the Blessed Virgin and Apostles (lst half of the 15C). In the *Carolingian Porch* on the W. side is the so-called *She-wolf* (Roman, 2C). The porch entrance has bronze doors from the time of Charlemagne.

Notable exhibits in the cathedral *Treasury* are: the so-called *Lothar Cross* (*c.*1000) with the Augustus Cameo (Roman, lC); the *Treasury Gospel* with the famous miniature of the Evangelists sitting at their writing-desks among the clouds (9C); the so-called *Charlemagne Hunting Horn* of ivory (the 'Olifant' of the Roland Legend, probably Sicilian, 11C). Further interesting pieces are a *golden book-cover* (*c.*1000) decorated

with Byzantine ivory; an *aquamanile bust* (representing Charlemagne, the eyes inlaid in silver, possibly commissioned by Frederick II in the coronation year 1215); the *Shrine of the Virgin Mary*, in the form of a church with the transept in silver, copper and enamel (1220–40). The *Reliquary Bust*, commissioned possibly for his coronation in 1349 by Charles IV and supposedly containing the skull of Charlemagne. The collection of altar-frontals and coverings for pulpits is also very fine.

**Abbey Church of St.John the Baptist** (Abteiplatz): situated on the Johannisberg in Aachen-Burtschied, it was established in 997 by Otto III as a Benedictine abbey and became a Cistercian nunnery in 1220. The abbey was built in 1730–54, on the

*The façade of the Gothic Rathaus, decorated* ▷
*with statues of German kings*

*Gobelin tapestry and reliquary bust of Charlemagne, Cathedral Treasury*

site of several earlier buildings, by the Aachen master builder J.J. Couven in collaboration with J.C. Schlaun of Münster. It was abolished as an abbey in 1802 and the abbey buildings were demolished; it is now a parish church.

**Rathaus** (Markt): Erected on the foundation walls of the Aula (Great Hall) of Charlemagne's palace, from which the Carolingian Grannus Tower has also survived.

In the 14C the city acquired the Aula and rebuilt it in the Gothic style as a battlemented Town Hall elaborately decorated with statues. On the upper floor is the Reichssaal for the coronation banquets of German kings and emperors. Baroque alterations were removed from the façade in the 19C (Gothic revival). The Karl Cycle by A.Rethel (1816–59) in the Reichssaal is the most important series of historical wall-paintings in 19C German art. Five of the original eight paintings (1840–51) still

exist, the best-known being '*Otto III opening the tomb of Charlemagne*'.

**Elisenbrunnen** (Friedrich-Wilhelm-Platz): The foundation stone of this fountain was laid in 1822, and it was built in 1825–7, after revision of an older design by Schinkel; it was restored after World War 2.

**Museums:** *Suermondt-Ludwig-Museum* (Wilhelmstrasse): Named after the Aachen collectors Suermondt and Ludwig, it houses Gothic altars, sculpture, household implements and, especially, ivories and 17C Flemish and Dutch paintings; there are also Impressionist and modern paintings, from Liebermann, Slevogt, Beckmann and Heckel to Klee, Picasso, Poliakoff, Antes and others. The core of the modern collection is on permanent loan from the Aachen *Ludwig Collection* (Kurhausstrasse 2). *Couven Museum* (17 Hühnermarkt): Interior furnishings of the

*Shrine of the Virgin Mary, treasury*

period 1740–1840. The *Heimat-Museum* (in the Burg Frankenberg) exhibits collections on town history. *Internationales Zeitungsmuseum* (13 Pontstrasse): 100,000 newspapers and periodicals from all over the world, particularly first, last, jubilee and special issues.

**Theatres:** *Stadttheater* (Kapuzinergraben): Built 1822–5 to a design by J.P. Cremer which was improved by K.F. Schinkel; rebuilt 1900. After its destruction in 1943, the façade with its columned portico and pediment was restored. 895 seats. *Studio theatre:* 99 seats. *Grenzlandtheater des Landkreises Aachen* (5/6 Friedrich-Wilhelm-Platz): This theatre was built in 1950, seats 199 and has its own company. The *Stadtpuppenbühne* (Kalverbenden) gives performances with Rheinland wooden puppets.

**Also worth seeing:** The city fortifications with the Marschiertor and the Ponttor

(built *c.*1300); the 18C parish church of St.Michael in Aachen-Burtschied; the 14C Minorite church of St.Nikolaus and the 1930 Fronleichnamskirke.

---

**Aalen 7080**
Baden-Württemberg                    p.422□H 17

The former imperial city on the Kocher has close connections with the settlements of Roman times (see Limes- Museum).

**Parish church:** The church was built in 1765–6. The ceiling painting (Resurrection, Ascension and Day of Judgement) by A.Wintergerst is the chief decorative feature (1767). The stucco is by M.Winnenberg.

**Half-timbered houses:** In the old town there are numerous handsome 16–18C half-timbered houses.

*Ruins of Nürburg near Adenau*

**Museums:** *Limes-Museum* (5 St. Johann-Strasse): This museum, unique of its kind in Germany, documents the occupation of Germany by the Romans. It was built on the site of a small Roman fortress. *Heimat- und Schubartmuseum* (Marktplatz): Collection of faience and porcelain and exhibits on the history of the town and the life of F.D. Schubart (1739–91).

## Adelsheim 6962
Baden-Württemberg        p.420☐G 16

**Protestant Church of St. James the Evangelist:** This plain, late-15C church is of exceptional interest because of the funerary chapel of the Lords of Adelsheim, an extension of the church to the S. None of the tombs is outstanding in itself, yet the 61 tablets show the development of this kind of memorial from the 14–18C. The finest of the series are the tombs of the founders of the chapel and the figure of Christoph von Adelsheim as a knight, all by the Master of Adelsheim, who is possibly identical with H.Eseler of Amorbach.

## Adenau 5488
Rheinland-Pfalz        p.416☐B 13

**The Nürburg:** Built in 1160 by Count Ulrich von Are, it was the official residence of the Electors of Cologne from 1290, but since its destruction by the French in 1690 it has fallen into decay. It is today owned by the province of Rheinland-Pfalz. The ruin of the Nürburg, with its late Romanesque keep and the remains of a castle chapel, towers about 1, 050 ft. above Adenau on one of the highest castle sites in the Eifel. The wooded hills around the castle became world famous as a result of the *Nürburg-Ring* racing circuit laid out by

*Ahaus Schloss*

O.Creutz in 1925–7 and later extended (a lap is 18.6 miles).

**Also worth seeing:** The catholic parish church (10C core, enlarged about 1200), with a commandery of the Knights of the Order of St.John; *Heimatmuseum* (local history) and *half-timbered houses* around the market place.

---

**Ahaus 4422**

Nordrhein-Westfalen                    p.414☐C 8

**Schloss** (Sümmermann-Platz): Built in 1689–95 as a palace for F.C. von Pletten-berg, Bishop of Münster, by the Capucin monk-architect A. von Oelde. It was sub-jected to bombardment during the Seven Years War and restored in 1766–7 by the episcopal court architect J.C. Schlaun (1695–1773). After burning down in 1945 it was rebuilt; work was completed in 1955.

The brick Schloss is a typical old West-falian moated Burg.

**Environs: Vreden** (16 km. W.): The former collegiate church of *St. Felicitas* (1060 – 1180) with *hall crypt* and *late Romanesque doorway* (*c.*1240) was altered in the Gothic style in the 15C. Despite ex-tensive bomb damage in 1945 the church was saved. Interesting features in the Cath-olic parish church of *St. Georg*, a late Gothic hall church which was also damaged, are a large *Antwerp carved altar*, a *figure of St.Catherine* (both 16C) and five late Gothic *Apostles*.

---

**Ahlen 4730**

Nordrhein-Westfalen                    p.414☐D 9

**St.Bartholomäus:** Nothing remains of the 9C baptismal church except the sacramental niche on the S. side. The present building dates from the late Gothic period, and is a hall church with attractive tracery on its wide windows. The tabernacle with small figures on the lower tier and a tower-like canopy with ironwork are by the Münster master B.Bunickman (1512).

**Heimatmuseum** (12 Wilhelmstrasse): The museum has exhibits on bourgeois and peasant life and culture in the SE Münsterland.

---

### Ahrensburg 2070
Schleswig-Holstein                    p.412 □ H 4

**Woldenhorner Kirche/Schlosskirche** (am Markt): The church was built at the same time as the Schloss in 1594–6. The name 'Woldenhorn' refers to the former village of Woldenhorn. The church has a fine coffered ceiling and is a long rectangular barn-like structure designed to emphasize the role of the preacher. The so-called *Gottesbuden* ('God booths') at the sides of the church are an unusual feature: they are a Renaissance version of council flats for the poor of the community.

**Schloss** (1 Lübecker Strasse): The N. German Renaissance style is cool and withdrawn, but the white Schloss in Ahrensburg with its four corner towers nevertheless has grace and charm; it is similar to the Schloss in Glücksburg (q.v.). Built in 1595 by P.Rantzau, it is the last product of the Rantzau era. A staircase, the panelling in the dining hall (French, *c.*1760) and the rococo ceilings are the best features of the interior, to which a ballroom was added in the 19C; the Schloss is now a museum.

**Also worth seeing:** Various 18C houses in the Markt (Nos. 10, 12, 15).

---

### Ahrweiler =
### 5483 Bad Neuenahr-Ahrweiler
Rheinland-Pfalz                       p.416 □ C 13

**Parish Church of St. Laurentius** (Marktplatz): Building started in 1269 using ideas from the Liebfrauenkirche in Trier (q.v.), and was completed in 1300. It is the earliest example of a hall church (in which nave and aisles are of equal height) on the left bank of the Rhine. The inward-

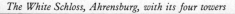

*The White Schloss, Ahrensburg, with its four towers*

sloping apses in the aisles are a striking feature, and the interconnected galleries in the three W. bays are unusual; they meet in the space under the tower. The early date of the building means that the heavy, massive style of Romanesque architecture is still present, despite the Gothic hall design. The traces of 14&15C *wall paintings,* some of which have later additions (Last Judgement, Seat of Mercy), are particularly fine. Other noteworthy features are the *baroque organ case* (1720), a wrought-iron *communion bench* (1779), the *gravestone* of Coen Blankkart (1561) and the early-16C sacristy door.

**Ahrgau-Museum** (5 Altenbaustrasse): Pre- and early history, 11–15C Christian art.

**Also worth seeing:** 13C town fortifications and the 15C Kalverienberg monastery.

---

**Aldersbach 8359**

Bavaria            p.422☐N 18

**Former Monastery Church of Mariae**

**Himmelfahrt:** Only the foundations of the tower remain from the original building, a late-11C Augustinian canonry taken over by the Ebrach Cistercians in 1146. The choir was built in 1617, the nave was completed in 1720 by D.Magzin, the façade and tower in the mid 18C and the Chapel of the Blessed Sacrament in the late 18C. The choir still has Gothic flying buttresses but the façade is late baroque, with ornate sculptural decoration over the doorway, above which there is a niche with an enthroned Virgin of the Immaculate Conception. The high altar by the Passau Master J.M. Götz, the side altars, pulpit, doors, choir stalls and tabernacle are all excellent. The finest feature of all, however, is the decoration by the Asam brothers of Munich, who were commissioned by Abbot Theobald I to decorate the church. E.Quirin, who worked in stucco, covered the lunette vaulting with swirling garlands of acanthus and foliage, and the capitals and pillars with more stylised designs in the Italian tradition; in the frescos on the ceiling of the nave, the walls and the choir C.D. Asam painted, as if in a heavenly theatre, scenes from the history of the Church: the Annunciation, Nativity, Passion, Resurrection and Ascension, Evan-

*St. Laurentius in Ahrweiler is regarded as the earliest hall church W. of the Rhine*

*Former monastery church, Aldersbach*

gelists and Church Fathers. Cloisters lead from the church to the *monastery buildings* which have an ornately decorated library, the Princes' or Solomon Room, a chapel by the gatehouse and also a musem of brewing.

---

### Alfeld an der Leine 3220
Lower Saxony                                    p.414☐G 9

**Alte Lateinschule/Altes Seminar:** This building, the Old Latin School or Old Seminary, is an especially fine half-timbered house in exposed brick; it dates from 1610, is completely detached and decorated on all four sides with poly-chrome carvings which form a frieze under the windows of the first and lower floors. On these carved bands, which are divided into individual panels, the subjects taught by the school are represented symbolically in a most unusual way in a colourful sequence of Roman generals and Christian evengelists, scenes from the Old Testament, Muses, the Arts and the Virtues. A *Renaissance doorway* with pilaster figures on either side leads into the municipal *Heimatmuseum* (local history).

**Karl Benscheidt Fagus-Factory:** The shoe-last factory is the first modern factory complex of its kind for which the design was thought through in artistic terms, and it pointed the way for later industrial architecture; the style was known in the USA as 'German Architecture'. The steel-frame construction built in 1911 – 14 by W.Gropius and A.Meyer allows the use of large expanses of glass, flooding the work-shops with light.

**Heimatmuseum** (4&5 Kirchhof): this local history museum is in an old half-timbered house (1610) with beautifully carved window balustrades; it specializes in the history of the town and the animal trade.

*Monastery church, Alpirsbach*

*Alpirsbach, Romanesque interior*

**Also worth seeing:** *St. Nicolai-Kirche* (Am Kirchhof): The present building is 15&16C, triumphal cross 13C, font 14C. The *Rathaus* in the marketplace: built in 1584–6, fine decorative gable.

---

**Allerheiligen =
Oppenau im Schwarzwald 7603**
Baden-Württemberg                    p.420☐D 18

---

**Ruins of the Monastery Church:** The ruined stone pillars and arches towering among the pine trees of a lonely Black Forest valley are the earliest example of Gothic architecture in central Baden. The former Premonstratensian monastery was founded by Duchess Uta von Schauenburg at the end of the 12C. The W. entrance and the porch, the so-called paradise, are still Romanesque but the main building is early Gothic *c.*1260–70; after a fire *c.*1470 it was rebuilt as a hall church. The monastery

was deconsecrated in 1803; some of the buildings survived and were restored, and are now used as spa accommodation. The early Gothic parts show strongly rounded lines, with an aftertaste of the Romanesque style. The connection with the stonemasons' lodge of Strasbourg Cathedral on the other side of the Rhine is clear in a number of the details, for example the tripartite arches in the main choir.

---

**Alpirsbach 7297**
Baden-Württemberg                    p.420☐E 19

**Former Benedictine Monastery Church** (Ambrosius-Blarer-Platz): The Romanesque basilica, today the Protestant parish church, is one of the most interesting examples of the Hirsau style of building (see Hirsau). There are summer *concerts* in the late Gothic cloisters.
The monastery was endowed in 1095 by

*Alsfeld, market place with Weinhaus*

three noblemen, consecrated in 1099, completed *c.*1125 and renovated in 1879 and 1957. The severe interior is defined by the cruciform ground plan and the flat ceiling. The nave is supported by massive columns; the E. capitals have motifs from the Physiologus. The lower parts of the fortress-like tower are also Romanesque, but the upper parts are Gothic with Renaissance additions; the sacristy, monastery buildings and cloisters were added at a later date. Traces of wall paintings in the choir niches, the altar niche, a bench from the old choir stalls and the furnishings of the W. door with bronze lion heads survive from the Romanesque period. The tympanum with Christ Pantocrator dates from 1130. The Swabian *altarpiece* of the Coronation of the Virgin (*c.*1520) is attributed to Syrlin the Younger. The *refectory* was extended to form the parish church in 1956.

**Market place and Rathaus:** The settle-

ment of Alpirsbach received its charter as a town in 1500, and many fine buildings, including the Town Hall (1566), have survived from this period.

---

### Alsfeld 6320
Hessen                                    p.416☐F 12

**Walpurgiskirche** (Kirchplatz): The little town is dominated by the tower of the Walpurgiskirche; Alsfeld was formerly important because of its position on the road from Hessen to Thüringen and is still one of the finest half-timbered towns in Germany.

The core of the church is an almost square early Gothic basilica (mid 13C), with new buildings added in 1393. The nave was frequently altered and raised, the last time being in 1732. The church is now the Protestant parish church. The pillars in the nave, the points from which the vaulting of the nave spring, some clerestory windows and the outer wall of the aisles have survived from the early Gothic building. The various styles of the many alterations to the church can be seen clearly inside and out. The contrast between the low, dark nave and the much higher, lighter choir is attractive: the opposite relationship is more usual. Individual *late Gothic wall paintings* survive of the furnishings, including a large early-16C St.Christopher on the E. wall of the N. aisle and an Annunciation on the gallery (*c.*1500). Rare items are the Romanesque *font*, a late Gothic *triumphal cross* and a 16C *carved altar* with a large Crucifixion.

**Rathaus** (Am Markt): Alsfeld Town Hall is one of the most important half-timbered buildings in SW Germany. It was built by Master Johann in 1512 – 16 (the half-timbered upper storeys in 1514) and restored in 1910–12. The stone lower storey with Gothic arches forms a hall, and above that are two half-timbered storeys with twin oriels rising through both storeys and topped with spires; the roof is a steep saddleback. Some techniques of construction reveal the Renaissance origins of the building, but the design is clearly late Gothic. The *council chamber* still has its 1577 and 1655 decoration, and the court room has a magnificent marquetry door.

**Market place and Old Town streets:** The *Weinhaus*, a three-storey early Renaissance stone building (defaced with round arched windows in the 19C) is next to the Rathaus in the famous market place with its many interesting buildings. The *Hochzeitshaus* (wedding house) is a Renaissance building (1564–71) with tall arched gables and a two storey corner oriel. In the old *inner town* the many twisty streets leading off the Marktplatz are worth seeing, for example the Rittergasse with the *Minnigerodehaus* and *Neurathhaus* of 1688 (Nos. 3–5, now the *Regionalmuseum*) and the *Stumpfhaus* with ornate carving and a portrait of the man who commissioned it. The half-timbered buildings show the development of half-timbered building from Gothic to neoclassicism.

**Also worth seeing:** Trinity Church in

Mainzer Strasse (14&15C); quite near is the Altenburg (12&18C) with a Schloss church (18C).

---

**Altdorf bei Nürnberg 8503**
Bavaria                    p.422☐K 16

**Former University:** The town of Altdorf, on the edge of the Franconian Alb, housed a University known throughout Europe from 1575–1809. This dated back to a grammar school, founded by a Nuremberg councillor at the time of the Reformation and moved to Altdorf, then in the territory of the Imperial City of Nuremberg; it then became an academy in 1578 and a university in 1622. Wallenstein was a student here from 1599–1600 and Leibniz received his doctorate in Altdorf in 1666.
In 1809 the university was closed and the greater part of its valuable libraries was sent to Erlangen.
*Building:* The smooth ashlar buildings (1571–82) are set round a rectangular inner courtyard closed to the N. by a wall and gatehouse. The three-storey main block has an open lower storey with round arches and a tall clock tower. In the centre of the courtyard inside an octagonal railing is the *bronze fountain* by G.Labenwolf of Nuremberg with rams' heads and spouting dolphins and a statue of Minerva on a small column.

**Also worth seeing:** Protestant parish church (choir and tower 14C; nave 18C); former Pfleg Schloss (1588), now the police headquarters.

**Environs: Grünsberg** (2.5 km S.): The ministerial Burg first mentioned in 1235 came into the possession of Nuremberg families in 1504 and was extended as a country seat in the 16&18C. There is notable stucco in the main building and in the gatehouse and tower.

---

**Altena 5990**
Nordrhein-Westfalen              p.416☐D 11

**Burg** (80 Fritz-Thomee-Strasse): The interesting feature of this medieval castle is its extent: the narrow barbican leads to the lower bailey, and the middle and upper gates to the keep and the upper bailey. Building is presumed to have begun in the 12C, it fell into disrepair in the 18C and was systematically rebuilt in 1907–16. There are Gothic altars from neighbouring parishes in the *Burg chapel*. In the new building is the *Märkische Schmiedemuseum* containing vessels in pewter, bronze, copper, brass and wrought iron from the Middle Ages to the present day. The old building contains a *collection of weapons*. The *Deutsche Drahtmuseum* (wire museum) is in the former commandant's house. (The Altena area was a centre for wiredrawers. The German *Youth Hostel movement* started its operations from this castle.

---

**Altenberg = 5068 Odenthal**
Nordrhein-Westfalen                                      p.416☐C 11

---

**Altenberg Dom/'Bergischer Dom':** This former monastery church of a Cistercian abbey in the wooded valley of the Dhünn in the Bergisches Land is one of

*Altena, Burg*

the greatest works of Gothic architecture on German soil. From 1400 the church was the goal of a major pilgrimage, the so-called Alsterberg Gottestracht. *Haus Altenberg* is the headquarters of the Federation of Catholic Youth in Germany.

*History:* In 1133 the Counts of Berg presented their old Burg retreat to the Burgundian Cistercians. The present Dom (cathedral) was built in 1259–1379 after the first Romanesque church collapsed in an earthquake in 1222. In 1803 it was deconsecrated, became privately owned and was turned into a factory; it burned down and the stone was removed for other buildings. King Friedrich Wilhelm IV had it restored in 1835–46, and it was completely rebuilt in 1895. It is now used for both Roman Catholic and Protestant services.

*Description:* The Dom is a good example of Cistercian austerity: a three-aisled basilica with transepts and elegant, undecorated buttresses. Simple columns instead of Gothic pillars with multiple ribs support the clerestory and only in the choir are the capitals ornamented with foliage. The grey friars did not build towers and made do with a turret for their bells. The Cistercian church in Royaumont NW of Paris was the model for the Dom in Altenberg.

*Interior and furnishings:* The finest features are the grisaille windows in the choir and a 14C *Annunciation* which was originally over the W. doorway. New Jerusalem of 1400–20; *Coronation of Mary altar*, S. German *W. window*, 2nd half of the 15C; 1490 tabernacle; altar cross *c.*1500; Flemish double Madonna *c.*1530; Herzogenchor and other tombs of Bergisch princes. Since 1980 it has had the Klais organ with 82 stops and 6034 pipes.

The 13C *monastery buildings*, altered in the baroque period, contain the Martin chapel.

---

### Altenstadt (bei Schongau) 8925
Bavaria                                    p.422 ☐ J 20

**Parish Church of St. Michael:** This is the only Romanesque vaulted basilica to have survived in Upper Bavaria, and is a most unusual feature in this stronghold of the baroque. The size and splendour of the building, which became a place of pilgrimage, are also unusual for a country parish church.

Early building details are missing, but the completion date is presumed to be *c.*1200. In 1826 the building was restored under King Ludwig I, and the most recent renovation began in 1961. Now the Catholic parish church.

It is built of tufa ashlars and is set on a hill and surrounded by a defensive wall; the two massive towers with stumpy tops add to the fortress-like impression. It is a three-aisled basilica with E. towers and 3 parallel apses. The only decoration on the heavy walls are the finely profiled cornices, archivolts and pilaster strips at the corners. As the interior is very plain the shallow *cushion capitals* decorated with ornaments, stylised foliage, palmettes and stars are particularly striking. The *Romanesque font* has exterior reliefs of John the Baptist, the Baptism of Christ, the Virgin Mary and St. Michael. There is an outstanding treasure in the nave: one of the few remaining Romanesque wooden triumphal crosses, with the original paint. The 'Great God of Altenstadt' wears a royal crown instead of the crown of thorns and the body keeps strictly to the shape of the cross, in the Romanesque tradition. It is over 10 ft. high and 10 ft. wide and dominates the otherwise undecorated space. Its attendant figures of Mary and John have been in the Bavarian National Museum in Munich (q.v.) for some time.

*Traceried window, Altenberg Dom*

*Altenberg Dom*

## Altomünster 8064
Bavaria                                          p.422□K 19

**Brigittine Monastery Church:** A Benedictine double monastery, for monks and nuns, was founded here by the hermit Alto shortly after 750. It later had exclusively monks, then only nuns, and was taken over by the Brigittines in 1485. It was secularized in 1803 and then reopened in 1842, and is today the only Brigittine house in Germany. Its church is the last work of the great baroque architect J.M. Fischer.

The choir dates from the early 17C, and the reconstruction of the nave on the medieval foundations was begun by Fischer in 1763 and completed after his death by his foreman in 1766-73. The sloping site and the nature of the double monastery led to a most unusual design with a floor on different levels and galleries on two storeys. The ornamentation is in the moderate, even severe spirit of late rococo, but nevertheless has elegance and grace; it is by the Augsburg stucco artist J.Rauch. Along with the ornate ceiling paintings, the altars in the lay nave (St.Augustine and St.Alto) are particularly noteworthy: they are late works by the Munich Master J.B. Straub and his studio, as are the figures of apostles, the upper high altar and the altars in the dividing choir.

## Altötting 8262
Bavaria                                          p.422□N 19

**Heilige Kapelle** (Kapellplatz): The chapel is one of the oldest churches in Germany. The House of Wittelsbach and indeed the whole of Bavaria is closely linked with the pilgrimage church of Altötting. The hearts of six kings, two queens, two electors and Field Marshall Tilly are committed here in the wall compartments opposite the miraculous image. More than 600,000 people make their pilgrimage to honour Mary here each year.

The chapel was first mentioned in 877, but could have existed as a heathen temple as early as the 7C. At the end of the 15C the central building of the old chapel became a pilgrimage shrine.

The miraculous image, a carving blackened with soot (hence 'Black Madonna'), was made c.1300 and probably comes from Lorraine. The figure, just over 2 ft. high, has been concealed in baroque splendour since the 17C. The interior walls of the octagonal room are also black, and the tabernacle with the miraculous image in the centre shimmers in silver against this sable ground. A life-size figure of Prince Maximilian of Bavaria kneels before it to the right: this was presented by his father as a thanks-offering for the deliverance of the ten-year-old child from a serious illness. To accommodate the flood of votive offerings the parish church of St.Philipp and St.Jakob made the sacristy into a *treasury*. The finest item is the so-called *Goldenes Rössl* (golden horse), a French piece made of gold, silver, ivory and jewels c.1400.

**Städtisches Wallfahrts- und Heimatmuseum** (4 Kapellplatz): Local pre- and early history and also extensive collections connected with the pilgrimage (including votive and devotional pictures).

**Also worth seeing:** Collegiate church of *St.Philipp and St.Jakob* (Kapellplatz): built 1599-1511, funerary chapel of Count Tilly, interesting treasure. Former Jesuit church of *St. Magdalena:* (16 – 18C). *St. -Anna-Basilica* (Konventstrasse): 1910-13 neo-baroque building.

## Alzey 6508
Rheinland-Pfalz                                  p.416□D 15

**Former St.Nikolai-Kirche** (Obermarkt): The church stands on the foundations of an old royal chapel and was built in 1476 as a late Gothic hall church. The nave was much altered after a fire in 1689. In 1844 –8 the church was rebuilt in Gothic style and even given rib vaulting, but the former flat ceiling was replaced in the restoration of 1905. In the tower porch is an *Entomb-*

*Altötting: Interior of the Heilige Kapelle* ▷

*The Heilige Kapelle in Altötting*

*ment:* seven life-size sandstone figures, dating from *c.*1430.

**Burg** (32–4 Schlossgasse): Volker von Alzey, the legendary minstrel of the Nibelungenlied, could not have been the lord of this Imperial castle, which was not founded until the 12C; however, as a vassal of King Gunther Volker was involved in the conquest in 406 of the Roman citadel in Alzey, which dates from *c.*365. In the entanglements of the interregnum of 1254–73 the castle of the Hohenstaufen princes was destroyed in 1260 as 'a den of thieves'. It was rebuilt in the 15&16C as a secondary residence of the Heidelberg Counts Palatinate. Local government departments are now housed in the various buildings. A 200 ft. square with walls 10 to 13 ft. thick marks the limits of the old moated Burg, to which corner towers with residences and wall passages were added by its various lords. The outer works, of which fragments still remain, were directly connected with the town fortifications.

*Museum Alzey-Worms* (41 Antoniterstrasse): The museum is housed in the former *Spital* (infirmary), a 16C Renaissance building with a round staircase tower and mansard roof (1747–8). It has Roman, Franconian, folklore and geological departments.

**Also worth seeing:** The Rathaus (3 Fischmarkt): built 1586; the Wartberg tower (Auf dem Wartberg): remains of the medieval town fortifications; former Roman citadel (Jean-Braun-Strasse).

---

**Amberg 8450**
Bavaria                    p.422☐L 16

The old ore-mining town, once the residence in the Upper Pfalz of the Counts

Palatinate of the Rhine, still looks like a fortified town with towers, electoral chancellery buildings, an old and a new electoral Schloss, Rathaus and many old houses. Gothic, Renaissance and baroque buildings crowd together side by side.

**Parish Church of St. Martin** (Marktplatz): Building began in 1421, the vaulting dates from 1483 and the tower was built 1509–34 and in the 18C. The flying buttresses support a continuous gallery for the first time in a Gothic hall church. After the Regensburg Dom (q.v.) this late Gothic church is the largest in the Upper Pfalz. With the exception of a bronze font the furnishings are 19C; the picture by C.Crayer, an imitator of Rubens, is important, however; it shows the Coronation of Mary with the Patron Saint (1658) and now hangs sideways over the sacristy; it was formerly on the high altar. The high tomb of Count Palatinate Ruprecht Pipan (d.1397) behind the high altar (15&16C) and the panel picture *Invention of the Cross by St.Helena* by J.Pollak (*c*.1500) are noteworthy. Outside in front of the N. wall by the E. doorway are Gothic console figures in sandstone (Mary with the Angel of the Annunciation), copies of the 13&14C originals which are kept at the rear end of the church for safety. The red marble grave of the cannon founder Martin Merz (d. 1501) is also notable.

**St. Georg** (Malteserplatz): The fortresslike exterior with massive W. tower is in stark contrast with the late baroque stucco of the interior. An earlier church is mentioned for the first time in 1094 but the present Gothic basilica was not built until 1359. The Jesuits took over the church from the Protestants at the time of the Counter-Reformation and added two side chapels (1656–76). The stucco is probably the work of Wessobrunn masters (A.Rauch and P.J.Schmuzer). The altars in the side aisles are also the work of Crayer (1668). Behind the choir is the long building of the *former Jesuit college* with a fine rococo library on the second floor.

**Deutsche Schulkirche** (Schrannenplatz): A monastery and originally oval church

*Marble tomb of Martin Merz*

built by W.Dientzenhofer at the end of the 17C, which did not attain its present distinctive form until 1738–58, when it was decorated with great lightness of touch in magnificent rococo style, and G.B.Götz painted the ceiling frescos. An ornate doorway with gable figures of St.Augustine and St.Francis de Sales has a lavishly carved wooden door. The finest points of the splendid decoration are the lively organ front with a tulip-like choir gallery below it, the pulpit and a broad wrought-iron tendril railing which forms the W. boundary of the church.

**Pilgrimage Church of Maria-Hilf:** A small rotunda was built on the hill above the town as a votive chapel after a plague in 1634, and it was replaced by a larger church by W.Dientzenhofer in 1697–1703. The stucco decoration (from 1702) is by the Italian G.B.Carlone and his pupil P.D'Aglio. On the mouldings and in front of the pillars are mariologically determined figures of saints and prophets. C.D.Asam's ceiling frescos of the story of the Amberg pilgrimage (1718) are the best feature of the interior decoration.

**Rathaus** (Marktplatz): The tall and slender gable, given vertical thrust by blind pointed arches, is pure, mature Gothic and was built in 1356. In the interior of the Rathaus, one of the finest in Germany, the small hall with its Renaissance panelling and the great council chamber are worth seeing.

**Townscape:** The present *Landratsamt* (local government office) was the former *Residence of the Counts Palatinate* designed by the Heidelberg architect J.Schoch (1602), and the present *Landgericht* (court building) was the *Government Chancellery*. Much of the *town fortifications* survives, including four of the original five town gates. An unusual feature is the point where the town wall crosses the river Vils on two arches: because of their appearance when reflected in the water they are known as the *'town spectacles'*. The former *Kurfürstliches Zeughaus* (electoral arsenal; 15C), the 18C *Ratstrinkstube* and a number of 15–18C *houses* are worth seeing. The Frauenkirche

*Rathaus stairs*

(15C) with a Gothic Annunciation group on the side portal, the former Franciscan church (15C, town theatre since 1803) and the 13–18C Dreifaltigkeitskirche (Trinity) are worth seeing.

**Heimatmuseum** (12 Eichenforstgasse): Collections on the history of the town including the 'Amberg song table'.

**Environs: Ensdorf an der Vils** (14 km. S.): P.J.Schmuzer (stucco) and C.D.Asam (ceiling frescos) were involved in the baroque refurbishment of the former Benedictine monastery church of St.Jakob (consecrated in 1123).

---

### Amelungsborn 3451
Lower Saxony                                    p.414☐G 9

**Former Monastery:** One of the oldest Cistercian monasteries in Germany was built here on a little hill in the 12C. The Romanesque nave of the monastery church and small sections of other parts of the building survive from the original building; most of the remainder dates from the Gothic period. Amelungsborn was the starting-point for other monastery foundations, including that of Riddigshausen, near Braunschweig (q.v.).

---

### Amorbach 8762
Bavaria                                          p.416☐F 15

**Former Benedictine Abbey Church of St.Maria:** Founded according to legend by the Abbot St.Amor in 734 and dedicated to St.Boniface a little later; large-scale rebuilding followed in the mid 9C, and the W. towers in the 12C. In 1742 the old basilica was demolished with the exception of the W. towers. The baroque rebuilding was completed by the Mainz architect M. von Welsch in 1747, and the church secularised in 1803. It is now the protestant parish church.
The massive Romanesque square towers

*Amberg, Rathaus* ▷

*'Town spectacles', wall across the Vils at Amberg*

with round arched windows on three storeys have survived in their old form; during rebuilding they were made to harmonise with the baroque façade placed in front of the older part of the church by the addition of graceful domes. There is a ceremonial staircase in front of this W. front which is decorated with pilasters and ornate sculpture and topped by a scrolled gable; the staircase emphasises the Schloss-like character of the buildings. The church is laid out as a cruciform pillared basilica and the former apse was widened to form a choir.

The rococo decoration ranks with that of the famous late baroque churches of Bavaria and Franconia. The decorations on wall and ceiling are by the Wessobrunn

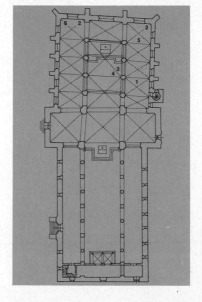

**Amelungsborn, former monastery church 1** Tomb of Count Hermann v. Everstein and his wife, 1375 **2** Romanesque piscinae **3** Sedilia **4** Figure of St. Bernard with reliefs on the rear side, 3rd quarter of the 14C **5** Font, 1592 **6** Tomb of Abbot Steinhover (d.1588).

stucco artists J.G.Üblherr and J.M.Feucht-
mayer, the latter being one of the most important S. German rococo artists; he and
his school were also responsible for the
high altar and various side altars. The
splendid pulpit is by the Würzburg court
sculptor J.W. van der Auvera. M.Günther
painted the high altar picture and the ceiling frescos. The wrought-iron railing
(1749–52) between the nave and the transept and the *organ* (1774–82) from the
workshop of the brothers Stumm are other
fine features. There are columns from the
Romanesque cloisters in the *cemetery*,
which was laid out in 1786 along the S.
side of the church. The *monastery buildings* on the S. side of the church date from
the 17&18C; the banqueting hall, called
the *Grüner Saal* because of its essentially
green colour scheme, is decorated with severe neoclassical stucco. There are unusual
wrought iron stoves under the musicians'
gallery. The *library* is also neoclassical,
with elegant ornaments on banisters and
balustrades. Finally the old *monastery mill*
with its steep step gable should not be
missed.

**Catholic Parish Church of St.Gangolf:**
The three-aisled hall was built in 1752–
4 to a design by J.M.Schmidt of Miltenberg. The frescos are by J.Zick (1753) and
the four statues on the high altar by J.Keil-
werth of Würzburg.

**Museum:** *Fürstlich Leiningensche Sammlungen Amorbach* (Leiningen Princes' collection; Kellereigasse): Local history,
medieval pottery, collection of devotional
pictures.

**Also worth seeing:** Fürstlich
Leiningsches Schloss (15C); Altes Stadthaus (15C); Templerhaus (1291); ruined
17C church on the Gotthardsberg.

**Environs: Amorsbrunn** (2 km. W.) The
1565 healing well in the pilgrimage chapel
of Amorsbrunn (first mentioned 1273)
goes back to a pre-Christian shrine with a
spring. Notable furnishings (16–18C) include a rare stone figure of St.Amor (1720).
**Wildenberg** (8 km. S.): The ruined Burg,
built *c.*1200 as a fortress by the Lords of

*Amorbach, aerial view*

Durn, was one of the most important Hohenstaufen castles and played a part in the
life of the medieval poet Wolfram von Eschenbach.

**Andechs = 8138 Erling-Andechs**
Bavaria                                p.422 □ K 20

**Pilgrimage Church Mariae Verkün-
diging (Annunciation) and Monastery:** The Benedictine monastery of
Andechs was a popular place of pilgrimage
as early as the 12C and still attracts a large
number of 'pilgrims', possibly to some extent because of the popular beer from the
monastery brewery, founded in 1455. St.
Rasso lived as Count of Andechs on
Bavaria's 2,400 ft. 'Holy Mountain' with
the relics which he is said to have brought
back from a pilgrimage to Jerusalem in
952.
The rediscovery of the lost '3 holy hosts'

in the year 1388 was the reason for the building of the late Gothic church (started 1420, completed 1448); it was badly damaged by lightning in 1669. In the mid 18C new vaulting was erected in the nave and choir, more windows were added and the church was refurbished in the rococo style, supposedly to designs by J.M.Fischer; the new choir altar was installed in 1759. The church was secularised in 1803, and in 1846 the entire monastery complex was bought by King Ludwig I and returned to the Benedictines. The church is set on a steep mountain slope and the exterior is that of a plain hall church with three aisles and a W. tower with an onion dome added at the time of the baroque reconstruction. The 18C renewal movement restricted itself to splendid redecoration of the Gothic building: walls, pillars and ceilings are covered with tendrils, acanthus and rocaille and the whole space is surrounded by a gallery which curves in waves. J.B.Zimmermann of Wessobrunn created the stucco and the ceiling frescos (scenes from the life of St. Benedict, Rasso's victory over the Magyars, pilgrimage scenes). The pilgrimage used to involve more than 200 parishes and centres on the miraculous image of the Madonna (*c.*1500) in the lower high altar and the Immaculata (*c.*1608) in the upper altar. The figures of Elisabeth von Thüringen and St. Nikolaus are by J.B.Straub. There are interesting votive panels on the W. wall. The *holy chapel* is reached from the gallery and contains the remains of the rich pre-secularisation monastery treasure. The most important items are the mid-15C *three hosts monstrance*, the 12C *victory cross of Charlemagne*, the *breast cross* of St.Elisabeth of Thüringen and her *wedding dress*.

---

### Andernach 5470
Rheinland-Pfalz                                    p.416☐C 13

**The Round Tower** (Dr.-Konrad-Adenauer-Allee): The tower was part of the town fortifications, which were partially built on the foundations of the old Roman town wall, and is an Andernach landmark and a reminder of the town's historic past. The town's original name, Antunnacum, points back to a Celtic settlement in which Drusus built a fortified citadel in 12 BC at the point where the Roman Rhine road crossed a road from the Eifel. In the Mid-

◁ *Abbey church, Amorbach*                    *Pilgrimage church, Andechs*

dle Ages and later Andernach was an important trading post. The Round Tower was built in 1448–52 and is 184 ft. high, 49 ft. in diameter and the walls are 16 ft. thick. Master Philipp, who is named as the architect, made the simple defensive tower into a work of art; it now houses a youth hostel. Parts of the town wall survive, and also the *Schuldturm* (debtors' tower), mentioned in 1340 and the *Rhine gate* with its Romanesque figures.

**Liebfrauenkirche** (Kirchstrasse): The church of *Mariae Himmelfahrt*, to give it its official name, is one of the finest Romanesque churches in the Rhineland. Building is said to have started in 1200, and it was restored in 1877–99 and is now the catholic parish church. The reputation of the four-towered basilica is based on the W. façade, which has round arches running the full length of all three storeys. The pointed lozenge roofs indicate Gothic influence. There are also Gothic elements in the interior, such as the pointed wall arches and the wooden keystones with episcopal, municipal and imperial coats of arms. The ornately carved 18C *pulpit* and the baroque *communion bench* came from Maria Laach. In the sacristy is a late Gothic *tabernacle* (*c.*1500). The 14C *branch crucifix*, a so-called Hungarian or plague cross, is notable. The *holy tomb* with larger-than-life figures is also worth seeing (1524).

**Stadtmuseum** (97 Hochstrasse): Exhibits on prehistory and the history of the town and region.

**Also worth seeing:** Former Minorite church (14&15C); town crane (16C); Rathaus (15&18C); ruined 17C Burg of the Archbishops of Cologne.

---

**Anholt=4294 Isselburg**
Nordrhein-Westfalen          p.414☐B 9

**Moated Schloss:** The Anholt Burg is a kind of island empire close by the Dutch border (Autobahn exit Bocholt/Rees/Isselburg). The round keep is 12C, the side buildings and staircase tower 14&15C. The

Burg was modified from the mid 17C in the Dutch baroque style. The park was laid out in the 18C and was extended by the addition of an English park in the 19C. The staircase in the main building dates from 1699 and has a monumental flight of wooden stairs. The stateroom with its ornate stucco is lined with tapestries designed by the Brussels artist L. van Schoor and the dining-room is decorated with tapestries showing peasant scenes based on pictures by the genre painter D.Teniers the Younger. The large *art collection* is notable and has 800 pictures (including an early Rembrandt), valuable tapestries and a great deal of porcelain.

---

**Annweiler am Trifels 6747**
Rheinland-Pfalz          p.420☐D 16

The village of Annweiler was declared an Imperial City in 1219 by the Hohenstaufen Emperor Friedrich II and the strong connection with the Trifels, the rock above the town, dates from this period.

**Imperial Burg of Trifels** (6 km. from Annweiler): The Burg (an Imperial Burg as early as 1081) is built on a sandstone outcrop above the green hills of the Pfälzer Wald. The imperial treasure was kept from 1124–1274 in the shallow oriel chapel on the E. side of the Burg, and the Norman treasure was also stored there in 1195. The fortress secured the road from Metz to the Rhine, and was never taken. It also functioned as a prison for distinguished men: the English King Richard Lionheart was kept prisoner here by Emperor Heinrich VI (1193–4), and Friedrich II kept his rebellious son King Heinrich here in 1235. In the Thirty Years War the Burg was a refuge for the populace; in 1662 much of it was destroyed by lightning. Rebuilding (since 1935) has raised the keep by one storey; the residence and knights' hall have been extended in the style of the original building.

There are two other ruined fortresses

*Hungarian cross, Andernach* ▷

nearby, Burg Anebos (12C) and Burg Scharfenberg (c.1200).

---

### Ansbach 8800, Mittelfranken
Bavaria                          p.422□J 16

**Former Collegiate Church of St. Gumbertus** (Johann-Sebastian-Bach-Platz): Some parts of the church are 13C but its present appearance is the result of much remodelling and extension in the course of the centuries; the nave of the new hall building was added in the last major phase of construcion in 1738. The church with its three towers has become the emblem of the town; it became important through its connection with the Knights of the Swan and contains 11 graves of individual Knights of the Order. The massive pulpit altar (to specifications by P.A.Biarelles) dates from 1738–9.

**Margrave's Schloss/Residenz** (am Schlossplatz): The Schloss is the principal attraction of this little Franconian residence town. It was built from 1713 onwards to plans by the Graubünden architect G. de Gabrieli on the foundations of a Renaissance building and work continued under the 'cavalier architects' J.W. and K.F. von Zocha and L.Retti from 1731–41.*Building:* The long façade has 21 bays and is the work of Gabrieli, who was also responsible for most of the courtyard with its chamfered corners and arcades. The SE façade is by K.F. von Zocha and the outer façades of the three wings are the work of L.Retti.

*Interior and furnishings:* The decoration is ascribed to L. Retti, who was one of the greatest designers of his time. Everything is tinged with the cool distinction of French rococo on the verge of neoclassicism. The finest feature is the Great Hall, which is two storeys high and has a musicians' gallery on its long side. The ceiling fresco by C.Carlone glorifies the young Margrave Carl Wilhelm Friedrich. One of the most distinguished rooms is the *Spiegelkabinett*: the mirrors have console frames arranged in steps and containing valuable porcelain groups and vases by many European manufacturers. Ansbach itself had a faience factory from 1709, and this provided the 3,000 tiles in the dining-room (1763–4). E. of the Residenz, though not directly connected to it, is the *Hofgarten*; this was first laid out in the 16C, but its

*Imperial castle of Trifels near Annweiler*

present design dates from the first half of the 18C. The *Orangery* (*c.*1726–43) is a 335 ft. long building in the N. of the Hofgarten.

**Also worth seeing:** Former Margraves' Chancellery (1594); Stadthaus (*c.*1532); Prinzenschlösschen (1699 – 1701); Protestant parish church of St.Johannes (15C); Heiliges Kreuz cemetery chapel (15C); synagogue (18C); Karlshalle (Catholic, 18C); grammar school (18C); many fine 16&18C houses and the Heimatmuseum (local history, 10 Schaitbergstrasse).

## Armsheim in Rheinhessen
Rheinland-Pfalz                     p.416☐D 15

**Former Pilgrimage Church of the Holy Blood:** The church was built from 1431 on older foundations as a three-aisled hall church; the W. tower was added in the late 15C, and the church rebuilt after a fire in 1852. The 230 ft. high W. tower can be seen for miles along the old Celtic road from Worms to Bingen. The late Gothic pulpit (*c.*1500, school of Riemenschneider) is decorated with symbols of the Evangelists and the Instruments of Christ's Torment.

## Arnsberg 5760
Nordrhein-Westfalen                     p.416☐D 10

**Priory Church of St.Laurentius:** Only the church remains of the Premonstratensian Abbey of Wedinghausen, founded in 1173 and dissolved in 1803; the tower complex dates from the 12C. The early Gothic choir was consecrated in 1253 and building of the present church continued into the 16C. The best furnishings are the early baroque high altar in marble and alabaster (actually the memorial tomb of Landrost Kaspar von Fürstenberg) by H. Grössinger and the tomb of Friedrich of Fürstenberg (*c.*1680); the double high tomb of Count Heinrich and his wife Ermengard von Arnsberg (14C) the pulpit and the pews (*c.*1740 are also notable.
S. of the church are remains of the *former monastery buildings*.

**Also worth seeing:** Hirschberg gate (1753) by the Priory Church; Altes Rathaus (1710); market fountain (1779);

*Ansbach, view of St. Gumbertus*

*Mystic wine-pressing, St. Gumbertus*

*Arcaded courtyard in the Margrave's Schloss, Ansbach*

Landberger Hof (1605, containing the *Sauerlandmuseum*) and half-timbered houses in the old town.

## Arnstein = 5409 Obernhof
Rheinland-Pfalz                                    p.416☐D 13

**Former Premonstratensian Abbey of St.Maria and St.Nikolaus:** Ludwig III, the last Count of Arnstein or Arnoldstein (d. 1185) founded a Premonstratensian monastery in his Burg in 1139 and later entered it as a monk himself. The abbey soon flourished and the buildings were greatly extended; the abbey church, consecrated in 1208, and the plain Romanesque refectory have survived. There was rebuilding in 1359, the baroque interior dates from the mid 18C and the church was secularised in 1803. The abbey church is a cruciform Romanesque pillared basilica with three aisles and vaulting, and has two choirs and two pairs of towers: the E. early Gothic towers are octagonal and the W. towers rectangular, with lozenge roofs. The high altar (1760) the pulpit (1757) and the gravestone of Ludwig IV (*c.*1320) are notable features of the interior.

## Arnstein 8725
Bavaria                                             p.416☐G 14

This little Lower Franconian town on the Wern was mentioned in 839 and received its charter in 1317; it is built around a central Schloss mound, and the main street, the Marktstrasse, follows the line of this mound and broadens into the market place, in which stands the 16C *Rathaus*.

**Catholic Parish Church of St. Nikolaus:** There are still some traces in the choir of the small Gothic chapel near the Rathaus which was extended in 1617;

in 1722–5 the nave was enlarged and a new tower erected. S.Urlaub was responsible for the ceiling paintings in the choir (1726) and the early neoclassical *side altars* are by G.Winterstein (1790). There is an ornately decorated *organ* (1610) by J.Hofmann and an elaborate pulpit (*c*.1700).

**Catholic Pilgrimage Church of Maria Sondheim** (on the S. edge of the town): This single-aisled church was built in 1440 on the site of an older church. Interesting features are the ceiling painting in the choir by P.Rudolf (1770, Mary above the Battle of Lepanto), the stained glass windows in the *choir* (r: *c*.1480, l: 1513), the *pulpit* with reliefs (*c*.1520) and a *Pietà* (*c*.1420) flanked by two late Gothic wooden figures in the N. chapel. A *sandstone Madonna* (*c*.1310) and the impressive 32 *memorial tombs* (15&16C) are also worth seeing. Of the 26 von Hutten memorial tombs those for Ludwig von Hutten (d. 1517), Konrad von Hutten (d.1502) and Philipp von Hutten (d. 1546 in Venezuela) are of particularly high quality. There are a further 9 *memorial tombs* outside the building and a *Mount of Olives chapel* by the N. apse.

**Schloss:** The Schloss was partially rebuilt as a prince bishop's *hunting lodge* after being destroyed in the Peasants War in 1540–4. Remains of the former *ring wall* are built into the surrounding buildings.

**Spital** (infirmary): The long two-winged building erected by von Greising in 1713 –30 was funded from an endowment by Moritz von Hutten (1546) and contains a *rococo altar* with a picture by J.M.Wolckrer (1748).

**Arnstorf 8382**
Bavaria                                    p.422☐N 18

**Oberes Schloss:** This Schloss is one of the few Bavarian moated Burg buildings. The oldest parts are presumably 15C, and there were major extensions in the 17 and early 18C. The rooms on the ground floor and the Schloss chapel with its baroque stucco date from the Gothic building

period, the upper storeys have baroque decoration. The decoration of the ballroom, the *Kaisersaal*, by M.Steidl (1714) is of great artistic merit. The fine *Theatersaal* (*c*.1700) is notable.

**Also worth seeing:** Unteres Schloss (17&18C); Parish Church of St. Georg (15&16C); Alt-Arnstorf-Haus (2 Vorderer Berg) which houses the local history museum.

**Arolsen 3548**
Hessen                                    p.416☐F 10

**Schloss** (27 Schlossstrasse): The complex is based on the Château at Versailles. As the Prince ordered the entire town to be designed on a drawing board, Schloss, church and houses form a unified whole. Count Anton Ulrich von Waldeck (Reichsgraf from 1711) founded the new town at the same time as he laid the foundation stone for the Schloss in 1713. Major J.L.Rothweil and his son Karl Friedrich were in charge of the project and they designed the Schloss and most of the buildings in the town. Building of the Schloss was essentially complete by 1720, though the interior decoration and the outer buildings were not completed until 1811.

The Schloss has a main courtyard and is horseshoe-shaped. Only one section of the rondel which was planned opposite the Schloss as a parade ground was completed. The moat which surrounds the whole complex is reminiscent of Westfalian moated Schloss design. The complex was more ambitious in conception, but was only partially completed because of financial difficulties.

The building is pure late baroque. The staircase, garden room, chapel and the conventionally classical great hall are the key rooms in the individual parts of the building, and are dominated by A.Gallasini's vivacious stucco work (1715–19). The rooms are furnished with pictures of local rulers from various periods (by Aldegrever, Meytens, Querfurt and J.H.Tischbein) and the well-known busts of Goethe and Frederick the Great by A.Trippel (1789);

*Arolsen, Schloss*

there are also sculptures by C.F.Rauch, who was born in Arolsen in 1777.

**Museums:** *Kaulbach-Museum* (3 Kaulbachstrasse) in the birthplace of W. von Kaulbach with memorabilia of the artist and his familly. *Christian-Rauch-Gedenkstätte* (6 Rauchstrasse): memorial museum in the sculptor's birthplace (1777–1857).

**Also worth seeing:** Government buildings and mews (1749–61); orangery and nursery garden (1819–22); neues Schloss (1763–78/1853); Protestant parish church (18C); houses; former Palais von Canstein (1743; now the Rathaus).

---

**Aschaffenburg 8750**
Bavaria                                     p.416☐F 14

When viewed from the bank of the Main the town is dominated by the four fortress-like towers of the sandstone Schloss Johannisburg.

**Collegiate Church of St. Peter and St. Alexander** (Stiftsplatz): First mentioned in documents in the 10C; building was started in 950 by Otto von Schwaben, who is buried in the church; in the early 12C the present nave was added as a pillared basilica; the W. doorway and the two side doorways on the N. side date from the early 13C; the E. choir, the transept and the cloisters are late Romanesque/early Gothic (*c.*1230–40). The N. tower was started in 1415 and completed in 1480–90; the *Maria Schee chapel* on the N side was built by Master Nikolaus in 1516; in 1618 16 Romanesque pillars from the Hohenstaufen Burg in Babenhausen were incorporated to support a W. gallery. St. Peter and St. Alexander is today the parish church.

**Interior and decoration:** The Romanesque nave with its short round arches contrasts with the pointed arches of the choir and transept. The leaf capitals on the pillars of the W. gallery are from the same workshop as the *tympanum* with Christ Enthroned on the W. doorway. The archaically severe *wooden crucifix* on the side wall of the nave was carved *c.*1200. The *Wailing over the Body of Christ*, the predella of a lost altar, is by M.G.Nithardt (M.Grünewald), who lived for many years in Aschaffenburg and nearby Seligenstadt; Grünewald created the altar whose component parts are now in Stuppach (q.v.) and Freiburg im Breisgau (q.v.) for the Maria Schee chapel. The bronze castings from the Vischer studio in Nuremberg were commissioned by Cardinal Albrecht of Brandenburg in Mainz, who fled to Aschaffenburg in the troubled Reformation period. There are notable jewels in the *treasury*. The late Romanesque *cloisters* on the N. side of the church contain a number of important tombs.

**Schloss Johannisburg** (Schlossplatz): The massive Renaissance Schloss was built by the military architect G.Ridinger of Strasbourg in 1605–14. It has four square towers at the corners, which were constructed around the original medieval keep. Ridinger was also responsible for the Schloss church in the N. wing. The Johannisburg was the first Renaissance Schloss in Germany in which the demonstration of power replaced the defensive function. The Schloss was very badly damaged in the Second World war. It houses an important branch of the *Bayerische Staatsgemäldesammlungen* (state picture collection).

**Pompejanum** (Pompejanumstrasse): King Ludwig I of Bavaria had the towerlike neoclassical Pompejanum built NW of the Schloss behind the Schloss garden by his court architect F.Gärtner in 1842–9 on the model of the house of Castor and Pollux in Pompeii.

**Cemetery** (Lamprechtstrasse): Wilhelm Heinse (1746–1803), the Sturm und Drang writer and author of 'Ardinghello', and Clemens Brentano (1778–1842), the Romantic poet and editor of 'Des Knaben Wunderhorn' are buried here.

*Collegiate church, Aschaffenburg*

**Museums:** *Staatsgemäldesammlung* and *municipal Staatsgemäldesammlung* (painting collections) and *Schloss museum* (in Schloss Johannisburg): local history, applied art (16–20C), painting and graphics (17–20C). *Stiftsmuseum* (former chapter house in the Stiftsplatz): pre- and early history, Roman finds, church art in the lower Main area.

**Environs: Schönbusch** (W. of Nilkheim): The *park* (18C) goes back to the Electors of Mainz, the neoclassical *Lustschlösschen* was built in 1778&9, and the various pavilions in the park between then and 1800 by E.J.d'Herigoyen.

---

**Aschau im Chiemgau 8213**
Bavaria                                p.422☐M 20

---

**Burg Hohenaschau:** The mightiest of the fortresses of the Chiemgau is set on a

*Schloss Johannisburg, Aschaffenburg*

cliff high above the countryside. One of the Counts of Freyberg, in whose possession Hohenaschau had been since the end of the 14C, transformed the uncomfortable Burg into a spacious Renaissance Schloss in 1561; it was rebuilt in the baroque style by the Counts Preysing, who lived in it from 1608–1853.

The main Burg, ring wall and keep date from the late 12C, the outer works are probably 13C and it was converted into a bastion-like fortress in 1561; there were further additions in the 17&20C. The chapel was rebuilt on medieval walls in 1637–9; the interior of the main Burg was decorated in 1672–86; the rococo interior of the chapel dates from the 17C.

The monumental Gallery of Ancestors in the state ballroom of the main Burg is fascinating: it consists of 12 larger-than-life-size stucco statues on pedestals. The ceiling, the walls above the doors and the marble fireplace are ornately decorated with stucco. The early baroque Italian high

altar from Verona was not placed in the chapel until the 20C. Other notable features are the two rococo side altars with paintings and stucco surrounds by J.B.Zimmermann and two wooden statuettes (1766) by I.Günther.

**Also worth seeing:** St.Mariae Lichtmess, parish church (15C,18C), and Chapel of the Cross (1753).

## Attendorn 5952
Nordrhein-Westfalen                    p.416□D 11

**Altes Rathaus** (Alter Markt): The open ground floor of this 14C building was a market hall and the upper storey a council chamber and ballroom. The step gables on the sides, the open arcaded hall and the Gothic arches in both the arcade and the upper windows are the dominant features. The interior has been modernised, and

*Altes Rathaus, Attendorn*

houses the *Heimatmuseum* (local history.)

**St.Johannes:** The square W. tower of the 14C Gothic hall church was taken over from an earlier Romanesque building. Near Attendorn is the 17C fortress *Schnellenburg*.

---

### Aufhausen, Oberpfalz 8401
Bavaria        p.422□M 17

**Pilgrimage Church Maria Schnee:** This collegiate church S. of Regensburg is visible for miles around; it is the work of the Bavarian master mason and architect Johann Michael Fischer, who designed 32 churches and 23 monasteries in S. Germany which are still standing.
The church was originally a wooden chapel, rebuilt in stone in 1672 and as a collegiate church by Fischer in 1736–51. After the plain walls of the exterior the in-

terior comes as a surprise: the spare lines of the building are redefined by the central rotunda, the chapel niches and the choir and anteroom with their round dome; a gallery is set like a wreath above the soaring rotunda. Elegant stucco work accentuates the area around the capitals of the double pilasters and the framing of the ambitious frescos. In the so-called *lady chapel* (left of the choir) is a Renaissance Augsburg altar panel (*c.*1510–15), possibly the work of Jörg Breu the Elder.

---

### Augsburg 8900
Bavaria        p.422□J 19

Augsburg, the city of the Fugger and Welser families, has produced many distinguished figures of which the best-known are Agnes Bernauer 'the angel of Augsburg' and Bertolt Brecht. Many writers have been inspired by the story of Agnes

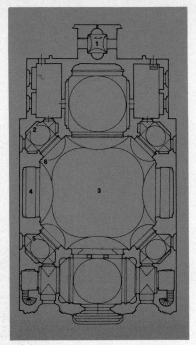

**Aufhausen 1** Statue of Virgin Mary (miraculous image), donated by Duke Wilhelm V of Bavaria **2** Image of Virgin Mary to design by Dürer **3** Ceiling painting to design by Asam **4** Side altar ('Death of St. Benedict') **5** Wooden relief of the Virgin Mary, Nuremburg school, late Gothic **6** Pietà

Bernauer and her love for Albrecht III of Bavaria. Brecht immortalised Augsburg in poems and ballads and dedicated the story of 'The Augsburg Chalk Circle' to the city of his birth.

**Dom St.Maria** (1 Frauenchorstrasse): A cathedral building was erected on the site of the first Roman settlement (Augusta Vindelicorum) under the Bishop and Saint Ulrich in the 10C. A late Roman baptismal pit has been discovered and also the walls of the cathedral's former baptismal chapel (pulled down in 1808).
*Building history:* The church was rebuilt as a three-aisled Romanesque pillared basilica with side towers under Bishop Heinrich II (1047–63) and from 1320 it was redesigned in the Gothic style and two more aisles were added; at the same time the E. section was demolished and replaced by a Gothic hall choir (consecrated 1431).
*Style of the building:* The most striking feature of the exterior is the contrast between the long, low Romanesque W. section and the tall Gothic choir building. The *choir*, which increased the length of the church by 123 yards, extends across the 'Via Claudia', the main Roman road which the first Roman camp was built to defend. The two doorways on the S. and N. sides of the choir, which also serve to mark the line of the old road, are Mary doorways, with two sections and a Madonna on the central pillar, dating from 1343 (N.) and 1356 (S.). The third doorway has the famous Romanesque bronze reliefs (*c.*1060).*Interior and furnishings:* The fact that the building is in two distinct sections means that the effects of space and light vary considerably. Under the very high W. choir is the Romanesque *crypt* (1060) and the 5 larger stained-glass windows in the nave date from the same period; they depict Jonah, Daniel, Hosea, Moses and David, and are the earliest *cycle of stained glass* in central Europe. The monumental *Bishop's throne* (probably *c.*1100) is made of stone and supported by two lions. The wall of the S. transept is painted with a 49 ft. high St. Christopher (1491). The most distinguished of the ornate furnishings are the 1493 paintings of the Life of Our Lady on the pillars of the nave by Hans Holbein the Elder, G.Petel's Man of Sorrows (*c.*1630, third N. pillar in the nave) and the bronze tombstone of Bishop Wolfhart Rot (d.1302) in the ambulatory by the Konrad chapel.*Also:* Andreas and Hilaria chapel by the S. transept (14C); Mary chapel in the cloister yard (18C); Katharine chapel (16C); cloisters and chapter house.

**St.Ulrich and St.Afra** (19 Ulrichsplatz): The two churches with their onion domes balance the Dom at the other end of the old town. The complex was formerly well

*Dom. St.Maria, Augsburg* ▷

outside the town, but is now the southernmost point of the Maximilianstrasse.

The first building was erected over the grave of St. Afra (martyred in 304) and Bishop Ulrich was buried here in 973. The late Gothic building dates from 1467–1526; the architects were V. Kindlin, B. Engelberg and H. König. Emperor Maximilian I laid the foundation stone for the choir in 1500. The preaching hall on the town side was built in 1710 in the baroque style as the protestant church of St. Ulrich.

The lofty interior (98 ft. high and 305 ft. long) is dominated by the three enormous altars in the choir. The architect, J. Degler the Elder of Weilheim, transferred the Christmas crib into the theatrical setting of an altar, and the two side altars are also reminiscent of Gothic shrines with figures. H. Reichle placed his cross altar with four monumental free-standing bronze figures in the crossing at the same time as Degler was working; it is a masterpiece of early baroque. In the various side chapels are the graves of some of the members of the Fugger family. In the W. the nave has a railing across its full width; the work is in wrought iron and wood and carries the

*Dom, S. portal*

St. Ulrich and Afra ▷

**Augsburg, Dom 1** Chapterhouse **2** Blasius Chapel **3** Catherine chapel **4** Virgin Mary chapel **5** Cloister **6** Andreas Hilaria chapel **7** Wolfgang chapel **8** Augustine chapel **9** Gertrude chapel **10** Konrad chapel **11** Anna chapel **12** Antonius chapel **13** Luke chapel **14** Bronze door, assembled from the doors of the Romanesque Dom **15** Bishop's throne, *c.* 1100 **16** Stained-glass windows with prophets, *c.* 1140 **17** Tomb of Konrad and Afra Hirn, 1423 **18** N. portal, 1343 **19** S. portal, 1360 **20** Altar panels by Jörg Stocker, 1484 **21** Altar panels by H. Holbein the elder, 1493 **22** High altar, Crucifixion by Jos. Henselmann, 1962

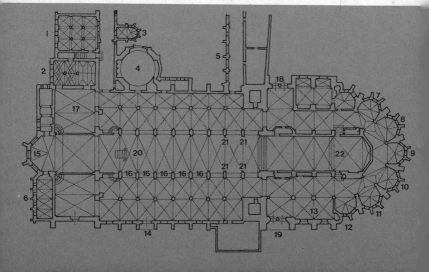

*The Zeughaus was built under the direction of E.Holl in 1602–7*

name of E.B.Bendel, an unknown smith and sculptor, as the carver. In the choir under the right side altar steps lead to the *vault* of St.Ulrich, the quarrelsome Bishop of Augsburg, decorated by P.Verhelst in exuberant rococo style (1762). The simple *Afra vault* with its late Romanesque sarcophagus stands in striking contrast.

**Church of St.Anna with Fugger Grave Chapel** (Annaplatz): The former Carmelite monastery is outwardly unassuming, but important because of its *Fugger burial chapel*, the first Renaissance building in Germany. The church was founded in 1321, rebuilt and enlarged in 1487–97 and restored by E.Holl in 1602–16; the tower in particular bears his stamp. The rococo interior dates from 1747–9. The Fugger chapel was endowed in 1509 by Jakob and Ulrich Fugger and consecrated in 1518; it was badly damaged in the War in 1944 and

in 1947 the vaulting was renewed and the grave reliefs were completed.

The original complex was transformed by baroque rebuilding, and the E. choir with its powerful buttresses is the only remaining late Gothic section. The Fugger chapel was added as the W. choir of the church, in the style of the Florentine and Venetian Renaissance. The central feature and most important work of art in the chapel is the late Gothic 'Wailing over the Body of Christ' group by H.Daucher in the sanctuary. S.Loscher was responsible for the four reliefs on the wall behind the altar. J.Breu the Elder painted the panels for the organ; they are all that remain of this valuable instrument, which was destroyed in 1944. The drawings for the reliefs on the graves of Jakob and Ulrich Fugger were by Albrecht Dürer. The *goldsmiths' chapel* on the N. side and the cloisters are also worth seeing.

**Former Dominican Church of St. Magdalena** (Dominikanergasse): Built 1513–15 as a hall church with two aisles, with rows of chapels on either side; there is fine, elegant stucco work with rococo designs by F.X. and J.M.Feuchtmayer (1716–249). The four bronze tablets on the long wall (for Emperor Maximilian I, his son and two grandsons) are evidence of the Habsburgs' prefererence for Augsburg at the time of the Renaissance. Prehistoric and Roman finds are on show in the building.

**Rathaus** (Ludwigsplatz): Built at the beginnng of the Thirty Years War by 'Stadtwerkmeister' (town superintendent) E.Holl (topping-out 1618). The interior was the work of M.Kager (to 1626), and centred on the *Goldene Saal* (Golden Hall); it was completely destroyed in the Second World War. The building in the Ludwigsplatz has seven storeys and is topped by a pine cone, the emblem of Augsburg, and framed by twin towers with verdigris-covered onion domes.

**Zeughaus (arsenal)** (Zeughausplatz): Built as town arsenal under the direction of E.Holl (1602–79), façade by J.Heinz. The Zeughaus predates the severe Rathaus

*The Rathaus (1618) was also built by E.Holl*

and is considered to be the earliest example of a baroque façade in Germany. The artistic centrepiece of the heavy design is H.Reichle's bronze group over the doorway showing Michael as Victor over Satan (1603 – 6), strongly influenced by the Michaelskirche in Munich.

**Rotes Tor** (Eserwall-Strasse): The wall and outer gate date from the mid 16C. The fortified tower was built by E.Holl in the first years of the Thirty Years War (1621&2). The tower is brick-built and has loopholes for artillery and firearms. It is often used as part of the setting for the summer *open-air opera festival* in the Wallgraben.

**Schaezler-Palais** (46 Maximilianstrasse): The Schaezler-Palais was commissioned by the banker B.A.Libert von Liebenhofen and built by the Bavarian electoral court architect K.A.von Lespilliez; it is the finest rococo building in the town. The focal point is the ballroom, which has carving by P.Verhelst and F.Xaver and stucco by S.Feuchtmayer. G.Guglielmi designed the decoration of the ballroom and also painted the allegory with figures on the oval ceiling. It represents the blessing of art and science by successful trade.

**Fountains** (Ludwigsplatz and Maximilianstrasse): The Augustus fountain outside the Rathaus and the Mercury and Hercules fountain in the Maximilianstrasse are the elegant punctuation of the city's show streets. The *Augustus fountain* by H.Gerhard, the director of the Munich court foundry, was erected to celebrate the 1600th jubilee of the city's founder, the Emperor Augustus. On the edge of the basin are 4 allegorical bronze figures symbolising the rivers of Augsburg: Lech, Wertach, Brunnenbach and Singold (1589–94). The merchant city celebrates the god of its principal trade in the *Mercury Fountain*. The figure of Mercury is a

copy (by Adriaen de Vries) of the Florentine Mercury group by Giovanni da Bologna. The *Hercules fountain* is also by de Vries (1595–1602).

**Fuggerei** (Jakobsplatz): In the Jakob suburb, below the Rathaus, is the so-called Fuggerei, the first estate for old people. It was endowed by Jacob Fugger the Rich in 1516–25. The estate is laid out at right angles and has 53 buildings containing 106 dwellings, and is reached through three gates which are closed at 10 p.m. Since 1521 the rent has been 'one Rhenish Guilder' per year, as laid down in the charter of endowment; that is DM1.71 in modern currency.

**Museums:** *Staatsgalerie* (46 Maximilianstrasse): includes pictures by Holbein the Elder, Burkmair and Dürer. *Barockgalerie* (46 Maximilianstrasse): rococo ballroom. *Maximilian-Museum* (24 Philippine-Welser-Strasse): Firearms of Emperor Karl V, architectural models by the famous architect E.Holl. *Mozart memorial* (30 Frauentorstrasse): original scores, Stein piano on which Mozart played.

**Theatres:** *Stadttheater* (1 Kennedyplatz): Opera and operetta; 994 seats. *Schauspielhaus* (Vorderer Lech): straight plays; 325 seats. *Augsburger Puppenkiste* (15 Spitalgasse): world-famous marionette theatre; 222 seats.

---

**Aumühle 2055**
Schleswig-Holstein                    p.414☐H 5

---

**Bismarck Mausoleum:** A mausoleum was built for Bismarck and his family in 1898 in the park at Friedrichsruh; it is a two-storey neo-Romanesque rotunda of Hohenstaufen type in which the marble sarcophagi are placed. *Friedrichsruh*, the former retreat of Otto von Bismarck, is now a museum with memorabilia of 'the grand old man of the Sachsenwald'.

◁ *Rotes Tor, Augsburg*

# B

## Babenhausen 6113
Hessen             p.416☐F 14

**Protestant Parish Church** (Marktplatz): This 14&15C church was restored in 1939. There is an important late Gothic carved altar in the choir (1515–18); the lavishly decorated central section has unmounted wooden figures of Pope Cornelius and Saints Nikolaus and Valentin, and the panels show other saints in relief. The altar

*Late Gothic carved altar in Babenhausen*

is generally considered to be the work of the Mainz Backoffen studio, but some scholars ascribe it to Matthias Grünewald, who was working in the nearby town of Aschaffenburg at the time. On the wall of the choir and in the S. aisle are paintings dating from the periods around 1400, 1480 and 1520 showing St. Nikolaus, Mary Magdalene's sea voyage and scenes involving martyrs. The decoration is 17C.

**Schloss** (1 Schlossweg): Originally a moated Burg; the old E. wing, an open hall with arches, dates from the Hohenstaufen period (*c.* 1210). The sculpturally remarkable capitals are copies; the originals are on show in the main building.

## Bacharach 6533
Rheinland-Pfalz          p.416☐D 14

*Baccaracum* (*altar of Bacchus*), the Roman name of the original Celtic settlement, comes from an altar stone in the Rhine which was blown up in the course of the regulation of the river in 1850. Bacharach, with its half-timbered houses and remains of town fortifications, features in more songs than any other town on the Rhine (Heine, Ricarda Huch, Victor Hugo among others).

**Ruin of Burg Stahleck:** It is only possible to gain an impression of the former castle, mentioned as early as 1135, from old prints. In 1194 the warring houses of Guelph and Hohenstaufen were reconciled by Agnes von Stahleck and Heinrich the Guelph. The remains of the splendid complex with keep, residence and fortifications were turned into a Youth Hostel in 1925–1926.

**Protestant Parish Church of St.Peter** (Marktplatz): The striking feature of this three-aisled late Romanesque basilica (1220–69) is the massive tower, which has castellations and a spire in its Gothic upper storey, and thus looks rather like a castle. The four-story interior, unusual in Germany, has the balance and vigour of early French Gothic. It was thoroughly restored after the town fire of 1872, and the paintwork was renewed in 1970 in the light of traces of the colour scheme of the original building.

**Werner Chapel:** Building began in 1289, the choir was consecrated in 1337 and building continued in 1426, but this splendid little work of art in red sandstone with a trefoil ground plan was never completed, and the lavish window tracery never glazed.

*Ruin of Burg Stahleck near Bacharach*

**Also worth seeing:** *Old house* and *Altkölnischer Saal* in the Marktplatz; *Alter Posthof*, with a Renaissace façade (1593–1594).

## Backnang 7150
Baden-Würrtemberg          p.420□G 17

**Rathaus** (Markt): Two half-timbered floors with a gabled roof are set on a stone lower storey; the stone mask corbels are particularly attractive. The Town Hall was built *c*.1600 and is a building of stately simplicity.

**Also worth seeing:** Former Parish Church/Former Collegiate Church of *St. Pankratius*, with Romanesque and Gothic elements; the choir of the former *Church of St.Michael* (13C) and the *Schloss* on the Schlossberg (1605, not completed); the *Heimatmuseum* in the Helferhaus (8 Stiftshof).

## Bad Bentheim 4444
Lower Saxony          p.414□C 8

**Prince's Schloss** (Schlossstrasse): The

Burg with its three castellated towers, once the seat of the Counts of Holland, stands on a steep cliff. The extensive complex includes buildings from the 13–19C. The keep and a round tower in the SW corner are Gothic, the so-called *Kronenburg* in the W. is largely neo-Gothic; it contains the residence, which has undergone neo-Gothic alterations, and the 12&13C ladies' quarters. On the steps of the S. terrace is the famous *Herrgott von Bentheim*, a 12C sandstone cross with a clothed figure of Christ; it was found near the Burg. The *Schloss Museum* shows local sculpture; the Schloss park is medieval and has been restored.

**Environs: Rheine** (23 km. E.): The *Church of St.Dionysios*, the *Hematmuseum* in the *Falkenhof* and *Schloss Bentlage* are all of interest.

---

**Bad Bergzabern 6748**
Rheinland-Pfalz                            p.420☐D 17

---

**Former Ducal Schloss:** The former Schloss of the Dukes of Zweibrücken is built on the site of a medieval moated Burg.

The S. building is the oldest of the four sections (1530) around the square courtyard; the other three were added in 1561 –79. The large complex started to look as it does today when its domes and baroque windows were added during rebuilding in 1725–30. The staircase tower on the courtyard side with the date 1530 on its doorway is a late Gothic relic of the period when the Schloss was built.

**Gasthaus zum Engel:** The former official residence of the Dukes of Zweibrücken is considered to be the finest Renaissance building in the Pfalz. The three-storey building (1556–79) with three gables enlivened with scrolls and obelisks, a lavishly decorated oriel at each corner, a spendid courtyard gate and two staircase towers is certainly the most beautiful of the many fine old houses in the town.

**Also worth seeing:** *Market Church* (after 1321; rebuilt in 1772, restored in 1896); *Protestant Schloss Church* (1720 – 30); *Lustschlösschen Zickzack* (17C, altered in the 19C); *Rathaus* (1705) and the towers (Dicker (fat) Tower and Stork Tower) which have survived from the town fortifications. *Heimatmuseum* with exhibits on history

◁ *Herrgott von Bentheim*                    *Ducal Schloss, Bergzabern*

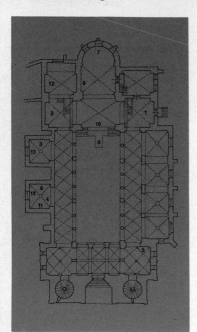

**Bad Gandersheim, canonry church 1** Stephen chapel **2** Virgin Mary chapel **3** Andreas chapel **4** Antonius chapel **5** Relief with God's hand blessing **6** Sculpture of Duke Lindolf, *c.* 1300 **7** Five-armed candlestick, early 15C **8** Bartholomew altar, *c.* 1490 **9** Three Kings' altar, late-15C **10** Triumphal cross, *c.* 1500 **11** Marienaltar, 1521 **12** Tomb of to 2 Mecklenburg abbesses, 1686 **13** Sarcophagus of Abbess Elisabeth Ernestine Antonie by Joh. Kaspar Käse, 1748 **14** Roswitha window

and crafts in the Bad Bergzabern and Wittgenstein area.

# Bad Berleburg 5920
Nordrhein-Westfalen                        p.416□E 11

**Schloss:** The present complex with three wings includes remains of a 13C Burg; the 16C building has a fine Renaissance doorway with coats of arms and a shell pattern on the top. The *red tower*, a low round building, also dates from this period. The baroque, three-storey middle section was

built in 1731–3, and the S. stable wing at the end of the 18C. The *music room*, with its fine stucco and gallery, has survived in its original form. The *Princes' Art Collection* with 17&18C furniture, weapons and portraits and the *library* with manuscripts and rare prints are open to the public. N. and S. of the Schloss are fine gardens with summer house and sculpture.

# Bad Dürkheim 6702
Rheinland-Pfalz                        p.420□D 16

Bad Dürkheim was already famous in Roman times for its woods, wine and spa; the 'Dürkheimer Wurstmarkt' (sausage market), despite its name the biggest wine festival in the world, takes place each year in September.

**Former Schloss Church of St. Johannes/Protestant Parish Church:** The three-aisled church is largely 14C (neo-Gothic tower 1865–6). The various tombs, including that of Count Emich IX and his wife, are notable.

**Also worth seeing:** On the Kästenberg near Bad Dürkheim are remains of a Celtic ring: 'Heidenmauer' (heathen wall). The rock drawings on the Krimhildenstuhl on the E. edge of the Kästenberg are evidence of the existence of a Roman quarry. Heimatmuseum (22 Eichstrasse): Local history.

# Bad Gandersheim 3353
Lower Saxony                        p.414□H 9

Bad Gandersheim was the home of Roswitha von Gandersheim (*c.*935–973), the first German poetess, who lived here as a nun and wrote spiritual plays, epics and legends in Latin.

**Münster/Former Canonry Church of St. Anastasius and Innocentius** (Wilhelmsplatz): The canonry was founded in 852 by Liudolf, the grandfather of Heinrich I, and rebuilt on various occasions af-

*Marienaltar, Münster, Bad Gandersheim*

ter destruction by fire. The church is unmistakeable because of the two octagonal towers which, along with a central section, form the façade. The towers were probably built in the course of alterations in the 15C, when five Gothic chapels were added to the original 11C building. The best features of the lavish furnishings are the *Bartholomäus altar* (*c*.1490) the *Marienaltar* (1521), the *Dreikönigsaltar (Three Kings altar)* (15C) and a five-branched *bronze candelabrum* (*c*.1425); in the Andreas Chapel is a *sarcophagus* for Princess Abbess Elisabeth Ernestine Antonie (mid 18C) and in the Mary Chapel *tombs* of two abbesses. In the E. of the Münster is the *Michael Chapel*, which dates from *c*. 1050 and is now used as a Catholic church. W. of this chapel is the Renaissance abbey *c*. 1600. The *Kaisersaal*, in a wing added in 1730, is well worth seeing; it is lavishly decorated with stucco and pictures of important ecclesiastical and secular figures.

**Georgskirche** (on the W. edge of the town): The original church was built long before the town, although some of the building is 15C and the half-timbered choir is 16C. The dour, peasant-like tendril decoration of the three-aisled interior is unorthodox; the high altar dates from 1711, and there is a life-size 15C wooden figure of St. George.

**Rathaus** (Am Markt): When the Town Hall, one of the finest Renaissance Town Halls in Lower Saxony, was rebuilt after a fire in 1580 the Moritzkirche was incorporated; this church was originally a filial church of the Georgskirche, which stood outside the town. The W. section of the Town Hall is a later addition. There are fine half-timbered houses around the market place (Nos. 8 and 9 among others) and the Heimatmuseum (No 10).

**Former Benedictine Monastery Church of St. Maria and Georg** (in

Clus): The three-aisled *basilica* of the former Benedictine monastery, dissolved in 1596, has survived. The central feature of the interior is the Lübeck *altar* (1487), a lavishly carved representation of the Coronation of the Virgin.

**Gandersheim Cathedral Festival:** The festival has taken place in June every year since 1959 outside the W. front of the cathedral (Münster).

**Environs: Brunshausen** (1 km. W.) On a spur W. of the Gande is the oldest monastery in S. Lower Saxony (780), subordinated to the nearby monastery of Clus in 1134 and turned into the *Benedictine Nunnery of Brunshausen* before 1200. The square, groin-vaulted 15C *choir* and the Romanesque *S. side apse* can still be discerned in the building, which is now used for commercial purposes.

---

**Bad Herrenalb 7506**
Baden-Württemberg                          p.420☐E 18

**Former Cistercian Monastery Church:** The monastery of Herrenalb was

*Münster, Bad Gandersheim*

founded to complement nearby Frauenalb. The minster sacristy, the old tithe barn and the *parvis* remain from the old building. In 1462 a steep *gable* with a Gothic window and a little ridge turret were added on the entrance side. In the Romanesque parvis the free-standing *groups of columns* and the stepped doorway in the W. are notable. Of the church itself, which was altered in the 15C, only the *choir* (1427) and its *side chapel* remain; the tower and the nave date from 1739. At the side of the Gothic choir is the *cenotaph* of Margrave Bernhard of Baden (1431), probably created by artists from the Strasbourg area. An exhibition on the history of the monastery and a collection of hand-made *roof tiles* can be seen on Saturdays from 10–12 in the *Heimatstube* in the Städtische Kurverwaltung building.

---

**Bad Hersfeld 6430**
Hessen                                      p.416☐G 12

**Stift ruins:** It was a good idea to hold the *Hersfeld Festival* in summer each year in the thousand- year-old Stift ruins (now weatherproof). If the church were still

standing it would be the largest Romanesque church in Germany. After the much-extended old church was destroyed by fire, the huge columned basilica with its long nave was started in 1040. In 1761 the church was burned down by the French during the Seven Years War, and it has been in ruins ever since. The *Städtisches Museum* is housed in a former 16C *monastery building*, and there are regular exhibitions in the former chapter house. The oldest bell in Germany, the 900 year old Lullus bell, hangs in the *Katharine tower*, built in the 12C and restored in the 19C.

**Rathaus:** The original Gothic building was rebuilt in 1597 as a three-storey building in two sections. The high roof has large stone gables in the Weser Renaissance style. The *council chamber* has a fine stucco ceiling and a door lavishly decorated with marquetry work.

**Old town:** Some stone Gothic and Renaissance buildings and numerous half-timbered houses (15–19C) remain in the centre of the old town.

**Also worth seeing:** The Gothic *Protestant Church of St. Vitus and Antonius* (1330–c.1500), thoroughly restored after a fire in 1952.

included 10 12C *double columns* from the cloisters of the monastery of Brauweiler.

**Protestant Erlöserkirche (Church of the Redeemer)** (1 Dorotheenstrasse): The main doorway of this domed church, built in neo-Romanesque and neo-Byzantine style in 1912–8, was modelled on St. Gilles near Arles. The interior is based on St.Mark's in Venice, and the furnishings are a lavish display of gold mosaic and marble.

**Saalburg Limes fort:** 7 km. NW of Bad Homburg is the best-preserved Roman fort in Germany. It was built in AD 120 to defend an important pass in the Taunus and could accommodate a cohort (c. 500 men). The original wooden building was replaced by a stone fortress in the 3C. From 1898–1907, as part of the wave of historicism encouraged by Kaiser Wilhelm II, the building was restored as the Romans would have left it: a stone ring wall with four gates, in the centre of the camp the main building with two courtyards, administrative buildings and the chapel where the

*Tomb of Margrave Bernhard von Baden (Strasbourg area, c. 1431) in the former Cistercian monastery church in Bad Herrenalb*

---

**Bad Homburg vor der Höhe 6380**
Hessen                                           p.416□E 14

**Schloss** (Schlossplatz): Landgraf Friedrich II von Homburg extended the medieval centre of the town by building a new town for the Huguenot refugees from France. He lived himself in the new Schloss, which he built in 1678 to replace the old Burg. The keep, the *White Tower* is the only surviving part of the 14C complex. The Schloss is an extensive but plain building; the only decorative features are the three lavish *doorways*. In a niche of the doorway of the archive building is a *bronze bust* by A. von Schlüter of Friedrich II, who was the original of Kleist's 'Prinz Friedrich von Homburg'. On the W. side of the upper courtyard is a hall, added in 1900, which

standards were kept. On the site of the stores and granary there is now a *museum* of archaeological finds, and around the fort are traces of the camp village and fort baths.

**Also worth seeing:** The *Heimat- und Hutmuseum* (120 Luisenstrasse) (local history and hats) and late neoclassical *houses and spa buildings*.

---

## Bad Iburg 4505
Lower Saxony                                           p.414 □ D 8

**Bishop's Schloss and Benedictine Monastery:** The Schloss and the monastery share the same site; there is only one distinct hill on the S. slopes of the Teutoburger Wald, and it was here that in the 11C Benno II, Bishop of Osnabrück, made the remains of a prehistoric fortress into a residence and founded the monastery of Iburg. The Bishop's palace is in the W., the monastery buildings are in the E., the monastery church is in the middle, and there used to be a jousting ground in front of the extensive complex. The *Bishop's palace* has the dimensions of a Burg, and as

time passed its defensive character became more important. (Bishop Konrad von Rietberg, 1482–1508, increased the height of the keep). The most attractive feature of the Schloss today is the *Rittersaal*; it was built from 1656 to plans by J.Crafft and the ceiling pictures with perspective, by the Italian painter A.Aloisi, were among the first in Germany. The *monastery church* is largely 11C, but it was altered in the 13C and (after a fire in 1349) in the 15&16C. The most striking feature of the furnishings is the *sandstone sarcophagus of the founder* Benno II but the 12C *gravestones* for Gottschalk von Diepholz in the N. transept and the 14C memorial to Ritter Ameling von Varendorf and his wife are of greater artistic significance. The *monastery buildings* face the town and the present three-wing building was built in 1751–3 to plans by J.C.Schlaun. The church is linked to the monastery buildings by the cloisters. The façade is decorated with larger- than-life-size sandstone figures of St.Clemens and Benno II. The fine stucco ceilings are by J.Geitner. The chapel is an important feature; it was built in 1665–7 by Ernst-August von Braunschweig-Lüneburg, the first Lutheran bishop. Abbot Norbert of Iburg wrote a biography of

*Stift ruins, Bad Hersfeld*

Benno II, the founder of Iburg; it is one of the most important ecclesiastical biographies of the period.

**Also worth seeing:** A little distance away from the Schloss is the little *Freudenthal hunting lodge*, completed in 1594. 13–14C *Catholic Fleckenskirche* with a 13C font and 17C sculptures and tombs.

# Bad Karlshafen
Hessen                  p.414☐G 10

Karlshafen lies at the confluence of the Diemel and the upper Weser and was founded in 1699 by Landgraf Carl von Hessen-Kassel as a Weser port; he introduced a population of Waldensians and Huguenots. It is the best surviving baroque town in Hessen built to a uniform plan. Landgraf Carl is said to have been personally involved in the design of the town, in co-operation with the Huguenot architect Paul du Ry. The rectangular harbour is the centre of the town, with large square blocks of plain two-storey houses on its long sides.

**Rathaus:** The Town Hall (1715–18) is on the S. side of the harbour; it was once a customs house and lodging for the Landgraf, and has a ballroom with fine stucco work.

**Other houses in the baroque town:** The *Invalidenhaus* (1714–10), SE of the harbour, has three storeys and a fine courtyard; opposite is the *Freihaus* (1723); to the NE the *Thurn und Taxis Post Office* (1768) is the last building in the older part of the town. Many other buildings survive from the time of the foundation of the town, all built to a uniform plan.

**Environs: Helmarshausen** (3 km. S.): The ruins of the *Krukenburg*, originally built in 1220 by Archbishop Engelbert of Cologne, are on a little hill. The tall, round *keep*, large parts of the defensive wall and towers and the 15C residence still stand. The ruins of the *Johannis chapel*, a Romanesque rotunda, have also survived; the chapel, which originally had a dome and four low barrel-vaulted transepts, shows the influence of the Near East (Church of the Holy Sepulchre in Jerusalem). The *former Benedictine Abbey of St.Maria and Petrus* (10C) was known in the 11–13C for its monastic craftsmen (goldsmiths and illuminators of manuscripts); little remains

*Bad Iburg, Schloss and Benedictine monastery*

*Rittersaal, Schloss Iburg*

of the building today except the sandstone E. wing of the abbey with 2 biform windows (capitals of the central columns *c*.1130) and an E. chapel with a semicircular apse and burial vault.

---

### Bad Kreuznach 6550
Rheinland-Pfalz                p.416□D 15

---

**Protestant Paulus Church** (auf dem Wörth): P.Hellermann incorporated earlier medieval buildings into his hall church with one aisle in 1768–81. The choir, transepts and W. façade remain of the Gothic church (1311–32); the nave and tower are baroque. In the choir the 14&15C *portrait tombstones* and in the nave the *altar* 1777 and the *pulpit* are worth seeing.

**Catholic Parish Church of St.Nikolai:** In 1281 the Carmelites enlarged a late Romanesque chapel built in 1266; it be-

came an early Gothic basilica with three aisles, consecrated in 1308. The interior has massive round pillars and groin vaulting. The gilded silver *crucifix reliquary* in the church treasure is worth seeing; its upper part was made *c*.1390 and its base by H. von Reutlingen in 1501.

**Nahe bridge:** Part of the bridge, which formerly had eight arches, and two of the houses built on it have survived between Badewörth island and the bank of the Nahe; it was mentioned in 1495, and has now become a symbol of the town.

**Ruins of the Kanzenburg:** The Burg was built *c*.1200, blown up by French troops in 1689 and redesigned by D.Böhm in 1971–2. The Kanzenburg is popular for its restaurant specialising in food cooked to medieval recipes.

**Kurhaus:** This neo-baroque building built in 1913 by Emanuel von Seidl was

*Krukenburg near Karlshafen*

an important headquarters in the First World War and in 1958 the meeting place of de Gaulle and Adenauer; it is now an hotel.

**Karl-Geib-Museum** (69 Kreuzstrasse): The municipal museum has housed the *gladiator mosaic* from the *Roman Villa* since 1968. The mosaic shows gladiators fighting with each other and with wild animals.

**Also worth seeing:** The *Salinental* with graduation works and medieval salt-mining buildings extends over several kilometres.

---

**Bad Mergentheim 6990**
Baden-Württemberg                    p.420☐G 16

From 1525–1809 Bad Mergentheim was the residence of the Teutonic Order, and the Grand Masters of the Order had great influence on the development of the town.

Its regular layout has been largely retained and the N. to S. and E. to W. axes are clearly recognisable. Many famous names are associated with Bad Mergentheim; perhaps the most famous is the Romantic poet Eduard Mörike (1804–75), who married Margarete von Speeth, the daughter of his landlady, in the town. Bad Mergentheim owes its present importance as a spa to the springs discovered in 1826.

**Catholic Münster of St. Johannes** (Kirchstrasse): The Münster was built in 1250–70 by the Knights of St. John of Jerusalem and taken over by the Teutonic Order in 1554. The vaulting was completed in 1584 and the princes' choir in 1617. The 17C marble relief, a monument to Marquard von Eck, Commander of the Teutonic Order, is a striking feature of the church.

**Former Dominican Church of St. Maria** (Hans-Heinrich-Ehrler-Platz): The church, started in 1312 and completed in 1388, lost a great deal in the neo-Gothic restoration of 1879; the *Eck chapel* (1607) remains. The *bronze memorial* for Grand Master Walther von Cronberg (d. 1543), thought to be by H.Vischer of Nuremberg, is really the only interesting feature. In the adjacent Mary chapel the 14C *frescos* on Dominican mystical themes are worthy of mention.

**Schloss:** The former moated Burg has been in the possession of the Teutonic Order since the 13C; the present building largely grew out of the modifications and extensions of 1565–70. The various towers, the 1626 entrance tower, the Blaser tower and keep in the main section, and the 1574 NW tower are the most distinctive features of this very varied complex. The lavishly decorated spiral staircase in the NW tower is notable; it leads to a hall on the second floor decorated in early classical style by F.S.Bagnato in 1778–82. F.J.Roth, B.Neumann and F.Cuvilliés were involved in the building of the *Schloss church* (today a Protestant church), although Neumann and Cuvilliés only provided a few designs. Striking features of the interior are the frescos by the Munich master N.Stuber

(1734); a vault houses tombs of various Princes of the Order.

**Market place and Rathaus:** The market place, which is surrounded by numerous fine old houses, is divided into an upper and a lower part by the Town Hall (1564); the Engelapotheke and the 'Straussen' inn, now a bank, are other impressive buildings.

**Deutschordens- und Heimatmuseum** (im Schloss): In the W. part of the Schloss, which is in the Renaissance style, is the museum, housed in the former Quarters of the Grand Master of the Teutonic Order. The exhibits include a collection of dolls, and memorabilia of the poet Eduard Mörike; the stucco in the museum is by F.Cuvilliés and most striking.

---

**Bad Münstereifel 5358**
Nordrhein-Westfalen          p.416☐B 13

**Former Collegiate Church of St. Chrysanthus and St. Daria** (Langenhecke): The most striking feature of this 10C building, restored in the 19C, is the massive W. front. The nave of the Roman-

*Schloss, Bad Mergentheim*

*Half-timbered buildings, Münstereifel*

esque pillared basilica is supported on plain arches; it contains the crypt, the graves of the church's patron saints Chrysanthus and Daria, F.Roir's 1480 tabernacle and the table tomb of Gottfried von Bergheim (d.1335). The font (1619) and the 14C carved wooden Madonna are two other important individual elements of the lavish furnishings.

**Rathaus** (Marktstrasse): The building has two distinct parts; on the left stepped gables and oriel turrets and on the right a loggia with three bays and a mansard roof. It was built in 1350 and 1550, but has been much extended and refurbished.

**Also worth seeing:** *Haus Windeck Orchheimerstrasse*: This 1644 half-timbered house is one of the finest and most important in the Rhineland. *Town fortifications:* 13&14C sections have survived in part; the best of the four gates is the NE *Werthertor*. The *Toni-Hurten-Heimatmuseum* is in a 12C Romanesque building; it covers the history of the town, medieval crafts and 14–16C furniture.

**Environs: Iversheim** (4 km. N.): there is a *Roman lime-kiln* in this suburb.

## Bad Nauheim 6350
Hessen                                    p.416☐E 13

Salt was mined on the site of the present town in Celtic times. From 1905 the town was replanned on a generous scale to produce what is probably the largest uniform complex of Jugendstil buildings in Germany.

**Kurhaus:** This set of buildings by W.Jost (1908–9) is a good example of Jugendstil architecture with neo-baroque ingredients. It consists of two main buildings with 16 small, differently-shaped *courtyards*, some of which are lavishly decorated. There are open arcades around the large *Sprudelhof* (fountain courtyard). In the *Kurpark* is the *Rabenturm* (1742–5).

**Also worth seeing:** On the 879 ft. *Johannisberg* are remains of a 2C Roman signalling tower and the 13C walls of the octagonal W. tower of a church. Today there is an *observatory* on the Johannisberg. The *Salzmuseum* (20–22 Ludwigstrasse) has exhibits on ancient and medieval salt-mining, and on the history of the town.

*Fountain courtyard, Bad Nauheim*

**Bad Orb 6482**

Hessen                   p.416□F/G 14

Bad Orb, set in a wooded valley in the Spessart, owes its prosperity and fame to the salt-water springs which made it a health resort for heart, circulatory and rheumatic diseases. The town grew round a rectangular market place and its distinctive appearance comes from the many half-timbered buildings (17–19C), particularly in the Lange Reihe, Am Tor, an der Weinreihe and below the church; the 13C town wall is largely intact. The *Salzmuseum* is in the *Sölder Tor* (1704–5), which has a little bell tower.

**Catholic Parish Church of St.Martin** (Pfarrgasse): The importance of this church derives from the centre panel (*c.*1440) of the *altar triptych* by the Master of the Darmstadt Passion, but this was destroyed along with other works of art when the church was damaged by fire in 1983; a reopening date has not yet been fixed.

**Spessart-Museum** (8 Villbacher Strasse): Minerals and fossils from Europe, Africa and North America; also exhibits on local history.

**Also worth seeing:** *Rathaus*: the *Rathaus* and the *Städtisches Heimatmuseum* are housed in the former administrative building of the salt works (19C); interesting salt-mining buildings such as the boiling houses have also survived in the town.

**Bad Reichenhall 8230**

Bavaria                    p.422□N 21

Bad Reichenhall was a settlement even before Roman times; it has large salt deposits and salt springs, and has thus become one of the most important health resorts in Germany; this fact is reflected in its architecture.

**Münster Church of St. Jeno:** The church was largely complete by 1208 and was dedicated in 1228; it is the largest Romanesque church in Upper Bavaria. The remarkable W. portal in red and grey marble is strongly influenced by the portals of Upper Italy (Trento and Verona). The outer pair of columns is supported by lions couchant and the tympanum shows

*St.Martin, Bad Orb*

Mary and the Christ Child with St.Zeno and St. Rupert. The interior was refurbished by P.Intzinger after a fire at the beginning of the 16C, and its distinctive Romanesque articulation was lost in the process. The Romanesque *cloisters* in the adjacent *monastery buildings* are worth a visit (open Sundays 11–12). On one of the columns is a relief of Friedrich I Barbarossa, a patron of the monastery. Another relief shows the fable of the fox, the wolf and the crane, an allegory of ingratitude.

**Heimatmuseum** (4 Getreidegasse): History of the town, collections of ecclesiastical art, folk art and peasant life.

**Also worth seeing:** Old salt works and spa buildings, parish church of St. Nikolaus (1181) and St. Agidi.

# Bad Säckingen 7880
Baden-Württemberg                   p.420□D 21

The 'Trumpeter of Säckingen', a verse epic by Victor von Scheffel (1854), brought the town literary fame. Scheffel, who lived and practised as a lawyer in Säckingen from 1849–51, told in his poem of the love of the bourgois Franz Werner Kirchhofer for the noble Maria Ursula von Schönauw. The story, which happened in Säckingen in the 17C, is commemorated by a gravestone in the Münster.

**Former Nunnery Church of St. Fridolin/Münster** (Steinbrückstrasse): The church started as part of a mission founded by the Alemannic apostle Fridolin on the former Rhine island in 522. Despite baroque additions the present building is essentially Gothic and dates from the 14C (nave 15C, towers 16C). Several fires led to considerable renovation and alteration, and the Münster is known particularly for the lavish rococo decoration which was added after the fire in 1751 by J.M.Feuchtmayer (stucco) and F.J.Spiegler (frescos); the high altar is by J.P.Pfeiffer (1721). Other notable features are some fine 17&18C tombs on the outer

wall of the choir, the choir stalls (1682) and the church treasure, which includes the shrine of St. Fridolin (Augsburg silver, 1764). There are remains of the old nunnery building around the church square.

**Schloss Schönau/'Trumpeter' Schlössle** (Schönaugasse): The romance which Victor von Scheffel used as the model for his epic 'Der Trompeter von Säckingen' was played out in this Schloss, which dates from 1500 and was built on the site of an earlier Romanesque building. It now houses the *Heimatmuseum*.

**Rathaus** (by the Münster): An early 19C building, attached to several houses which were built largely after the fire and subsequent plundering of 1678. The most important of the surviving houses is 15 Rheinbrückenstrasse with an 18C stucco façade.

**Rhine bridge:** The bridge is roofed throughout its length and is one of the oldest wooden bridges in the world.

**Hochrheinmuseum** (Schlossplatz): The museum is housed in the 'Trompeterschlössle'; it specialises mainly in primeval, pre- and early history and also has local and regional art-historical collections, including interesting collections of trumpets and watches and memorabilia of Victor von Scheffel.

# Bad Schussenried 7953
Baden-Württemberg                   p.420□ G 20

**Former Premonstratensian Monastery and Monastery Church:** The monastery was founded in 1183 but very little remains from this period; the original church was repeatedly altered, then destroyed and replaced by a new building; the present furnishings date from 1710–46. The dominant feature of the interior is the *nave fresco* by J.Zick (1745), showing scenes from the life of St.Norbert, the patron saint of the Order. The (1715–17) *choir stalls* are of particular interest: they show the development of the world in theologi-

cal terms, beginning with plants and animals and ending with the saints, carved with an exuberant delight in shapes and forms. The *high altar* and an Upper Swabian *statue of Mary* (*c.* 1450) in the side aisle are notable. The former monastery complex is famous above all for its *library* (1754–61), designed by D. Zimmermann. The space is enclosed by galleries on columns and the room is decorated with excellent stucco work, and grisaille and fresco painting. In front of the columns are figures of apostles in dispute with groups of putti, a symbolic representation of false doctrine. The spines of books behind the glass of the cupboards are painted dummies.

**Farmhouse museum** (in Kürnbach): Exhibits on the history of the town and peasant culture.

---

**Bad Segeberg 2360**
Schleswig-Holstein                     p.412□H 3

This salt and moorland resort on the Segeberger See has since 1952 attracted more than 100,000 spectators to the Karl-May festival in its open air theatre with a cliff as a natural stage set.

**Marienkirche/Former Monastery Church of the Augustinian Canons** (Kirchplatz): This brick church, one of the oldest in Germany, goes back to the 1260s. It has been much altered and extended but is still considered to be one of the finest examples of brick architecture in N. Europe. The capitals, transoms and archivolts were decorated with plaster even at this early period; the supply was assured by the nearby lime pit. The most important feature of the furnishings is the *carved altar* with many expressive figures representing the Passion. The altar dates from 1515. The *triumphal cross* above it is early 16C and the *pulpit* was added in 1612. An area with two aisles and fine rib vaulting N. of the choir is the only surviving part of the former *monastery*.

**Alt-Segeberger Bürgerhaus** (15 Lübecker Strasse): There are many old houses in the Lübecker Strasse including this 16C half-timbered house with gables, which now houses the *Heimatmuseum*.

**Environs: Bad Oldesloe** (16 km. S.):

◁ *St. Fridolin, Säckingen*                     *Library, monastery of Schussenried*

There is a 1634 altar with oak reliefs by H.Heidtrider in the 18&19C *Protestant Church of St. Petrus*.

**Altfresenburg** (14 km. S.): Interesting features are the so-called *Fresenburg Wallberg* by the Trave, the remains of a Slavonic rampart, and the manor house on the *Altfresenburg estate*, built by C.Hansen in 1791.

---

**Bad Urach 7432**
Baden-Württemberg                    p.420 □ G 18

**Former Collegiate Church of St. Amandus/Protestant Parish Church:** The core of the church dates from 1477–1500, when P. von Koblenz built a late Gothic basilica for Count Eberhard the Bearded. The tower did not reach its final height until the 19C and the choir arch was not painted until the 20C, but more important are the *furnishings*, which date from the time when the church was built. The lavishly carved *praying desk of Count Eberhard* dates from 1472. The *pulpit* was erected shortly after the completion of the church, but the sounding board was not added until 1632. The lower part of the pulpit is decorated with figures of the saints and the central section with church fathers; above that is ornate tendril decoration; this work is important 16C stonemasonry. The *choir pulpit* has to be seen in conjunction with this main pulpit. The choir stalls are notable despite a certain amount of renewal. The 1518 font in the baptistery between the choir and the aisle is by the sculptor Christoph von Urach. There is 15C stained glass at the end of the S. aisle, and there are memorial stones in the choir.

**Residenzschloss** (Bismarckstrasse): The Schloss, which was built from 1443, now houses a branch of the Würrtembergisches Landesmuseum in Stuttgart (q.v.). On the second floor is the *Goldene Saal* created by Duke Eberhard the Bearded in 1474 but not decorated as it is today until the 16&17C. The ceiling beams are supported by four Corinthian columns and the doors have ornate frames; another impressive feature is a lavishly decorated tiled stove.

**Rathaus and market place:** The fine half-timbered Town Hall is supported by free-standing wooden supports. The building was completed in 1562. The market

*Bad Segeberg, panorama with open-air theatre*

fountain in front of it is even older (1495 –1500) and is topped with a figure of St. Christopher (copy). The other half-timbered houses around the large market place are also hundreds of years old.

**Albvereins- and Historisches Museum** (Schloss): This has exhibits on the history of the town and a weapon collection from the Württembergisches Landesmuseum.

---

**Bad Waldsee 7967**
Baden-Würrtemberg                    p.420☐G 20

---

**Former Augustinian Canonry Church of St. Peter:** The body of the church, which dates from 1479, has survived but the building was so thoroughly restored in the 18C that it can almost be assigned to this period. This impression is confirmed by the two corner towers which frame the gracefully curving W. Façade. Only in the interior can traces of late Gothic be found, but here too the baroque is dominant; the finest feature of the ornate furnishings is the high altar by D.Zimmermann (1715), and its two splendid side altars with carved figures (between 1720–30). Another important feature of the furnishings is the bronze grave slab for Georg I Lord High Steward of Waldburg (d.1467), one of the most brilliant achievements of late Gothic pictorial art.

**Rathaus** (am Markt): The Town Hall, started in 1426, has been renovated on many occasions, most recently in 1975–7. Over the façade gable, which has blind niches with pointed arches and a tracery gallery, is a 1657 baroque bell gable. In the interior the Ratssaal (council chamber, wooden coffered ceiling) and the Ratszimmer (council room, remains of 1526 frescos) are worth a visit. The 19C *Kornhaus* is opposite the Town Hall.

**Schloss** (7 Schlosshof, W. of St.Peter): The former moated Burg, built in 1550, was considerably extended in 1745; the most important part is the Schloss chapel.

**Museums:** *Städtisches Heimatmuseum* (Kornhaus): 14–18C sculpture and domestic life in the 18C. *Kleine Galerie* in the Elisabethen-Bad: painting and sculpture.

**Also worth seeing:** There are remains of the 13C town wall of which the 1280 Wurzach gate was also a part.

*Carved altar of Augustinian Canons' church in Bad Segeberg*

## Bad Wildungen 3590
Hessen                                   p.416□F 11

**Protestant Parish Church of St.Maria, St. Elisabeth and St. Nikolaus** (Am Markt): The building was started in the first half of the 14C but not completed until the end of the 15C; the funerary chapel attached to the N. side of the tower was added in 1505. The tower dome was completed in 1811. In the almost square hall the groin vaulting is supported on slender pillars. The church is famous for the Wildungen altar by Konrad von Soest (see also Dortmund, Marienkirche). This cycle by Soest dating from the early 15C is one of the most important achievements of German painting. When closed the altar shows St. Katharine, St. John the Baptist, St. Elisabeth and St.Nikolaus and when open (it is then almost twenty ft. wide) it shows the Childhood, Passion, Resurrection and Ascension of Christ, the Miracle of Pentecost and the Last Judgement. Further interesting features: numerous tombs, including that of Samuel von Waldeck by A.Herber in 1579, a late Gothic crucifix above the altar (1518) and the Schmid organ (1982).

*Town church, Bad Wildungen*

**Also worth seeing:** Old town with numerous well-preserved or restored half-timbered houses, particularly in Brunnen-Hinter- and Lindenstrasse and the old town pedestrian area. *Schloss Friedrichstein* (in Alt-Wildungen): A Schloss going back to a *c.* 1200 Burg; the Schloss has an excellent baroque interior dating from the mid 18C. It was restored in 1976–80 and houses a *museum of weapons and uniforms.*

**Environs: Bergfreiheit** (10 km.S.): A restored *copper mine*, which gives an impression of the history of the trade in this area.

## Bad Wimpfen 7107
Baden-Württemberg                        p.420□F 16

Wimpfen lies at the confluence of the Jagst and the Neckar and was a fortress in Roman times; it has belonged to the bishops of Worms since the 9C. The Hohenstaufens built one of their largest palaces on German soil here. Wimpfen was a free imperial city from *c.*1350–1803.

**Former Imperial Palace (Kaiserpfalz):** This was built *c.*1180 on the Altenbeg, and is of sectional design, with a residence and splendid arches, and also a hall for use as a courtroom and for purposes of state. Beside it is the Gothic Steinhaus, the residence of the Burggraf. The palace chapel with its imperial gallery is worth seeing. In the W. is the Blue Tower, built of blue stone. The circular wall of the complex is still accessible to a large extent.

**Also worth seeing:** *Protestant Parish Church of St.Maria,* mentioned in documents in 1234; this is a large Gothic hall church, though the lower part of the building under the E. towers is Romanesque; *Benedictine Monastery of St.Peter,* the W. building and its two towers are Romanesque, the nave and E. parts 13C; the E. parts are perhaps the work of Erwin von Steinbach, who was responsible for Strasbourg Cathedral; the old furnishings are

*Bad Wurzach, staircase in the Schloss* ▷

notable. The *old town* has 15&16C houses and attractive fountains; the *Steinhausmuseum*.

**Environs: Mosbach** (20 km. N.): The old town of Mosbach still has numerous *half-timbered buildings* (15–19C), including the *Palm'sche Haus* (1610) and the *Rathaus* (1558&9); in the *cemetery chapel* (15C) are extensive cycles of late Gothic wall painting (1496).

**Gundelsheim** (10 km. N.): The 16–18C *Schloss Hornbeck* houses the *Heimatmuseum* (local history) and the *Siebenburgische Museum* with interesting collections of costumes, pewter and jewllery.

---

**Bad Wurzach 7954**
Baden-Würrtemberg                    p.420☐G 20

---

**Catholic Parish Church of St. Verena:** The three-aisled flat-roofed nave (1775–7) is predominantly in the classical French style. The most notable features are the *ceiling paintings* of Biblical figures and princes in contemporary costume and the *high altar* with a group of figures by J.A.Feuchtmayer in the upper niche.

**Nunnery of Maria Rosengarten** (next to the parish church): This institution was founded in the 16C by the High Stewardess of Waldburg and the building is of interest today for its attractive *staircase* (1764) and the little *rococo chapel*.

**Former Princes' Schloss:** The *Alte Schloss* has an 18C *chapel* giving access to a modern church. The *Neue Schloss* has three wings and a courtyard and was built in 1723–8, possibly by J.C.Bagnato. Its most remarkable feature is the 'finest *staircase* in Upper Swabia' in the gabled central pavilion; the staircase, lavishly but elegantly decorated, rises in graceful double flights around a trefoil centre space to the ceiling fresco of the Apotheosis of Hercules. It is assumed to date from the mid 18C but astonishingly it is not known who built it; regular *concerts* are held here.

*Also worth seeing:* The 1695 *Heilig-Geist-Spital* and the 1696 half-timbered *leper house*; the baroque *Pilgrimage Church of the Holy Cross* on the Gottesberg (1709–13).

**Events:** The *Wurzacher Blutritt*, a pilgrimage on horseback to the Gottesberg on the second Friday in July.

*Baden-Baden, ruins of a Roman bath*

**Environs: Arwach** (7 km. S.): *Catholic Parish Church of St. Ulrich and St. Margaretha:* A hall building of 1744–9 ascribed to J.G.Fischer, with a late Gothic tower from an earlier building (baroque spire 1761) and fine altars (Crucifixion group by J.F.Sichelbein on the 1700 high altar); the stucco and painting date in part from 1930.

## Baden-Baden 7570

Baden-Württemberg        p.420☐D 18

The Roman Emperor Caracalla bathed here in the Imperial Baths of 'Aquae Aureliae' in the year 213. In the 19C the baths became the meeting-place of Parisian society and the European and Russian aristocracy. Dostoevsky's novel 'The Gambler' is based on an experience in the casino at Baden-Baden, Gogol and Turgeniev wrote here and Balzac spent time with Mme Hanska, whom for most of his life he loved only from a distance. Mark Twain depicted life in this fashionable watering place in his book 'A Tramp In Europe'. As early as 1500 there were 12 bath houses here and 389 individual bathing cubicles, and the great doctor Paracelsus made use of the healing springs to save Margrave Philipp I from death in 1526.

**Former Collegiate Church of Our Lady/St.Peter and St.Paul** (Marktplatz): The church was built on imperial territory over the ruins of the Roman baths and was referred to as a parish church in 1245, but only the lower part of the tower has survived from the early building. The church was rebuilt in the 15C as a wide hall church with a high nave. A choir was built on to the N. aisle *c.*1460, and a complementary building in Gothic style was added to the S. aisle 200 years later; the upper storey of the tower dates from the 18C. The interior is dominated by an eighteen ft. high *sandstone crucifix* brought here from the old cemetery. It is a work of late Gothic naturalism by Nikolaus Gerhaert von Leyden, whose studio also provided the sculpted figures on the *tabernacle*. The splendid memorial tomb of Margrave Ludwig Wilhelm I (Louis the Turk) is the finest of the long series of *tombs* in the choir. The commander, his marshall's baton in his hand, stands on the altar tomb surrounded by allegories, trophies and emblems in honour of his victory over the Turks. An-

*Cistercian abbey of Lichtental in Baden-Baden*

The *municipal historical collection*, which includes archaeological finds from Roman times, is housed in two of the wings.

**Cistercian Abbey of Lichtental** (40 Hauptstrasse): The Nunnery of Lichtental is a little way outside the town; it was founded by Irmingard, the granddaughter of Henry the Lion, in 1243 and still functions as a nunnery. The building itself is 14&15C; Irmingard's gravestone is by the Strasbourg Master Wölfelin von Rufach. There are Gothic wall paintings (*c*.1330) in a grave niche in the choir. In the *Fürstenkapelle* (N. of the church) the panels of the 1496 altar are on show. The three sandstone figures over the entrance to the chapel (*c*.1300) are from the Black Forest monastery of Allerheiligen (q.v.).

**Kurhaus:** Baden-Baden became a fashionable resort at the beginning of the 19C. F.Weinbrenner of Karlsruhe, a strict neoclasical architect, transformed the 18C Promenade building into the present Kurhaus with its serene columned hall in 1821–4. He also modified the Capucine monastery bought from the monks by the publisher Cotta (now the *Badische Hof*) and built the *Palais Hamilton* (now the Städtische Sparkasse) in 1808.

*Lichtental*

other important feature is the niche grave of Philipp I, whose effigy lies on the coffin in his knight's armour.

**Niederbaden Neues Schloss** (Schlossstrasse): The Burg was the residence of the Margraves of Baden from 1479 but they moved their seat to Rastatt (q.v.) after the destruction of Baden-Baden in 1689. The late Gothic Schloss was built in the 16C under Margrave Philipp II. The so-called *Kavalierbau* (rebuilt in 1709) and the *Küchenbau* (from 1572), with a two-storey loggia and a storey with windows added in the 19C, are built around a courtyard in the shape of an irregular rectangle. The centrepiece is the main Schloss, the so-called *Renaissance Palace*, which has a portal and thermal baths on its ground floor. The architect of this rational and lucid building (219 ft. long) was K.Weinhart of Munich (1573–5). Only two of the many towers shown by Merian's 1634 engraving of the Renaissance Schloss have survived.

**Theatre:** *Theater Baden-Baden* (Goethe-Platz): The theatre was built in 1862 to plans by C.Couteau, and has its own company; 512 seats.

**Also worth seeing:** Altes Schloss Hohenbaden (12–15C, in ruins since 1590); the Fremersberg hunting lodge (1716–21) and the Protestant church on the Fremersberg built in 1958.

---

**Badenweiler 7847**

Baden-Württemberg                    p.420☐C 20

**Burg ruins:** Part of the 12C Hohenstaufen fortress has survived (residence and defensive walls); it was destroyed in 1678, but still attracts tourists with its fine views over the Rhine plain.

*Ruins of the former Hohenstaufen fortress, Badenweiler*

**Ruins of the Roman baths** (in the Kurpark): The thermal springs of Badenweiler have been flowing since Roman times. The ruins of the Roman baths were discovered by chance in 1784. Four bathing halls and side rooms with under-floor heating form the centre of the baths, which cover an area of 3,280 square yards. The extent of the baths suggests that they served a *Roman settlement* of considerable size.

**Also worth seeing:** *Kurhaus* (1972), built in terraces on the slopes of the Burg hill. *Kurmittelhaus* (1875; extended in 1906–8, 1954–8 and 1979–81). In the *Protestant Church* (1892–98) are 14C frescos (legend of the three living and the three dead men). The *Catholic Parish Church of St. Peter* (1960) is architecturally interesting; it has an elliptical ground plan and a free-standing tower. In the *Kurpark* (oldest parts 1758) is a memorial tablet to the Russian dramatist and writer of short stories Anton Chekhov, who died here in 1904.

**Baldern = 7085 Bopfingen**
Baden-Württemberg                    p.422□H 17

**Schloss:** The Schloss goes back to the mid 12C but the present building is essentially late baroque. Its best feature is the *Schloss church*, consecrated in 1725, for which G.Gabrieli provided the principal ideas; he was also responsible for the design of the three altars. The stucco work is by the Degging artists J.Jakob and U.Schweizer. Inside the Schloss the *Fürstenbau*, which also has lavish stucco work, is an important feature. The Schloss houses an important *collection of historical weapons*, ceramics and faience.

**Balingen**
Baden-Württemberg                    p.420□E 19

**Protestant Church:** The church has a

*Zollernschlösschen, Balingen*

massive tower based on the one at Rottweil (q.v.). The most striking feature of the interior is the stone *pulpit* by Master Franz (early 16C). The sounding board is by S.Schweizer of Balingen.

**Also worth seeing:** The 15C *Zollernschlösschen* was completely refurbished in 1930 and now houses the *Heimatmuseum* (local history, including a reconstructed dyer's shop) and the *museum of scales and balances*, which has exhibits from all over the world.

---

**Balve 5983**
Nordrhein-Westfalen                    p.416☐ D 11

---

**Catholic Parish Church of St.Blasius** (Am Kirchplatz): The plain hall church with three bays and a cross gable roof is typical of the South Westfalian Romanesque style. The overall impression of the complex is unfortunately impaired by the excessively large neo-Romanesque extension in the N. The transept and choir date from the end of the 12C and the nave, the W. tower and the sacristy from the mid 13C; the portals are without sculptural or other decoration. The heavy square pillars and dome vaulting in the nave also make a stern and serious impression. In the apses there are still remains of mid-13C *late Romanesque wall painting* (Christ as Judge of the World with saints and apostles) and early Gothic painting (1334, heavily restored in part). The furnishings also include a Romanesque censer, a late Gothic crucifix (late 15C) and a representation of St.Blasius (early 16C), the patron saint of the church.

**Balve cave** (1 km. N. on the B 229): This is the largest historically significant cave in Germany; neolithic tools have been found in it. They are on show, along with Bronze and Iron Age exhibits, in the *Vorgeschichtliches Heimatmuseum* (Museum of Local Prehistory).

---

**Bamberg 8600**
Bavaria                                p.418☐ J 15

---

Bamberg, the seat of the Counts of Babenberg, became a bishopric under Emperor Heinrich II (973–1024) and the spearhead of the Mission to the East; the Dom (cathedral) is its architectural and spiritual centre. Since the 14C the Rathaus has been the bottleneck between the ecclesiastic and secular parts of the town; it is now a baroque gatehouse tower with a solid mass of buildings on either side. The towers of the many churches soar above the confused mass of gables, some clad in pointed tiles and others in blue slate: a uniquely intact townscape, which also survived the last war without damage.

**Dom** (Am Domplatz): The present cathedral was built in the 13C on the site of an older building by Heinrich II; it owes

*Fürstenportal of the Dom in Bamberg* ▷

*Bamberg horseman*

*Empress Kunigunde, imperial tomb*

**Bamberg, Dom 1** Fürstenportal **2** Adamspforte, c. 1215-20 **3** Gnadenpforte **4** Screens of the Georgenchor choir, 13C a) Apostles b) Prophets **5** Figures from Fürstenportal, 13C a) Ecclesia b) Synagogue **6** Dionysius, 13C **7** Laughing angel, 13C **8** Virgin Mary **9** Elizabeth **10** Effigy of Clement II, 13C **11** Horseman **12** Annunciation relief **13** Altar tomb of Pope Clement II in the Peter choir, 13C **14** Monument to Prince Bishop Friedrich von Truhendingen, 1366 **15** Monument tp Prince Bishop Friedrich v. Hohenlohe, 1352 **16** Monument to Prince Bishop Albert v. Wertheim, 1421 **17** Monument to Prince Bishop Philipp v. Henneberg, 1487 **18** Monument to St. Heinrich and St. Kunigunde by Tilman Riemenschneider, 1499 ff. **19** Virgin Mary altar by Veit Stoss, 1523 **20** Painting of Georgenchor choir by K. Caspar, 1928

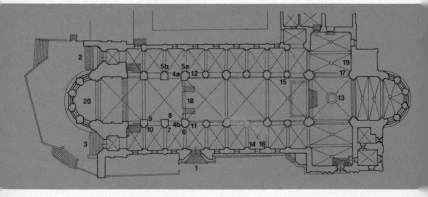

*Tympanum of the Marienportal*

its fame to its series of sculptures (Bamberg Reiter) and its portals.

*Building history:* The old cathedral was closed on all sides like a fortress. The new Hohenstaufen building (1215–37) was of a different design with four towers. The upper storeys of the E. towers and the spires of all four towers were added by J.M.Küchel (1766–8), a pupil of Balthasar Neumann.

*The building:* The Dom, with its four towers and three-aisled basilica, is a typical Romanesque building and even the Gothic parts follow the Romanesque design. It is a characteristic of German Romanesque architecture that the church has choirs in the E. and the W. (see Speyer and Worms).

*Interior and furnishings:* The E. choir has a dome above its windows with a fresco by K.Caspar (1928). In the W. choir and the W. transept there is deeply-incised groin vaulting. Under the E. choir is a three-aisled *crypt*. The portals on the E. side are

particularly attractive (the *Adamspforte* and the *Marienportal*, also known as the *Gnadenpforte*) and on the N. side (Fürstenportal, with Last Judgement), as are the pairs of Apostles on the walls of the Georg choir. It is probable that the famous *Bamberger Reiter* (left of the approach to the Georg choir), Maria, the 'laughing' angel, the norn-like Elisabeth, St. Dionysius and the statues of *Ecclesia* and *Synagoge* were originally on the portals. The oldest of the doorways is the *Adamspforte*; the figures of Emperor Heinrich, Empress Kunigunde, St.Stephanus, Peter and Adam and Eve, the first sculptures of the Middle Ages, were once on this portal, but are now in the *Diözesanmuseum* (5 Domplatz). In front of the E. choir is the *double sarcophagus* of Emperor Heinrich and Empress Kunigunde, a high tomb in Solnhofen slate with the imperial couple on the lid and reliefs on the side. It is a work of Riemenschneider (1499–1513) in late Gothic pleated style. On the last pil-

*Queen of Sheba, late-14C choir stalls, Bamberg Dom*

*Ratsstubenbau (1570–77) in the Alte Hofhaltung in Bamberg*

lar (left of the Peter choir) is the excessively thin figure of Bishop Friedrich von Hohenlohe as an old man, a work of the Würzburg Wolfskeel master (1352). The *Bamberg altar* by V.Stoss (1520–5) is now behind it on the wall at the W. end of the aisle; it is a Mary altar with the birth of Christ and reliefs on the panels, all in natural wood and unmounted. The third important sculpture in the W. choir of the Dom is the *Kreuzaltar* by J. Glesker (1648–53) with high baroque larger-than-life figures mounted in gold. The late 14C *choir stalls* are also notable. The *treasure* includes the imperial cloaks of Heinrich II and Empress Kunigunde, the imperial dalmatic (liturgical vestments) and the expensively mounted skulls of Emperor Heinrich and Empress Kunigunde.

**Alte Hofhaltung and Neue Hofhaltung** (8 Domplatz): The Alte Hofhaltung is attached to the N. side of the Dom, on the site where Kaiser Heinrich II built his palace in 1020, when the Dom was also under construction. The half-timbered wings in the courtyard, looking like a house on a country estate, are 15C. The *Ratsstubenbau* (1570–7) has pleasantly curving gables and an ornate oriel. Opposite the Renaissance building is the baroque *Neue Hofhaltung*, also known as the *Residenz*, largely built by J.L.Dientzenhofer (1697–1703) and housing a section of the *Bavarian State Painting Collection* and the *State Library*. In front of the building to the NE on a garden terrace is the *Rosarium*.

**St.Michael** (Michaelsberg): This church was founded by Emperor Heinrich II shortly after the Dom (1015), destroyed by an earthquake in 1117 and rebuilt in 1121 by Bishop Otto the Saint. The Romanesque apse was replaced by a narrow late Gothic choir in 1570, and in 1610 the upper parts of the towers were completed in the same style; in 1696 W.Dietzenhofer erected the W. Façade in front of the towers and in 1723 the wide steps and balustraded terrace were added. The flat ceiling was replaced in 1610 with vaulting painted with the 'botanical garden': the design in-

*Cloister, Carmelite church* ▷

cludes over 600 native and foreign plants. The high tomb of St.Otto (d.1189) is under the choir and an access 'tunnel' is provided for pious devotees of the saint. On the right and left of the narrow choir are rococo choir stalls with seats and panels by H.E.Kempel and Servatius Brickard.

**St.Martin** (Grüner Markt): G.Dientzenhofer and his son Johann Leonhard chose deeply incised arched niches, like those of 'Il Gesù' in Rome, as the distinctive feature for the façade of this church. The building dates from 1686 – 91, and was decorated and furnished by Italians. The central vault has a false dome painted on it. The Jesuit College attached to the church was a University for a time and once housed the *municipal library* (now in the new Residenz), which has a collection of manuscripts and drawings.

**Obere Pfarrkirche** (Unterer Kaulberg): The massive choir (with ambulatory), supported by arched buttresses, towers over the broken pattern of the chapel roofs. The church was first mentioned in the 11C; high Gothic new building (from 1338) in the style of the churches of the Mendicant Order; choir 1375–87; vaulting until 1421.

Access from the N. side is by the so-called Ehepforte (marriage doorway), a portal with Wise and Foolish Virgins and the Ascension and Coronation of Our Lady (*c.*1360). With the exception of the miraculous picture on the high altar (*c.*1330) the furnishings are essentially 18C. In the sixth ambulatory chapel is a fine *tabernacle* in sandstone with decorative reliefs.

**Baroque buildings:** Some of the baroque buildings in the town are of exceptional quality: *Rathaus* (Obere/Untere Brücke): the first river bridge was built at this point in 1157, and the first gatehouse in 1321. The present Town Hall building was erected in 1467 on a pile frame and given its baroque form by J.M.Küchel in 1744 –56. The curved mansard roof and openwork lantern with lavish balconies on either side are outstanding examples of the Franconian rococo of the Main area. The *Palais Concordia* (Concordiastrasse) was built in 1716–22, probably for Geheimrat Böttinger (now the State Research Institute of Geochemistry). Two wings at right angles form a garden parterre with a watergate on the Regnitz side. The *Böttingerhaus* (Judengasse) was built in 1707–13 for the same patron as the Palais Concordia and

*St.Michael*

*Old Rathaus with bridge* ▷

its exuberant décor has been accommodated to the cramped surroundings in a masterly fashion. The *Raulino-Haus* (1709–11) and the *Erbracher Hof* (1764–66), in which the Cash Office of the Superior Court (Oberjustizkasse) is housed today, are also worth seeing. Downstream of the Rathaus is an old row of fishermen's houses with geraniums on their wooden balconies known as *Little Venice*, and in this area old inns known as 'Schlenkerla' serve the famous Bamberg Rauchbier ('smoky beer'). *E.T.A.Hoffmann-Haus* (26 Schillerplatz): E.T.A.Hoffmann was conductor from 1804–14 at the theatre here (memorial in 26 Schillerplatz). This musical tradition is continued by the *Bamberg Philharmonic Orchestra*, who as the 'German Philharmonic Orchestra' moved from Prague to Bamberg.

**Museums:** The *Diözesanmuseum*, which houses the Dom treasure, is in the chapterhouse of the Dom. Other museums include: *Neue Residenz* (8 Domplatz): The Neue Residenz was built in 1599–1610 as the last residence of the Prince Bishops in Bamberg by J.Wolf the Elder and completed by J.Dientzenhofer in 1697–1703. This architectural monument houses exhibits on domestic life in the late baroque, rococo and classical periods. The *Staatsgalerie Bamberg* is also in the Neue Residenz; it is a division of the Bavarian Department of Castles, Gardens and Lakes, and shows 15–18C European painting. The *Historisches Museum* (7 Domplatz) has collections on art, crafts and anthropology. The *Karl-May-Museum* (11 Hainstrasse) is a memorial to the writer run by the Karl May Press, which is based in Bamberg; exhibits include May's study and library. The *Gärtner-und-Häcker-Museum (Museum of gardening and wine-growing)* (34 Mittelstrasse) has exhibits on the history of Bamberg's agricultural community and a collection of traditional costumes.

**Theatre:** *E.T.A.Hoffmann-Theater* (7 Schillerplatz): The theatre was reopened in 1958 after being damaged in the Second World War. It has its own company. 465 seats.

**Also worth seeing:** There are other fine churches in Bamberg, including *St.Jacob* (founded *c.*1070 and consecrated in 1111, altered in the 13&15C and also in the 18&19C); *St.Stephan* (consecrated 1020,

*Benedictine monastery, Banz*

altered at various times; the present building dates from the 17C), Protestant parish church since 1801; the *Karmelitenkirche* (13C, baroque reconstruction by J.L.Dientzenhofer); *St. Gangolf* (consecrated in 1063, extended in the 15C and altered subsequently) and the *former Dominican Church* (1310, with various later modifications), now used as a concert hall. *Also:* the former princes' Schloss *Geyserwörth* on the island in the Regnitz.

## Banz = Staffelstein 8623

Bavaria                                    p.418□J 14

**Former Benedictine Abbey:** The castle-like monastery in yellow sandstone with its twin-towered church is set on a plateau high above the Main and visible for miles around; it balances Vierzehnheiligen (q.v.) on the other side of the river. A fortified Benedictine monastery was founded by Countess Alberada of Schweinfurt in 1069; it was handed over to the Bishop of Bamberg in 1071, and a church was consecrated in 1114, but destroyed in the Thirty Years War. J.L.Dientzenhofer started to rebuild the monastery in 1695 and in 1710–19 his better-known brother J.Dietzenhofer was responsible for the church; the gatehouse wing in the main courtyard was built in 1752 to plans by B.Neumann.
The complex is approached from the Main side through a gate decorated with rococo tendrils and lively statuary; on its right and left are two-storey buildings, each ending in corner pavilions, as planned by B.Neumann. Beyond the steward's courtyard is the convent building, and then a little higher still comes the abbey building; this change of level causes a pleasing graduation of the various parts of the roof. The most important feature of the exterior design of the church is the vaulted façade between the two massive towers with their high curved domes. Figures of saints with dramatic expressions on their faces stand in the niches of the various levels and on top of the tower balustrades. The sculpture on the façade is by B.Esterbauer (1713). Despite the rectangular ground plan of the church the interior gives the impression of

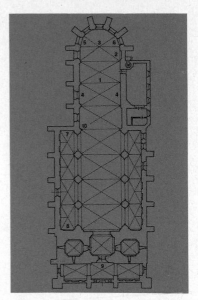

**Bardowick, Dom 1** Bronzefünte (font), 1367 **2** Tomb slab of Dean Hermann Schomaker, 1406 **3** Carved altar, 1425; pedestal *c.* 1404 **4** Choir stalls, late-15C **5** Tabernacle, late Gothic **6** Epitaph to Jakob Schomaker by Albert v. Soest, 1579 **7** Epitaph to Dr. Wilhelm v. Cleve (d. 1600) **8** Epitaph to Johannes Förster (d. 1547) **9** Portal, c. 1170 **10** Pulpit

being an elongated oval. The magnificent decoration was designed in part by Dientzenhofer. The most striking features are the *ceiling frescos*, the outstanding *choir stalls*, the *high altar*, the *choir altar* and the *pulpit*. In the abbey the *abbot's chapel* and the *Kaisersaal* can be visited.

## Bardowick 2123

Lower Saxony                               p.414□H 5

**Protestant Parish Church of St.Peter and St.Paul** (Dom): After the destruction of this once important trading centre by Henry the Lion in 1189 the Collegiate Church of St.Peter and St.Paul, known to local people as the 'Dom' (cathedral) was built. Of the late-Romanesque complex, built in 1220–30, the W. building in light

*Bardowick, St. Peter and St. Paul*

ashlar, another section with two towers and an inner porch, and the gallery remain. The nave was pulled down in 1380 and replaced with a Gothic brick hall which is entirely in harmony with the older parts of the building: it has a broad rib-vaulted nave and heavy round pillars. The two-panelled carved altar of 1425 is at the focal point of the very bright interior. The choir stalls were carved with reliefs of saints by two Lüneburg masters.

## Bassenheim 5401
Rheinland-Pfalz · p.416□C 13

**Catholic Parish Church:** The church was built in 1899–1900 and is of no architectural interest, but on the N. side altar is one of the finest works of German medieval sculpture the *Bassenheim Rider*, an almost completely three-dimensional relief in whitish-grey Main sandstone (3 ft. 9 ins.

by 3ft. 10 ins.) representing St. Martin sharing his coat with the beggar. The relief was not discovered by scholars until 1935, when they established that it had been brought to Bassenheim from Mainz, probably from the cathedral; it was identified as an early work of the Naumburg Master.

## Bassum 2830
Lower Saxony p. 414□F 6

**Collegiate Church:** The church is part of the Protestant charitable institution for ladies housed in the same complex. The former canonry was founded in the mid 9C by Ansgar, the famous Bishop of Bremen and Hamburg, but the present brick church was not consecrated until 1351. Its Romanesque origins can be discerned in

*Bassenheim Horseman* ▷

the squat shape of the buildings, and particularly in the heavy crossing tower, but the decoration on the E. gable and on the openings in the tower is definitely Gothic. The spacious transept and the light choir are impressive features of the interior.

## Baumburg (Chiemgau)
Bavaria                                    p.422□M 20

**Former Augustinian Canonry Church St.Margarethen:** The church with two towers and unusual pointed onion domes is visible for miles around. It stands on a steep bank on the site of a former Burg of

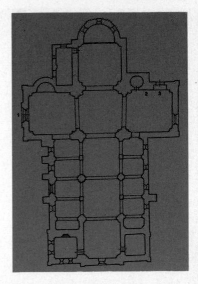

**Bassum, collegiate church 1** Main portal, so-called 'Brautpforte', 19C building, with some 13C sections **2** Monument of Abbess Anna, Countess of Hoya (d. 1585) **3** Figure of St. Mauritanius, 19C

the Counts of Chiemgau. The first building was consecrated in 1023 and the present church was built on the Romanesque foundation walls in 1754–57. The undecorated exterior does not prepare the visitor for the lavishness of the interior decoration: very fine rococo stucco work by the Wessobrunn School, excellent carving on the altars, pulpit and choir stalls, and putti all over the church. The ceiling paintings are by a Bohemian court painter, and those in the nave show scenes from the life of Augustine, the patron saint of the order (1756 – 7). The imposing high altar in stucco marble has 4 larger-than-life figures of saints and is considered to be one of the finest baroque altars in S. Bavaria. There are concerts of sacred music in the church in the summer.

---

**Bayreuth 8580**

Bavaria                                      p.418☐K 14

A settlement founded by the Counts of Andechs was first mentioned in 1194 and received its charter in 1231. It quickly recovered from being destroyed by the Hussites in 1430 and became a Margrave's residence at the beginning of the 17C. In the 18C Margrave Friedrich the Much-Beloved and his wife Wilhelmine, the favourite sister of Frederick the Great, completed several splendid baroque buildings, but they ran into financial difficulties, which were probably one of the causes of their subsequent decline. The town fell to Bavaria in 1810. In 1872 Richard Wagner added to Bayreuth's reputation by making it his home and founding the world-famous annual festival of his music.

**Protestant Parish Church of the Trinity** (Kanzleistrasse): This is one of the most impressive late Gothic churches in Upper Franconia; it was rebuilt in its present form in 1611–14 by M.Mebart, who retained many of the stylistic elements of the earlier building. The nave of the three-aisled basilica is supported by plain and flying buttresses. The staircase towers are baroque in character, and the building method and detail suggest the influence of disciples of Parler. The two towers, rising in massive cube-shaped sections with a linking bridge, have become one of the symbols of the town. The Renaissance *sacristy door* is the finest of the five portals; it has pilasters on either side and a triangular gable with obelisk above it. In the in-

*Festival theatre in Bayreuth*

terior the aisles are divided by Gothic arches supported on octagonal pillars. The church is evenly lit by high windows decorated with tracery. The baroque furnishings were for the most part removed by 19C purists. The *high altar* was built *c.*1615 to plans by H.Werner, who also worked with V.Dümpel on the carving; the pictures on the panels are 19C. Werner was also responsible for the reliefs on the font, which deal with the theme of baptism. There are numerous fine tombs.

**Villa Wahnfried** (48 Richard-Wagner-Strasse): Wagner had the large cube-shaped building built by J.Wölfel in 1847 in late neoclassical style. Outside the entrance is a bust of Wagner's patron Ludwig II, and Wagner and his wife Cosima are buried in the garden.

Richard-Wagner-Festspielhaus (Festspielhügel): The festival theatre was built in 1872–6 by G.Semper on the Green Hill NE of the town. The interior is based on the principle of the classical amphitheatre. The theatre has seats for *c.*1900 people and is noted for its excellent acoustics.

**Markgräfliches Opera House** (Opern-

strasse): The old baroque opera house first gave Wagner the idea of living in Bayreuth and establishing his festival here, but the theatre was used by the court for its own entertainment, and was the opposite of the democratic establishment which Wagner was looking for. The building, sandwiched between two houses, has an inconspicuous exterior; it was built in 1745–8 at the suggestion of Markgäfin Wilhelmine. The interior is by the famous Italian theatre architects G. and C.Galli Bibiena and is decorated with overwhelming magnificence in red, brown, green and gold. The stage perspective is interesting: the wings, designed by Galli Bibiena, go back almost 100 ft. The Bavarian State Theatre gives guest performances of opera and ballet in the summer.

**Altes Schloss** (Maximilianstrasse): The Altes Schloss can be recognised from a distance by its octagonal tower, which was built with a spiral ramp so that horses could be ridden up it (1565&6); there is a very good view from the top. The Schloss has three wings and was built in several stages in the 17C; the façade is decorated with unusual bust medallions created by E.Räntz of Regensburg in 1691. J.St.Pierre

*Villa Wahnfried*

added the *Schloss church* to the complex in 1753–6; it has been a Catholic church since 1813. It is a hall-like building with light-hearted rococo stucco work and contains the graves of Markgräfin Wilhelmine and her husband.

**Neues Schloss** (21 Ludwigstrasse): The fountain outside the Schloss is also by E.Räntz (1698). The New Schloss was commissioned from J.St. Pierre by the Markgräfin in 1753–4. The decoration of the rooms indulges Wilhelmine's taste for nature motifs: palms, cedars, birds, insects and dragons: China was in fashion at the time. On the ground floor the tufa grottoes, arbours and flower beds show a coquettish and sentimental view of nature which is typical of the 18C. The Neues Schloss houses the *Städtisches Museum (Municipal Museum)* (pre- and early history, local history, ceramics, faience, glass and tankards) and a branch of the *Bayrische Staatsgemäldesammlung (Bavarian State Collection of Paintings)* (16–18C painting).

**Eremitage (Hermitage)** (NE of the town): The first 'Hermitage' the *Altes Schloss* was built on the site of a former zoo; court society spent their time here pretending to be hermits and shepherds in the French fashion—an 18C social game. The complex was built in several phases between 1715 and 1750. Wilhelmine provided the creative ideas here too, and also had the *Neues Schloss der Eremitage* built close by. The *sun temple*, which has a gilded quadriga on top, has a neoclassical simplicity which makes it one of the finest rotundas of the late rococo period. In the park there are a natural theatre, a dragon's cave (1743), cascades and also a hermit chapel. Not far away is the grave built by Wilhelmine for her dog Folichon, in the form of an antique ruin.

**Museums:** *Städtisches Museum* and *Gemäldesammlung:* The Municipal Museum and a section of the Bavarian State Painting Collection are housed in the Neues Schloss (q.v.). *Deutsches Freimaurermuseum (Masonic Museum)* (1 Im Hofgarten): This museum has an exhibition and library devoted to the history of free-

masonry in Germany. *Richard-Wagner-Museum* (Villa Wahnfried): a collection and archives on the life and work of Richard Wagner.

**Also worth seeing:** The town has many fine patrician houses (particularly in Maximilianstrasse and Friedrichstrasse) and has retained much of its old Franconian charm. *Also:* The Schlösschen St.Georgen (1725) on a lake N. of the town and the Thiergarten hunting lodge (1715–20) S. of the town.

**Environs: Creussen** (9 km. S.): This little medieval town has walls and towers from the 15C *town fortifications* but is largely famous for its *Creussen stoneware*, which can be seen in the *Städtisches Krügemuseum*. The *church* dates from 1474–7 and has baroque redecoration and some *carved figures* (1703–9), by the Bayreuth court sculptor E.Räntz, on the pulpit and the organ.

**Lindenhardt** (16 km. S.): The *Protestant parish church* went through various late Gothic building phases. The 1687 choir altar, endowed by Bindlach in 1687, is worth seeing for its early works by M.Grünewald (1503): the *tempera pictures* show the *14 Auxiliary Saints* (inside the panels) and the *Man of Sorrows* (back of the shrine) There is also an interesting pictorial grave, with portraits of the priest Degen and his wife (c.1703), by E.Räntz in the choir.

---

**Beckum 4720**

Nordrhein-Westfalen　　　　　　　p.414☐D 9

**Catholic Priory Church of St. Stephanus:** The foundations of 3 earlier buildings have been excavated under the present church, a Gothic hall church begun at the end of the 13C and completed in 1516; the nave includes the W. tower of the Romanesque building. Among the furnishings are an octagonal 13C *font* with reliefs in the Romanesque monumental style. One of the treasures is the *Pruden-*

*tia shrine* consisting of a wooden core covered with embossed silver, gilded and lavishly decorated. On the sides of the saddle-roofed shrine Christ, Mary and the 12 apostles are depicted, standing between double columns with trefoil arches (1240).

---

### Bedburg 5012
[Nordrhein-Westfalen          p.416☐B 11

**Wasserschloss:** The almost square complex with an inner courtyard and corner towers was one of the earliest brick Burg buildings in the Rhineland and, despite the fact that it was built in various periods (1300–1600), it forms a unified whole. The two-storey column arcades which form the boundary of the inner courtyard are considered an architectural masterpiece.

---

### Beilngries 8432
Bavaria          p.422☐K 17

**Schloss Hirschberg** (3 km. NW): Behind the two late medieval gatehouses, with tor-

ture chamber and dungeon, is the former summer residence of the Prince Bishops of Eichstätt, a serene rococo building. Prince Bishop Anton of Strasaldo had the fortress redesigned by M.Pedetti in 1760 –4. Behind the rococo railing is the main courtyard with two long wings; it has a gatehouse arch decorated with amusing gnomes. The great hall, study and oriel room among others are decorated with cheerful stucco work. The two-storey *baronial hall* is hung with portraits of Anton von Strasaldo and paintings of the most important places in the diocese. The Prince Bishop had a fresco of the sacrifice of Iphigenia painted on the ceiling (1774 by M.Franz). The Schloss is now a centre of spiritual exercise for the Eichstätt diocese.

**Also worth seeing:** The 15C ring walls and and nine defensive towers are still largely intact. The Mary Chapel was built in 1683 and enlarged in 1753, the former Franciscan monastery was built in 1763 and the cemetery church of St.Lucia dates from 1469–76. In *Köttingwörth* there are *frescos* (*c*.1300) in the baptismal chapel of the Catholic Parish Church of St.Vitus which are worth seeing.

*Prudentia shrine, Beckum*

## Beilstein 5591
Rheinland-Pfalz                    p.416□C 14

**Catholic Parish Church** (am Josefsberg): The three-aisled hall church was built over a period of almost fifty years and was finally completed in 1738; it has strikingly fine *baroque furnishings*.

**Burg Metternich:** The Burg, which dates from the 12–15C, was inherited by Freiherr von Metternich in 1637; he was an ancestor of the Prince and Austrian chancellor who brought about the renewal of Europe after the Napoleonic Wars. The Burg has been in ruins since it was sacked in 1689. There is an interesting Merian engraving of 1689, which gives a good impression of the former extent of the complex.

## Benediktbeuren 8174
Bavaria                           p.422□K 21

**Former Benedictine Monastery:** The monastery of Benediktbeuren, with the craggy Benediktinerwand as a backdrop,

not only drew attention to itself as a considerable architectural achievement, but also as a cultural centre. The text of the 'Carmina Burana', set to music by Carl Orff in 1937, was written here in the 12–13C. Benediktbeuren has been a Salesian monastery and college since 1930. There are concerts in the summer.

**Church of St. Benedikt:** This church and monastery are the oldest foundations of the Benedictine Order in Upper Bavaria. The present early baroque building dates from 1680–6, and is on the site of a late Gothic complex. The nave is a broad pilastered hall which gives the impression of being rather squat; it has a shallow barrel-vaulted roof and deep side chapels with low galleries above them. The whole building shows Italian influence, but this is most evident in the lavish stucco decoration on the pilasters, arches and vaulting. H.G.Asam, the father of the famous Asam brothers, was responsible for the ceiling frescos and his son Cosmas Damian painted the picture on the Antonius altar. J.M.Fischer's oval *Anastasia chapel* N. of the sanctuary is a jewel of baroque architecture (1750–8). Two stucco marble pilasters joined by cornices give the small

*Schloss Hirschberg near Beilngries*

space a monumental look. The side altars are ascribed to I.Günther. The silver gilt bust reliquary of St. Anastasia is by E.Q.Asam. Some of the lavishly decorated rooms in the monastery are the work of J.B.Zimmermann.

**Museum:** *Historische Fraunhofer-Glashütte* (126 Fraunhoferstrasse): The collections trace the development of the optical industry.

---

## Bensberg = 5060 Bergisch-Gladbach 1
Nordrhein-Westfalen                 p.416☐C 11

**Neues Schloss** (Schlossstrasse): This was once a hunting lodge, but has now been turned into a barracks. Elector Johann Wilhelm von der Pfalz commissioned his court architect Count M.Alberti to build a palace on the model of Versailles. It was a large, symmetrical complex with loosely related buildings rendered in white. Plain two-storey constructions purpose-built in 1838, the height of Prussian guard houses, have replaced the single-storey pavilions with mansard roofs. Only a few pieces of

stucco work and painting remain of the former furnishings.

**Alte Burg** (Engelbertstrasse): The Alte Burg dates from the 12&13C and was the favourite home and dower house of the Counts of Berg, but fell into disrepair after the Neues Schloss was built. Three towers of this Romanesque building and parts of the outer walls were skilfully included in the modern Town hall complex.

**Museum der Stadt** (17 Burggraben): Collections include the history of Bensberg, anthropology, geology and mining and the paper and leather industries.

---

## Bensheim 6140
Hessen                              p.416☐E 15

**Catholic Parish Church of St. Georg** (Am Marktplatz): This neoclassical church was built in 1826–30, in the early Christian and Roman basilica style, on the site of a Romanesque church. When it was rebuilt after the Second World War the Romanesque tower which had been incorporated into the 19C building was replaced

*Former Benedictine monastery, Benediktbeuern*

by a modern façade with two towers, and two new side towers were added to the choir. The interior is also freely based on early Christian church architecture. The tall, slender columns, the barrel vaulting in the nave and the flat coffered ceilings in the aisles are all neoclassical (renewed 1963 on the basis of old plans). Notable features of the furnishings are the paintings on the side altar and a late Gothic *tower monstrance* (15C).

**Houses:** 16–18C half-timbered buildings are the characteristic feature of the town, which was a settlement in pre-Roman times and was later owned by the monastery of Lorsch. Remains of the town fortifications have survived.

**Auerbach Schloss** (in Bensheim-Auerbach): The Burg in Bensheim-Auerbach was built by the monastery of Lorsch in the 13C to protect its estates. It was in ruins from the French incursion of 1674 until it was restored in 1903. There is a 246 ft. well-shaft in the courtyard.

**Fürstenlager:** The former spa complex of the court of Hessen-Darmstadt is also in Bensheim-Auerbach. A remedial spring was discovered in 1738 and pavilion-like buildings were grouped around it; they were all completed by the end of the 18C.

**Bergsträsser Heimatmuseum** (Marktplatz): Pre- and early history, peasant and bourgeois domestic culture, crafts, guild life.

**Environs: Heppenheim** (5 km. S.) has kept its medieval appearance; it has many 15–18C *half-timbered houses*, including the 13C *former Mainz Amtshof* (5 Amtsgasse) which houses the *Volkskundemuseum für Odenwald, Bergstrasse and Ried* (folklore museum). The so-called *Schindersburg* (122–124 Siegfriedstrasse) and the *Rathaus* (1551) are stately half-timbered buildings.

---

**Berching 8434**
Bavaria                                    p.422☐K 17

This 'Rothenburg of the Upper Pfalz' in

the valley of the Sulz, with its almost unchanged medieval façade, is a major tourist centre with the newly-founded *Heimatmuseum* as an additional attraction. The *town fortifications* are intact and even the oak doors of the four town gates are still in existence. The *Chinese tower* is the most important of the nine *defensive towers*.

**Parish Church Mariae Himmelfahrt:** The early Gothic parts of this church, renovated in 1983&4, were considerably extended by the Eichstätt court sculptor M.Seybold from 1756 onwards. The dominant features of the interior are the *ceiling paintings* by J.M.Bader and the lavish *rocaille stucco work* (1758).

**Church of St.Lorenz:** The walls of the nave suggest an earlier, 11C building. The lower parts of the tower are 13C. The church's present appearance was determined by rebuilding work started *c.*1680; it was renovated in 1982. The furnishings include the *high altar*, with carving on the Nuremberg model (1500–20), and the *side altars* with first-class *panel paintings* of the Laurentinus legend.

**Pilgrimage Church of Mariahilf** (on the road to Beilngries (q.v.), which is 8 km. away): The present building was built in 1796 on the site of a former field chapel. There is a *Man of Sorrows group* in the church which is said to date from 1480–90.

---

**Berchtesgaden 8240**
Bavaria                                    p.422☐N 21

**Former Augustinian Canonry Church of St.Peter and St.Johannes** (Schlossplatz): The first church was dedicated to St.Peter and St.John the Baptist in 1122. The second building, of which the W. part and the cloisters have survived in excellent condition, followed in the early 13C. Prior Johannes added the slender early Gothic choir in 1283 – 1303, and *c.*1470 the Romanesque nave was pulled down and replaced with a pillared hall. The early-13C towers were built in reddish-grey ashlar in the Italian Romanesque fashion and rebuilt in the 19C; the spires are, however, a solecism. The broad Gothic hall nave with circular columns and sharp-edged net vaulting comes as something of a surprise after the porch, which is sandwiched between the heavy shapes of the towers, and the round arch of the portal, which is inside and down a few steps. The choir slopes upwards at the end of the nave and is a unique example of early Gothic in Bavaria. The W. portal is Romanesque and the N. portal Gothic; there are striking gravestones of the Prince Priors in red Untersberg marble, in particular the high tomb of Prior P.Peinzenauer (1432), by the W. entrance. The choir stalls, with intertwining animal designs on the sidepieces, (1436–43) are a notable feature. On the canonry building side of the church are rococo prayer niches in the shape of swallows' nests (c.1750).

**Stift/Residenz:** The residential building of the canonry (Stift) later became the Residenz and is now owned by the Wittelsbachs; it is set around the monastery courtyard and built on Romanesque foundations. It has been much changed in the course of the centuries. The stucco façades on the Residenzplatz side were added in the 18C. In the interior the Romanesque *cloisters* are among the best of their kind. The canons' dormitory (c.1410) is now part of the *Museum*, which shows mainly the excellent art collection of the former Crown Prince Ruprecht, who lived here for many years.

**Museums:** As well as the *Schlossmuseum* (see Stift/Residenz) the *Heimatmuseum* (local history) is also recommended. Its exhibits come largely from the college of wood carving. *Salzmuseum* (83 Bergwerkstrasse): This is a specialist museum dealing with the development of salt- mining and the customs of the salt-miners; it works in close co-operation with the Berchtesgaden salt-mine, which was opened in 1517 and still operates today.

**Also worth seeing:** Frauenkirche am Anger (16C), pilgrimage church Maria-Gern (1709), N. of Berchtesgaden, and the pilgrimage church of Kunterweg, W. of the town (1731–3).

## Berlin (West) 1000

p.418

The tiny market towns of Colonia (1237) and Berlin (1244) are first mentioned in the 13C. In 1307 the two communities were combined as a double town, in 1359 Berlin joined the Hanseatic league and in 1488 became the residence of the Margraves of Brandenburg. Its rise to eminence began after the Thirty Years War with the Great Elector Friedrich Wilhelm (1640–88), who had Berlin extended as a walled fortress. At the beginning of the 18C Berlin was transformed into a baroque residence town. The city achieved architectural unity under Elector Friedrich III (1688–1713), who was King Friedrich I from 1701 and in the same year made the combined Prussian state into the Kingdom of Prussia. The Stadtschloss was built in its final form, the Arsenal and Schloss Charlottenburg came into being, and the Academies of Arts and Sciences were founded. Friedrich Wilhelm I, the soldier king, laid down outlines for the city's future development, and Berlin became one of the most important royal residences of the rococo period. The city became the spiritual and intellectual centre of Germany: the Enlightenment and Romanticism were discussed in its salons. By 1871 the King of Prussia was Emperor of Germany and Berlin was the capital of the German Empire. Finally in the 'Golden Twenties' the area around the Kurfürstendamm, the Memorial Church, the Kaufhaus des Westens and the Tauentzienstrasse became the centre of social and intellectual life in Germany. The 'Romanische Café' by the Zoo, the meeting place of intellectuals and poets, took over from Lutter & Wegner's wine cellar in the Gendarmenmarkt, where 100 years before Chamisso, E.T.A.Hoffmann, Fouqué, Brentano and many other of the leading lights of Berlin had met. Much which was important in Berlin's past is now in the E. part of the city.

**Kaiser-Wilhelm-Gedächtniskirche** (Breitscheidplatz am Zoo): The new centre of W. Berlin has developed around this church, which was built in 1891–5 in late

Romanesque style; the bombing of the Second World War left only the W. tower as a memorial. The new Gedächtniskirche building (1961–3) is by E.Eiermann; it is a low octagon in blue glass bricks, known to Berliners as the 'prayer gasometer'.

**Catholic Church of Maria Regina Martyrum** (Heckerdamm): This memorial church to the victims of the Hitler dictatorship was built in 1960–3 by the architects H.Schaedel and F.Ebert, not far from the place of execution in Plötzensee prison. The complex consists of a large courtyard, a community centre, a towerlike concrete framework with belfry and the gigantic block which houses the upper and lower churches. In the lower church are the three martyrs' memorial graves, and in the upper church is a fresco of the Apocalypse by G.Meistermann.

**Protestant Church in the Hohenzollernplatz** (Wilmersdorf): This is a lucidly organised clinker design on a generous scale (1930–3), the work of the Hamburg architect Höger, who was responsible for the Chile-Haus in Hamburg (q.v.); his intention was to aim 'for a heightened effect of sanctity and space using modern construction methods in a spare and functional way'.

**Church of St. Matthäus** (Tiergarten, next to the new National Gallery): The builder of this church, F.Stüler, was a pupil of K.F.Schinkel. The three-aisled church, completed in 1846, was rebuilt in its original form after the war as a sensitive testimony to the architectural style of historicism. The strips of coloured brick and the three E. apses are reminiscent of early Christian architecture and the churches of Ravenna.

**Former village churches:** Numerous village churches have survived in Berlin, where 59 country parishes were among the communities brought together in 1920 to form Greater Berlin. The *St.Annen-Kirche* (Königin-Luise-Strasse) in Dahlem was mentioned as early as 1300. The church was built of large rough bricks on a rock base in the 13C and later; The first trans-

mission station for optical telegraphy between Berlin and Koblenz was installed on the turret of the gable in 1832. *Tempelhof* got its name from the Knights Templar and two churches of the Order have survived in the suburb. The first is in the park opposite the Rathaus; it is an undecorated low granite building with a 13C Romanesque apse, and is now the oldest building in Berlin. The *Templerordenskirche in Marienfelde* dates from the early 13C; it is a square hall with a W. tower, a typical Brandenburg village church of the Hohenstaufen period. There are similar village or small town churches in many parts of Berlin, in Steglitz, Zehlendorf, Schöneberg, Lichterfelde, Rudow, Britz, am Stölpchensee and in Lübars, to mention just a few places. Somewhat larger is the *St.Nicolai Church in Spandau* (Carl-Schurz-Strasse). This Brandenburg brick church from the high Gothic period (c. 1400) has a Gothic font, a baroque pulpit and an interesting Renaissance stone altar (over the family vault of the fortress builder Rochus zu Lynar, who endowed the altar in 1582 and is represented on the panels with his family).

**Zitadelle Spandau:** The Italian Count Rochus von Lynar rebuilt the old moated Burg at the confluence of the Spree and the Havel in 1578–94. Included in the new complex (a 350 yard square with four bastions) were the manor house (1512) and the old, early-14C keep ('Julius tower') which from 1874–1919 housed the 'Imperial war treasure' of 120 million gold pieces.

**Grunewald hunting lodge** (am Grunewaldsee, Pücklerstrasse): Elector Joachim II Hektor (1505 – 71), who introduced the Reformation to his principality in 1539, called the small hunting lodge which he commissioned from C.Thiess in 1542 'Zum Grünen Wald' ('In the Green Wood'). The lodge has looked as it does today since the 18C and houses a fine collection of 17C Dutch painting.

**Schloss Charlottenburg** (Spandauer Damm): The massive central tower of the Schloss is set precisely on the line of the Schlossstrasse and dominates the broad

*Kaiser-Wilhelm-Gedächtniskirche with Europa-Center*

main courtyard and low wings of the long building. At the rear the Schloss park extends along the Spree to the N. The main Schloss was built in several stages; the original complex (the central building without the tower) was commissioned by Elector Friedrich III (King Friedrich I from 1701) in 1695 for his wife Sophie Charlotte, the friend of the philosopher Leibniz. The wings were not added until 1701–7 by the Swedish architect Göthe. He also completed the central building with its massive tambour, lantern and figure of Fortuna. During the 1950 rebuilding operation the figure (recreated by R.Scheibe) was redesigned as a weathercock. After the Queen's death the W. wing (Orangerie) was finished and the Schloss was given the name 'Charlottenburg'. Frederick the Great then continued to extend it: G.W. von Knobelsdorff built the section which balances the Orangerie for him in 1740–43; it is a long building with two storeys, the so-called *Knobelsdorff*

*building* with the 'Golden Gallery' as its main room; the decoration is rococo. On the ground floor of the Knobelsdorff wing is the important *Kunstgewerbemuseum* (applied art, including Guelph treasures). In the main courtyard is the equestrian statue of the Great Elector (see under monuments). The park has three architectural attractions: the *Belvedere*, a three-storey, early neoclassical Schlösschen (late-18C, by G.Langhans, the creator of the Brandenburg Gate). The next interesting feature is the *Schinkel Pavilion* just to the E. of the main Schloss. It is in the style of a summerhouse which Friedrich Wilhelm II, who commissioned it, had seen in Naples; it was built in 1824 to designs by K.F.Schinkel: a simple cube with balcony railings all the way round and central loggias in the upper storey. On the W. side of the park is the *Mausoleum*. This building (by H.Gentz, 1810) was altered first by Schinkel, and then again in 1841. The sarcophaguses of Queen Luise and Friedrich

Wilhelm III are by the sculptor C.D.Rauch (1842-6).

**Schloss Bellevue** (Spreeweg): The Schloss and its fine park were designed and built by P.M.Boumann in 1785-6 for Old Fritz's youngest brother Prince Ferdinand of Prussia. The building is set around a courtyard and has the cool restraint of early neoclassicism. Bellevue was formerly a princely residence, museum and government guest house, and is now the Berlin home of the President of the Federal Republic.

**Schloss and Kavaliersbau on the Pfaueninsel** (Wannsee): The Schloss was built in 1794-7 for Friedrich Wilhelm II as a summer Buon Retiro for himself and Countess Lichtenau; in the sentimental spirit of early Romanticism it was designed to look like a ruin. The great hall is lined with costly wood of various types and the crystal chandeliers and wall mirrors show a taste for comfort in neoclassical Schloss style. On the ceiling is a copy of Guido Reni's famous 'Apollo in the Chariot of the Sun'. The *Kavaliersbau*, built in 1804 at a discreet distance from the Schloss, was refurbished as a princely residence by K.F. Schinkel in 1824 - 6. The Gothic façade comes from a patrician house in Danzig (*c.*1400): it was bought by the King and incorporated into the building by Schinkel. The dairy, the cowshed in the form of a chapel, the peacock house and a large aviary built by Lenné are other features which might intrigue the visitor.

**Humboldtschlösschen 'Schloss Tegel'** (Carolinenstrasse): W. von Humboldt inherited the old Renaissance country house (*c.*1550), formerly the property of a secretary at the Elector's court, and had it extended as a neoclassical Schlösschen in 1820-4. Schinkel quadrupled the number of towers and commissioned reliefs of the four winds from C.Rauch for the corner towers, on the model of the tower of the four winds in Athens. In the upper storey are the *Blaue Salon* and the *Grosse Antikensaal* with originals and copies of antique sculpture and Thorvaldsen's 'Mercury with Syrinx'. Chamber concerts are some-times put on in the Antikensaal in the summer. At the end of the Schlosspark by the lake is the Humboldt tomb, designed by K.F.Schinkel in 1829 (with a column in the middle on which there is a copy of B.Thorvaldsen's 'Hope'; the original is in the Schloss.

**Schloss Kleinglienicke** (Kleinglienicker Brücke, Königstrasse): The Schloss consists of living, state and farm accommodation built by K.F.Schinkel for Prince Karl of Prussia in 1824-6; the buildings are distributed throughout the park. An old villa was modified to form the main Schloss, with a golden lion-fountain in front of it. The most unusual building is the so-called *Kasino*, consisting of three adjacent cubes with terrace and pergola, in the style of an Italian country house. There is a covered viewing platform on the bank of the Havel.

**Reichstag building** (Platz der Republik): This building was considered 'modern' when it was erected in 1884-94 in pompous high Renaissance style by P.Wallot as an impressive monument symbolising the power and grandeur of the new Reich. The building was partially destroyed by fire in 1933 and badly damaged in 1945. It has

*Zitadelle Spandau*

been rebuilt without the gigantic glazed dome on the central section and is now used for party and committee meetings.

**Renaissance-Theater** (6 Hardenberg-strasse): The theatre was built by O.Kaufmann, a well-known theatre architect who was also responsible for the *Volksbühne* (in East Berlin) and the *Komödie* (206–7 Kurfürstendamm).

**AEG turbine house** (12 – 16 Huttenstrasse): Peter Behrens (1868 – 1940), architect and industrial designer, became artistic adviser to AEG in 1906 and designed the turbine house, originally 360 ft. long and one of the earliest modern industrial buildings. The long sides consist largely of glass and are apparently only supported by the heavy jointed pillars at the corners.

Berlin, Schloss Charlottenburg 1 Porcelain Cabinet 2 Chapel 3 Apartments of Frederick I. a) Bedroom b) Study c) Braid room d) Audience room 4 Apartments of Sophie Charlotte a) Audience room b) Hallway c) Residential rooms 5 Garden room 6 Vestibule 7 Anteroom 8 Glass bedroom 9 Audience room 10 Mecklenburger room 11 Oak gallery 12 Panelled corner tower

**Druckhaus Tempelhof** (Mariendorfer Damm): The 236 ft. high Druckhaus (printing house) office building towers up to the S. of Tempelhof airport. The window niches, rising to a height of six storeys, and the ribs on the tower and the main building have earned the clinker-clad printing house of the former Ullstein Press (now Axel Springer) the name 'newspaper cathedral'. The building dates from 1926&7 and was designed by E.Schmohl.

**Shell-Haus** (Reichpietsch-Ufer/Hitzigallee): The Shell-Haus was built in 1926 – 31 by the Düsseldorf architect E.Fahrenkamp and now houses BEWAG. The building consists of eight tall, staggered towers with rounded corners, which unfurl along the Landwehr canal like a folding screen. It was the first high-rise ferro-concrete building in Germany.

**Olympic stadium** (Heerstrasse/Jesse-Owens-Allee): The stadium was built for the XI Olympic Games in 1936 on the 'Reichssportfeld', and holds 100,000 people. The whole complex, including swimming pools, Maifeld, equestrian stadium and open-air stage, is lavishly decorated with sculpture. It was built by Werner

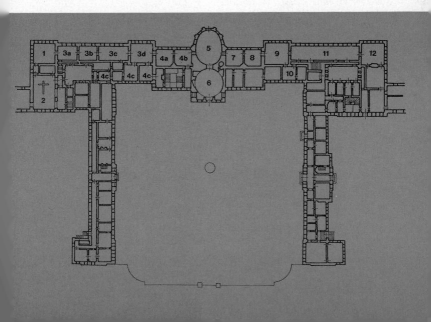

March, whose father Otto March built the 'Deutsches Stadion' on the same site in 1913.

**Corbusier-Haus** (Jesse-Owens-Allee/Heerstrasse): The French architect Le Corbusier based this unusually large high-rise block, his contribution to the International Building Exhibition in Berlin in 1957, on the model of his Unité d'habitation in Marseille; it is built on concrete stilts and is 150 yards long and 184 ft. high, has 17 storeys, contains 530 flats, and houses 1,400 people.

**Hansaviertel** Altonaerstrasse/Bartningstrasse): A team of 48 German and foreign architects was brought together for the International Building Exhibition in 1957 and designed modern high-rise flats for the site of the old Hansaviertel, which had been devastated in the war. Despite the differing personalities involved (they included architects. W.Gropius, O.Niemeyer, A.Alto and H.Luckhardt) the modern suburb was successfully built and served as a model for modern urban domestic architecture.

**Kongresshalle** (John-Foster-Dulles-Allee): The Kongresshalle was the American contribution to the 1957 Building Exhibition. The congress hall, oval in shape and seating 1,300 people, is set on a rectangular base containing conference rooms, restaurant, post office, office accommodation etc. The roof is a boldly designed curve, which has earned the building the nickname 'pregnant oyster'. (Because of the partial collapse of the roof in May 1980 the building is likely to be closed until 1985.)

**International Kongress-Zentrum 'ICC'** (Messedamm): Berlin's most modern conference centre is opposite the Funkturm and the Messegelände (exhibition site), to which it is joined by a covered bridge. The building has been used since 1979 for concerts, theatrical performances and shows as well as congresses and conferences.

**Deutsche Oper** (Bismarckstrasse): F.Bornemann designed the present building in 1961 to replace the old Deutsches Opernhaus destroyed in the Second World War; the auditorium has 1900 seats. The windowless façade covered with river pebbles caused the building to be christened 'Sing-Sing' by the people of Berlin.

*Schloss Charlottenburg*

**Europa-Center** (Breitscheidplatz, am Zoo): The 20-storey Europa-Center was built in 1963–5 on the site of the former 'Romanisches Café' and houses cinemas, shopping areas and arcades on several of its floors. Berliners call it 'Pepper's Manhattan' after its architect K.H.Pepper.

**Philharmonie** (Tiergarten, am Kemper-Platz): The new Philharmonie, an asymmetrical tent-like building, was built in 1960–3 by H.Scharoun as the first phase of the planned artistic and cultural centre. The concert hall is a distorted pentagon with boxes rising in irregular terraces and a centrally-placed orchestra; it seats over 2, 300 people. The acoustic problems caused by the unusual shape were solved by using pads of material. The Philharmonie is the home of the Berlin Philharmonic Orchestra (principal conductor Herbert von Karajan) and is popularly known as the 'Circus Karajani'.

**Grosser Kurfürst (statue of the Great Elector)** (in front of Schloss Charlottenburg): This monument used to be on the Lange Brücke by the Stadtschloss on the Spree, but came to the W. part of the city as a result of the war and is now in the main courtyard of Schloss Charlottenburg. It is one of the great European equestrian statues and was designed by architect and sculptor Schlüter and cast by J.Jacoby.

**Brandenburger Tor:** The gate at the W. exit from old Berlin was a customs point until the 60s of the 19C, and is now a visual link between the two halves of the city. The Propylaea of the Acropolis were architect C.G.Langhans' model for the building at the end of Unter den Linden (1788–91).The quadriga with the goddess Victory is almost 20 ft. high and the work of the sculptor G.Schadow (1789–93); it was removed by Napoleon in 1806–7 but brought back again in 1814. The sculpture was recast in 1956 and replaced on the reconstructed gate.

**Kreuzberg monument** (Viktoriapark): The cast-iron mock Gothic monument was erected on the Kreuzberg by K.F.Schinkel in 1813–15 to commemorate the Wars of Liberation.

**Siegessäule** (Grosser Stern): The Siegessäule (victory column) was erected in front of the Reichstag in 1872&3 to commemorate the wars and victories of 1864,

*Schloss Bellevue*

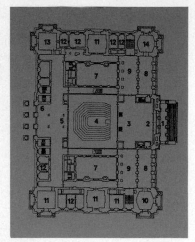

**13 Berlin, Reichstag 1** W.portal **2** Reception hall **3** Sculpture by B.Heiliger **4** Plenary assembly room **5** E. portico **6** Triptych by A.Camaro **7** Inner court **8** Presentation room **9** Lobby **10** Leisure room **11** Assembly room **12** Office room **13** Reception room **14** Reading room

form with columns; there is a gilded goddess of Victory on top of the column, and steps inside lead to a viewing platform.

**Lilienthal monument** (Lichterfelde-Ost, Lilienthal-Park): A monument to air pioneer Otto Lilienthal was erected in 1914 in S. Berlin on the artificial hill from which he made his first attempts at flight from 1891 onwards; it consists of a wide flat circular roof on eight supports, reached by an ashlar staircase.

**Luftbrückendenkmal (airlift monument)** (Platz der Luftbrücke): The city erected a memorial to the blockade imposed by the Soviet government in the winter of 1948 – 9; the monument is by E.Ludwig, and was the first abstract work of this kind in Berlin; it is popularly known as the 'hunger rake'.

**Museums:** Berlin's art treasures are at the time of writing still spread around the city: the *Gemäldegalerie* (paintings), *Skulpturensammlung* and the world-famous *Kupferstichkabinett* (engravings) are in Dahlem and the *Völkerkundemuseum* (anthropology), the *Ostasienmuseum* (Far East) and the *Museum für Indische und Islamische*

1866 and 1870&1 (the Reichstag building itself was not started until 1884). The stone column is 223 ft. high and stands on a plat-

*Reichstag building*

*Olympic stadium*

*Kongresshalle*

*The Philharmonie building in the Tiergarten, with its tent-like concrete roof, was built by H.Scharoun in 1960–3*

*H.Scharoun describes the terraces of seats for the spectators in the Philharmonie as rising up around the orchestra like vineyards*

*Victory column*

*Kunst* (Indian and Islamic art) are at 8 Landstrasse. The second centre is around Schloss Charlottenburg, which houses the *Kunstgewerbemuseum* (applied art) in its E. wing, while the *Museum für Vor- und Frühgeschichte* (pre- and early history) is in an adjoining building to the W. In the pavilion (formerly a barracks) at the end of the Schlossstrasse, opposite the Schloss, is the *Antikenmuseum* (classical antiquities), dealing with smaller items (the larger sculpture is in East Berlin). The *Ägyptische Museum* (Egyptology) in the E. pavilion is world-famous for the head of Nefertiti and portrait sculpture of the Amarna period. In the third centre is the *Nationalgalerie* (50 Potsdamer Strasse), close to the Philharmonie and the State Library, and the first building of the new Museum Centre to be completed. It has exhibitions of 19&20C art in an underground complex with many galleries, and an open-air courtyard for sculpture. The unusual building by Ludwig Mies van der Rohe (1965–8)

was originally planned as an office block for a Central American tobacco company and has a sloping glass pavilion (164 by 164 ft.) above the storey which serves as a base (295 by 295 ft.); the glass pavilion is intended for temporary exhibitions of modern art. The *Berlinmuseum* in Kreuzberg (14 Lindenstrasse) is accommodated in the only remaining baroque building in Berlin and shows the history of the city in documents (it also has a portrait gallery and graphics by Menzel).

As well as the above-mentioned museums there are a number of specialist museums of which only a few can be mentioned here: *Botanischer Garten und Botanisches Museum* (6–8 Königin-Luise-Strasse): the Botanical Garden in Dahlem was established in 1897–1909 by A.Engler, and has been augmented with various academic collections. The *Brückenmuseum* in Dahlem (9 Bussardsteig) was founded in 1966–7 and shows work by artists of the 'Brücke' group, founded in Dresden in 1905. The

*Berliner Post- und Fernmeldemuseum* (15 An der Urania) deals with postal history, post in Berlin, television and stamps. The *Deutsches Rundfunkmuseum* (1 Hammarskjöldplatz) deals with the technolgy and history of German radio and television since 1923. The *Museum für Verkehr und Technik* (9 Trebbinerstrasse) deals with steam engines and robots, motor bikes and cars, model ships and shipping routes, typewriters and print technology, the history of calculation and data storage, and principles of physics and technology. The *Staatliche Porzellanmanufaktur* (Wegelystrasse and 48 Budapesterstrasse) has a collection of historic porcelain and arranges guided tours of the famous Berlin porcelain factory.

**Theatres:** As well as the theatres which have been mentioned for their architectural merit (see *Renaissance-Theater, Deutsche Oper* and *Philharmonie*) there are many other theatres in the city. The *Schiller-Theater* (110 Bismarckstrasse), was destroyed in the Second World War and reopened in 1951; it has 1, 186 seats; the *Schiller-Theater-Werkstatt* is a studio theatre behind the main building); the *Schlosspark Theatre* (48 Schlossstrasse) was reo-

pened in 1945 and has 479 seats; these are the three auditoriums used by the Berlin State Theatre. The *Freie Volksbühne Berlin* (24 Schaperstrasse) has its own company, performs straight plays and has 1,017 seats. The *Hansa-Theater* (47 Alt-Moabit) performs straight plays and has 570 seats. The *Theater am Kurfürstendamm* performs light plays and seats 785. The *Theater des Westens* (12 Kantstrasse) performs operetta and musicals and seats 1,400. The *Tribüne* (18 - 20 Otto-Suhr-Allee) performs straight plays and seats 313. The *Berliner Kammerspiele/Theater der Jugend* (99 Alt-Moabit) performs largely for young people and seats 420. The *Schaubühne am Lehniner Platz* (153 Kurfürstendamm) is devoted to progressive straight theatre and seats 450. The *Vaganten-Bühne* (12a Kantstrasse) performs modern plays and seats 100. The *Grips-Theater* (22 Altonaer Strasse) is a children's theatre with 360 seats.

**Bernkastel-Kues 5550**
Rheinland-Pfalz                    p.416☐B 14

**Catholic Parish Church of St.Michael**

◁ *Brandenburg Gate*                    *National Gallery*

(S. of Bernkastel): St.Michael, along with the *Ruined Burg Landshut*, the many fine *half-timbered houses*, the *Michaelsbrunnen* and the decorative *Renaissance Rathaus* is one of the principal sights of this little town on the Mosel. The heavy ashlar tower (early 14C, once part of the town wall) with its eight small oriel-like side towers looks like a defensive tower. The nave of the church was extended in the 17C, and the baroque façade dates from this period; it was restored in 1968. The most striking of the lavish furnishings are the Triumphal Cross group with life-size wooden figures (*c.* 1440), the Mary Altar with alabaster figures and reliefs (1750) and the 18C organ front and choir stalls.

**St.-Nikolaus-Hospital** (in Kues): Kues owes its fame to Nicolaus Cusanus, cardinal, philosopher and theologian, who endowed his birthplace with a hospital for 33 old and ailing men in 1447. After his death his heart was buried in the chapel; his body is in Rome. The late Gothic hospital complex consists of cloisters around a square courtyard, the rooms or cells are on the S. and W. sides, the refectory on the N. and the chapel on the E. side. In the chapel choir is the grave of Nicolaus von Kues with the particularly attractive late Gothic gravestone of his sister beside it (d.1473). The library with over 400 manuscripts (some by Cusanus) and incunabula is now above the sacristy. There is a wine museum in the *hospital*. The birthplace of Nicolaus von Kues, also called the *Kardinalshaus*, has a permanent exhibition devoted to his life and work.

---

## Besigheim 7122
Baden-Württemberg                    p.420 □ F 17

The unique appearance of this little town, with its old bridge over the Enz (1581) and brightly-coloured roofs, has become well-known from the work of G.Schönleber, the Swabian painter. The town lies between the Enz and the Neckar, and is protected to the N. and S. by two gigantic round Romanesque towers, the surviving parts of the old Burg. They are called the 'Roman towers', and are respectively 38 and 41 ft. in diameter and have entrances 36 ft. above ground level.

**Protestant Church:** There is a 1380 Passion cycle in the nave of the 14&15C

*Michaelsbrunnen fountain with half-timbered houses*

church. In the choir is the high altar, which is a shrine with carved figures of the two Johns, busts, and a scene in the middle representing a miracle by St.Cyriakus. The whole thing is surrounded by foliage and tendrils through which the figures seem to peer, as if in an arbour. The shrine and panels are the work of Christoph von Urach (1520), a sculptor who worked between the Gothic and Renaissance periods.

**Also worth seeing:** The Rathaus (1459), the Marktbrunnen (fountain) (late 16C) and the bridges over the Enz (1581 and 1833).

---

**Beuron 7792**
Baden-Württemberg                    p.420☐F 20

**Benedictine Abbey of St.Martin and Maria:** The abbey of Beuron stands in a loop of the Danube among the towering limestone cliffs of the Schwäbische Alb. It is the chief abbey of the Benedictine Congregation and, in the spirit of the ancient rules of the order, has great achievements to its credit in the field of liturgical reform and, in contrast with the baroque splen-

*Benedictine abbey church of St.Martin and Maria in Beuron*

*Ceiling painting in the Beuron church, by J.I. Wegscheider*

dour of its own church, has sought to establish a new language of religious architecture based on the early Christian and Romanesque styles; an interesting product of 'Beuron art' is the *St.Maurus Chapel*, 3 km. away, built by Father D.Lenz in 1868–70. In 1732–8 there were strenuous attempts to make the baroque abbey church itself look like an early Christian place of worship, but since then the building with its pillared balconies has been restored, although the baroque high altar by J.Feuchtmayer had been so much changed in the 'purification' of 1872 that it could not be returned to its former magnificence. The *Gnadenkapelle*, added to the N. side of the church in 1891, with a 15C Pietà, is an exemplary specimen of the artistic endeavours of New Beuron. The extensive new monastery buildings house a theological college and various research institutes as well as the *Bible museum*.

striking 16C houses: *15 Markt* (former standards office), *22 Markt* (former salt store) and *4 Markt* (former merchants' hall).

**Town fortifications:** The fortifications were in good condition until 1782 but were then largely removed. The *Ulmertor* remained: this was built in 1410 to secure the town from the E; the *Gigelturm* and the *Weisse Turm* also survived, and have been partially renovated.

**Museums:** *Städtische Sammlungen/Braith-Mali-Museum* (6 Museumstrasse): The museum includes the *Alte Spital* (rebuilt in 1519). It has collections on pre- and early history, the history of the town, arts and crafts and 15–20C sculpture; it also houses memorabilia and the studio of the animal painter A.Braith (1836–1905) and of Ch.Mali (1832–1906); *Wieland Museum* (17 Marktplatz).

---

**Biberach an der Riss 7950**
Baden-Württemberg                    p.422 ☐ G 20

The writer Christoph Martin Wieland (1733–1813) was born in Biberach (more precisely: in Oberholzheim). In his Weimar period he was in close contact with Goethe and Schiller. His summerhouse still stands in the garden of 10/1 Saudengasse, which now accommodates the *Wieland museum*.

**Parish Church of St. Martin** (Kirchplatz/Am Marktplatz): The Gothic basilica dates essentially from the 14&15C; the interior was refurbished in the baroque style in 1746–8. The most striking features are the large *fresco* in the nave (J.Zick, 1746) the *high altar* (1720) with a painting by J.Bergmüller, the filigree *choir screen* (1768) and the pulpit (1511). J.Esperlin was responsible for the oil paintings in the nave.

**Houses:** Many old houses, most of them with massive lower storeys and protruding half-timbered upper sections, have survived and give the town its characteristic appearance. There are three particularly

---

**Bielefeld 4800**
Nordrhein-Westfalen                  p.414 ☐ E 9

**Neustädter Marienkirche** (Kreuzstrasse): This Gothic hall church (completed 1330) was badly damaged in the Second World War; the towers were completely burned down. The three-aisled nave contrasts strongly with the long narrow choir, which has a rectangular E. end and is lit by a lavish tracery window. There are important works among the furnishings, including an *altarpiece* in the choir which is a major example of Westfalian Gothic painting in the so-called 'Soft Style' (11 of the 18 missing panels are to be found in German and foreign museums). It is by the 'Master of the Berswordt altar', who also painted the Crucifixion altar in the Marienkirche in Dortmund (q.v.). There are 15 sandstone figures from the former choir screen of the church (c. 1320) on the altar cornice. The same artist was probably also responsible for the memorial tomb of Otto III of Ravensberg with wife and child on the N. side of the choir, one of the most important works of 14C German sculpture.

**Altstädter Nicolaikirche** (Postgang): A 16C Gothic carved altar with 250 sculpted figures from an Antwerp studio takes pride of place in this church (1330–40).

**Sparrenburg** (Am Sparrenberg): The town of Bielefeld, which grew in size and reputation through its membership of the Hanseatic League and the linen trade, was formerly protected by the Sparrenburg, particularly during the Thirty Years War. Count Ludwig of Ravensberg had the Burg built between 1240 and 1250; its principal attractions today are a 121 ft. high look-out tower and the 300 yards of tunnels under the fortifications.

**Museums:** *Kunsthalle Bielefeld* (5 Artur-Ladebeck-Strasse): The new building, endowed by the Dr. Oetker company, was built by P.Johnson in 1966–8. It collects international painting, graphics and sculpture of the 20C. *Kulturhistorisches Museum* (61 Welle): Art and cultural history in E. Westfalia and Lippe, applied art. *Bauernhaus-Museum* (82 Dornbergerstrasse): farmhouse museum.

**Theatres:** *Stadttheater* (27 Niederwall): The theatre was opened in 1904 and performs opera and operetta; 775 seats. *Theater am Alten Markt* Alter Markt: straight plays; 339 seats. *Rudolf-Oetker-Konzerthalle* (Stapenhorststrasse): Concerts by the Philharmonic Orchestra and the Bielefeld children's choir.

---

**Billerbeck 4425**
Nordrhein-Westfalen                    p.414☐C 9

**Catholic Parish Church of St. Johannes:** St.Ludger, the first Bishop of Münster, who died in Billerbeck in 809, said his last mass in the Johanniskirche, which was founded 800 years ago. A later building was consecrated in 1074, and the lower storeys of its W. tower are incorporated in the tower of the present church, which was built *c.*1234. It is considered to be one of the most important late Romanesque hall churches in the Münster region, although it differs from the Münster pattern and inclines towards the style of the Rhineland in its more ornate exterior, most strikingly in the accentuation of the N. doorway and the decorative friezes on the round arches. In 1425, in the Gothic period, alterations were made: tracery was

*Sparrenburg, Bielefeld*

added to some of the windows, and the spire probably also dates from this phase of building. The interior is also lavishly decorated. The furnishings include an octagonal, late *Gothic font* (1497), a late Gothic hanging *double Madonna* and stone sculptures of Our Lady and the Saviour (1618).

**Ludger-Brunnen-Kapelle** (Ludgeristrasse): In a square surrounded with lime trees by the spring in which St.Ludger is said to have been baptised is a small open brick building with ornate sandstone decoration, built, according to an inscription, in 1702 and containing a recumbent figure of the Saint.

### Bingen 6530
Rheinland-Pfalz                                      p.416□D 14

**Mäuseturm (mouse tower)** (in the Rhine): The legend that the wicked Bishop Hatto of Mainz came to a terrible end by being eaten by mice in this tower on the cliffs in the middle of the Rhine probably has its origin in a linguistic confusion: the customs tower which Bishop Hatto used

to make a great deal of money from the traffic on the river was called 'Mautturm' (toll tower), which local dialect turned into 'Mäuseturm' (mouse tower).

**Burg Klopp** (reached via the Mariahilf road): The Archbishops of Mainz, who controlled movement on the Rhine and the Nahe crossing, had a garrison here from the 13C, and a Canon of Mainz lived here as Lord of Bingen from 1438. The Burg was often burned down, and finally blown up in 1711. The new building, for which foundations of old Romanesque sections were used, dates from 1875–9. The *Heimatmuseum* (local history) is now in the Burg tower.

**Catholic Parish Church/Former Collegiate Church of St.Martin** (Zehnthofstrasse): The present building dates from the early 15C; there is a crypt from the Salesian period (11C) under the E. section of the nave, and the late Gothic hall is also of architectural significance. The two figures on the side altars in the nave (St. Barbara and St.Katharina) are in the so-called 'Soft Style' (c.1420).

**Also worth seeing:** The *Rochus chapel*

*Chapel of St. Roch near Bingen*

above Bingen (1895, earlier buildings dating from 1666 and 1814 were destroyed), the 16C *Rhine crane*, the *Drusus bridge* over the Nahe with bridge chapel (10 or 11C, partially renewed after 1945), 17&18C houses and remnants of the town fortifications.

### Birstein 6484
Hessen                                    p.416□F 13

**Schloss:** The Schloss stands high above this bracing resort in the Vogelsberg hills. The oldest parts of the involved complex date back to 1279. The most impressive section is the *Neues Schloss* (1764) (it is stressed that this is not open to the public), which conceals a large part of the older building. It is built in uniform baroque style and has lavish *interior decoration* (stucco, painting).

### Bischmisheim 6601
Saarland                                  p.420□B 16

**Protestant Parish Church:** This church, an octagonal, symmetrically articulated rotunda, is an example of sober, functional neoclassicism. It was built to a design by the Berlin architect K.F.Schinkel in 1822 on the model of the Palatinate chapel in Aachen (q.v.), with a tent-like pyramid roof and a lantern over the octagon. The interior is that of a typical protestant preaching church with the altar, pulpit and organ set in line one above the other.

### Blaubeuren 7902
Baden-Württemberg                         p.422□G 19

**Former Monastery Church:** This outwardly plain church with its numerous *monastery buildings* stands below the limestone cliff, close by the Blautopf, the deep blue source of the river Blau. Only parts of the tower remain of the building established by the Hirsau Benedictines in the

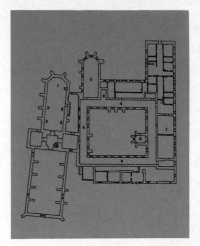

**Blaubeuren, monastery 1** High altar, 1493; woodwork by Jörg Syrlin the younger, figures by Gregor Erhart **2** Choir stalls by Jörg Syrlin the younger, 1493 **3** Sedilia by Jörg Syrlin the younger, 1496 **4** Cloister **5** Chapterhouse **6** Fountain chapel **7** Refectory **8** Margarethenkapelle

11C. Generally speaking the complex dates from the late Gothic period and shows remarkable unity (1491–9, by P.Koblenz). The high altar is a major example of late Gothic carving in Germany. The monastery is still a Protestant theological seminary.

**Interior and furnishings:** The interior of the church is split into two by the lower part of the tower; it was formerly connected in the middle by arched openings on two levels, but the *nave* is now totally closed off, and used as a parish hall. The most important architectural feature is the system of ribs rising to meet above the *choir*; they have been much too brightly painted. The figures of the 12 Apostles between the windows are protected with baldachins. The lavishly carved *choir stalls* with busts by the Ulm 'master cabinet maker' Syrlin the Younger (1493, some added later) are arranged in a horse-shoe pattern at the W. end of the choir: all the stalls face the choir and the large high altar, which takes up the entire width of the narrow choir and is as high as the ribs of the

*Renaissance Rathaus, Bocholt*

vaulting. It is a double *polyptych* with reliefs on its inner panels and with outer panels painted on both sides. The five larger-than-life figures on the central shrine are by the carver G.Erhart (1493): the Madonna on the Crescent Moon in the middle has its original colouring.

**Also worth seeing:** Heimatmuseum (local history, in the Klosterhof), the early-15C Protestant parish church, the late-16C infirmary with its museum of primeval history, an 18&19C drop forge and the 1593 Rathaus.

---

**Bocholt 4290**
Nordrhein-Westfalen                              p.414☐B 9

---

**Catholic Parish Church of St. Georg** (Kirchstrasse) This church has a raised nave and is one of the step churches (Stufenkirchen) which are a feature of the Münster area. The high baroque dome, which was once a dominant feature of the skyline, was destroyed in the war.
Building began in 1415 on the site of a late Romanesque church and was completed in 1486. The late Gothic hall church has five bays, short transepts and a choir with a five-sided apse. The W. side of the tower, with its huge six-part tracery windows reaching right to the ground, forms a magnificent façade. In the Kunstkammer (art storeroom) is a late Gothic Crucifixion picture of the Life of Our Lady by the Cologne Master (viewing by appointment only).

**Rathaus** (Marktplatz): The Town Hall is one of the finest Renaissance buildings in Germany; it was begun in 1618, and the decoration of the façade is extremely varied. The two upper storeys are built in brick and decorated with Corinthian half-columns and pilasters. The ground floor is in the form of a hall with arches and the

*Lamentation, priory church of Bochum*

first floor has lavishly decorated oriels. It was rebuilt to the original design after the Second World War.

**Also worth seeing:** The *Efing* (1665) and *Woord* (1792–95) *town houses*; the former has an octagonal staircase tower.

---

**Bochum 4630**
Nordrhein-Westfalen                          p.416☐C 10

**Priory Church of St.Peter and St.Paul** (Brückstrasse): This church is one of the few buildings which remain of the former small agricultural town which in 1850 only had 5,000 inhabitants. The tower dates from the first building phase (14C). The nave is in the form of a late Gothic hall church (building began in 1517). A late-12C Romanesque font with scenes from the Life of Christ in relief has survived from the original furnishings, and also a

Wailing group dating from *c.*1520 (see illustration).

**Museums:** *Deutsches Bergbaumuseum* (Am Bergbaumuseum): The museum has collections on the history of mining and its depiction in art from AD 150 to the present day. A special attraction is a working model of a mine with full machinery, which visitors are free to enter. *Kunstsammlungen der Ruhr-Universität* (150 Universitätsstrasse): antiquities, coins, painting and 20C sculpture. *Bochum Museum* (147 Kortumstrasse): art collection and temporary exhibitions of post-1945 art. *Stadthistorische Sammlung* (10 an der Kemnade) in the moated Burg known as Haus Kemnade.

**Theatre:** *Schauspielhaus/Kammerspiele* (15 Königsallee): The Schauspielhaus was founded in 1919 and is one of the most important German-speaking theatres; 900 seats.

## Bonn 5300
Nordrhein-Westfalen                    p.416□C 12

The former Roman citadel of Castra Bonnensia saw a great deal of action and sustained heavy damage during its time as a fortified town; in the 18C Bonn became the baroque residence of the extravagant Electors of the House of Wittelsbach, who took great delight in building and shaped the visual personality of the town; its appearance has changed completely since Bonn was declared capital of the Federal Republic of Germany in 1949, and government buildings began to dominate the town.

**Münster of St.Martin/former Collegiate Church of St. Cassius and St. Florentinus** (Münsterplatz): According to legend St.Helena, the mother of Constantine the Great, endowed a little Collegiate Church, and it was on these foundations that the Münster was built; it is still the centre of Roman Catholic worship in Bonn.
c.1065–75 a three-aisled cruciform basilica with crypts and two towers was built; after a fire in 1239 the church was rebuilt and the E. apse, E. towers and cloisters were added. After 1200 the present transept was built (restored 1883–9 and 1934); there was general restoration after Second World War bomb damage).
The formal variety of the Münster makes it a good example of late Romanesque architecture in the Rhineland. The elevation is determined by five towers of differing heights; the impressive spires replaced the original roofs at a later date. The flying buttresses of the nave are among the oldest in Germany. The W. part of the *crypt* has survived from the 1060–70 building. The figures of the recording angel and the Devil with a roll are the only surviving early-13C stone *choir stall ends*; they are probably the work of the Samson master of Maria Laach (q.v.). In the choir is a tall Renaissance *tabernacle*, and in the nave a bronze figure of St. Helena (1600 – 10). The surviving 13&14C *wall paintings* have been heavily restored. S. of the church are the three-sided, two-storey *cloisters*.

**Ramersdorfer Kapelle** (Bornheimer Strasse): This former chapel of the Teutonic Order, built c.1250, was originally in Ramersdorf at the foot of the Siebengebirge. To save it from demolition it was rebuilt in 1846 in the Old Cemetery in Bonn. The building is distinguished by its airy grace — slender columns with shaft rings and ornamented capitals.

**Old Cemetery** (Bornheimer Strasse): The cemetery was established in the 18C for soldiers and foreigners, and many famous people were later buried here (including E.M.Arndt, A.W.Schlegel, Tieck, Beethoven's mother, Schiller's wife Charlotte and his son Ernst, Adele Schopenhauer and Robert and Clara Schumann).

**Jesuit Church** (Bonngasse): The present Catholic University Church was used as a stable during the French period, and its old furnishings were destroyed. Building started in 1688, the façade was completed in 1692, and the church was dedicated in 1717.
The church is a late mannerist building with five bays, based on the medieval hall church design. The magnificent façade is supported by 4 massive buttresses with Corinthian capitals and has a statue of the Saviour at the top. The two five-storey towers have onion domes. Of the original furnishings only the 1698 pulpit remains; the altars came from other churches.

**Rathaus** (Markt): The Town Hall is a baroque building from the period of the Wittelsbach Electors in Bonn. It was built in 1737–8 to a design by M.Leveilly. The façade was restored after the war. A double open staircase with a particularly fine iron railing leads up to the doorway. The mansard roof has a coat of arms and a clock.

**Electoral Residence and Hofgarten** (Am Hofgarten): The town's most impressive public building is the baroque Schloss, now the University. Kurfürst Joseph Clemens had his residence built by E.Zuccalli of Graubünden in 1697–1702 to replace the 13&16C building demolished in 1689. Zuccalli's building was remodelled by

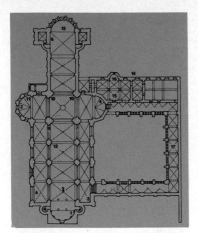

**Bonn, Münster 1** Tombs slab of Engelbert v.Falkenstein, last quarter of 14C **2** Monument to Ruprecht of the Palatinate (d. 1480) **3** Altar of Mary Magdalene, c. 1600 **4** Altar of the Blessed Sacrament, 1608 **5** St. Helena by Hans Reichle, c. 1600-10 **6** Tabernacle, 1619 **7** Altar of Christ's Nativity, donated in 1622 **8** Altar of the Trinity, 1704 **9** Altar of the Magi, 1713 **10** Side altars by Johannes Damm and Josef Metzler, 1735 **11** All Souls' altar, 1699, antependium, 1761 **12** Pulpit **13** High altar, 1863 **14** Chapter Building **15** Chapterhouse **16** Cyriacus chapel **17** Cloister

Louis XIV's director of building R.de Cotte in 1715. The *Schloss chapel* was added in 1777, and in 1818 the *Rheinische Landesuniversität* took the buildings over. At the heart of the complex is a closed baroque building on the Italian palazzo pattern, with several storeys and corner towers, around two courtyards. Additions in 1715 formed a Schloss with three wings, open to the SE. The Residence also includes the Koblenzer Tor, which as a former seat of the Order of St.Michael is also known as the Michaelstor.

**Poppelsdorf Schloss/Electoral Schloss/Schloss Clemensruhe:** This small Schloss was formerly part of the Electoral Residence and was connected with it by the Poppelsdorfer Allee. It was partially rebuilt on a reduced scale after the Second World War. Only four wings with a circular courtyard and a gallery with round arches have survived of French architect R.de Cotte's original building. The

baroque flower and vegetable gardens became the *Botanical Gardens* in the 19C. The Schloss houses the *Zoological* and *Mineralogical and Petrological Institutes* of the university.

**Kreuzberg Church** (Poppelsdorf): The interesting feature of this pilgrimage church, renovated in 1714, is the 'House of Pilate', an extension of the choir, with a 'Holy Ladder' on the pattern of the 'Scala Sancta' in Rome. It is probably based on a design by B.Neumann. The middle section of the staircase can only be ascended kneeling. On the balcony, above the central doorway of the three, are figures of Christ, Pilate and a soldier. Neumann also worked on the baroque interior of the church, so the double-sided high altar with the praying Electors is probably by him.

**Beethovenhaus** (20 Bonnstrasse): The 18C house in which Beethoven was born in 1770 and in which he lived until he was 22 has been a museum since 1889, and houses the largest and most valuable Beethoven collection in the world: memorabilia, a Beethoven archive and a library of about 20,000 volumes.

*Ramersdorfer chapel*

**Villa Hammerschmidt** (Adenauerallee): The Villa Hammerschmidt dates from 1963–5, and was named after the industrialist who lived there; it is upstream on the Rhine in the Adenauerallee villa suburb, which became the government quarter after 1949; the Villa Hammerschmidt is now the home of the President of the Federal Republic, and contains valuable 18–20C paintings.

**Palais Schaumburg** (Adenauerallee): The Palais in which the Chancellor's Office was housed until 1976 was formerly the residence of Princess Viktoria zu Schaumburg-Lippe, the sister of Wilhelm II. It was rebuilt in Renaissance style in 1858–60.

**Double Chapel in Schwarzrheindorf:** Opposite Bonn on the other side of the Rhine there used to be a Roman guardhouse on a little hill, and it was on this site that the double chapel, one of the finest examples of Romanesque architecture in the Rhineland, was built; it is now the *Catholic parish church of St. Clemens* in Schwarzrheindorf.

The building was used as a Burg chapel under Graf Arnold von Wied, later Archbishop of Cologne, and consecrated in 1151; it was extended in 1173 and restored by Clemens August after damage in 1747–52. In 1803 it was secularised and used as a barn and stable. The upper storey was handed back to the church in 1832 and the lower storey in 1865.

The double chapel design (two rooms one above the other, connected by a central opening) was common in Romanesque Burg chapels; the upper church was intended for the lord of the castle and the lower church for the congregation. The original rotunda with 4 transepts was later enlarged by the addition of the W. facing nave, and at the same time the tower was raised by one storey; the tall spire is a Gothic addition.

The important Romanesque wall and ceiling paintings date from the time when the chapel was built. The pictures are painted on a dull blue ground in thin red, yellow and grey fresco; some of the wall paintings were restored in the 19C. The carved wooden Madonna of the 17C Swabian school should be mentioned.

**Museums:** *Rheinisches Landesmuseum* (16 Colmanstrasse): Since its reorganisation in 1969 this has been one of the largest

*Electoral Residence*

*Poppelsdorf Schloss*

*Palais Schaumburg*

*Godesburg, Bad Godesberg*

museums in the Rhineland. It offers a survey of Rhineland Roman art of all periods and also exhibits early Christian finds, Roman weapons and altars, Christian art, 16C Dutch panel painting and modern painting and sculpture. *Städtisches Kunstmuseum Bonn* (7 Rathausgasse): 20C art and particularly the Rhenish expressionists and painters of the 'Brücke' and 'Blaue Reiter' groups. *Ernst-Moritz-Arndt-Haus* (79 Adenauerallee): The house where Ernst Moritz Arndt lived and died (1769 –1860); paintings of Bonn and Rhine landscapes. *Kasimir-Hagen-Sammlung* (34 Wilhelmstrasse): German Jugendstil and Rhenish Expressionism. *Akademisches Kunstmuseum der Universität Bonn* (Am Hofgarten): This is the oldest systematic university museum in Germany, founded in 1819. Exhibits include copies of antique sculpture, antique applied art, and coins and glasses. *Postwertzeichen-Museum* (81

◁ *'Holy Staircase', Kreuzberg Church*

Adenauerallee): Up-to-date collections of new issues of German stamps (prearranged visits only).

**Theatres:** *Theater der Stadt Bonn* (1 Am Boeselagerhof): Plays, opera, operetta, ballet, musicals; 896 seats. *Contra-Kreis-Theater* (3–5 Am Hof): Progressive drama; 200 seats. *Theater der Jugend* (Beuel, 50 Hermannstrasse): school performances; 420 seats. *Stadttheater Bad Godesberg* (Bad Godesberg, 9 Am Michaelshof): touring performances by German and foreign companies; 519 seats.

**Godesburg** (Bad Godesberg, Am Burgfriedhof): Christian missionaries built a chapel dedicated to St.Michael on the basalt peak, and in the year 1210 a typical summit Burg on an oval ground plan was erected. In 1583 the Burg was blown up during a siege, and it has been in ruins ever since. Only the defensive walls of the Romanesque residence with its round staircase tower, the ring walls and the somewhat later keep have survived. In the *Michaelskapelle* the Romanesque apse is the oldest section to survive; the baroque nave with lavish stucco vaulting was built in 1697–9. A striking feature is the high altar with a gilded figure of St.Michael.

**Also worth seeing:** *Redoute*, built in 1790 for Elector Max Franz of Cologne. The old Catholic *Martinskirche* (12C, altered in 1746) in Muffendorf and the 12C *Turmhof* (altered in the 18C) in Friesdorf.

---

**Bopfingen 7085**
Baden-Württemberg                    p.422☐H 17

**Protestant Parish Church** (1 Kirchplatz): This Romanesque building shows Cistercian influence; it has a nave with a flat ceiling and a rectangular 13&14C Gothic choir. The lower parts of the tower are early Gothic and the upper parts baroque. The paintings (1472) on the high altar, a late Gothic carved altar with Madonna and figures of Saints are, according to the signature, by the Nördlingen painter F. Herlin. The most important of the tombs is that of Wilhelm von Bopfin-

gen (1287), an outstanding work of the mid 14C. In the nave and choir are remains of old wall paintings, and in the sacristy a fresco fragment, in good condition, of Women and Angels at the Tomb (late 14C).

**Also worth seeing:** The 1586 Rathaus with pillory, and the pilgrimage church on the Flochberg (1741–7.

---

**Boppard 5407**
Rheinland-Pfalz                    p.416☐C 14

**Church of St.Severus** (Marktplatz): The Roman citadel of Bodobriga is one of Drusus' *c.*20 BC Rhine fortresses, and the town built on that site continued to be of historical significance. In the 10C the relics of St.Severus were brought here from Trier. The Romanesque building dates from the early 12C, the towers were faced and incorporated into a new building *c.*1200 and the church was dedicated in 1225; further extensions followed immediately: the nave was raised and in 1236 the apse was extended; the spires date from 1605.

The two towers, which are very close together, are set between the nave and the choir, so that from the outside they look

*Church of St.Severus, Boppard*

like a transept. There is a Romanesque portal in the W. façade. The choir has a wealth of architectural detail: slender columns with blind niches supporting a dwarf gallery. There are rosette windows at the points from which the Gothic vaulting springs, while the arches and galleries of the lower parts of the nave have the bulkier quality of the Romanesque period. As well as the paintwork, which was revealed in 1890, an enthroned Madonna (1280–1300) and a triumphal arch cross have survived from the first half of the 13C.

**Former Carmelite Church:** The monastery was founded as early as 1265 (the present building dates from 1730) but the church was not started until 1319, and extended in 1439–44. It has a plain exterior but is notable for its fine furnishings: the *choir stalls* (*c.*1460), the baroque high altar (1699), Renaissance wall graves (16C) in the choir and a wall painting (1407).

**Museums:** *Städtisches Heimatmuseum* (Alte Kurfürstliche Burg): Pre- and early history, finds from Roman graves, geological and mineralogical collections and also weapons, weights and measures, coins and jewellery. *Wald- und Holz-*

*museum/Thonetmuseum* (Burgstrasse): Forestry and woodwork of all kinds; collection of butterflies.

**Environs: Kamp-Bornhofen** (3km E. on the r. bank of the Rhine): The 13C ruined castles of Liebenstein and Sterrenberg, known as the 'warring brothers', are above the Franciscan monastery and pilgrimage church of *Bornhofen*, mentioned as early as 1224. In the Von-der-Leynschen-Hof (1594) is a *Museum of rafts and navigation.*

---

**Bordesholm 2352**
Schleswig-Holstein                              p.412☐H 3

---

**Collegiate Church/Former Monastery Church of the Augustinian Canons:** This church on a peninsula in the Bordesholm lake was a popular centre of pilgrimage in the Middle Ages because of its relics and the tomb of Bishop Vizelin. A church of St. Mary was begun in 1322 and dedicated in 1332, from 1450–2 the nave vaulting was constructed and the building extended by a hall nave with a single bay, and in 1490–1509 it was again enlarged by two hall bays.

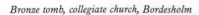

*Bronze tomb, collegiate church, Bordesholm*

The plain building, with only a ridge turret, is typical of N. German Gothic. The choir and walls are undecorated and only broken by windows and shallow wall bands. The canons' choir dominates the E. section, and the galleries were also originally intended for the canons; the late Gothic lay church is in the W. section. In the sacristy, the so-called *Russian chapel*, is the sarcophagus of Duke Karl Friedrich (the father of Tsar Peter III). The most famous item of the former furnishings, the *late Gothic carved altar* by H.Brüggemaann (1514–21) was moved to Schleswig cathedral in 1666. The present high altar is baroque (1727). The Gothic *choir stalls*, the important *bronze tomb* of Duchess Anna of 1514 and an altar with paintings showing Dutch influence have survived.

## Borken 4280
Nordrhein-Westfalen                    p.414☐B 9

**Catholic Priory Church of St. Remigius** (Mühlenstrasse/Remigiusstrasse): There has been a church since the Carolingian period on this site where once-important roads met. The lower storeys of

*Gothic triumphal cross, Bosau*

the W. tower of a hall church built *c.* 1150 have survived. The present church dates from 1433, and the numerous chapels were added subsequently. The rebuilding of the church after it had been badly damaged in the last war was completed in 1954. The most famous items of the lavish furnishings are a Romanesque font (*c.* 1200) with human and animal figures, a 14C *forked crucifix*, two pictures of *the Virgin and Child and St. Anne* and a 15C *Entombment*.

**Environs: Gemen** (2 km. N.) The Burg Gemen complex was built on four islands in the 15C; the main Burg was completed in 1411.

## Bosau 2422
Schleswig-Holstein                    p.412☐H 3

**Vizelinkirche:** In the year 1150 the Wendic missionary bishop Vizelin began to build a small bishop's church on the Plöner See. When, shortly after that, the see was moved to Oldenburg and later to Lübeck, the building was reconstructed as a late Romanesque village church with choir and round apse. The church was heavily refurbished in the 19C; some of the *Gothic paintwork* has survived in the apse. An *altar with figures* and a *Gothic triumphal cross* date from the first half of the 14C.

## Bottrop 4250
Nordrhein-Westfalen                    p.414☐B 10

**Heilig-Kreuz-Kirche:** The church, built by R.Schwarz in 1957, is considered to be one of the most successful examples of modern ecclesiastical architecture. The supports are made of reinforced concrete and the walls of exposed brick. The whole building is constructed on a ground plan in the shape of a parabola. The stained glass wall is by G.Meistermann.

**Heimatmuseum** (20 Im Stadtgarten):

*Marksburg near Braubach* ▷

The museum has exhibits on local history and prehistory, and the history of the Ruhr.

## Braubach 5423
Rheinland-Pfalz                                   p.416☐D 13

**Marksburg:** This is the only Burg on the Rhine which is still intact; it is set above the town on a 560 ft. high mound. In the so-called Kaiser-Heinrich tower, in which legend has it that Emperor Heinrich IV took refuge while fleeing from his son, there was from 1437 a chapel of St.Mark the Evangelist, from which the castle gets its name. The heavily fortified complex consists principally of a citadel, keep, residence and 'Rheinbau': three 12–14C wings around a triangular courtyard in which the square 13C *keep* stands. The inner bailey is reached through a gatehouse, several bastions and three further massive gates; it contains the Gothic *residence*, the most important part of the castle, amd the *Kaiser-Heinrich tower*. The ring walls of the *citadel* are 13C, from the 15–17C numerous walls, battlements, round towers and bastions were added. The so-called *Rheinbau* consists of 18C half-timbered buildings.

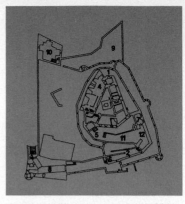

**Marksburg 1** Chapel tower, first half of 13C **2** Inner tower, c. 1500 **3** Drawbridge gate, 1st half of 15C **4** Great hall, late 14C **5** Iron gate, late 14C, altered in the 17/18C **6** Fuchstor gate, late 14C **7** Cannon house, 16C **8** Tunnel corridor, 1643-45 **9** Scharfes Eck (sharp corner), 1643-45 **10** Pulvereck (powder corner), 1643-45 **11** Small battery, 1643-45 **12** Large battery, N. section, 1643-45 **13** Castle keep

The castle is the property of the Deutsche Burgenvereinigung and houses their offices. It is run as a *museum* and is open to the public throughout the year.

*Schloss of the Counts of Solms-Braunfels*

## Braunfels 6333

Hessen                                      p.416☐E 13

**Schloss:** The former Burg of the Counts of Solms-Braunfels was captured on various occasions in the Thirty Years War and badly damaged by two fires. The dominant features now are the 19C extensions. At the NE corner of the complex, which is presumed to have been founded in 1260, although large-scale building did not start until the 15C, are the rectangular three-storey *residence* and the somewhat older *Friedrichsturm*. On the E. side the site is dominated by a 15C *semicircular tower*. The former *main tower* has a late Gothic upper section (the present main tower was built in 1884). On the S. side of the main courtyard is a late Gothic *hall* with a 15C frieze on the archway. The *kitchens* were built in 1710–12. The Schloss is reached via the ring walls and battlements and four late Gothic gates. There is now a *museum* in the residence with a collection of 14–18C sculpture and painting and also numerous old weapons and pieces of furniture.

**Heimatmuseum** (Obermühle): Local history, paintings.

**Also worth seeing:** Unified townscape. The numerous half-timbered buildings are interesting, particularly the *Fürstliche Rentkammer* (c.1700). Ruined 14C Burg Philippstein.

## Braunschweig 3300

Lower Saxony                               p.414☐J 8

Henry the Lion (1129 – 95), whose influence extended into the 13C, put his stamp on the appearance of the city of the Guelphs. Braunschweig, around which two branches of the Oker flow, originally consisted of a series of small settlements brought together and extended by Henry the Lion. At their centre was the village of

Braunschweig, cathedral 1 Imerward crucifix, c. 1160 2 High altar, dedicated in 1188 3 Bronze candlestick donated by Henry the Lion 4 Tomb slab of Henry the Lion and Duchess Mathilde, c. 1250 5 Albrecht the Fat (d. 1318) 6 Heinrich III, Bishop of Hildesheim (d. 1362) 7 Duke Otto the Mild and Duchess Agnes, 1346 8 Scourging column 9 St.Blasius and John the Baptist, early-16C 10 Tomb of Duke Ludwig Rudolf (d. 1735) and Duchess Christine Louise, tin figures by H.M. Vetten.

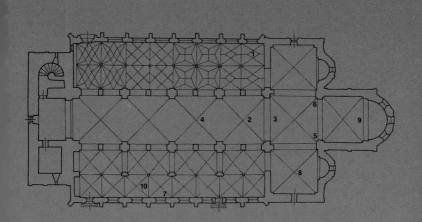

Bruneswiek, mentioned as early as 1031. In the year 1260 Braunschweig joined the Hanseatic League. All the important secular and ecclesiastical buildings date from the 12–14C. The cathedral built by Henry the Lion served, more or less obviously, as a model for the seven parish churches of the town. The gables with lavish tracery on the Altstadtrathaus and the church buildings are a typical Braunschweig feature. The old town was 90% destroyed in the Second World War, but although the demands of a modern city militated against complete restoration, the most important old buildings were rebuilt.

**Dom/Former Collegiate Church of St.Blasius** (Burgplatz): The cathedral was begun by Henry the Lion in 1173 and largely completed by 1195, when Henry died and was buried here. A Gothic belfry was placed between the two octagonal upper towers of the W. front in 1275. In the 14C a row of Gothic gables was added to the S. aisle. The Romanesque N. aisle was replaced by a two-aisled hall in the late 15C. The E. exterior of the building is to a large extent original.
*Interior and furnishings:* A surprising feature, new for the period and the region, is the *vaulting of the nave* (by architects from Lombardy?). Under the E. part a *crypt* has survived, which has been the princely burial vault since the Guelphs returned from Wolfenbüttel in the 18C. Not until the 19C was it discovered that the walls and vaulting of the church had originally been covered with a set of religious pictures. Restoration work after the Second World War has revealed these uniquely beautiful paintings dating from 1220–40; they are reminiscent of enlarged illustrative miniatures. An archaically severe *crucifix* (c.1160) was taken over from the collegiate church which preceded Heinrich's cathedral; it bears the inscription 'Imevard me fecit' (Imerward made me). The seven-branched *candelabrum* in the choir was endowed by Henry the Lion. There are larger-than-life figures of the Duke himself and his wife Mathilde on the *tombstone* in the nave: these are idealised portraits in the courtly Hohenstaufen style; the model of the cathedral held by the Duke is an interesting feature (c.1250).

**Burg Dankwarderode** (Burgplatz): The area around the Dom was formerly the moated Burg of Heinrich's predecessors. Heinrich built his own Burg of Dank-

*Dom, effigies*　　　　　　　　　*Dom, N. side aisle* ▷

*Burg Dankwarderode; in the foreground is the Lion of Braunschweig*

*Portal of the Protestant parish church*

warderode here, and some sections of this fortress have been included in the faithfully restored building. In the 17C the Burg served as an arsenal and later, after modifications, as a barracks. It was not until the end of the 19C that its historical importance was recognised and it was saved from further damage. On the Burgplatz looking E. is the famous *Lion of Braunschweig*, which Henry the Lion had placed here in 1166 as a symbol of his power. The formerly gilded monumental lion is the oldest example of a free-standing sculpture in Germany.

**Protestant Parish Church of St. Martin** (Altstadtmarkt): The principal parish church of the old town was begun only a few years after the Dom and follows its design in almost every particular; like the Dom St. Martin it was also changed from a basilica to a hall church. Above the bays of the aisles are Gothic tracery gables, some of which have lavish sculptural or-

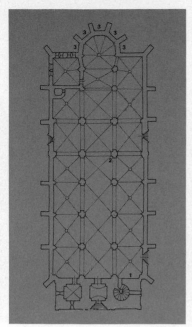

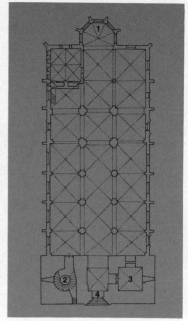

**Braunschweig, Katharinenkirche 1** Tomb of Jürgen v.der Schulenburg (d. 1619) and his wife Lycia by Jürgen Röttger and Lulef Bartels **2** Pulpit, 1890 **3** Choir window by H.-G. v.Stockhausen, 1959

**Braunschweig, Protestant parish church of St.Andreas 1** Choir with high altar **2** N. tower **3** S. tower **4** W. portal

namentation on the model of the Dom (*c.*1320–30). The tracery gables on the entire E. side were put there to harmonise with the Gothic Town Hall. There is an interesting late Gothic bronze *font* supported by four men representing the rivers of paradise (1441, by B.Sprangken).

**Protestant Parish Church of St. Katharina** (Hagenmarkt): St.Katharina was built *c.*1200 on the pattern of St. Martin (and indirectly of the Dom) in the settlement of Hagen, which was incorporated into the Guelph town under Henry the Lion. It too was transformed from a basilica to a hall church, in 1275. A large belfry with Gothic tracery was built between the octagonal towers *c.*1300.

**Protestant Parish Church of St. Andreas** (Wollmarkt): This late-12C church also follows the design of the Dom and St.Martin, and was turned into a hall church in the late 13C. Similarity with the Dom is also shown in the gables added above the windows of the new aisles.

**Protestant Parish Church St. Magni** (Am Magnitor): The old church in the former village of Altewiek was replaced in 1252 by a new building planned from the outset as a hall church. It was restored after the last war according to modern ideas. The writer and critic *G.E.Lessing* (1729–81) is buried in the *St. Magnus cemetery.*

**Former Benedictine Church of St. Aegidien** (Aegidienmarkt): after a fire in the year 1278 (the monastery church had been consecrated in 1115) the E. sections of the church were rebuilt and completed in the late 13C, but the W. section was not

*Altstadtrathaus, with the Marienbrunnen fountain in the foreground*

finished until 1437, then consecrated in 1478. The tower, which was never completed, was pulled down in 1817. The *interior* makes the building 'the most beautiful hall church in Braunschweig'. The high choir with its Gothic windows and a small gallery is built to an expressive design. The baroque *pulpit* has shallow figure reliefs by the great late Gothic sculptor Hans Witten, whose principal works are in the Harz and Saxony. The Braunschweig Landesmuseum für Geschichte und Volkstum (State Museum of History and Folklore) was housed in the church from 1906; it is now in the Paulinerkirche. *Monastery buildings:* the sacristy, chapterhouse, parlatorium and monks' hall, all in the E. wing, have survived.

**Former Cistercian Church in Riddagshausen:** This typical Cistercian church is striking for the ascetic simplicity and severity of its design. It has no choir, but a straight apse with 14 small chapels round

it for private worship and atonement. Tracery, sculpture or pictorial decoration were forbidden for the windows, which are set in pairs. The Order was opposed to earthly splendour of any kind, and forbade ostentatious towers, and so Riddagshausen only has a single ridge turret above the crossing; the turret was renewed in the Renaissance period. The church is strikingly long (91 yards); nothing remains of the old furnishings.

**Altstadtrathaus** (Altstadtmarkt): After the devastation of the Second World War the *Altstadtmarkt* was restored as an 'island of tradition'. The stone tracery on the gables of the Town Hall (only the façade is original) above the arcades is the dominant feature of the square. On the upper floor between the gallery openings are stone statues of Guelph princes under baldachins.

**Gewandhaus (Cloth Hall)** (Altstadtmarkt): The Gewandhaus, mentioned as early as 1303, served as a warehouse and market hall for cloth merchants. Its magnificent gables were added in the late 16C: the splendid façade facing the Kohlmarkt was designed by the town's chief architect H.Lampe in 1590–1. The eight storeys have nothing to do with the distribution of the floors behind them, they are simply show façades. The topmost gable is crowned with a figure of justice; there is a recurrent three-centred arch motif in the central series of windows, which decrease in size. There is a restaurant in the cellar of the present building.

**Houses:** Despite war damage (over 800 stone and half-timbered houses were destroyed) some houses in the old town survived or were restored. The *Huneborstelsche Haus* (2a Burgplatz) and close by the neoclassical *Haus Vieweg* are notable. The *Haus Salve Hospes* (12 Lessingplatz), which now houses the Kunstverein, is in the same spare, neoclassical style.

**Schloss Richmond** (Wolfenbüttelerstrasse): Built on a terrace above the meadows in the valley of the Oker in 1768–9 for Duchess Augusta by K.C.W.Fleischer in severe late baroque style inclining to the neoclassical (Louis Seize), the square Schloss is unusual in

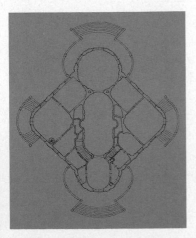

having its approach stairs at the corners. The ground plan shows an unusual mixture of round, oval or irregular rooms (see illustration).

**Museums:** *Herzog-Anton-Ulrich-Museum* (1 Museumstrasse): This houses an applied art section and a major collection of paintings. The most famous item is the 'Family Group' by Rembrandt, the painter's most important work on German soil. There are also pictures by Rubens, van Delft, Steen etc. *Staatliches Naturhistorisches Museum* (10a Pockelstrasse): The exhibits in this museum, the oldest scientific museum open to the public, go back to the collections of the Guelphs; it was founded in 1754. *Städtisches Museum* (Am Löwenwall): A museum dealing with the history of the town and the surrounding area. *Wilhelm-Raabe-Gedächtnisstätte* (29a Leonhardstrasse): Memorabilia of the writer Wilhelm Raabe, in the house in which he lived. *Landesmuseum für Geschichte und Volkstum* (1 Mönchstrasse): Houses collections on regional and general history and on folklore.

**Theatres:** *Grosses Haus* (Am Theater): Theatrical tradition in Braunschweig goes back to visits by English actors in the 17C. The former Grosses Haus was destroyed in the Second World War and its restoration was completed in 1948. It presents opera, operetta and plays, and seats 1186. *Kammerspieltheater Kleines Haus* (Grünewaldstrasse): Presents only straight plays; 350 seats.

---

**Brauweiler 5026**
Nordrhein-Westfalen                    p.416☐B 11

**Former Benedictine Abbey Church** (Ehrenfriedstrasse): This building is on the site of a Roman settlement, on which the sister of Emperor Otto III and her husband Ezzo founded their Palatinate monastery and church in 1024. The upper church was consecrated in 1061, the W. building, the nave and the group of three towers date from the first half of the 12C; the towers were left incomplete and not finished until the 19C, along with the octagonal crossing tower, which was part of the original design. The tall spire was built in 1629 and rib vaulting added in 1514.

The three-towered W. building with central tower is impressive; the long porch dates from 1780. The surface of the building is elaborate and detailed, and the windows and decorations are uniformly distributed, making Brauweiler a text-book example of Romanesque architecture.

The *main doorway* of the W. building with its ornamental animal figures is presumably the work of a Lombard artist; the *S. doorway* is guarded by two lions. Above the doorways of the side choirs are tympanum figures of the founders Ezzo and Mathilde. The cycle of *relief tombstones* with figures in the lapidarium (collection of stone monuments) are of particular distinction (1065–1084; some copies). The *ornate furnishings* include the choir screens (1174&1201) the founders' high tomb (*c.*1200), an important stone retable with Madonna and saints (*c.*1190), 2 early Renaissance altars and the wooden figure of Nikolaus, the patron of the church, enthroned (late 12C). Also 18C confessionals and organ case.

---

**Breckerfeld 5805**

Nordrhein-Westfalen                    p.416☐C 11

**Protestant Parish Church** (Schulstrasse): The church, which is dedicated to James, the pilgrim Saint, was on the pilgrimage route from N. Germany to Santiago de Compostela in Spain. It was built in the 14C but its principal item of decoration dates from the period of the Reformation: a *carved altar* in oak with Mary, St.James and S.Christopher in the central shrine. It is the work of an outstanding Lübeck artist, perhaps from the studio of B.Dreyer.

---

**Breisach 7814**

Baden-Württemberg                    p.420☐C 20

**Stephansmünster:** The Münster is set on a rocky hill above the town and has seen

and survived countless wars and political upheavals. It had to be completely rebuilt after 1945.

The nave, transepts and E. towers date from *c.*1200, the S. tower, the choir and the W. bay from about 1300–30, the vaulting, sacristy and interior furnishings are 15C. The various phases of building can be clearly discerned: each of the symmetrical towers has a Romanesque and a more elaborate Gothic section. The addition of the choir made the Münster into a hall church *c.*1300.

15C rebuilding brought Gothic elements to the fore. N. Italian influence can be seen in the Romanesque nave. A late Gothic *choir screen* (*c.*1500) divides the choir from the nave: the Madonna, standing between Joseph and the Three Kings and the church's patron Stephen, is framed by slender tracery arches with baldachins. The W. hall is dominated by a monumental *fresco* by M.Schongauer (Judgement of the World, *c.*1490). The most valuable feature

*Breckerfeld, carved altar, parish church*

of the interior furnishings is the famous *Breisach altar* by the master HL, dating from 1523–6. The Madonna appears on the central shrine of the carved altar between God the Father and Christ. The late Gothic design shows signs of incipient baroque. The martyrs Stephen and Laurentius are depicted on one panel, the other shows the town's patrons Gervasius and Protasius, whose bones rest in a silver shrine in the church treasury.

## Breitenburg = Itzehoe 2210

Schleswig-Holstein                    p.412 □ G 3

**Schloss:** The foundations of this building go back to the Gothic period. In the 16C the statesman, scholar and distinguished art collector Heinrich von Rantzau extended the Schloss and made it into a centre of humanism in the north. The complex was destroyed in the Thirty Years War by Wallenstein's soldiers; the new buildings are essentially 19C, but the 1592 *well* is a reminder of the older building. The *Schloss chapel* with its ornate furnishings (rebuilt 1965) is worth seeing. The *art collection* includes a silver relief of Heinrich Rantzau (1577) and paintings by L.Cranach, H.Holbein the Younger, Herkules Seghers, J.Owens and copies of works by Thorwaldsen.

## Bremen 2800

Bremen                                p.414 □ F 6

The free and Hanseatic city of Bremen stands on a ridge by the banks of the Weser; its sole allegiance to the Empire was not recognised until 1646, but it was a member of the Hanseatic league from 1358 and even before that, in centuries of struggle with the ruling archbishops, Bremen had achieved democratic independence as the

*Breisach altar*

second oldest republic in Europe. Archbishop Ansgar, the 'Apostle of the North', who moved the see from Hamburg to Bremen in the 9C, and Adalbert von Bremen, who wanted in the 11C to make Bremen into the 'Rome of the North', had a profound influence on the appearance of the older part of the town. Even today it combines the roles of ecclesiastical centre and rich and prestigious Hanseatic town. The figure of Roland by the Rathaus faces the cathedral and symbolises civic freedom, and the statue of the 'Bremen town musicians' in the yard of the church of Our Lady is also famous. The 'Musings in the Bremen Ratskeller', with which Wilhelm Hauff showed his respect for the Hanseatic town in 1826, are illustrated in murals in the Ratskeller by M.Slevogt.

**Dom St.Peter** (Marktplatz): Cathedral and Town Hall stand side by side in the same square and enjoy equal esteem. The cathedral was started in 1042, but the impressive W. façade and towers were not completed until the 13C. The chapels in the S. aisle were built in the 14&15C, and the N. aisle was raised and modified in the late Gothic period by C.Poppelkern. After destruction and decline in the 16&17C the rebuilt N. tower was given a baroque top. From 1888–1901 the Dom was restored with great sensitivity in the Romanesque style, and the exterior in particular was given striking stylistic features, but also the unsuitable crossing dome. The Dom is today Bremen's principal Protestant church.
*The building:* The impression made by the exterior of the building is determined by the the early Gothic W. towers, most forcefully in the upper sections. The 2 crypts in the W. and E. go back to the earliest stage of the building and are a reminder that the original Romanesque church was intended to have two choirs. The W. crypt was reduced in size by the later addition of the towers, but the E. crypt, 75 ft. long and 36 ft. wide, makes an impressive lower church. The vaulting of the Romanesque pillared basilica, which originally had a flat ceiling, was added in 1230–40 and a complex system of pillars and half-pillars with capitals had to be developed to support it.

The swollen ribs and engaged columns in the S. aisle are particularly impressive. The N. aisle was renewed in the late Gothic period and fine net vaulting was added. The paintwork in the church was the result of restoration in the late 19C.
*Interior and furnishings:* The oldest and most important item is the *Enthroned Christ* in the SE crypt (*c.*1050). In the W. crypt, which serves as a baptismal chapel, is a *bronze font*: a bowl decorated with arches and figures and supported by 4 men riding on lions. It is a masterpiece from the period *c.*1220–30, in the great tradition of bronze casting of the Harz region. The most important pictorial decoration in the nave is provided by the nine almost 16 ft. high oak ends remaining from the *choir*

*Dom of St.Peter* ▷

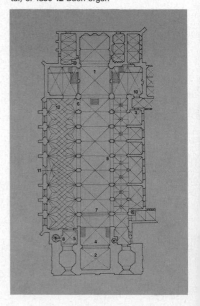

*N. aisle of the Dom St. Peter in Bremen*

*stalls* (*c.*1400) destroyed in 1828, and the organ gallery with figures, the work of the Münster artist H.Brabender, known as 'Beldensnyder'; the work, completed in 1518, has sandstone niches containing figures of Charlemagne (with a model of the cathedral) and the builder of the cathedral in the middle, and to the right and left canons, patrons and knights. This arrangement of figures is the last demonstration of the power of the church before the onset of the Reformation. The same sculptor was responsible for the stone Madonna on the last pillar before the crossing in the N. aisle.

**Rathaus** (Marktplatz): The Gothic Town Hall, built 1405–10 as a kind of municipal fortress with battlements and wall passage, was altered in appearance when the Reformation ended the tension between town and church; the façade facing the square was opened up with tall windows and the roof was given three gables and a cornice balustrade. The former wall passage was replaced on the main façade by an arcade of almost Italian lightness and an excessively lavish stone balcony-balustrade (1608–12). The seven Electors with Charlemagne and, in each case, four

*E. crypt in Dom St. Peter in Bremen (c. 1050)*

figures (prophets and sages) under baldachins, on the narrow side of the building, date from the period of the building's origin (c. 1410, school of Parler), but fit into the overall picture very well. The protuberant central gable, which reaches right down to the arcade, is a masterpiece of the 'Weser Renaissance', which found its motifs and ideas in Holland.

*Interior and furnishings:* The lower of the two halls set one above the other is a purely Gothic room (apart from the doors and spiral staircase) which was formerly used as a market and assembly hall, and even for theatrical performances. In the *upper room* Gothic and Renaissance combine, particularly in the windows. The finest feature of this councillors' banqueting hall is the *Güldenkammer*, a small room within the hall which was once decorated with golden leather wall coverings, and was used for confidential sessions; there is a glazed musicians' gallery above it. A wealth of figures, symbols, ornaments, cartouches and columns combine to form the most lavish wood carving of the N. German Renaissance. The allegorical frescos on the long wall opposite (including the Judgement of Solomon ascribed to the painter M.Bruyn) date from 1532. The *Ratskeller*

is worth visiting for the huge 18C painted barrels which form built-in 'drinking niches', and also for the 400 different wines which are served here.

**Roland** (Marktplatz): The almost 33 ft. high stone figure of Roland is the property of the Town Hall and citizens of Bremen; it was placed there in 1404 to replace a wooden Roland which had been burned by the Archbishop's faction. It is a symbol of civic freedom, and was the model for all the other Rolands in N. Germany; it expressed to the ruling archbishops the people's claim to sole allegiance to the Empire, and the very fact that the knight is turned to face the Dom symbolises protest and resistance. The Roland was venerated by the citizens of Bremen as 'a safeguard and a secular shrine'. The sword of justice in his hand stresses the city's independent jurisdiction, and a Platt (low German) inscription on the shield speaks of the freedom which 'Karl' (the Emperor) had granted to the city.

**Parish Church of Our Lady** (on the NW side of the Town Hall): The most striking features of this hall church are the three transverse gable roofs over the nave. The

*Rathaus and Dom*

squat towers of differing height show the phases of the building: the S. tower is Romanesque (*c.*1130), and was incorporated into the new W. tower complex in 1229. The hall church with three aisles has fine tracery windows (today in plain brick, formerly painted). The church of Our Lady is the Protestant parish church.

**Parish Church of St.Martin** (Martinistrasse): This church stands close by the Weser and its façade and four gables face the river. It was originally a three-aisled basilica, but was made into a hall church after being badly damaged by floods in the 14C, and was the Bremen merchants' place of worship. It was rebuilt after the Second World War. Interesting features of the furnishings are the Crucifixion reliefs and a 14C fresco. The Neander window (see ground plan) commemorates the well-known writer of hymns; his work includes 'Lobet den Herren'. There is a Glockenspiel in the tower, and the Neander house is attached to the church.

**Stadtwaage (Office of Weights and Measures)** (Langenstrasse): The three-storey building is made even higher by a five-storey step gable. It was built in 1587–88, totally destroyed in the Second World War, but rebuilt in 1958–61.

**Schütting** (Marktplatz): To show its importance in the eyes of the city, the merchants' hall stands immediately opposite the Town Hall: 'Schütting' is a Platt word for 'accumulating money'. The impressive façade with steep window axes was built in 1536–8 by the Antwerp architect Johann den Buscheneer. Decorative gables (with a Hanseatic merchant ship) and the cornice balustrade were added in 1594. The 1565 E. side gable is by a third hand, and is a step gable of the kind used on the Stadtwaage. The heavy portal with steps and balustrade was added in the late 19C and does not suit the aristocratic elegance of the façade.

**Schnoor** (near the Weser in the E. part of the old town): The 'Schnoor', a petit bourgeois residential area with picturesque small houses and courtyards was formerly

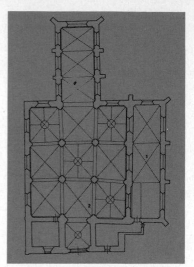

**Bremen, Unserer Lieben Frauen 1** 14C paintings, with retouched remains in the aisle (now the community hall) **2** Pulpit, 1709

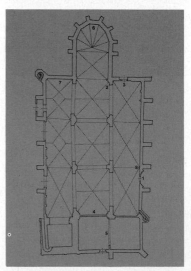

**Bremen, Martinikirche 1** Tympanum with Christ, 13C **2** Pulpit by H.Wulf, 1597 **3** Epitaph to Mayor Zobel, 1598 **4** Organ front by H. Wulf, 1603 **5** Relief of St. Martin, 1626 **6** Choir window by E.Steinecke, 1959 **7** St.Martin window **8** Neander window

inhabited by fishermen and workmen. The houses date from the last four centuries and have names like 'Behind the Wooden Door', 'Shady Place' or 'Castle of Torments'. The Schnoor is the only quarter of the city which has survived as a coherent whole.

**Böttcherstrasse:** This name is part of the cultural history of Bremen: in 1926–31 Ludwig Roselius, a coffee merchant and patron of the arts, commissioned contemporary artists to redesign an old street in a strange combination of medieval and expressionist styles. There are sculptures by B.Hoetger on the façades of the houses, some of which were badly damaged in the Second World War. The central feature is the *Roselius-Haus*, which contains the Roselius art collection.

**Villa Ichon** (24 Goetheplatz): This house, built in 1852, was rebuilt in 1871&2 in the historicist style. In 1982 the house, which since 1965 had fallen increasingly into disrepair, was taken over by a group of Bremen businessmen and architects and restored, largely in its original style. Since October 1982 various artistic groups have used the villa and many cultural events have taken place here; the house also presents temporary exhibitions, and has awarded a Villa Ichon culture peace-prize since 1983.

**Museums:** *Kunsthalle* (Am Wall): The collection of paintings includes works by Delacroix, Corot, Manet, Monet, Leibl and the German Impressionists. The graphics collection contains about 200,000 items (drawings and prints) and, despite heavy losses in the war, is one of the most significant in Germany. The sculpture collection is also worth seeing. The *Focke-Museum* (240 Schwachhauser Heerstrasse): The new building was designed by Prof. Bartmann in 1964, and houses the collections from the historical and applied art museums. *Übersee-Museum* (13 Bahnhofsplatz): In this museum, founded in 1896, are models of Chinese and Japanese houses and Japanese temple gardens, and also exhibits on ethnography. Within the Übersee-Museum is a *Children's Museum*

which deals predominantly with indigenous animals. *Bleikeller im St. Peter Dom* (Am Markt): Storage in lead has permitted the survival of *c.*500-year-old mummies. *Deutsches Schiffahrtsmuseum:* The German Maritime Museum is in the museum dock in Bremerhaven (60 km. N.).

**Theatres:** *Theater am Goetheplatz:* Opera, operetta, straight plays, musicals and dance; 989 seats. *Schauspielhaus:* Straight plays, musicals; 400 seats. *Concordia* an der Schwachhauser Heerstrasse: open stage for modern and experimental theatre; 100 seats.

---

**Brenz an der Brenz=Sontheim 7927**
Baden-Württemberg                    p.422☐H 18

There has been a church on the site of the *Protestant Parish Church and Former Collegiate Church of St. Gallus* since the 7C; it is a Romanesque pillared basilica which has an 8C choir in the shape of a parallelogram with apse, and also side aisles with side apses. The 1170–90 westwork was raised in 1631 and is unusual in having three towers. There is elaborate *decoration* on the consoles and arches of the exterior, on the tympanum (Christ teaching with Mary and John) and on the capitals of the Romanesque groin-vaulted *paradise porch*. In the interior the 13C *column capitals*, the medieval *tombstones* and a *Christ with Mandorla* (*c.*1250) in the S. apse are worth seeing.

---

**Bronnbach=Wertheim 6980**
Baden-Württemberg                    p.416☐G 15

**Former Cistercian Monastery Church of St.Maria:** The present Catholic parish church in the Tauber valley is one of the most interesting early Cistercian churches in Germany, showing Provençal and Burgundian influence. Building began in 1157, modifications took place in 1166 and the church was consecrated in 1222; the baroque interior dates from the

17&18C. The spare Cistercian style is evident in the exterior: a long cruciform three-aisled basilica, with a ridge turret above the crossing as the only decoration. The high aisles still have late Romanesque round arches, but those in the barrel-vaulted nave are Gothic.

The lavish *baroque altars* with twisted columns do not fit in with their dry, severely Cistercian surroundings, but are nevertheless of artistic merit. The high altar, the four side altars and the pulpit were created in 1712 by the Würzburg Master B.Esterbauer. The former high altar and the Magdalene altar are 17C. The *monastery buildings*, including *c.*1230 cloisters, 12C chapterhouse with late Romanesque rib vaulting on four columns, and 1727 Josephssaal are also worth seeing.

---

**Bruchsal 7520**
Baden-Württemberg                                   p.420☐E 17

---

**Schloss** (Schönbornstrasse): This magnificent Schloss was built under the aegis of one of the prince bishops of Schönborn, as were many other fine baroque buildings in the diocese; the bishops were consis-

tently skilful in their choice of architects, sculptors, painters and stucco workers. The building contains one of the most important works of baroque architecture in Europe, Balthasar Neumann's *Bruchsal staircase*. The Schloss complex consists of 50 individual buildings, and was completely destroyed in an air raid in 1945; it has been meticulously and painstakingly rebuilt by notable artists, largely in its original form. The well-known *Bruchsal Schloss concerts* take place annually in the Louis Seize chamber music room.

Building in the main courtyard with corps de logis, residential wing and church wing began in 1722; in 1730 the fresco painter C.D.Asam was involved in the decoration of the church (destroyed); the staircase dates from 1731 and the bell tower from 1738; decoration continued in the interior until 1760 and in the chamber music room until 1776.

The horse-shoe shaped complex is completed on the road side by connecting buildings. The two corner pavilions and Neumann's gatehouse are notable features. The gate leads straight to the impressive columns and pilasters of Neumann's façade.

*Interior and decoration:* Behind the splen-

*Schloss in Bruchsal*

did façade is the *staircase*. The stairs leap in a magnificent arch from a grotto-like space on an oval ground plan to the landing, which has a broad dome. A delightful feature is the change in the quality of light from the darker grotto to the light upper storey with stucco decoration beneath the glowing dome with frescos by J.Zick; these show scenes from the history of the building and the see. The landing leads to the restored *Fürstensaal*, which has portraits of the bishops of Speyer, and an allegorical ceiling fresco. Exhibited in the *corps de logis* are tapestries, paintings and furniture which survived the war, and also porcelain, faience, hunting weapons and gold objects. The *Hofgarten* to the W. of the Schloss is in the severe French style.

**Badische Landesbühne** (6 Klosterstrasse): The company performs in the Bruchsal theatre (280 seats) and in a number of places in the surrounding area.

**Museums:** The *Städtisches Museum* (in the Schloss) has exhibits on pre- and early history and medieval and modern history and painting, and the *Heimatmuseum Heidelsheim* (16 Merianstrasse) shows items on local history and crafts.

## Brüggen 3211
Lower Saxony                               p.414☐G 9

**Schloss:** This splendid baroque building with English park was largely built between 1686 and 1716 for a Braunschweig-Lüneburg court official. From the spacious entrance hall a double staircase leads to the upper storey, where the *banqueting hall* is decorated with pilasters, Corinthian capitals, stucco and putti. The central painting on the flat ceiling shows 'Apollo above the Circle of the Seasons' (1705).

## Brühl 5040
Nordrhein-Westfalen                        p.416☐B 12

**Schloss Augustusburg:** The country seat and hunting lodge of the Elector Clemens August was built on the foundations of a heavily fortified moated Burg blown up in 1689; it was originally to have been a moated Schloss, but in the second phase of building the design became Bavarian-French rococo under the Bavarian court architect F.de Cuvilliés. The Schloss, 'the finest rococo achievement in the

*Schloss Augustusburg, Brühl*

Rhineland', is now used by the Federal government for state purposes.

The foundation stone was laid and building began under J.C.Schlaun of Münster in 1725; Cuvilliés' removal of the towers and moat, reworking of the façade and introduction of a broad terrace took place in 1728–40. The Schloss was completed in 1754–70, with neoclassical touches. Repairs to war damage were finally completed in 1961.

Schlaun's baroque conception can still be seen from the E. aspect; Cuvilliés made the S. side the most important and with his spacious terrace transformed the complex into a garden Schloss.

The entrance hall is dominated by the *staircase*, which was designed by Balthasar Neumann. The grey, greenish blue and pink shimmer of the stucco marble columns and architraves, the white of the figures, the gold tones of the wrought iron banister and the bright stucco on a coloured ground make a fascinating blend of colours. The staircase leads to the *Guard Room* in light French rococo with a neoclassical flavour. In the N. wing are other

**Brühl, Schloss Augustusburg 1** Staircase **2** Garden room **3** Dining and music room

state rooms, like the *Blue Winter Quarters* 18C and above that is the *Yellow Appartment* with the Cuvilliés dining room.

**Also worth seeing:** The *Falkenlust* hunting lodge (built in 1729–40 to Cuvilliés' design). Former court and monastery church of *Maria zu den Engeln* (1491, rebuilt in 1735).

---

## Bückeburg 3062
Lower Saxony                                    p.414☐F 8

**Protestant Parish Church** (Lange Strasse/Schulstrasse): This church of the former Schaumburg-Lippe residence is one of the earliest large Protestant buildings and Herder, who was in charge of the parish from 1771–6, used to preach here.

The most splendid feature of the church (1611–15) is the *façade*, which rises from a plain base with ever-increasing elaboration of design and ornament and brings together a variety of stylistic elements.

The interior was designed as a Protestant preaching church and has wooden galleries on all sides, rib vaulting like a Gothic hall church and tall, slender columns with

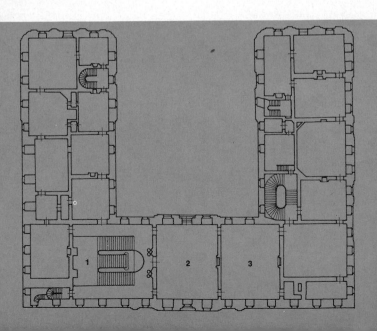

Corinthian capitals; the baroque paint-work has been renewed and the fine baroque *organ* was reconstructed after a fire in 1962, using the old carvings. The *pulpit* is also elaborately carved, with an elegant prince's box on the W. wall; there is a famous *bronze font* by A.de Vries (1615).

**Schloss** (Schlossstrasse): The present Schloss is on the site of a moated Burg built c.1300 by Graf Adolf von Schaumburg and modified in 1370–1404; the keep and the chapel of the older building have survived. The Schloss was rebuilt in Renaissance style in 1560–3 with four wings around a rectangular courtyard, a staircase tower and a court gallery on two sides. The baroque alterations were even more radical. The *Schloss gate*, a baroque triumphal arch in the same style as the church, shows a tendency to ostentation. The old *keep* was included in the baroque façade. In the *Schloss chapel* the altar table supported by two angels, the prince's box and the finely-carved pews are notable. The *goldene Saal* is also worth a visit (1605 coffered ceiling).

**Museums:** *Schaumburg-Lippisches Heimatmuseum* (22 Lange Strasse): This museum, founded in 1890, documents the

*Götterpforte in the Goldene Saal of the Schloss in Bückeburg*

*Bückeburg, moated Schloss*

*Bücken, carved altar, collegiate church*                    *Protestant parish church* ▷

history of the former principality of Schaumburg-Lippe and has exhibits on bourgeois and peasant domestic life and a collection of national costume. Other collections are housed in the *Schloss*.

## Bücken, Kreisgrafschaft Hoya 3091
Lower Saxony                                      p.414□F 7

**Protestant Collegiate Church:** Materials as well as style show the evolution of this 11–13C Romanesque basilica with two towers: in the first phase of building sandstone was used, in the second ashlar and granite, and in the third brick. The excellent furnishings include a 16 ft. high *triumphal cross* (1270). The *stained glass* with representations of the Life of Christ and legends of the saints is early Gothic. A late Gothic *carved altar*, the 13C stone *pulpit*, the 14C *choir stalls* and a 32 ft. high

*tabernacle* are particularly worthy of attention.

## Büdingen 6470
Hessen                                          p.416□F 13

**Schloss:** The formerly moated Schloss of the Princes of Ysenburg and Büdingen is a good example of an old, compact Herrenburg; Büdingen's medieval fortifications are still in excellent condition, and Schloss and town form a satisfying visual whole. The entire fortress complex was formerly surrounded by a double moat; the Burg is in the unusual shape of an irregular polygon with 13 sides; the surrounding walls are built of convex ashlar and are up to 6 ft. thick. Traces of the Romanesque complex can be seen everywhere, for example in the round arches of the former windows and the remains of an archivolt from the *residence*. The lower floor of the *chapel* and

the originally detached *keep* are also Romanesque and the *gatehouse* is Gothic with a late Gothic porch, but the overall impression is determined by the later buildings (late Gothic and Renaissance). Some groin-vaulted rooms in the Burg (some 16C wall paintings have survived), the furnishings of the late Gothic chapel (1495 – 7) and also the exhibits in the *Schlossmuseum* are of interest.

---

### Büren 4793
Nordrhein-Westfalen                    p.414☐E 10

**Former Jesuit Church of Maria Immaculata:** Bavarian and Tyrolean artists co-operated on this southern-looking baroque church—a rarity in Westfalia; it is also unusual to find the choir in the W. and

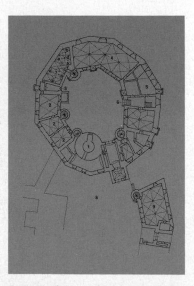

**Büdingen, Schloss 1** Castle keep, lower tower 13C, upper tower 15C **2** Great hall **3** Chapel, early 13C **4** Crooked hall, 15C **5** Kitchen **6** Baroque portal by Bartholomäus Schneller, 1673 **7** Schloss chapel, 1495-7 a) Choir stalls by Peter Schantz and Michel Silge, 1497-9 b) Tomb of Johann v. Ysenburg and Sophie v. Wertheim, *c*. 1400 c) Pietà, late-15C d) Pulpit by Konrad Büttner, 1610 **8** Castle outworks **9** Watch-tower

the façade in the E. The Elector of Cologne Clemens August, also Bishop of Paderborn, sent his Bonn court architect Roth to Büren to design the church, which was built in 1754-60. J.D.Winck, a pupil of the Bavarian rococo artist C.D.Asam, was responsible for the ceiling paintings. The stucco work dates from 1767-71 and the sculptures were finished a little later. The ornate and lavishly decorated *façade* and the crossing with its massive *dome* are the dominant exterior features; in the interior the splendour of the *stucco work* forms a fascinating contrast with the pink and blue tones of the walls. The *ceiling paintings* show scenes from the Life of Our Lady.

---

### Burghausen 8263
Bavaria                    p.422☐N 19

**Burg:** The six sections of the ancient Burg of the Dukes of Bavaria extend for 1200 yards along a narrow ridge between the Salzach and the Wöhrsee to form the largest castle complex in Germany; Emperor Heinrich II, also Duke of Bavaria, held court in a fortress here. The present building dates from the 13–15C. To the N. the site is flat and protected by numerous ditches, gates and courtyards; the final courtyard is a narrow gorge. The S. buildings tower over the town like the bow of a ship and include the three- storey *Dürnitzstock*, in which there is a storage hall with two aisles. Above that is the heated *dining- hall*, also with two aisles; both rooms have fine 15C groin vaulting. The upper storey was formerly the ballroom for the numerous inhabitants of the Burg. The choir of the St.Elisabeth *Burg chapel* was built as Romanesque architecture gave way to Gothic (*c*.1255) and the nave with its net vaulting *c*.1475. The Fürstenbau of the Burg of the Bavarian Dukes of Burghausen today houses a department of the *Bayrische Staatsgemäldesammlungen* (state painting collection).

**Also worth seeing:** 14C Rathaus; 16C government building; *Municipal Photographic Museum* at the entrance to the Burg; *Municipal Heimatmuseum* (local his-

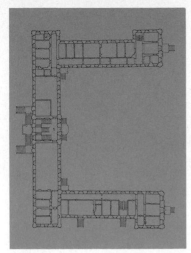

**Büren, Jesuit seminary 1** Carved staircase, 1727

tory) in the inner courtyard of the Burg; houses in the Inn quarter; parish church of St.Jakob (1360, with various modifications); Hospital Church of St.Jakob (1360, with various modifications); Heilig Geist Hospital Church (1st half of the 14C, baroque modification in the 18C); outside the town the 15C *Heiligkreuz* (Tittmoninger Strasse).

---

### Burglengenfeld 8412
Bavaria                                    p.422□L 16

**Burg:** Much remains of the Wittelsbach Burg dating back to the period around 1100 *(walls, keep, Friedrichsturm)*; several buildings were added in the 12C.

**St.Veit:** In this little church refurbished in the rococo style is the *memorial tomb* created by L.Hering for Bernhard von Hyrnheim (d.1541).

---

### Bürresheim
Rheinland-Pfalz                            p.416□C 13

**Burg:** Some of the Schloss is occupied; the rest is owned by the Land and used as a museum. It is easy to follow the stages by which the medieval fortress developed into a Gothic and then a baroque residential

*Burghausen, Burg*

building. The oldest part, the so-called Kölner Burg in the W. of the complex, still has a tall rectangular 12C *keep*; for Schloss Bürresheim see Mayen.

## Butzbach 6308
Hessen                                    p.416□E 13

Like many other towns Butzbach claims to have been Goethe's model for the epic 'Hermann und Dorothea'. The town has a large number of half-timbered houses built before the Thirty Years War.

**Markus church** (Kirchplatz): When the Markuskirche was built in the 14&15C the *Michael chapel* was incorporated and surrounded by walls, like the rest of the churchyard. Despite many alterations the character of the complex has been maintained. A striking feature of the interior furnishings is the *baldachin memorial tomb* of Landgraf Philipp von Hessen-Butzbach (1622); there is a 1614 *organ*.

**Rathaus and market place:** The *clock* was installed in the 1560 *Rathaus* in 1630. The finest buildings in the market place are the *Alte Post* (1636) and the *Goldene Löwe*.

**Heimatmuseum** (18 – 20 Griedelerstrasse): (local history).

## Buxtehude 2150
Lower Saxony                             p.414□G 5

Buxtehude was once a port and Hanseatic town. Only the *Marschtorzwinger* remains of the fortifications (arms granted 1539).

**Protestant Petrikirche** (Kirchenstrassen): The Petrikirche, which was presumably built in the mid to late 14C is a typical example of N. German brick Gothic. The three-aisled basilica was refaced in the 19C and the upper part of the tower was renewed, but in the style of the older parts of the building. The interior is particularly attractive: it has ornately profiled Gothic arches, six-part rib vaulting and high, light walls on the window sides. The most famous item of the interior furnishings, the late-14C *Buxtehude altar*, a Mary altar by Master Bertram, is on loan to the Hamburg Kunsthalle. The present *high altar* dates from 1710, the *pulpit* from 1674 and there are lavishly carved *pews* in the side aisles.

*Bürresheim, Burg*

**Also worth seeing:** The foundations of the *Benedictine monastery* (Altkloster) of 1197 have been excavated and reconstructed. The old port (Fleth) and parts of the former town fortifications like the moat (Viver) and fortified tower (Zwinger) still determine the layout of the Old Town. Medieval buildings such as 3 Fischer-strasse, 6 Abtstrasse and the house at 25 Lange Strasse have been outstandingly well restored.

**Heimatmuseum** (9 Petriplatz): Extensive local history collection. Altland filigree, figure of the Madonna and Passion altar (Flemish wood carving).

*Petrikirche, Buxtehude*

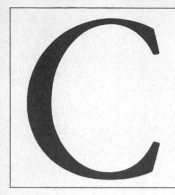

## Cadolzburg 8501

Bavaria                                     p.422□J 16

**Zollernburg** (reached by Marktstrasse
and the outer castle gate): The castle was
first mentioned in 1157, but its origins
probably date further back. It was extensively rebuilt in the 16–19C. In spite of the
numerous alterations and the damage
which it suffered at the end of the war, the
typical features of this medieval family seat
are still easily discernible. The outer
works, the towers, the gates and their
defences give an impression of a stronghold
from the high Middle Ages. The extensive
castle was formerly the residence of the
Counts of Zollern, who were the Burggrafen of Nuremberg, and in 1415–56 it
was the seat of the Electors of Brandenburg. Albrecht Dürer painted two watercolours of the courtyard.

## Caldern=3551 Lahntal 2

Hessen                                     p.416□E 12

**Protestant parish church:** The present
parish church was built in the mid 13C and
was linked to the Cistercian monastery
which had been founded a short time before. The building shows typical late
Romanesque features. As was usual at that
time in the village churches of the Dill district, the *pavement* in front of the high altar

is decorated with pebbles in a fishbone pattern. The *crucifix* dates from the first half
of the 14C. The richly decorated *organ* was
added in *c.* 1700.

## Calw 7260

Baden-Württemberg                          p.420□E 18

Calw is the birthplace of the novelist Hermann Hesse (1877 – 1962). The house
where he was born stands in the market
place. He is commemorated by a plaque
and a memorial in the museum. In his
'Gerbersau', Hesse collected all his stories
set in Calw and Swabia.

**Nagold bridge and Nagold chapel** (over
the river Nagold): The Gothic chapel of
St. Nikolaus was built above the middle
pier of this picturesque bridge in the 14C.

**Market square** (Markt): The town hall
(1673) bears witness to the affluence which
Calw enjoyed as the medieval meeting
point of clothiers from all over Europe.
The upper storeys were added in 1726.
The town has numerous well-preserved
*half-timbered houses,* most of which were
erected after the great fire which the town
suffered in 1692. The *market fountain* was
built in 1686.

**Local museum and Hermann Hesse
memorial** (Bischofstrasse 48): Folk art,

*Calw, chapel on bridge over the Nagold*

costumes, peasants' furniture, pewter, religious art, old furniture, and mementoes of the author Hermann Hesse, are on display here.

## Cappenberg = 4714 Selm
Nordrhein-Westfalen    p.414☐C 10

Gottfried von Cappenberg and his brother Otto turned the castle into a Premonstratensian monastery. Gottfried did this in order to atone for taking part in the campaign waged by the Saxon Duke Lothar, who took the city of Münster in 1121, setting the cathedral on fire in the process. Annette von Droste-Hülshoff, the Westphalian poetess, composed a ballad on the subject.

**Catholic parish church of St.Johannes** (Am Schloss): This church, with its rich *decorations*, is one of the most important religious sites in Westphalia. After Cappenberg castle had, in 1122, been converted into a house for the poor of Christ, work on building the church and monastery was begun (completed in 1149). The entire complex was secularized in 1803, and in 1816 it was acquired by Baron von Stein, who died here in 1831. The original appearance of the building was subsequently altered. The pillared basilica, which has a nave and two aisles and originally possessed a flat roof, was given a Gothic vault in *c*. 1387. The basilica has a cruciform ground plan, typical of the period. The exterior walls are undecorated, and this accords with the severity and spirit of the Premonstratensians. Despite the Gothic vaults, the interior is characterized by Romanesque features. The *church treasure* includes the famous gold-plated copper head of Frederick Barbarossa, a *reliquary* said to be the first image of an emperor to have been made in Germany (mid to late 12C). The precious stones used for the eyes have been lost. Also note the *Cappenberg*

*Double monument, St. Johannes, Cappenberg*

## Castell 8711
Bavaria                                    p.418□H 15

**Upper and lower castles** (on the Herrenberg/Schlossberg): These two ruined castles are the remains of the ancestral seats of the Castell counts. The upper castle was built in 1258, but its basic features probably date back to the early 9C. The lower castle was completed in 1497.

**New Schloss** (N. of the village): The new, baroque Schloss (begun in 1687) was the residence of the counts of Castell until 1806. Occupying three sides of a courtyard, it was built of rough masonry.

**Protestant parish and Schloss church:** The church (built 1780–92) is one of the major examples of Protestant architecture in Bavaria. The interior is late rococo and the galleries blend in well with the rest of the church, and they also extend around the choir.

*crucifix* in the transept (12C), an important example of late Romanesque German sculpture. The *double monument* to Gottfried and Otto von Cappenberg, the two founders, is a masterpiece of the high Gothic and is to be found in the choir. Dating from *c*. 1330, it is the work of unknown Westphalian sculptors. The founders are seen carrying a model of the church between them. The 16C *choir stalls* are richly carved. In the S. transept is a larger-than-life *effigy* of the knight Gottfried von Cappenberg, who was later canonized.

**Schloss:** This former provost's residence was built in 1708, although the S. wing dates from 1684 and the two gatehouses from 1840; and it is approached along an oak-lined avenue. It now houses the *Baron von Stein Archive*. The main sections of the *park* surrounding the Schloss were laid out by Baron von Stein. E.M. von Arndt was a frequent guest here.

## Celle 3100
Lower Saxony                               p.414□H 7

Adolf von Knigge wrote in 1793 that Celle 'was adorned with charming plantations in the English taste,' and that 'despite the desolate surrounding region, Celle unites the amenities of country life with the companionable joys of town life'. Hermann Löns praised Celle as a 'very beautiful town', and Hans Fallada described his visits to his grandmother in Celle in his memoirs 'Those times we spent at home'.

**Schloss** (Schlossplatz): This Schloss stands on a rise and is surrounded by old moats. The building was originally the centre and focal point of the town. Its present form goes back to Duke Georg Wilhelm (1665–1705). However, some parts of the building can be traced back to the late 13C. The oldest room is the *Schloss chapel* in the SE tower. This chapel was

*Head reliquary, St. Johannes* ▷

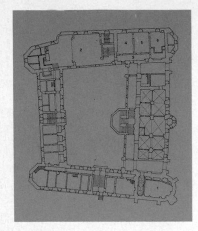

**Celle, Schloss 1** Schloss chapel **2** Schloss theatre **3-6** Ducal state rooms

built in 1485 and rebuilt in the 16C. The numerous alterations and rebuildings have only slightly changed the overall impression made by the building. The heavily articulated façade, with its gables, oriels, portals and the distinctive corner towers, is a masterpiece of German Renaissance architecture. Behind the façade there is an inner courtyard and the NW tower houses the *castle theatre* (completed in 1695), the oldest surviving theatre in Germany. There are splendid baroque rooms in the N. wing.

**Town church** (An der Stadtkirche): Originally Gothic, now a three-storeyed 17C baroque hall church with a wealth of stucco and sculpture. In the choir, several 16&17C *tombs* and *epitaphs* of the Guelph counts remind one of the original interior. Note the *wooden barrel-vault*, the *altar* (1613) and the *princes' crypt*.

**Old Rathaus** (Market): Begun in the 14C,

*The Schloss in Celle is a German Renaissance masterpiece*

the Old Rathaus was enlarged in Renaissance style in 1573–9. The façade was altered in neoclassical style in the 18C. A W. extension was added in 1938.

**Old town:** *Kalandgasse, Kanzleistrasse* with the *Higher Regional Court, Schuhstrasse, Am Heiligen Kreuz, Poststrasse* and *Grosser Plan* with some beautiful, well-preserved *half-timbered houses* are all interesting streets in the old town. There is also a baroque *prison* on the Trift. Most of the town houses are richly decorated and display features dating from the late Gothic up to the baroque. The small oriels (Ausluchte) are typical.

**Bomann Museum** (Schlossplatz 7): The collections are devoted to the rural life on Lüneburg Heath, and the history of the town and surrounding country. A fully furnished 16C farmhouse from Narjesbergen has been set up in the museum.

**Schloss theatre** (Schlossplatz 1): The main theatre seats 330 and there is also a studio theatre with 55 seats. Each of these theatres has its own company.

*Cismar, Benedictine monastery church*

---

**Cham 8490**

Bavaria                                      p.422□M 16

**Rathaus** (Marktplatz): The 15C town hall has been altered several times, and in 1875 a neo-Gothic extension was added to it.

**Parish church of St.Jakob** (Stadtplatz): The substructures and towers date back to the 13C but the nave was rebuilt several times prior to 1900. The fine *stucco* and *paintwork* are from around 1760, as is the *tabernacle* in the sacristy.

**Fortifications:** The oldest sections of these well-preserved fortifications are 13C. The *castle gate,* with its four massive, round towers, is worth seeing.

*Heimatmuseum* (Ludwigstrasse 1): Collections devoted to the history of the town and countryside, as well as folklore.

---

**Cismar=2433 Grömitz**

Schleswig-Holstein                           p.412□J 3

**Former Benedictine monastery and church:** A number of Benedictine monks were banished from Lübeck by the archbishop because of their behaviour and were sent to what was then the remote town of Cismar (now a district of Grömitz). Today, there are only remains of the comprehensive 13C monastery, and these have been incorporated in more modern buildings and are now barely recognizable. The single-aisled brick church, which was completed in *c.* 1250, although subsequently enlarged and rebuilt several times, survives. Its interior is clearly modelled on the Marienkirche in Lübeck (q.v.). The most important feature is the carved *altar* (1310–20), which is probably by a Lübeck workshop. The reliefs show scenes from the life of Christ, and there are other pictures in their original frames. The wings

*Clausthal-Zellerfeld, parish church*

depict the lives of John the Evangelist and St.Benedict.

## Clausthal-Zellerfeld 3392
Lower Saxony                          p.414☐H 9

**Protestant parish church of the Holy Spirit** (Hindenburgplatz): This church completed in 1642 and built of spruce is one of the largest wooden churches in Europe (the tower is of oak). The interior is dominated by the *pulpit* and the *altar* (1641), the *brass chandelier* (1660), some very fine 17C *memorials,* and the *organ* (1770).

**Oberharzer Museum** (16 Bornhardtstrasse): A museum devoted to the history of mining in the Harz. It includes an underground mine gallery, horse-operated gins, and many other items of mining equipment.

## Cloppenburg 4590
Lower Saxony                          p.414☐D 6

**Museumsdorf** (Museumstrasse 13): The foundation stone for what is today the largest open-air museum of its kind in Germany was laid in 1934 by H.Ottenjann, an expert on the local history of Cloppenburg. It covers 37 acres and features 16–19C peasant's houses from Lower Saxony, which have been faithfully re-erected in the museum and furnished accordingly. The village, a popular tourist attraction, today contains a total of 80 buildings. The *Quatmannshof* (1805), with its half-timbered façade and projecting gable, is among the finest houses in the Museumsdorf.

## Coburg 8630
Bavaria                               p.418☐I 14

The former residents of Coburg include: Martin Luther (who, in 1530, spent over five months here waiting for an opportunity to be heard by the Augsburg Imperial Diet), the poet Friedrich Rückert (from 1820 until his death in 1866) and the novelist Jean Paul (who was here as a ducal councillor in 1803–4).

**Veste Coburg** (Veste): The Veste is among the largest castles in Germany and is regarded as the 'Franconian crown'. It stands above the valley of the Itz and commands a view over Thuringia and Franconia.
*History:* The castle occupies an impregnable position on a spur which falls steeply on three sides. It appears to have been begun in the 11C—the chapel of St.Peter and St.Paul—the Fürstenbau with the adjoining kitchen and the Steinerne Kemanate (Stone Bower) which Luther later made famous, were added in the 12&13C. The medieval castle was expanded into a provincial fortress in the 16&17C.
*Architecture:* The extensive alterations, rebuilding and additions, mean that there is no uniform architectural style. The *Blaue Turm* shows late Romanesque features, the *Hohe Haus* with its many oriels

*Museum village of Cloppenburg*

were added in the early 15C. The nave was probably not completed until the 16C. The baroque interior dates from the 18C. Much of the church is late Gothic. The two towers, which are dissimilar, are a conspicuous feature. One of them is square and almost unadorned apart from the baroque calotte and the Gothic turrets of the top storey. It is much shorter than the second tower, which has balustrades and pinnacles. A prominent feature of the interior is an *alabaster monument* (1598) to Duke Johann Friedrich II by N.Bergner, the Thuringian sculptor. The monument rises through five tiers to a height of 39 ft., and is among the most significant and splendid Renaissance monuments in Germany. The figures on the main tier depict members of the Duke's family, while the central relief shows Joseph being transported to the tomb of the Canaanite. The outstanding *tombstone* of the knight Bach is medieval and is situated in the basement of the tower.

**Schloss Ehrenburg** (Schlossplatz): The name of the building (Ehrenburg means honoured castle) dates back to a visit paid by Emperor Charles V in 1547.
In 1543–7, the original Franciscan monastery was expanded into a town Schloss by order of Duke Johann Ernst. In 1586, Duke Johann Casimir gave the order for extensive alterations and enlargements. Further work was carried out in the 17&18C after a fire. The wing leading towards the Steingasse is today all that survives of the Renaissance Schloss built by Duke Johann Ernst. The main part of the Schloss was rebuilt after the fire, and its main front, some essential features of which are baroque, faces N. (some sections are neo-Gothic). The *court chapel*, which can scarcely be recognized as such from the outside, is part of the W. wing. It was completed in 1701 and has lavish stucco and a gallery that runs virtually the whole way round it. The *Giants' Hall*, named after the 28 giants in heavy Italian stucco, is on the floor above the church. The *White Hall* (on an upper floor of the central section), the *Red Room* and the *Gobelin Room* also have richly stuccoed ceilings. The decoration of some of the other rooms is neoclassical,

is late Gothic, and the *Ziehbrunnen* is Renaissance. There are several courtyards, surrounded by up to three rings of walls. The *Fürstenbau*, the *Steinerne Kemanate*, and the new guests' building, are grouped around the E. courtyard.
*Interior and decoration:* Today the Veste contains extensive *art collections* from nine centuries of European art and culture. The focal points are: the collection of Cranach's paintings, the largest collection of arms in West Germany, and a coin cabinet with some 20,000 coins and medals. There is a world-famous collection of drawings and prints (300,000 sheets). The *Luther Room* in the Steinerne Kemanate commemorates Luther's stay here in 1530.

**Protestant parish church of St.Moriz** (Pfarrgasse): The parish church contains significant Renaissance cultural monuments and is the oldest surviving building in the town centre. Work began in the 12C, and large sections, such as the two towers,

*Veste Coburg*

the most typical example being the *Throne Room* in the E. wing. Large parts of the schloss are today a *museum,* displaying the town's history, 19C domestic décor, and baroque tapestries.

**Rathaus** (Marktplatz): The town hall in its present form was rebuilt in the 16C and in *c.* 1750 it was extended. The two-storeyed *oriel* in the SE corner of the building depicts St. Moriz, the town's patron saint. Underneath this, there is a smaller statue of H.Schlechter, the *architect,* in his hands he is holding a small sign on which the architect's symbol and the initials of his name can be seen. On the upper storey of the town hall is the *Great Hall,* with a massive timber ceiling.

**Cantzley and town houses:** The *Cantzley,* which is the town law court (1600), is on the N. side of the market square. Some fine town houses survive in the Ketschengasse (the *mintmaster's house,* No. 7),

in the Bürglass *(Hahnmühle),* and in the Steingasse (where the court pharmacy is to be found among other buildings). Houses No. 4 (tourist office) and No. 17 in the Herrngasse, and also the *secondary school,* are interesting.

**Regional theatre** (Schlossplatz 6): This theatre was opened in 1840 and has 550 seats. Today it has both its own company of actors and its own group of musicians.

---

**Cochem 5590**
Rheinland-Pfalz                    p.416□C 14

**Reichsburg Cochem** (Schlossstrasse): Built in 1072, enlarged in the 14C, destroyed in the 17C, rebuilt in 1869–77, damaged again in World War 2 and subsequently repaired. Only the octagonal lower storey of the keep survives from the original castle and the main elements of the present building are neo-Gothic (the castle is open to the public).

**Catholic parish church of St.Martin** (Kirchplatz): This church dates back to a Franconian foundation. It was rebuilt in *c.* 1500. Large parts of the building were destroyed in World War 2, but the choir and the S.wall of the nave survived. The *reliquary bust* of St.Martin (*c.* 1500) is an interesting feature.

**Old houses:** Some of the houses in the *Moselpromenade* (12 and 36) were spared 'modernization'. They evoke the colourful history of the town, whose first mention, in the 9C, states that it is the property of the Holy Roman Empire. There are some more fine old houses on the *market square*, together with the Rathaus (1739).

---

**Coesfeld 4420**
Nordrhein-Westfalen                      p.414□C 9

---

**St.Lamberti** (Marktplatz): The present church was originally a late Romanesque hall church, which was altered and decorated in late Gothic style in 1473–1524. The W. end and the tower were built in 1703, replacing some sections of the old building which had fallen down. Apart from the late Gothic elements, Dutch classical influence can be seen in the *tower* (sandstone with brick facing). The most important decoration is the early-14C life-sized *crucifix*, made of wood. The 11 life-sized *Apostles* on the pillars (1506–20) are by J.Düsseldorp. There are also *paintings* by the Antwerp school, and some *wrought iron*.

**Catholic parish church of St.Jacobi** (Jacobikirchplatz): The late Romanesque hall church, which dates back to 1195, was destroyed in World War 2 and replaced by a modern building. The famous and richly decorated 13C *portal* has survived and is typical of Münsterland portals. Of the old furnishings, the late Romanesque *font* (*c.* 1240) and the Flemish *carved altar* (*c.* 1520) have survived.

**Münsterland town houses:** Most of the fine town houses were destroyed in World War 2. Some have survived in *Mühlenstrasse* (including 3 and 15), in *Süringstrasse* (9, 14) and in *Walkenbrücker Strasse* (4, 29).

**Also worth seeing:** The *Walkenbrücker Gate* (Mühlenplatz), which was rebuilt after the war, and the *Pulverturm* (Schützenwall), are remnants of the town's massive 14C *fortification*. The *Heimatsmuseum* is devoted to local history.

---

**Comburg = 7170 Schwäbisch Hall**
Baden-Württemberg                        p.420□G 17

---

**Former monastery of Gross-Comburg:** The former monastery is in the Kochertal valley on the SE edge of the town of Schwäbisch Hall. The monastery castle is one of the most important buildings of this kind in Germany. It was founded in the 10C by the Franconian Count von Rothenburg, and was later rebuilt, probably in 1087. The overall complex is a mixture of buildings from eight centuries.

**Monastery church of St.Nikolaus:** The present church was erected in 1707–15 on the foundations of an older one, some sections of which survive (W. tower and choir towers). The restrained style of the older building contrasts with the baroque splendour of the new church. The influence exerted at that time by artists from Würzburg is unmistakable (Joseph Greising was the architect).
*Interior and decoration:* The long hall is rich in baroque treasures. The *high altar* is by the Würzburg artist B.Esterbauer (1713–17). The *antependium,* consisting of a wooden panel with gilt copper (*c.* 1140), is more significant than the high altar itself. The antependium and the enormous *wheel chandelier* both probably originate from the Comburg workshop. The ring symbolizes the wall of Jerusalem with its twelve towers, and the lanterns are in the form of gatehouses. Apostles and prophets are depicted in embossed medallions. There are similar wheel chandeliers in the

*Reichsburg, Cochem*

Münster in Aachen (q.v.) and in the cathedral in Hildesheim (q.v.). The Romanesque *tomb of Burkhard II,* the church's founder (*c.* 1220), is in the nave. The *monument* to Provost Neustetter dates from 1570 and is a Renaissance masterpiece.

**Monastery:** The numerous additions and alterations to the monastery mean that it no longer displays any uniformity. The most important part is the hexagonal *Erhard chapel,* a massive building whose origins can be traced back to 1230 and earlier. The third of the three *gates* is early-12C Romanesque and houses the *St. Michael chapel.*

**Klein-Comburg:** Probably a convent, Klein-Comburg was erected in the first half of the 12C on the slope of the valley opposite Gross-Comburg. Its central feature is the former *monastery church of St. Ägidius,* only the choir of which is vaulted. Some remains of the 12C paintwork have

survived, but most of it was replaced in the 19C.

---

**Corvey = 3470 Höxter**
Nordrhein-Westfalen                         p.414☐G 9

**Former Benedictine abbey of Corvey:** In 822, after the unsuccessful founding of a settlement known as *Hethis* in 815, the brothers Adalhard (the abbot of Corbie) and Wala, both of whom were cousins of Charlemagne, founded the Benedictine abbey of *Corvey* on a bend in the river Weser. The monastery soon became an intellectual centre. It was here that Widukind wrote his history of the Saxons. The richly stocked *monastery library* contained the Annals of Tacitus, which still survive, and several works by Cicero. The poet Hoffmann von Fallersleben worked here on the library of the Count of Corvey from 1860 –74, although this was long after Corvey had been secularized. Fallersleben's tomb

*Chapterhouse, Comburg monastery*

is in the monastery graveyard. The abbey was rebuilt in baroque style after being destroyed in the Thirty Years' War. The extensive complex forms a long rectangle and is entered through a stone gateway. Today, nothing remains of the moats and drawbridges. The E. wall with a parapet walk, has survived.

**Former monastery church:** A basilica with a nave, two aisles and an outside crypt was built in 822–44 and was also destroyed in the Thirty Years' War. It stood on the site of the present parish church of St. Stephanus. The present building, a Gothicized hall church, was constructed in 1667 – 71. The W. end of the original church was incorporated in the new one, and has survived all the ravages of war. The dimensions of the previous church were also largely retained. The *Benedictus Chapel* (1727) is E. of the choir, and on the S. side of the nave is the *Lady Chapel*, which was also added later (*c.* 1790). The church was extensively restored after World War 2. The W. end, built 873–85, was used for the German emperors, who attended the monks' divine service from here (there is documentary evidence for 24 royal visits up to the mid 12C). The function of the W. end corresponded exactly to that of the Palatine Chapel in Aachen (q.v.). The particularly large central arch was for the emperor, the smaller ones were for the retinue. The new Gothic section, built 1667–71, adjoining the W. end is the most important part of the church.

*Interior and decoration:* The church's decoration is characterized by what is known as Paderborn baroque. This is more pompous and robust in its forms than the baroque of S. Germany. The *high altar* and both *side altars* are bright red, and the *choir stalls* are richly carved. The *organ* on the W. wall is borne by four angels. In the W. end, a much-damaged *fresco* from the time of the church's foundation depicts the battle between Odysseus and Scylla.

**Schloss:** The Schloss developed from the former abbey and was built in 1699–1721. It surrounds the *cloister* and a second large *inner courtyard*. The *W. façade* is 650 ft. long and has five portals of different sizes. The *Corvey Festival* is held annually in the *Kaisersaal*.

## Crailsheim 7180
Baden-Württemberg　　　　　　p.422□H 17

**Town church of St. Johannes Baptist:** An inscription on the tower gives 1398 as the year when the church was begun, but there are documents which mention the building as early as 1289. Work was not completed until the mid 15C. The late Gothic church is similar in form to the Franciscan church in Rothenburg (q.v.). The central feature of the interior is the *high altar* dating from 1486. The *tabernacle*

Corvey, former abbey church of St. Stephanus and Vitus 1 W. end 2 High altar, c. 1675, designed by Johann Georg Rudolph, carved by Johann Sasse 3 Side altars, c. 1675 4 Choir stalls, c. 1675 5 Organ: works by Andreas Schneider, 1681; organ front attributed to Sasse 6 Memorial to abbot v. Bellinghausen (d. 1696) 7 Memorial to abbot v. Velde (d. 1714) 8 Memorial to abbot v. Horrich (d. 1721) 9 Memorial to abbot v. Bittersdorf (d. 1737)

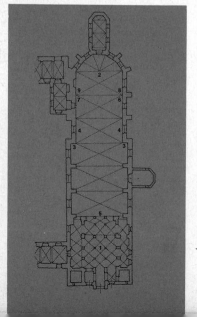

(1499) and the *baroque organ* (1709) are both worth looking at. There are numerous *tombs*, the finest being those of Wendel von Schrotzberg, on the S. wall of the nave, and Anna Ursula of Brunswick and Lüneburg, on the W. wall.

**Fränkisch-Hohenlohesches Heimatmuseum:** (Spitalstrasse 2): This museum in the former hospital chapel has collections relating to the town's history, arts and crafts, violins and faience.

## Creglingen 6993
Baden-Württemberg　　　　　　p.416□H 16

**Herrgotts chapel:** The gentry of Brauneck ordered a Herrgotts chapel to be built S. of the town of Creglingen in 1399. It was erected on the site of a miracle of the Host (a peasant had found a Host while ploughing). It became a much-visited pilgrimage church in the late Middle Ages. This chapel consists of a single area incorporating both the nave and choir. Thanks to first-class restoration, the beauty of the original building can still be seen.

*Interior:* The *altarpiece of the Virgin* is especially fine. It stands above a stone altar table in the nave, on the exact site of the miracle of the Host. T. Riemenschneider carved this Lower Franconian masterpiece in 1502–5. It is comparable with the Altar of the Holy Blood in St. Jakobs in Rothenburg (q.v.), but it is superior in its arrangement. The central scene of the Assumption depicts the Virgin Mary being borne to heaven by the angels. The Apostles may be seen below her. The wings show scenes from the life of the Virgin. The Coronation of the Virgin is shown at the top, with the Saviour floating above. The individual figures are either not coloured or only very slightly. The rear of the central scene and of the Coronation of the Virgin is pierced by holes and the light coming from behind gives rise to a highly unusual shadow effect. The two *side altars* date from c. 1460, the *high altar* from c. 1510. There are *tombstones* in the pavement of the church.

*Corvey, monastery church from ground* ▷
*floor of W. end*

# D

## Dachau 8060
Bavaria                                      p.422□K 19

Ludwig Thoma lived in Dachau (Augsburger Strasse 13, 1893–7) and was the town's 'first resident advocate'. In his stories about peasants, he described the town as possessing a 'rough, old Bavarian zest'.

**Schloss** (Schlossstrasse): The building which preceded the present Schloss was an 11C castle, replaced under Duke Ernst by a new building constructed in 1546–73. Rebuilding was carried under Max Emanuel in 1715. The Schloss fell into disrepair in 1806–9, and only the SW section survived. The high point of the Renaissance building was the old *Festsaal* with its splendid coffered wooden ceiling. A notable staircase leads up to it, and is the work of J.Effner, who also drew up the plans for the rebuilding. In the Festsaal it-

*Dachau, Schloss*

self there is a grisaille frieze painted by H.Thonauer in 1567.

**Court garden:** A baroque garden, only sections of which survive, it originally descended to the Amper valley in series of large terraces.

**Parish church of St. Jakob:** Built 1584 –1629, damaged by war in 1648 and subsequently repaired. Later several additions were made and the height of the towers was increased. The most important item of decoration is a chased silver figure of St. James dating from 1690.

**Concentration camp memorial** (Alte Römerstrasse 75), with exhibits relating to the history of the concentration camp and of persecution under the Nazis.

---

## Darmstadt 6100

Hessen                 p.416☐E 15

From 1567 onwards Darmstadt was the seat of the Landgraves of Hesse-Darmstadt. Large parts of the town were destroyed in World War 2 when buildings of architectural importance were lost and the former plan of the town was obliterated. The town was a cultural centre in Hessen from the 18C onwards, and possibly even before. Karoline von Hesse-Darmstadt, Goethe's 'Grosse Landgräfin', maintained contacts with the major figures of her time, including Goethe, Herder, Wieland and Frederick the Great. However, Darmstadt is also associated with such names as Georg Büchner, the dramatist who lived here in 1816–31 and 1834 – 5, the poet and journalist Matthias Claudius (1776), the poet Ferdinand Freiligrath (1841–2) and Theodor Heuss (1st President of the Federal Republic). Around the turn of the century an artists' colony developed on the Mathildenhöhe. Darmstadt is the home of the German Academy for Language and Poetry and the Georg Büchner prize, the most important German prize for literature, is awarded here every year.

**Schloss** (Marktplatz): The Schloss now houses the Province and Hochschule (Technical University) library, the State Archive, the Schlossmuseum, and some Hochschule departments.
The origin of the present building dates back to 1331. There was a fire in 1546 and

*Darmstadt, Ernst-Ludwig-Haus*

*Russian chapel*

*Portal of the Hochzeitsturm*

rebuilding began in 1557. Ten years later, the Schloss was extended and converted into a Residenzschloss. L.R. Delafosse drew up plans to make the building a showpiece of baroque style. In 1944 the entire castle complex was burned down but was subsequently rebuilt to the original plan. The complex is divided into the Altschloss and the so-called Neuschloss. The Altschloss consists of simple, mainly three-storey buildings of different styles around three inner courtyards. The oldest section, the Herrenbau, developed from the 14C palace although alterations were made right into the 20C. The *Weissesaalbau* (1501–12, altered in 1716) adjoins the Herrensaal to the S. The S. end of the complex is formed by the *Kaisersaalbau* (1595–7). On the E. side (1595–7) there is a Renaissance church. The church entrance facing the court was rebuilt in 1709 from plans drawn up by Delafosse. The *Paukergang* (1595–7) forms the N. end of the Altschloss and above the gate there are very fine double-arched loggias in both upper storeys. The Altschloss is connected to the Neuschloss by the *Glockenbau* (1663–71). The lantern of the square, four-storeyed, staircase tower contains the carillon cast by S.Verbeek in 1670. According to Delafosse's plans, the Neuschloss was to be extended into a great castle, but this project was only partly realized. The Neuschloss surrounds the old castle building with two long wings to the S. and SW and these make a monumental impression, the focus of attention being the projecting entrance on the side facing the market.

*Interior and furnishings:* Parts of the rebuilt castle are used as an archive, library and museum, and also for some departments of the Hochschule, and the original furnishings have had to be moved. However, the atmosphere of the former residence is recreated in the Schlossmuseum—whose most important possession is the *'Darmstadt Madonna'*, by Holbein the younger. The Hesse *Landesmuseum* (entrance in the

*Protestant parish church*

*St. Ludwig*

Friedensplatz) houses art and science under a single roof and its most interesting section is the *Sammlung Ströher,* one of the world's most important collections of pop art.

**Herrengarten with the Prinz-Georg-Palais** (Schlossgartenstrasse.): In step with the changes in court taste, the former castle grounds were redesigned to form a French pleasure garden (1681 under Elisabeth Dorothea) and an English garden (1766). In the Herrengarten there stands the Prinz-Georg-Palais, which Delafosse probably built around 1710 as a summer residence for the court. The orangery and coach house, which are separate wings, extend in front of the simple baroque palace. The palace has been used as a *porcelain museum* since 1907.

**Mathildenhöhe** (from the city centre via Dieburger Str.): The Mathildenhöhe, a park created in 1830 by Grand Duke Ludwig II and named after his daughter-in-law Mathilde, became an artists' colony in 1901, establishing itself with a sensational exhibition. It was as a result of this and the following art exhibitions that Darmstadt became a centre of the German Jugendstil (Art Nouveau). Famous artists designed buildings on the Mathildenhöhe. The Viennese artist Josef Maria Olbrich, who was in charge of the work of extending the Mathildenhöhe into an artists' colony, designed the *Ernst-Ludwig-Haus* (today the seat of the German Academy for Language and Poetry). Peter Behrens, an artist from Hamburg, built a house for himself on the Alexandraweg. Olbrich's group of three houses on the Prinz-Christian-Weg was built for the exhibition held in 1904. The *Hochzeitsturm,* one of the town's landmarks, was designed by Olbrich and completed for the 1908 exhibition. The *Russian Chapel,* which was consecrated in 1899, is also located on the Mathildenhöhe.

**Rosenhöhe** (near the Ostbahnhof): Formerly a vineyard on the estate; a park was laid out here in the early 19C. The *Mausoleum* of Princess Elisabeth (designed by G. Moller in 1826) is in the middle of the park. The *Löwentor*, originally on the Mathildenhöhe, was built by A.Müller and B.Hoetger for an exhibition given by Darmstadt artists in 1914. An altered version was erected on the Rosenhöhe.

**Luisenplatz:** The distinguishing feature of the Luisenplatz in the town centre is the *Ludwigssäule (Ludwig Column)*, 95 ft. high, built in 1844 as a monument to Grand Duke Ludwig I. The *Kollegienhaus* (1777 –80) was rebuilt after being destroyed in World War 2. Once an administrative building, it is today the seat of the President of the Government.

**The principal Protestant Church** (Kirchstrasse.): All that remains of the original Marienkapelle, which dates from the 13C., is the five-storey W. tower (upper storey 1627–31, lantern and belfry 1953). The long choir was probably built in 1419–31. Originally built in 1685–7, the late Gothic nave was altered in 1844–5. After being destroyed in World War 2, the church was rebuilt (1952–3), with alterations. It has unique Renaissance tombs, the most important of which is the three-tiered monument in the form of an altar, showing Landgrave Georg I and his wife Magdalena zur Lippe. It was the work of P.Osten in 1588–9 and, together with the monument to Philipp the Magnanimous in Kassel, is the oldest monumental tomb in Hesse, dating from the post-Reformation period.

**The Catholic St.-Ludwigs-Kirche** (Wilhelminenplatz): Behind the monument to Grand Duchess Alice. The large rotunda was erected in 1822–38 to a design by G.Moller (1820) and rebuilt by C.Holzmeister (Vienna) after being completely destroyed in World World 2. This building was built in imitation of the Pantheon of Rome and is regarded as a typical German classical building. The dome is 48 ft. high and its diameter is 95 ft.

**Altes Landestheater** (between Schloss and Herrengarten): Built as a court theatre by G. Moller in 1818–19 it was rebuilt in 1875–9 with slight alterations after a fire in 1871. It finally burned down in 1944. The portico of columns has survived.

**Museums:** *Hessisches Landesmuseum* (Friedensplatz 1): Painting, sculpture, and examples of applied art etc. are held in the museum, built by A.Messel in 1896–1906. *Hessische Landes- und Hochschulbibliothek* (in the Schloss): The collection on display includes valuable early printed books, manuscripts, music manuscripts and letters written by musicians. *Schlossmuseum* (Residenzschloss): Interior furnishings and paintings of the 17 – 20C, carriages, costumes and uniforms. *Grossherzogliche Porzellan-Sammlung* (in the Prinz-Georg-Palais in the Herrengarten): European porcelain and faience of the 18&19C. *Kunsthalle* (Steubenplatz): Temporary exhibitions of art from all periods. *Stadtmuseum* (Grosse Bachstrasse 2): Local history.

**Theatres:** A large and small theatre with workshop (both opera and drama) are housed under one roof in a modern building designed by R.Prange in the Marienplatz. The large theatre has 956 seats, the small one 482, and the workshop 150. *Theater am Platanenhain* (Georg-Büchner-Platz 3): A small theatre.

**Environs: Kranichstein,** (8 km. NE) It was built by Jakob Kesselhut in 1572 for Landgrave Georg I as a castle with three wings in the Renaissance style. A striking feature is the sturdy round tower in the NW corner. A building was added at right angles in 1863. Today the castle is a *hunting museum* and a hotel.

---

**Dausenau 5409**

Rheinland-Pfalz                    p.416☐D 13

**Protestant parish church of Maria and St.Kastor:** The church was first mentioned in 1319. The tower is Romanesque, while the short nave is a 14C Gothic hall structure. The cathedral in Trier (q.v.) served as the model for this type of galleried hall church, which is found quite frequently in the Middle Rhine and Lahn region. Some remains of the 14C paintwork survive in the main choir, in the S. side choir, and in the vault of the S. aisle. The late Gothic winged altar (*c.* 1500) depicts the Virgin Mary, and the wings depict scenes from the life of the Virgin.

**Also worth seeing:** *Pilgrimage church of Ave Maria* (1716–18), with an unusual altar by the Schweizer family of sculptors. There is a miraculous image dating from the 15C.

### Deggendorf 8360
Bavaria        p.422☐N 17

**Parish church of Mariae Himmelfahrt:** This church, whose origins go back to a Romanesque structure burned down in 1240, has been altered on many occasions. Today there is a tympanum relief (1242–50) on the wall of the *Wasserkapelle* (beside the parish church). The high altar has a baldacchino and was originally made by M.Seyboldt in 1749 for the cathedral in Eichstätt. It was moved to Deggendorf in 1884.

**Also worth seeing:** *Church of the Heiliges Grab:* A Gothic basilica with a nave and two aisles dating from 1360. *Bürgerspital church of St.Katharina:* Interesting ceiling paintings by F.A. Rauscher. The *Rathaus* in the Marktstrasse dates from 1605 and has the chapel of St.Martin (1296). In the market square there are two *fountains* dating from the 16&18C. The *pilgrimage church of the Schmerzhafte Muttergottes* (Geyersberg) is 15C.

### Deggingen 7345
Baden-Württemberg      p.420☐G 18

**Parish church of the Heiliges Kreuz:** The church was rebuilt in 1700, although the 14C Gothic tower was retained. The massive high altar is by the local Schweizer family of sculptors. The focal point is the Crucifixion, which has Longinus on horseback and mourning women. The figures at the sides depict Helena and Constantine. In the upper section are God the Father with the Apostles John, Peter, Paul and James, and also the hosts of Heaven.

### Deidesheim 6705
Rheinland-Pfalz       p.420☐D 16

Deidesheim, a small, old town on the Weinstrasse (wine route), is full of stories about wine. These start from the entry made by Alexander von Humboldt in a book at the still-surviving 'Zur Kanne' inn while he was staying in Deidesheim, and continue up to the famous 'History of Wine-Growing', the standard work by Friedrich Armand von Bassermann-Jordan.

**Catholic parish church:** (Marktplatz): This important late Gothic Palatinate church was built in 1464 – 80 and was rebuilt in 1689 after being destroyed. A basilica with a nave and two aisles, it contains a number of fine old items. The most important of these are the busts of the Apostles and prophets which formerly crowned

*Deggingen, Heiliges Kreuz church*

the choir stalls and which are today attached to the pillars of the gallery (*c.* 1480). The high altar has a crucifix dating from about 1510, and the two angels hovering around the altar were added in the 18C and are attributed to the followers of Verschaffelt. A good relief of St. George has also survived.

**Rathaus** (Marktplatz): The town hall has a striking exterior, columned staircase (1734), which leads from the exposed 16C basement up to the 18C upper storey, which was added at a later date. It has a fine canopy.

**Heidenlöcher** (N. of Deidesheim): This stone rampart was probably built in the prehistoric period and used as a refuge. Only ruins survive today, but there are traces of houses and gates.

**Also worth seeing:** *Spitalkirche* (Weinstrasse): A chapel (1496), with adjoining 16–18C hospital buildings. *St. Michael chapel* (wall): A late Gothic building dating from 1662 (restored in 1951 after being destroyed in World War 2). *Museum of modern ceramics* (Stadtmaurergasse 17).

## Denkendorf 7306
Baden-Württemberg                    p.420□F 18

**Former monastery church:** The main sections of this building date back to the 12&13C. The ponderous groin vault in the portico is supported by two powerful pillars. The flat-roofed basilica also rests on massive pillars. The *crypt* (1515) below the floor of the church has wall paintings and is reached by descending 23 steps. This crypt is a relic of the cult of the Holy Sepulchre, which developed at the time of the Crusades. There are fine tombs in the portico and the S. aisle.

**Also worth seeing:** Graveyard church (*c.* 1500).

## Detmold 4930
Nordrhein-Westfalen                    p.414□F 9

Malwida von Meysenburg, in her 'Memoirs of an Idealist' (1876), described Detmold in the following enthusiastic terms: 'It was a clean, pretty town, located in one of the most picturesque parts of

*Residenzschloss of the zur Lippe princes, Detmold*

*Denkendorf, monastery church*

Northern Germany, surrounded with hills which are covered in magnificent beech forests and are associated with historic memories of the far-distant past.' These memories are mainly of the German chieftain Arminius, who broke the Roman supremacy in AD 9 by defeating the army of the Roman legate Varus. The site of the battle was probably in the immediate vicinity of Detmold. The town's famous sons include the dramatist Christian Dietrich Grabbe (1810 – 36), the poet Ferdinand Freiligrath (1810 – 76), Georg Weerth (1822–56), the essayist and poet, and Theodor Althaus (1822–52). Albert Lortzing lived here from 1826–33.

**Residenzschloss** (Ameide): A moated medieval castle (the massive castle keep survives), which was only occasionally used as a residence by the Lippe princes. In 1528–36 it was enlarged into the strongest fortress in the principality. In 1549, J.Unkair, who was also the architect of the Schloss in Tübingen, designed the present building, which has characteristic staircase towers and is built around a courtyard. It was not completed until 1621 and the SW wing was added in 1670.

The Residenzschloss is regarded as one of the most significant works of the so-called Weser Renaissance, even though not all the alterations are particularly sympathetic. The Schloss was originally much fortified, but parts of the ramparts and moats were removed. The building was completed by C.Tönnis, the Weser Renaissance architect, to the plans of J.Unkair.

The most valuable items of the rich decoration are the eight *tapestries* on the walls of the king's room. These are devoted to the subject of Alexander and were woven around 1670 by Jan Frans van den Hecke in his Brussels workshop. The original decoration of several drawing rooms and other living rooms survives. The *art collections* can be visited and are part of the *Schloss museum.*

**Lippisches Landesmuseum und Heimathaus** (Ameide 4): The museum of the principality of Lippe now occupies two historic half-timbered houses, a tithe barn and granary, which are connected by a bridge. The two houses originally stood in the Falkenhagen monastery and in the courtyard of the Schieder property respectively, and have been re-erected here. The

*Hermannsdenkmal on the Grotenburg in the Teutoburger Wald forest (monument to Arminius)*

museum also deals with the art of the principality of Lippe.

**Westfälisches Freilichtmuseum** (Krummes Haus, on the S. edge of the town): Peasants' houses and farmsteads have been brought here and faithfully rebuilt.

**Landestheater** (1 Theaterplatz): Opera house and theatre with 676 seats.

**Also worth seeing:** Market square. The 16C Renaissance Markt church. The Neues Palais (new palace), built 1706–18.

---

**Dettelbach 8716**
Bavaria                                    p.416☐H 15

**Pilgrimage church of Maria im Sand** (Wallfahrtsweg): A Pietà, which became a miraculous image in 1505, was the starting point of a pilgrimage. Julius Echter, a Prince Bishop of Würzburg who was fond of building, commissioned this Lower Franconian pilgrimage church (1610–13).

It is still much visited today. The choir of the original, smaller church was incorporated in the new one, which is regarded as a typical example of the so-called Julian style, which sought to combine late Gothic, Renaissance and baroque elements. The W. façade, and the lavish portal, which is the work of M.Kern, are characteristic of this style. Inside, the altar of mercy, with its unusual dimensions, captures the onlooker's attention. This stuccoed marble altar and baldacchino is by A.Bossi (1778–9). The pulpit, which was also made by M.Kern (1626), is regarded as one of the major pieces of Renaissance stone sculpture.

**Catholic parish church:** The main tower and the round staircase tower are linked by a wooden bridge—a most unusual arrangement. Some parts date from 1489, while other sections were rebuilt in 1769. The tower is surrounded by eight apsidal

*Mater Dolorosa from the mid-Rhine (c. 1420)* ▷
*in the pilgrimage church of St.Maria,*
*Dieburg*

*This monument in memory of Kaiser Wilhelm I was erected in 1896 on the Wittekindberg in the Wiehengebirge at the Porta Westfalica, where the river Weser runs between the Wiehengebirge and the Weserkette range*

chapels which open off the choir through round arches.

**Town walls and Rathaus:** When Dettelbach was made a town in 1484, work immediately began on building a town wall, large parts of which still survive. The three-storeyed Rathaus (*c.* 1500) is worth seeing for its gable and the outside staircase of its façade.

## Dieburg 6110
Hessen                                    p.416☐F 15

**Pilgrimage church of St. Maria:** The present building is essentially baroque and dates from when it was enlarged in 1697–1715. Its origins are pre-Carolingian. The main feature of the interesting interior is a Middle Rhine Pietà (*c.* 1420). This forms part of the high altar by J.P.Jäger (1749), whose design for the altar and columns is very similar to the one he made in St. Quintin in Mainz. The miraculous image is made of leather, mortar and linen—a rarely used technique.

## Diessen am Ammersee 8918
Bavaria                                   p.422☐K 20

**Church of St. Maria, formerly a collegiate church of Augustinian canons** (above the town): The present church was preceded by the St. Stephan convent, founded in *c.* 1100, and by the collegiate church of Augustinian canons (*c.* 1122–32). Work on the present building was begun in 1720. When the shell was almost complete it was torn down and restarted to plans by J.M.Fischer, the baroque architect from Munich. It was completed in 1739.
It is the first of a series which later included Fürstenzel (q.v.), Zwiefalten (q.v.) and Ottobeuren (q.v.). The harmonious façade is crowned by a finely curved gable. Augustine, the patron of the order, appears in the niche below the Eye of God. The original upper storeys of the tower were destroyed and replaced in the neo-Gothic style.

*Interior and decoration:* The church is one of the most important baroque buildings in Bavaria. When drawing up his plans, Fischer was restricted by a stipulation compelling him to make extensive use of the existing foundations, but he nevertheless achieved a centralized effect. The interior is a pilastered hall and the altars stand at the end of a processional route which leads between the wide, massive pillars. The best artists of the period worked on the interior: the stucco is by the brothers F.X. and J.M. Feuchtmayer, and J.G.Üblherr from Wessobrunn (q.v.). Some of the sculptures were designed by François du Cuilliés the elder and made by J.Dietrich. The pièce de résistance is the high altar, which stands at the top of a flight of steps. Four church fathers flank the altar table. The altarpiece, which can be lowered, depicts the Assumption of the Virgin. Behind the altarpiece, which is by B.A. Albrecht (1738), there is a platform which can be fitted with different pictures to suit the various holy days (theatrum sacrum). Artists such as E.Verheist, F.X. Schmädl, G.B. Pittoni, G.B. Tiepolo, J.G. Bergmüller and J.B. Straub worked on the side altars. It was Straub who made the pulpit. The angel hovering above the font in a side chapel

*Collegiate church, Diessen*

was not originally part of the decorative scheme It is attributed to the followers of I.Günther (*c.* 1760). The rich frescos are by Bergmüller (1736).

**St.Georgen** (on the W.edge of the town): This 15C church was enlarged in 1750. Among the artists involved in the decoration were such famous names as F.X. Feuchtmayer (stucco), J.Zitter (frescos), M.Günther (parts of the altar).

**Also worth seeing:** The cemetery church of St.Johannes.

were returned to their original state. It is one of the few Romanesque buildings whose original structure has survived to the present day. The closely set towers, which are entirely plain up to the level of the top of the nave, are a typical feature. *Interior:* The compact piers and vaulting are indicative of the Romanesque. Interesting features include the early Gothic *font* (*c.* 1220) and the 16C Renaissance tomb of Philipp Frey von Dehrn. The church treasure contains a fine reliquary of St. Lubentius (the head probably dates from *c.* 1270, the bust from *c.* 1447).

---

**Dietkirchen = 6520 Limburg**
Hessen                          p.416□D 13

**Former collegiate church of St. Lubentius and Juliana:** The church occupies a picturesque site on a limestone rock in the valley of the Lahn. Some parts of this important Romanesque church, such as the towers and transept walls, date from the mid 11C. The nave was widened in the 12C. As a result of restoration work carried out in 1958, some of the alterations were eliminated and parts of the building

---

**Dietramszell 8157**
Bavaria                         p.422□L 20

**Former collegiate church of Augustinan canons:** This is one of the most important baroque churches in Upper Bavaria. In the early 19C, Dietramszell became a collective convent for nuns who had become homeless as a result of secularization. The present monastery church was constructed as a new building in 1729–41 and was consecrated in 1748. A chapel of St.Martin with a small monastery attached

*The church in Diessen is among the most important baroque buildings in Bavaria*

*Hovering angel, Diessen*

*Dietkirchen, former collegiate church*

was founded on the same site by the Tegernsee monk Dietram in the 12C. Designed by an unknown architect, the exterior of the church gives no hint of its rich decoration: fine stuccoes and pastel-coloured frescos by J.B. Zimmermann. The centrepiece of the massive high altar is a painting of the Assumption of the Virgin Mary, another work by Zimmermann (1745). The paintings in three side altars are also by him.

**Church of St. Martin:** Consecrated in 1722, it adjoins the collegiate church to the N. and can be entered from the first bay of the nave. The stucco and paintings are again by J.B. Zimmermann.

**Pilgrimage church of St.Leonhard** (N. of Dietramszell): This late rococo church was consecrated in 1774. It makes a particularly romantic impression against the background of the mountains. Finely decorated.

**Diez 6252**
Rheinland-Pfalz                           p.416 □ D 13

**Schloss Oranienstein** (on a rocky slope N. of the town): Princess Albertine Agnete of Orange had the Schloss built in 1672–84. The five-winged building is grouped around a principal courtyard open towards the S. D.Marot, an architect at the Dutch court, was employed to rebuilt it in 1697–1709. Today the Schloss is used by the Federal German Armed Forces. Richly decorated, the outstanding features are the stucco ceilings by E.Castelli and the fine ceiling paintings. The *Schloss chapel* is in the E. side wing. The organ, unusually, is above the pulpit.

**Schloss Diez:** Standing on a rock above the town, the castle's Romanesque keep is visible from afar, with its helm roof and four Gothic corner towers. The original building dating from the second half of the

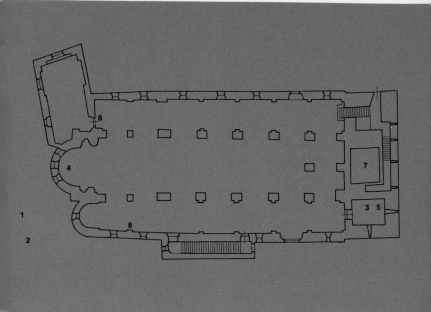

**Dietkirchen, former collegiate church 1** Dreifaltigkeitskapelle (Trinity chapel) **2** Michael-skapelle chapel **3** Stone sarcophagus of St. Lubentius, 10C inscription **4** Paintwork in crossing vault, 2nd quarter of 13C **5** Head reliquary of St.Lubentius, head c. 1270, breast section 1447 **6** Iron mounting and door knocker of sacristy door (copy, original, 13C, in the cathedral treasure) **7** Organ front, c. 1695 **8** Monument to Philipp Frey v.Dehm (d. 1550)

11C was enlarged in the 14C and rebuilt in 1732.

**Also worth seeing:** *Diezer Heimat-museum* and *Nassau museum* in the *Schloss Oranienstein:* Mememtoes of the Nassau-Oranien family, prehistory, geology, folklore. Fine half-timbered buildings, and remains of the town walls. The 13C *Protestant church.*

**Environs: Balduinstein** (6 km. SW): Ruined castle.
**Schaumburg** (7 km. SW): Schloss and museum.

**Dillenburg 6340**
Hessen                                    p.416□E 12

In 1568, on the square beneath the 'Wilhelmslinde' (William's linden tree), which is still alive (Schlossberg), William of Orange was asked to lead the struggle for independence from Spain. William of Orange is commemorated in Goethe's play 'Egmont', where he appears as Egmont's adviser.

**Protestant parish church** (Kirchberg): Built 1489–1524, it contains 15 tombs of the Nassau-Oranien family. The dominant feature of the interior is the late Renaissance double gallery which runs around three sides. The monument for the heart of Count Johann of Nassau (d.1475), is in the choir.

**Also worth seeing:** The *Wilhelmsturm* (a tower in the courtyard of the former

*Augustinian canons' church in Dietramszell*

Schloss): A Dillenburg landmark, built in 1872–5. Only a few remnants, including certain vaults ('Kappeskeller'), survive from the Schloss built in 1240. *Old Rathaus* (Hauptstrasse): Rebuilt after 1723, with two stone storeys and a half-timbered one. Many fine half-timbered houses from the 16–18C survive all over the town. The *Oranien-Nassuischen Museum* in the Wilhelmsturm tower has collections relating to early history, as well as ceramics, porcelain, pewter, graphics, and weapons.

---

**Dillingen an der Donau 8880**

Bavaria                                      p.422□I 18

---

This medieval fortress town gained in importance in the 15C after Augsburg had escaped the domination of the bishops. From then until the 18C, Dillingen was the residence and administrative seat of the former bishopric of Augsburg. In 1549, Cardinal Otto Truchsess von Waldburg founded a theological college here, which was raised to the status of a university in 1554. As a result, Dillingen developed into an intellectual centre of the Counter-Reformation in Germany.

**Studienkirche Mariae Himmelfahrt** (Kardinal-v.-Waldburg-Strasse): This church forms part of the complex of monastery and university buildings. It was built in 1610–17 and was altered in rococo style in 1750–68. The basic features of the church can be compared with those of St. Michael in Munich (q.v.). However, there are no galleries, transept or hall-type choir, and this accords with the so-called Vorarlberg pilaster scheme, which is also to be found in Ellwangen (q.v.) and Obermarchtal (q.v.). The otherwise solemn atmosphere is made more cheerful by the rich decoration and lustrous frescos. The high altar is the work of the local artists

J.M. Fischer (the sculptor) and J.Hartmuth. The altarpiece depicts the Assumption and is by J.G. Bergmüller. The painting on the SE side altar is also by Bergmüller (1756).

**Papal basilica of St.Peter** (since 1979) (Klosterstrasse): This hall church, with its nave and two aisles, was built by J.Alberthal from Graubünden (1619–28). In 1643 the arcades were removed. The stucco is by J.Feistle (1734).

**Monastery and university buildings** (Kardinal-v.-Waldburg-Strasse): These comprise the Alter Regentiebau of the former seminary (1619–21), the former university (1688/9) with the 'Golden Hall' whose gorgeous rococo decoration dates from 1713–38, and the former Jesuit college (1713–38) with its baroque library. Opposite is the *Gymnasium* (secondary school) of 1724.

**Schloss** (Schlossstrasse): This former fortress was initially used only as a refuge for the bishops who had been driven out of Augsburg. After a fire in 1595, rebuilding began and numerous extensions were made, and in the 18C it took on its magnificent, Schloss-like appearance.

**Also worth seeing:** The *Spitalkirche Hl. Geist* (c. 1500, altered in 1687) and the *St.Wolfgangs chapel* (1536, rebuilt in 1591 and 1725) in the former graveyard. The *Franciscan convent church of Mariae Himmelfahrt*, which adjoins St.Peter's basilica, is the work of J.G.Fischer, and has a crucifix dating from about 1520. It is also worth walking round the town.

**Environs: Lauingen** (5 km. W.): A medieval town with the *Catholic parish church of St.Martin*, one of the last Gothic hall churches (completed in 1518); monuments and the remains of frescos.

---

**Dingolfing 8312**
Bavaria                                    p.422☐M 18

**Parish church of St. Johannes:** This brick building was completed in c. 1490, having probably been begun in 1467. It is one of the most beautiful surviving Gothic churches in Bavaria. Only some of its original furnishings have survived, including two carved figures of St.John (c. 1520).

*Schloss Oranienstein, Diez*

*Dillingen, St. Peter*

**Schloss** (Upper town): This 15C rectangular brick building replaced the original castle (1251). The seat of a duke, it has a captivating and richly adorned stepped gable. Today the Schloss houses the *Heimatmuseum* (local history).

## Dinkelsbühl 8804
Bavaria             p.422☐H 17

Dinkelsbühl became important in the early Middle Ages as a result of its position and it was because of this that Goethe stopped here in November 1797 after returning from his third journey to Switzerland. J.P.Hebel featured the town in his 'Zwei Postillione' ('Two Postillions'). The novelist and essayist Kasimir Edschmid compared Dinkelsbühl with Rothenburg, but stated that Dinkelsbühl 'does not have the sound of trumpets in the air, or the bloody drama, or the ghosts of history...'

**Parish church of St.Georg** (Marktplatz): This important Gothic building was designed and built in 1448–99 by Nikolaus Eseler (father and son). A hall church with a nave and two aisles, it is 252 ft. long and 74 ft. wide. The interior is dominated by the slender pillars which support the compact net-vaulting. Most of the decoration is later. A late Gothic panel of the Crucifixion was incorporated in the neo-Gothic high altar (1892). In contrast, the altar beneath a baldacchino at the entrance to the choir dates from around 1470, and the tabernacle, the pulpit and the font are also contemporary with the church's building.

**Half-timbered medieval houses** (Segringer Strasse and Nördlinger Strasse): The 12–15C town has survived almost untouched. The four gates: Wörnitztor to the E., Nördlinger (S.), Segringer (W.) and Rothenburger (N.)., have survived from the town's fortifications. There is a mixture of Franconian and Swabian elements in the excellently preserved half-timbered buildings. The house known as the *Deutsches Haus,* in the Marktplatz, was built in 1440 and is considered to be one of the finest half-timbered houses in southern Germany. The traveller should also visit the 16C *Ratstrinkstube,* which is the former councillors' taproom, the *Kornhaus* (granary) dating from 1508, and the *Schranne* (c. 1600). The *Palais des Deutschen Ordens,* built in 1761–4 as a house of the Teutonic Knights, forms an exception among these old German town houses. Churches worth mentioning include *St. Ulrich* (c. 1700), the 17C *Kapuzinerkirche,* and the *Dreikönigskapelle* (14C, secularized in the 19C).

**Historisches Museum** (6 Dr.-Martin-Lutherstrasse): Collections devoted to the history of the town, arts and crafts, and folklore.

## Donaueschingen 7710
Baden-Württemberg       p.420☐E 20

This town, where the rivers Brigach and

*Deutsches Haus, Dinkelsbühl* ▷

*Donaueschingen, Schloss*

Breg meet to form the Danube (see the 'Donauquelle' or 'Source of the Danube' in the Schloss courtyard), owes its cultural importance to the stimulus provided by the Princes of Fürstenberg. The court library, which has some 130,000 volumes, is a special feature. The poet Joseph Victor von Scheffel was librarian here in 1857–9. The Donaueschingen *music festival* is held each autumn.

**Catholic parish church of St.Johannes Baptist/Johanneskirche** (71 Karlstrasse): A baroque church with twin towers (1724–47), an impressive façade and lavish interior. The twelve Apostles in the nave are worth viewing but the most important feature is a Madonna (1525–30) attributed to the artists who created the Breisach altar (q.v.).

**Schloss** (2 Fürstenbergstrasse 2): This plain baroque building dating from around 1723 was extensively rebuilt in 1893–6 and

the interior was changed considerably. Next to the Schloss is the source of the Danube, for which A.Weinbrenner built a circular fountain with an allegorical marble group. There are significant *collections* of Renaissance and baroque domestic décor and arts and crafts. The collections of the Fürstenberg Princes are in the *Karlsbau* behind the Schloss. The main element is the collection of works by German artists (H.Holbein the elder, Lucas Cranach the elder and younger, B.Strigel, B.Beham and others) displayed in the *picture gallery*.

**Hofbibliothek** (3 Haldenstrasse): The library's most valuable item is a copy of the Nibelungenlied (Hohenemser manuscript C) from the first half of the 13C.

**Environs: Pfohren** (5 km. SE): The Entenburg, a moated cube-shaped castle with four massive round corner towers, was built by the Counts of Fürstenberg in 1471.

**Neudingen** (8 km. SE): A centrally planned church with the Fürstenberg vault, it was built by T.Diebold in 1853–6 in the form of a Greek cross crowned by a slender dome.

---

## Donaustauf 8405
Bavaria                                    p.422☐M 17

**Castle:** Only fragments survive of the 12C castle destroyed in 1634. These include parts of the 11C chapel, and the great hall. The history of the castle is associated with such names as Frederick Barbarossa (1156) and Henry the Lion (1161).

**Walhalla** (above Donaustauf): Ludwig I of Bavaria dedicated this white marble building to the 'Germans who had distinguished themselves by glorious deeds'. However, the idea of a national monument barely proceeded beyond the initial decoration. The temple, built by Leo von Klenze in 1830–41, is based on Greek models. It measures 410 x 165 ft., and it has a peripteros of 52 Doric columns. Crown Prince Ludwig contributed some 120 busts, including those of Erasmus of Rotterdam, Goethe, Hutten, Kant, Klopstock, Lessing, Luther, Schiller, Wagner, Wieland and Winckelmann. Six Valkyries and the marble statue of Ludwig I were added after 1945.

---

## Donauwörth 8850
Bavaria                                    p.422☐I 18

Donauwörth's position between Swabia, Franconia and Bavaria has made the town a crossroads and has influenced its history and culture. The well-preserved 13C town was devastated in 1945, but most of it has been rebuilt. The central feature is the famous Reichsstrasse, which is part of the road from Nuremberg to Augsburg. Situated along its length are the parish church, the Reichsstadt fountain (1977, Professor Wimmer), the Rathaus, the town tollhouse, several interesting half-timbered houses and the Fuggerhaus. Until the 19C,

the Danube was not navigable beyond here. Werner Egk, the composer, was born in the Auchsesheim district of the town in 1901. His tomb is in the town cemetery.

**Parish church of Mariae Himmelfahrt** (Reichsstrasse): Built in 1444–61 as a late Gothic hall church. Its massive tower soars above all the roofs of the town. The central point of the rich decoration, which includes 15C stained-glass windows, is the *tabernacle,* built by stonemasons from Augsburg in *c.* 1500. It is a canopied late Gothic structure, and the figures carved in relief make a very natural impression. In the *sacristy* is a painting by the Danube school (1515).

**Former Benedictine monastery of the Heiliges Kreuz** (Heiliges-Kreuz-Strasse): This baroque monastery was built on the site of a 12C structure of which the lower storeys of the tower survive. J.Schmuzer from Wessebrunn (q.v.) built the present church in 1717–20. Built without arcades, it has fine galleries and the focus of attention inside is the high altar by F.Schmuzer (1724). The side altars and the crypt chapel (underneath the organ gallery) are also notable. The most important paintings are by J.G.Bergmüller (the altarpiece of the high altar being one).

**Fuggerhaus** (Reichsstrasse): The Swedish King Gustav Adolf (1632), and Emperor Charles VI (1711), were among the guests in this famous house, built by the Augsburg Fuggers in 1543. An interesting feature of this beautiful Renaissance building is the large portico.

**Gerberhaus with Heimatmuseum** (Im Ried 103): The 15C Gerberhaus (tanner's house), one of the oldest half-timbered houses in the town, contains the Heimatmuseum, with exhibits relating to domestic life in town and country, votive tablets and verre églomisé.

**Also worth seeing:** Remains of the town fortifications, with the *Riedertor* and *Färbertor* (both facing the Danube) gates. The *Tanzhaus* (Reichsstrasse) with the Archaeological Museum. The *Rathaus* (Reichs-

*Walhalla near Donaustauf*

strasse), which has elements from various periods. The neoclassical former *Deutschordenshaus* (Kapellstrasse), which contains the Werner Egk meeting point. Numerous old houses. The *Fischerbrunnen* fountain in Ried.

## Dornum 2988
Lower Saxony                              p.414☐D 4

**Moated Schloss:** This baroque schloss (1668 – 1717) built around a courtyard replaced a 14C fortress of the Häuptling family. It stands in the park next to the Beninga castle in the town centre, and is the only one of the three fortresses the Häuptlings originally held to have survived.

**Protestant parish church/Bartholomäuskirche:** Like some 100 East Frisian one-roomed churches, this 13C brick

church was built on a Dutch model. The tombstones and memorials on the inside walls show the close relationship which existed with the Häuptling family. Features worth noting: the pulpit with its rich figurative decoration (*c.* 1660), the font (*c.* 1270), and the altar (1683). The Crucifixion is a copy of the famous painting by van Dyck. The monument in front of the altar depicts Gerhardt II von Kloster (1594).

**Windmill:** This windmill (1626) is the last surviving one of its kind in East Friesland.

## Dortmund 4600
Nordrhein-Westfalen                       p.416☐C 10

Dortmund is the economic and cultural centre of the E. Ruhr. Today an industrial town, it was formerly a member of the

Hanseatic League and a free imperial town. The Hellweg, which is today the main shopping street and is divided into the Westen- and Ostenhellweg, is a famous military and trade route (it was along the Hellweg that Charlemagne marched from the Lower Rhine to the Weser). After 1945, the members of the Dortmund *Gruppe 61* wrote about the problems of the Ruhr district. In 1961, the town of Dortmund was awarded the Nelly Sachs prize, one of the most important German cultural prizes.

**Reinoldikirche** (Ostenhellweg/Friedhof): This church, a spacious basilican structure built in 1260–80, is dedicated to Reinoldus, the town's patron saint. Legend has it that when he was slain by stonemasons from Cologne during the building of a church, the bells of all the churches rang of their own accord and his hearse rolled to Dortmund by itself. He is depicted by a 15C wooden figure on the pillar of the triumphal arch. The counterpart to this depicts Charlemagne, who is described as the town's founder. The late Gothic choir dates from 1421–50, while the W. tower, which is 330 ft. tall and was formerly the 'wonder of Westphalia' and the town's landmark, was completed in its present form in 1701. The late Gothic *carved altar* (1420–30), and the choir windows behind it are also of interest. These windows were made by Gottfried von Stockhausen during the post-1945 rebuilding. There is an unusual brass *eagle lectern,* which was probably made in Belgium in *c.* 1450.

**Marienkirche** (Ostenhellweg): The small 12C Romanesque church is probably the oldest vaulted building in Westphalia. The interior of the church is dominated by the compound piers with clusters of delicate columns, which form the arcades. The panels of the famous *Marienaltar* have not survived intact. Conrad von Soest, a son of the ·town, painted these panels in *c.* 1420. They are amongst the most important pieces of Gothic painting in Germany. The pictures in the wings of the altar were rather unsuccessfully trimmed in 1720 when being incorporated into a baroque altar. The old panels have been reassembled in Landesmuseum (provincial mu-

seum) in Münster. The central picture depicts the death of the Virgin, the Nativity of Christ is on the left, and on the right the Adoration of the Magi. An artist known as the master of the *Berswordt altar,* who was an older contemporary of Conrad von Soest, was responsible for the altar in the N. aisle in 1390. The altar was donated by Councillor Lambert Berswordt. Christ is at the centre of each of the three paintings (Christ bearing the Cross, Crucifixion, Deposition). On the N. side is the *reliquary,* which was only finished 100 years after the choir had been completed. Reliquaries were a feature of Westphalian churches of this period. Today, an oak figure 36 in. tall, with a coloured mount, is preserved here. The richly carved oak *choir stalls* (1523) are typical late Gothic.

**Protestant church of St. Petri/Petri-Kirche** (Westenhellweg): The main sections of this church were built in 1320–53. The church was almost entirely destroyed in World War 2, but by 1963 it had been rebuilt. From the outside, the distinguishing feature of this almost square church, which has a nave and two aisles, is its ponderous W. tower. The enormous Antwerp *carved altar* (*c.* 1520) is a well-known feature; it was installed here in the 19C. This altar is 24 ft. 4 in. wide and 18 ft 5 in. tall. It has 633 carved, gilt figures grouped in 48 scenes.

**Catholic priory church of St. Johannes der Täufer** (Silberstrasse): This 16C church is famous for its massive *winged altar,* which is the masterpiece of D. Baegert from Wesel (1470–80). It depicts the Crucifixion of Christ, while the subjects represented in the wings include the Holy Family and the Adoration of the Magi. The oldest view of the town of Dortmund is to be found on the panel with the Holy Family. The 15C *tabernacle* is also worth seeing.

**Parish church of St. Peter** (Syburg): Interesting features include the foundations of a church which was probably built by Charlemagne in 799 and was discovered whilst the church was being rebuilt after

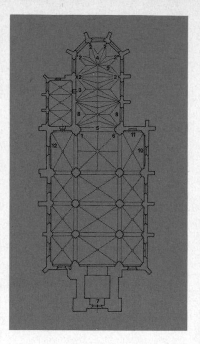

*Reinoldikirche, Dortmund*

the war. The small graveyard surrounding the church has numerous 16–18C tombstones.

**Westfalenhalle** (Rheinlanddamm): The pre-war building dating from 1925 measured 245 ft. across and was a brilliant architectural achievement of international quality. After being destroyed in World War 2, it was replaced in 1955 by a new building designed by Walter Hötje, the architect from Dortmund. This hall, which is used for sports and many other purposes, can hold up to 23,000 spectators and is one of the largest in Europe. Several smaller halls, with a total area of 323,000 sq. ft. were added in the 1970s. The Westfalenhalle complex also includes an ice rink and a riding stable. The two large football stadiums are in the immediate vicinity.

**Theatres:** The *Grosses Haus* theatre was opened in 1966. Both musical and theatrical performances are held here. There are

**Dortmund, Reinoldikirche 1** Statue of St. Reinoldus, early-14C **2** Apostles on the engaged columns in the choir, c. 1420-30 **3** Virgin Mary **4** Altar, probably Burgundian, c. 1430-40 **5** Lectern, Belgium, c. 1450 **6** Statue of Charlemagne, mid-15C **7** Stained-glass window with the four Church Fathers, mid-15C **8** Choir stalls, c. 1470 **9** Font by J.Winnenbrock, 1469 **10** Crucifix, 2nd half of 15C **11** Panel painting of Christ bearing the Cross, early-16C **12** 'Last Judgement', study by Volterra, early 16C

1160 seats. Next to it are the *Kleines Haus* and the *Schauspielstudio* (both these are in 15 Hitropwall), with 498 and 99 seats respectively, and also the *Children's and Young People's Theatre* (in the Ostwall, with 514 seats).

**Museums:** The *Museum am Ostwall* (7 Ostwall) mounts temporary exhibitions of modern art, as well as the Karl Gröppel collection (German Expressionists) and

*Marienaltar by Conrad von Soest in the ▷ Marienkirche*

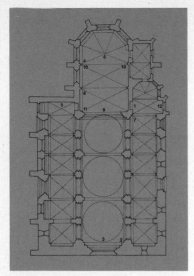

**17 Dortmund, Marienkirche 1** Romanesque choir column **2** Virgin Mary Enthroned, c. 1230 **3** Archangel Michael, 1320 **4** Tabernacle, late-14C **5** Berswordt altar, donated c. 1390 **6** Marienaltar by Conrad v.Soest, c. 1420 **7** Virgin Mary, c. 1430 **8** God the Father in Judgement, c. 1470 **9** Triumphal cross, c. 1520 **10** Choir stalls, 1523 **11** Eagle lectern, c. 1550 **12** Font, 1687

other exhibits. *Museum für Kunst- und Kulturgeschichte* (3 Hansastrasse): Prehistory, early history, history of the town, folk art, cultural history, and arts and crafts (12–20C), picture collection. The famous gilded copper *reliquary* in the form of the head of Frederick Barbarossa, originates from the cathedral treasure of *Cappenberg* (q.v.), and is said to be the earliest image of an emperor to have been created in Germany (mid- to late-12C).

**Haus der Bibliotheken** (Markt): The *municipal and provincial library* with over 300,000 volumes, the *town library* and the *Institute of Journalism* are all housed in one building. The Institute of Journalism is of international importance, with newspapers from before and during the March revolution of 1848, early printed journals, cartoons, and posters. *Archiv für Arbeiterdichtung* (Archive of Workers' Poetry 56–58 Ostenhellweg).

**Duderstadt 3408**
Lower Saxony                                    p.418□H 10

**Catholic priory church of St. Cyriakus/Oberkirche** (Marktstrasse):

*Petrikirche, carved altar*

The present building, a large hall church with six pillared bays in the nave, was begun in 1394, but was not completed until the early 16C. Only some parts survive of the Gothic and the later baroque decoration. The high altar was redesigned in 1874–7, with a Passion of Christ, carved in *c.* 1500, being included. The 15 baroque figures on the pillars include the twelve Apostles.

**Rathaus** (Marktstrasse 6): The 13C half-timbered town hall combines elements of the Lower Saxon and Hessian-Franconian styles. It was originally a market hall, and its upper storey included the double-aisled citizens' hall. The building was enlarged in the 15&16C.

**Half-timbered houses:** Numerous fine half-timbered houses from various periods have survived in the old part of town. 91 Marktstrasse was built in 1752, and is known as the *Steinernes Haus*. The main feature of the old *town fortifications* is the Westertorturm gate tower, which is surmounted by an affected Mannerist spire.

**Heimatmuseum** (3 Oberkirche): The Eichsfeld local history museum is in the town's former school, a half-timbered building dating from 1767, with a fine baroque portal.

## Duisburg 4100
Nordrhein-Westfalen      p.416☐B 10

Duisburg is the centre of the W. Ruhr. Its position was one reason why steel production developed here (20 of the Ruhr's 35 blast furnaces are in Duisburg). The port of Duisburg, with a total area of 2,235 acres and a turnover of 50 million tonnes, is the largest inland harbour in Europe and the largest river port in the world. Gerhard Mercator, the geographer and cartographer, lived in Duisburg from 1512–94.

**Salvatorkirche** (Salvator-Kirchplatz): This 15C tufa basilica was enlarged in neo-Gothic style in 1903–4. Note the memorial stone to G.Mercator, who worked for the Duke of Jülich and founded the science of cartography.

**Also worth seeing:** The Catholic church in Duisburg-Hamborn (a 12C hall church

*Westfalenhalle*

*Rathaus, Duderstadt*

*St. Cyriakus, Duderstadt*

built of tufa). The Catholic parish church of St.Dionysius in Duisburg-Mündelheim (a 13C tufa basilica, with decorative paintwork and some notable wooden sculptures). The Mercator Halle (a modern multi-purpose hall in König-Heinrich-Platz, with 2,500 seats and an exhibition area of 7500 sq.ft.).

**Museums:** The *Niederrheinische Museum* (64 Friedrich-Wilhelm-Strasse) developed from private collections kept in Duisburg and today, in addition to temporary exhibitions, it has collections relating to the town's history, the history of cartography, prehistory and early history. In the *Wilhelm-Lehmbruck-Museum* (51 Düsseldorfer Strasse) there is a collection with works by W.Lehmbruck, the sculptor from Duisburg.

**Environs: Broich** (8 km. E.): The 11C *Schloss Broich* stands opposite Mülheim an der Ruhr. The *palast* of the 12C *Hochburg*

was built in *c.* 1400. The towers which flank the gate, and various other annexes, are 17&18C.

---

**Düren 5160**

Nordrhein-Westfalen    p.4416☐B 12

**Protestant parish church:** Built in 1954, this church is an outstanding piece of modern religious architecture. In it, the architects, Hentrich and Petschnigg, have adhered consistently to the principle of the centrally planned building.

**Catholic parish church of St. Anna:** The former parish church of St.Anna was destroyed in World War 2, as indeed was most of the town. The new building by R.Schwarz is divided into three main sections: portico, weekday chapel, Sunday church.

**Leopold-Hoesch town museum**

(Hoeschplatz 1): Items relating to prehistory, early history and 20C art are on display in this building dating from 1905, which is transitional between the neobaroque and Art Nouveau.

**Environs: Langerwehe** (10 km. W.): An interesting *Töpfereinmuseum* (museum of pottery) has been installed in the parish house. **Nideggen** (15 km. S.): *Ruins* of the 12C castle of the Counts of Jülich. The oldest part of the castle, which was restored in 1960, is the four-storeyed *keep* to the E.; the palas to the S. dates from the 14C. **Zulpich** (20 km. SE): Finds from the *Tolbiacum* mentioned by Tacitus in AD 70, including a small *Roman bath*, can be seen in and near the *Heimatmuseum* (8 Mühlenberg). In addition, the 13&14C *town fortifications*, the 14&15C *Kurkölnische Landesburg*, (castle) and the *crypts* (c. 1060) of the *Catholic parish church of St.Peter* are of interest.

---

**Düsseldorf 4000**

Nordrhein-Westfalen                  p.416□B 11

Düsseldorf combines Rhineland charm with the atmosphere of a metropolis. But it is also a town of castles (in Kaiserswerth and Benrath), the home of important theatres, museums and galleries, and the birthplace of such famous Germans as Heinrich Heine, who was born here on 13 December 1797. The Königsallee and Hofgartenstrasse are examples of German classicism, and the new theatre, the Thyssen high-rise office building and the plethora of post-war buildings are fine examples of modern town planning. The town awards two prizes for significant achievements in the field of art and culture, the Heinrich Heine Prize and the Grossen Kunstpreis of the state of North Rhine-Westphalia.

**Collegiate church of St. Lambertus** (Altstadt): This Gothic hall church replaced the original Romanesque basilica in 1288–1394. The W.tower, 235 ft. tall, has made the church into a landmark of the

town. Only a small part of the medieval decoration has survived. Special attention should be paid to the remains of the Gothic wall paintings, and also a late Gothic *tabernacle* (1475–9) with an abundance of figures. The monument to Countess Margarethe von Berg (1388) and the wall tomb (behind the baroque high altar) to Duke Wilhelm V (1594–9) are outstanding (the church was the burial site of the princes until St.Andreas was built). Most of the furnishings, namely the high altar, four side altars, the pulpit and the pews, were installed in 1650–1712. The church treasure contains fine pieces of silver.

**Catholic parish church of St.Andreas** (Andreasstrasse): Wilhelm von Neuburg, a count palatine, ordered the church to be built from 1622–9 as a Jesuit monastery church, and also as a court church and burial place for the counts of Neuburg. The choir includes the *mausoleum*, which was added in 1667 and contains the body of Prince Elector Joh. Wilhelm II. This is the finest 17C building in the Lower Rhine area, and was modelled on the court church in Neuburg an der Donau and on Roman buildings of the late Renaissance and early baroque. In the aisles are life-sized wooden figures of Apostles and Saints, and the bust of Count Palatine Wolfgang Wilhelm is to be seen above the W.portal. The first-class stucco is also worth mentioning.

**Catholic parish church of St. Maximilian/Maxkirche/Former Franciscan monastery church of St. Antonius von Padua** (Zitadellenstrasse): Built 1736 in the style of a Lower Rhine hall church, the stuccoed interior has choir stalls, pulpit, pews and organ gallery. One of the finest items is a brass eagle lectern, which was cast in Maastricht in 1449.

**Former collegiate church/parish church of St.Margaretha** (Gerresheim district): Completed in 1236, it appears severe from the outside. It is 155 ft. long and the interior is almost undivided. The decorative paintwork has been renovated. There is a larger-than-life wooden *crucifix* from the last third of the 10C above the high altar. The late Gothic *tabernacle,* whose five-sided housing is surrounded by a wrought-iron grille, dates from the 15C.

**Former collegiate church of St. Suitbertus/Catholic parish church** (Kaiserswerth district): This imposing early Romanesque pillared basilica has a nave and two aisles (223 ft. long and 75 ft. wide). The choir was added in 1230–40. The main item in the church treasure is the *shrine of St.Suitbertus.* This box, 5 ft. 2 in. long, is made from gilded copper plates and bears some fine figures. The Apostles, the Virgin Mary and St.Suitbertus occupy the arcades of the side sections.

**Schloss Jägerhof and Hofgarten** (Jägerhofstrasse): This Schloss to the E. of what is today the Hofgarten (court garden) was built in 1748–63 by order of the Prince Elector Carl Theodor zu Pfalz as a resi-

Düsseldorf, basilica of St.Lambertus **1** Our Lady of Sorrows, c. 1420, on a stela of shell limestone by K.M. Winter, 1975 **2** Font, 15C **3** Choir stalls **4** Tabernacle, late Gothic **5** Pulpit **6** St. Christopher, early-16C **7** High altar, 1688-98 **8** Wall tomb of Duke Wilhelm the Rich by G. Scheben, 1595-99 **9** Bronze portal by Prof. E. Mataré, 1960

dence for the Head Bergisch Huntsman. The architects were J.J. Couven and N. de Pirage, who designed the building in the style of a maison de plaisance. There are art collections (see museums). The court garden was laid out by N. de Pirage in 1769 on the orders of Prince Elector Carl Theodor, and is the first public municipal park in Germany. After being destroyed, it was planted anew by M.F. Weyhe in 1796 and, along with some new gardens on the ramparts which had been torn down, it was redesigned from 1804 onwards and expanded to the N. in 1811 under Napoleon. There is a monument to Heinrich Heine on the Napoleonsberg hill.

**Schloss Benrath** (Benrath district, Schlossallee): This Schloss, built by N. de Pigage in 1755–73, shows clear parallels with those of Mannheim and Schwetzingen, which were also built by de Pigage. In the latter two buildings, he had to incorporate existing structures, while in Benrath he was given a free hand. The result is one of the finest hunting lodges in the Rhineland. The building comprises a total of 84 rooms. But only the vestibule, garden room and drawing room are actually as tall as they appear from outside. Inside,

*St. Lambertus*

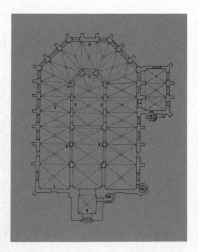

the building is divided into four storeys facing the two oval patios. The rooms are in Louis XVI style. Most of them were designed by the same artists who worked on the castle in Mannheim (stucco by G.A. Albuzzio, wood carvings by M.van den Branden and A.Egell, woodwork by F.Zeller). There are two *cavaliers' houses* to the left and right of the main building. The park, part of which was laid out anew to form an English garden in the 19C, was also part of the overall plan. To the E. of the Spiegelweiher lake is the *Prinzenbau* (prince's building), erected by Duke Philipp Wilhelm in 1651–61.

**Kaiserpfalz** (Kaiserwerth district): The Kaiserburg was rebuilt by Frederick Barbarossa. Only parts survive today, such as the outer wall, facing the Rhine, of the former palas hall. This wall is 165 ft. long, 43 ft. high and 20 ft. wide. The castle was originally on an island formed by an artificial loop of the Rhine.

**Modern architecture:** The town's modern architecture matches the importance of Düsseldorf as the headquarters of numerous major companies. These buildings begin with the *Tietz department store* (today

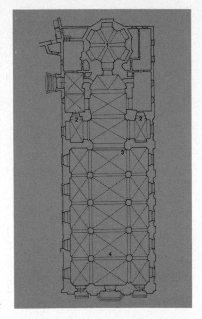

**Düsseldorf, St. Andreas 1** Mausoleum with sarcophagi of the Neuburgers **2** Side altars, 17C **3** Pulpit, mid-17C **4** Organ front, 2nd half of 18C

*Choir of Andreaskirche*

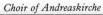

*Andreaskirche*

the Kaufhof department store) in the Königsallee. This was built by J.M. Olbrich in 1907-9 as a four-storeyed complex. It marks the end of Art Nouveau and the beginning of Functionalism. In 1911-12, P.Behrens built the *Mannesmannhaus,* a monumental, highly functional building situated directly on the Rhine. The *Ehrenhof-Anlage* was completed in 1925 as an exhibition hall designed by W.Kreis, and is also by the Rhine. It comprises the *Tonhalle* (a round building with a dome), the building of the former Reichsmuseum of Economics and Sociology, and the Ehrenhof (with a museum of art). The whole complex reflects the strong urge towards modern functional buildings, but at the same time it also shows that the architects are not thereby schematized or constricted. One of the buildings which were erected after World War 2 and established a trend in modern architecture is the *Thyssen-Haus* between the Hofgarten and the business centre. It was built by the architects H.Hentrich and H.Petschnigg in 1957-60.

**Classical houses:** Numerous classical buildings, which were formerly a feature of Düsseldorf, were destroyed in the war, and only some of them have been rebuilt with their old façades. Good examples are to be found in the Bastionstrasse (3-11a and 13-23), in the Bilkerstrasse (particularly 24-26, 32, 36-42, 46) and in the Elisabethstrasse, especially 18.

**Also worth seeing:** *Königsallee:* one of the best-known shopping streets in Europe, laid out in 1801 to plans by C.A. Huschberger, the Munich court architect. *Schlossturm* (Burgplatz): Remains of the 13C Schloss burned down in 1872. *Ratinger Tor:* Part of the classical town gate built by A. von Vagedes in 1811-14.

**Theatres:** The *Dt. Opera am Rhein* (Heinrich-Heine-Allee 16a) dates from 1875 and was completely rebuilt in 1954 -5. Today the company of the Düsseldorf-Duisburg theatrical association performs operas and ballets here. There are 1,342 seats for spectators. The *Düsseldorfer Schauspielhaus* (theatre) (Gustaf-

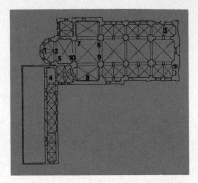

**Düsseldorf-Gerresheim, former Damenstift-skirche 1** Crucifix, last third of 10C **2** High altar with Romanesque altar table **3** Sarcophagus of St.Gerricus, 14C **4** Monstrance, c. 1400 **5** Tabernacle, late 15C **6** Virgin Mary, early 16C statue **7** Candlestick of the Virgin Mary, early 16C **8** Choir stalls, early 18C **9** Pulpit, early 18C **10** Reliquary niche, c. 1500

Gründgens-Platz 1) is one of the most important German theatres. The present building, designed by B.Pfau, was opened in January 1970. There are 1,036 seats. The *Kom(m)ödchen* (Hunsrückenstrasse) is one of the best-known German cabaret theatres.

*Collegiate church of St.Margaretha*

*Schloss Jägerhof*

**Museums:** The *Düsseldorf Art Museum* (5 Ehrenhof) has temporary art exhibitions, a picture gallery with 16–20C works, and several specialist departments (graphics collection, arts and crafts, glass collection). The *Landesmusem Volk und Wirtschaft* is an economics museum, unique of its kind in Germany. The *Kunstsammlung Nordrhein-Westfalen* (5 Grabbeplatz) has 20C paintings, with a significant collection of works by Paul Klee. The *Schloss Benrath* displays the domestic décor of the rococo and late baroque, and also porcelain and objets d'art. The *Heinrich-Heine-Institut* (14 B Bilker Strasse) has a library, an archive and a *museum*. The *Goethe Museum* (Jägerhofstrasse 1) originated from the private collection of Anton Kippenberg, the former owner of the Insel-Verlag publishing house. It has a total of some 35,000 exhibits and is the third largest Goethe museum after the collections in Frankfurt and Weimar. The *Haus des Dt.Ostens* (Bismarckstrasse 90) has collections relating to the customs, domestic interiors and history of East Germany, with a chart of those expelled from the former East German and Sudeten territories, and also a weapon collection. The *Hetjens-Museum/Dt. Keramikmuseum* (in the Palais Nesselrode, Schulstrasse 4) displays ceramics from eight millennia and china from all over the world. *Ernst Schneider Stiftung* (Schloss Jägerhof): Furniture, silver and porcelain from the 18C, especially Meissen.

**Environs: Ratingen** (10 km. N.): The parish church of *St.Peter and St.Paul* was allegedly founded by St. Suitbert in the early 8C and is of interest not only for its Romanesque towers but also for its early Gothic hall structure. The *church treasure* includes one of the earliest monstrances in Europe (1394). Among the exhibits in the *Stadtgeschichtliches Museum* is a collection of works by the porcelain modeller J.P.Melchior (1747–1825).

## Eberbach = 6228 Eltville

Hessen                                    p.416☐D 14

**Former Cistercian Monastery:** These monastery buildings dating from the 12–14C have survived in the lonely Taunus mountains in the heart of the Rheingau. The buildings are considered to be a classic specimen of a reformed monastery in the high Middle Ages. The Cistercians, who were entirely self-sufficient, estab-lished a considerable reputation for the wines of the area and also gave the monastery its place in the history of art. As there were up to 300 monks and lay brothers living in the monastery at the height of its fame the establishment very quickly took on the character of an independent community. In about 1215/20 the Cistercians even built a hospital of their own, with all the necessary buildings for the supply of food and drink. After secularization in 1803 the monastery was a prison

*Cistercian monastery of Eberbach, dormitory*

and lunatic asylum for almost 100 years (1813–1912), and then a military rehabilitation centre (1912–18). The former monastery buildings are now maintained and used by the state wine authorities of the Rheingau. The historic site can be visited (guided tours are available at weekends if arranged in advance).

*The buildings:* The monastery site is surrounded by a 12&13C wall approximately 1,200 yards long by 16 ft. high, all of which has survived, with the exception of the gates and doors. The church is the focal point of the site. It was consecrated in 1186 (building commenced in 1145). The interior of the basilica is essentially Romanesque and this plain, spare style determines the shape of the pillars and arcades of rounded arches, and the block-like design of the walls. Very little remains of the original lavish decoration. This makes the *tombs* all the more striking, especially that of the Cantor of Mainz Cathedral, Eberhard von Oberstein (d.1331), which is at the E. end of the S. aisle. The tombs in the first chapel on the S. side depict Wigand von Hynsperg (d.1511) and Adam von Allendorf (d.1518) and his wife. They are the work of the famous Rhenish sculptor H. Backoffen or his pupils and have some Gothic and some Renaissance ornamentation. N. of the church are the *retreat buildings*, which are grouped round the *cloister* and lawn. The only striking room in this complex, which was kept very spartan in the Cistercian manner, is the *refectory*; the splendid Baroque stucco ceiling was added in 1738. West of the retreat rooms is the *convertite* building, which was built in the 12&13C and provided accommodation for the lay brothers. These lay brothers had fewer spiritual duties than the monks and performed tasks which took them outside the monastery grounds. The rules of the Order required them to live in strict separation from the monks.

**Ebersberg 8017**
Bavaria                                    p.422☐L 20

**Former Monastery Church of St.**

*Monastery church of St. Sebastian, Ebersberg*

**Sebastian:** Only the foundations of the original building (completed in 1312, the towers are part of an earlier building) can be distinguished. As so many alterations have been made no uniform architectural scheme can be identified. The church is dedicated to St.Sebastian, whose skull was brought from Rome to Ebersberg in 931. The high altar (1773) shows the figure of Sebastian between Ignatius Loyola, Peter, Paul and Francis Xavier. The tombs in the *funerary chapel* N. of the chancel are important examples of late Bavarian Gothic. The *sacristy* is also finely decorated with carved figures from the workshop of I.Günther, and the *chapel of St.Sebastian* above it has excellent stucco and a reliquiary bust of St.Sebastian (late 15C).

**Also worth seeing:** Town hall built in 1529 with net vaulting and carved wooden ceiling; market place with baroque and Biedermeier houses.

## Ebrach 8602
Bavaria                                        p.418□I 15

**Former Cistercian Monastery:** In the 12C Ebrach was the Cistercians' first house in Franconia (and their third in Germany). New foundations spread from here and Ebrach became the spiritual centre of the Order. The aim of retaining autonomy and thus being independent of the Bishops of Würzburg was not achieved, however. The monastery today occupies a large site with five courts. The first phase was built to the plans of J.L.Dientzenhofer and the second phase was designed by H.J.Greising. The influence of Greising can be seen above all in the façades, in the staircase of the N. part of the abbey, and in the design of the principal courtyard. The involvement of Balthasar Neumann, who was little known at the time, is questionable. In 1851 the monastery buildings were turned into a prison.

**Monastery church:** This basilica with three aisles is one of the largest churches built by the Order in Germany (277 ft. long, 76 ft. wide, 71 ft. high). Twelve chapels open off the chancel of this impressive building. The most striking feature of the interior is the stucco (1773–91) by M.Bossi. The W. wall has a fine rose-window. In the choir is a *marble stucco altar*, also by Bossi. The lavishly decorated *choir stalls* and the *organ* are also worth seeing. The most important tomb is that of Queen Gertrud and her son, King Friedrich of Swabia. The *chapel of St. Michael*, which has Romanesque elements, was completed in 1207.

## Ebstorf 3112
Lower Saxony                                  p.414□H 6

Ebstorf is famous for the 'Ebstorf map of the world'. Today one can only see a copy of the map, as the original was destroyed by fire in 1943. This map of the world— considered to be the finest medieval specimen—consisted of 30 parchment sheets and has an overall size of 42 sq. ft. It is in the shape of a disc held by Christ and places Jerusalem at the centre of the world. This 13C world picture is based on the descriptions of Gervasius of Tilbury and other sources and consists of a number of details drawn from geography, medicine, world history and Greek mythology.

*Rose-window, Ebrach*

*Virgin Mary (13C), Ebstorf*

*Sections from the 13C map of the world in the monastery of Ebstorf*

**Ebstorf convent:** In approximately 1160 a Premonstratensian Canonry was founded here and converted in 1197 into a Benedictine convent which became extraordinarily wealthy as a centre of pilgrimage in the Middle Ages. The *convent buildings* (14&15C) contain a large number of chests and cupboards originally brought by the novices as their dowry. They form a small-scale documentary history of *Lüneburg furniture*. The monastery has been an institution for gentlewomen since 1555.

**Convent church:** This is a large, late Gothic church of the type also found in Lüneburg, Uelzen and Verden (qq.v.) The *nuns' gallery* occupies a large part of the nave, and is decorated with sculpture, including two *Madonnas*, a life-size *St. Maurice* (1300), a *Madonna with halo*, and a 15C painting of the *Virgin Mary*. The interior is dominated by a *Triumphal Cross group* above the altar and a 15C three-branched candelabrum. Particularly nota-

ble are the *bronze font* (1310), the *Apostles' frieze* (1400), and—as in other parts of the monastery — the many pedestals and keystones which show occasionally amusing scenes from monastery life, the lives of the saints, and mythology. In the church and in the S. and W. cloisters are splendid *stained-glass windows* (c.1400).

## Eckernförde 2330
Schleswig-Holstein          p.412□H 2

This former fishing village developed into a town in the 13C and is today the economic and cultural centre of the Landkreis Rendsburg/Eckernförde. The rectangular market place was the centre of the medieval town.

**Nikolaikirche** (Nikolaistrasse): This brick Protestant church (nave and two aisles) is based on a 13C church with one aisle (the

*Adoration of the Shepherds, 1515, Eckernförde*

*Altarpiece by Gudewerdt the younger, 1640*

chancel and parts of the W. tower remain.) The unassuming exterior does not prepare us for the splendour of the interior decoration, which makes this church one of the most important in Schleswig-Holstein. The most striking feature is the altarpiece: created by H.Gudewerdt the Younger *c.*1640, it is the finest baroque altar in Schleswig-Holstein. The carvings on the pulpit are by H.Gudewerdt the Elder. The church is also well known for its tombs, particularly that of Thomas Börnsen (1661) by H.Gudewerdt. The *bronze font* (1558) is lavishly decorated.

**Borby Protestant church:** This basically single-aisled stone church (*c.*1200) has an early-13C Gotland limestone font, and a carved altar influenced by the work of H.Gudewerdt the Younger (1686).

**Houses:** There are fine, largely unspoiled old houses in Kieler Strasse (No. 48), and in Nikolaistrasse, Gudewerdtstrasse and Gaethjestrasse.

**Heimatmuseum** (59 Kieler Strasse): Collections on the history of the town and folklore of the Gettorf and Eckenförde areas.

---

**Eichstätt 8833**
Bavaria                                    p.422□K 17

In the Renaissance Eichstätt's importance extended beyond its immediate surroundings. Eichstätt today is essentially baroque in appearance: this is a consequence of the fire of 1634, which almost entirely destroyed the town, which was then rebuilt in the baroque style. The town wall is still largely intact. The strong influence of the Church in the town, the seat of a bishop, is shown by the presence of the Dom, the Benedictine monastery of St.Walburg and a Catholic seminary.

**Dom** (10 Domplatz): The cathedral dominates the town. Of the original Romanesque buildings the cruciform ground plan and the towers remain. The building is principally 14C: (building began again in 1256 with the choir, and the pillared Gothic nave and aisles were added in 1380–96). The most important feature of the Dom is its interior decoration, and in particular the *Pappenheim altar* in the N. transept. Kaspar von Pappenheim, a canon, endowed the altar, almost 32ft. in height, in 1489. It is presumed to have been created by the Nuremberg sculptor V.Wirsberger, one of the most important artists of his time. In the Willibald choir is the famous *stone Madonna* (1297). Opposite is the tomb of the founder of the monastery, Willibald (Willibaldstumba, *c.*1269). The altar in the choir was rebuilt on several occasions and is today largely neo-Gothic. The statue of St.Willibald, a work of the local sculptor L.Hering, is one of the most important sculptures of the Renaissance. Hering was also responsible for the *Wolfstein altar*, which is now on the W. wall of the S. aisle. The *Mortuarium* (Hall of the Dead), on the W. side of the cloisters, also contains striking tombstones. The columns which support the eight double bays include the *[schöne Säule*, a masterpiece of German stonemasonry. The stained glass representing the Last Judgement (designed by Hans Holbein the Elder) in the four windows on the E. side of the Mortuarium, is also artistically significant.

**Parish church of St.Walburg** (Walburgiberg): The church is named after St. Walburg, the sister of Willibald, the founder of the monastery. She lived in the convent of Heidenheim, founded by her brother, but her remains were brought to Eichstätt in the 9C. After the Dom this is the dominant building in the town; it was built in 1626–31, and has not been significantly altered. A high porch leads to the nave. The pilastered interior is decorated in Wessobrunn (q.v.) stucco. Behind the 18C high altar is the *Confessio of St. Walburg* (vault altar), a rare combination of tomb and altar.

**Former Prince Bishop's Residence** (Residenzplatz): The restoration of the present buildings was begun in 1704 after the great fire of 1634, and completed in 1791. They have housed state offices since 1817. The *staircase* by M.Pedetti is of ar-

*Schutzengelkirche, Eichstätt*

chitectural significance. The main hall (also called the *hall of mirrors*) is on the second floor. It has ornate stucco, and decorative mirrors on the walls. In front of the Palace in the Residenzplatz is the notable (1775–80) *Marienbrunnen* (fountain). The square is one of the finest baroque squares in Germany. The adjoining buildings were also designed by the well-known architect G.Gabrieli.

**Former Summer Residence** (26 Ostenstrasse): The Summer Palace was built in the first third of the 18C by G.Gebrich. It is more than 75 yards wide and the interior is highly decorated. It now houses the administrative offices of the Eichstätt Gesamthochschule.

**Jesuit Church/Schutzengelkirche** (Leonrodplatz): Most of this church, first consecrated in 1620, had to be rebuilt in 1661 after the great fire. There is strikingly ornate stucco by F.Gabrieli, brother of the Prince Bishop's architect G.Gabrieli. The high altar is by the court sculptor M.Seybold, and the altar panel is by the Augsburg artist J.E.Holzer.

**Bishop's Palace** (5 P.Philipp-Jenningen-Platz): A distinguished 18C building occupied by the Bishop from 1817. The architect was G.Gabrieli. The building contains numerous outstanding 15&16C works of religious art.

**Willibaldsburg** (on the SE edge of the town): The castle, founded in the 14C, is on a ridge outside the town gates. The *Gemmingen building*, designed by E.Holl, was the only part of a 16–17C plan for an extension in the style of a Renaissance palace to be realized. The part of the building which remains today houses the *Jura Museum in der Willibaldsburg*, which contains some exhibits from the prehistoric and early periods, but deals principally with history of the town, and late Gothic painting and sculpture.

**Former Augustinian Canonry** (in Rebdorf): The pillared basilica with a nave and two aisles is the product of rebuilding in 1732–4. The W. section is in the Roman-esque style of the earlier building. The stucco is by F. Gabrieli. To the SE lies the *monastery*.

**Former Augustinian monastery** (in Marienstein): The only remaining buildings are the priory and the kitchens.

**Museums:** As well as the Museum in the Willibaldsburg (q.v.) and the Diocesan Museum (5 Residenzplatz), Eichstätt has the *Sammlungen des bischöflichen Seminars* and the *Berger Museum* (Harthof), which specializes in fossils from the Franconian Jura, and the important *cathedral treasure* (in the sacristy of the chapterhouse).

**Also worth seeing:** There are a number of extremely well-decorated smaller churches, which tend to be neglected in favour of the cathedral, the parish church and the Jesuit church. These include the *Capuchin Monastery of the Sacred Cross* (17C), with its fine 'Holy Sepulchre', the former *Dominican Church* (13C, rebuilt 1713–23), the late Gothic *Mariahilf Chapel* (with baroque elements), the former *Notre Dame monastery church* (c.1720), and the *Frauenberg Chapel* (1739; near the Willibaldsburg). The *Dompropstei* (1672; Jesuitenplatz), which has exceptional stucco decoration, and the *Coblenzl-Schlösschen* (post 1730) are also worth a visit.

**Einbeck 3352**

Lower Saxony                                   p.414☐G 9

Einbeck, which became a member of the Hanseatic League in 1368, is known for its furs, linen, wool and beer, and also for its well-preserved half-timbered houses. Well-known citizens include Friedrich Sertürner, who discoverd morphia in 1805 and who is buried outside the Altenberg Gate. Till Eulenspiegel is said to have worked here as a builder's apprentice and there is a monument to him.

**Former Collegiate Church of St.**

*Stained-glass window in the Dom ossuary* ▷

**Alexander** (Stiftplatz): At the beginning of the 12C the town and the church were centres of pilgrimage to the Holy Blood. In the 13&14C a new building was erected on the site of the former church, incorporating parts of the older building. Little of the former decoration remains: the *choir stalls* (1288), the *tombstone* of Provost Johann (d. 1367), and a *font* (1427). The Romanesque *chandelier*, 11 ft. in diameter and probably mid 15C, is also worth seeing.

**Protestant Church of St.Jakob** (Marktplatz): Little remains of the original 13C building. The ornate baroque W. façade was an attempt to develop stylistic elements which were already present. The pulpit with its simple carvings dates from the year 1637. There are striking 16&17C tombs.

**Town Hall** (6–8 Marktplatz): The three round-pinnacled front sections make a curious architectural effect. By the Town Hall (1593) is the *Ratswaage* (1565). The highly decorated woodwork on the ground floor is the principal feature of this unusual building. The *Ratsapotheke* (1562), and the *Brodhaus* are also in the Marktplatz. The Brodhaus was built by the Einbeck Bakers' Guild in 1552, ten years before the Ratsapotheke.

**Half-timbered houses:** More than 100 well-preserved late Gothic houses are to be found inside the ramparts. There are particularly fine houses in Steinweg, Tidexerstrasse and Marktstrasse, almost all dating from the 16C.

**Museums:** The *Städtisches Museum* (11 Steinweg) is in one of the fine old houses. The main features of the collection are exhibits on the cultural history of Einbeck, mould engraving, wallpaper printing and brewing. The historical *bicycle collection* (1-3 Papenstrasse) is also of interest.

---

**Eining = Neustadt 8425**
Bavaria                                    p.422□L 17

**Kastell:** In 1879 ruins of a Roman fort

were discovered S. of this small town and excavated between then and 1920. It is called Abusina (after the river Abens). The development of the citadel up to the 1C can be seen. The site, which can be visited, is 160 by 136 yards, and must therefore have been the small fort of a cohort. Features which can be distinguished are towers, gates, the central building (praetorium), the atrium, the arsenal, and the administrative complex and its adjacent buildings. In the 2C the Romans began to build the *limes* near to Eining (the 'dry limes' as opposed to the 'wet limes', which was formed by the Danube). The Raetian limes was 103 miles long in all; its walls were 6–10ft. high, and up to 4ft. thick. Watch-towers were placed at regular intervals.

---

**Ellingen 8836**
Bavaria                                    p.422□I 17

**Schloss** (NW of town): After Emperor Friedrich II presented Ellingen to the Teutonic Knights in 1216, the Order first of all established a commandery. The commmander of the Ballei (Province) of Franconia had his residence here, and became German Master of the Order in 1788. In 1708 the Schloss was built around a courtyard, the church forming the N. side. The S. side is the most striking feature. Its façade has three projections. The building was designed by F.Keller, and the stucco is by the Viennese artist F.Roth. The buildings today contain the Ellingen *Residenzmuseum* and the *East Prussian Cultural Centre*. The collection displays classical and French Empire domestic items and also has rooms devoted to the Teutonic Order. N. of the Schloss is the lavishly decorated *riding school*, and to the S. is a brewery.

**Schloss church** (in the Schloss): Important features are the baroque decoration, the stucco and the lavish frescos (1718). The high altar was created by the distinguished Augsburg artist F.X.Feuchtmayer. The carved prayer desks are of outstanding quality.

**Rathaus** (Hausnerstrasse): The Ellingen

*Ratsapotheke and Brodhaus, Einbeck*

architect F.Roth, who designed the Schloss, was also responsible for the Town Hall (completed 1774) which was originally intended as a court of justice. It is one of the finest rococo buildings of the period.

**Also worth seeing:** Little remains of the town fortifications except the *Pleinfelder Tor* (1660). The *Rezat bridge* (1728) with its 8 saints, the *Catholic Parish Church of St. Georg* (1729 – 31), and the *Mariahilf Chapel* (begun 1676, completed *c.*1730, by the cemetery), are also of interest.

---

**Ellwangen, Jagst 7090**
Baden-Württemberg                    p.422☐H 17

---

Ellwangen (not to be confused with Ellwangen bei Biberach an der Riss) is in the beautiful Jagst valley, where the foreland of the Swabian Alb meets the Ellwangen hills. The town developed from 1146 on-

wards around the former monastery and the collegiate church. In the surrounding hills are the Provosts' Schloss and the pilgrimage church of Schönenberg.

**Former Collegiate Church/Catholic Parish Church of St.Veit** (Marktplatz): The present building was largely built in 1233 on the site of earlier 8&11C buildings; it has had a turbulent history. Alterations were made in almost all periods before it assumed its present baroque style under Prince Provost Georg von Schönborn in 1737–41. The exterior is dominated by the two large towers and five apses. Basic Romanesque features are particularly apparent in the *crypt*, which is under the crossing and differs strongly from customary designs. *Tombstones* and *memorials* remain from the earlier interior. The bronze casts of the founders Hariolf and Erlolf (in the S. transept) and Albrecht von Rechberg (in the N. transept) are attributed to the Nuremberg sculptor P.Vischer. The tomb of the knight Ulrich von Ahelfingen (d. 1339) in the W. porch is one of the finest Gothic tomb carvings in Swabia. Baroque alterations have completely changed the dominant features of the church. The sandstone *altar of the Holy Cross* (in the porch) dates from 1610. The altar in the S. arm of the transept is early 16C and the altar in the N. arm dates from 1613. The E. high altar was restored in 1910 and the high altar in the crossing in 1952, both using original materials. The *chapter building*, with its late Gothic *cloisters* and Mary Chapel (*c.*1470), is at the N. end of the church.

**Jesuit Church** (1 Marktplatz): The Jesuit church is close by the former collegiate church. It was completed in 1721, and is particularly important because of its vaulting, painted by C.T.Scheffler of the Asam school. It shows scenes from the life of the Virgin and architectural structures. It is Scheffler's first major work; he was also responsible for the frescos in the Congregation Hall of the *Jesuitenkollegium* (1720 –2).

**Pilgrimage Church of St. Mary** (21 Schönenberg): The *Loreto chapel* was built in delightful surroundings in 1639. It is part of the pilgrimage church built by V.M.Thumb in 1682–95, and survived a fire in 1709. The dominant feature of the interior is the huge blue and black marble altar. Stucco (1683 and 1709) and frescos (1711) are largely by M.Paulus.

**Schloss** (Schlossstrasse): This building, high above the town, was based on the original 13C Burg, which was later extended as an abbot's residence and fortress, and in 1608 took on its present form as a four-sided Fürstenschloss in the late Renaissance style. In 1720–6 the interior was refurbished in baroque style. Today it houses the *Schlossmuseum*, with exhibits on pre- and early history, church art (baroque cribs), valuable faience, prints, and baroque drawings.

**Also worth seeing:** The *canons' curias* (17&18C) can be recognized by their statues of Our Lady. The *Landgericht* (3– 7 Marktplatz, formerly the Town Hall) was

built in 1748 to plans by B.Neumann. The *Palais Adelmann* (6 Obere Strasse) is based on Italian models and was probably built by M.Thumb in 1688. Also note the former governor's building (1591); the Marienkirche (1427 with baroque alterations in 1735); the cemetery church of St.Wolfgang.

---

## Eltville 6228

Eltville, a charming little town on the right bank of the Rhine, is the oldest town in the Rheingau; its economy is based on wine and Sekt (sparkling wine). Its history can be traced from the time of the barbarian invasions, when an old Alemannic settlement became the core of the town, which has been the scene of many battles. In 1332 Eltville officially became a town. Thomas Mann brought literary fame to the town when the hero of his novel 'Felix Krull' invented the brand 'Loreley extra cuvée' for the firm of Engelbert Krull, which was based in Eltville. There is a memorial to Johannes Gutenberg, the inventor of printing, in the keep of the Burg. It was in Eltville that Gutenberg was granted the title of courtier in 1465 by the Archbishop of Mainz and Elector Adolf of Nassau; this was incidentally the only honour which Gutenberg received in his lifetime.

**Catholic Parish Church of St. Peter and St.Paul** (5 Rosengasse): This church was begun in the middle of the 14C on the site of the 12C Romanesque basilica; building was completed in 1686. During restoration work in the years 1932–4 a fourth E. aisle bay and a new sacristy were added. The striking tower is a masterpiece of late Gothic art in Hessen. On the E. wall of the tower interior is a fine 15C wall painting, which was only revealed in 1961. The generally lavish interior furnishing includes a *font* (1517), decorated on its base with figures from the gospels. The font was made in the workshops of the Mainz artist H.Backoffen. Another masterpiece is the *Crescent Moon Madonna* (16C), which is also presumed to be the work of a Mainz

*Former Collegiate Church of St. Veit, Ellwangen*

artist. The best of the various *tombstones* and *tombs* is the memorial to Agnes von Koppenstein (d.1553). The *Mount of Olives* (c.1520) and the *Crucifixion* (c.1505) in the cemetery chapel (1717) are also worthy of note.

**Burg ruins:** The 14C moated Burg is built on a square ground plan. One side is directly on the Rhine, the other sides were formerly protected by barbicans. In the 14&15C the Burg is presumed to have been the residence of the Electors.

**Houses:** There are numerous houses in a good state of preservation in the Hauptstrasse; they give a clear picture of the history of the town. The baroque Madonnas and statues of the saints on houses are typical. There are also attractive houses in the side streets. The Stockheimer Hof (16C), the Gräflich Eltzsche Hof (16C) and the Bechtmünzer Hof (15C) are the most striking.

**Emden 2970**
Lower Saxony                              p.414☐C 5

Emden has always been dominated by the North Sea. The town has the third largest harbour on the North Sea, and an important shipbuilding industry. This tradition can be traced back to the Middle Ages, when Emden became one of the most important dock and shipbuilding towns of its period, as a result of receiving refugees from the Dutch Wars of Religion.

**Great Reformed Church of St.Cosmas and St.Damian** (Kirchstrasse): The original hall church with three aisles was begun in the 12C and much rebuilt later, and then almost totally destroyed in 1944. It is still a ruin, and is to remain in its present condition as a memorial to the unification of the reformed churches of Lower Germany and the Netherlands. We are reminded of this connection by a ship carved in sand-

*Ellwangen, Schloss*          *Font (1517), Eltville* ▷

stone (1660; above the door to the N. transept), whose crew of refugees from the Netherlands on their way to Emden are seen desperately battling with a stormy sea.

**Reformed New Church** (Brückstrasse): This church also has strong connections with the Dutch Wars of Religion. It was built in the years 1643–8 on the model of the Noorderkerk in Amsterdam, and was used by the refugees as a house of prayer. Four large gable roofs give the church its unorthodox appearance.

**Town Hall** (Am Delft): L. van Steenwinkel built for Emden a copy of the Town Hall in Antwerp, for which he was also responsible. The building, with its classic Renaissance façade, was completed in 1576. It was rebuilt after being badly damaged in the Second World War. Today it houses the *Ostfriesisches Landesmuseum* and the *Städtisches Museum*. The Ostfriesisches Landesmuseum specializes in

artistic and cultural history (docks and navigation), paintings and local history; the Städtisches Museum has an armoury with historical weapons. The *town silver* is also in this museum.

**Also worth seeing:** Few of the houses survived the air-raids of the Second World War. One which did is *12 Pelzerstrasse*, which has a fine Dutch Renaissance façade.

**Theatre:** The Emden New Theatre (12 Theaterstrasse) was opened in 1970. It has 681 seats and takes productions from nearby theatres and touring groups.

---

**Emkendorf 2371**
Schleswig-Holstein       p.412☐H 2

Count Fritz Reventlow and his wife Julia made the Herrenhaus on the Emkendorf estate a centre of North German artistic life

*Emmendingen, Schloss*

at the beginning of the 19C. From 1794 onwards the formerly baroque Herrenhaus was rebuilt in early neoclassical style. The rooms are decorated with Pompeian and Etruscan motifs. Literary figures who gathered here included Friedrich Gottlieb Klopstock, Matthias Claudius, Christian and Friedrich Leopold zu Stolberg and numerous other intellectuals of the time. Claudius is said to have written his famous 'Abendlied' here.

## Emmendingen 7830

Baden-Württemburg                    p.420☐D 19

Emmendingen is proud of its connections with Goethe: Johann Georg Schlosser, a magistrate in Emmendingen (1774–87), married Goethe's sister Cornelia in 1773 and they lived there until her death in 1777. She is buried in the Old Cemetery. Goethe himself stayed in the Schlossers' house on numerous occasions in 1775 and 1779. The annals of the town mention Jakob Michael Reinhold Lenz, one of the leaders of the Sturm und Drang movement, the historian Johann Daniel Schöpflin and the author Johann Peter Hebel. The writer Alfred Döblin died in the state hospital here.

**Former Schloss:** The Margraves' Schloss, which has been much altered in the course of time, today houses the *Heimatmuseum*. This deals with the history of the town, Goethe memorabilia, and works of the painter Fritz Boehle.

**Also worth seeing:** *Catholic Church of St.Boniface* (19C) with early Gothic altarpiece by the Nördlingen master Friedrich Herlin (c.1470), the Rathaus (1729) and the Town Gate (18C).

**Environs: Kenzingen** (13 km. NW): In the *Catholic Parish Church of St.Laurentius* in the S. baptismal and funerary chapel of the von Hürnheim family the *portrait tombs* are worth seeing; in the N. chapel there is now a *Mount of Olives* (1734), which used to be outside in the choir.

## Emmerich 4240
Nordrhein-Westfalen                    p.414☐A 9

Emmerich was very badly damaged in the Second World War, but was rebuilt very much in the original style. Its closeness to the Rhine and the Dutch border has made Emmerich essentially a trading town. The town's coat of arms is the oldest in Germany.

**Former Collegiate Church of St. Martin:** Building was begun in the 11C, but not completed until the 15C (the church was rebuilt in a simplified form after its destruction in the Second World War). The *choir* shows traces of the original Romanesque building. The *crypt* with its six Romanesque columns is also preserved. In the two chapels adjacent to the crypt there are *Romanesque wall paintings* (12C). The original lavish furnishings are only partially preserved: parts of the late Gothic *choir stalls* (1486) and a carved *crucifix* (c.1200). In the *treasury* are valuable gold figures of St.Martin and St.Vitus (Hochelten). The most important item is the *Ark of St.Willibrord*, which was originally (11C) a richly decorated oak chest-reliquary; the top was added c.1400 and the whole thing was remade c.1520 in the form of a monstrance.

**Parish Church of St.Aldegundis** (St. Aldegundis Kirchplatz): After being destroyed in the Second World War the 15C church was faithfully rebuilt. Some of the late Gothic interior furnishings are worth seeing: the silver-gilt monstrance (16C), and several sculptures. An ascent of the tower is also recommended (good views of Emmerich).

**Rhine bridge:** The Rhine bridge is 1343 yards long and thus the longest suspension bridge in Germany.

**Museum:** The Rhine Museum (2 Martini Kirchgang) is an important museum, with exhibits on the history and development of shipping on the Rhine.

## Enger 4904
Nordrhein-Westfalen                    p.414☐E 8

**Protestant Parish Church/Former Collegiate Church of St. Dionysius:** Duke Widukind, leader of the Saxons in the struggle against Charlemagne, is said to have founded a church on this site in 785, and to have been buried here after his death in 807. The Saxon Prince is commemorated by the Tumba in the choir of the present-day church. It now forms part of a Renaissance Tumba (c.1590), but the actual portrait slab probably dates from c.1090. It is one of the most important sculptures remaining from the Salic period. The church contains a *carved altar* by H.Stavoer (Hildesheim). It was completed c.1525. The design was influenced by Dürer and his pupils.

**Also worth seeing:** *Wittekind Memorial* (10 Kirchplatz): This small museum is

*Ark of St. Willibrord, Emmerich*

*Erbach, Schloss*

largely devoted to the Saxon leader Widukind. There are also copies of the *treasure* from the church of St.Dionysius (the originals are in Berlin museums).

## Enkenbach = Enkenbach-Alsenborn 6753

Rheinland-Pfalz                    p.420□D 16

**Former Premonstratensian Monastery Church of St. Norbert/Catholic Parish Church:** The foundation of a Premonstratesian monastery was mentioned in documents as early as 1148, well before the monastery church was added in 1220–72. The church is a mixture of various styles. There is a notable Romanesque porch, which is one of the most beautiful in Germany. Despite some Gothic elements the building is essentially Romanesque.

**Also worth seeing:** In the *Protestant Par-*

*ish Church* is an organ by the brothers Stumm, and in the Hauptstrasse there are some fine old houses. The Cistercian Monastery Church in *Otterberg* is also worth a visit.

## Erbach im Odenwald 6120

Hessen                              p.416□F 15

Erbach is the administrative centre of the Odenwald district and the centre of German ivory carving. The town developed under the protection of the former Burg, a forerunner of the present Schloss.

**Schloss:** There was originally a medieval moated castle on the site of the present building; of this only the keep remains (1200). Count Georg Wilhelm had the long, plain Schloss built in 1736. The baroque elements come from rebuilding work in 1902. In the Schloss is the *Count's Collection*; this was assembled by Franz I,

*Wallfahrtskirche Heiliges Blut in Erding*

Count zu Erbach-Erbach (1754-1823), and contains medieval weapons, an arsenal, armour, busts of Greek and Roman emperors and soldiers, and an antler gallery.

**Museums:** The Erbach Ivory Museum (1 Otto-Glenz-Strasse) is unique of its kind. It has displays of German ivory work since the 18C and is to be extended.

**Also worth seeing:** 16C Rathaus; Protestant Parish Church, built 1749–50 to plans by F.J.Stengel; Burgmannenhöfe in the Städtel (row of fine old buildings, mainly 16&17C).

---

**Erding 8058**
Bavaria                                    p.422☐L 19

The origin and development of the town has been influenced by its position on the main road from Munich to Landshut.

There was a royal court here in the 9C, but the town was refounded by Duke Otto II of Bavaria in the 13C.

**Parish Church of St.Johann:** The main parts of the building are 14&15C, but the furnishings predominantly 19C. The 16C Town Hall was originally built on to the bell tower, which is 16 ft. away from the church. The Town Hall was separated in 1866, but the tower is now connected to the neo-Gothic Schrannenhalle. The interior of the church is dominated by slender columns which confirm the influence of the Landshut (q.v.) school. The contents include the *Leinberger Crucifix* by H.Leinberger (1520). Wooden figures from the late 15C have been incorporated in the neo-Gothic high altar.

**Pilgrimage Church of the Holy Blood** (Heilig Blut 4): This church on the edge of the town did not take its present form until 1675–7 at the hands of the Erdingen master mason H.Kogler. The cruciform crypt on the site of the Miracle of the Host is a reminder of previous buildings and the origin of the pilgrimage. The stucco decoration by the Munich craftsman J.G.Bader is unusually imaginative. The delicate gallery is particularly striking.

**Museum:** The *Heimatmuseum* (from 1986 in the Antoniusheim, Prielmayerstrasse) has exhibits on pre- and early history and displays of 14–18C sculpture and everyday peasant life.

**Also worth seeing:** *Hospital Church of the Holy Spirit* (12 Landshuterstrasse): 1444 with stucco from 1688 and a fine high altar (1793); 17C *Rathaus*; numerous well-preserved 17&18C *houses*. The Landshuter Tor (known as the *Schöner Turm* (15C) remains from the original town wall.

**Environs:** There are various fine village churches nearby (including Altenerding, Gross-Thalheim, Hörgersdorf and Oppolding) which are worth visiting for their lavish furnishings.

---

**Eriskirch 7991**
Baden-Württemburg                    p.420 □ G 21

**Parish and Pilgrimage Church of Our Lady:** This lavishly decorated church (*c.*1400) has unique treasures, including stained glass and frescos in the nave and choir. The frescos (15C) are particularly distinguished works of the so-called Lake Constance school. In the choir are the stained-glass windows endowed by Count Heinrich de Montfort in 1408. The three Gothic Madonnas (two in the choir and one on a side altar in the nave) are also worth noting.

---

**Erlangen 8520**
Bavaria                              p.418 □ I 15

Erlangen is part of the Nuremberg-Fürth-Erlangen industrial complex, and the site of the University of Nuremberg-Erlangen

(founded in 1743, with more than 16,000 students) and many internationally important firms. The great period of the town's development began when Emperor Karl IV took over in the year 1361 and laid out the present-day Old Town. Margrave Christian Ernst von Bayreuth introduced the second stage of the town's development with the Huguenot settlement of 1686. At this time the building of the rectangular new town began. Professors at the University have included Johann Gottlieb Fichte (1805–6), Friedrich Rückert (1826–41) and Ludwig Feuerbach (1828); former students include Johann Peter Hebel.

**Church of the Trinity in the Old Town** (Martin-Luther-Platz): The church was built in its present form in 1721 after the great fire of 1706. The interior is surrounded by balconies, and there is an unusual pulpit-altar. The tower, which is an integral part of the façade, is an emblem of the town. The organ case is by F.P. Diefenbach.

**Protestant Reformed Church** (Hugenottenplatz): The skilful design of the wooden gallery makes the interior of the church, which was built 1686–93, appear round. Both the exterior and interior of the building are very plain; only the pulpit is ornately decorated.

**Schloss** (Schlossgarten): The foundation-stone for this long, three-storey building was laid by Prince Georg Wilhelm in 1700; it was completed four years later. The furnishings were destroyed by fire in 1814. The Schloss is now used by the University. The *Schlossplatz* is dominated by the *Hugenottenbrunnen* (fountain). The allegorical designs commemorate Margrave Christian Ernst.

**Orangery** (Schlossgarten): The Orangery was built in 1706–8 to plans by G. von Gedeler, who also designed the Schloss. It is in the middle of the Schloss garden, which was laid out in 1704–5, and maintained in the French style until 1785–6. The orangery building is semicircular in form and has a central hall with fine stucco decoration.

*Huguenot fountain (1706), Schloss garden*

*Orangery and Schloss garden*

**Margraves' Theatre** (2 Theaterplatz): At the NE corner of the Schloss garden is the Margraves' theatre, which was built on the orders of Margrave Friedrich Wilhelm in 1517–19, and rebuilt and refurbished by the Venetian G.P. Gaspari in 1742. There are nowadays about 130 performances per year by touring groups in the theatre, which has 664 seats.

**Also worth seeing:** The *Palais-Stutterheim* in the Marktplatz, built 1728–30, is now the municipal library. The *Neues Rathaus* was built by H.Loebermann in 1970–1, together with the Congress Centre and Stadthalle; these buildings are all in concrete. The *Parish and University Church in the New Town* (consecrated 1737; Neustädter Kirchplatz) has interior stucco and ceiling paintings by C.Leimberger and a pulpit altar supported by an angel by E.Räntz.

**Museums:** Various museums were established in conjunction with the University. The *Archäologische Sammlung* (4 Kochstrasse) has copies of Greek and Roman statues. The *Gemäldesammlung* (1 Schlossgarten in the Orangery) deals with all aspects of art and art history. The *Geographische und Völkerkundliche Sammlung* (4 Kochstrasse) concentrates on geography and anthropology. The *Graphische Sammlung* shows drawings, engravings and wood carvings by major artists (including A.Dürer and M.Grünewald), and also coins and medallions. *Other museums:* Musical instrument collection (4 Schlossplatz), prehistoric collection (4 Kochstrasse) and the *Stadtmuseum* (9 Martin Luther Strasse), which has collections on the history of the town, crafts and folklore.

---

## Erlenbach bei Bad Bergzabern 6749

Rheinland-Pfalz                    p.420☐D 17

**Burg Berwartstein:** Emperor Frederick I presented the Burg to the Bishop of Speyer in 1152. It has been largely in ruins since it was destroyed in 1591, although parts of it are still occupied. The building is one of the many rock fortresses found in the Wasgau, and is divided into an upper and lower Burg and outer works. The upper Burg is built on a steep cliff and has rooms and passageways hewn from the

*Markgrafen-Theater, Erlangen*

rock. The cannon emplacements in the outer works of the Burg show its defensive capability. To the S. is the *ruined Burg Kleinfrankreich* with its distinctive round tower (*c*.1480).

## Erwitte 4782
Nordrhein-Westfalen                  p.414☐E 10

Because of its favourable position at the junction of the Hell and Lippe roads a royal court was founded in Erwitte and Heinrich I (935) and other Saxon kings lived here.

**Catholic Parish Church of St. Laurentius:** The imposing tower was built in the mid 13C and is hardly less impressive than the tower buildings in nearby Soest (q.v.). The baroque spire was destroyed by fire in 1971 and rebuilt in Romanesque style on the model of the St.Patrokli tower in Soest. The reliefs in both transept doorways and on the columns of the triumphal arch are particularly striking. The tower interior has a small second choir. The decoration includes nine almost life-size wooden Apostles (1763), the 'Madonna of the Seven Swords' and a 13C wooden crucifix.

**Schloss:** The long, two-storey building was built as a moated Burg in the 17C and rebuilt in 1934. The influence of the Weser Renaissance is apparent. The Schloss is now owned by the town of Erwitte.

**Also worth seeing:** 16–18C half-timbered houses in and around the Marktplatz; the former Rathaus (1716) by the Marktplatz; the former residence of the Droste family (completed 1703), taken over as the Marienhospital in 1859.

## Eschwege 3440
Hessen                              p.418☐H 11

**Protestant Parish Church of St.Dionys in the Old Town** (Marktplatz): The church was built in the 13–16C. The al-

most square hall has striking baroque decoration; the best feature is the carved 17C pulpit. The organ (1677 – 9, by J.F. Schaffer), with its 'gnarled' ornamentation, is worth seeing. The *Princes' Vault*, in which Mad Fritz (Landgrave Friedrich of Hessen) is buried, is under the altar.

**Schloss** (1 Schlossplatz): The Schloss was founded in 1386, but most of the surviving buildings were not begun until 1581. The principal room in the severe Renaissance building is the former knights' hall. This was mainly used as a Catholic chapel to the Schloss, but it is now available for formal occasions. The Schloss is occupied by the Landratsamt.

**Also worth seeing:** *Altes Rathaus* (Am Markt): a half-timbered building built in 1660; half-timbered buildings in the market place; the *Hochzeitshaus* (1578): Renaissance building with a step gabled tower; *Heimatmuseum* (14a Vor dem Berge): local history; the nearby double town of Bad-Sooden-Allendorf, which has a complete set of half-timbered houses in Allendorf, among which is the *Odenwaldt Haus*.

## Essen 4300
Nordrhein-Westfalen                  p.416☐C 10

Essen, one of the towns between the Rhine and the Ruhr, has in the last hundred years become an industrial and cultural centre with almost 700,000 inhabitants. The history of the town was dominated until the 17C by the convent founded *c*.850 by Altfried, later Bishop of Hildesheim, in which he placed his sister as the first abbess. Until 1670 the abbess of the time had total control over the town, which was thus unable to develop until that date.

**Münster/Former Convent Church of St.Maria, St.Cosmas and St.Damian** (Burgplatz): The Gothic hall church with two aisles was built over the 11C late-Ottonian crypt in 1276-1327. Damage sustained in the Second World War was made good in 1951-9. There are many outstanding works of art from the Ottonian period in the richly decorated interior. In the W. Building are some remains of 11C *wall paintings*. The *cross column* was erected during rebuilding in the 10C behind the bishop's throne in the choir. The *seven-branched candelabrum* which is now in the W. building was made *c.*1000. The most outstanding item is the *Golden Madonna*, which was carved before 1000, and is the oldest free-standing figure of the Madonna in the West. The *Theophanu Cross*, which was made in the 11C, is hardly less important. It is now kept in the Münster Treasure, along with the crown of the Golden Madonna. In the *crypt* is the tomb of Altfried, Bishop of Hildesheim (d.874). The richly decorated stone sarcophagus is 14C work, and it was not tranferred into the crypt until the 19C. In the *Münster Treasure* are outstanding works by German goldsmiths of the Ottonian period.

**Former Parish Church of St.John the Baptist** (Burgplatz): This hall church with two aisles was built in 1471 and decorated in the baroque style *c.*1700; it is today part of the Münster, to which it is connected by the *Atrium*.

**Church of the Resurrection** (Kurfürstenplatz): An interesting idea by O.Bartning in 1929, modelled on the baroque galleried church: it is a steel construction on a circular ground plan. Half the area is intended for the congregation, and the other half for the celebration of Holy Communion.

**Abbey Church of St.Ludger** (Werden, Abteistrasse): The church, founded in 796 by Ludger, the first Bishop of Münster, was built in its present form in the period 1156–75. It is essentially Romanesque. A square tower and the massive crossing tower dominate the building. The interior is a mixture of Romanesqe and Gothic features. The furnishings are late baroque (1706–18). The imposing high altar occupies the entire height and width of the late Romanesque choir. In the N. transept is a life-size figure of the Virgin, which was made in the early 14C in a Lüttich workshop. The many tombs are also striking.

The *church treasure* was considerably reduced by secularization, but is still full of priceless items. The most important include: a bronze crucifix (1060), which is one of the finest in the world; the chalice of St.Ludger (*c.*900), which is the oldest in Germany; an 8C Franconian reliquary chest; late Romanesque sandstone reliefs (originally part of the covering of the sarcophagus for the tomb of Ludger).

**Catholic Parish Church of St.Lucius** (Werden, Heckstrasse): The church was built in 995–1063, and is the oldest parish church N. of the Alps. It was restored in its original form in 1965.

**Collegiate Church** (Essen-Stoppenberg): This little church, a 12C Romanesque pillared basilica, has been much altered over the centuries.

**Villa Hügel** (across the Baldeneysee, can be reached via Haraldstrasse): The Villa Hügel was built on this charming site for industrialist Alfred Krupp in 1870–2. It has been open to the public since 1953. Major art exhibitions are occasionally held here. The contents of the house include three important sets of Gobelins.

**Schloss Borbeck** (Schlossstrasse): The earlier buildings were replaced by the present late baroque moated Schloss in the 18C; the Great Hall is the residence of the abbesses of the convent and various municipal organizations are also accomodated in the building.

**Museums:** *Folkwang Museum* (64–66 Bismarckstrasse): The museum is based on the Municipal Museum of Art, founded in 1906, and on the collection of Dr.Hans Goldschmidt, presented to the town in 1920. The collection includes art and cultural history, Oriental sculpture, Christian art, ceramics, glass and porcelain, Javan shadow puppets, engravings, drawings and prints; a highlight is the collection of 19&20C German and French painting and sculpture. *Deutsches Plakatmuseum* (2 Rathenaustrasse): Includes more than

*Münster, Essen* ▷

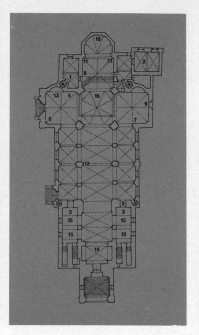

*Bronze crucifix (1060), St. Ludger*

15,000 posters from many countries, and specializes in political and artistic posters. *Ruhrland- und Heimatmuseum* (62 Bismarckstrasse): Collections on science and pre- and early history, and the history of the Ruhr and the town of Essen. *Halbach hammer* (im Nachtigallental): The hammer comes from a 16C smithy in the Siegerland and was erected in Essen in 1936. It is one of the most important specimens of industrial archaeology in Germany.

**Theatres:** The old Schauspielhaus, which was destroyed in the Second World War, was not rebuilt, but the *Opernhaus* (opened 1892) was rebuilt in 1950, and today presents both opera and straight theatre. It has 637 seats. A second auditorium in the *Humboldtaula* (Varnhorststrasse), which has 546 seats, is used only for straight theatre; this is also the case in the *Studio Theatre*. There is also a *mobile theatre*, which gives guest performances in various parts of Essen.

**Essen-Werden, former abbey church of St. Ludger 1** Sacristy **2** Treasury **3** Wall paintings, mid-10C **4** Virgin Mary, 13C **5** Our Lady of Sorrows, early-16C **6** Rain of manna, 16C **7** Elijah and the angel, 16C **8** Tombstone of abbot Grimhold (d. 1517) **9** Last Supper c. 1705 **10** High altar, 1710 **11** Choir stalls, 1710 **12** Pulpit, 1710 **13** Marienaltar, 19C; painting by T. Mintrop **14** Organ, 1910 **15** Stained-glass window by de Graaf, 1957

**Also worth seeing:** *Marktkirche* (Pferdemarkt): This church, first mentioned in 1058, was the centre of the Reformation in Essen. Only the E. part was restored after the church was destroyed in the Second World War. *Gruga Park* (Norbertstrasse): The present-day Gruga Park (179 acres) was developed from the Old Gruga Park (1929) and the Botanical Gardens (1927) into a modern recreation centre. Directly adjacent to the Gruga Park is the *Gruga-Halle*, a modern building with a capacity of 8,500 spectators.

*Villa Hügel above Baldeneysee*

## Esslingen am Neckar 7300
Baden-Württemberg                    p.420□F 18

There were settlements in the central area of the present town even in prehistoric times. In about 800 Esslingen became a market and in 1212 a town. The town has largely survived in its old form. The Andreas Gryphius Prize for eastern German literature and since 1963 the Georg Dehio Prize for History have been awarded in Esslingen.

**Protestant Church of St. Dionysius** (Bahnhofstrasse): The present church was built in the 13C on the site of earlier 8–11C buildings, and has suffered much modification in the course of the centuries. The two E. towers were built c.1230 and are essentially Romanesque; the S. tower has Gothic elements. The interior is a basilica with seven bays, dominated by lofty arches and the choir screen (1486–9 by

L.Lechter, Heidelberg). The *Ark of the Sacrament* on the left wall of the choir and the *font* are also striking works by Lechner. The *high altar* by P.Riedlinger (Ravensburg) was built in 1604 and depicts scenes from the Life of Christ. The *stained-glass windows*, representing scenes from the Old and New Testaments, are of a high order.

**Dominican Church of St.Paul** (Mettingerstrasse): This church, consecrated in 1268 by Albertus Magnus, is the oldest remaining church of the Order in Germany. It is a long basilica with fine rib vaulting and a polygonal choir. Its severe form and plain decoration reflect the ideals of the mendicant Order.

**Former Franciscan Church of St. Georg** (Franziskanergasse): The church was originally built by the mendicant brothers in 1237. The nave was pulled down in 1840 as it was becoming derelict. The partially Gothic choir remains.

**Church of Our Lady/Protestant Parish Church** (Mettinger Strasse): The Gothic tower is one of the finest in Germany. U. and M.Ensinger and the Böblinger family were involved in the construction of the church. There are excellent reliefs and sculptures over the doorways, and Apostles by J.Töber on the pillars of the nave. The stained glass dates from 1320–30.

**Altes Rathaus** (Rathausplatz): This fine building is based on a half-timbered structure of 1430. The façade is in Renaissance style. The clock by J.Diem of Tübingen is the central feature of the ornate Dutch gable. The carved figures (c.1440) on the consoles in the *Bürgersaal* portray saints, emperors and electors.

*Neues Rathaus* (Rathausplatz): The building was originally constructed as a private house for J.C.Palm in 1747. It has been the Town Hall since 1842.

*Burg* (Burgsteige): All that remains of the once imposing buildings (originally constructed in the 12&13C and extended 1515–27) are parts of the walls and the *Dicke Turm*. The Burg was once the westernmost part of the town's fortifications. The *gatehouse on the Pliensau bridge*, the *Schelztor* and the *Wolfstor* have also survived.

**Neckar Bridge:** The Neckar bridge, which originally led to the Pliensau island, was in existence by 1286 and is one of the oldest bridges in Europe. The smaller of the two Neckar bridges is known for the Gothic Nikolaus Chapel (c.1430).

**Theatre:** The Schauspielhaus (1 Strohstrasse) has a main house with 300 seats and a studio with 65 seats.

**Museums:** The Stadtmuseum is in the Altes Rathaus (Rathausplatz). It specializes in local history, as well as art history and antiquities.

**Also worth seeing:** There are many 16 –18C houses, the majority of which are half-timbered.

**Environs: Plochingen** (9 km. E.): the late Gothic *Protestant parish church* (1481–8) has a choir with net vaulting and late Gothic *choir paintings* (c.1485) with *symbols of the Evangelists*; there is also an interesting *pulpit column*.

## Ettal 8107
Bavaria                                      p.422 □ K 21

Ettal, the 'Bavarian Temple of the Grail', is a popular place of pilgrimage 5 km. from Oberammergau (q.v.) and 15 km. from Garmisch-Partenkirchen (q.v.).

**Benedictine Monastery Church:** A religious institution was founded in 1330 by Ludwig der Bayer on a road off the trade route from Augsburg to Innsbruck; it was intended to house 22 monks in a Benedictine monastery, 13 knights with their wives, and several widows. A Madonna by G.Pidano, brought from Italy by the Emperor, soon made the church the most important centre of pilgrimage in the Alpine foreland. In 1370 the Gothic monastery church was completed as a twelve-sided building, modelled on the Church of the Holy Sepulchre in Jerusalem. In 1710 E.Zucalli and F.Schmuzer remodelled the building in the baroque style, but preserved the original core. The baroque dome was added, after a fire, by F.Schmuzer in 1745–52. The highly decorated façade and another choir were added in the 18C. The twelve-sided section is 83 ft across, and is dominated by the gigantic dome fresco created by J.J.Zeiller in 1746. The organ loft and the stucco were by J.B. Zimmermann, and the altars and pulpit by J.B.Straub. This involvement of the finest artists made the central part of the monastery church one of the masterpieces of German rococo.

## Ettlingen 7505
Baden-Württemberg                            p.420 □ E 17

Finds from the Bronze Age and Roman

*St.Dionysius, Esslingen*

*Benedictine monastery of Ettal*

times show the importance of Ettlingen in the distant past.

**Catholic Parish Church of St. Martin** (Kirchenplatz): The original building (12 –15C) burned down in 1689 and only the tower choir (12&13C) and the high choir with its fine stellar vault (1459–64) remain. A striking feature is the façade, which is divided into three by three large pilasters. The interior is a plain single space with some decorated wall recesses.

**Schloss** (Schlossplatz): This building with four wings dates from 1728–33. Its finest section is the lavishly decorated *Schloss chapel*, which was later converted into a concert hall, and reduced from three to two storeys. C.D.Asam was responsible for the design of the chapel, and also the ceiling paintings. St.John of Nepomuk is the principal subject. In the *courtyard* is the Delphinbrunnen (1612), and in front of the Schloss the Narrenbrunnen (1549). The

*Albgau Museum* of the town of Ettlingen is now housed in the Schloss complex, and in the summer there is a Schloss Festival.

**Rathaus:** The Town Hall dates from 1737 - 8, and was built to plans by the Baden-Baden master stonemason A.Mohr. As a reminder of the Roman period a copy of the Roman Neptune stone, washed up from the Alb in 1480, has been incorporated in the wall.

---

**Eutin 2420**
Schleswig-Holstein                    p.412□1 3

This former residence town on the Grosser Eutiner See has maintained its reputation as a 'rose town' until the present day. Eutin likes to be known as the 'Weimar of the North'. In the reign of Duke Peter Friedrich Ludwig a number of famous men worked here, among them Goethe's

*Ceiling painting in Ettal church*

*Schloss chapel, Ettlingen*

friend Leopold Count Stoltenberg, Johann Heinrich Voss, the translator of Homer, and the painter Friedrich Wilhelm Tischbein. The most distinguished son of the town is the composer Carl Maria von Weber, in whose honour the *Eutin Summer Festival* is organized each year in July and August in the Schlosspark.

**Protestant Church of St. Michaelis** (Marktplatz): This vaulted brick basilica dates from the first third of the 13C, (much altered in later years). The parts of the original building which remain show clear traces of early Gothic work. The furnishings include a seven-branched candelabrum (1444), a bronze font (1511), and two tombs (*c.*1670) in the 'gnarled' style (ornamentation characterized by gnarling and knotting).

**Schloss** (Schlossplatz): The present-day building with four wings developed from the former Burg of the bishops of Lübeck. The most striking part of the Schloss is the *Blaue Saal* in the W. wing. The contents of the Schloss include the largest collection of Princes' portraits in N. Germany, among them portraits and historical paintings by Wilhelm Tischbein and landscapes by Ludwig Philipp Strack. There are also exhibits on domestic life in the late baroque, Regency, and classical periods, porcelain and tapestries from Brussels, and model ships. The Schloss is surrounded by a fine park, originally in the French style, but later redesigned in the English manner. There is a Schloss festival in the summer.

## Fallersleben = 3180 Wolfsburg 12

Lower Saxony                              p.414□I 8

Fallersleben became well-known through Hoffmann von Fallersleben (1798–1874), the author of the 'Deutschlandlied', who was born here. The author is commemorated at his birthplace (4 Westerstrasse) and by a *museum* (5 Schlossplatz).

**Protestant Church:** This classical church with uniform interior decoration was built in 1804, and designed to place emphasis on preaching. The gallery running right round the church and the pulpit altar are typical of this type of building.

**Schloss** (Schlosspark): All that remains of the 16C building is a two-storey half-timbered wing with an imposing staircase tower (early 17C).

## Faurndau = Göppingen 7320

Baden-Württemburg                          p.422□G 18

**Parish Church of St. Marien:** 'Furentowa' was once the name of the monastery which, at the time of the Hohenstaufen Emperor Frederick II, contained the church (*c.*1230) which still stands today. The building is decorated with fine *masonry*, which is at its best outside the church on the apses. The interior of the church is also decorated with cornice mouldings and ornamental friezes. The six columns and four half-columns in the central part of the building have excellent *capitals*. The early Gothic *wall and ceiling paintings* were revealed during restoration work. The roof was raised in the Gothic period, and it is possible to see both the old and new levels from the ridge.

## Fehmarn (island)

Schleswig-Holstein                         p.412□1/K 2

**Protestant Church of St. Johannes** (in 2448 Bannesdorf): The plain, early Gothic building (13C) was originally built of dressed stone and partially rebuilt in brick in the 19C. An impressive feature of the interior is the warm red colour of the lower areas of the brick walls. There are remains of late Gothic *wall paintings* on the N. wall of the choir. The former *rococo high altar* (1777) with side columns and putti is now on the S. side.

**Nikolai Church** (in 2448 Burg): This brick church in Fehmarn's principal village was built in the middle of the 13C. The E. half and the choir are later additions. The *high altar* (14C), the late Gothic *Blasius Altar* and *Gotland font* (mid 13C) remain of the original medieval furnishings.

**St. Peter** (in 2449 Landkirchen): This

mid-13C hall church with two aisles is similar to the church in Burg in its dimensions and some individual features but differs in its chapel, a late Gothic addition, and the free-standing wooden bell tower.

**St. Johannis** (in 2449 Petersdorf): The high W. tower of this imposing village church became a landmark for seafarers. The church was built in various periods up to 1567. There is a *carved altar* (pre 1400) which, with the altar by Meister Bertram in the Hamburg Church of St.Petri, is considered to be the finest 14C work in the Hanseatic area.

**Also worth seeing:** 3 km. S. of Burg is *Burg Glambek*, one of the few large ruined castles in Schleswig-Holstein.

**Feuchtwangen 8805**
Bavaria                                    p.422☐H 17

**Former Collegiate Church** (Marktplatz): This church, dating back to the 8C and rebuilt in the 13C, was much altered in subsequent centuries. The most significant furnishings are the high altar (1483 by M.Wohlgemut of Nuremberg), the choir stalls (*c.*1510, but reduced in extent and modified later), and numerous tombs, (including the life-size figure of S.von Ehenheim, 1504).

**Heimatmuseum** (19 Museumstrasse): Folk art and folklore, craft workshops (in the cloisters) and a special collection of fire-fighting equipment.

**Fischbeck = 3253 Hessisch Oldendorf 2**
Lower Saxony                           p.414☐G 8

**Former Augustinian House of Canonesses:** The focal point of this charming site with its 13 – 18C buildings is the Romanesque cloister with its double arcades and Gothic tracery.

**Protestant Collegiate Church:** This church is one of the most significant and interesting Romanesque buildings in the Weser region. The ponderous, tower-like W. building, dominating the nave with its five storeys, is reminiscent of a fortified castle. The choir and the apse have round arches and friezes, slender roundels and Rhenish windows. The 12C work in the interior can still be recognized despite restoration: the crypt is the best example of this style. The most valuable item is the bronze-gilt reliquary (probably *c.*1200, original in Hannover (q.v.)).

**Flensburg 2390**
Schleswig-Holstein                    p.412☐G 1

This town on the Danish border grew up from a late-12C trading settlement with market and mooring facilities. The rise of Flensburg as a centre of trade and culture began at the end of the 13C. The town is dominated by solid, late Gothic *gabled brick buildings*, which began to take over from half-timbered buildings in the 15C.

*Head reliquary, Fischbeck collegiate church*  ▷

*Renaissance altar, Marienkirche, Flensburg*

There are also *Renaissance*, and 17&18C houses with 'Utluchten' (oriels), and noteworthy classical buildings. There are also traces of the Middle Ages and the Renaissance in the *town walls*, above all the *Nordtor* of 1595, a wide, round-arched gateway with a brick stepped gable.

**Church of St. Marien** (Nordermarkt): Building of the two-aisled Gothic hall began in 1284, and in the 13&14C the E. chancel was extended and the side chapels added. The furnishings include an unusually large, carved and painted wooden *Renaissance altar* (by H.Ringering in 1598), a *bronze font*, on which the 4 Evangelists carry a bowl decorated with 8 reliefs, and one of the most important Renaissance tombs in Schleswig-Holstein, the grave of *Anna von Buchwald* (1597), on the E. wall of the S. transept.

**Church of St.Nikolai** (Südermarkt): This

*Monument to Anna v. Buchwald, Marienkirche*

large Gothic brick building dates largely from 1390–1480. The most important feature of the furnishings is the lavishly carved *organ* with its Renaissance front by H.Ringering (1604/9). The *rococo high altar* (1749) is also noteworthy; it has twisted columns and life-size representations of the virtues.

**Church of the Holy Spirit** (Nordergraben): This plain building erected in 1386 was later enlivened with a baroque gable, and has an eight-sided lantern dating from 1761.

**Flensburg, Marienkirche 1** Ceiling paintings a) Legend of the Virgin Mary, c. 1400 b) Old Testament, c. 1400 c) Last Judgement, late-15C **2** Crucifix, 15C **3** Pulpit, 1579 **4** Font by Michael Dibler, 1591 **5** Memorial to Jürgen Beyer, 1591 **6** Monument to Anna v.Buchwald, 1597 **7** Altar by H. Ringerink, 1598; paintings by Jan van Enum **8** Memorial to Evert Vette by Jan van Enum, 1601 **9** Memorial to Niels Lorentzen, 1642 **10** Memorial to Carsten Beyer, 1644 **11** Memorial to Niels Hacke, 1648; Entombment by H.Jansen **12** Organ; front dates from 1731 **13** Crucifixion by M.Kahlke, 1920 **14** Glass paintings by K. Lassen, 1946-56 a) Christmas b) Good Friday c) Easter d) Ascension e) Last Judgement f) Whitsun **15** Glass paintings by G. v.Stockhausen, 1959-60 a) Creation b) Moses and Elijah c) Trinity d) Samaritans and Good Shepherd

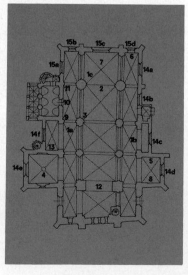

**Städtisches Museum** (1 Lutherplatz): Collections on the artistic and cultural history of Schleswig, sculpture and furniture, and rooms from sea-faring, middle class and peasant households.

**Landestheater** (22 Rathausstrasse): This theatre with 601 seats houses performances of opera and straight theatre and was built by Fielitz in 1893&4 on the site of the old theatre of 1795.

**Also worth seeing:** The *Church of St. Johannis* in the E. part of the town has interesting paintings on its vaulting. *Old Cemetery*, historic *public buildings* and *private houses*.

**Flossenbürg 8481**
Bavaria                                    p.418□M 15

**Ruined Burg of Flossenbürg:** As well as the memorial to the victims of the former concentration camp there is an imposing ruined Burg (12C). The oldest part is the keep on the topmost point of the rock. Lower down are the residence and the tower, dating from the beginning of the 13C. The freestones, up to 7ft. long, show how the ashlar technique had been perfected.

**Forchheim, Oberfranken 8550**
Bavaria                                    p.418□K 15

The town stands at the confluence of the Wiesent and the Regnitz, and was founded on the site of a 6C Frankish settlement. In the 9C Forchheim became a royal court and finally a Palatinate. Kings were elected here on three occasions. Extensive building began in the town from 1300. It has retained its medieval appearance to a large extent, and this makes it particularly attractive.

**Catholic Parish Church of St.Martin** (Kirchenstrasse): The influence of the Bamberg Association of Cathedral Builders (Dombauhütte) can be seen in the oldest, Romanesque parts of the church. The present-day, essentially Gothic, ashlar sandstone building was built in the 14C, and in 1670 the cupola was added. On the exterior wall of the chancel is an excellent *Mount of Olives* by the Bamberg sculptor H.Nussbaum, who also carved the fine *wooden relief* (Christ taking leave of Mary) inside the church on the W. wall of the N. transept; the influence of Dürer is clear.

**Pfalz** (16 Kapellenstrasse): The moated Burg, presumably built on the site of the Carolingian Kaiserpfalz, dates from the 14C. The picturesque complex consists of a late Gothic *gateway*, the rugged *palas*, a gabled building (16C), and the *staircase tower* in the courtyard (17C). Inside are late Gothic *frescos* and the *Pfalzmuseum*, which shows pre- and early historical finds, and folk art.

**Rathaus** (Rathausplatz): The Town Hall

*Johanniskirche, Flensburg*

*Forchheim, Rathaus square*

(14–15C) is near the Pfalz by the typical Franconian marketplace, among other imposing half-timbered buildings. It has fine decorative half-timbering, and balustrade columns with carved wooden figures on the capitals.

**Also worth seeing:** Remains of the *fortifications* (16–18C) which formerly surrounded the town in the SW and N.

---

### Frankenberg/Eder 3558
Hessen            p.416□F 11

Frankenberg has maintained its medieval appearance to the present day. It was largely re-built after a fire in 1476.

**Protestant Parish Church/Former Church of Our Lady** (Auf der Burg): In the 14C Tyle von Frankenberg rebuilt parts of the church, which was begun in 1286.

He was responsible for new building work in the chancel, consecrated in 1353, the tower, parts of the transepts and the *Mary Chapel*, built on to the S. transept and a jewel of Gothic architecture. In reshaping the formerly two-aisled hall he followed to a large extent the model of the Church of St. Elizabeth in Marburg (q.v.). The exterior is severe early Gothic, with buttresses and cornices, but the doorways are more lavishly decorated, particularly the W. doorway. In the interior, lit by high windows, the leafwork on the *capitals* and the masks and animal heads on the *columns* in the nave and chancel are striking features. The vaults are decorated with tendril motifs, blossoms, fruit and birds (*c.*1480, revealed in 1962). The *stone figures*, now in the sacristy, the *stone pulpit* and the *stone reredos* in the Mary Chapel are noteworthy.

*The Rathaus (1509) in Frankenberg* ▷
*exerted a wide influence on other half-timbered buildings in Hessen*

*Marienkapelle in the Liebfrauenkirche*

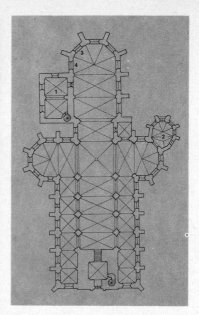

**Frankenberg, Marienkirche 1** Sacristy **2** Marienkapelle **3** Tabernacle, c. 1350-60 **4** Christ on the Mount of Olives, relief, 14C

**Rathaus** (Marktplatz): The Town Hall was built in its present form in 1509. It has spires on its eight oriel turrets, a ridge turret and a staircase tower, and was of similar significance for the development of half-timbered building in Old Hessen as the Town Hall in Alsfeld (q.v.). The splendidly carved *corbels* over the doorways are particularly striking. On the S. side the figure of a kneeling man can be made out; he has a fool with cap, bells and flute sitting on his shoulder.

**Also worth seeing:** 16–18C *houses*, which still dominate the townscape; the *Kreisheimatmuseum* (10 Bahnhofstrasse): local history; an important Cistercian Monastery in nearby *Haina*.

**Frankfurt am Main 6000**
Hessen                                  p.416☐E 14

Frankfurt was for many centuries the city in which Kings and Emperors were elected and crowned. It is also the city of Goethe, and of the German National Assembly in the Paulskirche; trade fairs have been held here since 1240, and it is the home of the Stock Exchange. Frankfurt was a magnificent and dignified medieval city, but the original townscape was lost in the bombing and fires of 1944: almost 2,000 medieval houses were destroyed and not rebuilt. In modern Frankfurt the remnants of the past are simply islands with the rush and confusion of a busy commercial city seething around them; cultural life is taken seriously, however, as we see from the existence of 22 theatres, 12 museums, and important galleries, libraries and universities, above all the *Johann Wolfgang Goethe University*, founded in 1914.

**Dom/Former Collegiate and Catholic Parish Church of St. Bartholomäus** (Domplatz): *Building history:* In the Carolingian period a church of St.Salvator stood on the site where German Emperors were elected from 1356 and crowned from 1562; remains of this church have been discovered. The present building dates largely from the 13, 14&15C; its architect was M.Gerthener, who also designed the high W. tower with its rare and unusual pinnacle (1415). This phase of the building took more than 100 years, and in fact the topmost pinnacle was not placed on the tower until work of extension and renewal was undertaken in the 19C.

*The building:* The various phases of the Gothic extensions to the building can be seen in the capitals, tracery and vaulting. The most striking feature of the interior is the almost equal length of nave and transept; the vaulting was not raised to a unified height until the 19C. The hall design, supporting columns and intimate adjacent

**Frankfurt, Dom 1** S. portal of tower, 1422 **2** S. portal of transept **3** N. portal of transept **4** Tower **5** Dividing chapel with font **6** Holy Sepulchre chapel **7** Selection chapel **8** Portico by Denzinger, 1879-80 **9** Choir stalls, 1352 **10** Tabernacle from the workshop of Madern Gerthener, 1415-20 **11** Maria-Schlaf-Altar, 1434 **12** High altar, 2nd half of 15C **13** Crucifixion by H.Backofen, donated by J.Heller in 1509 **14** Bartholomew, relief by H.Mettel, 1957

chapels are the dominant features of the interior.

*Doorways and furnishings:* The doorways leading into the interior from the N. and S. are decorated with figures from the earliest period of the building's history. The *column Madonna* in the N. doorway is particularly fine. The S. doorway has on its gables and consoles a whole collection of figures including the Adoration of the Magi, a Crucifixion, prophets and saints. This work is by the upper-Rhenish master Antze (*c.1350*), *who was also responsible for the very fine choir stalls.* One bench end shows Emperor Ludwig the German with a model of the church. Under the tower is the most important feature of the furnishings, a life-size *Crucifixion group* consisting of seven people with three crosses; it is a stone sculpture by H.Backoffen of Mainz (1509). The *Dormition altar* in the Mary Chapel (which can be reached from the N. transept) is also in stone, and is the realistic and excellent work of a mid-Rhenish master (1434). The *wall paintings* (1427) over the choir stalls, depicting the legend of St. Bartholomew, ascribed to S.Lochner, are very faded. Two *gravestones,* which, like the rest of the furnishings, were put in store during the war, are of partic-

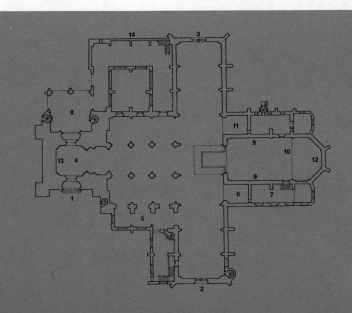

*Crucifixion, Dom*

ular interest: a knight with his helmet under his arm (Günther von Schwarzburg, anti-king to Karl IV), and in the N. transept the double grave of the Holzhausen family (late 14C).

**Catholic Parish Church of St. Leonhard** (Alte Mainzer Gasse, by the Main): Emperor Frederick II presented this site by the river Main for the building of a church (1219), of which the two octagonal chancel towers and two doorways with ornate capitals and Norman arches with pediments remain. The choir between the towers was added in 1430 and two further N. and S. aisles in the early 16C. The *Salvator-Chörlein* is a masterly piece of craftsmanship.
*Buildings:* The Romanesque origins of the *towers* are clearly visible. The lavish tracery of the *choir* (by M.Gerthener) is predominantly Gothic. The stellar and net vaulting of the picturesque interior became more and more elaborate in the 15C and

reached its decorative peak in the *Salvator-Chörlein*, the tomb of the Holzhausen family (1516).
The most important feature of the furnishings is a *painting* of the Last Supper (by H.Holbein the Elder) in the N. aisle. It is part of the predella of an altar which is now in the Städel Museum (q.v.).

**Catholic Church of Our Lady** (Liebfrauenberg): Little remains of the original house of worship, now used by the Capucines as a monastery church. The most important surviving feature is the *tympanum relief* over the S. doorway with its lively Adoration of the Magi in a three-dimensional landscape, a major work of the so-called 'Soft Style' (*c.*1420), probably created by M.Gerthener (cf. Cathedral and St.Leonhard). Only a few figures remain (in the chancel and the nave) from the ornate *rococo furnishings*.

**Paulskirche (Church of St.Paul)** (Paulsplatz): This sober, neoclassical church, started in 1787 and completed in 1833 (with the construction of the tower), must have looked strange among the patrician and bourgeois houses of old Frankfurt. It was originally built as a Protestant preaching church, but it was used as the meeting place of the German National Assembly in 1848&9. The building burned down in the Second World War, and when it was rebuilt in 1948&9 it was intended as the Parliament building for the Federal Republic. It is today used by the city on formal occasions, such as the presentation of the Goethe prize, the Peace Prize, the German Book Trade Prize etc.

**Former Carmelite Monastery** (5 Karmelitergasse): Only the chancel and nave remain of the *Church of St.Mary*, which was part of the original complex; the monastery buildings have been partially rebuilt. In the former *refectory* the 262 ft. long *fresco cycle* by *J.Ratgeb* of Herrenberg (1514–23) has survived only in part. Ratgeb, who with Grünewald was the great expressive painter of the late Gothic period, died by quartering in 1526 as a revolutionary in the Peasants War.

*St. Leonhard* ▷

**Church of the Teutonic Order St. Maria** (in Sachsenhausen, Brücken-strasse): The present Catholic parish church has a bright, pure Gothic interior with a single aisle (consecrated 1309). A small S. side chapel was added c.1520 and the baroque façade in the 18C.

**Römer** (Römerberg): The *Rathaus* of the old Coronation City consisted of eleven separate houses joined together by a complicated system of courtyards. It took its name from the oldest of the gabled houses, the house 'Zum Römer', mentioned by this name as early as 1322. The lower storeys on the Römerberg were formerly open trading halls. In the upper storey is the restored *Kaisersaal*, the former hall for coronation banquets, with *portraits* of the German Emperors. The few surviving sections of the *Kaisertreppe* (imperial steps) and their wrought-iron banister are worth seeing. Of the five gables which make up the famous façade of the Römer three were restored and two are modern copies. In 1938 rebuilding of the houses opposite the Römer was completed, and the half-timbered houses *Wilder Mann, Goldener Greif* and *Schwarzer Stern* were reconstructed; they had been destroyed by bombing in 1944.

**Leinwandhaus:** M.Gerthener built this former merchants' hall for textiles and raw materials of the textile trade SE of the Dom in 1399. It has been rebuilt, and since 1984 has housed the *Kommunale Galerie* and the *Fotografie-Forum-Frankfurt*.

**Hauptwache** (Hauptwache): The former guard house, a single-storey baroque building with a high mansard roof, has been rebuilt at the beginning of the *Zeil*, Frankfurt's principal shopping street; it now houses a café.

**Steinernes Haus** (Alter Markt): This is one of the few houses which at least partially survived the last war. The imposing Gothic patrician building is easily recognised by its turrets and the battlements on the roof cornice. The restored building is now used for exhibitions by the *Frankfurt Kunstverein*.

*Marienaltar, Deutschordenskirche*

**Goethehaus** (23 Am Grossen Hirsch-graben): Goethe's birthplace, a building with three storeys, was completely destroyed in the war and rebuilt in 1946–51. It was furnished with the original contents, which had been put in store. The study in which Goethe wrote 'Götz', 'Werther', and parts of 'Faust', the fine staircase, the courtyard, the reception room and Frau Aja's kitchen can all be seen in their original form. The house is connected with the *Goethe Museum*, which belongs to the Freie Deutsche Hochstift.

**Saalhof Chapel** (31 Saalgasse): By the *Eiserne Steg* bridge over the Main is the *Rententurm* with its four slated pinnacles. It was formerly part of one of the *city gates*. Behind the tower remains of the former royal moated Burg have survived, particularly the small 12C *Romanesque chapel*, which is the oldest building in the town.

**Town fortifications:** The *Rententurm*, the

*Römer*

*Galluswarte*, the *Bockenheimer Warte*, the *Sachsenhäuser Warte* and the *Friedberger Warte* remain of the ancient fortifications, as does the *Eschenheim gate tower*. The latter was built in 1426–8 by Frankfurt's principal Gothic architect M.Gerthener as a round tower with wall passage and pinnacles. The composer Paul Hindemith lived from 1923 – 5 in the *Kuhhirtenturm* (cowherds' tower) in Sachsenhausen (Deutschherrenufer).

**Theatres:** The **Alte Oper** (Opernplatz) was reopened in 1981 after war damage had been repaired; it has 2,500 seats. The *Städtische Bühnen* for opera, straight theatre and small scale performances are in a single complex (11 Untermainanlage). The *Fritz Rémond Theatre in the Zoo* (16 Alfred Brehm Platz), the *Komödie* (18 Neue Mainzer Strasse) and the *Theater im Turm* (2 Eschersheimer Landstrasse) are straight theatres presenting wide-ranging programmes.

**Museums:** All the Frankfurt collections were brought into being by private initiative. The *Städelsche Kunstinstitut* (63 Schaumainkai) shows European painting from the 14C to the present day. Its most distinguished works are van Eyck's *Madonna of Lucca* and Rembrandt's *Blinding of Samson*. The collection also includes works by Cranach, Dürer, Holbein, Rubens, Hals, Schongauer, Manet, Renoir and Picasso. The *sculpture collection in the Liebighaus* (71 Schaumainkai) is one of the most important in Europe. The *Museum für Vor- und Frühgeschichte* (pre- and early history; 5 Justinianstrasse) is in the charming *Wasserschlösschen Holzhausensche Oede*. The *Museum für Kunsthandwerk* (15 Schaumainkai) has a collection of European and Asiatic arts and crafts. Also: the *Bundespostmuseum* (53 Schaumainkai), the *Historisches Museum* (19 Saalgasse), which is a local history museum, the *Museum für Völkerkunde* (29 Schaumainkai), an anthropological museum, the *Architektur-*

*Hauptwache*

*museum* (43 Schaumainkai) and the *Filmmuseum* (41 Schaumainkai).

**Cemeteries:** There are famous people buried in all the Frankfurt cemeteries. Goethe's parents are in the *Petersfriedhof*, the great medical researcher Paul Ehrlich is buried in the *Jüdischer Friedhof* (Jewish cemetery, Rat-Beil-Strasse); in the *Hauptfriedhof* are the philosopher Schopenhauer and Goethe's 'Suleika' (Marianne von Willemer, the banker's wife). In the tradition of princely burials the *Grabkapelle Reichenbach* was built here in 1843, and this funerary chapel has recumbent effigies of Elector Wilhelm II of Hessen-Kassel and his wife, Countess Reichenbach.

**Church of St. Justinus** (Höchst, Hauptstrasse): The *leaf capitals* in the arcades of the nave are Carolingian. After 1431 the *sacristy* was added in place of the S. transept. A few decades later the slender Gothic *E. chancel* was added, along with

the *W. doorway*, with its splendid *stone figures* of St. Paul and St. Anthony.

**Bolongaro Palace** (Höchst, Hauptstrasse): The palace, with its 130 yards of street façade, was built in 1772–5 for the tobacco manufacturers and bankers J.P. and J.M.M. Bolongaro. It is used today as a local government office. The pointed obelisk which forms the ridge turret on the central part of the building is unusual. This building with its baroque fountain and fine flights of steps faces the Main.

**Farbwerke Höchst: Administrative Building:** This building by P. Behrens (1920–4) is a typical example of expressionist industrial architecture in the 1920s; it has a tower and cathedral-like staircase with pillars in the shape of stalactites.

**Centenary Hall of the Höchst AG**

*Behrens-Bau, offices of Farbwerke Hoechst* ▷

*Funerary chapel of Reichenbach, main cemetery*

(Höchst, Pfaffenwiese): Symphony concerts are performed here as well as opera, ballet and straight theatre by German and foreign touring companies.

**Also worth seeing in Höchst:** The *Renaissance Schloss*, which was built on the site of the medieval *Burg*; also the *Heimatmuseum* (local history) in the old *Customs Tower* (13 Schlossplatz).

**Environs: Dreieichenhain** (9 km. S): In the *Dreieich-Museum* (52 Fahrgasse) are archaeological finds from the ruins of the *Hain moated Burg*, a 10&11C royal hunting lodge originally protected by a marsh moat. The Old Town has striking 17&18C half-timbered houses and is surrounded by 12–15C town fortifications.

---

**Frauenchiemsee 8211**
Bavaria                                      p.422☐M 20

**Benedictine Nunnery Church of St. Maria:** The foundation of the nunnery *c.*782 on this island in the Chiemsee was the work of Duke Tassilo III, but Irmingard, a granddaughter of Charlemagne, was also of central importance in its history. The Patroness of the Chiemgau was abbess here (her grave (866) was discovered in the course of excavations in 1961). The church was built on the foundations of an older church dating from 866 which was destroyed by the Hungarians in the 10C. The present-day Romanesque building is essentially 11C. The lower storeys of the free-standing, octagonal bell tower were also built at this time; the tower, originally a refuge tower, is now the emblem of the island. Its upper storeys were added in the Gothic period and in 1626 the onion dome was built. Copies of the Romanesque

**Frankfurt, Alte Nikolaikirche 1** Memorial to Siegfried zum Paradies by Madern Gerthener, c. 1410 **2** Memorial to Katharina zum Wedel (d. 1378) **3** Stone figure of St. Nicholas in external niche on N. side, late Gothic **4** Rococo pulpit by J.D.Schnorr, 1761-71 **5** Tympanum with St. Nicholas between two crippled beggars, Gothic **6** Tympanum with scene similar to 5, probably originating from W. portal

frescos (*c.*1130) from the presbytery of the Münster can be seen in the Carolingian gatehouse (*c.*850) in the summer months. This Salzburg work shows Christ, Martha and Mary, angels, and the tree and fountain of life.

The *furnishings* of the church are all baroque and date from the 17C. Most important elements: the baroque *high altar* (1694, restored in 1980), the *ceiling paintings* and the *carved Madonna* (mid 16C). There are numerous Gothic and baroque red marble *gravestones* in the chancel galleries. The nunnery now houses a boarding school.

---

**Freckenhorst = 4410 Warendorf 2**
Nordrhein-Westfalen                      p.414☐D 9

**Catholic Parish Church of St. Bonifatius:** The former collegiate church took its name from the relics of St. Bonifatius which were kept here. Its W. façade, which is like a massive town gate, makes it one of the most important early Romanesque churches in Westphalia. The mother of the Westphalian authoress Annette von Droste-Hülshoff was one of the canonesses, and Annette von Droste-

Hülshoff wrote some chapters for L.Schücking's novel 'The Canoness' on the basis of the stories her mother told her. *Building history:* As the result of a fire only the present W. part remains of the original 11C building. The new building was consecrated in 1129 (inscription on the font). In the subsequent centuries the church was extended, and the towers were raised and provided with windows. In 1670 the baroque pyramid roof of the tower was built.

*Buildings:* The spaciousness of this plain building, a cruciform basilica, is its most impressive feature. It is unusual to find this combination of five towers in Westphalia. The church is essentially *Romanesque*, only the vaulting in the nave is *Gothic*. The *columned arcades* in the aisles are of interest: the *capitals* are decorated with tendrils and human heads. Only part of the 13C *cloisters* remains of the original nunnery building. *Furnishings*: The famous Freckenhorst *font* is one of the most important 12C German stone fonts. The two bands of reliefs show couchant lions and scenes from the life of Christ. The *grave slab* of Geva, who founded the church in the 13C, is of interest: the life-size figure is shown in a closely-draped gown with elaborate folds.

*St. Maria, Frauenchiemsee*

## Fredelsloh = 3413 Moringen 3

Lower Saxony　　　　　　　　p.414☐G 9

**Former Monastery Church of St. Blasii:** The present-day Protestant parish church is an impressive if somewhat bleak building in heavy reddish ashlar sandstone. The apse-like bay between the two massive W. towers is unusual. The 12C church also has an austere interior: there is no sculptural decoration. Of the old furnishings, apart from a badly damaged *font* only the *sandstone reliefs* with figures of the 12 Apostles in the chancel remain.

## Freiburg im Breisgau 7800

Baden-Württemberg　　　　　　p.420☐D 20

Freiburg, which stands on the Dreisam between the Black Forest and the Upper Rhine, is dominated by its Gothic *Münster*. The *Schauinsland* hill (funicular railway) gives a good view across the town.
This essentially bourgeois town has resisted every pressure to make it noble and dignified; flowing through its centre is the rapid *Bächle*, a medieval sewerage system, which cools the town in oppressive summer weather and into which every genuine citizen of Freiburg must have fallen at least once. Its independent tradition goes back to Duke Konrad of Zähringen, who in 1120 presented plots of land 50ft. wide and 100ft. long to 'respectable tradespeople'. Independence of spirit has long been a characteristic of the town. It was conquered in 1515 by peasants in revolt, in 1632 and 1638 by the Swedes, in 1644 by the Bavarians and in 1677, 1713 and 1744 by the French. Its buildings remained essentially unchanged until the Second World War. The bomb damage of 1944 has been almost entirely made good, and the fine old town now looks very much as it always did.

**Freckenhorst, parish church of St. Bonifatius, former collegiate church 1** Font, 1129 **2** Lions' heads on the sacristy doors, Romanesque, probably from the former main portal **3** Tombstone of Geva, early-13C, in the crypt **4** Standing candlestick, 15C **5** 3 tabernacle, c. 1500 **6** Virgin Mary mourning, c 1520 **7** Former high altar and memorial to Abbess Maria v. Plettenberg by W. Spannagel, 1646 **8** Figures of the Virgin and Joseph by C.X. Stippeldey, 1791-3 **9** High altar by H.G. Bücker **10** Ambo by H.G. Bücker **11** Shrine of St. Thiatildis; casing by H.G. Bücker

*St. Bonifatius, Freckenhorst*

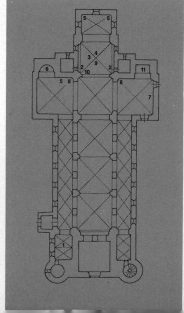

**Münster Church of Our Lady** (Münsterplatz): Only the *transepts* and the two adjacent *Hahnen towers* (*c.*1200, though the upper parts and the open Gothic spires are later) remain of the original Gothic building. The second building phase included the nave (1220–60), and the third the high Gothic W. tower (1260–1350). Subsequently the old Romanesque choir, which had become too small, was pulled down and replaced by a longer Gothic *choir*. This work began after the completion of the tower and was not finished until 1515.

The *Romanesque* parts of the transepts and the two side towers stand in clear contrast to the Gothic work. The nave is in the severe Gothic tradition of the Minster in Strasbourg. The light choir and its galleries and series of chapels is reminiscent of St. Vitus Cathedral in Prague. The architect of the chancel was J. von Gmünd of the school of Parler. The tower (1260–1350) is in three sections: a square lower building, above that the octagon and finally the steep pyramid of the spire. Instead of a roof, openwork ornamentation in red sandstone was used. This was the first Gothic single tower, and it has been much copied.

*Interior:* On the gables of the *W. doorway*, which leads into the *porch*, are friezes representing the Life of Christ, the Last Judgement, the twelve Apostles and the Ecclesia with synagogue. On the porch walls are the wise and foolish virgins, the 'Prince of the World' as seducer, naked lust, and also saints and angels; the sculptors and stonemasons responsible were from Strasbourg. The porch, formerly used as a courtroom, has stone benches and standard measurements for the ell and the barrel (on the left and right by the entrance). The *Madonna* inside over the doorway (*c.*1270–80) is the finest of the figures in this cycle. It was presumably on the *high altar* before this was decorated in 1516 with the Crowning of Mary and wing pictures by H.Baldung, called Grien. Grien was also responsible for the painting of the famous *Schnewlin Altar* (now in the 9th from the left of the 16 chapels surrounding the chancel). Instead of the 15th chapel (S., close by the transept) a *sacristy*

*Freiburg Münster*

was erected; in it is a Man of Sorrows by L.Cranach (1524). H.Holbein the Younger combined the two wings of the Oberried Altar (1521) into one in the *University Chapel* (11th from the left). In the adjacent *Cyriak Chapel* is a font by the Freiburg sculptor Chr.Wenzinger (1768). It is rococo work, at once pious and light-hearted. In the fourth chapel from the left, the *Locherer Chapel*, is a Virgin of Mercy (1521–24), carved in wood and entirely unpainted. The *Chapel of the Tomb* (1340) is contemporary with the nave, and runs back along its S. side. Christ lies on a tumba, and the watching disciples crouch along its side. Behind the grave the figures of the three women can be made out. In the body of Christ is a small iron door which conceals the Host until Good Friday. The *pulpit* on the S. side of the nave is Gothic in form, but was in fact made in 1559–61 in pastiche late Gothic style by J.Kempf, who portrayed himself on its base. He is wearing Renaissance dress and looking out of

the window. The best feature of the interior is the *stained glass*, which unfortunately has survived only in part. The panes are 13–15C with some later additions.

**Former Franciscan Monastery Church of St. Martin** (Rathausplatz): This church was destroyed in the Second World War and rebuilt (completion 1953) in its original form as a Gothic church of the Mendicant Order. Earlier alterations were removed. The nave is dominated by broad arches borne on undecorated round columns. The only decoration in this otherwise plain, austere and ascetic building is in the chancel.

**Former Church and Monastery of the Augustinian Eremites** (22 Salzstrasse): This church dates back to the year 1278 and is built round a hall-like nave (later rebuilt in baroque style). The *monastery* was built on to the S. of the church in the 14C, and has accommodated the municipal *Augustinermuseum* (q.v.) since its inception in 1923.

**University Church/Jesuit Church** (Bertholdstrasse): This church, built in 1685–1705, burned down in a Second World War air raid, and the valuable furnishings were lost. The new building has no stucco and very plain altars.

**Adelhauser Church** (Adelhauser Platz): After many attacks and much destruction the Dominican Order moved the church and the monastery into the town, where the new building was begun in 1687. The most important items in the church, which is presumed to have been built by a French architect and has many French features, are the *sandstone figure of St.Katharina* and the famous *Adelhauser crucifix* (both 14C). There is also a notable *Picture of the Virgin* (14C) and a *Madonna figure* by H.Wydyz (*c.*1500).

**Protestant Church of St.Ludwig** (Stadtstrasse): The present-day church was erected on a different site from its predecessor, the Tennenbach monastery church,

*Freiburg Münster*

*Martinstor*

which had been moved into the town; it was destroyed on 27.11.1944. St.Ludwig is a good example of *modern church architecture*. The altar and the congregation placed around it are the focal point of the church.

**Kaufhaus** (Münsterplatz): The Münsterplatz came into being in the early 16C on the site of the old cemetery around the Münster, and the Kaufhaus was built *c.*1520 on its S. side. This is a *late Gothic* building with pinnacles and coloured tiled roofs at the corners, painted blood red and decorated with gold. The arcade on the ground floooor was a market hall, and the upper storey served as a banqueting hall for the town. The imperial protectors of the town were honoured with *statues* on the façade (by S.von Staufen, 1530).

**Town fortifications:** Remains of the 13C fortifications can be seen in the Kaiser-Josef-Strasse and the Oberlinden area; they are the *Martinstor* and the *Schwabentor*.

*Kaufhaus (1520) in Münsterplatz*

The Martinstor was completed *c.*1230, but was raised by 68ft. in 1900. The Schwabentor was restored in 1953.

**Basler Hof** (167 Kaiser-Josef-Strasse): The head of the town government is accommodated here today; previously the building housed representatives of the cathedral chapter and the Austrian government, and the district office. It was built in 1500–10 to plans by Imperial Chancellor Stürzel.

**Haus zum Schönen Eck** (8 Münsterplatz): This baroque house was built next to the late Gothic Kaufhaus in 1755–65 by the Frankfurt architect and sculptor Chr.Wenzinger. The most striking feature of the building is the staircase with large ceiling paintings in the upper storey.

**Fountains:** Fountains are a notable feature of the Freiburg townscape. They include the *Bertholdsbrunnen* (at the junction of Kaiser Josef Strasse/Bertholdstrasse/Salzstrasse), the *Georgsbrunnen* (Münsterplatz) and the *Fischbrunnen* (Münsterplatz).

**Museums:** The *Augustinermuseum* has one of the finest art collections on the Upper Rhine. Paintings by H.Baldung and M.Grünewald are the most precious possessions of the gallery, alongside Romanesque and Gothic stained glass, sculpture and tapestries. *Museum für Ur- und Frühgeschichte* (housed in the Colombischlösschen, Rotteckring; primeval and early history). The *Museum für Völkerkunde* (32 Gerberau; anthropology) the *Stadtarchiv* (18 Salzstrasse; town archive), the *Deutsches Volksliederarchiv* (13 Silberbachstrasse, folk-song archive), the *Münstermuseum* (4 Schoferstrasse) and the *Zinnfigurenklause* (pewter figures) in the Schwabentor are all of interest.

**Theatre:** The *Städtische Bühnen* (46 Bertholdstrasse) present opera, operetta and studio work in three venues and in the open air in the Rathaushof.

**Also worth seeing:** *Altes Rathaus* opposite St.Martin, *Neues Rathaus* (former Old University), the rebuilt *university buildings*, the *Münsterbauhütte* and private houses from the Gothic to the rococo period.

---

**Freising 8050**
Bavaria                                    p.422□L 19

The town developed at the foot of the Domberg above the Isar, one of the spiritual and ecclesiastical centres of South Germany. Freising was a cathedral town from the 8C until the see was moved to Munich in 1821. Churches, chapels, clergy residences and the buildings of the bishop's palace on the ridge remain.

**Dom St. Maria and St. Korbinian** (Domberg): Shortly after the death of Bishop Otto, the great mediaeval historian and uncle of Frederick Barbarossa, an endowment by this emperor made possible the rebuilding of the *Romanesque Dom* (1160), which remains in its essentials today. The interior was however decorated by the brothers Asam in 1723–4 with extravagant *rococo paintings* and lavish *stucco*. 100 years before this the Romanesque building had already been altered by Renaissance rebuilding and additions. The original flat ceiling disappeared at the end of the Gothic period (vaulting by Meister Jörg, the master of the Frauenkirche (q.v.) in Munich, 1481&2). The *choir stalls* also date from this period. The *high altar*, erected during the Renaissance alterations of 1625, has today only a copy of the 'Woman of the Apocalypse' by Rubens (the original is in the Pinakothek (q.v.) in Munich). There are fine paintings on the *side altars*. Frederick Barbarossa (with Otto von Freising?) and opposite them the Empress Beatrix, are portrayed on the columns of the porch doorway. The most interesting part of the cathedral is the four-aisled *crypt* with the famous *beasts' column* un-

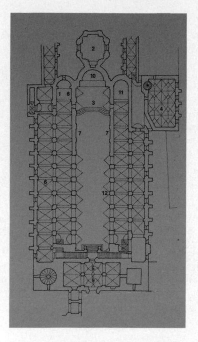

Freising, cathedral of St.Maria und Korbinian 1 Stephanuskapelle 2 Maximilianskapelle 3 Crypt containing beast's column, stone coffin of St.Korbinian, tombstone of bishop Hitto (d. 835) 4 Sacristy, treasury in upper storey 5 Portal, c. 1190 6 Virgin Mary on the stairs, 1461 7 Choir stalls, 1484-5 8 Lamentation by E.Grasser, 1492; Christ, 1440 9 Portico 10 High altar 11 Chapel of the Blessed Sacrament 12 Pulpit, 1624

der the raised altar. The *Chapel of the Sacrament* is at the end of the S. aisle.

**Chapel of St. Benedict:** Behind the Dom, with which it is connected by *cloisters*, is the little church of St.Benedict, the so-called *Old Dom*, a work of the high Gothic period (1346). The ribs and columns were, however, covered with baroque stucco work at the beginning of the 18C.

**St.Johannes** (on the W. side of the Dom): The new building (1319–21) is excellent high Gothic, and was erected on the site of the original baptismal chapel. Above the

*Adoration of Christ, Dom, Freising*

N. aisle of the cathedral the Prince Bishop had a private passageway built, connecting the cathedral directly to his residence.

**Bishop's residence:** There is now an education centre in this building, which was partially decorated by F.Cuvilliés and J.B.Zimmermann.

**Neustift former Monastery Church:** NE of the Domberg is the Neustift Monastery Church, a product of co-operative work by distinguished 18C artists. G.A.Viscardi's building was decorated by J.B.Zimmermann and F.X.Feuchtmayer. The finest piece is the high altar from the studio of I.Günther (1765), who was also responsible for the carved choir stalls with their sequence of lively putti.

**Museums:** The *Museum des Historischen Vereins* (7 Mittlere Hauptstrasse) has exhibits on pre- and municipal history. The *Diocesan Museum* behind the Residence (21 Domberg) has fine sculpture and paintings.

**Also worth seeing:** The oldest brewery in the world, founded in 1040, is near Freising in the former Benedictine Abbey of *Weihenstephan*.

---

**Freudenstadt 7290**
Baden-Württemberg                p.420□E 18

**Market place:** Freudenstadt was designed and built in 1599 at the command of Duke Friedrich; it stands at a height of 2,400ft. in the Black Forest, and was intended for silver miners and, from 1603, for Protestant refugees from Austria. The plan foresaw an open rectangle of 718 ft. by 708 ft., like a Roman camp, around which the streets were to be laid out as in a board game, but it was only partially realised. Of the public buildings intended to

*Right-hand screen, Dom*

*Johanneskapelle, Dom*

stand at the four corners of the square only the church and, diagonally opposite, the Town Hall were built. The low houses around the square are connected by arcades. There was to have been a Schloss in the middle of the square, but it was not built. The town, which has been a popular spa since the 19C, was badly damaged in 1945, but has been completely restored.

**Church** (Marktplatz): This church, which was destroyed in the war but rebuilt, consists of two wings meeting at right angles, as demanded by the layout of the square. One was intended for men and the other for women. It is one of the most unusual ecclesiastical buildings of the Renaissance. False vaulting of planking and stucco unites the two wings. The furnishings for this austere building, designed to stress the importance of preaching, were collected from other churches. The most striking piece is the *lectern* (*c.*1180) with the four Evangelists. It still has its original highly-

coloured paintwork, and is presumed to be from the monastery of Alpirsbach (q.v.) or Hirsau (q.v.). The relief frieze of entwined animals on the 12C *font* is open to many interpretations.

**Also worth seeing:** The *Heimatmuseum* (local history) in the Stadthaus and the *Dorfmuseum* (village museum) in Dietersweiler.

**Freystadt 8431**
Bavaria                                    p.422□K 16

**Pilgrimage Church of Maria-Hilf:** This rotunda with its imposing dome was built from 1700–10 by G.A.Viscardi. The fine stucco work is by F.Appiani (1707) and the frescos, (which were painted over but then revealed during thorough restoration work in 1950–9), are the work of H.G.Asam and his sons Cosmas Demian and Egid Quirin, who were later to become

*Freudenstadt*

famous. The stucco figures on the narrow walls of the transepts are striking.

## Friedberg 8904
Bavaria                                  p.422☐I 19

Friedberg, the old Bavarian ducal town on the Lechrain, is dominated by its Burg, dating from the 30 Years' War.

**Pilgrimage Church of the Peace of Our Lord:** An avenue of trees leads to this baroque church E. of the town. The broad 18C building looks dour and dumpy, but it is a unified artistic whole. The spacious, light interior is clearly based on the model of St.Michael (q.v.) in Munich. The *decoration* is unusually ornate: there are massive, reddish-grey marble stucco columns with gold capitals, delicate pink stucco work by F.X.Feuchtmayer and a protruding organ loft with a half-dome. The dome painting in the chancel is by C.D.Asam (1738), and the ceiling painting in the nave is by his pupil M.Günther. The N. side altar has a late Gothic miraculous image.

**Rathaus:** The two-storey Town Hall (1680) is in the Marktplatz, and is based on buildings by E.Holl in nearby Augsburg (q.v.).

**Burg:** Almost nothing remains of the original 13C building; only the enclosing walls could possibly be original. The tower was added in 1552, and the rest of the building in the mid 17C. The *Heimatmuseum* (local history) is housed here today.

## Friedberg 6360
Hessen                                   p.416☐E 13

An imperial Burg was erected by the Emperor Barbarossa in the 12C on the site of the Roman fortifications. From it grew up an imperial town which was not overshadowed by nearby Frankfurt (q.v.).

**Protestant Church/former Church of our Lady:** This extraordinarily spacious church, one of the largest hall churches in Hessen, shows the ambition and drive of the citizens of this little town. An order by King Ruprecht of the Pfalz caused the W. façade, which should have had two towers, to remain incomplete. He forbade the raising of the building in 1410, because the towers could have been used as a bulwark against the Burg. The building of the nave dragged on from 1260–1370. In the interior the cylindrical columns and the rib vaulting were picked out in red with white joints. The capitals and keystones are brightly coloured. The 13C middle-Rhine sandstone statue known to art historians as the *Friedberg Madonna* is near the late Gothic choir screen. An early Gothic *altar pyx*, a *tabernacle* and a Gothic *font* are other outstanding features of the furnishings.

**Burg:** The Burg was built on the rectangular ground plan of the ancient Roman fort in the 12C. The massive 16–18C fortifications with gateways, towers and keeps remain. The *Burgmannenhäuser*, residential buildings which are part of the inner Burg, are like a town in themselves (16–18C). The emblem of the Burg and the town of Friedberg is the *Adolfsturm*, built in 1348 with the ransom money of Count Adolf of Nassau, who was once held prisoner here. The tower is 164ft. high and has a second wall passage above the four bartisans. The spire was added in the 19C.

**Judenbad** (20 Judengasse): This Jewish ritual bath for women, some 80 feet below ground level, consists of a square shaft running down to the water and seven flights of stairs; the archways have columns with fine leaf capitals. According to an inscription the bath was built in 1260. There are few Jewish baths remaining in Germany, and this is a particularly fine specimen.

**Also worth seeing:** The *Wetterau-Museum* (16 Haagstrasse) shows interesting exhibits on local history.

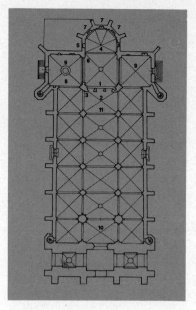

Friedberg, town church, Unserer Lieben Frau 1 Rood screen 2 Crucifix on the rood screen, earlier than 1500 3 Virgin Mary, c. 1280 4 High altar table, 1306 5 Sacristy door 6 Tabernacle, 1482-84 7 Choir window with stained glass, 1472-82 8 Font, c. 1230-60 9 Brass chandelier 10 Organ, 1964-5 11 Bronze cross by Karl Hemmeter, 1971

---

## Friedrichshafen 7990

Baden-Württemberg                    p.420☐G 21

*Lake Constance*, at its most attractive around Friedrichshafen, has inspired many visitors to write poetry. The author Martin Walser, who lives nearby, wrote 'It is astonishing how many people who are not poets at all have written poems about Lake Constance.' The rider who rode over the frozen lake (an opportunity which only seldom occurs) has been immortalised by many authors.

**Protestant Schloss Church** (in the Schloss): The former Benedictine Priory Church of St.Andreas was originally part of a monastery, which was rebuilt as a

Schloss in 1824–30. The church dates from 1695–1701, and was built by C.Thumb on the Vorarlberg pattern (a nave with side chapels, galleries between the pilasters and a twin-towered W. façade). The *stucco decorations* are by J.Schmuzer and his two sons, all masters of the famous Wessobrunn School (q.v.). Blossom, garlands, fruit, vine-leaves and shells in dazzling white and early baroque shapes cover the vaulting like a thickly woven tapestry.

**Museums:** In the Town Hall is the *Städtisches Bodenseemuseum* with art treasures from Upper Swabia and a *Zeppelin section*. *Oberschwäbisches Schulmuseum* (school museum) in the school house in the Schnetzenhausen district of Friedrichshafen.

---

**Friedrichstadt 2254**
Schleswig-Holstein                          p.412□F 2

---

Duke Friedrich III of Gottorf founded and gave his name to the town in the 17C; it was intended for Dutchmen driven out of Holland because of their faith.

**The town:** The town, largely built by

*Schlosskirche, Friedrichshafen*

Dutch craftsmen, still looks like a country town in N.Holland: it has tree-lined thoroughfares and brick houses with stepped gables and large windows. The most elaborate façade is that of the *Old Mint* (2 Mittelburgwall) of 1626, a narrow building with statuary and tiled ornamentation. The *Paludanushaus* (28 Prinzenstrasse) is quite different, with baroque scrolls on the three-storey gables and a broad, light façade with regularly placed windows, which give it a rather stately look. In the *Catholic church* (1853) is a fine 13C *crucifix*.

---

**Fritzlar 3580**
Hessen                                       p.416□F 11

---

This town above the Eder was given a royal palace at the time of Charlemagne. Later it was a fortified base for the Archbishop of Mainz in his feud with the counts of Hessen-Thüringen; some walls and towers remain from this period.

**Dom St.Petri/Catholic Parish Church** (Domplatz): In 724 St.Boniface felled a sacred oak on the site of the present-day ca-

*Dom Fritzlar*

thedral. In 732 a stone building replaced the original wooden church. Of the subsequent building (1085 – 1118) only the *crypts* and the *westwork* remain. After 1180 the cathedral began to be rebuilt in its present form. The partially Romanesque, partially Gothic *parvis* dates from 1232 or later. The long Gothic windows in the E. and S. of the choir were added in the 15C, and the *roter Hals* at the N. entrance in the 18C. The spires on the towers are 19C. The general impression given by the cathedral is late Romanesque, but on the E. side one can detect in the two remaining apses of the chancel the clash of Romanesque decoration (Zwerchgalerie) with Gothic windows and Renaissance tracery. *Interior:* The three spacious *crypts* with their short, sturdy pillars are noteworthy. The shrine of St. Wigbert with a seated figure (1340) and a larger-than-life-size relief of St. Peter with a key (12C) are to be found here. There is also a Romanesque stone deacon as *supporter for a lectern*. The *triumphal cross* over the chancel, the multitiered *pyx* in the N. transept, the fine *wall paintings* in the S. transept, a stone *Holy Trinity group* and an expressive *Pietà* are all Gothic of various periods. The rest of the interior is baroque. In the *treasury* of the cathedral (entrance through the cloisters) the principal exhibits are: the *Emperor Heinrich cross*, which is set with precious stones, pearls and gems (12C), a *portable altar* (12C) and a *circular reliquary* with gilded metal reliefs and enamel.

**Historic Rathaus:** (Markt): An earlier building was largely destroyed by fire in the 15C; the present Town Hall was completed shortly after that. It is one of the oldest Town Halls in Germany still being used for its original purpose. It is also the focal point of the medieval town, which has a particularly attractive, untouched *market place*. The *Marktbrunnen* dates from the year 1564.

*Fortifications:* The town wall, which dates from the 12-14C, remains almost in its entirety; the most striking feature is the *Graue Turm* by the Burg moat (13C).

**Also worth seeing:** In the Protestant *Fraumünster Church* there are wall paintings (*c.*1300), and the *Church of the former Minorite Monastery* also has 14C wall paintings. The old town has a large number of very fine *mercantile* and *private houses*. The *Fritzlar Museum* in the 16C

*Kaiser Heinrich cross, Dom*

*Chalice with paten, Dom*

Hochzeitshaus has pre- and early historical collections, rural domestic equipment
and chests from six centuries.

## Fulda 6400

Hessen                                  p.416☐G 13

This town on the edge of the Rhön has
been a centre of religious life in Germany
since the 12C. This ecclesiastical tradition
extends from St. Boniface to the modern
conference of Catholic bishops. The conversion of central Germany to Christianity
in the 8C was based on Fulda. The monastery school was pre-eminent in the illustration of manuscripts, and the
Hildebrandslied was copied here. Einhart,
the biographer of Charlemagne, and Otfried von Weissenburg came from the
school at Fulda. Hrabanus Maurus, in his
time as abbot, initiated church and monastery building in and around Fulda. In the
18C the abbots were raised to the rank of
imperial princes, Fulda flourished again
and the town was given its exuberant baroque exterior. The architectural range of
the town is demarcated by severe, heavy
Romanesque building on the one hand and
the glamour of baroque and rococo on the
other.

**Dom St. Salvator and St. Boniface**
(Domplatz): A flat-roofed basilica used to
stand on the site now occupied by the
Dom. The basilica, which was of gigantic
proportions, grew out of two churches and
contained in its W. chancel the tomb of
St. Boniface (whose remains were brought
here in 819). In 1704 the old, much modified basilica was so derelict that Prince Abbot Adalbert von Schleiffras commissioned
a new building from his court architect
J. Dientzenhofer. The ground plan and line
of the walls followed the previous building to a large extent.
The exterior, with its twin towers and ornate lines, is reminiscent of Franconian baroque churches. The building dates from
1704–12, that is to say from a period when
the rococo architecture familiar to us from
later 18C buildings was unknown. The architect had a model of the dome of St.
Peter's in Rome sent to Fulda.
*Interior:* The interior is dominated by the
massive *crossing dome* through which light
floods into the building. The *stucco decoration* has strong profiles, cornices and
arches; Italian masters were involved in the

*Dom, Fulda*

work. The large *niche statues* are also from an Italian workshop. The *high* and *side altars* almost all date from 1700–15. The *Boniface vault* in the W. under the monks' chancel has 16 sandstone figures and an altar which represents the death and resurrection of the saint. In the *cathedral treasury* is a manuscript (*c.*700) said to have belonged to St.Boniface.

**Chapel of St.Michael** (on the Michaelsberg): N. of the Domplatz is the Catholic Priory Church of St.Michael, which was built in 820–2 by the monk-architect Racholf, but only the crypt remains from this period. Along with the basilica in Seligenstadt (q.v.), parts of St.Justinus in Frankfurt-Höchst (q.v), the churches on the island of Reichenau (q.v.) and the Marienkapelle in Würzburg (q.v.) the sepulchre chapel of St.Michael is the oldest church building in Germany. It is a circular building with eight columns and a gallery originally on one level, a replica of the Church of the Sepulchre in Jerusalem. The building was rebuilt in the 11C to a Carolingian plan. The capitals from the earlier church were used again, but a second level was added. At the same time the building took on a defensive role and the nave was extended. The characteristic rounded roof was not added until the baroque period.

**Schloss/Former Residence of the Prince Abbots** (Schlossstrasse): The originally medieval Abbots' Burg, rebuilt as a Renaissance Schloss and developed into a magnificent baroque building by J.Dientzenhofer in 1707–34, now accommodates sections of the *Vonderau Museum*. The building, with its open *principal courtyard* on the town side is arranged round an *inner courtyard*, which was also rebuilt in baroque style by Dientzenhofer. Even the former keep was incorporated into the new building. On the ground floor is the *Kaisersaal* with its heavy stucco decoration. The *Fürstensaal* on the second floor (former banqueting hall) is reached by the main staircase. The Fürstensaal has lavish stucco work and is ornately painted. The most interesting room in the Schloss is the *Spiegelkabinett*, whose walls, doors and

mirrors are decorated with flamboyant rococo ornamentation and frames. Opposite the Schloss on the N. side of the *park* is the *Orangery* (1722-30), built by Dientzenhofer to plans by the Mainz court architect M.von Welsch. It is the finest baroque palace in Fulda. J.Fr.Humbach's Flora vase (1728) is like a fountain of stone in the centre of the building.

**Petersberg near Fulda:** This former Benedictine Monastery, standing on a hill

**Fulda, Dom 1** High altar with carved Ascension by Neudecker, and above this a stucco Trinity by Artari **2** Benediktusaltar, alabaster statue by Neudecker, remaining design by Artari **3** Sturmiusaltar; alabaster statue by Neudecker, altar by Artari **4** Relief of Charlemagne, early-15C, from the former collegiate church **5** Altar of the Magi by J.W. Fröhlicher with altarpiece by J.Albin **6** Pulpit by A.B. Weber, c. 1712 **7** Choir organ by J.Hoffmann, 1719 **8** Organ by A.Oehninger, 1708-13; carvings on the organ front by A.B. Weber **9** Monument to Adalbert v.Schleiffras by J.H.E. Mockstatt, 1719-22 **10** Monument to Adolph v.Dalberg by C.J. Winterstein, 1729–34 **11** Memorial to prince-abbot Placidus v.Droste by J.Valentin Schaum, 1741-3 **12** Memorial to Amand v.Buseck, 1756

*St. Michael*

*Crypt*

and visible over a long distance, is one of the four monasteries around Fulda set symbolically in the shape of a cross, and dating back in part to Hrabanus Maurus; the others are the Andreasberg, the Johannesberg and the Frauenberg. Only the *crypt* with its three apses is Carolingian. It contains the tomb of St. Lioba, a relation and fellow-worker of St. Boniface.

**Schloss Fasanerie near Fulda:** In the 18C the Prince Abbots of Fulda had an older small Schloss SE of the town extended as a pleasance. The transition from the *front courtyard* through the large *central pavilion* to the *old Schloss* is impressive. The decoration conveys even today the splendour of the baroque. The Landgraves of Hessen have their art treasures here; the *antiquities* and the *porcelain collection* are particularly worth seeing.

**Museums:** In the *Vonderau-Museum* (in the Schloss and in the former Jesuit Seminary in the Universitätsplatz) there are exhibits of prehistory, anthropology, craft and natural lore, and also numismatics, sculpture, painting, graphics, faience work, porcelain and domestic culture. The *Deutsches Feuerwehr-Museum* (6 Universitätsstrasse) covers the entire history of the fire-fighting service. The *Permanent Exhibition of the Hessische Landesbibliothek*, (12 Heinrich von Bibra Platz) shows Fulda's tradition as a centre of manuscript illustration (see introduction to this entry).

**Also worth seeing:** On the site of the original market church the Catholic Parish Church of St. Blasius was built from 1771–86 in rococo style; its interior suggests the classical severity which was to follow. Striking secular buildings include the *Paulustor* (moved here in 1771), the *Hauptwache* (1757–9), the *Palais Buseck* (1732) and the *Altenstein Palais* (1752).

*Orangery, Schloss* ▷

*Kaisersaal, Schloss*

## Fürstenfeldbruck 8080
Bavaria                                    p.422☐K 19

**Former Cistercian Monastery Church
of the Ascension of the Blessed Virgin**
(Fürstenfeld): The monastery church,
which is one of the most important sacred
buildings in Upper Bavaria, is a clear
demonstration of the relationship between
Bavarian baroque and Italian art. The new
building (1701) was designed by G.A.Vis-
cardi, who began to build the chancel and
towers. The War of the Spanish Succession
brought building to a halt, however, and
it did not start again until after the death
of Viscardi, (consecration in 1741), and so
German elements began to creep in. The
exuberance of the exterior is concentrated
largely in the façade. Its two storeys are
each lightened by six columns, and above
them is the gable, decorated with columns
and flanked with scrolls. On the balustrade
are figures of St.Benedict and St.Bernard,

and in the central niche is a statue of Christ
the Redeemer. The interior has a broad,
barrel-vaulted nave and a chancel with a
semi-circular apse. There is a fascinating
multiplicity of colours on the columns,
walls and vaulting. The *stucco decoration*
is by the brothers Appiani, the *vault painting* by C.D.Asam. The *side altars* and probably the *high altar* were designed by
E.Q.Asam. Among the splendid features of
the decoration the *choir stalls*, the *pulpit*
and the *enthroned Madonna* in the sacristy
(a particularly fine late-15C wood carving)
are most striking.

## Fürstenzell 8399
Bavaria                                    p.422☐O 18

**Former Cistercian Monastery Church
of the Ascension of the Blessed Virgin:**
The famous Bavarian architect
J.M.Fischer had to come to the rescue of

*Monastery church, Fürstenfeldbruck*

*Rococo figure, library, Fürstenzell*

a highly unsatisfactory project started by a Passau sculptor in 1739 on the site of the original 14C church. Fischer took over the existing rectangular building and transformed it into a living, soaring space. The façade is unusually wide, but perfectly proportioned, with two towers and a protruding central section. To relieve the square effect of the interior the corners are slanted and rounded. The galleries move in convex curves from one pilaster to the next. The lavish *decoration* in stucco and frescos heightens the soaring effect. The frescos on the vaulting are by the Tyrolean painter J.J.Zeiller, who also painted the *high altar* panel with the Ascension of the Blessed Virgin. The altar itself with its twisted columns and very fine tabernacle angels is by the Munich master J.B.Straub. One of the *monastery buildings* which is attached to the S. of the church is the *library*, a gem of Bavarian rococo. The galleries are supported by figures of Atlas, and have carved lattices. The *Fürstensaal* and the

*dining-room* are of similar quality to the library, but rather more restrained.

**Füssen 8958**

Bavaria                                    p.422☐1 21

**Former Benedictine Monastery Church of St.Mang** (Magnusplatz): The massive early medieval tower is the most striking feature of this church, which stands high above the town. A 12C Romanesque building over the tomb of St. Magnus, the Apostle of the Allgäu, previously stood on the site of the present church, which was designed in 1701 (consecrated 1717) by the local architect J.J.Herkomer. The building shows a strong Venetian influence (Herkomer studied in Venice) in the organisation of the space in the hall nave, and in the juxtaposition of the intersection dome and smaller shallow domes. The semicircular windows divided into three are an idiosyncrasy of this architect. He also designed the *stucco work* and *frescos* which show the life of the church's patron Magnus (St. Mang), and to a large extent the *altars* as well. The ornamentation with its dense webs of stucco and frescos set in medallions also shows the influence of N. Italy. The *monastery* and its interior decoration are also by Herkomer. Its fine *banqueting hall* is a companion piece to the Kaisersaal in Ottobeuren (q.v.).

**Hohes Schloss** (10 Magnusplatz): A Schloss with the character of a domestic residence developed from Duke Ludwig of Bavaria's 13&14C medieval defensive Burg in a period of considerable building activity from 1490–1503; its interior was partially refurbished in the 17C at the same time as the building of the *chapel of St. Veit.* In the N. wing there is a section of the Bayrische Staatsgemäldesammlungen (State collection of paintings).

**Spital Church:** The completely painted façade of this small baroque church (1748&9) with its huge figures of St. Florian and St. Christopher is a fine example of Bavarian *Lüftlmalerei.*

**Heimatmuseum** (3 Lechhalde): A collec-

*Spital Church, Füssen*

tion of local sacred and secular arts and crafts, including early violins and lutes (18C).

**Gaibach 8721**
Bavaria                                    p.418□H 15

**Catholic Parish Church:** The church
was built by no less an architect than
Balthasar Neumann in 1742–5; it was commissioned by Prince Bishop Carl of Schönborn. The four-storey tower is 16C and was
included in the new building. The layout
is cruciform, with a large dome.

**Schloss:** Valentin Echter of Mespelbrunn
had the Burg rebuilt as a Renaissance
Schloss about the end of the 16C.
J.L.Dientzenhofer was responsible for the
more recent baroque building (1694–1710).
Further rebuilding in the early 19C was in
the neoclassical style. The 'Konstitutions-
säule' in the park in front of the Schloss,
designed by von Klenze and built in
1824–8, commemorates the first Bavarian
constitution, approved by Max I. Joseph
in 1818.

---

**Garmisch-Partenkirchen 8100**
Bavaria                                    p.422□K 21

Garmisch-Partenkirchen is one of the most
important holiday resorts in the German
Alps. Its twisty streets and Romantic nooks
and crannies are a constant reminder of the
high level of popular artistic activity. Folk
theatre and festivals of traditional costume
are central to the cultural tradition. The

composer Richard Strauss lived in a villa
in the street named after him until his
death on 8.9.1949.

**Old St. Martin** (Garmisch, 2 Pfar-
rhausweg): Little remains of the original
building (c. 1280) except the lower part of
the tower. The church was extended in
1446, when the spire and the fine net vaulting in the nave were added. The interior
is dominated by a central column, probably built on the pattern of the rotunda in
Ettal (q.v.). The *Gothic wall paintings* are
historically significant: they include a
larger-than-life-size figure of St.
Christopher (13C), and scenes from the
Passion (15C).

**Pilgrimage Church of St.Anton** (Partenkirchen): Building work on this church
lasted from 1704–39. The older part is octagonal, and the later building (probably
by J.Schmuzer), is elliptical (S. side). Seen
from the outside the two parts of the building look like plain squares, but they merge
with considerable architectural charm in
the interior. The most striking feature is
the ceiling painting by J.E.Holzer (1739).

**New Parish Church of St.Martin** (Garmisch): This church, built by J.Schmuzer
in 1730–4, has stucco work by J.Schmuzer,
M.Schmidt and L.Bader, all of Wessobrunn; the ceiling frescos are by M.Gün-
ther, and the high altar panels by M.Speer
(after van Dyck).

**Schachen hunting lodge** (N. of Garmisch over the Elmau): Ludwig II (1864 –86) had this hunting lodge built in a picturesqe situation as a retreat. The *Moorish room* is particularly worth seeing. There is now a museum of local history in the lodge.

**Werdenfels Museum** (47 Ludwigstrasse): The museum was founded in 1895 to show the work of the technical school for wood carvers and cabinet-makers. It includes exhibits on folk culture, costume, ceramics, glass, carnival customs, graphics and 16–18C sculpture.

**Theatres:** There are touring performances in the Kongresshaus (Dr-Richard-Strauss-Platz); the *Kleine Kurtheather* presents straight theatre throughout the year and in the season there are performances of folk drama by the Peasant Theatre in the Gasthof 'Zum Rasen' (45 Ludwigstrasse).

**Also worth seeing:** Parish Church of the Ascension of Our Lady (Partenkirchen, 1865–71 after a fire) with paintings by the Venetian B.Letterini (1731); Plague Chapel (1634–7) with a 16C Rochus figure.

---

**Geilenkirchen 5130**
Nordrhein-Westfalen                    p.416□A 11

**Schloss Trips:** The buildings, former seat of the counts of Berghe von Trips, consist of a main section with several outer works dating from the 15–18C. The centre of the extensive moated Burg is the *Herrenhaus* with its massive tower.

**Schloss Breill:** Building started in the 16C, and was continued and completed in the 18C.

**Also worth seeing:** *Parish Church of the Ascension of Our Lady:* The neoclassical central part of the church (1822–5) was built on a cruciform ground plan. *Burg Geilenkirchen* (1 Markt): Ruin of the keep of the former Burg of the Lords of Heinsberg (14C).

---

**Geisenheim 6222**
Hessen                                   p.416□D 14

Geisenheim, on the right bank of the Rhine, was once the end of the trade route which lead from Lorch to Geisenheim, avoiding the rapids at Bingen. The present-day prosperity of the town is based on wine-growing. It is the home of the Research Institute and Technical College for wine-, fruit- and vegetable-growing.

**Catholic Parish Church of the Holy Cross** (Kirchplatz): The present Gothic hall church was erected on the site of the earlier Romanesque building in 1510–20. In 1838–41 the building was considerably modified under the direction of P.Hoffmann. The twin-towered façade, the new galleries and the vaulting in the nave were particularly successful parts of this operation. The interior decoration has striking altars and tombs of noblemen. The baroque high altar (1700, with Crucifixion group) is now on the W. wall of the S. aisle. The neo-Gothic high altar is 19C. There are several 16–18C tombs.

**Former Stockheim Hof** (62 Winkelerstrasse): The three-storey stone building dating from 1550 is typical of the openplan hall of the Main and middle-Rhine region. Its lines are broken by the staircase tower on the S. side and the large oriel. The text of the Peace of Westphalia, which was to end the Thirty Years War a year later, was drafted here in 1647.

**Other halls:** As well as the former Stockheim Hof there are numerous other halls in Geisenheim. They include the former von der Leyen Hof (on the road out of the town to the W; 1581), the former Ingelheim Hof (1 Bahnstrasse; 1681), the former Oststein Palais (34 Rüdesheimer Strasse; 1766–71).

**Schloss Johannisberg** (4 km. NE. of Geisenheim): This Schloss was presented to Prince Metternich by the Austrians in

*Memorial to Friedrich von Stockheim in the ▷*
*Heiliges Kreuz church, Geisenheim*

*Schloss Johannisberg near Geisenheim*

1816, and is now in the possession of his successors (tours of parts of the building are possible).

**Environs: Eibingen** (4 km. NW): The former *Benedictine nunnery* was founded in 1148 as an Augustinian double monastery; St.Hildegard of Bingen installed Benedictine sisters here in 1165.

**Marienthal** (3 km. N.): The medieval furnishings of the *monastery and pilgrimage church* include, as well as the late Gothic *W. portal* with Annunciation tympanum, a fine 14C *picture of the Virgin* and *tombstone* of H.von Hohenweiser (d.1485), and outside a wooden *Crucifixion group* dating from *c*.1520.

---

**Geislingen an der Steige 7340**
Baden-Württemberg                p.420□G 18

---

The town has developed on a rectangular core, intersected by the Marktstrasse and formerly surrounded by fortifications. Little of this medieval centre now remains: there are some multi-storey half-timbered buildings, like the *Alte Zoll*, a timber building in the Alemannic style.

**Protestant Parish Church** (1 Kirchplatz): This church, a late Gothic columned basilica built 1424–40, is worth seeing for the choir stalls of 1512 by J.Syrlin of Ulm (see inscription), and D.Hennenberger's pulpit (1621).

**Burg Helfenstein** (3 km. E.): Little remains of the former Burg since its demolition in the 16C except the Öden tower, said to be 14C.

**Museums:** The *Heimatmuseum* (11 Moltke Strasse) with exhibits on the history of the town and the Land is in the *Alte Bau* (16C), one of the town's former fruit stores.

## Gelnhausen 6460
Hessen                                    p.416☐F 14

Barbarossa is said to have founded the town
in 1170. Its favourable position at the junction of important routes led to its being a
popular stopping-place for Emperors (30
recorded visits by Hohenstaufen Emperors; in 1180 the Reichstag met here).
The decline of the town, which ran parallel with the decline of the Stauffens, was
accelerated by pillaging in 1634–5.

**Protestant Marienkirche** (above the
Untermarkt): This many-towered church
is visible over long distances because of its
raised position. It was built in five stages.
It started as a small 12C church which was
much extended in the course of the centuries. Last to be built was the *processional
chapel* S. of the chancel in 1467. The best
interior feature is the high altar. The shrine
was built on a 13C altar table by N.Schit
of Seligenstadt in 1500. It depicts the
Madonna with four saints. As well as this
masterpiece of late Gothic carving there are
four other altars (St.Anne's altar *c.*1500,
the N. side altar *c.*1480, the altar of the
cross *c.*1500 and the altar in the S. aisle
*c.*1490). The ornately carved *choir stalls*
and unusual 14C music stand are also
worth seeing. The furnishings also include
the well-preserved Mary tapestry (*c.*1500)
and the Passion tapestry (15C). There are
numerous stone coats of arms on the exterior walls.

**Former Kaiserpfalz:** The palace on the
Kinzig island was presumably completed
for the Gelnhausen Reichstag in 1180. The
Emperor Barbarossa commissioned it personally as an important link in the chain
of palatinate buildings which he was then
erecting in rapid succession. After Barbarossa the palace sheltered numerous
other emperors before it began to fall into
decline in the 15C. The buildings have
been extremely well restored. The palace
is surrounded by a circular wall built partially of 5ft. ashlar blocks with unusually
ornate ornamentation. The outer works
and the former Town Hall stood in front
of the Burg.

*Marienkirche, Gelnhausen*

**Romanesque house** (Am Untermarkt):
The house was built *c.*1180, probably for
imperial officials, and restored in the 19C;
it later served as Town Hall and today it
is the Protestant community hall. The
most important room in the three-storey
building is the 16ft. high hall on the first
floor.

**Heimatmuseum** (2 Kirchgasse): There
are exhibits on the history of the town and
pre-historic archaeological finds, and collections on Hans Jakob Christoph von
Grimmelshausen (1622 – 76, author of
'Simplicissimus') and on the teacher and
inventor Philipp Reis (1834–74; pioneer
of the telephone), both born in Gelnhausen.

**Also worth seeing:** *Catholic Church of
St. Peter* (Am Obermarkt): The original
building was 13C, but was used for secular purposes and then extended for use as
a Catholic church in 1932–8; *Johanniterhof*

(Holzgasse): house of the Order of the Knights of St. John from the early 14C; *Arsburg Klosterhof* (Lange Gasse): stone building rebuilt in 1743 in the baroque style; it has a fine porch with columns; *Rathaus* (14C), containing the *Meerholzer Heimatmuseum* (local history); *town fortifications:* the town walls date from the Stauffen period and are in good condition; notable features are the Hexenturm (15C), the Halbmond and some gates.

---

## Gelsenkirchen 4650

Nordrhein-Westfalen                    p.414☐C 10

This industrial town in the centre of the Ruhr has six harbours and is a centre of coal-mining and the iron, steel, glass, clothing and chemical industries.

**Moated Schloss Horst** (Horst, Schmalhorststrasse): This 1570 Renaissance Schloss served as the model for numerous moated Schloss buildings in Westphalia. It was commissioned by the Elector Governor of Cologne Rutger von der Horst, and consisted originally of four wings round a large inner courtyard. In the 19C the largely derelict Schloss had to be demolished; only the servants' wing and the ground floor of the former Herrenhaus remained. Some of the fine old fireplaces are being transferred to Schloss Hugenpoet in Kettwig (q.v.).

**Artists' Colony in Halfmannshof** (Halfmannsweg): This colony was founded in 1931 in a former farmhouse. It holds regular exhibitions of modern art.

**Museums:** *Städtische Kunstsammlung* (5 –7 Horster Strasse): temporary exhibitions of modern art, and also a permanent exhibition of modern works; there is a specialist department of kinetics. *Heimatmuseum* (Buer, (5–7 Horster Strasse): collection on municipal and cultural history and the history of the Land.

**Theatres:** *Musiktheater im Revier* (Kennedyplatz): The old municipal theatre was destroyed in 1944 and rebuilt in 1959 by a team of architects under the direction of W. Ruhnau. The *Grosse Haus* has 1044 seats and the *Kleine Haus* 353 seats. Since October 1965 the cities of Gelsenkirchen and Bochum have worked together: the Musiktheater (opera, operetta and musi-

*High altar, Marienkirche*

*Romanisches Haus*

cals) regularly makes guest appearances in the Schauspielhaus in Bochum (q.v.) and the Bochum ensemble regularly performs in Gelsenkirchen.

**Also worth seeing:** *Schloss Berge* (Buer, Adenauerallee) is a plain building (16C, mentioned in the 13C) with three wings, a moat and a park.

## Gelting, Angeln 2342
Schleswig-Holstein p.412□H 1

**Protestant Church:** This is a square, late baroque hall church (1793) with four boxes for the nobility and an altarpiece with five panels (1793). There is an octagonal *wooden font* (1653) by H.Gudewerdt with a lid and carved 'gnarling'. There are metal and sandstone Regency and rococo sarcophagi with ornate decoration in the Rumohr vault.

**Herrenhaus Gelting:** The history of this estate can be traced back to the 13C. The house was built in its present form in 1770. The house is of some architectural distinction, and has a notable collection of fur-

niture and paintings (privately owned; viewing by arrangement only).

## Germerode 3447 Meissner bei Eschwege 2
Hessen p.416□G 11

**Former Premonstratensian Monastery and former Monastery Church of St. Mary and St. Walburg:** After the foundation of the monastery (1144&5), building of the basilica with columns began; the original design was re-established in the course of thorough restoration work in the fifties. The crypt, the only one in N. Hessen, is in four sections. The interior is dominated by the oak galleries on the W. and N. sides. The organ casing, built in 1700 by Altstetter, the Mühlhausen organ builder, is carved in the 'gnarled' style.

## Geseke 4787
Nordrhein-Westfalen p.414□E 10

Geseke grew up on the Hellweg, one of the most important medieval routes between E. and N. in Germany. It is built on an oc-

*Former Kaiserpfalz palace, Gelnhausen*

tagonal ground plan; the ramparts remain in their entirety, the rest of the fortifications only in part. The town was granted its charter in 1217.

**Catholic Parish Church of St Peter/Stadtkirche** (Marktplatz): The church goes back to a 12C basilica with columns, but was largely built in the 13&14C and later much modified. The most important part of the interior is the pulpit (18C), which is lavishly decorated with reliefs and figures, the octagonal font (1576) and the earliest surviving European *reliquary monstrance* (12C).

**Catholic Parish Church of St. Cyriakus/Collegiate Church** (Auf dem Stift): The church was built in several phases in the 10–13C, and was much modified in the 19C, but the massive W. tower and the sturdy E. building with two towers remained largely untouched, and these are the most important exterior features of the church today. The oldest interior furnishings are the *pyx* (early 16C) and a wooden image of the Virgin (early 15C). The *high altar* (1717) and the two *side altars* (1729 and 1731) are striking: they are lavish works in marble and alabaster with columns and ornate decoration with figures and reliefs. The Romanesque chapterhouse, now used as a sacristy, is one of the former *monastery buildings* which survive.

**Houses**: Böddeker Hof (2 Wigburgastrasse): This is the oldest secular stone building in the town and it was built between 1350 and 1450. There are fine half-timbered houses at 1 Markt, 13 Hellweg (now a museum, see below), 40 Hellweg, 10 Kleiner Hellweg and 6 Kirchplatz (by the Collegiate Church).

**Städtisches Heimatmuseum/Hellweg Museum** (13 Hellweg): This local history museum, which has collections on the history of the town and the Land is now housed in the Dickmannsche Haus, which was built in 1664 for commercial purposes. In the interior are the courtroom, a kitchen with fireplaces and the barrel-vaulted cellar.

---

**Gettorf 2303**
Schleswig-Holstein                    p.412□H 2

**Protestant Church:** This early Gothic

*Shrine, Herrenhaus Gelting*

church (13C, completed in 1424) is one of the largest churches in the former Duchy of Schleswig. It has a fine interior, with a late Gothic carved altar (*c*.1510) and an ornately carved Renaissance pulpit by H.Gudewerdt the Elder (1598). The bronze font (1424) is also striking.

## Giessen 6300
Hessen                                    p.416□E 13

This old university town on the Lahn was badly damaged in the Second World War, but the most important buildings were rebuilt from the original plans. The university, now named after Justus Liebig, was founded in 1607.

**Former Augustinian Canonry Church** (in Schiffenberg, 5 km. SE): The church is presumed to date from the foundation of the former Augustinian Canonry in 1129, and it has remained essentially unchanged. It has a flat roof, fine Gothic vaulting in the E. chancel and seven arches on each side of the nave. On the S. side of the courtyard is the former *commandery*

*Premonstratensian canonness's church, Germerode*

(1493). The *new building* was added *c*.1700 in the W., and the *deanery* (1463) forms the W. end of the complex. It has been state property since 1809, and in 1972 Giessen took the buildings over from the Land.

**Neues Schloss** (Brandplatz): The half-timbered Neue Schloss was built in the 16C and restored in 1899–1907; it is not far from the Alte Schloss, which is largely in ruins; the keep (*c*.1330) was known as the 'Heidenturm'. The Neue Schloss has five oriels and a staircase tower (on the courtyard side). The university now uses the great hall on the ground floor, which has been divided up for this purpose. The *arsenal* (1585–9) forms the NE side of the courtyard of the Schloss.

**Museums:** *Liebigmuseum* (12 Liebig-strasse): The Liebig memorial is now in the rooms of the 'Chemical Laboratory', set up in 1824 in the former town guard house. *Oberhessisches Museum:* The department of pre- and early history and anthropology is in the *Wallenfelshaus* (opening late 1985); the department of local history and folklore is in the *Burgmannenhaus* (2 Georg-Schlosser-Strasse), a restored half-timbered building (1350); the department of painting and arts and crafts is in the *Alte Schloss* (2 Brandplatz), and includes a coin collection and a definitive collection of the works of the engraver J.G.Will (1715–1808).

**Giessen Stadttheater** (Berliner Platz): The theatre has its own company for the performance of plays, opera and operetta. It was built in 1907 and has 662 seats. The *Theaterstudio* is in an old cigar factory in the Kennedy-Platz; it was opened in 1974 and has 200 seats.

**Also worth seeing:** the *Leibsche Haus* was built in the 14C as a vassal house for the former Burg of Gleiberg (1197) and is one of the oldest half-timbered buildings in Germany (14C; badly damaged in 1944; rebuilt 1976&7). *University:* The Justus Liebig University was founded in 1607 and rebuilt in 1880; it is in the S. of the town. The building burned down in 1944 and was rebuilt in 1950–5. The *university library* has more than 400,000 volumes, including valuable manuscripts, incunabula and first editions. The *Röntgen memorial* (by the Stadttheater) was created in 1962 by E.F.Reuter. Wilhelm Conrad Röntgen (1845–1923) became professor in Giessen in 1879 and is buried in the *Alte Friedhof*.

## Gifhorn 3170

Lower Saxony         p.414☐J 7

The town of Gifhorn has stood since the 13C on this site at the confluence of the Aller and the Ise and on the crossroads of the Salzstrasse (from Lüneburg to Braunschweig) and the Kornstrasse (from Magdeburg to Celle).

**Schloss** (Schlossstrasse): The building of the Schloss, planned on a lavish scale and originally heavily fortified, started in 1525 during the joint reign of Otto and Ernst von Braunschweig, Dukes of Celle. The architects were M.Claren and his son who had made their reputation with the Schloss in Schwerin and the Fürstenhof in Wismar. The surviving parts of the building are the *gatehouse*, which shows the transition from the Gothic to the Renaissance style, the *staircase tower* (1568) the *Schloss chapel* (c.1547) and the adjacent *commandant's house*, in early Renaissance style. The Kavalierhaus is also worth seeing, along with several 16–18C houses.

**Museums:** *Kreisheimatmuseum* (in the Schloss): Collections on pre- and early history, folklore, and arts and crafts. *Wind- und Wassermühlen Museum* (by the Schloss lake): wind- and water-mills.

## Glücksburg 2392

Schleswig-Holstein        p.412☐G 1

**Schloss:** From the year 1209 a monastery stood on the site now occupied by the white-walled moated Schloss. Duke Johann von Sonderburg the Younger had the old building pulled down in 1583 and the present day building by N.Karies was completed in 1587. The Schloss was also a tem-

porary residence of the Danish King Friedrich VII, who died here in 1863. The otherwise severe façade is relieved by three gables. The state rooms are in the central section, and the living rooms are on the right and left. The interior was to a large extent refurbished in the baroque style (chapel 1717) and houses important collections, which can be seen in the *Schloss museum*. There is a *picture gallery*, a collection of *leather wall coverings*, an excellent *Gobelin collection*, and there are also exhibits on the development of the applied arts. The *Schloss library* has *c.*10,000 volumes.

## Glückstadt 2208

Schleswig-Holstein        p.414☐G 4

The Danish King and Duke of Holstein Christian IV, who founded Glückstadt in 1617, wanted to establish a town with a fortress and harbour to rival Hamburg. It is a perfect example of a town of the early modern era planned and built under royal patronage.

**Lutheran Church/Stadtkirche** (Am Markt): This whitewashed brick building with a single aisle was built in 1618–23 and modified to its present form in 1650&1. The square W. tower with its arched doorway and unusual baroque dome is a striking feature. The interior is also baroque; the most impressive furnishings are: the altar with alabaster work by H.Röhlke (1696), the choir screen (1708), the pulpit (17C), a font dating from 1641 and several brass chandeliers (c.1650). The galleries were painted in the 17C.

**Former Wasmer Palais** (36 Königstrasse): The palace, a building with three wings dating from 1728, stands out among the other houses belonging to officials and the nobility. The most striking features are the staircase and the banqueting hall (1729). The late baroque stucco work is by the Tessin artist A.Maini. *Also worth seeing:* Königshof (17C, rebuilt 1840), former

*Pulpit, Protestant church, Gettorf*

*Moated Schloss, Glücksburg*

Provianthaus (storehouse, 1705), Toll- und Zuchthaus (madhouse and prison 1738), harbour with row of historic houses.

**Detlefsen Museum** (43 Am Fleth): The museum is in a house built in 1631&2, the *Brockdorff Palais*. It deals with the history of the town, the cultural history of Elbmarschen, local crafts and also whaling and navigation.

## Gmund am Tegernsee 8184
Bavaria                          p.422□L 20

**Parish Church of St. Ägidius:** The present church was built in 1688–93 to plans by L.Sciasca; its predecessor had been badly damaged in the Thirty Years War. The paintings on the high altar are by G.Asam (1692) and the gilded wooden relief on the N. side altar is by I.Günther (1763).

## Goch 4180
Nordrhein-Westfalen              p.414□A 9

The town grew up at the junction of several Roman roads which led over the river Nier.

**Parish Church of St.Mary Magdalene** (10 Kirchhof): The church was largely completed in 1323, but went through a second phase of building in the late 14C and was also modified *c.*1460. Together with the churches in Kalkar (q.v.) and Kleve (q.v.) it is one of the most important brick churches of the N. lower Rhine. The building is dominated by the five-storey tower in the W. On the N. side are five gables. The main interior space is now the side aisle added in 1460; it is 170ft. long. The stellar vaulting is supported by late Gothic pillars. There is a notable 15C sandstone *tabernacle*.

**Also worth seeing:** The 14C *Steintor* is

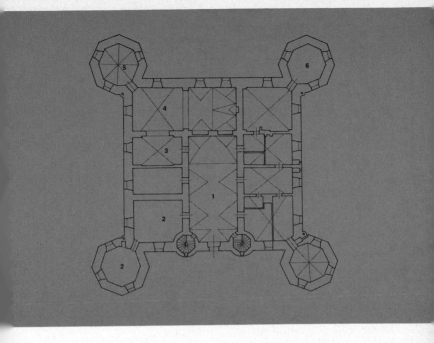

**Glücksburg, Schloss 1** Green entrance hall **2** Office **3** Ducal family pew **4** Chapel, design of 1717 **5** Archive **6** Prince's crypt

the last of the original 28 towers and gates of the *town fortifications* and houses the *Steintor Museum* with prehistoric and Roman archaeological finds, pewter vessels, church art, Gothic carved wooden figures and rare stained glass. *Haus zu den fünf Ringen* (1 Steinstrasse): The three-storey brick façade of this 16C house is topped by a stepped gable and flanked with square turrets.

## Göppingen 7320
Baden-Württemberg                    p.420☐G 18

Hermann Hesse spent part of his schooldays (1890&1) in Göppingen an der Fils. Extensive damage in 1425, 1782 and 1945 has led to continual rebuilding of the Hohenstaufen town, and consequent alteration of its appearance.

**Oberhofenkirche/Former Collegiate Church of St.Martin and St.Mary** (Ziegelstrasse): Building began in 1436, but the original plans have still not been realised. The influence of the Ulm (q.v.) school can be seen in many details. Various additions and renovations (especially in 1853, tower and wooden gallery) have changed the church considerably. Features which survive from the time of the church's foundation are the wall paintings in the chancel (1449), the oldest surviving picture of the Hohenstaufen Burg of 1470 in the transept, the choir stalls (1500) and a carved crucifix (*c.*1520).

**Museums:** *Städtisches Museum* (36 Wühlestrasse): The museum is housed in the former town Schloss of the Freiherr von Liebenstein, a half-timbered building dating from 1536. The museum specialises in

*Red Room, Schloss Glücksburg*

the history of the town and the Hohenstaufens. *Schönhengster Archiv und Volkskundliche Sammlungen* (33 Nördliche Ringstrasse): collections and documentation on the Schönhengstgau, formerly the largest German-speaking enclave in Bohemia.

**Theatres:** *Stadthalle* (41 Blumenstrasse): Touring companies perform in the Grosse Saal, which has 813 seats and in the Kleine Saal with 437 seats. *Deutsches Theater* (11 Theaterplatz): built in 1889&90 by Schnitger; it has 640 seats.

**Also worth seeing:** *Protestant Parish Church* (Pfarrstrasse): This plain church was built in 1618&19 to plans by H.Schickhardt; it has a painted wooden ceiling. The tower was not added until 1838. *Schloss* (25 Pfarrstrasse): This Renaissance building with four wings dates from 1555–68 and was built by A.Tretsch and M.Berwart. The façades were much altered in the 18C,

and only three of the four staircases remain. The main staircase or 'Rebensteige' (1562) has ornate reliefs of plants and animals and is a mixture of Gothic and Renaissance design. The *Rathaus* (1783) with its two wings is built on neoclassical lines.

## Goslar 3380

Lower Saxony         p.414☐H 9

Goslar, now a popular holiday resort in the Harz, has always been an important town and has had an eventful history. The discovery *c.*968 of silver in the Rammelsberg, which made Goslar 'the treasury of the German Emperors' was crucial in the decision to build an imperial palace. After the imperial period the town was dominated by merchants; it became an imperial bailiwick as early as 1290 and a free imperial town in 1340. The merchants encouraged mining and started a second major period of building, which produced a number of important buildings *c*.1500. The town got into economic difficulties when the Guelphs took over the mine, and because of fires in 1728 and 1780.

**Former Church of the Cistercian Convent of Neuwerk** (Rosentorstrasse): The oldest parts of the church (in the E.) date from the 12C, and the nave and the vaulting in the side aisles were added in 1200 –50. The most striking external features are the two W. towers, and lavish ornamentation and exceptional sculpture make it one of the most beautiful churches in Lower Saxony. The most important interior furnishings are the late Romanesque painting in the chancel (*c*.1225) and the choir screen (*c*.1225); the pulpit was incorporated into the organ loft in 1950. The convent building, a fine half-timbered construction, dates from 1719.

**Protestant Parish Church of St.Peter and St.Paul** (Frankenbergerplatz): The parish church became part of the Convent of Mary Magdalene in 1236. An earlier church was replaced by a new building in 1140–50; this building was later much altered and extended, and then disfigured in 1787 by the demolition of its towers. Points

of connection with the town wall can be seen on the left and right of the W. building. The tympanum in the S. doorway, the columns of the nuns' gallery and the wall paintings which have survived in outline on the upper clerestory of the nave are reminders of the Romanesque first phase of the building. The baroque altar (1675) is by H.Lessen the Elder. The gallery balustrade was completed in 1690, and the pulpit is by J.Lessen the Younger (1698).

**Catholic Parish Church of St.Jakobi** (Jakobi-Kirchhof): The W. tower was built in 1140 on to a pre-1073 basilica and at the beginning of the 16C the N. and S. aisles were added. The original Romanesque design was replaced to a large extent by Gothic elements in this process. The most striking interior feature is the famous *picture of the Virgin* by H. Witten (*c*.1525). The wall pictures in the chancel (13C), the stone relief on the W. wall of the N. aisle (Coronation of the Virgin, *c*.1513), the organ (1640), the font (1592) and the ornately carved pews are notable features.

**Protestant Parish Church of St. Cosmas and St.Demian/Marktkirche** (Marktkirchhof): The N. tower was built

*Gmund, view*

*Oberhofenkirche, Göppingen*

in its present form after a fire in 1593, and after the fire of 1844 both towers again had to be renewed; the style of the towers conceals the fact that the basilica dates from as early as 1150. The most important interior feature is the stained glass showing the martyrdom of St. Cosmas and St. Demian (*c.*1250). The bronze font by M.Karsten (1573), the Renaissance pulpit (1581) and a fine altar panel (1659) are also notable.

**Imperial Palace with Ulrich Chapel and Cathedral Porch** (Kaiserbleek): The palace at the foot of the Rammelsberg was built in the 11C as a symbol of imperial power. The first assembly of princes took place here in 1009 at the invitation of Heinrich II. Emperor Heinrich III (1039 –56) was responsible for the impressive dimensions of the typically Romanesque buildings, which have largely survived until today. At its centre is the *Reichs- und Kaisersaal*, which occupies the whole of the upper floor of the former palas and is the largest room in a German imperial palace. Pictures by H.Wislicenus (1879–97) show episodes from German history. On the S. side the two-storey *chapel of St. Ulrich*, also a Romanesque masterpiece, is attached to the main building. Its lower storey is in the form of a Greek cross, and the upper floor is octagonal. Beneath the memorial (*c.*1300) to the founder Heinrich III the Emperor's heart is kept. The Chapter of St.Simon and St.Judas, the so-called Dom, 'the Chapel of the Empire' is also part of the palace complex. The only part of the Dom which remains — it was demolished in 1820 — is the porch, in which the imperial throne (11C) can be seen. The throne has bronze arms and is a masterpiece of medieval craftsmanship. Kaiser Wilhelm I sat on this throne to open the first Reichstag of the new German Reich in Berlin in 1871.

**Rathaus** (Markt): The 15C Town Hall

shows the power of the bourgeoisie, who since the 13C had taken over the role of the Emperors in Goslar. The central feature is the late Gothic *Ratsherrenzimmer* (council chamber) with unique wall paintings, some of the most important works of art in Lower Saxony. The upper storey is reached by an open air staircase (1537). The Romanesque *Marktbrunnen* (1st half of the 13C) in front of the Town Hall is notable: it has two large bronze basins surmounted by an imperial eagle.

**Museums:** *Goslarer Museum* (1 Königstrasse): Artistic and cultural history, animal life in the Harz, coins. *Sammlung Adam* (1 Gemeindehof): manuscripts, pictures, coins and 5–20C documents, collections on mining, forging and silver-mining in Goslar. *Mönchehaus* (3 Mönchestrasse): collection of modern art.

**Also worth seeing:** *Siemenshaus* (12 Schreiberstrasse): This splendid building, which dates from 1693, is the seat of the Siemens family of industrialists. It is one of the most important merchant houses in Goslar. Of the *guild houses* built at the height of the bourgeois era in Goslar only two survive in reasonable condition. They are the clothiers' house (known as *Kaiserworth*, am Markt) and the *Bäckergildehaus* (corner of the Markt and Bergstrasse), both of which date from *c*.1500. The clothiers' house has been known as Kaiserworth since the 14C because of the carved figures of Emperors standing on corbels in the narrow late Gothic niches. The corbels are supported by various figures; the naked man ('Dukatenmännchen') is particularly unusual. Many *private houses* survive from the medieval period; they are to be found above all in Marktstrasse, Gosestrasse, Schreiberstrasse and Königstrasse; these are mostly stone houses. There are fine half-timbered houses in Schreiberstrasse, Gosestrasse, Bergstrasse, Bäckerstrsse, Kreuzstrasse and Kornstrasse. *Town fortifications:* The massive fortifications with the *Breite Tor* and the *Rosentor* were built *c*.1500, principally to protect the town from the Dukes of Braunschweig-Wolfenbüttel.

**Environs:** *Former Canonry of St.Peter* (on the Petersberg, E. of Goslar): Foundations of a *c*.1050 canonry. *Former Augustinian Canonry of St.George* (on the Georgenberg, N. of Goslar): foundations of a canonry completed in 1150 with an 11C Münster

*Cistercian convent, Neuwerk*

*Marktkirche*

on the Aachen pattern. *Former Augustinian Canonry in Grauhof* (1701–17). *Ruin of the Former Augustinian Canonry of St. Mary* (12C) (in Reichenberg). *Herzberg* (10 km. E.): This little town at the edge of the Harz is worth seeing for its fine *half-timbered buildings* and for *Burg Herzberg.*

---

## Gössweinstein 8551
Bavaria                                    p.418☐K 15

---

**Catholic Parish and Pilgrimage Church** (Balthasar-Neumann-Strasse): This impressive Balthasar Neumann church was consecrated in 1739 after a building period of only nine years. Its connections with a Holy Trinity pilgrimage can be traced back to the 15C. The most important feature of the interior decoration is the stucco work by the Bamberg master F.J.Vogel. The high altar was designed by J.M.Küchel. The altar of the cross and the Mary altar are worth seeing, as are the courtyard (also by Küchel) and the adjacent cemetery with its massive monument to the parents of Prince Bishop Ernst von Mengersdorf.

**Burg** (1 Burgstrasse): The originally Gothic Burg was rebuilt in its present neo-Gothic style at the end of the 19C.

**Environs: Kohlstein** (2.5 km. N.): In the 18C *Schloss chapel of St.Maria* of the beautifully sited 15C Schloss are a fine altar and choir stalls from the studio of G.Reuss.
**Ebermannstadt** (15 km. W.): The furnishings of the *Catholic Filial Church of the Birth of Our Lady* include works by F.A.Thomas and G.Reuss and a Madonna with halo (1797) by F.Theiler.

---

## Göttingen 3400
Lower Saxony                               p.418☐H 10

---

Göttingen grew up at the junction of two old trading routes, the Hellweg and the Königsstrasse. In 1737 the town became a centre of learning because of the university founded there by the Elector Georg August of Hannover, after whom it is named. The university brought many famous artists and scholars to the town: the mathematicians and physicists Abraham Gotthelf Kästner and Georg Christoph Lichtenberg, the poets Gottfried August Bürger and Friedrich Wilhelm Gotter, Johann Heinrich Voss, the translator of Homer, and also Wilhelm and Alexander von Humboldt, the brothers Grimm, Heinrich Heine and Hoffmann von Fallersleben. Göttingen was also the centre of the Hain-Bund (1772), an emotional protest movement against the rationalism of the Enlightenment.

**Protestant Church of St. Jakobi** (Jakobikirchhof): Building started in 1350 and was completed in 1433 with the extension of the tower, which is 243 ft. high. The church was rebuilt after a fire in 1555. The most important feature of the lavish interior decoration is an *altarpiece* (1402).

**Protestant Church of St. Albanus** (Geismarstrasse, near the Stadthalle): The most striking feature of this church, dating to a large extent from the 15C, is the

*Cathedral porch, imperial throne*

*altarpiece* showing the beheading of Albanus and eight scenes from the life of the Virgin Mary. It was created by H.von Geismar in 1499.

**Protestant Church of St.Johannis** (Am Markt): The most impressive feature of this church, started in the 13C and completed by the addition of the two towers in the 15C, is the massive undecorated W. façade. The plain expanse of masonry stretches unbroken to the top of the walls of the nave; the doorway was pierced at a later date.

**Protestant Church of Our Lady** (Groner Torstrasse): This 14C building was later much extended and the bell tower was not added until the 15C. The *altar panels* painted in the 16C in the workshop of B.Kastrop are a striking feature; the individual panels are set up in various parts of the church. There is a gatehouse between the church and the prebendary built in the 14C for the Knights of the Teutonic Order.

**Paulinerkirche/former Dominican Monastery** (Paulinerstrasse): The monastery was completed in 1304, and the church in 1331. In 1737 the university moved into the monastery buildings, which later became the university library. The church has an unusually spacious interior which is severe in design and reminiscent of the churches of the mendicant Order in central Germany.

**Altes Rathaus** (Markt): The historic Town Hall, which has survived in its original form, is the dominant building in the Marktplatz. The larger N. part and the S. extension stand in stark contrast to each other. The loggia at the entrance to the S. building is striking. Inside the building the Rathaushalle, the Ratskeller and the guardroom are worth seeing. The Gänseliesel fountain (1901) is in front of the Town Hall.

**University buildings:** The new building in the N. of the town brought together many of the departments of the university, founded in 1734 and formally opened in 1737. At first the university used the *Dominican monastery* (see Paulinerkirche) and then spread to buildings in various parts of the town. In 1816 the *observatory* was completed, and in 1837 the *Aula (great hall) building* (1 Wilhelmsplatz) was

*Kaiserpfalz with Ulrichskapelle*

opened. The *lecture theatres* (2 Weender Landstrasse) followed in 1865.

**Niedersächsisches Staats- und Universitätsbibliothek** (State and university library, Prinzenstrasse): The library has well over 1.5 million volumes (including more than 10,000 manuscripts, 6,000 incunabula and a Gutenberg Bible (*c.*1455), and is one of the largest in the German-speaking world.

**Museums:** *Städtisches Museum* (7–8 Ritterplan): in the Hardenberg Hof, a Renaissance palace, are collections on pre- and early history, the history of the Land, the town, the university and student institutions, and also faience work, porcelain, pewter, weapons, musical instruments and graphics. *Kunstsammlung der Universität Göttingen* (10 Hospitalstrasse): important paintings, graphics and sculpture from Italy, the Netherlands and Germany from the 14–20C.

**Theatres:** *Deutsches Theater* (11 Theaterplatz): This theatre was built in 1889&90 by the Oldenburg court architect Schnittger. *Junges Theater* (1 Hospitalstrasse): This communication and activity centre with its large and small auditoria was set up in the former Otfried Müller House (mid 19C). The *Junges Theater* founded in 1957 is also housed here. There is an annual *Handel Festival* in Göttingen.

**Also worth seeing:** *Houses:* The oldest surviving house in Lower Saxony (25 Rote Strasse; 1276); there are also fine houses in Johannisstrasse (No. 33), Burgstrasse (No. 1) and in the Barfüsserstrasse (No. 12). They all date from *c.*1540 and are largely unaltered. *Bismarckhäuschen and ramparts* (Wall): All that remains of the fortifications is this tower in which future Chancellor Otto von Bismarck lived as a student in 1833.

**Environs: Nikolausberg** (6 km. NE): former Augustinian Nunnery Church (12C), with a heavily restored high altar (*c.*1490); the painted N. altar dates from *c.*1400.
**Bursfelde** (24 km. W.): This *Benedictine*

*monastery* on the Weser, founded by H.von Northeim in 1093, was the spiritual centre of the *Bursfelde Congregation* under Abbot J.Hagen (1439–69); this was a group of monasteries wishing to live more closely to the original Benedictine Rule.
**Plesse** (8 km. N.): the ruined Burg Plesse has a massive 11C keep.

---

### Greifenstein 6349
Hessen                                    p.416☐E 12

**Burg Greifenstein:** The Burg, which is in ruins, originally consisted of a keep and outer works. The central part of the site is 12C. The Burg was rebuilt in its present form in 1919, and has housed the German bell museum since 1973. The grounds have been redesigned on various occasions. The *Burg Chapel of St.Katharina* is now the Protestant parish church.

---

### Gross-Gerau 6080
Hessen                                    p.416☐E 14

**Protestant Parish Church/former Church of Our Lady** (Kirchplatz): The new building dating from 1470–90 burned down in the Second World War, but has been rebuilt using the old outer walls. The W. doorway with a 15C middle-Rhine Madonna on its central column is notable.

**Rathaus** (Frankfurter Strasse): A half-timbered building dating from 1578&9. The building has been much extended and restored and has lost its original appearance. There are other *half-timbered buildings* in Mainzer Strase, Burggraben and Kirchstrasse. In the Town Hall is the *Heimatmuseum* with exhibits on the history of the town, archaeological finds and a collection of household implements.

**Environs: Dornberg** (5 km. S.): The 12C Schloss residence of the Counts of Katzenelnbogen is now used as a conference centre.

*Homage room, Rathaus, Goslar* ▷

*Winged altar, Jakobikirche, Göttingen*

## Grossgründlach = 8500 Nürnberg 1
Bavaria                                    p.422 □ K 16

**Parish Church:** There are eight windows in the parish church (1681) from the cycle created by H.B.Grien from 1504 onwards for the cloisters of the Carmelite Monastery in Nuremberg. The *baroque Schloss* on the outskirts is worth seeing; it was built in 1685–95 and is surrounded by a landscaped park.

## Günzburg 8870
Bavaria                                    p.422 □ H 19

**Frauenkirche** (Frauenplatz): D.Zimmermann built the church from 1736–41. Many of the details show parallels with the church in Wies. The decoration was carried out by artists of distinction: the frescos are by A.Enderle (1741).

**Also worth seeing:** The *Schloss* (1580) in which the Austrian administration was housed until 1805 stands above the town. In the Schlosskapelle the *W. chapel* (1754) by Zimmermann's pupil J.Dossenberger is important. The frescos are by A.Enderle. The *former mint* opposite the Schloss and several houses were also designed by Dossenberger. The *Heimatmuseum* (2 Rathausgasse) has exhibits on pre- and early history, folklore, ceramics and sculpture.

## Gutach/Schwarzwaldbahn 7611
Baden-Württemberg                          p.420 □ D 19

**Vogtsbauernhof Open Air Museum:** Several Schwarzwald farmhouses are grouped around the thatched *Gutacher house*. The houses date largely from the 16&17C and show old furniture and farm equipment. All the machines on the site are water driven and still work.

## Hagen 5800

Nordrhein-Westfalen                    p.416□C 10

**Jugendstil buildings**: (*Jugendstil* is the German version of art nouveau.) At the beginning of this century Hagen, through the initiative of the industrialist and patron Karl Ernst Osthaus, was a centre of early modern art; architects like H. van der Helde and P.Behrens, and the painter Thorn Prikker were some of the artists who lived and worked here, and their thinking and artistic attitudes have had a marked influence on the townscape. A clear example is the *Hauptbahnhof* with its monumental entrance hall *windows* depicting 'The Obeisance of the Crafts before the Artist', Thorn Prikker's first work as an artist in glass, and the *Eduard Müller Crematorium*, an important Jugendstil building by Peter Behrens (in Hagen-Delstern). In the cemetery is the grave of the painter Ch.Rohlf with a plain tablet by E.Mataré and a bronze sculpture of Christ teaching by Ernst Barlach. Osthaus had plans for a *Hohenhagen Garden City* which was to be in the modern suburb of Emst. The plans were only partially realised, but the completed projects were the work of artists of distinction: from 1906 onwards the row of houses known as the *Stirnband* (Lauweriks) and the *Hohenhof* (van der Velde) were built. The Hohenhof, which is now owned by the town, has been re-stored and contains some of the surviving furnishings designed by van der Velde. The interior decoration includes contributions by Hodler, Vuillard and Matisse. The painting of the study was carried out to designs by Thorn Prikker, who was also responsible for the glazing of the staircase.

**Schloss Hohenlimburg** (20 Alter Schlossweg): The Schloss includes parts of the Burg founded in 1230, which can still be recognised in the present building. The Schloss was frequently modified, especially in the mid 18C. The *outer works* date from the 14C along with the outer courtyard, which has been rebuilt to an irregular plan and has a surrounding wall. The central feature is the *inner courtyard*, which has a high wall with wall passages and turrets. The inner court also includes the *old* and the *new palas*, in which the *Heimatmuseum* is housed. The fine *half-timbered oriel* and the wrought-iron *fountain* are picturesque features.

**Museums:** The *Karl-Ernst-Osthaus-Museum* (73 Hochstrasse) was originally privately founded by Osthaus as the Folkwang Museum, but the outstanding modern art collection was acquired by the city of Essen (q.v.) in 1922. The present museum has a collection of 20C art. The *entrance hall* is the only surviving part of van der Velde's interior. In the *Hagen Open Air Museum* (in Hagen-Selbecke) technical devices of historical importance have been collected from various parts of Germany.

**Theatre:** The *Städtische Bühnen* (65 Elberfelder Strasse) have their own company for the performance of opera and operetta on an excellently equipped stage; the auditorium has 804 seats.

---

**Haigerloch 7452**
Baden-Württemberg                    p.420☐E 19

**Schloss and Schloss Church:** The plain, unadorned buildings make an effect solely because of their situation on rising ground and their unusual grouping. The Schloss dates mainly from 1580, when it was built using the surviving parts of a *c*.1200 Burg. Baroque rebuilding gave the Schloss its present appearance. Parts of the building, restored in 1975–81, are now used as an hotel and for exhibitions and seminars. The *Schloss church* (now the Catholic parish church of St.Trinitatis) was built in 1584 –1609 in mock Gothic style. The excellent *rococo stucco work* in the interior is by a Wessobrunn master. Only a wrought-iron *choir screen* and the *c*.1500 *crucifix* in front of it survive of the old furnishings. The *high altar* suffers from early baroque congestion. The other seven stucco altars were added in the mid 18C.

**Pilgrimage Church of St.Anne:** The church was built in 1753–5 on an artificial terrace on the E. edge of the upper town, probably to a design by J.M.Fischer, the architect responsible for the famous baroque buildings in Zwiefalten (q.v.) and Ottobeuren (q.v.). It is a hall church without towers and with slightly protruding transepts and a short choir with a semi-circular apse. J.M.Feuchtmayer was reponsible for the excellent *stucco decoration* and the design of the side altars. The *frescos* were painted by M.von Ow. On the *high altar* is a pilgrimage image of the Virgin and Child with St.Anne dating from the second half of the 14C.

**Atommuseum** (in the former Bierkeller): The atomic researchers Heisenberg, von Weizsäcker, Bothe and Wirz attempted in 1945 to produce energy by splitting the atom in the first nuclear reactor in this cellar cut into the rock.

---

**Hamburg 2000**
Freie und Hansestadt Hamburg        p.412☐H 4

At the centre of Hamburg is a lake: the Alster river was dammed as early as the 13C and around the lake which was formed are set the Kunsthalle, St.Jacobi, St.Petri, the Rathaus, the Jungfernstieg, the Gänsemarkt and, a little further away, the opera house. Hamburg, originally 'Hammaburg', was founded in the 9C by Emperor Ludwig the Pious on the sandy spit of land between the Elbe and the Alster. The Pressehaus, St.Petri, and St. Nikolai stand on this site today, and the tower in which the 11C Bishop Bezelin lived was also here; its foundations can still be seen in the cellar of the building at 10 Speersort. The Hanseatic League developed in the 13C as the result of a community of interest with Lübeck. In the 17C Hamburg was a centre of international trade and the most powerful fortress in Europe. The city's reputation as a commercial centre was confirmed in the 19C despite the fact that a quarter of the old Hanseatic buildings burned down in the 'Great Fire' of 1842. Heavy damage was also suffered in the Second World War. Hamburg has many famous connections: G.E.Lessing, who is commemorated in the Gänsemarkt, was literary manager of the Deutsches Nationaltheater from 1767. Matthias Claudius published his 'Wandsbeker Bote' here from 1771–5. Klopstock completed 'Messias' in Hamburg in 1773, and Heine was trained as a banker in his uncle's business from 1816–18. Hebbel completed the tragedies 'Judith' and 'Genoveva' here, and H.H.Jahn played an important part in the town's literary life in the 20C. C.von Ossietzky, the publisher of the pacifist periodical 'Weltbühne' and Wolfgang Borchert were born in Hamburg, as were the composers Mendelssohn and Brahms. Long before them Handel, Telemann and C.P.E.Bach worked in

*Schlosskirche, Haigerloch*

Hamburg, which still has a flourishing cultural life. The university was founded in 1919.

**Protestant Parish Church of St.Petri** (Mönckebergstrasse): This is the oldest church in Hamburg, and its green spire set on red brick walls has become an emblem of the town. Although the present building is largely neo-Gothic (1844–9) a fine old *stone Madonna* (c.1470) and Meister Bertram's famous *Grabow Altar* remain of the older furnishings. The altar is now in the Hamburg Kunsthalle.

**Protestant Parish Church of St.Jacobi** (Steinstrasse): This 13–15C Gothic hall church is on the same sandy spit of land as the Petri church and only a few hundred yards away; it was much extended in the Renaissance and baroque periods. After the Second World War only the outer walls and a stump of the spire remained. The *furnishing* had been put in store, however,

and survived, including the baroque *pulpit*, three late Gothic *altars* (of which the best is the Lukas altar), and the unique *organ* by Arp Schnitger, which is now back in the church; the baroque front of the latter masterpiece had to be restored.

**Protestant Parish Church of St. Katharinen** (bei den Mühren): This church, first mentioned in the 13C, was largely built in the 14&15C, and lavishly decorated in the Renaissance and baroque periods. In 1944 the church burned down completely, but its most distinctive feature, the tower with green copper spires, was rebuilt on the 16C model. A few older works of art were added to the *modern furnishings* (crucifix c.1300, and a c.1400 St. Katharina).

**Protestant Parish Church of St. Michaelis** (Neanderstrasse): This broad oval building with its enormous tower (the *Michel* is 433 ft. high and a symbol of the town) is the most important surviving Protestant church in Germany designed to lay emphasis on preaching. It is baroque, and after the fire of 1906 and its destruction in the Second World War it was built for a third time to the original plans; (architects J.L.Prey and E.G.Sonnin (1754–7)).

**St.Nicolai tower** (Ost-West-Strasse): Only the neo-Gothic tower of the former Protestant parish church of St.Nicolai survived the Second World War; the church was completed in 1882 and, in a fit of romantic nationalism, the tower was based on Cologne Cathedral and the Münster in Freiburg. At 475 ft. it is one of the highest church towers in Germany. The space under the tower is a *Memorial for the Victims of Persecution and War 1933–45.*

**Horner Weg Protestant Trinity Church:** An old village church bombed in the Second World War was replaced by a *modern building* which consciously avoids any hint of conventional church architecture. The bell tower is a tall concrete framework shaped like a letter A at the end of a low steeply sloping oval drum with a copper roof. It was built in 1953–7 by the Munich architect R.Riemerschmid.

**Billwerder Protestant Trinity Church** (Allermöhe): This 17C half-timbered hall church is typical of a number of *village churches* in the Hamburg area. The *wooden barrel-vaulted roof* was painted in the 18C with clouds, angels and scenes from parables. The *altarpiece* is an unusual mannerist work with one main and seven subsidiary scenes carved in relief from copper engravings.

**Christianskirche** (Klopstockplatz in Altona): This church at the beginning of the Elbchaussee is an 18C *brick building* with a rounded mansard roof. It stands in a *cemetery* which has been turned into a small public park. Among the neoclassical *tombstones* is the grave of the poet and dramatist Klopstock (1727–1804) and his two wives.

**Krameramtshäuser** (11 Krayenkamp): This is a piece of old Hamburg as it was before the Second World War and the rebuilding of the old town in the 30s. The *brick and half-timbered houses* were built in 1676 for the widows of former members of the Grocers' Company.

**Nicolaifleet** (35–49 Deichstrasse): This

*Lukasaltar, St.Jacobi*

*St. Michaelis*

*Dreifaltigkeitskirche*

is a complete row of 17&18C gabled houses which have *half-timbering* on their *waterfront* side. The sides facing the street are solidly built in stone and some have simple decorative gables.

**Rathausmarkt:** This group of buildings near the Kleine Alster on the site of two former monasteries is reminiscent to a limited extent of St. Mark's Square in Venice. The *Rathaus* (built by an architects' co-operative from 1886–97) is a lavish municipal and representatve building with staircases and rooms in various imitative styles; the late neoclassical (1839–41) *Börse* (Stock Exchange) behind the Rathaus in the Adolphsplatz is architecturally more satisfying.

**Kontorhäuser** (office buildings): These were built after the First World War between the Steinstrasse and the Messberg by city architect F.Schumacher. The involvement of F.Höger in this project was

significant: he applied traditional brick building techniques to modern, multi-storey office buildings; the most striking example of this N. German brick expressionism is the ten-storey *Chilehaus*, built by F.Höger in 1922–4; its pointed end on the Buchardplatz looks rather like a gigantic ocean liner.

**Gasthof Stadt Hamburg** (Hamburg-Bergedorf, 2 Sachsentor): This was built *c.*1600 as an inn and is now a restaurant. The *half-timbering* is lavishly decorated with rosettes and figures and the bricks between the timbers form elegant patterns. A gabled building giving vehicular access to the courtyard was added *c.*1700 and the whole building was moved back 23 ft. in 1958–9 as part of a road-widening scheme.

**Palmaille** (in Altona): Some of the *neoclassical palaces* survive which once stood alongside a court, originally 700 yards long, intended for the game of 'palla a maglio (an Italian version of croquet); they were built *c.*1800 by the Dane C.F.Hansen (Nos 49, 112, 116 and 120).

**Elbvororte** (suburbs by the Elbe): From the beginning to the middle of the 19C rich citizens of Hamburg built white-painted villas and country houses with park-like gardens high above the banks of the Elbe; they stretch from the beginning of the *Elbchaussee* through the suburbs of *Othmarschen*, *Kleinflottbek* and *Nienstedten* as far as *Blankenese*, and many of them were designed by the architect C.F.Hansen. One of the finest is the *Jenischhaus* in the Jenischpark (50 Baron-Voght-Strasse), which was built to an amended plan by K.F.Schinkel. It is now a *museum* of 16–20C domestic life and furniture.

**Cemeteries:** The *Ohlsdorfer Friedhof* is one of the largest parkland cemeteries in the world; it is over two miles long and three quarters of a mile wide. It was laid out in its present form in 1897–1913, and extended on many occasions. Among the many mausoleums, gravestones and sculptures is G.Marcks' *Memorial to the Victims of Bombing in Hamburg* (1950–1). The *Judenfriedhof* (Jewish cemetery) laid out in

1611, in Altona (Königstrasse) also survived the Second World War. The memorials are decorated in styles appropriate to their period.

**Museums:** *Kunsthalle* (Glockengiesserwall): This old brick building on the site of a former defensive wall is a good example of the imitation Italian Renaissance style (1863–8); the extensions on the Hauptbahnhof side were built in 1914–19. The collection of paintings includes masterpieces from the 14C to the present day and is one of the best in Germany; there are also remarkable collections of sculpture, coins and graphics. *Museum für Kunst und Gewerbe* (Steintorplatz): Painting and sculpture from the Middle Ages to the rococo period, antique art, prehistoric and European implements and Far Eastern applied art. The carpet, tapestry and textile collection is particularly fine. *Museum für Hamburgische Geschichte* (24 Holstenwall): Built in 1913–23 by the Hamburg city architect F.Schumacher, whose exemplary town-planning skills gave whole areas of the town their unmistakeable appearance; it contains collections on local history, models of docks and railways, costume, the Hamburg guilds, domestic

*Panorama with Rathaus*

culture, theatre and academic life. *Hamburgisches Museum für Völkerkunde* (14 Bindestrasse): Sections on the anthropology of Africa, Eurasia, Central and South America, the Far East and the Pacific. *Barlach-Museum* (Jenisch Park): contains the famous H.F.Reemtsma collection. *Altona Museum* (Altona, 23 Museumstrasse): This is devoted to NW German popular art and navigation. Notable open air museums: Rieck-Haus (284 Curslacker Deich), Museumsdorf Volksdorf (46 Im Alten Dorfe) and the am Kieckeberg open air museum in Ehestorf.

**Theatres:** *Staatsoper* (34 Grosse Theaterstrasse): The first permanent opera house in Germany was opened in Hamburg in 1678 in the Gänsemarkt, quite near to the present building. The acoustics are excellent in the new opera house, built in 1953–5; the otherwise austere auditorium has unusual tiered balconies. The *Deutsches Schauspielhaus* (by the Hauptbahnhof, 39 Kirchenallee) continues the tradition of the German National Theatre founded in Hamburg in 1767, for which Lessing wrote his famous 'Hamburgische Dramaturgie' from 1767 – 9. Also: *Thaliatheater* (Alstertor), *Kammerspiele* (9 –11 Hartungstrasse), *Theater im Zimmer* (in a pretty, neoclassical building at 30 Alsterschaussee) and the *Ohnsorg-Theater* (22–5 Grosse Bleichen), which presents plays in Hamburg dialect.

**Also worth seeing:** *Pöseldorf* with its old villas, antique shops, narrow streets and pleasant eating and drinking houses. Down the Elbe from Blankenese is the famous *Schulau ship-greeting station* in *Wedel*, the birthplace of the sculptor and dramatist Barlach, with a 16C *Roland*.

**Environs:** The fruit- and vegetablegrowing area of the Vierlande, the Altes Land (downstream on the Elbe) with its old farm houses; Altengamme, Neuengamme and Ochsenwerder, with their fine village churches.

---

**Hameln 3250**
Lower Saxony                                  p.414□G 8

This medieval town on the right bank of the Weser owes its early economic expansion and importance to this favourable geographical position. It started *c.*800 as a

*Monument to the dead by G. Marcks, Ohlsdorf graveyard*

monastery around which a trading settlement soon formed. Organised expansion of the town began *c.*1200, and there was a great deal of building during the prosperous period from the Middle Ages to the Reformation. The most striking buildings are those in the *Weser Renaissance* style. The town is known in literature through the legend of the Pied Piper.

**Protestant Münster Church of St. Bonifatius** (am Münsterkirchhof): The oldest parts of the much rebuilt and extended Münster are the late-12C octagonal Romanesque *lantern tower* and the *crypt*, which must date from about 100 years earlier. The rebuilding of the nave to form a unified Gothic *hall* began in the middle of the 13C; the *Elisabeth Chapel* was also added to the transept at this time. All that remains of the old *furnishings* are the founder's stone on the crossing column with the date of foundation according to legend (712), a relief tablet with the Virgin Crowned by Angels (1415) and a Gothic tabernacle on the high altar.

**Protestant Church of St. Nikolai** (Markt): The original Romanesque church was greatly extended in the 13C and the narrow spire was added in 1511. After the destruction of the Second World War it was rebuilt as a mock basilica with gables on its S. side.

**The Osterstrasse:** The Osterstrasse has many fine old *houses*. The *Hochzeitshaus* (2 Osterstrasse) was built in 1610–17 for solemn and festive municipal occasions. On the ground floor were the public scales, the apothecary's shop and the wine shop, and on the third floor was the town armoury. The most striking features of the building are the gables decorated with scrolls. The *Pied Piper Plays* are enacted from the end of May to the end of September on the terrace between the Hochzeitshaus and S.Nikolai. The *Rattenfängerhaus* (Pied Piper House) did not acquire the name until the 19C; it is now a restaurant. It has particularly detailed design and lavish decoration: the gable is densely covered with embellishments of all kinds. The *Demptersche Haus* in the market place is much more austere. The tall, half-timbered triangular gable with symmetrically carved bays only has sculptural decoration on the top of the two-storey oriel. The *Leistsche Haus* contains the *Heimatmuseum* (9 Osterstrasse). The most striking feature of this

*State opera house*

building is a two-storey oriel (Utlucht). There is a figure of Lucretia on the gable, and the relief frieze between the storeys represents the virtues. The most important items in the museum are concerned with the legend of the Pied Piper.

**Theatres:** There are touring productions by various companies in the *Weserbergland-Festhalle* in the Rathausplatz.

---

### Hämelschenburg = Emmerthal 3254
Lower Saxony                                p.414☐G 9

---

**Schloss:** The Hämelschenburg is the foremost example of the so-called *Weser Renaissance* style. The horseshoe-shaped *S. wing*, which faces the street, was begun in 1588 and is architecturally the most interesting feature. The division into storeys is emphasised by horizontal bands, an oriel marks the central point and the façade is enlivened by ashlar decoration and copper gargoyles. The *courtyard* with octagonal *staircase towers* is reached via a sloping bridge and a *magnificent door* (1613) bearing the name and arms of von Klencke, who commissioned the building. The former Schloss chapel, dating from the 16C, is now the *Protestant village church*. In the sanctuary is the wooden *Renaissance memorial tomb* of the man who commissioned the Schloss, which is still owned by the family. Above the slab there is a late Gothic representation of the *Garden of Paradise* in lime wood, showing Our Lady surrounded by 6 Holy Women (late 15C).

---

### Hanau 6450
Hessen                                       p.416☐F 14

---

The older parts of Hanau, the town where the first German faience was manufactured, were largely destroyed in the Second World War. It is the birthplace of the brothers Grimm (bronze memorial in the Neustädter Marktplatz) and has for centuries been the centre of the goldsmith's art.

**Protestant Marienkirche** (Altstädter

*Pied Piper's house, Hameln*

Markt): This former Cistercian monastery church was rebuilt after the Second World War, but the effect of a 15C Gothic hall was not entirely achieved. The valuable *stained glass* portrays St. George, the Holy Kindred, Our Lady, and other saints. In the choir are notable *gravestones*.

**Deutsches Goldschmiedehaus** (Altstädter Markt): The former *Altstädter Rathaus* was built in 1537–8. Above the massive ground floor are two half-timbered storeys with oriels and high stone step gables at the side. The fine *rococo sandstone doorway* was formerly part of another building. Originally the ground floor had an open hall with scales for flour and tobacco, and a tobacco press. In the Deutsches Goldschmiedehaus is a *craft museum* showing interesting jewellery and artefacts made from precious metals.

**Wilhelmsbad** (2 km. N. in a park): Prince Wilhelm von Hessen-Kassel had the Wilhelmsbad built in 1777–82 over a medicinal spring discovered in 1709. The focal point is the *Kurhaus* and its symmetrical side buildings, and beyond that is the *English park*, containing unusual pastiche buildings: an artificial Burg ruin, a suspension bridge over a ravine, a hermitage and a roundabout. The *Brunnentempel*, with decorative figures on its roof and balustrade, has some artistic value. The *Hessen Dolls' Museum*, established in 1983, is also worth seeing.

**Schloss Philippsruhe** (in the suburb of Kesselstadt): The *Historische Museum* is now in the Schloss; it shows local historical and cultural collections and also Hanau faience. It was built in 1701–12 in the French manner as a two-storey, horseshoe building, but was radically altered in the 19C. The *Weisse Saal* with its stucco work is worth seeing.

---

# Hannover 3000

Lower Saxony                                p.414□G 8

The capital of Lower Saxony has a well-known Technical University as well as a School of Human and Veterinary Medicine. Hannover became an important cultural centre when the town became the summer residence of the Guelphs in 1636. The Electorate of Hannover was combined with the Principality of Lüneburg in 1705. From the accession of George I in 1714 until 1837 the Electors of Hannover were Kings of England. Hannover was the birthplace of A.W.Iffland (1759–1814, actor and dramatist), F.Schlegel (1772–1829, poet and academic) and F.Wedekind (1864–1918, actor and dramatist) and many other famous figures. Charlotte Kestner née Buff, and Julie Schrader have also gone down in literary history: Charlotte was immortalised by Goethe in 'Leiden des jungen Werthers' and was the inspiration for Thomas Mann's 'Lotte in Weimar', and Julie Schrader, the 'Welfischer Schwan', was the toast of poets and artists at the beginning of the present century. The city was designed by two important town planners: G.F.Laves, who developed the neoclassical areas in the 19C and R.Hillebrecht, who redesigned the town after the Second World War, when many historic buildings were rebuilt from the original plans. At the end of April or the beginning of May each year Hannover is host to the world's largest industrial fair.

**Protestant Church of St. Georg and St. Jacobus** (2 Am Markt): This 14C church is one of the most important examples of N. German *brick Gothic*; it was rebuilt after 1945 to the original plans. The *hall church* has 3 *choirs* at its E. end. The most important interior feature is a *c.*1490 late Gothic *carved altar* in the main choir. The *tower* with its ridge turret above the steep gables on all four sides is a symbol of old Hannover.

**Protestant Church of St. Johannis** (5 Rote Reihe): Shortly after the foundation of the new town this *Neustädter Hof- und Stadtkirche* came into being as a centre of Protestantism. It was built to a design by the court architect H.Sartorio, a Venetian. It was originally a hall church with a vaulted wooden roof and two galleries; the position of the windows on the E. side confirms the earlier existence of these galleries, removed during rebuilding work *c.*1870. After the war the exterior and the W. tower were restored but the interior was modernised. The philosopher *Leibniz* is buried here: the vault is full of rubble, but the shattered tombstone is in the SE corner of the church.

**Church of St.Clemens** (Clemensstrase): This Catholic priory church was built to plans by the Venetian T.Giusti at the beginning of the 18C, but the dome was not added until the church was rebuilt after the Second World War. Giusti's model is in the Historisches Museum (q.v.).

**Altstädter Rathaus** (Marktstrasse): The exterior of this 15C building was restored after the Second World War. The *façade* with its *step gable* is one of the most important secular Gothic buildings in N. Germany. The colourful tiles with their red and green glaze, and the play of shapes in the various patterns and friezes are nowhere else found in such perfection.

**Leinschloss** (Friederikenplatz): A first castle with three courtyards was built by Duke Georg von Calenberg in 1640 on the site of the former Minorite monastery in the S. corner of the old town; the theatre, the church and the baronial hall were added later. G.Laves altered and extended the building *c.*1826 in classical style. The building was rebuilt in 1959 – 62 and modernised for the *Assembly of Lower Saxony.*

**Opernhaus** (1 Opernplatz): The opera house, which today seats about 1600 spectators, was built as the *Court Theatre* by G.Laves *c.*1850 in a mixture of classical and Renaissance styles, but burned down in the Second World War. The exterior was rebuilt in its old form and the interior modernised to conform with modern theatrical requirements.

**Wangenheim-Palais** (17 Friedrichstrasse): This palace, built in 1832, is the most balanced work of the Hannover architect G.Laves. The central building with its gable in the antique style is neoclassicism at its most perfect.

**Modern Architecture:** In the early 20C some exemplary specimens of modern architecture were built in Hannover. These include the *Stadthalle* (Corvinusplatz), a massive circular building with asymmetrical wings which was completed in 1914 to plans by P.Bonatz. The ten-storey *Anzeigerhochhaus* (9 Goseriede) is a brick-clad reinforced concrete building with mock Gothic and expressionist features. This building, with its round copper dome, has become the emblem of modern Hannover; it was created in 1927–8 by F.Höger.

**Herrenhausen** (Herrenhäuser Strasse): A quadruple *avenue of lime trees* more than a mile long leads from the Königsworther Platz directly to the buildings of Herrenhausen. More than 1400 lime trees were planted in 1726 to form the avenue, which ends in the famous rectangular *Great Garden.* The gardens, which are among the most important of their kind in Europe, were laid out in the Dutch style and have a strictly geometrical ground plan which has remained unchanged to the present day. The hedges, if placed end to end, would be over 13 miles long. The baroque style of the gardens is emphasised by the fountains, including the highest on the Continent, grottoes, sculpture and urns.

*Altstädter Rathaus, Hanau*

*Schloss Philippsruhe, Hanau*

In the summer there are theatrical performances and concerts in the former *garden theatre*, the first of its kind in Germany. The long *Gallery*, which was used as a temporary opera house after the war, is the only remaining building. T.Giusti decorated the walls with scenes from the Aeneas legend and the patterns on the stucco ceilings reflect the layout of the flower beds. In the *Berggarten*, now the *Botanical Gardens* on the other side of the Herrenhäuser Strasse is an early work of G.Laves, the *Library Pavilion*; he created the *Mausoleum c.*25 years later. In the SE is the *Georgengarten*, a park in the English landscape style laid out in 1779 and enlarged in 1816. A 1790 *Leibniz Temple* was moved here from the town. The *Georgenpalais* (1780–96) in the middle of the park today houses the *Wilhelm-Busch- Museum* (q.v.).

**Museums:** The *Niedersächsische Landesmuseum* (5 Am Maschpark) shows fine art from the 11C to the present day; it has the finest Impressionist collection in Germany, and also sections on primeval history, natural history and anthropology. The *Kestner-Museum* (3 Trammplatz) has permanent exhibitions of ancient Greek, Roman and Egyptian art, and also shows medieval applied art, miniatures and coins; there are also first-class temporary exhibitions. The *Kestner-Gesellschaft* (16 Warmbüschenstrasse) mounts exhibitions of modern and ultra-modern art. The *Herrenhausen-Museum* (14 Alte Herrenhäuser Strasse) in the 1721 *Fürstenhaus* shows paintings and furniture from the collection of the House of Braunschweig-Lüneburg. The *Wilhelm-Busch-Museum* (1 Georgengarten) in the former Georgenpalais (q.v.) is largely devoted to Wilhelm Busch, who was born in Hannover, but also shows works by H.Zille, and modern caricatures. The *Historische Museum am Hohen Ufer* (6 Pferdestrasse) offers a survey of local history and folk art.

*Herrenhausen, Hannover* ▷

*Panorama with Rathaus*

*Protestant Marktkirche church of St. Georg and St. Jacobus*

**Libraries:** The *Niedersächsische Landesbibliothek* has over 600,000 volumes. The manuscripts include a copy of the oldest German translation of the Bible (*c.*800). The *Stadtbibliothek* has over 400, 000 volumes, and many manuscripts and incunabula.

**Theatres:** The operatic section of the *Niedersächsische Landestheater* (1 Opernplatz) has been back in the old Opernhaus (q.v.) since 1950. The *staatliche Schauspiel* performs in the *Ballhof* (5 Ballhofstrasse), the old Ballspielhaus, built soon after the Thirty Years War, and in the *Theater am Aegi* (2 Aegidientorplatz). The latter theatre presents guest performances by the state *Landesbühne Hannover,* who also play in the *Gartentheater* and the *Galerie Herrenhausen.*

**Also worth seeing:** The artificial *Maschsee* S. of the *Neues Rathaus* is a popular place for relaxation; it was laid out in

*Leineschloss, portico*

1934–6 and there is a fine view from the dome.

## Hannoversch Münden 3510
Lower Saxony                    p.418□G 10

Alexander von Humboldt (1769–1859) is said to have considered Münden to be one of the seven most beautifully situated towns in the world. It is attractively placed at the confluence of the Werra and the Fulda with the Weser; the late medieval Old Town consists almost entirely of half-timbered buildings and the town has received many awards in recent years for its work of preservation and restoration.

**Protestant Church of St. Blasius** (Kirchplatz): The present Gothic hall church was begun in the late 13C to replace two previous Romanesque buildings; the first stages included the choir, the side apse, the sanctuary and the E. bays of the three aisles. In a second phase from 1487 work continued towards the W., and was temporarily completed in 1519 with the building of the vaulting under the tower. The church was not completed until 1584, when the tower was raised above the ridge of the saddle roof and given its present outline by the addition of the dome ('Welsche Haube'). The finest features of the interior are the pulpit (1493), the 1645 organ front (the organ itself is modern), the baroque altar (1700), and especially the font (1392) by N.von Stettin, the bronze door (c. 1400) to the sacrament niche in the choir and the representation of 'St.Anne with the Virgin and Child' (early 16C) in the arch above the altar.

**Rathaus** (Am Markt): The new Town Hall was built by G.Crossmann in 1603–9 in the 'Weser Renaissance' style to replace parts of a previous Gothic building of which the door jambs and step gable on the S. side survive. In the asymmetrical fa-

*Anzeigerhochhaus*

çade is a lavishly decorated *portal* with double Ionic pillars; in front of it is a terrace with steps (1605).

**Schloss** (Schlossstrasse): The Schloss was built in early 'Weser Renaissance' style in the 1560–80 after an earlier medieval building (11–13C) was destroyed by fire; the *staircase tower* in the NE corner of the courtyard and the part of the chapel with ogival windows still survive from the Guelph Schloss. The *wall paintings* with which Herzog Erich II von Calenberg-Göttingen had the Schloss decorated in the course of new building (especially in the 'White Horse Chamber' and the 'Roman Chamber') are, alongside those in Burg Trausnitz in Landshut, the most important Renaissance frescos in Germany. Today the Schloss houses the *Heimatmuseum* of pre- and early history and the history of the town.

**Also worth seeing:** Many 15&16C *half-*

*timbered buildings* and the *Werra bridge*, the oldest remaining stone bridge in the Upper Weser and Werra area. Five arches of the old bridge, mentioned in 1329, survive. By the *Aegidenkirche* is the tombstone of the celebrated but notorious Dr.Eisenbart, who died in 1727.

---

**Harburg,Schwaben 8856**
Bavaria                                         p.422□I 18

**Schloss:** The Burg above the Wörnitz valley belonged *c.*1150 to the Hohenstaufen Emperors, and in 1295 it came into the possession of the Counts of Oettingen, whose princely successors still own it. Originally the building, surrounded by an unusually high wall and secured only on the vulnerable side by a second ring wall, was intended to protect the imperial road from Nördlingen to Donauwörth. The date of building is not known, but the *inner wall*, the *keep* the *residence* and the remains of the *well* suggest that work started in the 12&13C; the frontal *defensive wall* in the SW with semicircular towers was a 14&15C addition. Around the middle of the 16C the *bailey*, the *NE tower*, the *new building* (also known as the 'Kastenhaus' (box house), the oriel in the *Princes' Building* and the *water-supply fountain* were added. A covered way leads from the second floor of the Princes' Building to the *Schloss Church of St.Michael*. Its earliest parts are Romanesque, it was extended in the 14C and completed and the stucco work added in the baroque period. On the walls of the choir are outstanding *late-Gothic carvings*: a Madonna (1480) and St.Michael (*c.*1510). There are also some worthwhile works among the numerous Oettinger tombs. The Princes' Building contains the *art collection*, in which the most important pieces are a 12C ivory crucifix and the side wings of a Riemenschneider altar.

---

**Hassfurt 8728**
Bavaria                                         p.418□I 14

This town between the Hass hills and the

*Panorama with Schloss, Harburg*

Steigerwald shows by the regularity of its streets (alleyways crossing at right angles) that it was planned as a unified whole in the 13C. A *stretch of wall* and three *town gates* remain of the 16C buildings, along with *half-timbered houses* and the *Rathaus* (1521).

**Catholic Parish Church:** Building of the nave of the hall church, the choir and the two towers began in 1390 and continued until the end of the 15C. In the 19C the baroque interior decoration was removed and the building refurbished in neo-Gothic style. On the N. wall of the choir are three remarkable late Gothic wooden figures (St. Kilian and companions, *c.*1500). The figure of *John the Baptist* on the choir arch is an outstanding piece of work by Riemenschneider.

**Ritterkapelle** (in the town behind the Bamberg gate): Artistic activity in this church, which was built for Franconian no-

bility at the same time as the Parish church, was concentrated in the *choir*. Under the roof ridge is a three-tiered *frieze of coats of arms* consisting of 248 shields. There are also coats of arms on the keystones of the arches. The church has many 19C mock-Gothic additions, including the gallery, the pinnacles in the choir and the ridge turret. Above the SW *doorway* is a 1455 Crucifixion in relief.

**Stadtmuseum** (Herrenhof, 22 Zwerchmaingasse): This has exhibits on the history of the town and also a collection of 19C moulds used by chandlers and gingerbread-makers.

---

**Havixbeck 4409**
Nordrhein-Westfalen                      p.414☐C 9

**Haus Havixbeck** (1 km. SW of Havixbeck): This *moated Burg*, a plain manor house, developed from a Westphalian farmhouse; there is added Renaissance decoration. A *bridge with three arches* leads over the moat to the *gatehouse*. The three-sided complex, open to the S., dates from various periods. The octagonal *staircase tower* is part of the original 11&12C building. The E. part of the house dates from 1562. The baroque *bridge columns* and *garden columns* with putti and urns, and the curved retaining wall of the island were constructed *c.*1733 and in 1759 to designs by the famous Münster architect J.C.Schlaun.

**Haus Stapel** (2 km. N. of Havixbeck): Haus Stapel is based on a moated Burg mentioned as early as 1211. The *outer works* and the neoclassical *manor house* (1819–27) are on a large island. The wide outer works were completed in 1719. From 1801 the house was owned by the Freiherren von Droste zu Hülshoff, relations of the poetess, who paid visits here. Her effects were kept here until 1970.

**Also worth seeing**: The *Catholic Parish Church of St.Dionysius* has a 12C W. tower and 14C nave, and is lavishly decorated.

There is a *plague chapel* in the church square inscribed with the date 1664.

**Environs:** *Haus Hülshoff* (10 km. E.): This is the third and best known Havixbeck moated Burg and was the birthplace and residence of the poetess Annette von Droste-Hülshoff. The 17C *outer works* are fortified with square corner towers. The decoration in the *upper Burg*, a plain brick building with two wings (1545), dates from 1789. In some rooms there are pictures of the poetess and her family, and memorabilia.

---

**Hechingen 7450**
Baden-Württemberg                    p.420□F 19

---

**Burg Hohenzollern** (6 km. S. of Hechingen): There is documentary proof of the presence of the Counts of Zollern in Hechingen since the 13C. From 1623 they lived as Princes of Hohenzollern in the Burg, which was rebuilt from 1850–67 to an old site plan by the military architect von Prittwitz and the civilian architect Stüler in mock Romantic style with bat-

*Moated castle, Haus Havixbeck*

tlements and seven towers. It is well sited on a hilltop and visible for miles around. The 15C *Catholic St.Michael Chapel* is all that remains of the old Burg; it has three Romanesque sandstone reliefs and Gothic stained glass. In the neo-Gothic *Protestant chapel* are the coffins of Frederick the Great and Friedrich Wilhelm I (brought here from Potsdam). The *Hohenzollerische Landessammlung* and the *Heimatmuseum* are also in the Schloss. There are various memorabilia and the Prussian crown of 1889.

**Former Collegiate Church of St.Jakob** (Kirchplatz): The present Catholic parish church, designed by the French architect M.d'Ixnard and dedicated in 1783, is a fine example of early *neoclassicism*. Traditional baroque forms are retained in the exterior, but the new, more austere style can be seen in the urns and garlands, above all on the W. tower. The interior, elegant in white and gold, is sober and without undue adornment. The only traces of baroque are the *Atlas figures* supporting the prince's gallery and the *ceiling paintings* in the side chapels. The *altars* are plain slabs with tabernacles, and only on the N. side altar is there a figure of the Virgin. In the *choir* is an early German Renaissance bronze

casting, the *grave slab* of Graf Eitel-friedrich von Zollern and his wife (1512). It is probably by P.Vischer of Nuremberg.

**Former Franciscan Monastery Church of St.Luzen** (St.-Luzen-Weg): At the N. extremity of the lower town a 17C pilgrims' way leads to the monastery church, a very long plain building dating from 1586–9. The *interior* is an extremely interesting example of the *late Renaissance* style. The vault decoration and the keystones still show traces of Gothic. Beneath them are beams supported by richly decorated half columns and pilasters in pure Renaissance style. Between the columns are shell-shaped niches with Apostle figures. They, like the ornaments on the stucco, show Dutch influence. The pulpit and the choir stalls (1587–9) are by H.Amann of Ulm.

**Villa Eugenia:** This villa in the Zoll-strasse was built in 1786–9 as a 'Lustgar-tenhaus'. The austere side wings were added to the attractive central building in the 19C, and have a deleterious effect on its appearance. There are other classical *park buildings* in the *Fürstengarten*.

*Burg Hohenzollern*

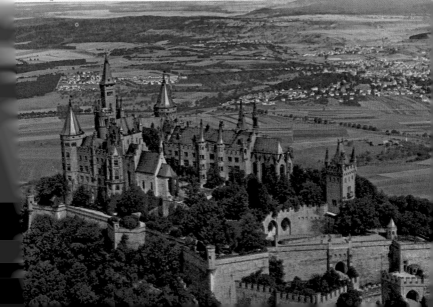

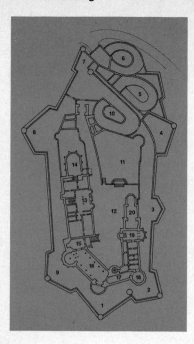

**Burg Hohenzollern 1** Der Spitz (peak) **2** Scharfeckbastei (bastion) **3** Gartenbastei **4** St. -Michaels-Bastei, crown prince's burial site **5** Lower outworks **6** Wilhelmsturn **7** Schnarr-wachtbastei **8** Neue Bastei **9** Fuchslochbastei **10** Rampenturm **11** Castle garden **12** Castle court-yard **13** Castle inn **14** Protestant chapel **15** Family tree hall **16** Counts' hall **17** Library **18** Mar-grave's tower **19** Queen's room **20** Michaels-kapelle

---

## Heidelberg 6900
Baden-Würrtemberg                    p.420☐E 16

Only the lower jaw remains of the earliest inhabitant of this region; he was homo heidelbergiensis, a man from the inter-glacial period about 500,000 years ago. On the Heiligenberg in the 1C BC, on the site of the present-day open-air theatre, there was a Celtic shrine which later became a Romano-heathen place of worship. The ac-tual history of Heidelberg began when the Wittelsbach Ludwig the Kelheimer be-came Count Palatinate in 1226. The Wit-telsbachs lived here until they they moved their residence to nearby Mannheim in 1720. Elector Ruprecht III founded the second German university (after Prague) here in 1386. The red sandstone Heidel-berg Schloss went through three major building periods: the Gothic, until approx-imately 1500, the first Renaissance period and thirdly, and perhaps most importantly, the period from 1544–1632, in which the Burg was transformed into the princely Schloss which gave Heidelberg the appear-ance the world knows today. Literary Heidelberg is well represented by 'Des Knaben Wunderhorn', which Arnim and Brentano edited in 1805–8 at 151 Haupt-strasse. Old Heidelberg was spared in the Second World War; only a few bridges were blown up during the retreat as a matter of routine.

**Schloss** (Schlossberg): The oldest parts of the Schloss are the Roman granite pillars which Elector Philipp (1476–1508) caused to be brought from the Imperial Palace of Charlemagne in Ingelheim; they are in the *Brunnenhalle* (on the right after the *tower gate*). Before that Elector Ruprecht, later German Emperor and founder of the university, fortified the building and ad-ded the three E. towers. The *Ruprechtsbau* (on the left after the gate) by the Frankfurt architect M.Gerthener also dates from this period; it was refurbished in Renaissance style in the 16C. The warlike atmosphere at the time of the Peasants' Revolt and the Reformation led to further fortification. At the same time the *Bibliotheksbau* on the S. side and the *Frauenzimmerbau* on the E. side were added, along with the *Gläserne Saalbau* (Hall of Glass, so called because of the mirrors set in its columns). The period in which the ancient fortress was tranformed into a magnificent residence began in 1530 and ended with the outbreak of the Thirty Years War. This phase saw the addition of the *Ottheinrichsbau* (1556 –9), the first palace building of the Ger-man Renaissance; it combines horizontal

*Burg Hohenzollern, counts' hall* ▷

ordering of storeys in the Italian manner with exuberant decoration in the tradition of Germany and the Low Countries; the architect is unknown. The Ottheinrichs-bau today houses the *Deutsches Apotheken-museum* (q.v.). Half a century later this tour de force found a powerful competitor in the *Friedrichsbau* (1601–7), though decorative exuberance got a little out of hand in this case, and this was not helped by the decision to extend the mock ruin *c.*1900. The series of figures in the niches is interesting: it shows the princes from Charlemagne to the builder of the Schloss Friedrich IV (low down on the right). The Friedrichs-bau has two showpiece façades, facing the courtyard and the town, and a broad terrace on the N. side. A final flicker of Renaissance delight in building shows in the *Englischer Bau* (in the NW of the complex, near the *Dicke Turm*, which was blown up), built by the 'winter king' Friedrich IV for his English wife. He also brought his gardener from England; on the terraces he created the *Hortus Palatinus*, a mathematically laid-out garden in late Italian Renaissance style. The famous *Heidelberg Tun* is in a building near the Englischer Bau; it was constructed under Karl Theodor to hold a tenth of the Pfalz wine yield as a tribute to the Elector; it has a capacity of 220,000 litres.

**Haus zum Ritter** (178 Hauptstrasse): The Renaissance architectural style spread from the Schloss to the town. The Huguenot merchant Bélier had his Haus zum Ritter designed on the pattern of the Ottheinrichsbau in 1592; it is topped by a figure of Ritter Georg. There are two rows of oriels on the five-storey façade, which has extremely ornate gables.

**Church of the Holy Spirit** (Hauptstrasse): Building of this church was started at the time of the foundation of the university; the church is surrounded by a series of delightful shops set between its buttresses. There are unusual *galleries* in the side aisles of the nave; these were intended as library space for the University and were supposed to house the famous *Bibliotheca Palatina* which was, however, sent to Rome as a gift and as booty of war in 1622; 100 German manuscripts were returned by Pope Pius VII in the 19th century. The Gothic church gained its *mansard roof* in 1698 and the characteristic *baroque dome* on the tower in the early 18C; as a result of the Reformation the interior was divided

*Heidelberg, panorama with Schloss*

by a wall until 1936: Catholics on one side, Protestants on the other. An interesting item among the furnishings of the church is the *gravestone* of the founder of the university Ruprecht III (d. 1410) and his wife Elisabeth of Hohenzollern.

**Former Jesuit Church** (Schulgasse): The present Catholic parish church was built in 1712 to a design by J.A.Breunig, the Heidelberg architect responsible for many important early-18C buildings in the town, including the nearby *Jesuitenkolleg*, the *Hospital mit Annakirche* (104 Plöck), the *university buildings*, the building occupied by the *Kurpfälzisches Museum* (97 Hauptstrasse) and the *Haus zum Riesen* (52 Hauptstrasse). An *open hall* is unusual for the period of origin, and it seems cool, almost neoclassical. The *stucco capitals* with rococo decoration are very fine. There are three *sculptures* ascribed to the Mannheim baroque sculptor P.Egell (1691–1752): a Salvator Mundi and two Saints.

**Catholic Parish Church of St.Vitus** (in Handschuhsheim): This church, built in the Gothic period and much altered later, contains a number of important *tombs*, of which the best is that of Johann von Ingelheim and Margarete von Handschuhsheim in the E. transept. The sculptor, who initialled and dated his work (M.LSP.VH 1519), was from the school of H.Backoffen of Mainz; the portrait heads of the figures are of outstanding quality.

**Alte Brücke** (Karl-Theodor-Brücke): This bridge, arching gracefully over the Neckar towards Neuheim and Handschuhsheim, is at least the fifth on the same site. It was blown up in 1945, but rebuilt to its original plan. The *Brückentor* with its two round towers was built in 1786–8 under Elector Karl Theodor, after whom the bridge is named.

**Berg Cemetery:** A number of well-known people are buried in this cemetery, laid out in 1844. They include the chemist R.W.Bunsen (d.1899), the writer J.H.Voss (d.1826) and the conductor Wilhelm Furtwängler (d.1954).

**University Library:** This is one of the most important libraries in the German-speaking world, and houses 1, 120, 000 volumes and a famous collection of manuscripts (open to the public daily). The collection includes the *Manessische Liederhandschrift*, containing 137 Minnesänger miniatures (*c.*1320), the second version of Otfried von Weissenburg's *Evangelienharmonie* and the 13C *Sachsenspiegel*.

**Museums:** The *Kurpfälzische Museum* (97 Hauptstrasse) in Heidelberg architect Breunig's 1712 baroque building (see above) has an exhibition including pictures by the artists who discovered Romantic Heidelberg (Fohr, Rottmann, Fries, Blechen). The collection also includes Riemenschneider's Windesheimer Zwölfbotenaltar, which was covered with a thick layer of oil paint and not recognised as a work of the great wood carver until after the Second World War. The *Deutsche Apothekenmuseum* in the Schloss shows the development of pharmacy from ancient herbal pratice to the present day.

**Theatre:** Heidelberg owes its theatrical fame to the Heidelberger Festspiele in the

*Hotel Haus zum Ritter*

*Schloss Hellenstein, Heidenheim*

*Rathaus, Heilbronn* ▷

courtyard of the Schloss. The *Städtische Bühnen* present opera, operetta and straight theatre. 590 seats.

## Heidenheim an der Brenz 7920

Baden-Württemberg   p.422☐H 18

**Schloss Hellenstein:** Although the Burg survived attack and plunder in the Thirty Years War relatively unscathed there were plans to pull it down in 1820, but it was in fact restored later in the century and its picturesque appearance retained; the most striking features are the *defensive walls and towers, the stepped gables* and a domed *octagonal tower*. There are still medieval remains in the *Upper Schloss*, but the buildings date largely from the 17C.

**Museums:** *Heimatmuseum* in the Schloss Chapel (consecrated 1605). *Römerbadmuseum:* An AD 2 Roman bath excavated in 1980–1.

## Heilbronn am Neckar 7100

Baden-Württemberg   p.420☐F 17

The town takes its name from a sacred spring (Helibrunne) which used to rise near St. Kilian's church. Thanks to its favourable position at the junction of two important trade routes Heilbronn quickly became rich and powerful. Little remained of the original town after the Second World War; the older buildings were almost all destroyed, and only the most important ones have been rebuilt.

**Protestant Parish Church of St.Kilian** (Kaiserstrasse): Particular difficulties arose in reconstructing this church, which was started in the 13C and destroyed in the Second World War; the Gothic decoration alternating with Renaissance work in mock-antique style called for painstaking attention to detail. The *tower*, originally built in 1508–29 by H.Schweiner of Weins-

berg, is unusual in design (see illustration); at the top is a soldier bearing the town banner. The most important feature of the furnishings is the 1498 *high altar*; the 13 figures and the side pieces were put in store during the war and therefore survived, but the shrine had to be renewed.

**Rathaus** (Marktplatz): The Town Hall is a Gothic building dating from 1417; the magnificent Renaissance façade was not added until the late 16C. An open-air staircase leads to a gallery running the full length of the building and supported by five arches with Ionic columns. The pride of the town is the *Town Hall Clock*; it has two faces and was designed by J.Habrecht, who created the famous clock in Strasbourg Cathedral.

**Götzenturm** (Untere Neckarstrasse): The tower is a remnant of the town fortifications. Tradition insists that Götz von Berlichingen was held here in 1519, but at that time the prison was in the *Bollwerksturm*, which also survives.

**Käthchenhaus** (Marktplatz): On the W. side of the Marktplatz is a much modified aristocratic house in which the original of Kleist's 'Käthchen von Heilbronn' is said to have lived; it was rebuilt after the Second World War.

**Historisches Museum** (1 Eichgasse): This little museum is devoted to cultural and historical collections on Heilbronn and environs.

**Theater Heilbronn** (64 Gartenstrasse): The theatre was opened in 1951 as the Kleines Theater Heilbronn; it has its own company and seats 375.

---

**Heiligenberg 7799**
Baden-Württemberg                       p.420☐F 20

**Schloss:** N. of Überlingen, high above Lake Constance, is the Renaissance Schloss of the Princes of Fürstenberg, extended in the 16C: galleries four storeys high were placed in front of the Gothic *Kemenatenflügel* on the courtyard side (1594–1604); the *Rittersaal*, along with the Goldene Saal in the Augsburg Rathaus (q.v.) one of the most splendid and stylistically significant buildings of the German Renaissance, was added from 1580–4 opposite the residen-

*St. Kilian, Heilbronn*                       *Coffered ceiling, Schloss Heiligenberg* ▷

tial wing. The richly carved coffered ceiling (118 by 36 ft.) is suspended in the roof space and supported by columns between the high circular windows. Sandstone fireplaces with figures on the columns and in the niches face each other at the narrow ends of the room (1584). The tall, narrow 17C *Schloss Chapel* in the W. wing is three storeys high and reminiscent of a theatre with its galleries and boxes. There are notable 14C *windows* (taken from the Dominican Church in Konstanz), *carvings* and *wall paintings*.

---

## Heiligenstadt 8551

Bavaria                                    p.418☐K 15

**Schloss Greifenstein** (2 km. N. of Heiligenstadt): This impressive set of buildings was designed by the baroque architect L.Dientzenhofer. The *collection of weapons*, featuring hand weapons from the Middle Ages to the present day, and the *Wappensaal*, displaying the coats of arms of all the women who married into the Stauffenberg family, are both of considerable interest.

---

## Heiligkreuztal=Altheim 7940

Baden-Württemberg                          p.420☐F 19

**Former Cistercian Convent Church:** The church was consecrated in 1256 but transformed into a basilica and completed in 1319. Further reconstruction followed in the 16,17&18C and the retreat building, the abesses' building and the pharmacy were restored very recently. The most striking feature is the *interior furnishings*: the large, splendidly-coloured E. window is one of the most important surviving works of the high Gothic period. The choir walls have frescos by the Master of Messkirch (1533). Of the many sculptures the most striking is the fine painted group on the E. wall of the choir (*c.*1340), showing Christ with John resting on his breast. The *c.*1515 Adoration of the Magi by M.Schaffner, now in the Germanisches Nationalmuseum in Nuremberg, was originally

in this church and there is a copy on one of the side altars.

---

## Heilsbronn 8802

Bavaria                                    p.422☐I 16

**Former Cistercian Monastery Church:** The church was consecrated in 1150; it was formerly part of a monastery, which was used as a Fürstenschule from 1581 and later amalgamated with the Gymnasium in Ansbach; it was commissioned by the powerful Bishop Otto of Bamberg. In 1333 the Zollern Burggrafen of Nuremberg became patrons of the monastery, and more than 20 of them were buried here from then until the 18C. The church was rebuilt after the Second World War and as far as possible the original style of decoration was retained. The *nave* has a great deal of masonry, clumsy cubiform capitals and short, stumpy columns in the original heavy style. In contrast to this are the light, early Gothic *E. choir* (*c.*1280) and the *S. aisle* (1412–33). The apse of the *Heideck Chapel* (S.transept, late 12C) is also in the robust and simple earlier style. Of the original 29 *altars* 9 remain. The high altar, a carved, late Gothic Adoration of the Magi, is the work of a Nuremberg master (1502–22). The side altars are partially based on the work of Dürer (e.g the Martyrdom of the 11,000 Virgins, Mary with Saints, 1511). The numerous *tombs* give the church something of the character of a museum; the wall grave of the Margraves Friedrich and Georg (d.1543) in the S. aisle is a fine example of the German Renaissance style. The 12 Apostles carved on the *pulpit* are late Gothic. In the choir is a 1515 *tabernacle*. N. of the church is the mid-13C *former refectory*, a late Romanesque hall. The richly decorated doorway to the church is in the Germanisches Nationalmuseum in Nuremberg (q.v.).

---

## Helmstedt 3330

Lower Saxony                               p.414☐I 8

Helmstedt is today the central crossing point for traffic between the Federal

Republic and Berlin. It flourished from 1576-1810 when one of the main post-Reformation German universities, the Academia Julia (the Guelph university), had its seat here, but the town was already significant at the time of the evangelisation of Eastern Europe in the 9C and the old mission chapel in the courtyard of the Monastery of St.Ludgeri is a reminder of this period.

**Juleum** (Juliusplatz): The Guelph Duke Heinrich Julius founded the Academia Julia in a dissolved Cistercian Monastery, the Graue Hof, but commissioned several other university buildings at the same time. In 1592-7 the Aula building and the *Auditorium Maximum* were added. The *library* in the upper storey, today a multipurpose foyer, was not built until the 16C. The light-coloured sandstone which outlines the windows, doorways and tower is in marked contrast with the dark colouring of the rest of the building. The *main doorway*, formerly the students' entrance, has the university coat of arms of Samson with the Lion above it and on the *tower doorway*, used by non-academics, is the ducal coat of arms. In the cellar of the university, which today houses the Kreisheimatmuseum, the duke set up a *Trinkstube*, so that the students could learn that 'Bacchus must be trodden underfoot'.

**Former Monastery Church of St. Ludgeri and Double Chapel of St. Peter and St.John the Baptist** (on the way into Ostendorf): This old Benedictine monastery, which was directly subject to the Empire, was founded in the 9C in close connection with the Abbey of Essen-Werden (q.v.) and existed until the secularisation of 1803; today St.Ludgeri, which suffered heavily in the war (burned down 1942), is the Catholic parish church. The E. parts of the building show traces of its 11C origins: the most important feature is the *Felicitas Crypt* under the E. building, which is half underground and supported in the middle by columns and diagonally placed members. The shape of the *capitals* is of interest, and on the W. wall there are remains of a *plaster floor* with a representation of the 7 Wise Men of Antiquity. The

*double chapel* in the courtyard of the former Ludgeri monastery (the upper part is dedicated to John and the lower part to Peter) is probably the oldest building in the complex: 9C walls have been excavated. The exterior of the double chapel, with the exception of the dome and lantern (1666), is mid 11C. Inside, the Romanesque vault has been covered with baroque stucco decoration; the columns still have their original capitals.

**Former Monastery of Marienberg** (Klosterstrasse): A Gothic *choir* was added to the *Romanesque nave* in the 14C and rebuilt in 1488; the fine *doorways* with tendril ornamentation are late-12C. The two chapels under the incomplete tower have early Gothic *wall paintings* (1256), and in the N. transept the *Romanesque stained glass* representing the Apostles has survived. The most valuable piece of embroidery from the former Augustinian Nunnery in the *former convent building* is the embroidered linen antependium with Christ, apostles, saints and symbols (*c.*1250). The valuable work of the parament workshop is exhibited in the *Schatzkammer* (treasury).

**Town fortifications:** One of the former town gates, the *Hausmannsturm* still stands in Neumärker Strasse.

**Lübbensteine** (Braunschweiger Landstrasse): The two *dolmen* date from the neolithic period.

**Kreisheimatmuseum** (2 Bötticherstrasse): The most important collections in this museum in the Juleum are on palaeontology, biology and numismatics.

**Brunnentheater** (7 Brunnenweg): This theatre with 813 seats, opened in 1815 and rebuilt 1924 - 7, presents touring productions.

**Environs:** *Schöningen* (11 km. S.) has notable 16&17C *half-timbered buildings* and the *former Augustinian Canonry Church of St. Lorenz*, an 11C Romanesque church with late-12C vaulting; the nave and late Gothic net vaulting were added in 1491&2. The

*Juleum, Helmstedt*

*St. Ludgeri*

*Protestant Parish Church of St. Vinzenz*, a hall church (1429–60) with a late Gothic stellar-vaulted sanctuary and fine 17C furnishings is also worth seeing; the *Schloss*, a rectangular Renaissance complex (1568&9) with an inner courtyard, is a fine building.

---

**Herborn (Dillkreis) 6348**
Hessen                                    p.416☐E 12

Herborn's historical importance rests on the Protestant theological university which functioned here from 1584 – 1818 and which has continued as a seminary in the Schloss since 1886.

**Schloss** (Am Schlossberg): This was built in the second half of the 13C and later extended. The picturesque complex with its high *saddle roofs* and three slender round

*corner towers* dominates the skyline of the town.

**Former Hohe Schule** (University; 5 Schulhofstrasse): This was the Town Hall until 1588 and is now the *Heimatmuseum*. It is a two-storey stone building with a fine *half-timbered gable* and a distinctive *oriel*; the courtyard façade has a striking *staircase tower*. The former *Aula* (great hall) with portraits of Princes and professors indicates the earlier use of the building.

**Rathaus** (Marktplatz): Under the windows of the second storey of this 1589–91 Renaissance building is a set of carved family coats of arms; the originals are in the Heimatmuseum.

**Also worth seeing:** The *Old Town* with its medieval alleyways, slate-clad half-timbered houses and remains of the town fortifications is the core of this attractive

*Münsterkirche, Herford*

*Johanneskirche*

place. The *Kornmarkt* is the most interesting area.

## Herford 4900
Nordrhein-Westfalen        p.414☐E 8

The town developed from four settlements, each with a place of worship; by the Middle Ages the proliferation of churches and monasteries had led to the nickname 'Holy Herford'. Today the principal churches are Protestant. Herford is the birthplace of the great baroque architect Pöppelmann, who was responsible for the Zwinger in Dresden.

**Protestant Münster Church** (Münsterplatz): This is the former collegiate church of a convent for noblewomen founded in 790. It was replaced by a new building started in 1220. The last part to be built

was the two-towered façade; only the S. tower was completed. This late-Romanesque church is the oldest example of the great Westphalian *hall churches*. In the interior the buttresses, the vaulting and above all the *capitals* show how styles developed during the building period: in the E. there are still Romanesque cushion capitals but the nave has crocket capitals; the *tracery windows* also show Gothic influence. The most important feature of the furnishings is the *font* (1500), with statuettes of the saints and very lively biblical scenes on the reliefs.

**Protestant Marienkirche** (Stiftberg): This church also was once part of a convent and was built as a *high Gothic hall church* on an almost square ground plan; the diagonal saddle roofs are the characteristic feature of the exterior. The slender soaring pillars make the broad interior seem unusually light. A late Gothic *reliquary* serves as altar furniture; another

*Herrenchiemsee, Neues Schloss*

striking feature is a 1330–40 stone standing figure of the *Madonna*.

**Protestant Church of St. Johannes** (Neuer Markt): The *stained glass* in the choir is the best feature of this Gothic hall church. 18 medallions (*c.*1300) tell the story of the Life of Christ; the windows in the two diagonal sides have high Gothic designs. In the middle window is a Crucifixion (with pictures of the founder; 1520). The *pews* and the *galleries* are also notable.

**Also worth seeing:** The Gothic *Protestant Jakobikirche* has unified furnishings with late-Renaissance wood-carving, an inlaid pulpit and wall panelling. There are 16C *half-timbered buildings* in the Elisabethstrase (No 2), the Brüderstrasse (Nos 26 and 28), and the Neue Markt (No 5). The *Städtisches Museum* (2 Deichtorwall) has collections on local culture and history.

## Herrenchiemsee = Prien 8210
Bavaria                                      p.422 ☐ M 20

There was originally a canonry on the island (to complement the nunnery on the neighbouring island of Frauenchiemsee (q.v.)) but it was largely destroyed in the course of secularisation. All that remained was the *parish church* and the E. section of the monastery, the so-called *Altes Schloss* (with library and Imperial Hall *c.*1700), and also parts of the *nave* of the former monastery church and the vaults, which were used as a brewery and beer cellar after secularisation.

**Neues Schloss:** Ludwig II, wishing to protect the island from speculators, bought it and realised his dream of sun-kingship in the manner of Louis XIV: he built the Schloss in the French baroque style in imitation of Versailles. The King, at whose death in 1886 building was halted for financial reasons, never lived in the state rooms but only in a side wing. The craftsmanship in the interior is exquisite (*bedroom, gallery of mirrors* and the *gardens* in the style of Versailles with the Latona fountain are very striking. Plans and models of the additional buildings planned by Ludwig can be seen in the adjacent *König-Ludwig-II-Museum*.

## Hersbruck 8562
Bavaria          p.422☐K 16

**Protestant Parish Church** (Untere Lohe): This church founded in the 10C was completed as it stands today in the 15&18C. An important feature of the *furnishings* is the high altar, ascribed to the 'Herford master' (probably Nuremberg school). The ceiling paintings were by the local artist J.C.Reich; some 15&17C glass has survived in the choir windows.

**Heimat- und Hirtenmuseum** (7 Eisenhüttlein): The most important feature is the unique collection on the history of shepherds. Other collections include: local history, guilds and crafts, folk art.

**Also worth seeing:** The *former hospital church* (Spitaltor), built 1406–23, was later brought within the ring wall; it has a fine baroque altar. *Schloss* (Unterer Markt): Built in 1618–22 around a main courtyard, an unusual pattern for the period.

## Herten 4352
Nordrhein-Westfalen      p.414☐C 10

**Moated Schloss:** The brick Schloss burned down a number of times between 1530 and 1702, but was repeatedly rebuilt. The three stocky towers at the corners of the fortified building are striking, and it had rooms which could be heated, a novelty at the time. The Schloss stands in a large English park in which there is also the ruin of a former *rococo orangery*.

## Heusenstamm 6056
Hessen          p.416☐E 14

**Catholic Parish Church of St.Cäcilia and St. Barbara:** Important artists worked on this church, which was origi-

*St. Cäcilia and St. Barbara, Heusenstamm*

nally built as a burial place for the von Schönborn family. Balthasar Neumann was responsible for the design of the nave with a characteristic *tower* set into the façade. The *decorative coats of arms* on the *doorway*, the *statue of the Redeemer* and the *urns* on the façade side are by the Würzburg sculptor J.W.van der Auwera. He also created the *pulpit* and the *high altar* in the spacious interior. The *ceiling paintings* with the Awakening of Lazarus, the Resurrection of Christ and the Adoration of the Lamb indicate by their themes the church's intended function as a place of burial. The baroque *gateway* by the church was commissioned by Erwin von Schönborn for a visit by Emperor Franz I and his son King Josef II.

**The Schönborn Schloss:** This was planned as a large, square moated Burg, but only the façade on the front side and the two massive round corner towers with domes were completed (1663–8). The solemn, fortress-like complex is typical of the period after the Thirty Years War; the new Rathaus building now forms the fourth side.

**Heimatmuseum** (64 Jahnstrasse): The collection of seals of the Archbishops and Electors of Mainz is important, and there are exhibits on the history of the town.

---

### Hiddesen = Detmold 4930
Nordrhein-Westfalen                    p.414□F 9

**Hermannsdenkmal:** The Grotenburg, a hilltop in the Teutoberger Wald on which the monument built by E. von Bandel stands today, is supposed to be the place at which Arminius (Hermann the Cheruscan) defeated the Romans under Quintus Varus in AD 9. At the summit of the hill remains of the so-called *great Hun ring* survive. In 1838–46 a masive round temple with Romanesque arches and domed roof was built; it serves as a base for the colossal figure of Arminius erected in 1875 (height including supporting building 111 ft.). The memorial is an example of German historicist sculpture and architecture.

---

### Hildesheim 3200
Lower Saxony                           p.414□H 8

The town is dominated by its Romanesque churches; the outstanding ones are *St. Michael*, a perfect example of the Lower Saxon Romanesque style, and the *Dom*. Both churches have a proven connection with St.Bernward (*c.*960–1022). He was the initiator of the new strict style of building and the founder of a workshop for sculpture, painting, founding and goldsmiths' arts, which produced some very important work. The *thousand-year rose tree* by the apse of the Dom is also famous. It goes back to the legendary foundation of Hildesheim by Ludwig the Pious (son of Charlemagne) who was hunting near 'Hildwins Heim' and is said to have been given a wondrous sign to found a town there.

**Dom St.Mariae** (Domhof): This Catholic church and its baroque furnishings were completely destroyed in the Second World War but rebuilt from the old plans, so that it is today much as it was in the 15C. A spare mock-Romanesque style was considered acceptable for the interior of the basilica, which was rebuilt with a flat wooden ceiling. With the exception of the *chapels* in the side aisles and the *parvis* by the N. transept the architecture is Romanesque, with strictly mathematical proportions. The square of the crossing is repeated six times in the choir, transept and nave and the so-called Lower Saxon support pattern (pillar-column-column) is followed. In the two-storey Romanesque cloister by the chancel apse the *thousand year rose tree* is still alive; it has been proved to have been there since the 13C. The most valuable of the Dom furnishings are the 11–13C works from the Hildesheim foundry: in the W. doorway are the *bronze doors*, actually cast for St.Michael, with Old and New Testament representations in 16 reliefs. These masterpieces of foundry technique (each 15 by 4 ft.) were made in 1015. The 12.5 ft. *Christussäule* was intended as an imitation of Trajan's Column in Rome; it is also by St.Bernward and has a spiral band of reliefs showing scenes from the Life of Christ. A successor of Bernward presented in 1061 the *Hezilo chandelier*, which is named after him; it is a massive wheel chandelier 19.5 ft. in diameter with the battlements and towers of the New Jerusalem in silver, gold and copper plate. The 13C *bronze font* supported by four kneeling men with pitchers (the rivers of Paradise) shows biblical and symbolic baptismal scenes. In the *Dom treasure*, one of the most valuable collections in Germany, the main items of interest are Bernward's silver cross (1007), the Oswald Reliquary (*c.*1160), crosses, evangeliars and ritual objects (mainly from Bernward's workshop).

**St. Michael** (Michaelisplatz): The principal Protestant church in Hildesheim was built by Bishop Bernwald on a hill on the N. edge of the settlement and rebuilt in its original form after the Second World War. It has 6 towers and 2 apses and is a perfect example of a 'fortress of God', as built on the E. frontiers of the Ottonian empire as a symbol of resistance to the approaching heathen.
*History:* The foundation stone was laid by Bishop Bernward in 1007. The crypt was completed in 1015, and the whole building was finished in 1033, 11 years after the death of Bernward. Later alterations include the removal of the cubiform capitals (only two remain), the erection of the angel closures (only the N. remains), and the addition of a painted wooden ceiling. *Building:* The Romanesque parts of the church were built in two stages, and this is seen most clearly in the different *capitals*: cubiform capitals alternate with leaf capitals. A *high choir* was added above the *crypt* (extended 1193) with its famous *sarcophagus* of the canonised Bernward. The late-12C *closures* of the W. crossing are important German stucco work. The dimensions of the church are based on mathematical calculations: the crossing square is repeated 16 times in the nave, transepts and choir; the same balanced dimensions are found in the height of the building, to which attention is drawn by the red and white paintwork of the bearing arches. The three-storey N. gallery is perfect in its beauty. Late Gothic *tracery windows* were put into the S. aisle in the 15C. The *painted*

*Bronze door (1015), Dom*

*ceiling* is unique of its kind; its eight panels show the the story of God's saving acts from the Fall and the Tree of Jesse to Mary, and are a rare example of late Romanesque monumental painting.

**St. Godehard** (Godehardsplatz): This Catholic basilica was built from 1133–72 as a memorial church for Godehard, the successor of Bernward; he was also canonised. It survived the war largely unscathed and is a particularly pure example of Romanesque architecture. The exterior is dominated by the octagonal, pointed *crossing tower*. The *stucco tympanum* (*c.* 1205) on the N. door (Christ blessing between two saints) confirms the link with Upper Italy (Civate). The tall, slender nave has a flat ceiling, and the E. choir was extended by an ambulatory with altar niches on the French pattern: Godehard was canonised in Reims. The *capitals* are particularly lavishly decorated with figures, scenes and ornaments. In the W. part between the towers there are two *chapels*, one on top of the other. The *choir stalls* (*c.*1466) are good late Gothic work. The *Albani Psalter* in the *treasury* is a famous piece of 12C European book illustration.

**St.Mauritius** (Moritzberg): This church was built in the W. of the town by Hezilo, one of Bernward's successors. The *crypt* is under the E. *tower*. The Romanesque building, which includes very fine *cloisters* (12C with slight alteration later), was decorated in the baroque style in the 18C. Under the W. gallery is the *sarcophagus* of the founder of the church.

**Catholic Heiligkreuzkirche** (Kreuzstrasse): This church was originally a town gate with openings to the E. and W. The cube-shaped building was extended and altered under Bishops Bernward, Godehard and Hezilo in the 11C and completed in its present form by the addition of the Romanesque galleries, the transept and the choir. The Romanesque E. part of the church stands in contrast with the baroque W. organ wall. In 1712 the church was given a baroque façade on the pattern of the principal church of the Jesuit Order in Rome, Il Gesù.

**Protestant Church of St.Andreas** (Andreasplatz): The church and its high tower burned down in the Second World War but were rebuilt in a new and impressive way. The steep E. choir (14C) with its ambulatory, chapels and total height of 88.5 ft. is reminiscent of French cathedrals. The Romanesque lower part of the *tower* survives; it was raised in the late Gothic period but did not reach its present height of 377 ft. until the 19C.

**St. Magdalena** (Mühlenstrasse): This Gothic church, rebuilt after the Second World War, has in its *treasure* the famous Bernward cross, which the bishop is said to have made with his own hands. The two Bernward candlesticks (cast silver, *c.*1000) are from the saint's grave.

**Rathaus and Tempelhaus** (Markt): Only a few houses survived the Second World War. The *Rathaus* was rebuilt with its old proportions and Gothic exterior. The so-called *Tempelhaus* was named after a nearby synagogue. The 1457 ashlar building almost miraculously survived the war. The tall central section is framed by two decorative circular towers.The Renaissance oriel was added in 1591.

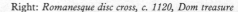

*St. Godehard*          Right: *Romanesque disc cross, c. 1120, Dom treasure*

*Tempelhaus by the Markt*

*St.Michael*

**Roemer- and Pelizaeus-Museum** (1 Am Steine): This has one of the most important *ancient Egyptian collections* in Germany and a collection of Chinese porcelain.

**Theatre:** The *Stadttheater Hildesheim GmbH* (6 Theaterstrasse) has a main house with 697 seats and a studio theatre.

### Hirsau = Calw 7260
Baden-Württemburg                              p.420□E 18

Hirsau, in the dark Black Forest valley of the Nagold, was in the 11C under Abbot Wilhelm the starting point of the reform movement which has gone into history as the *Hirsau Reform*. This was based on the principle of the monasteries' complete independence from all secular powers and utter submission to the power of the Pope. The Hirsau Reform influenced many existing and newly founded monasteries.

**Ruins of the Monastery of St. Peter and St.Paul:** The *church* was built under Abbot Wilhelm in 1082–91 on an eminence on the left bank of the Nagold as a

model building for the reform movement emanating from Cluny. Only the NW tower, the so-called 'Owl Tower' has survived; it was built *c.*1100. From the ground plan, revealed by thorough excavation, the large scale of the complex can be clearly seen. Alpirsbach (q.v.) gives the best impression of the normal dimensions of a church in the Hirsau style; the size of the Hirsau complex itself is unusual: it was more than 100 yards long and 24 yards wide. Parts of the *cloisters* (*c.*1490) and the *Mary Chapel* (1508–16) in the SE of the building survive from the Gothic period.

**St.Aurelius:** The older of the two Hirsau churches is in the lower part of the village on the right bank of the Nagold. It was built in the 11C on Carolingian foundation walls, partly demolished in the 16C and used as a barn and gymnasium in the 19C. Since 1955 it has been available for Catholic worhip again.

*Ducal Hunting Schloss:* This ruined Schloss was built in 1586–92 by G.Beer in typical Stuttgart Renaissance style; it was destroyed in 1692.

## Hirschhorn 6932

**Cemetery Chapel:** The Old Town between the Neckar bank and the steep hillside was so cramped that the church had to be built on the other side of the river in Ersheim. The Gothic *nave* with late Gothic window tracery and high beamed ceiling was consecrated in 1355; the choir, with its lavish tracery and net vaulting, was added in 1517. The furnishings include a late Gothic *tabernacle niche*, several 15C *wooden pictures* and numerous 14–17C *tombs*. There are also fragments of Gothic *wall paintings*.

**Former Carmelite Monastery Church:** The Carmelite monastery is on a slope above the town. The *wall paintings* in the church were heavily restored at the end of the 19C. On the neo-Gothic high altar is a Gothic *Madonna*, excellent 1510

–20 Nuremberg work. The *Anna Chapel* on the S. side has survived in good condition. It is equally richly furnished and has among other things a larger-than-life-size *Crucifixion Group*, a wood carving of *the Virgin and Child with St.Anne* and a *stone pulpit* on a twisted column (1618).

**Burg and Schloss:** The Burg and Schloss, built by the lords of Hirschhorn and now a hotel and restaurant, have been combined into a satisfactory unit. The oldest part is the powerful *curtain wall* (*c.*1200); the early Gothic *residence* was extended in 1583 – 6 into a splendid Renaissance building. The former *Burg chapel* (1346), with traces of wall paintings, is notable.

## Hirzenrain, Wetteraukreis 6476

**Protestant Parish Church/Former Monastery Church of St.Maria:** From 1431 the Augustinian canons extended a late-14C chapel and erected the building around the present nave. The most interesting feature is the late Gothic rood screen with its particularly striking figures of St. Peter, St. Paul, the Madonna and St. Augustine which make it one of the most important of this period in Germany. One of the sculptures is a Crescent Moon Madonna (*c.*1460).

## Hof an der Saale 8670

**Protestant Parish Church of St. Michaelis:** A fire in the town left only the foundation walls of the hall church built in the 14C and modified in the 15&16C. The exisiting neo-Gothic building is clearly the work of G.E.Saher. The decoration is exclusively 19C, the wooden cross in the nave 15C.

**Protestant Church of St.Lorenz:** This

*Ruined monastery, Hirsau* ▷

13C hall church was modified in the 16&17C and in 1813; the roof and ridge turret are the most striking features of the exterior. The pulpit altar is the work of P.Hetzel (1822). The Hertnid altar, a late Gothic altarpiece with side wings and painted panels was endowed in the 15C by the Dean of Bamberg Cathedral Hertnid von Stein, and was originally in St. Michael's. There is a notable 16C wooden cross and an 18C tomb.

**Protestant Hospital Church:** This rectangular church dating back to the 14C was modified in the 16&17C, given a neo-Gothic exterior in 1836 and restored in the 20C. The ceiling paintings and the pictures on the galleries are by H.A.Lohe. The 1511 altarpiece came from St.Michael's. The sounding-board of the 1561 pulpit is by J.N.Knoll (1693).

**Also worth seeing:** *Catholic Parish Church of St.Maria:* A 19C neo-Gothic building with furnishings from the same period. *Luther Church:* Built in 1936 by R.Reissinger. *Old Gymnasium* (Grammar School): The largely late Gothic Franciscan summer residence was modified in the 16C and extended to three storeys with ridge turrets. *Rathaus:* The three-storey building with its square staircase tower was modified in the 16C and then in 1823. The *houses* in the town were rebuilt in their original Biedermeier style after the fire. The façades in the Ludwigstrasse are particularly attractive. *Theresienstein Park:* The Heerdegen summer house, an artificial ruined Burg and the late Gothic gate can still be found in this park, laid out in 1815.

**Environs: Pilgramsreuth** (19 km. S.): *Protestant Parish Church* (15&16C), altar and pulpit by E.Räntz, late Gothic wall paintings and figures.
**Regnitzlosau** (11 km. E): One of the finest country churches in the area. Painted ceiling and gallery balustrade: the paintings are by H.A.Lohe (in the nave, 1672) and J.N.Walther (E. part of ceiling and galleries, 1744–7). The lavish baroque pulpit altar is framed by an equally magnificent structure with four columns and figures by W.A.Knoll (1743). Gravestone of C. von Reitzenstein (1655, studio of J.Brenck).

---

**Hofgeismar 3520**
Hessen                              p.416☐G 10

---

The town, presumed to originate from a former court of the Kings of Franconia, was an early centre of Protestantism in Germany. Independent Huguenot and Waldensian settlements were established here after 1685.

**Former Collegiate Church Liebfrauen** (Kirchplatz): The present Protestant parish church is a Gothic *hall church* but the tall W. tower and the W. doorway are part of the original Romanesque building. The earlier style can also be seen in the interior nave pillars with their decorated *corbels* (Adam and Eve can be seen at the S. end) and cushion *capitals*. Gothic features are the tall bi- and tripartite *tracery windows*, the decorated *doorway with columns* with the Coronation of the Virgin (*c.*1330) and the *groin vaulting*. A particularly interesting feature of this church is the *Hofgeismar Altar*, an important early German panel

*Pilgramsreuth (court), parish church*

*Gesundbrunnen, Hofgeismar*

painting. Only the side pieces have survived, and they have been combined to form a single panel. They show scenes from the Passion (*c.* 1310), and are of a high standard of design and colouring.

**Gesundbrunnen:** The part of the town known as Gesundbrunnen (lit. 'health spring') is a reminder that Hofgeismar was a spa until 1866. The *circular temple* was designed by S.L. du Ry. It is balanced in the W. by the *Wilhelmsbad* (extended in 1960–3 for the Protestant Academy) and in the E. by the *Friedrichsbad* (today a training centre for Protestant preachers). There is an old peoples' home in the former *stables* (1747). The *Schlösschen Schönburg*, a beautifully proportioned building (1787–9) by S.L. du Ry, is in the fine English park. The symmetrically arranged rooms are well decorated and furnished.

**Regional Museum:** The almost 1,000-year-old groin-vaulted Rathaus houses worthwhile exhibits on the town of Hofgeismar and the Diemelland.

---

## Höglwörth = Anger 8233

Bavaria                              p.422☐N 20

**Former Augustinian Canonry of St. Peter and St. Paul:** This monastery, charmingly situated on a peninsula, once an island, was refounded in 1125 by Archbishop Konrad of Salzburg. It fell into disrepair again, however, and was rebuilt once more in the 17C. The church was consecrated in 1689; its most striking features are the stucco work by B.Zöpf of Wessobrunn (1765) and the ceiling painting by F.N.Streicher (1765). The monastery was dissolved in 1817.

**Environs: Anger** (2 km. SE): The *parish church of St.Peter and St.Paul* (*c.*1450) has a *Madonna with Rosary* (*c.*1680) and a 16C

*Pietà* on the high altar, *2 rococo sculptures* (on the left side wall of nun-benefactress Ellanpurg and on the right a Good Shepherd), both by I.G.Itzlfeldner, who was also responsible for the 5 sculptures in the *upper chapel*.

## Hohenkirchen = 2941 Wangerland 1
Lower Saxony                              p.412□D 4

**Protestant Parish Church:** This typical *Frisian granite ashlar church* dates from the 13C, and houses some remarkable works of art. The finest feature is the *font* with relief figures (Mary and Magi); the stone trough, supported by 4 heavily-maned lions, has been in the same place since the church was founded *c.*1250. The *altar* and the *pulpit* are by L.Münstermann, a Master between the periods of Renaissance mannerism and early baroque.

## Hohenschwangau = Schwangau 8959
Bayern                                    p.422□IK 21

**Schloss:** Hohenschwangau is essentially a 13C building which had fallen into disrepair. It was rebuilt as late as 1832 by the scene painter and stage designer D.Quaglio for Crown Prince Maximilian of Bavaria as a summer residence in the English Tudor style and furnished according to the prevailing Romantic taste. The rooms are *painted* with remarkable courtly and legendary designs by M. von Schwind.

**Also worth seeing:** N. of the Schloss in the direction of Schwangau is the pilgrimage church of *St. Koloman* (1673; stucco by J.Schmuzer).

## Holtfeld = Burgholzhausen 4807
Nordrhein-Westfalen                       p.414□E 8

**Schloss** (8 km. S. of Burgholzhausen): This *moated Schloss* on two islands was built in 1599–1602 in the so-called Lippe

Renaissance style. A striking feature is the *Herrenhaus* with its fine S. gable. The *stone coats of arms* on the various buildings and gatehouses are notable.

## Homberg an der Efze 3588
Hessen                                    p.416□G 11

**Protestant Church/Former Church of St.Maria:** The church is on a raised terrace above the market place; only the foundations of its Romanesque predecesor were included in the present building, which dates mainly from the 14C. The tower is a later addition. Like many other churches in Hessen this church is related to the Elisabeth church in Marburg (q.v.). In the interior the *original paintwork* has been restored on the basis of traces of the old paint. The *relief heads* (God the Father, Holy Ghost, Lamb of God) on the keystones of the vaulting and the *capitals* with their lavish wreaths of interest. In the N. aisle are 7 late Gothic *Stations of the Cross* which were previously on the terrace of the Rathaus. The lavish decoration on the 18C *organ front* and various *tombs* are also remarkable.

**Townscape:** Homberg is one of the most interesting-looking towns in Hessen. The *Gasthaus zur Krone* (1480) is one of the striking 15–19C *half-timbered buildings*, of which the best are in the market place. The *Heimatmuseum* is housed in the *Hochzeitshaus* (26 Pfarrstrasse).

## Höxter 3470
Nordrhein-Westfalen                       p.414□G 9

Höxter grew in competition with the powerful monastery of Corvey (q.v.), which wanted to direct travellers on the old trade route between Rhine and Elbe over its own Weser bridge. Höxter joined the Hanseatic League and became a flourishing merchant town; it has now assimilated the former monastery of Corvey.

*Schloss Hohenschwangau* ▷

*Kilianikirche, Höxter*

**Protestant Kiliani Church** (An der Kilianikirche): The present building originated from an 11C flat basilica, vaulted in the 12C. The best feature is the *W. façade* with a raised central section, based on the westwork of its neighbour and rival Corvey. The spires are a later addition to the two dark red Sollingen sandstone *towers*. The S. aisle was replaced by a *hall* in the 15C. The altar is decorated with a late Gothic *Crucifixion Group* (c.1500), and the 1597 *pulpit* has alabaster reliefs.

**Townscape:** Old municipal buildings and a large number of splendid houses have survived from the period of the town's greatest success. In the entrance hall of the half-timbered *Rathaus* (1610–13) with its carved oriel is a *Romanesque relief* of the public weighmaster. The *Deanery* with its double gable, oriel and belfry is one of the finest half-timbered buildings in Germany (Markt). Other largely Renaissance buildings are to be found in *Westerbachstrasse*

(Nos 2, 10&34) and in *Nikolai-, Markt- and Stummrigestrasse.*

**Also worth seeing:** The *Höxter-Corvey Museum* in the Corvey Schloss (q.v.).

**Environs: Brakel** (15 km. S.): The *Catholic Parish Church of St.Michael and John the Baptist*, much modified from the 12–18C, has remarkable *baroque furnishings*. The *former Capuchin Church of St. Franziskus* (1715–18) is the earliest church building by J.C.Schlaun and contains good *rococo sculpture*, including a *St.Nepomuk*. **Beverungen** (20 km. SW): Striking features are the numerous 17C *half-timbered gabled houses* and the carved wooden *baroque decoration* in the *Catholic Parish Church of St.John the Baptist* (1682–98) and the *Burg* (c.1330), a former moated Burg with a six-storey *residence*.

---

## Hugenpoet (bei Kettwig)=Essen 4300
Nordrhein-Westfalen                    p.416☐B 10

**Schloss Hugenpoet:** This moated Schloss in the Ruhr valley was built in 1647–96 on the foundations of an earlier building and thoroughly restored in the early 19C. The *Renaissance fireplaces* on the ground floor from Schloss Horst an der Emscher are worth seeing. The three finest are named Cain and Abel fireplace, Lot fireplace and Troy fireplace, after the themes which they depict.

---

## Husum 2250
Schleswig-Holstein                    p.412☐F 2

The 'grey town by the sea' owes its fame to two men: Theodor Storm, who is buried here, and C.F.Hansen, the leading Danish classical architect, whose family came from Husum.

**Marienkirche:** This was one of the most important late Gothic buildings in Schleswig-Holstein, but it was pulled down in 1807 and replaced with a *classi-*

*cal*, severely Protestant *preaching church* (1829 – 33) by the above-mentioned C.F.Hansen. Only a *bronze font* remains of the furnishings of the former church, which were auctioned in 1807.

**Schloss** (Schlossstrasse): The Schloss was once a large complex with buildings in Dutch Renaissance style, but it was largely demolished in the 18C; 4 *sandstone fireplaces* with alabaster reliefs are among the surviving features.

**Museums:** There is a museum of N. Frisian local history in the so-called *Nissenhaus* (25 Herzog-Adolph-Strasse). The *open-air museum in the Osterfeld Farmhouse* (11 Nordhusumerstrasse) has exhibits on peasant life and crafts.

**Also worth seeing:** There are many fine *merchants' houses* and the modified *Rathaus* in the Grosse Strasse (Nos 15 and 30), at 21 Norderstrasse, 3 Hohlengasse (one of Theodor Storm's houses) and in the Markt (Nos 1–3). Theodor Storm, who set many of his Novellen in Husum, is buried in the *St. Jürgen Cemetery*.

## Idar-Oberstein 6580

Rheinland-Pfalz           p.416☐C 15

In 1933 13 districts at the confluence of
the Idar brook and the Nahe joined to form
the town of Idar-Oberstein. The appearance of the town is determined by geographical factors: between the Nahe and
the Burgberg there was little room for extending the Old Town, with the result that
the houses are huddled closely together and
in many cases intricately interlocked.

**Protestant Felsenkirche** (rock church;
in Oberstein): This was built in 1482–4 in
a niche carved out of the rock. Falling rock
necessitated fundamental renovation in
1742 and 1927–9. The valuable *altarpiece*
on a gold background dates from *c.*1420.
Below the church a row of 16–18C houses
has survived.

**Castle Ruins:** On precipitous crags above
the rock church stand the ruins of the Altes
Schloss (*c.*1000; keep and remains of
curtain-wall survive) and of the Neues
Schloss (*c.*1200; surrounding walls of the
residential buildings and parts of round
towers survive). The Neues Schloss was
destroyed by fire in 1865.

**Also worth seeing:** The *Weiherschleife*
(Tiefensteiner Strasse) is the last jewel-
cutting shop still to be powered by water.

The shop cut mainly agates; according to
recent research they were being mined in
Roman times in the *Steinkaulenberg,* the oldest jewel mine in Europe which is still accessible. *Museum unter der Felsenkirche* (in
Oberstein): exhibits on the jewellery and
precious stone industry. *Deutsches Edel-
steinmuseum* (on the 1st floor of the 22-
storey Diamant- und Edelsteinbörse,
Schleiferplatz): All known precious stones
are displayed both uncut and cut in this,
the largest exhibition of its kind in Europe.

*Idar Oberstein with Felsenkirche*

*Unionskirche, Idstein*

## Idstein 6270
Hessen                                    p.416 □ E 14

**Former Collegiate Church of St. Martin/Protestant Parish Church/Unionskirche** (Martin-Luther-Strasse): This church has a varied architectural history. It is based on a 12&13C building, of which only the lower part of the tower on the N. side of the choir has survived. Most parts of the present Gothic building resulted from rebuilding in 1328 –40. Later the *Reiterchörlein* (family vault at the E. end of the S. aisle, 15C) and the *Sebastianskapelle* (now the sacristy, 1509) were added. In 1655-77 Count Johann had the church converted into a court church designed to set an emphasis on preaching, and provided unusually lavish interior furnishing. The interior is full of *canvases* from the Antwerp School of Peter Paul Rubens, which make it look rather like a gallery of baroque painting. The ceiling painting was added in 1725 by M.Pronner of Giessen. There are numerous Gothic, Renaissance and baroque *tombs*. By the N. wall of the choir is the tomb (1721) of Prince Georg August Samuel and his wife, made to a design by M.von Welsch by the Mainz court architect M.Hiernle in 1728 -31. The *high altar* was built by A.Harnisch in 1673. The wrought-iron *choir screen* (1726) was made in the workshop of J.U.Zais. The organ is by J.H.Stumm. The church's name commemorates the *Nassauische Union* concluded by Lutherans and members of the Reformed Church.

**Former Burg and Schloss** (Schlossgasse): The *Burg* was founded in the 12C. The massive gatehouse was completed in 1497, the keep ('Witches' Tower') around 1400. The chancellery building (1565), with its Renaissance half-timbered gable, is now used by the civic authrities. The *Schloss* was built in 1614-34 and acquired the court chapel in 1717. Inside the Schloss the stucco-work, in particular, in the two Imperial rooms is lavish and extravagant. The former bedroom is arranged in Pompeian style with alcoves and ornate ceiling painting. A grammar school is now housed in the palace.

**Also worth seeing:** *Rathaus* (König-Adolph-Platz): The Town Hall, built in 1898, was destroyed by a landslide in 1928, but was rebuilt in 1932–4. *Half-timbered buildings:* Amongst the numerous half-timbered buildings, which often date from the 16C, but mainly from the 17C, the best are the houses on König-Adolph-Platz (numbers 2,3,5,11 and 15) the so-called *Killingerhaus* with symbolic carvings on the Franconian oriels and the gable-point, in the Obergasse (1,2,4,5,14,15,16,18, 20,24), in the Borngasse and on the Weiherwiese.

---

**Ilbenstadt=Niddatal 6361**

Hessen                                     p.416□F 14

**Former Premonstratensian Monastery with Monastery Church of St. Mary and St.Peter, St.Paul:** Gottfried v. Kappenberg founded the monastery, one of the first of this Order in Germany, in 1123; it flourished in the 12&13C. The *former monastery church* is one of the most important Romanesque churches in Germany. It was started in 1139 and consecrated in 1159. The superb stonemasonry (such as the battling lions and centaurs) was executed by the same Italian craftsmen who worked on the imperial cathedrals in Speyer and Mainz. The Romanesque attains its ultimate perfection in the two towers, the upper storeys of which have remarkable corner pilaster strips, round-arch frescos and two tiers of arches at the level of the bells. Of the furnishings, the 14C wall paintings on the S. side of the choir (including that of the founder, Gottfried v. Kappenberg) are worthy of mention. The *tomb* of the founder was complete at the end of the 13C, but was later reworked. By the nave pillars are large *Apostle figures* and a *Madonna* (by C.L.Werr; 1700). Another fine feature is

the *organ*, with its splendid carved front by J.Onymus (Mainz) (1733–5). Organ gallery and parapet were made by F.Vossbach (1732). The *monastery buildings* now house the Charity of St.Gottfried (the monastery was dissolved in 1803).

**Also worth seeing:** The *Ritterhof* dates from 1742, while the *Nidda Bridge* was completed in 1745.

---

**Indersdorf = Markt Indersdorf 8062**

Bavaria                                    p.422□K 19

**Former Augustinian Canonry with Church:** The canonry was founded in 1120, at the insistence of the Pope, in exchange for the lifting of the excommunication of Pfalzgraf Otto IV. The church was completed by 1128, then rebuilt after a fire in 1264 and modified in the baroque period. Of importance are the lavish stucco by F.X.Feuchtmayer and frescos by M.Günther (1755); the frescos depict scenes from the life of St.Augustine. A *Rosary Chapel* was added to the S. aisle at the time of the baroque modifications; this also acquired lavish stucco and fresco decorations in 1755. In spite of these baroque additions the Romanesque design of the elongated basilica is still easily recognizable. Part of the monastery complex (1693 –1704) is the *Nikolaus chapel*.

---

**Ingelheim 6507**

Rheinland-Pfalz                            p.416□D 14

**Protestant Burg Church:** This 14&15C Gothic church (12C tower) has survived in excellent condition and can be considered a perfect example of a fortified church building. It is surrounded by a graveyard and the whole complex is protected by walls and towers 26–30 ft. high. The exterior of the church is dominated by the 4 roofs of varying height and design. The lavish furnishing includes *glass painting* (middle window in the choir; 15C) and numerous *tombs* of the local nobility (along the walls of the nave). *Late Gothic tendril*

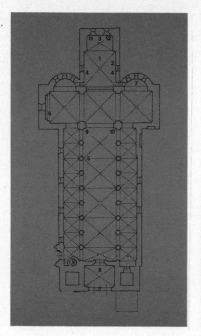

*Former monastery church, Ilbenstadt*

**Ilbenstadt, former monastery church 1** Tomb of Gottfried von Kappenberg, late 13C **2** Remains of 14C wall paintings **3** Virgin Mary seated, 1st half of 14C **4** Choir stalls, 1677 **5** Pulpit, 1690; figures by Joh. Wolfgang Fröhlicher **6** St. Gottfried by J.W.Fröhlicher, 1695 **7** Crucifixion by J.Friedrich Strassmayer, 1700 **8** Organ by Johann Onymus, 1733-35; casing by Franz Vossbach **9** Luke by M.Bitterich, 1742 **10** Mark by M.Bitterich, 1742 **11** Augustine by B.Zamels, 1744 **12**Norbert by B.Zamels, 1744

*paintings* were discovered on the vaulting during restoration work.

**Kaiserpfalz** (Im Saal): Ingelheim is considered to be the birthplace of Charlemagne, and it is said that he commissioned a Kaiserpfalz of especial size and splendour to show reverence for the town of his birth. Very little has survived of this building, which in the Middle Ages was frequently used for important gatherings. A reconstruction of the complex, which was burned down by the French in 1689,

is now to be found in the Städtisches Museum (Rathausplatz).

**Also worth seeing:** The Romanesque *Protestant parish church* of *c.*1100 has been altered many times. The most recent extension was begun in 1961.

## Ingolstadt 8070

Bavaria                                    p.422□K 18

The first official reference to Ingolstadt was made in 806. Duke Ludwig the Severe built a Burg after 1255. In 1472 Duke Ludwig the Rich founded the University and helped the town to attain a special position in spiritual and cultural life. Ingolstadt was also a centre of the Counter-Reformation, under the leadership of Petrus Canisius. Until the 17C the town drew its economic importance from its position on the Danube. Ingolstadt is now an important in-

*Liebfrauenmünster, Ingolstadt;* Right: *Detail from the high altar*

dustrial town (including automobile industry, large refineries).

**Town fortifications:** Since 1430 Ingolstadt has been enclosed by 3 rings of walls, giving it the reputation of being the best-fortified town in S. Germany. Even Gustav Adolf stormed the town in vain during the Thirty Years War. The walls, equipped in many places with semi-circular brick towers, have largely survived intact, although of the great main gates there remains only the Heiliges-Kreuz-Tor (Kreuzstrasse), one of the most striking gates of its period. Directly behind it, towards the town centre, is the Liebfrauenkirche.

**Parish Church of Our Lady/Liebfrauenmünster** (1 Kreuzstrasse): This plain brick building is one of the most beautiful achievements of the late Gothic period in Bavaria. The church was started in 1425 under Duke Ludwig the Bearded

and work continued until 1536. The nave is 267 ft. long, 101 ft. wide and 90 ft. high. Pillars and net vaulting show characteristic late Gothic design. Showpiece of the *interior decoration* is the *high altar* (1572; late Gothic and Renaissance) by the Munich painter H. Mielich. It is nearly 30 ft. high and contains 91 paintings. The *choir stalls* and the *pulpit* are very fine; they are probably by the Munich joiner Wenzel. The individual *side chapels* are also richly furnished.

**Parish Church of St.Moritz** (4 Moritzstrasse): The first church was built here in Carolingian times. A late Romanesque building, consecrated in 1234, was incorporated into the new buildings of the 13&14C. During the 18C the church acquired excellent stucco by J.B. Zimmerman and frescos by P.Helterhof (removed in the 19C, partially renewed in 1946). Inside the basilica the *high altar* with tabernacle (1765) deserves particular attention.

*Liebfrauenmünster, choir*

There are also numerous figures in wood and stone. The altar on the E. wall of the N. aisle has a very fine silver statuette of the *Immaculata* (1760 by J.F.Canzler, Munich).

**Minorite Church** (Harderstrasse): This basilica, dating back to the 13C, is famous for its numerous tombs and powerful high altar. Among the best *tombs* are that of Elisabeth and Dorothea Esterreicher (at the entrance: *c.* 1522) and of Herr and Frau Esterreicher (in the Montfort Chapel, which was added around 1700). The Tettenhammer (1543) and Helmhauser (1548) tombs on the S. wall are by the famous sculptor L.Hering of Eichstätt. The *high altar* (1755) dominates the interior. Since the Second World War the *Lichtenau Chapel* (added 1601) has contained the miraculous image of the Schutter Madonna (15C) and the Preysing epitaph, made by I.Günther in 1770 for the (destroyed) Franciscan church.

**Asam Church of Maria Viktoria** (1 Neubaustrasse): This building was consecrated in 1736 as a prayer room for the Marianist student congregation; there are similar rooms in Munich, Augsburg, Landshut, Amberg and Dillingen. It has not been clarified whether the famous C.D.Asam was himself the architect, but it is certain that he created the frescos. Asam is said to have taken only 8 weeks to complete the frescos and to have been paid 10,000 guilders for them; he immediately returned the money as a donation, however. In the centre is the enormous *ceiling painting*, a fresco of unusual wealth of colour. Several excellent *oil paintings* hang on the walls. The *high altar* is by J.M.Fischer (Dillingen, *c.* 1763). Also of interest are the *wall seats* (1748) and the inlaid *cupboard doors* . A particularly valuable piece is the *Turkish monstrance* (1708), in which the Battle of Lepanto is depicted.

**Neues Schloss** (Paradeplatz): This

*Altes Schloss/Herzogskasten*

Schloss, built in 1418–32 at the behest of Ludwig the Bearded, acquired several extension buildings over the succeeding centuries and in 1539 the existing moat ramparts were strengthened by formidable bastions. Thorough restoration was undertaken after the Second World War. The Schloss now houses the *Bayerische Armeemuseum* (q.v.).

**Altes Schloss/Herzogskasten** (Hallstrasse): After 1255 Duke Ludwig the Severe had a first Burg built at the SE corner of the little town; its main features have survived. The nickname 'Herzogskasten' means something like 'Duke's hovel'. After the completion of the Neues Schloss (see above) the Herzogskasten was used as a granary.

**Theater und Werkstattbühne** (1 Schlosslände): The Ingolstadt Theatre has its own company, which plays in this building designed by H.-W.Hämer and opened in 1966; the main house has 671 seats, while the workshop has 99.

**Museums:** *Bayerische Armeemuseum* (Neues Schloss, 4 Paradeplatz): This Bavarian Army museum was opened in 1881 in the arsenal on the Oberwiesenfeld in Munich, and moved to Ingoldstadt after the Second World War. The collections include weapons and uniforms from 1500, and also military equpment and other associated exhibits (graphics, paintings, tin figures). *Deutsches Medizinhistorisches Museum* (18–20 Anatomiestrasse): exhibits on the history of anatomy and surgery and also pictures of doctors and a garden of medicinal plants.

**Also worth seeing:** The Gnadental Chapel (1487) in Harderstrasse, the 14C Hospital Church of the Holy Ghost in Donaustrasse, the Hohe Schule, built in 1438, the Anatomie building (after 1723), the Konviktbau (seminary) of the Jesuit

*Marienaltar, Isenhagen convent*

College (1583), town houses and the Altes and the Neues Rathaus.

---

### Irsee (über Kaufbeuren) 8951
Bavaria                                    p.422□I 20

**Former Benedictine Monastery Church Mariae Himmelfahrt:** The present church was built from 1699–1702 to plans by the Vorarlberg architect F.Beer on the site of a medieval church. The two towers were completed a good 50 years later. The interior is dominated by the lavish stucco of members of the famous Wessobrunn Schmuzer family. The unusual pulpit (1725) is in the shape of a ship, with a swelling sail as sounding-board. Putti are discernible in the rigging.

**Environs:** In Eggenthal (N. of Irsee) a rotunda was built as the Pilgrimage Chapel

Mariae Seelenberg in 1697. Here too there is lavish stucco by the Wessobrunn School.

---

### Isen 8254
Bavaria                                    p.422□L 19

**Former Collegiate Church:** The present church was preceded by a monastery foundation of the 8C. The essentially late Romanesque pillared basilica with three aisles was decorated with lavish stucco and frescos in 1699; in the 18C two further stucco altars were added. A larger-than-life-size *crucifix* survives from earlier times (1530). The *crypt* is also of interest.

**Museum:** The local history collection in the Altes Rathaus documents the Battle of Hohenlinden (1800) and shows rustic and craft instruments.

---

### Isenhagen = Hankensbüttel 3122
Lower Saxony                               p.414□I 7

**Convent:** W. of Wittingen, between Gifthorn and Uelzen, lies this former Cistercian convent (founded 1243), which from 1540 was run as a Protestant institution for ladies. The convent has varied and interesting furnishings (frescos, embroideries, old furniture). The outstanding pieces in the *Collegiate Church* are the high altar (altarpiece *c.*1420), a Renaissance pulpit (1683), the Marienaltar (*c.*1520) and a lectern (*c.*1200). Also of interest are the cloisters and the library.

---

### Iserlohn 5860
Nordrhein-Westfalen                        p.416□D 10

The iron industry, still an important part of the economy of Iserlohn, has been established here since the Middle Ages.

**Upper Town Church/St. Marien** (Am Poth): Most parts of this late Gothic hall church date from the 14C. Outstanding is the carved altar (*c.*1400; probably from a

Dutch workshop), one of the most important works of this period in Westphalia.

**Protestant Pankratius Church/ Bauernkirche** (3 Inselstrasse): This originally Romanesque pillared basilica was altered in late Gothic style. The principal feature of the furnishings is an altar shrine (mid 15C).

**Haus der Heimat** (1 Fritz-Kühn-Platz): Near the Pankratius church a patrician house with open-air steps was built in 1763 (19C alterations); it houses the town administration and the interesting *Heimatmuseum* (local history).

**Parktheater** (Alexanderhöhe): This building, opened in 1964, seats 805. Iserlohn does not have its own company.

## Isny 7972
Baden-Württemberg                    p.422□H 21

This former imperial town is now a spa and winter-sports resort. In the 13C Isny acquired its ring of walls, still largely intact. The Blaserturm in the market place was once the town watchtower.

**Former Benedictine Monastery Church of St. Jakob and St. Georg/Catholic Parish Church** (Schloss): The earlier 11C buildings were destroyed by fire in 1631 and replaced from 1661 by the present church, a hall complex of unusual uniformity. The opulent rococo decoration dates from the 18C (stucco by H.G.Gigl, frescos by J.G.Holzhey). The massive high altar was made by J.Ruetz (1758), who was also responsible for the side altars and the pulpit. The former monastery buildings (17C, with refectory and Chapel of the Virgin Mary) now house a *hospital*.

**Rathaus** (Espantor): After the old Town Hall burned down in 1631 several town houses were combined to form a new Town Hall; generally they have survived in good condition. The Wassertorturm now houses the *Heimatmuseum* (local history).

## Itzehoe 2210
Schleswig-Holstein                    p.412□G 3

A fire in 1657 destroyed large parts of this town, which has had a rich and varied history. Itzehoe's wealth was established in the Middle Ages as a result of its favourable position on trade routes. In the 17C it became a garrison and fortress town. In 1627 Wallenstein prepared for the capture of the Breitenburg from Itzehoe.

**Protestant Church of St. Laurentius** (Kirchenstrasse): This massive brick building dates from 1716. Of interest are the numerous *vaults* in which Holstein nobles are buried in metal sarcophagi. A late Gothic cloister linked the church with the former *Cistercian convent*. Outstanding among the furnishings are the carved altar (1661), the wooden pulpit (1661) and the organ front (1718).

**St.Jürgen Chapel** (Sandberg): After the fire of 1657 the chapel was rebuilt. The interior paintwork dating from 1657–72 has survived intact.

**Schloss Breitenburg** (4.5 km. SE of Itzehoe): This Schloss, once attacked by Wallenstein, was rebuilt in the 18&19C. Preserved are a 1582 well and the *castle chapel* of 1634 (interesting altar and sarcophagus).

**Also worth seeing:** *Heimatmuseum Prinzesshof* (20 Viktoriastrasse): This two-storey 17C house was the residence of Elector Wilhelm I in 1804. Today local history collections and also prehistoric finds and excavations are displayed here. *Germanengrab* (Am Lornsenplatz): Bronze Age stone tomb. *Rathaus* (Neustädter Markt) dating from 1695, *houses* (particularly in the Breite Strasse, Krämerstrasse and Kapellenstrasse).

*St. Jürgen chapel, Itzehoe* ▷

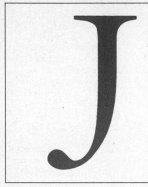

# J

## Jagsthausen 7109
Baden-Württemberg       p.420□G 16

**Schloss:** In the 14C the lords of Berlichingen took over an old castle and its estate. Götz von Berlichingen (the 'Knight with the Iron Hand') was born here in 1480; he entered literary history as a result of Goethe's play 'Götz von Berlichingen'. Residence, Rittersaal and almost all the other rooms of the *Götzenburg* have survived in good condition. Every summer an extremely well-attended festival is held in the castle courtyard. Apart from the Götzenburg a red and a new Schloss exist, although these are of lesser importance.

## Jever 2942
Lower Saxony       p.414□D 4

This little town (pop. 13,000) was of particular importance even in Roman times because of its proximity to the sea; later it played a significant role in Frisian coastal shipping. Motto in hard times: 'Godes fründ, aller wereld fiand' ('friend to God, foe to all the world').

**Protestant Town Church** (16 Kirchplatz): A 10C church burned down, and so did several medieval successors. After a further fire in 1728 a new building was built, which in 1959 also fell victim to the flames. The *funerary chapel*, containing the *tomb* of the Frisian chief *Edo Wiemken the Younger* (d.1511) was undamaged. The monumental tomb is an unusual combination of wood and stone by Antwerp artists (1561–4). It has an impressively large number of individual figures, hardly equalled by any other tomb.

**Schloss:** Building began in the 14C, although the present complex dates largely from the 15&16C. The Schloss consists of

*Tomb of Edo Wiemken, Jever*

4 irregular wings around a keep, which is visible for miles (baroque upper part, 1736). The audience chamber is worthy of particular attention, with coloured leather wall-hangings and a splendid coffered ceiling (1560–4). Today the Schloss houses the *Heimatmuseum* (local history).

**Also worth seeing:** *Rathaus* (Kirchplatz): This was built by A.von Bentheim as Town Hall and wine tavern (1609–16). The council chamber has fine panelling. The distinctive front sections of the building date mostly from a later period. The town has many old houses with fine doorways, often colourfully painted.

**Environs: Gödens** (11 km. S.): Moated Schloss Gödens.

---

**Johannisberg 6225**
Hessen                                     p.416☐D 14

**Schloss Johannisberg** (4 km. NE of Geisenheim): Benedictine monks founded a double monastery on the site of the present Schloss in the 11C; the last abbot stood down in 1563. The Prince Bishops of Fulda had the complex extended in baroque style in 1718–25. During the Franco-Prussian war the Schloss was temporarily in the hands of the French and fell when peace was made to the Austrians, who gave it to Prince Metternich. Schloss and church were modified in the neoclassical style in 1826. The complex was rebuilt following its destruction in the Second World War. 'Schloss Johannisberger', one of the finest wines of the Rheingau, can be drunk in the Schloss, which is surrounded by vineyards

**Former Monastery Church:** Rebuilding after the Second World War restored the 11&12C design to a large extent; it had suffered over the centuries in the course of numerous alterations.

---

**Jork 2155**
Lower Saxony                              p.414☐G 5

This charming little community (pop. 8, 500) is at the heart of the 'Altes Land', a region near Stade known for its fruit-growing.

**Farmhouses:** These half-timbered

*Audience chamber in the Jever Schloss*

houses, nearly all thatched, date for the most part from before 1800. Of interest are the front doors, which are splendidly decorated with lavish carving. Some of the richly ornamented 'bridal doors' are also preserved; there is an old custom that these doors should only be opened to admit the newly-wed bride, or at her death. The barrel-vaulted *brick church* was first mentioned in the 13C.

## Jülich 5170

Nordrhein-Westfalen                    p.416□A 11

The Roman fort of Juliacum lay at the important junction of the Cologne-Aachen and Cologne-Tongern-Bavai roads. The town was later fought over by the Normans, as well as the Guelphs and Hohenstaufens and the Archbishop of Cologne. The town was damaged by several terrible fires as well as by all these quarrels, and in 1944 it was almost totally destroyed in an air-raid.

**Priory Church** (Markt): The W. tower recalls the original 12C church, replaced by a neo-Gothic building in 1878. The lower floor of the tower forms a porch leading into the nave, while the two upper storeys combine to form a high domed space.

**Citadel and Schloss** (Schlossstrasse): This extensive complex was built from the 16–18C, altered, partly dismantled, and then finally destroyed in the Second World War. The original design of this once-famous Renaissance fortress is still discernible, however.

**Römisch-Germanisches Museum** (Altes Rathaus, Kölnstrasse): Finds from the time of the Romans are the focal point of the collection.

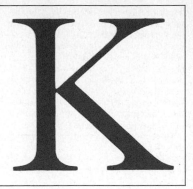

# K

## Kaiserslautern 6750

Rheinland-Pfalz          p.416☐D 16

The 'Kaiser' prefix probably goes back to the Emperor Frederick Barbarossa, who built a Burg in the the River Lauter here in 1152; it was blown up by the French in 1703, during the War of the Spanish Succession. The Schloss of Pfalzgraf Johann Casimir (1570–80), which stood near the old Hohenstaufen castle, also fell victim to the same attack.

**Former Premonstratensian Church/Collegiate Church of St. Martin und St.Maria** (Marktstr.13): The narrow, single-aisled choir was built for the monastery church in early Gothic style in 1250–90. The three-aisled nave, making this the first hall church in the Pfalz, was not added until around 1320 as a lay church. Over the W. part of the old choir is the octagonal early Gothic tower, which was rebuilt after bomb-damage. The W. towers were added in the 16C.

**Former Minorite Church/St.Martin's Church** (4 Klosterstrasse): The former Minorite church and present Catholic parish church of St.Martin was built around 1300. As a church of the mendicant Order it is extremely plain; the flat stucco ceiling of the nave was created in 1710.

**Fruchthalle** (Fruchthallenstrasse): Built by A. von Voit in 1843–6. This three-storey building with round-arch windows was temporarily seat of the provisional government following the 1848 revolution. On the upper floor there is a large banqueting hall.

**Rathaus** (Rathausplatz): With its 24 storeys and height of 260 ft. the Town Hall is an emblem of the town. Incorporated into the complex is the *Casimirsaal*, which belonged to the erstwhile Schloss of Pfalzgraf Johann Casimir and was built on the foundations of the even older Barbarossa Burg.

**Museums:** The *Pfalzgalerie* in the Pfälzische Landgewerbeanstalt (Museumsplatz 1): 19&20C art and temporary exhibitions. *Theodor-Zink-Museum* (Steinstr.48): Local history collections.

**Theatres:** *Pfalztheater am Fackelrondell* with opera, operetta and straight plays. *Kammerbühne* in the Kreissparkasse.

## Kaisheim 8851

Bavaria          p.422☐I 18

**Former Cistercian Monastery Church:** This late high Gothic building (274 ft. long, 78 ft. wide) dating from 1352–87 is the most beautiful of its kind in the Bavarian-Swabian plain. In accordance with the rules of the Order there were originally no towers on the W. front, but a century later the wide crossing tower was added (1459). The spire and the interior were converted to baroque in the 18C. Of particular interest is the chancel with its double ambulatory. The most valuable item of the interior furnishings was once the late Gothic altar by H.Holbein the Elder, now in the Alte Pinakothek in Munich (q.v.), which was replaced by the present baroque altar in 1673. Worthy of note is the *tomb slab* of the monastery's founder Heinrich von Lechsgemünd (1434).

---

## Kalkar 4192
Nordrhein-Westfalen                        p.414□A 9

In the late Middle Ages Kalkar was an important trading town and member of the Hanseatic League. At the same time it developed into an artistic centre (carved altars of the 'Kalkar School').

**Parish Church of St.Nikolai** (Jan-Joest-Strasse): This three-aisled brick building with 3 parallel saddle-roofs is a Lower Rhenish version of the Gothic hall-church (see Kleve). The tall narrow windows and graduated buttresses emphasise the Gothic tendency to the vertical. The building was started in the early 15C, but more than a century passed before the various chapels, porches and the sacristy were complete. The really important feature of the church is its furnishing. Pride of place goes to the *high altar* (1448–1501), carved by Meister Loedewich with 208 three-dimensional figures. J. Joest of Wesel painted the 20 pictures on the panels; their colourfulness and lively depiction of the Passion are both of a high order. The most important figure of the Kalkar School was H.Douvermann. His *Altar of the Seven Sorrows of the Virgin* dates from 1519–22 and stands in the S. side choir. In the middle of the carved altar is a wonderful Pietà framed with scenes from the Life of the Virgin Mary and surrounded, as in Xanten (q.v.), with lavish tendril work. One of Douvermann's later works, the *Altar of the Holy Trinity*

(1528), stands at the entrance of the S. side choir. The church also contains many superb sculptures, including the *Altar of the Seven Joys* (1507–9), the *Altar of St.Anne* and the *Altar of St. John*, a *Crucifixion group* and the graceful *Virgin candelabrum* with the double figure of the Madonna.

**Städtisches Museum** (5 Hanselaerstrasse): Local history, manuscript collection with an edition of the *Sachsenspiegel* (1390–1400).

**Also worth seeing:** *Rathaus* (1438–46) with tall hipped roof, battlements with corner towers and an octagonal staircase tower. *Beginenhof* with medieval wall and ceiling paintings. *Church of St.Anthony* (14&15C). Romanesque twin-towered basilica of *St. Clemens* (12C).

---

## Karden=Treis-Karden 5402
Rheinland-Pfalz                           p.416□C 14

Karden, together with Treis, now forms the double town of Treis-Karden on both banks of the Mosel. Karden (on the left bank), as Vicus Cardena, is supposed once to have been the base of St.Castor and his companions during their mission to the area around Trier.

**Former Collegiate Church of St. Castor:** The present Catholic parish church shows 3 recognisable building stages. Three storeys of the W. tower and the substructure of the church survive from the earliest building, consecrated in 1121. In 1183 the choir, transept and E. towers were renovated after serious damage by fire, and in 1260 the nave was converted into a Gothic groin-vaulted basilica. Inside one can follow the development from early Romanesque design on the E. side, through late Romanesque in the choir apse to early Gothic elements in the nave. The most valuable of the furnishings is the *high altar* (early 15C), made entirely of baked clay. Apart from remains of the *cloister*, various buildings from the former *collegiate area* are still preserved, the finest of which is the late Romanesque *Propsteihaus*

*High altar in St.Nikolai, Kalkar*

(priory house, *c.*1200, known as 'Korbisch', because the Chorbischof of Trier once resided there). Of cultural and historical interest are the wall paintings in *Haus Boosfeld,* the former seminary. 8 pictures illustrate the saga of Henry the Lion according to a poem by Michael Wyssenhere, and 9 pictures depict the story of Susanna in the Bath.

## Karlsruhe 7500
Baden-Württemberg                              p.420☐E 17

After the Durlach Burg of the Margraves of Baden had been destroyed by the French in 1689, Margrave Karl Wilhelm laid the foundation stone for his new residence in Hardtwald, his hunting-ground S. of Durlach, in 1715: the focal point was to be the palace, for which first the octagonal tower was built and from which 32 streets radiate. Only nine of these lead into the

town, the other 23 fan out to the adjoining woods. The line of the palace and its side-buildings is continued by other buildings of controlled height and design. The founder of 'Carols Ruhe' (Charles' Rest) Karl Wilhelm invited people of all denominations from all over Germany to settle in the town. The town design described above also determined the further enlargement of Karlsruhe after his death (1738) by his successor Karl Friedrich (1738–1811), who in 1800 took the architect F. Weinbrenner into his service. Weinbrenner laid out the *Kaiserstrasse,* which runs parallel to the palace as precisely as if drawn by a ruler. From the palace the *Karl-Friedrich-Strasse* joins the Kaiserstrasse at right angles and leads over Rondellplatz to the *Ettlinger Tor.* In the *Marktplatz* stands the *Pyramid,* originally built of wood, but later rebuilt in stone, beneath which is the tomb of the town's founder Karl Wilhelm. Famous people who were either born in Karlsruhe or lived here for a long time include the

*Panorama with Ducal Schloss, Karlsruhe*

writer Johann Peter Hebel and the poet and novelist Joseph Victor von Scheffel (1826–86). Scheffel and the painters Karl F.Lessing, W.Trübner and H.Thoma are buried in Karlsruhe's *Hauptfriedhof*. The actor Eduard Devrient made the Badische Hoftheater one of Germany's finest theatres from 1852–70. Since 1956 the *Hermann Hesse Prize* for literary and academic work, worth DM 10, 000, has been awarded every 3 years in Karlsruhe.

**Former Ducal Schloss** (Schlossplatz): Only the Schloss tower (1715), focal point of the town's fan-shaped plan, survives of the old Schloss. The other buildings were replaced from 1749–81 by conversions or new buildings, which nevertheless exactly followed the original ground plans. Designs by many architects (including several projects by Balthasar Neumann) were incorporated into the final plan by F.v.Kesslau. The Schloss buildings form a right angle and, along with the adjoining side

buildings, enclose the large gardens in front of the Schloss. The Schloss was badly damaged in the Second World War, but restored to the original design. The interior was expansively redesigned as a modern museum (see below.

**Catholic Parish Church of St.Stephan** (Erbprinzenstrasse): The architect F.Weinbrenner took the Pantheon in Rome as his model for this church (1808–14). He built a rotunda with a massive wooden dome (98 ft. span) and a columned portico on a Greek cruciform ground plan. The church was rebuilt in a simplified form after the Second World War. The dome is now made of reinforced concrete.

**Protestant Stadtkirche** (Marktplatz): From 1807 – 11 Weinbrenner built this church for the Protestants, parallel to St. Stephan's, with a columned portico like a Roman temple. The interior, redesigned after the war on modern lines, used to have

*Marktplatz with Pyramid, Karlsruhe*

three aisles with two-storey galleries on the left and right.

**Other Weinbrenner Buildings:** Weinbrenner's buildings, characterized by formal austerity, also include the former *Margräfliches Palais* on Rondellplatz (1803–14), connected with a bank since rebuilding, the *Rathaus* (Marktplatz, opposite the Stadtkirche and the *Mint* (Stephanienstrasse), completed in 1826, after Weinbrenner's death.

**Museums:** The *Badische Landesmuseum* (in the Schloss, Schlossplatz) includes collections on pre- and early history, folklore, Greek, Etruscan, Roman and Egyptian art, and sculpture and craft from the Middle Ages to the present day. The *Kunsthalle* (2–6 Hans-Thoma-Strasse), in a building of 1838–46, is one of Germany's principal picture galleries with important works of early German painting, baroque and Romantic painting (including Grünewald,

Holbein the Younger, Lucas Cranach, Dürer, H.B.Grien, Boucher and particularly Chardin). Hans Thoma, who has a section to himself, was director of the gallery from 1899–1919. Housed in the neighbouring *Orangerie* is the Modern department with works by Courbet, Manet, Monet, Cézanne, Trübner, Liebermann, Kokoschka, the Brücke artists and other Moderns. *Städtische Galerie* (10 Karlstrasse): 19&20C painting and sculpture. *Verkehrsmuseum* (63 Werderstrasse): With Drais's foot-propelled bicycle. *Oberrheinisches Dichtermuseum* (6 Röntgenstrasse): This museum is devoted to writers of the Upper Rhine region, and based on inherited memorabilia of the writer Joseph Victor von Scheffel, since supplemented by nearly 5000 volumes, and complemented by paintings, illustrations, manuscripts and books.

**Theatres:** The *Badische Staatstheater* (11 Baumeisterstrasse) was opened in 1975 and

*St. Stephan, Karlsruhe*

is now a home for opera and straight theatre. The *Grosse Haus* seats 1002, while the adjoining *Kleine Haus* takes a maximum of 550. *Die Insel* (14–16 Wilhelmstrasse) (180 seats) is reserved for straight plays. The *Kammertheater* (79 Waldstrasse) is privately owned and has 143 seats.

**Also worth seeing:** (in Durlach): The former Margrave's Schloss (16C) with Prinzessinnenbau and Schloss chapel (now Pfinzgaumuseum).

---

**Kassel 3500**

Hessen                      p.416□G 11

Kassel was a prince's seat as early as 1277. The grandson of St. Elisabeth built his Burg on the high bank of the Fulda; remains of the fortifications of a later building can still be seen at the 'Rondell'. Friedrich II of Hesse-Kassel (1760–85),

who hired out 12,000 of his countrymen as mercenaries to the English in the N. American War of Independence, together with his predecessors Wilhelm VIII and Landgrave Karl, made Kassel one of the finest residences in Europe with the Karlsaue, the Orangery, Wilhelmshöhe Park, the Gemäldegalerie, Friedrichsplatz and numerous palaces and mansions. The heavy damage sustained during the last war has altered the appearance of the town, but not destroyed it completely: the principal features, from the Hercules statue in Wilhelmshöhe to Friedrichsplatz and the Karlsaue, have survived.

**Protestant Brüderkirche** (Brüderstrasse): This church (built from 1292–1376) belonged to the former Carmelite monastery (1292) and is a typical building of the Mendicant Order: there is only one aisle, on the N. side. Above the N. portal is a beautiful relief of the 'Wailing over the body of Christ' (*c.* 1500).

*Löwenburg, Wilhelmshöhe*

**Former Collegiate Church of St. Martin and St.Elisabeth** (Luther-Platz): The present Protestant parish church was once the main church in the 'Freiheit' area established by the Landgraves. The Gothic choir was completed in 1367, but the rest of the building not until 1462. The church was gutted during the last war, but has been rebuilt. The choir is closed off by a glass screen for worship; the newly-vaulted nave is equipped for musical performances. All that survives of the interior furnishings is the splendid 39 ft. high *alabaster tomb* of Landgrave Philipp the Magnanimous (who introduced the Reformation in Kassel) and his wife Christine (1567 – 72). The artists were E.Godefroy and his pupil A.Liquier Beaumont. In the *vault* below the sacristy is the magnificent sarcophagus of the creator of the baroque residence of Kassel, Landgrave Karl (d.1730).

**Karlskirche** (Karlsplatz): The reformed Karlskirche looks somewhat lost since its rebuilding; it stands in the middle of the destroyed old Huguenot quarter, built for the French Protestants by Landgrave Karl in the upper New Town to a plan by Paul du Ry. This octagonal rotunda was built by P.du Ry in 1698–1710. It was rebuilt with a simple tent roof topped with a little cage-like bell tower instead of a dome.

**Elisabeth Hospital** (Oberste Gasse): This was built around 1300 on the SW edge of the medieval town and outside the old walls. After the war it was authentically rebuilt and now houses a large number of wine bars. In a wall niche stands the sandstone figure of St.Elisabeth (early 15C).

**Ottoneum** (Steinweg): Opposite the Elisabeth Hospital stands the *Kunsthaus*, which has been the *Museum fü Naturkunde* (natural history) since 1884. It was built in 1602–6 as Germany's first theatre and named after the Landgrave's son Otto. The

*Ottoneum, Kassel*

Renaissance building by W.Vernukken is impressive for the variety of its window grouping (conversion by P.du Ry) and the gable scrolls.

**Fridericianum** (Friedrichsplatz): Landgrave Friedrich II had this early neoclassical building (1769–79) built by S.L.du Ry on the edge of Friedrichsplatz for his art collections and library. In 1955 the first *documenta* — moved into the burnt-out ruins of the Fridericianum; this was a trend-setting exhibition of modern art, and became a recurrent event (1959, 1964, 1968 and 1972).

**Friedrichsplatz and Karlsaue:** Friedrichsplatz (380 yards long, 163 yards wide) is one of the largest squares in Germany. The later Opernplatz is also part of it; it is a terraced balcony over the lower-lying Karlsaue (now cut off by Frankfurter Strasse). The whole complex was originally conceived as a green area, in the middle of which was to stand the marble monument of the Landgrave Friedrich II. The *Karlsaue* is a symmetrical park laid out by Landgrave Karl. Five paths radiate from the ruined *Orangery* (1702–10); together with the parterre lawn in front of it, the Orangery is used for open-air statuary exhibitions which are part of the 'documenta'. The middle path leads to a pond laid out to a symmetrical design; beyond this and on exactly the same line is a raised square (now called 'Siebenbergen'), which is a paradise for horticulturalists. The whole complex once had grottoes, cascades, mazes and a garden theatre, but the French garden style died out in the 19C. Next to the Orangery stands the reconstructed *Marmorbad* (1722–28), a cube topped by a balustrade with figures. Inside is a marble pool, around which runs an ambulatory with figures and reliefs.

**Wilhelmshöhe, Park and Schloss** (Wilhelmshöher Allee): The park in the Wilhelmshöhe district, planned by Landgrave Karl and architect G.F.Guerniero, is unique among European baroque gardens. The original plan was that water from the highest point of the Habichtswald, where an enormous octagon with the giant statue of *Hercules* was built (total height 235 ft.), should flow down a cascade to the palace below (height difference of 770 ft.). However, only a third of these plans could be realised under Karl. The English style, which replaced the French style in the 2nd half of the 18C, altered the plans: sentimental-romantic chapels, ruins, waterfalls, pyramid aqueducts, pavilions and fountains were distributed over the whole area. The last point in this development is the *Löwenburg*, conceived from the start as a ruined Burg, which the later Elector, Landgrave Wilhelm had built by H.C.Jussow. In its lavish rooms, furnished in the style of medieval knights, Wilhelm used to withdraw to lead a temporary existence as a hermit. Elector Wilhelm also commissioned *Schloss Wilhelmshöhe* (1786 –1803) by S.L.du Ry and H.C.Jussow. This neoclassical building, originally a central building with 2 oblique wings, loosely connected to the main building by terraces, was seriously marred when the height of the terraces was increased. The building now houses the famous *Staatliche Gemäldegalerie*, after a long period in provisional quarters in the Landesmuseum in Brüder-Grimm-Platz. It is the most important gallery in Germany, alongside those in Munich, Dresden and Berlin, and has paintings by Rembrandt (18), Rubens (21), van Dyck (12), Titian, Frans Hals, Terborch, Poussin, Dürer, H.B.Grien, Altdorfer and many others. The *Antiques Department* with the famous 'Kassel Apollo' is ranked third after Berlin and Munich.

**Wilhelmshöher Allee:** Habichtswald residence, park and town, were all linked together under Landgrave Friedrich II by the dead straight Wilhelmshöher Allee (designed by S.L.du Ry, 1781). The *statue of Hercules* high above Wilhelmshöhe Park marks its line. It starts from Brüder-Grimm-Platz at the Königstor with the 2

*Alabaster tomb of Landgrave Philipp the Magnanimous and his wife Christine, St. Martin and St. Elisabeth, Kassel*

Wachhäuser, where the Brothers Grimm lived from 1814–22 and wrote down their fairy tales. The *Murrhard Library* opposite (324,000 volumes and 4500 manuscripts) possesses Germany's oldest literary monument, the manuscript of the 'Hildebrandslied' (*c.* 800).

**Museums:** The *Brüder-Grimm-Museum* (4a Brüder-Grimm-Platz): Autographs, prints and secondary literature on the works of the brothers Jacob and Wilhelm Grimm. *Neue Galerie* (1 Schöne Aussicht) with 19&20C painting and sculpture. *Staatliche Kunstsammlungen:* in Schloss Wilhelmshöhe (see above). *Deutsches Tapetenmuseum* (in the Hessisches Landesmuseum) with exhibits from 7 centuries.

**Theatres:** The *oper* of the State Theatre (15 Friedrichsplatz) have long had a fine reputation. The same building is also the

*Fridericianum, Kassel*                    *Schloss Wilhelmshöhe* ▷

home of *straight theatre*. The *Komödie* plays at 39 Friedrich-Ebert-Strasse (145 seats).

**Also worth seeing:** Palace of *Bellevue* (2 Schöne Aussicht). Remains of the old *town fortifications*.

**Environs: Wilhelmsthal** (9 km. N.): Near Wilhelmshöhe, reached via Rasenallee, is the rococo Schlösschen of *Wilhelmsthal*, built for Landgrave Wilhelm VIII. The architect was F.Cuvilliés the Elder, who here created his most beautiful and elegant building.

---

**Kastellaun 5448**
Rheinland-Pfalz                          p.416☐C 14

This is probably Trigorium, first mentioned in 820; it achieved the status of a town in 1305 and again in 1969. Of interest

are the ruins of the *Burg* (W. wall of the residence of the upper Burg), destroyed by the French in 1689.

---

**Kastl bei Amberg 8455**
Bavaria                                  p.422☐L 16

**Former Benedictine Monastery Church of St. Peter:** The monastery, built around 1103 on the site of a Burg, was founded by Count von Sulzbach and Countess Luitgard (statues next to the entrance to the paradise). The three-aisled essentially Romanesque church with partly Gothic apses was consecrated in 1129. The barrel vault over the choir (*c.*1400) is one of the oldest in Bavaria. The *pillar frescos* were revealed and extended in 1906. Of interest are the numerous *tombs* (since 1964 in the paradise porch). The great majority of the furnishings were not brought into the church until the 18C. The two monu-

*Former Benedictine monastery church of St. Peter, Kastl*

*Interior of St. Peter, Kastl*

ments to Abbot Menger (d. 1554), which depict him at the feet of the Virgin and praying before the Cross, were made by L.Hering. The former *monastery buildings* have survived in part; they were used from 1636 by the Jesuits, from 1825 to 1929 by the local authority and now house a Hungarian grammar school.

**Environs: Pfaffenhofen** (1.5 km. W.): Along with the *Schweppermann Collection* in the Schweppermannburg (13&14C) there is also the Romanesque *Catholic parish church of the Assumption of the Virgin* with an early-13C *Karner* (two-storey graveyard chapel) from the start of the 13C. Fragments of the *interior painting* (1400–20) have survived.

---

**Kaub 5425**

Rheinland-Pfalz                        p.416 □ D 14

---

**Burg Gutenfels** (above the town): From

*Pfalzgrafenstein castle, Kaub*

the 12–19C a toll was exacted from ships passing through the narrow part of the Rhine by Kaub by the ever-changing Lords of Burg Gutenfels. The castle (13C core), in which Gustavus Adolphus lived for a lengthy period during the Thirty Years War, was rebuilt at the end of the 19C. It is a stately complex with 2 long parallel wings, battlements, gatehouse, keep and wooden arbours in the courtyard.

**Pfalzgrafenstein:** This place became famous because of the castle, known as the 'Pfalz bei Kaub' ('imperial palace of Kaub') or the 'Steinernes Schiff' ('stone ship') and standing on an island in the Rhine. In 1327 a five-cornered toll tower was first built, around which a 3-storey defence wall was built in late Gothic times. With the bastion added in 1607 the complex resembles a stone ship in the river. The 'Pfalz' went down in history when Blücher crossed the Rhine at Kaub in the course of his campaign against Napoleon.

**Blücher Museum** (Metzgergasse 6): The collection, brought together here in 3 departments since 1935, commemorates Blücher's crossing of the Rhine (see above) and the Field Marshal's life.

### Kaufbeuren 8950
Bavaria                                   p.422☐I 20

In 1713 Sophie von La Roche was born in the former free Imperial city of Kaufbeuren. She was engaged to the writer C.M.Wieland and considered 'Governess of the Daughters of Germany', as well as 'Poet Mother' of the Sturm und Drang (Storm and Stress) movement. Kaufbeuren is also the birthplace of Ludwig Ganghofer (1855–1920), who wrote novels set in the Alps and became one of the most successful German writers ever; commemorating him are collections in the *Heimatmuseum* (12–14 Kaisergässchen) and a memorial

*High altar by J.Lederer (1436) in St. Blasius, Kaufbeuren*

plaque on the house where he was born (Kirchplatz).

**Fortified Church of St. Blasius** (13 Blasiusberg): This chapel on a hill in the NW of the town is built on the old town wall. The original wall passage leads right through the nave (1484) and the tower is actually a defence tower. The *high altar* made by J.Lederer for the choir (1436) is one of the major works of Upper Swabian late Gothic (1518). Some of the figures were taken from an older shrine, the panels were painted by J.Mack. The walls are decorated with 5 groups of *late Gothic painting cycles.* Also worthy of mention amongst the valuable furnishings in the stylistically uniform chapel are the *choir stalls* and an expressive *crucifix* on a processional cross (*c.*1350).

**Also worth seeing:** Former Franciscan church (1315, greatly altered several times);

St.Cosmas and St.Damian (1494; arrangement in the 17&18C).

---

**Kelheim 8420**

Bavaria                                    p.422☐L 17

Evidence of the settling of the area goes back to the Old Stone Age. 'Cheleheim' was first documented in 866 but the town was laid out as it is now (*c.* 1206) by Duke Ludwig II, the Severe. The pattern of right-angled streets and right-angled surrounding walls is known in the history of town planning as the Wittelsbach type (Wittelsbacher Stadtgründungstyp). At the junction of the principal longitudinal and latitudinal roads stood, until 1824, the Rathaus (now in the former town clerks' building at the NE corner of the junction). Very little remains of the old town walls, but 3 town gates (Donautor, Altmühltor, Mittertor) have survived from the 13&14C.

**Liberation Hall:** This 150 ft. high monumental building was built on the 325 ft. Michelsberg, the site of an old Celtic place of worship. The building was intended to commemorate the Wars of Liberation against Napoleon in 1813–15 and was initiated by Ludwig I of Bavaria following his Greek journey in 1836. Begun in Byzantine style by F.Gärtner (1842), it was altered, after the latter's death, by L. von Klenze in 'Antique-Roman' style (completed 1863). On the outside there are similarities with the Tomb of Theoderich in Ravenna, and inside with the Pantheon in Rome. The two enormous pillared colonnades are topped by a coffered dome. 34 marble Victories (for the 34 German states) are set in a wide circle with 17 plaques between them inscribed with the names of the battles (figures by L. von Schwanthaler). In the architrave above the gallery, borne by 72 granite columns, are the names of towns captured or recaptured in the war. The interior is clad in the finest materials, while the building itself is executed in rendered brick.

**Also of interest:** The *Parish Church of the Assumption of the Virgin* (NE side of the

*Liberation hall near Kelheim*

Marktplatz) dates from the 15C and has a late Gothic Madonna (*c*.1440, over the S. side portal). The *Hospital Church of St. Johannes/Otto Chapel* goes back to the murder (1231) of Duke Ludwig ('The Kelheimer'); it was built by the murdered man's son. The *Herzogskasten* ('Duke's Box') has survived from the Middle Ages and now houses a grammar school.

**Archäologisches und Heimatmuseum** (11 Ledergasse): Pre- and early history, folk-lore.

## Kempen 4152

Nordrhein-Westfalen                     p.416☐B 10

This little town on the Lower Rhine became known through its great son Thomas à Kempis (1380–1471), theologian, mystic and author of the 'Imitation of Christ', one of the most important works of late medieval religious literature.

**Catholic Parish Church of St. Maria/Propsteikirche** (Kirchplatz): The Marienkirche is in the centre of the town, which was built to a circular design. The four-cornered Romanesque W. tower with its round-arched portal and the nave (on the foundations of an older building *c*.1200) were built in the 13C. The Gothic S. aisle, hall choir and nave vaulting were added in the 14C. The N. aisle was added in 1453–60. The lavish late Gothic furnishings come from Cologne, Antwerp and the Lower Rhine. Important pieces include: the tower-like *tabernacle* (1461), particularly valuable carved *choir stalls* (1493) and a splendid wrought-iron *Mary candelabrum* (1508). Of the 20 documented altars there remain 3 from the Antwerp School (high altar, 1513; altar of St.George, 1525, and altar of St.Anthony, 1540).

**Städtisches Kramer Museum** (21 Burgstrasse): The former Franciscan monastery (18C) contains a collection on Lower Rhine interior decoration. The monastery church contains the *Museum für niederrheinische Sakralkunst:* sculpture collection, objects used in churches and paraments (14–20C).

**Also worth seeing:** Parts of the *town fortifications* (c.1370) are still preserved in Kuhstrasse (Kuhtor), the Möhlenring and in the Hessenring. The former *Burg* of the Electors of Cologne (1396–1400) was altered several times, but is nevertheless of importance as a Lower Rhine brick building. *St.Peter's Chapel* (12C) and *Chapel of the Holy Ghost* (1421).

---

**Kempten 8960**

Bavaria                                    p.422□H 21

Remains of the walls of *Oppidum Cambodunum* (basilica, baths, forum etc.), first mentioned in AD18, excavated in the district of Lindenberg (restarted in 1982), recall the Roman period. The later history of the town was greatly affected by the parallel existence of the Imperial City, Protestant since 1527 and the Benedictine Abbey, directly subordinate to the Emperor; during the Thirty Years War, with the help of the Swedes and Imperial troops they destroyed each other to a large extent.

**Collegiate Church of St.Lorenz** (Stiftsplatz): This was Germany's first large church building after the Thirty Years War. In 1651 M.Beer of Bregenz wanted to create a massive building on the N. Italian pattern; J.Serro took over from 1654 and completed the building in 1670. Inside the church the vaulting catches the visitor's attention. The *stucco* is by G.Zuccalli, the *paintings* by A.Asper. The fine *choir stalls* (1669) are embellished with polychrome scagliola work. The altars date from the 17&18C. Below the W. gallery is a *fork crucifix* (c.1350): Tree of Life.

**Former Prince Abbots' Residence** (Residenzplatz): Prince Abbot Roman Giel von Gielsberg had a new Residence built by M.Beer at the same time as the church (1651–70). The interior is particularly fine; the stucco decoration shows the develop-

ment from 1683 (Fürstensaal) to around 1760 (Gästezimmer). In the 18C the area around the great *State Rooms* was extended in S. German rococo style (1734–42). Master architect was J.G.Üblherr, who borrowed ideas on ornamentation from such masters as Cuvilliés and J.B. and D.Zimmermann.

**Museums:** The Allgäuer Heimatmuseum (1 Grosser Kornhausplatz) is housed on 3 floors of the former Prince Abbots' Kornhaus. The Römische Sammlung Cambodunum (31 Residenzplatz; Roman remains) is housed in the Zumsteinhaus, a neoclassical building of 1802.

**Also worth seeing:** *St.Mang,* the old town church, is modest in comparison with the dominant collegiate church. It is a late Gothic brick building (1427), the nave of which (flat basilica ceiling) is vaulted and decorated with rococo-style stucco (1767&8). The Gothic *Rathaus* (1474) with its onion tower and double flight of steps conceals the roofs of the former Weavers' Guildhall. — The *Rathausbrunnen* was created by the brass-founder H.Krumpe, who operated in Augsburg and Munich (1601). Also: The *Londoner Hof* (2 Residenzplatz) of 1764 with rococo façade, the late Gothic *Weberhaus* (20 Gerberstrasse) and the beautiful Ponikau House (10 Rathausplatz) have preserved their beautiful rococo furnishings, also by I.G.Üblherr. *Keck Chapel* (Kaufbeurer Strasse) with choir frescos (c.1460).

---

**Kevelaer 4178**

Nordrhein-Westfalen                        p.414□A 10

**Gnadenkapelle** (Kapellenplatz): Since the Thirty Years War the Gnadenkapelle has been the goal of countless pilgrimages to the 'Madonna von Kevelaer'. In 1642, after a vision, the pedlar Hendrick Busman had a shrine built for a miraculous image, a small Antwerp copper etching with a so-called Luxemburg Madonna. In 1654 the shrine was modified as a small, hexagonal domed building of simple rural baroque design. In 1643–5 H.van Arssen built a first

*Stateroom, Residenz, Kempten*

pilgrimage church, the so-called *Kerzenkapelle*. In 1858–64 the new *Pilgrimage Church of St.Maria* was built in neo-Gothic style, a basilica holding 5000 people, annually visited by more than half a million pilgrims.

**Museum für niederrheinische Volkskunde** (Hauptstr.18): In a Lower Rhine town house of 1704, with collections on pre-history, local arts and crafts and Lower Rhine sculptures.

## Kiedrich 6229

Hessen                               p.416☐D 14

The church precinct, surrounded by a high wall enclosing parish church, funerary chapel and some beautiful half-timbered buildings, is the lively centre of this former place of pilgrimage; also attractive are the Town Hall (1585) and numerous fine houses in the Markt-, Kammer-, Sutton-, Scharfenstein- and Oberstrasse .

**Parish Church of St. Dionysius und St. Valentinus:** The church was built in various stages in the 14&15C, and certainly influenced by the Frankfurt architect M.Gerthener. There is interesting stellar vaulting in the choir and the nave (1481, by a Bavarian master from the school of H.Stethaimer). The stonemasonry is of a lavishness hardly equalled elsewhere in the Rheingau. The relief above the beautiful W. portal, 'Annunciation and Coronation of the Virgin Mary', is a charming work of the Soft Style (*c.* 1420). The church was authentically restored by J.Sutton in 1857 –76. Amongst the diverse and valuable furnishings the most beautiful pieces are a *seated Madonna* (Cologne, *c.*1330, below the choir-screen), the nave *pews*, which have survived in their original form (*c.*1510) and the refurbished *organ* with a casing which can be closed (*c.*1500).

**Funerary Chapel of St. Michael:** A
slender, lofty building (c. 1440) with the
mortuary on the lower ground floor. On
the upper floor hangs a beautiful wrought-
iron *chandelier* with a life-size *double
Madonna* on a crescent moon (c. 1520), a
carving from the Backofen workshop. The
chapel leads to a sort of loggia with a
Gothic tracery sandstone screen; from here
the relics of St. Valentine are displayed to
the pilgrims.

**Scharfenstein Castle Ruins:** First mentioned in 1211, once inhabited by the
Archbishops of Mainz, ruined since the
17C.

---

**Kiel 2300**
Schleswig-Holstein                    p.412☐H 2

---

In the Middle Ages and subsequently sea
trade meant little to this town, which was
very much in the shadow of Lübeck and
Hamburg. Kiel did not begin to grow
rapidly until the 19C, when it fell to the
Prussians and became the naval port of the
Empire. Docks sprang up on the E. bank
of the firth and the Kiel Canal (Nord-
Ostsee-Kanal) was built, considerably
changing the appearance of the town. After the Second World War Kiel, the capital of Schleswig-Holstein, was replanned
on a generous scale. The cultural history
of Kiel, apart from its buildings, museums
and theatres and the annual 'Kieler
Woche', is connected above all with the impressionist poet Detlev Lilliencron, born
in 12 Herzog-Friedrich-Strasse, the narrative authors Timm Kröger, Theodor
Storm and the brothers Tycho and Theodor Mommsen, who together with Storm
compiled the 'Liederbuch dreier Freunde'
in Kiel. The *Kulturpreis der Stadt Kiel* is
awarded annually during the 'Kieler
Woche' to deserving creative artists or patrons of the arts. At irregular intervals the
*Internationale Scheersbergpreis* for acting
and amateur theatre is also awarded in
Kiel.

**Protestant Church of St. Nicholas** (Alter Markt): This Gothic hall building,
built from the mid 13C onwards, was converted 100 years later along the lines of the
Church of St. Peter in Lübeck (q.v.) and
given a long choir. In the 19C the church
acquired a neo-Gothic shell and after the
Second World War it was rebuilt to a partly
modern design with concrete pillars and
reinforced concrete ceiling. The carved and
painted *high altar* survived, along with the
Patriarchs' Altar (1460), the *bronze font*
(1344), a monumental *triumphal cross*
(1490) and the baroque pulpit (1705). In
front of the NW corner of the church
stands 'der Geistkämpfer', by Ernst
Barlach.

**Rathaus** (9 Fleethörn): This building
(1907–11) has an art nouveau ashlar façade
and a massive tower with a pointed copper
spire.

**Former Franciscan Monastery** (Falck-
strasse): This is the city's oldest building
(1240–46); the *refectory* (now a theological
seminary) and the W. wing of the *cloister*
have survived. Let into the cloister wall is
the tombstone of the city's founder, Count
Adolf von Schauenburg (d. 1261.

**Former Schloss** (Schlossstrasse): The
13C Schauenburg castle was converted
into a Renaissance palace in the 16C. After its destruction in the Second World War
a section was rebuilt in an authentic style
(1961–5). It houses a local history collection and a cultural centre (see below).

**Museums:** *Stadt- und Schiffahrtsmuseum*
(19 Dänische Strasse and 65 Wall): local
history, history of shipbuilding and navigation. *Landesgeschichtliche Sammlung*
(Schloss): regional history and folklore,
music and manuscripts. *Kunsthalle und
Archäologische Sammlung* (1 – 7
Düsternbrooker Weg): casts of Greek
sculptures, collection of Greek vases,
painting and graphic arts (16–20C). *Völkerkundemuseum* (3 Hegewichstrasse): ethnography of the South Seas, E. Asia and
Africa. *Stiftung Pommern* (44 Dänische
Strasse): painting, and cultural history of
Pomerania.

**Theatres:** *Opernhaus am Kleinen Kiel:*

*W. portal, parish church, Kiedrich*

*Naval monument in Laboe near Kiel*

Built in 1905 – 7 and restructured in 1952&3; 869 seats. *Schauspielhaus* (103 Holtenauer Strasse); 540 seats.

**Also worth seeing:** Catholic Church of St.Nicholas (1891) with Virgin Mary Altar of *c.*1515.

**Environs: Laboe** (19 km. N.): Naval Monument (1927 – 36) by G.A.Munzer. **Rammsee** (6 km. SW): *Schleswig-Holsteinisches Freilichtmuseum* open-air museum of farmhouses and agricultural implements.

---

## Kirchhain
Hessen        p.416☐F 12

**Protestant Parish Church of St.Jakob** (in Langenstein): The 13C church is historically important because of the late Gothic double-net vaulting in the choir,

dating from 1522; there is also late Gothic vault painting. The other parts of the church are in rustic baroque style.

---

## Kirchheim am Ries 7081
Baden-Württemberg      p.422☐H 17

This little village still has 3 churches: the large church of the former Cistercian convent, the 15C Protestant parish church of St.Jakob and the Church of St.Martin (now the Protestant cemetery chapel); its walls contain stones from the Roman period. The altar table in the choir is supported by an inverted Roman votive altar.

**Catholic Parish Church/Former Cistercian Convent Church of the Assumption of Mary:** This typical High Gothic building was built around 1310. In the 18C it acquired rococo decoration and baroque altars. The high altar (1756) in

*Marienaltar (c.1515) in Nikolauskirche, Kiel*

particular is in stark contrast with the linear austerity of the Gothic architecture. The side altars with their twisted columns, as well as the pulpit, are also baroque (17C). Of interest is a Soft-Style *pietà* (*c.*1420).

### Kirchheim, Schwaben 8949

Bavaria                                        p.422☐I 19

**Fuggerschloss:** On the gently sloping bank of the Mindel there stood a knight's Burg, which Hans Fugger, heir to the wealthy Fugger family in Augsburg (q.v.), had extended as family Schloss in 1578–85. The best artists of the age created a princely residence here, and it has survived as one of the finest Renaissance buildings in Swabia. The most important part of the complex is the *Banqueting Hall*, for which W.Dietrich made superb door frames and the lavish *coffered ceiling*. The dark figures

in the wall-niches are striking, but the finest feature is the *chimney-piece* with seated and recumbent figures by H.Gerhart and C.Pallago (1582 – 5), based on Michelangelo's Florentine Medici tombs. The use of space is reminiscent of Heiligenberg (q.v.) and of the now destroyed Goldene Saal in the Augsburg Rathaus (q.v.). Hans Fugger commissioned a grandiose *altar tomb* in multi-coloured marble from H.Gerhart and A.Colin. This stood for a long time in St.Ulrich's in Augsburg, but was recently installed in the 16C *Schloss chapel* in Kirchheim.

### Kirchheimbolanden 6719

Rheinland-Pfalz                              p.416☐D 15

The town of Kirchheim owes its distinctive appearance to an 18C Schloss, 2 churches, a series of uniformly elegant baroque houses and remains of town fortifications with 3 towers and 2 town gates; it acquired the second part of its name in the 19C.

**Former Lutheran Schloss Church/Protestant Parish Church of St. Paul** (Marktplatz): This church was built together with the castle in 1739–44. It is a hall building set on the diagonal with lofty, 62 ft. high vaulting and galleries on the narow end walls; altar and prince's box are face to face on the broad sides. During a visit in 1778 W.A.Mozart played on the organ (1745), made by master organbuilder J.M.Stumm.

**Schloss** (Marktplatz): The architect of the Schloss in Mannheim was responsible for this building (1738–40), which has survived only on part and has been much altered. A few beautiful portals in the garden (c.1750), outbuildings such as the coach house, orangery and former tennis court give an indication of the size and style of the complex.

**Protestant Parish Church of St. Peter/formerly St. Remigius:** This building dates back to the 12C (choir tower). In the 18C the dome was added and the church furnished in baroque style. By the SW corner of the tower is an interesting sundial (probably 13C).

**Also worth seeing:** *Town fortification:* The Apothekerturm, the Graue and the Rote Turm (restored) are part of the former town fortifications and are linked by an roofed wall passage along which it is still possible to walk. The Upper and Lower town gates are also in good condition. The two-storey *houses* in the Amtsstrasse are set out in such a way that no individual house looks more important than its neighbour, in the spirit of 18C egalitarianism. The *Heimatmuseum* (14 Amtsstrasse) includes mementoes of the period of the volunteer corps of 1848&9.

---

**Kisslegg 7964**
Baden-Württemberg          p.420□G 20

---

**Parish Church of St.Gallus:** The Füs-

*Monastery church, Kirchheim am Ries*

sen architect J.G.Fischer skilfully modified the original 9&10C church in 1734–8. The ceiling, arches and walls are decorated with lavish *stucco* by J.Schütz. Outstanding items of the furnishings are the *pulpit,* the *sounding-board* and the *font,* all by J.M.Hegenauer, c.1740–5. The sacristy *silver* includes 21 statues and reliefs by the Augsburg goldsmiths Mittnacht and Mader.

**Gottersackerkappelle St. Anna** (NW, above the village): This baroque cemetery chapel (1718&19 has fine Wessobrunn stucco.

**Altes Schloss:** The Schloss of the Princes of Waldburg-Wolfegg has tall stepped gables on both sides and four round corner towers (early 16C). Fine wall paintings (c.1580) have been uncovered in the NE corner tower. Many of the rooms were redecorated by J.G.Fischer during the baroque period.

**Neues Schloss:** Amongst the artists who built and arranged this 3-storey building in 1721-7 to the design of J.G.Fischer was the famous J.M.Feuchtmayer, who made the 8 *stucco figures of Sybils* on the staircase. Also of interest is the *chapel*. The *Schlossmuseum* is interesting and there is a *broom museum* in the former kitchen buildings.

**Environs: Bärenweiler** (4 km. SW): The *high altar* by K.Hegenauer in the *Kapelle zur Heiligen Dreifaltigkeit* is worth seeing. **Rötsee** (8 km. NE): There are 18C *ceiling paintings* by A.Wiedemann and a 15C *statue of the Madonna* from the Multscher studio in Ulm in the *pilgrimage church of St.Maria* .

---

**Kitzingen 8710**
Bavaria                                    p.418□H 15

---

Kitzingen is one of the oldest towns on the Main. The Benedictine monastery was founded in 745, and the walled settlement grew up around it. The methodical right-angled layout of the town dates back to the 12&13C and is linked with the need to protect the Main crossing. This more recent part of the town was also surrounded by a wall, built in 1443, which has survived in part.

**Protestant Parish Church** (Kaiserstrasse): The German-Italian architect A.Petrini, who operated in Würzburg (q.v.), built the church for the Benedictine nuns in the style of the Italian baroque in 1686-99. The massive façade is dominated by a very tall tower, which now balances the later tower of the Chapel of the Holy Cross (see below). After secularization the monastery church was taken over by the Protestant community in 1817.

**Chapel of the Holy Cross** (Balthasar-Neumann-Strasse in Etwashausen): Balthasar Neumann's chapel (1741-5) was built with an eye to the Petrini church on the other bank of the Main. The tower soars high above the façade and has a bulbous top. Neumann wanted the architecture to speak for itself, and therefore

omitted the lavish decoration usual in the late baroque period.

**Catholic Parish Church of St.John the Baptist** (7 Obere Kirchgasse): This 15C hall church with three aisles was restored with some authenticity at the end of the Fifties; the 19C neo-Gothic furnishings were removed, and *late Gothic wall paintings* in the N. aisle were revealed and the *tabernacle* (1470-80) restored to its original condition. The fine *choir-stalls* date from the 15C. The depictions of the *Passion story* over the modern high altar are parts of an altar of *c.*1480.

**Museum:** The *Deutsches Fastnachtsmuseum* in the Falterturm belongs to the German Carnival Guild and shows carnival masks, costumes and accessories, as well as the relevant literature. The *Städtisches Museum* and the *Städtisches Archiv* (21-3Landwehrstrasse) show contributions on the town's history, viticulture and crafts.

**Also of interest:** The *Falterturm* and the *Grosslangheimer Tor* (1565) (in Etwashausen) have survived of the 15C town fortifications. The *Main bridge*, which in its present form dates back to the 17&18C, is first mentioned around 1300. The *Rathaus* (Untere Marktgasse) is a fine 3-storey Renaissance building (1561-3); its gable has complex patterns.

---

**Kleve, Niederrhein 4190**
Nordrhein-Westfalen                        p.414□A 9

---

**Former Collegiate Church St.Mariae Himmelfahrt:** Meister Konrad of Kleve was the architect of this Gothic church with three aisles; the choir was consecrated in 1356 and the nave and W. towers completed in 1426. The extremely high (originally windowless) nave is the first example of a so-called *Kleve stepped hall*. The church was almost totally destroyed in the Second World War and the interior subsequently redesigned. The *altar of the Virgin Mary* by H.Douverman and J.Dericks (1510-13) with a 14C Madonna figure, along with various tombs of Kleve famil-

*Catholic parish church of St. John the Baptist, with the old town*

ies (14–16C) have survived of the original lavish furnishings; there is a *church treasury*.

**Former Minorite Church St. Mariae Empfängnis** (Tiergartenstrasse): The present Catholic parish church (*c.* 1440) is characteristic of the Gothic architecture of the Mendicant Order: two very long aisles, with simple tracery and ornamentation. On the other hand, the two rows of oak *choir stalls* (1474) are unusually richly decorated

**Schwanenburg:** Nothing remains of the 11&12C Burg of the Counts of Kleve. The Schwanenturm dates from the extension of the castle in the early 15C; it is a Gothic building with parapet, corner towers and spire, and the Spiegelturm on the S. side (1429). Fragments of a Romanesque wing dismantled in 1771 were incorporated into the newer sections of the castle. Today the castle is the seat of the *district court*.

**Tiergarten:** The new Tiergarten in the NW is reached by 12 radial avenues; there are also fine parks and gardens in the SE of the town. In a natural gorge below the Tiergarten is the so-called *amphitheatre* (1656), a terraced garden based on Italian models with a statue of Pallas Athene (1660) in the centre. The whole park (1656) was created by Johann Moritz of Nassau.

**Städtisches Museum** (33 Kavarinerstrasse): The museum is accommodated in the house of the landscape painter B.C. Koekkoek (19C) and contains Lower Rhine art from the Middle Ages and modern times.

---

**Klosterlechfeld 8933**
Bavaria                                    p.422□I 19

---

**Pilgrimage and Monastery Church of Maria Hilf:** On the historic site of the bat-

*Marienaltar in collegiate church in Kleve*

tle with the Hungarians in 995, where later the German emperors also gathered their armies for their Italian campaigns, the widow of an Augsburg patrician Regina Imhoff founded a votive chapel, which was built by the Augsburg architect E.Holl (1603). Holl based the cylindrical design and the half dome on the Pantheon in Rome. A nave was added in 1656–9 and two round chapels in 1690 – 1. All the towers have the onion domes which are so popular in Swabia. Church and monastery buildings (Franciscans built a monastery next to the chapel in 1666–9) form a group which is visible for miles around. The interior was uniformly painted and decorated with stucco in the rococo style. *Pulpit* by the Augsburg sculptor E.B.Bendel.

**Knechtsteden 4047 = Dormagen 6**
Nordrhein-Westfalen                          p.416☐B 11

**Former Premonstratensian Church of**

**St.Maria und St.Andreas:** The Romanesque vaulted basilica of the monastery founded in 1132, with its double choir (E. and W.) was intended both as a collegiate and as a parish church (1138–62). The W. parts are preserved, the E. choir is renovated in Gothic style (1477). The wall painting in the curve of the apse dates from 1162 and is one of the most important monumental paintings of the period. The church interior is of impressive simplicity with round and semi-circular columns. The finest feature of the furnishings is the *capital sculpture* on the S. portal and on the choir-screens.

**Kobern = Kobern-Gondorf 5401**
Rheinland-Pfalz                          p.416☐C 13

**Matthiaskapelle:** Above the town, where the *Oberburg* and the *Unterburg* once stood, is the Chapel of Matthias (1230–40), where the head of the Apostle Matthew, proba-

*Klosterlechfeld, pilgrimage church of Maria Hilf*

*Klosterlechfeld, church of Maria Hilf*

bly brought from a crusade by Heinrich II of Isenburg-Kobern, was kept until 1422, when the relic was moved to Trier. The unusually small interior of the chapel, which is obviously reminiscent of the Church of the Holy Sepulchre and the Dome of the Rock in Jerusalem, is borne by 30 columns in six groups. They are much lower towards the outer wall, creating the impression of a spider's web. Kobern is the most beautiful example of a Romanesque chapel in the Middle Rhine area.

**Dreikönigskapelle:** In the cemetery stands the Chapel of the Magi of 1426–30; the original interior painting (*c.*1450) is of a very high quality.

**Goloring:** Outside the town is one of the most remarkable pre-historic monuments, the Goloring: a circular tomb, 650 ft. in diameter, dating from 1200–600 BC. It was probably used as a place of worship (now ammunition store).

---

## Koblenz 5400

Rheinland-Pfalz    p.416□C 13

A Roman camp was established under Tiberius (AD 14–37) at the confluence of the Mosel and the Rhine; a Roman trading town developed, which was destroyed at the time of the Barbarian Invasions. In the presbytery of the Liebfrauenkirche and below the choir of St. Florin are remains of the settlement. The *Burg* was built on the site of the Roman fort in 1276–89 and was later extended as the Elector's castle (now town library). Next to it was built the much admired *Balduinsbrücke* between 1332–8; some of the 14 arches over the Mosel have disappeared as a result of the regulation of the Mosel. The heyday of the town of Kobenz was the 12–14C, when the great religious buildings, which are still its most striking feature, were built. In the 17C, with the move of the Electors of Trier to Ehrenbreitstein, Koblenz enjoyed a second heyday in the baroque period.

**Deutschordenskommende** (Rheinufer): The spit of land between the Mosel and

the Rhine acquired the name 'Deutsches Eck' through the presence of the Knights of the Teutonic Order (1216). Of this complex, which was badly hit in the last war, the Renaissance building of the *Komturswohnung* with the charming floral courtyard behind it was rebuilt in its old form.

**Former Collegiate Church of St. Florin/Protestant Parish Church** (Florinsmarkt): This Romanesque building was built around 1100 (after a preceeding building of the 10C), and acquired a Gothic choir in 1356. Further Gothic alterations followed in the 17C (flat ceiling replaced by Gothic vaulting; Gothic windows in W. tower front). The tower walls are divided by dark bands of basalt and in the 5th storey the openings at the level of the bells are set under arches which in the S. tower are alternately light and dark. Of interest are the Gothic wall paintings in the niches of the ante-choir (14C).

**Former Collegiate Church of St. Kastor/Catholic Parish Church** (7 Kastorstrasse): On the spit of land between the Mosel and the Rhine, very near the Deutschordenshaus, lies St. Kastor, the most important church in Koblenz. In the two lower storeys of the W. towers remains of the preceding building, an old Carolingian church, are discernible. The current church originated during the course of the 12C and was consecrated in 1208. The nave and crossing were vaulted in 1496–9. The four-towered complex has a similar W. front to its neighbour church of St. Florin. The church interior is both Romanesque and Gothic: the Romanesque arches are topped by broad Gothic stellar vaults (1496–9). To the left and right of the choir stand 2 *altar tombs* under Gothic wall canopies. Preserved in the niche behind the tomb of Kuno von Falkenstein (with the recumbent figure of the dead man, who died in 1388) are early *Gothic wall paintings*. The expressive crucifix on the high altar was made by G.Schweiger of Nuremberg (1685). The *pulpit* with the 4 Evangelists was probably the work of the Koblenz artist P.Kern (1625).

**Liebfrauenkirche** (Am Plan): This has

*Panorama, Koblenz with Ehrenbreitstein*

been the principal parish church of the town since the Middle Ages. It was built on Roman and Carolingian foundations from 1180, and completed in the early 13C. Three architectural periods can be clearly recognised: the original Romanesque W. section includes the nave and the first part of the choir, the main part of the choir is very fine late Gothic (15C), and the upper parts of the towers date from the baroque period (1693–4). Striking features of the somewhat spare furnishings are some fine *Renaissance tombs*, an elegant *Immaculata* and a *St.Joseph* (both *c.* 1750). In the S. aisle is a Dutch marble bust of the *endower of the altar* (1693).

**Former Residence Schloss** (Clemensplatz): This town Schloss was built by P.M.d'Ixnard in the New Town of Koblenz for Clemens Wenzeslaus von Sachsen, the last Elector and Archbishop of Trier, who lived in Ehrenbreitstein. The neoclassical building was completed in 1791, but only

three years later the Elector fled to Augsburg before the French Revolutionary armies—the same armies who were greeted as forces of Libration by J.Görres, the great publicist of the Napoleonic era, born in Koblenz in 1776. The Schloss became a French military hospital until 1813, was then a barracks, a law court and a residence for King Friedrich Wilhelm IV of Prussia. The building was completely destroyed by fire in 1944; in the interior only the staircase has survived in its old form. All the other sections were adapted to the needs of the offices of the local authority which they now house.

**Ehrenbreitstein:** The first fortifications were built on this long ridge as early as 1100. The first bastions were built in the 16C; they were extended in the 17&18C, with the result that Ehrenbreitstein became one of the most important German fortresses in the 19C; it was never taken, though its garrison was often defeated by

*Tomb of Kuno von Falkenstein*

(corner of Löhrstrasse and Marktstrasse) were built in the 17C and gained their name because of the four stone oriels. The *Clemensstrasse*, which came into being when the town was extended in the 18C, shows signs of early neoclassicism; the finest features are No. 2, now a bank, a fine three-storey corner building with a lavishly carved door, and the balcony rail. The oldest surviving building is the house at *2 Kastorstrasse*, c.1520. The present *Gasthof Deutscher Kaiser* (Kornpfortgasse) is also medieval; it is a tower-like five-storey build-

**Liebfrauenkirche, Koblenz 1** Crucifix, mid 14C **2** Stained-glass window with Crucifixion, c.1460–70 **3** Tombs of the v.dem Burgtorn family **4** Altarpiece by Silvester Baumann, 1680 **5** Bust of Johann Crampich von Cronefeld (d.1693) by Jan Blommendael **6** Langnas tomb (d. 1711) **7** Immaculata, mid 18C, on the chancel arch **8** Niche with Virgin Mary in W., 1702 **9** Sacristy by Nicholas Lauxern, 1776

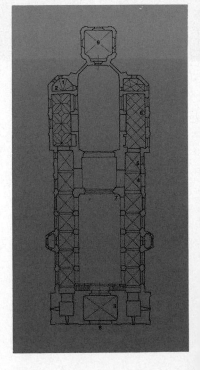

starvation. Forts and batteries were added in the style of the old baroque buildings, covering a large area of the ridge. The *fortress church* is worth seeing; it is a gigantic building like a barracks, with galleries and barrel vaulting. The *Museum für Vorgeschichte and Volkskunde* (prehistory and ethnography) and the largest *Youth Hostel* in the Federal Republic are now housed in the fortress.

**Houses:** The 17&18C *Bürresheimer Hof* and the *Dreikönigshaus* (15 Kornpfortstrasse), a baroque building dating from 1701, are both striking. The S. wing of the *von der Leyenschen Hof* is 16C, the left half was modified in the 18C. The adjacent *chapel of St. Jacob* (now used for the old Catholic mass) was once a cemetery chapel and dates from the 14C; it was rebuilt after the war. The great diplomat of the Congress of Vienna, Clemens Wenzeslaus von Metternich, was born in the *Metternichsche Hof* in 1773. The *Vier Türme* (four towers)

*Residenzschloss*

ing built in the 16C for the master of the Archbishop's mint.

**Kurfürstliche Residenz:** The court of the Electoral Residence (built in 1626–32 for Elector Philipp Christian von Soetern, below the fortress by the Rhine) was a lively intellectual centre in the last decades of the 18C. Goethe and Wieland were guests ofthe authoress Sophie von la Roche, Beethoven's mother was one of the court staff and Clemens Brentano was born here in 1778. The most important section built when the Elector moved his court to Koblenz (see above) is the so-called *Dikasterialgebäude*; the courthouse (now financial office) was built by Balthasar Neumann in 1739 and is reminiscent of the Residence in Würzburg (q.v.) and the baroque Schloss buildings of Franconia.

**Deutsches Eck** (Moselstrasse am Rhein): An equestrian statue of Kaiser Wilhelm was built in 1897 on this tongue of land at the confluence of the Rhine and the Mosel. It was destroyed amidst the confusion of war in 1945; the base has been set up again as a monument to German unity.

**Koblenz-Moselweiss:** The Catholic parish church of *St.Laurentius* is around the first bend in the river, an area which is now part of Koblenz. It is a 13C Romanesque basilica with contemporary paintwork (freely renewed); its finest feature is the *stone pulpit* with figures of Christ and the Evangelists: a wonderful piece of sculpture dating from 1467.

**Museums:** The *Mittelrhein-Museum* (15 Florinsmarkt), originally in the Schloss, is now housed in the Bürresheimer Hof, the town's old Merchants' Hall. Its collections include pre- and early history, Middle Rhenish art of the medieval period, 20C Rhenish art and modern graphics. The *Mittelrheinische Postmuseum* (14 Friedrich-Ebert-Ring) has exhibits on the history of

*Rittersaal, Schloss Stolzenfels*

transport, postage and telecommunications.

**Theatre:** The theatre has a fine neoclassical façade and was built at the same time as the Schloss (2 Deinhardplatz). 500 seats. The *Studiobühne* is in the Bürresheimer Hof (13 Florinsmarkt). 150 seats.

**Environs: Stolzenfels** (5 km. S.): K.F.Schinkel designed the new Schloss, which was built on the site of an old knights' Burg dating from 1242; this building was destroyed by the French in 1688. King Friedrich Wilhelm IV lived here and gave many large-scale receptions. The Schloss is noted for its lavish furnishings; the finest areas are the *Rittersaal*, the king's *residence* and the courtyard and *chapel*.

**Rhens** (9 km. S.): This little town was mentioned as early as 874 and most of its *medieval fortifications* and many *late Gothic half-timbered houses* have survived (includ-

ing 7–9 Markt, 20 Hochstrasse) and also the fine *Rathaus* (*c.* 1560).

---

## Köln/Cologne 5000
Nordrhein-Westfalen            p.416□ B 12

Cologne was the major town on the Rhine even in Roman times. The original native settlement was called Oppidum Ubiorum, and the Romans based a legion here. The camp covered an area of about one square kilometer, and its central street was built on exactly the same line as the Hohe Strasse in the modern pedestrian precinct. Around AD 50 the Empress Agrippina, the wife of Claudius and born in Germany, made the camp a 'Colonia', a town for retired legionary veterans, and gave it the name Colonia Claudia Ara Agrippinensium. The town's monogram CCAA appears repeatedly on old Roman stones and inscriptions. The extent of the Roman town can still be clearly seen from the remains of fortifications. For example the 1C *Römerturm* on Zeughaus- and St. Apern-Strasse was at the NW corner of the Roman town. The S. boundary of the town ran along the line of Bachstrasse to Maria im Kapitol. The fort of Divitia (Deutz) on the other side of the Rhine was linked to the town by a bridge. There are remains of the *Praetorium* and the *Imperial Palace* under the Rathaus in the Kleine Budengasse. The area of the post-1200 medieval town was bounded by the 'Wall' streets (Eigelsteintor, Hahnentor, Severinstor). Some 40,000 people lived in Cologne in the 12&13C and about 150 churches were built (47 of these were knocked down during secularization alone). The 'Ring' streets mark the line of the fortified walls which surrounded the city from the time of the Hohenstaufens; they were not pulled down until 1881. Still further out the city is surrounded by a green belt 550 yards wide and over six miles long: here the Prussians built their fortresses, dismantled in 1911. When the city developed beyond the 'rings' in the 19C, it enjoyed a new period of growth. In 1880 the cathedral was completed after a building period of 600 years, and this triggered off considerable activity; the New Town grew up between the 'Wall' streets and the fortress ring. After 1919 the old university, the oldest in Germany (1388 – 1798), was refounded. The Second World War left ninety per cent of the centre of Cologne in ruins, but nearly all the valuable monuments have been rebuilt. With its museums, collections, theatres, auction houses and art markets Cologne is now one of Germany's most important cultural cities. Numerous notable scholars, churchmen and artists have lived and worked in Cologne: Albertus Magnus, one of the greatest scholars of the 13C, Thomas Aquinas, Meister Eckhart and also Karl Marx (editor of the 'Neue Rheinische Zeitung' 1848&9) and novelist Heinrich Böll, the winner of the Nobel Prize for Literature. The Westdeutsche Rundfunk, the Deutschlandfunk and the Deutsche Welle have made Cologne a centre for famous artists and journalists since the war.

**Dom St.Peter und Maria:** Building history: The reliquary containing the bones of the Three Kings, brought to Cologne from Milan as a gift from the Emperor Barbarossa to Reinald von Dassel, made the city one of the most popular places of pilgrimage in the whole of Europe. It was decided that a new shrine should be built in the High Gothic style of N. France on the site of the old cathedral. The cathedral chapter appointed Master Gerhard, an architect of this new Gothic school. His successors were Master Arnold (1271–1308) and his son Johann (1308–1331). The foundation stone was laid in August 1248 and the choir was finally consecrated in 1322. The transept was then begun, work on the nave continued and the S. tower built as far as the bell cage; all work was then halted in 1559. The E. Choir, temporarily walled up on the W. side in 1322, remained in this state for the next five hundred years. The crane on the half-completed S. tower was part of Cologne's silhouette for centuries. At the start of the 19C a romantic enthusiasm for the Middle Ages and the 'German style' (meaning the Gothic) lead to renewed progress. Some of the original plans for the W. façade of the cathedral were discovered in the granary of the Gasthof 'Zur Traube' in Darmstadt, and others 2 years later in Paris, and in 1842 building at last began again. On the 15th of October 1880 the cathedral was consecrated in the presence of Kaiser Wilhelm I. With its 515 ft. high towers the cathedral was not only at that time the highest stucture in the World, but also one of the largest churches in Christendom. Proportions: 470 ft. long, 147 ft. wide, interior height 140 ft., length of transepts 245 ft. *The building:* Cologne Cathedral was modelled on Amiens Cathedral, but with 5 aisles (also in the nave), a transept with three aisles, a two-aisled ambulatory around the choir, opening into 7 radiating chapels in the apse and 2 adjacent chapels in the ante-choir. This unusually large space was intended to accommodate the streams of pilgrims, and to allow them to walk round the Reliquary of the Three Kings in the crossing. The choir remains unaltered from the time it was built (some exterior masonry had to be replaced be-

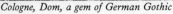

*Cologne, Dom, a gem of German Gothic*

cause of industrial pollution). The cathedral was provided with only 3 portals instead of the 5 originally planned. These are huddled between the massive towers; the gables at each level of the towers overlap the next higher storey. *Interior and furnishings:* Apart from 5 late Gothic stained-glass windows, the furnishings of the nave date from the 19C; it seems like a long narrow ravine when entered from the W., being 3 times higher than it is wide. The furnishings of the main choir on the other hand, the statuary on the pillars and tall windows, date from the 13&14C. The transept also contains old items, such as the stone figures on the pillars of the cathedral choir (*c.*1320) and the *Virgin of Milan* (in the Sakramentskapelle). The glass in the main choir and radiating chapels dates from 1260 onwards. The *choir stalls* are the largest of the German Middle Ages (with special seats for Pope and Emperor). Above the stalls are old wall paintings (*c.*1330). The *high altar* (*c.*1320) is a block with

figure decorations on all sides. Positioned behind it is the valuable *Reliquary of the Three Kings.* This most famous medieval reliquary (begun by N. von Verdun in 1181 and not completed until 1220), made of wood clad in gold and silver plate, is in the shape of a basilica with nave and side-aisles with raised groups of figures and tendril decorations on the end-walls, sides and roofs. The *Gero Cross* in the *Kreuzkapelle* (first on the N. ambulatory) is one of the oldest and most important works of European monumental sculpture (commissioned around 970 by Archbishop Gero). The *Marienkapelle* (last in the S. ambulatory) contains the famous *Stephan Lochner Dom picture,* the Adoration of the Magi with Saints Gereon and Ursula and virgins (1440). In front of this is the *Tomb of Archbishop Friedrich von Saarwerden* (d.1414). In the S. transept stands the emotive stone figure of *Christopher* by the Cologne master T. van der Burch (*c.*1470), also a *Madonna* (*c.*1420) and the *Agilolphus Altar*

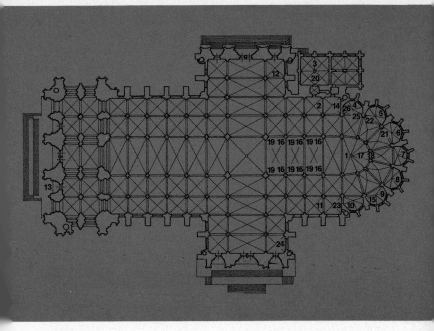

**Cologne, Dom 1** High choir **2** Kreuzkapelle **3** Sakramentskapelle **4** Engelbertuskapelle **5** Maternuskapelle **6** Johanneskapelle **7** Dreikönigskapelle **8** Agneskapelle **9** Michaelskapelle **10** Stephanuskapelle **11** Marienkapelle **12** Treasury **13** Petrusportal **14** Gero cross, donated c.970 **15** Sarcophagus of Archbishop Gero, c.970 **16** Choir screen **17** Altar **18** Shrine of the Magi, 12-13C **19** Choir stalls, c.1320 **20** Milan Madonna **21** Monument to Archbishop Konrad v.Hochstaden, c.1320 **22** Tomb of Archbishop Philipp v.Heinsberg, c.1360 **23** Picture of cathedral by S.Lochner, c.1440 **24** Agilolphusaltar, c. 1520 **25** Georgsaltar, early 16C **26** Tomb of Archbishop Anton v.Schauenburg (d. 1558)

(*c.*1520). P.P. Rubens designed 11 *tapestries* for the cathedral ('Triumph of the Eucharist'), but these only hang in the nave at Whitsuntide and Christmas. The *Treasury* is one of the richest in Europe with its manuscripts, vestments and implements from all centuries.

**St.Andreas** (Komödienstrasse): After various earlier buildings this late Romanesque basilica with its massive crossing tower was built around 1200 in the city fortification ditch at the N. wall of the Roman town. The Gothic hall, which provides an impressive contrast with the Romanesque nave, was built in 1414–20 in place of a choir. In a Roman sarcophagus in a *Funer-*

*ary Chapel* adjoining the reopened *crypt* lie the bones of *St.Albertus Magnus*, the great Scholastic and polymath (d.1280). The W. portico and the *Löwenportal* (now in the Gothic sacristy) with old decorations (*c.* 1200) are Romanesque. The beautiful two-rowed *choir stalls* date from the Soft-Style period (*c.* 1420–30). The *high altar* is one of the later works of the Cologne painter B.Bruyn Jr. (*c.*1550). Of interest in the W. side-chapel is the *winged altar of the Brotherhood of the Rosary,* founded in 1474, by the 'Master of St.Severin' of Cologne (1474).

**St. Aposteln** (Neumarkt): This church was built on the W. periphery of the old

*Dom, S. portal*

*Dom, looking east*

city (begun around 1030) with 3 conchae (niches in the choir and transepts). These conchae and the group of towers provide an unusual picture of Romanesque architecture (1192–1240) when seen from the Neumarkt side. The church was obviously modelled on Byzantine domed churches. Adjacent is the W. nave with its massive tower (called the 'Apostelklotz'). During rebuilding in 1955 an old crypt (*c.*1150) was revealed below the W. tower. In 1956 a modern week-day chapel was added to the S. aisle; it has an altar made up of 12 statuettes of the Apostles (from an altar in the church, *c.*1330). The most valuable item in the *Church Treasury* is the *Heribert Chalice* (*c.* 1190).

**St. Georg** (Georgstrasse): This church at the S. gate of the Roman town of Colonia was built above the ruins of a Roman guardhouse. A later Merovingian building was replaced by a new church (1059–67) when a canonry was established. The E. choir and transept, together with the five-aisled *crypt,* date from this stage of construction. 100 years later (1188) the square W. choir was added. A plump, cuboid building from the outside the cube-like building looks clumsy; it was originally conceived as the lower storey of a tower, with 16 ft. thick walls. The interior comes as a surprise, being richly articulated and of balanced proportions. The *forked cross* in the W. choir is from the period of mysticism (*c.*1380). The *Wailing Altar* (before 1558) was made by B. Bruyn the Younger, and the *font* dates from around 1240. The *stained-glass window cycle* by J. Thorn Prikker (1930) was reconstructed to the original designs after the war.

**St. Gereon** (Gereon-/Christophstrasse): In Roman times this site was a burial ground. In the 4C a Christian martyr church was built here. This late-antique oval building with niches still forms the core of the church. Choir and crypt were added in the 11&12C in the course of extensions. From 1219–27 the antique oval building, formerly clad in gold mosaics, was extended into a massive 4-storey decagon. 10 free-

*Dom, view of the choir* ▷

*Roman N. gate with a view of the Dom*

standing pillars with flying buttresses surround the tower-like building and support the 110 ft. high stellar dome (outer size: 156 ft.). The decagonal awning-roof was originally gilded. St.Gereon is one of the most unusual and excellent medieval buildings in the West, comparable with Florence Cathedral (dome) or Hagia Sophia in Istanbul. Inside there are still remains of the Roman masonry to be seen. Of interest in the *crypt* are the pavement mosaics (1156, now renewed. The *baptistery* was built at the same time as the upper storeys of the Roman building. The famous *wall paintings* of this chapel (St. Gereon and other martyrs of the Theban Legion) originated a little later. The high Gothic *sacristy* (1315) contains important *glass paintings;* the delicate figures of saints are similar to the sculptures in the cathedral choir, which date from the same time. The artists A.Manessier (1964), G.Meistermann (1980 – 84) and W.Buschulte (1983&4) created the new

*window-glass* in all parts of the church, which was reconsecrated in 1984.

**Jesuit Church of St.Mariae Himmelfahrt** (Marzellenstrasse): Begun in the first year of the Thirty Years War to plans by C.Wamser of Aschaffenburg (1618), consecrated in 1678 and completed in 1689, the church is the most important Jesuit building in NW Germany. The façade with the great 'Gothic' central window and 'Romanesque' towers shows the tendency of the Counter-Reformation to revive 'holy' architecture. Pointed-arch vaulting, tracery windows and arches inside are neo-Gothic adaptations. The baroque furnishing was mostly destroyed in the last war and almost entirely reconstructed afterwards. The most artistically notable piece is the *pulpit* by the Augsburg sculptor J.Geisselbrunn (1634). The building, proclaimed the 'Temple of Reason' in the French Revolution, is now a Catholic parish church.

**St. Kunibert** (Konrad-Adenauer-Ufer): This church, completed a year before the cathedral was begun (1247), is the last and most lavish of the city's late Romanesque churches, built in succession with St. Gereon and St. Aposteln. As there the decorative choir is flanked by towers. The architecture, however, is more slender and narrow than in St.Aposteln, a suggestion of early Gothic. The interior is characterized by the *stained-glass window cycle* in the choir and E. transept (1220–30), the most important of the late Romanesque in Germany. Also of interest are the *wall paintings* in the S. (baptistery) and N. choir area (c.1250, in zig-zag style). The *Annunciation* (on the pillars in the crossing) the church is an important work of Gothic sculpture; the angels and Mary on the lectern were commissioned in 1439 by Canon Hermanus de Arcka. The *church treasure* includes a Sassanid silk with hunting scenes (7C) and the Ewaldi Cloth (10C), the pall of St.Ewald, once used as an altar cloth.

**Maria im Kapitol** (Pipinstrasse/Eichhof):

*Shrine of the Magi, Dom* ▷

*The choir stalls in the Dom, with their 104 seats, are among the largest of their kind*

On the site of the present church there stood in Roman times a temple to the Capitoline Gods Jupiter, Juno and Minerva. In the 7C St.Plektrudis, whose tomb slab is preserved from around 1160, established a convent. The present W. building with the central building and the staircase towers (and a ladies' gallery inside) probably dates from the 10C. The rest of the building with the nave and trefoil chapel (to the E., N. and S.) was built in the 11C. The choir became the model for several churches in Cologne (St.Aposteln, Gross St.Martin) and in the NW of the Empire. The *crypt* is the largest in Germany after Speyer(q.v.). In the Gothic epoch chapels were added next to the E. choir and Gothic windows were pierced in various places. The church was badly damaged in the Second World War and the old design was simplified to some extent in the rebuilding; in place of the Gothic vaulting the nave acquired a flat ceiling.

The finest feature of the furnishings are the two wooden *doors* (16 ft.); the reliefs were originally painted (*c.* 1050). The W. part is reminiscent of the rotunda of the Münster in Aachen (q.v.). The *rood screen*, made by the Belgian master J. van Roome in black marble and alabaster and endowed in 1523, is now repositioned before the crossing. Notable, along with the *tomb slab* of Plektrudis, is a *forked cross* (1304). Also of importance are the stone *Enthroned Virgin*, from around 1160, and a standing *Madonna* (Byzantine, *c.* 1180–90). A master from the workshop of the great Strasbourg sculptor N.G. van Leyden made the *Virgin and Christ Group* (1466) for the Hardenrath Chapel. The *Mourning Woman*, made by G.Marcks in 1949, stands in the rebuilt cloister as a memorial to Cologne's war victims.

**St. Maria Lyskirchen** (Am Leystapel): This church, also called the 'Church of the

*Detail from Stephan Lochner's 'Adoration of the Magi', c.1440, in the Marienkapelle in the Dom*

Rhine Boatmen', was built in the 13C (preceding building in the 10C). The Second World War left the church almost unharmed, but it has been greatly altered by Gothic-style window insertions and vaulting (17C) and by neo-Romanesque restorations (19C). The most important features of this building are the *paintings* in the nave vaulting (*c.*1250): 24 pictures of biblical scenes. The Adoration of the Magi above the main entrance and the scenes from the legend of St.Nicholas in the S. tower vault were painted somewhat earlier. The church's main sculpture is the *Boatmen's Madonna,* over 6.5 ft. high, a work of the Soft Style (*c.* 1420). Also of interest are the *glass paintings* (1520–30) in the N. aisle, and the *church treasure.*

**Gross St.Martin** (Am Fischmarkt): The present building, which again has the typical Cologne triple-concha layout (c.f. Maria im Kapitol, St.Aposteln), was be-

gun in 1150, after a fire. The massive crossing tower (274 ft. high) was built together with the nave between 1185 and 1220 and is one of the city's emblems. The spire was added in the Gothic epoch (and rebuilt in the same style), but the 4 other towers have Romanesque roofs.

**Former Minorite Church of Mariae Empfängnis** (Minoritenstrasse): Parallel to the building of the Gothic cathedral the Minorites began their church without a tower, also Gothic and modelled on the church of St.Elizabeth in Marburg (q.v.). Although the building looks entirely unified, additions were made from 1244 to the mid 14C. Tufa and trachyte were used to create the strongest possible impression. The vaulting above the aisles represents an early stage of the Gothic system. The mendicant Order did not permit a tower: it was replaced with a graceful ridge-turret. Pillars and vaulting are of great simplicity.

*St. Gereon, wall painting in the baptistery*

*Wall paintings in the baptistery of St. Kunibert*

Buried in the church is the theologian and scholar *Duns Scotus* (1260 – 1308). The modern sarcophagus of the 'Doctor subtilis' was made by J.Höntgesberg (1957).

**St.Pantaleon** (between Am Weidenbach and Waisenhausgasse): This is a large church of the late imperial period, comparable with Corvey or Essen-Werden (qq.v.). The two-storey building with its monumental westwork was used not only for worship, but was simultaneously a lawcourt, baptistery and singers' meetingplace. Adjacent to the W. tower, which on the inside rose like a shaft right up to the roof, was a flat-ceilinged hall building, to which side aisles were added in 1152. The 17C baroque vaulting was replaced by the original flat ceiling after the Second World War. The late Gothic rood screen on the E. side of the church is a cycle with many figures. The Roman *sarcophagus* with the bones of Archbishop Bruno (in the *crypt*) and 2 valuable *reliquaries* for the St. Maurice and St.Albinus (1170–90, now in the Treasury) are among the most important parts of the furnishings, as is the altar-tomb of Empress Theophanu.

**St.Peter** Jabachstrasse): This late Gothic basilica (1515–30, after an earlier building of the 12C) has wide galleries on 3 sides above the low aisles. After the heavy damage of the last war the church was not revaulted, but given a flat ceiling. The most valuable item of the furnishings is a work by P.P.Rubens, originally painted for the high altar and now in a special chapel. This *Crucifixion of St.Peter* was one of the last works of the great painter (*c.* 1639–40), who was born in the parish of St.Peter and whose father lies buried here. Also of interest is the church treasure. The church used to be connected to the Cecilian foundation and church (now housing the Schnütgen Museum) by a passage.

**St. Severin** (Severinskirchplatz): The choir is late Romanesque (1230 – 7), the nave late Gothic. Excavations revealed the foundations of an old 4C sepulchre church. This was probably built for St. Severin,

*Mariae Himmelfahrt* ▷

*Door, Maria im Kapitol*

*Severinstor*

Bishop of Cologne, who lived around 400 and is buried in this church. The *crypt* below the main choir was built in 1043 and enlarged when the choir was extended in 1230–7. The tomb of St.Severin is marked by a memorial plaque. Of the late Romanesque furnishing a *Crucifixion* has survived in the choir vault (*c.*1260). The two-rowed *choir stalls* with animals, human heads and leaf-work were carved from hard oak at the end of the 13C. The 20 pictures above them depict the *Legend of St.Severin* and were painted in the Cologne workshop of the 'Master of St.Severin' (*c.*1500). In the built-on *sacristy* (Chapel of St.Margaret) there is a *wall-painting* with a Crucifixion, the work of the famous 'Veronika Master' of Cologne (1441). In the same room there are panels by the 'Master of St.Severin', who also created the *glass paintings* (Crucifixion) in the S. aisle. The large limestone figure of a *Madonna* (*c.*1290) is in the French style. A *crucifix* on the forked cross was made around 1330.

**Trinitatiskirche** (Filzengraben): This Protestant church was built to the design of the late neoclassical Berlin architect F.A.Stüler in the style of an early Christian basilica, in order to 'avoid comparison with the excellent Romanesque and Gothic works in Cologne' (1857–60). The church façade is jammed between the house fronts of the street. Gallery arches open out on 3 sides above closely-placed pillars on the ground floor. The cool, light, festive building, destroyed but for the walls in the last war, was rebuilt in the sixties.

**St.Ursula** (Ursulaplatz): On the S. wall of the high Gothic choir (1287) is an inscription about Clematius, a citizen who had a chapel rebuilt here around 400 on the site 'where holy virgins spilt their blood for the name of Christ'. Originally there were 11 virgins, although legend increased the numbers to 11,000, with St. Ursula at their head. Nave and W. end were completed in 1135, the tower above

*Gürzenich*

*Rathaus*

in the 13C (baroque spire 17C). Next to the Romanesque porch in the W. stands the high second S. aisle, in the Gothic style. Notable among the furnishings are the larger-than-life-size stone figures of Ursula in the Protective Coat (N. side apse),the Virgin Mary and the Redeemer (S. aisle, c.1490). These are attributed to the Cologne stonemason T. van der Burch. In the *Goldene Kammer* the walls are full of reliquary niches and human bones, decoratively arranged to form inscriptions and symbols. The most important item is the Romanesque *Aetherius Shrine* (c.1170; according to legend Aetherius was the betrothed of St. Ursula).

**Gürzenich** (Gürzenichstrasse): The city's banqueting hall and ball-room, built in 1441–7, has a fine tracery façade above a dour lower storey. This façade was authentically rebuilt after the Second World War; the interior was redesigned in modern style.

Adjoining the Gürzenich are the ruins of *Alt St.Alban* (11C, with numerous modifications up to the 17C), in which a copy of the *Mourning Parents* by Käte Kollwitz has been set up as a memorial to Cologne's dead from the last war.

**Altes Rathaus** (Alter Markt): The five-storey *Rathausturm*, which was built with the confiscated assets of the patricians after the victory of the guilds (1407–14), has been rebuilt after being totally destroyed in the last war. Parts of the *Hansa Saal* (c.1330) with the stone figures of the *9 Good Heroes* (c.1360) survived, however. Also undamaged was the lavish two-storey vestibule, the *Doxal* on Rathausplatz, a splendid loggia building in the style of the Italian-influenced 'Dutch Renaissance' (1569–73).

**Overstolzenhaus** (Rheingasse 8): This late Romanesque residential house with step gable (13C) was reconstructed after the war. An early Gothic fresco (jousting) survives inside. The building now serves the city as *Kunstgewerbe-Museum*. (Arts and Crafts).

**Museums:** The *Wallraf-Richartz-Museum* (An der Rechtschule) owes its basic stock of paintings to a donation by Canon Ferdinand Franz Wallraf (1748–1824) and to the merchant Johann Heinrich Richartz (1795–1861), who provided the building. Today it covers European painting with major works by Rembrandt, Courbet, Manet, Corot, Renoir, Sisley, 30 paintings by W.Leibl, who was born in Cologne in 1844, Liebermann, Slevogt and others. It also contains the Haubrich Expressionist collection. The modern *Sammlung Ludwig* is housed on the upper floor. In the *Schnütgen-Museum* (29 Cäcilienstrasse) are sculptures, implements, glasses and vestments from the Cologne area dating from the Middle Ages to the 18C. The Romanesque former Cäcilienkirche (12C) has been converted to house this unique collection. *Römisch-Germanisches Museum* (4 Roncalli-Platz): This new building by H.Röcke and Kl.Renner (1970–4) is technically one of the best-conceived museums to have been built in post-war Germany.

*Overstolzenhaus*

The most important exhibits are the Dionysos mosaic and the Poblicius tomb which towers up through several storeys. The collection was greatly extended after the war, as many new finds were made beneath the debris. The *Rautenstrauch-Joest-Museum für Völkerkunde* (45 Ubierring 45) has 60,000 exhibits of exotic art from all parts of the world, particularly pre-Columbian American art and African art (Benin bronzes). The *Museum für Ostasiatische Kunst* (Universitätsstr.100) has a fine collection of Chinese, Japanese and Korean art. The *Kölner Stadtmuseum* (Zeughausstr.1) in the Renaissance brick building of the old arsenal (1594) contains documents on the city's history from the 14–20C; one of the most interesting exhibits is the 1571 Mercator model of the city.

**Theatres:** *Opernhaus* (opera, 1346 seats) and *Schauspielhaus* (drama, 920 seats) in Offenbachplatz. *Kammerspiele* (Ubierring). 313 seats. *Theater am Dom* (Glockengasse): Drama. 376 seats. *Pantomimentheater* (Aachener Str.24): W. Europe's only mime theatre. 86 seats.

**Also worth seeing:** Bastei (restaurant on old city tower with views of the city; Kaiser-Friedrich-Ufer); Fairground on Köln-Deutz (built for the 'Pressa' by A.Abel in 1925–7); Städtische Bühnen, Grosses and Kleines Haus (Offenbachplatz). This theatre was built by W.Riphahn in 1954–62.

---

· **Königsbach = Königsbach-Stein 7535**
Baden-Württemberg                p.420☐E 17

**Protestant Parish Church/formerly St.Mariae:** In the late 15C a church was added to an early Gothic defence tower (choir rebuilt in 1625–7, upper tower storey, 1782). The churchyard wall is also fortress-like and dates in part from Romanesque times. There are fine *tombs*, particularly that of Venningen (1599–1602) and that of the later master of the Schloss Colonel Rollin von St.André (1661–8).

*Schnütgen-Museum*

**Wasserschloss:** The 3 wings of this Renaissance building with four round corner towers are set round a courtyard; the Schloss was built in the 16C on the site of a 15C moated Burg and partly rebuilt in baroque style in 1623–50. The gate with the large coat of arms of the castle founder Erasmus von Venningen is preserved unaltered (1551—86). The main portal dates from the 18C.

**Rathaus:** This 18C half-timbered building has a striking and unusual gable supported by wooden columns.

## Königsberg in Bayern 8729
Bavaria                                    p.418☐I 14

Many old half-timbered buildings and old town gates have survived in this picturesque place on the edge of the Hassberg mountains; it probably dates back to a Frankish royal estate and was granted its charter in 1358. The finest old buiildings are grouped around the focal point of the town, the Salzmarkt. One of the most beautiful houses stands at 111 Marienstrasse (clock-maker's house). A monument in front of the Town Hall commemorates the town's most famous son, the astronomer Johann Müller (Regiomontanus; 1436–76), who was born here.

**Also of interest:** Protestant parish church (Am Markt): This high Gothic church, one of the most attractive Frankish hallchurches, was begun in 1397. Following a fire in 1640 temporary wooden accommodation had to suffice until the church was extended in 1894.

## Königslutter 3308
Lower Saxony                               p.414☐I 8

**Former Benedictine Abbey Church of**

**St.Peter and Paul/Kaiserdom:** In 1135
Emperor Lothar III founded a Benedictine
monastery not far from his ancestral castle Süpplingenburg. The principal part of
the E. end, the cloister and the Löwenportal on the N. side were built during the
Emperor's life-time (he died in 1137). In
the mid 15C the bare Romanesque westwork, broken only by 3 window-cavities,
and the Romanesque crossing tower, were
provided with towers decorated with
Gothic spires. The aisles were vaulted by
the mid 14C, while the nave acquired its
Gothic-style vaults (after the collapse of a
flat ceiling) at the end of the 17C. The
westwork is a Carolingian structure, formerly perhaps a fortified church, baptistery or burial place; inside, above a low
passage to the church, is a gallery with a
wide opening into the nave: the place for
the Emperor and his entourage at mass.
There are apses at the E. end. The main
central apse is lavishly decorated with a foliage frieze, mask consoles and symbolic
hunting scenes. For these works and for the
Lion Portal on the N. side the Emperor
summoned N. Italian stonemasons. The
E. end is the most impressive part of the
interior with its 5 apses and passages between choir, side apses and transept. The
vaulting in this part is Romanesque, in the
aisles Gothic and in the nave (with the
original head consoles) baroque. The wall
paintings (1894) were based on surviving
fragments of the originals. The *Tomb of
Emperor Lothar* and his wife (which was
destroyed by the collapse of the ceiling) is
a historical reproduction (1708) of the baroque original. The N. part of the *cloister,*
borne by 10 central columns, has two
aisles. It is the most important masterpiece
of the stonemasons of Königslutter; not a
single motif is repeated.

**Museum:** *Sammlung Klages:* This small
collection, in of a former brewery, displays
minerals and fossils.

---

**Königstein im Taunus 6240**
Hessen                                    p.416□E 14

---

**Catholic Parish Church St. Mariae:**

*Stone Virgin Mary, Königstein im
Taunus*

Königstein, a popular residential town, has
had a charter since 1313. Dating from that
time is the parish church, now a baroque
hall building with a double W. gallery
(built in 1744–6). Preserved in the NW corner and N. wall are remains of Romanesque walls, while in the choir and in the
tower are sections of a late Gothic addition
(walled-up portal). The *High altar* and
*pulpit* are among the best rococo works in
the Middle Rhine. Of the old furnishings
a *stone Virgin Mary* (1440) with its original painting has survived. The tombs date
from the 15–18C.

**Burg ruins** (Oberstadt): This Burg was
the largest and most impressive fortification in the Taunus area, until it was blown
up by the French in 1796 and used as a
quarry in the 19C. It probably originated
in the 2nd half of the 12C. The foundations of the central core are Romanesque,
the massive outer works date from after

1535, while the rest of the building is 14&15C.

**Stadtmuseum** (in the Altes Rathaus): Pre- and early history and craft (16–19C); model and plans of the former Burg.

---

### Königswinter 5330
Nordrhein-Westfalen                    p.416☐C 12

---

The town's main industry was once the trachyte quarries on the Drachenfels, which until the mid 17C provided the material for many important Rhineland church buildings, including Cologne Cathedral. In 1836 the quarries were abandoned in order to preserve the ruins of the Drachenfels castle.

**Catholic parish church of St. Remigius:** A new building with a nave, two aisles, semi-circular apse and five-storey E. tower was begun in 1779 to replace a Romanesque church. The neoclassical interior has been redesigned on neo-baroque lines. Only the high altar, parts of the baroque pulpit and the organ front survive from the time of construction. A rare piece is the reliquary of St. Margaret (14C).

**Kloster Heisterbach:** This ruined church in a remote wooded valley is an expression of the Cistercian wish to live apart from the world. The ruins became widely known through the German Romantics, who related many versions of the legend of the 'Monk of Heisterbach'. In 1809 the massive basilica, begun in 1202 and consecrated in 1237, was blown up, together with the monastery. Apse and ambulatory survived, however, as the explosive placed there did not go off. Even the ruins show how fine the late Romanesque church must have been; from the outside the choir seems to be built in layers: the radiating chapels, set into the thick wall from the inside, are like a base with little windows and a roof, then come the windows of the *ambulatory*, and in the 3rd storey are the high *round-arched windows* of the high choir. From the inside everything appears

lighter and more elegant. Today there is a *Cellite convent* near the ruins; the buildings date from the 18C.

**Drachenfels Castle:** Archbishops of Cologne built this castle on a summit of the Siebengebirge in the 12C. The castle was captured several times and badly damaged by the stonemasons' lodges of the Lower Rhine. The Romanesque keep and outer ring wall survive. According to the saga the dragon killed by Siegfried was supposed to have lived in a cave here.

**Environs: Oberpleis** (to the NW): **Former Priory Church/Catholic Parish Church:** Oberpleis was an independent priory in the 12C. The present church was built in the 12&13C. The dominant feature is the five-storey W. tower. Romanesque and Gothic design mingle in this columned basilica. Romanesque and Gothic wall- and *vault-paintings* and a *depiction of the Cosmos* on the floor have survived in the interior. The *crypt*, built in the second half of the 12C, has beautiful groin vaults, borne by 16 columns. The gem of the furnishings is a *retable* from around 1150–60 depicting the Virgin Mary, 3 virgins and the Magi. The tufa retable is one of the most important works of high Gothic sculpture in the Rhineland.

**Siebengebirgsmuseum** (Kellerstrasse): This refined two-storey building (1732) contains architectural fragments from the Heisterbach monastery (4 km. N. of Königswinter) and a missal (13C) with lavish initial ornamentation from the castle chapel on the Drachenfels.

---

### Konstanz (Constance) 7750
Baden-Württemberg                    p.420☐F 21

---

Emperor Constantine Chlorus, father of Constantine the Great, is supposed to have founded the city in the late 3C (wall remains found in the Münsterplatz). Around 600 Constance became a bishopric, from 1192-1548 the city on Lake Constance was a Free Imperial City and in 1414–18 the first Council on German soil was held

*Holy Sepulchre, Münster, Konstanz*

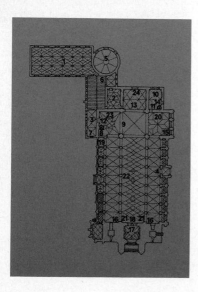

here; it condemned the Reformer J.Hus to be burned at the stake as a heretic and had him executed outside the city gates in 1415.

**Münster Unser Lieben Frau** (Münsterplatz): The cathedral stands on the site of a sunken Roman fort and has a long and complicated building history. One of the oldest parts (10C) is the *crypt*. The church to which it belonged collapsed in 1052 and was immediately replaced by the present church (consecrated 1089). This was a large flat-ceilinged columned basilica with transept and closed choir. The nave was not vaulted until 1679 – 83. The aisle chapels date from the 15C. The W. double-tower façade dates from the 12C. N. and S. tower were altered several times. *Inside,* the choir, redesigned on neoclassical lines in 1775–7, and the stucco decorations in the choir and transept do not fit in with the medieval character of the church. The *Grosse Herrgott von Konstanz,* a 15C crucifix, carved *doors* (1470), each with 10 scenes from the Life of Christ, and a lavishly articulated *late Gothic staircase* (1438) in the N. transept have survived. The staircase shows Burgundian influence and is decorated with scenes from the Old and New Testaments. The most famous item is the *Holy Sepulchre* in the *Mauritiuskapelle,* a 16 ft. high duodecagonal sandstone structure (*c.*1280) of high Gothic design with tracery windows, 12 figures of Apostles and figures from Christ's childhood. Inside the building is the actual tomb, which is surrounded by watchmen.

**Former Dominican monastery** (now is-

**Konstanz, Münster 1** Chapterhouse **2** Sacristy **3** Alte Nikolauskapelle **4** Gold discs, 11-13C **5** Holy Sepulchre in the Mauritius rotunda, 1303 **6** Crucifixion picture, 1348 **7** Wall paintings, c.1425 **8** Schnegg (staircase tower), 1438 **9** Choir stalls, 1465-70 **10** Stained-glass window, mid 15C **11** Wall painting, mid 15C **12** Death of the Virgin Mary, 1460 **13** Tomb of the Archbishop of Salisbury (d.1417) **14** Tomb of Bishop Otto v.Hachberg (d. 1434) **15** Tomb of Bishop B.v.Randeck (d. 1466) **16** St.Christopher pictures, 15C **17** Main portal, 1519 **18** Organ, 1517-20; probably designed by Peter Flötner **19** Altarpiece, 1524 **20** Mariae-End-Altar, 1637; altarpiece by J.Rieger, 1710 **21** Image of death, 1659 **22** Pulpit, 1680 **23** Thomasaltar, 1682 **24** High altar with Assumption, 1774

*Kaufhaus am Hafen, Konstanz*

land hotel, Auf der Insel): The church, now also part of the hotel, forms the S. part of the monastery buildings, grouped around the 4 walks of the cloisters. The architecture of the cloisters is very beautiful early Gothic (1260–70). In the vestibule of the cloisters, now the hotel office, there are still 16C wall paintings (Dance of Death and Mirror of the Virtues).

**Former Augustinian Church of the Holy Trinity** (Rosengartenstrasse): This Gothic basilica (with baroque additions), built in the 2nd half of the 13C, is famous for its 1417 cycle of wall frescos on the history of the Augustinian Order. The patron, Emperor Sigismund, had figures of saints from his Bohemian home placed in the arch spandrels; the architecture also shows a close connection with Bohemia.

**Kaufhaus am Hafen/Konzilgebäude** (Am Hafen): This building, once used for the linen trade, was built in 1388. The massive building with 2 halls, one above the other, large hip-roof and crane oriels at the corners is wrongly supposed to have been the scene of a conclave of cardinals in 1417 to choose the new pope (Martin V), hence the name Konzilgebäude. In fact the Konzil met in the Münster.

**Museums:** *Kunstverein Konstanz/Von Wessenberg Picture Gallery* (41 Wessenbergstrasse): paintings and graphics from the Lake Constance area (19&20C). The *Rosgartenmuseum* (3–5 Rosgartenstrasse) has collections on pre- and early history, cultural history, folklore, crafts and numismatics.

**Stadttheater** (11 Konzilsstrasse): This is one of the oldest theatres in the Federal Republic; it was opened in 1609 in a former monastery building. It has its own company. 400 seats.

**Also worth seeing:** Parish church of *St.*

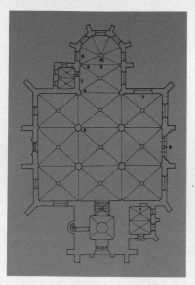

**Korbach, Parish church of St. Kilian 1**
Marienkapelle **2** Crucifix, early 14C **3** High altar
table, c.1340 **4** Font, 14C **5** Pulpit, late 14C **6** Lectern support, early 15C **7** Adoration of the Magi,
early 15C **8** S. portal with figures, early 15C **9** Tabernacle by B. and J.Bunkeman, 1525 **10** Altarpiece, 1527

*S.portal of St. Kilian, Korbach*

*Stephan,* a late Gothic building (1428; not
completed until 1845) which replaced a
12C building; former Jesuit church of *St.
Konrad* (1604 – 7), the church of *St.
Katherina* of the Dominican convent of
Zoffingen (1257) with a *Mater Dolorosa* by
C.D.Schenk (1684), the late-16C *Rathaus*
the former *Kanonikushaus* of the canonry
of St.Johann (5 Münsterplatz) with 14C
frescos and the *Haus zum Schafhirten* (6
Zollernstrasse).

**Korbach 3540**

Hessen                                    p.416□F 11

The craftsmen's town of Korbach, the oldest town in the Waldeck, was granted a
charter in 1188 and for a time was a member of the Hanseatic League. Its favourable position on the old Cologne-Leipzig

and Frankfurt-Bremen roads helped its development. It was badly damaged in the
Thirty Years War and the Seven Years War;
it is now a local administrative centre and
thriving economically and culturally.

**Protestant Parish Church of St.Kilian**
(Altstadt, 5 Kilianstrasse): This spacious
late Gothic hall church (1335–1450) is influenced by the style of Westphalian
churches. The nave and two aisles are of
equal width. The hall is almost square and
is supported by 4 pillars. On the S. side is
the *Marienkapelle,* built in 1340, which has
been a war memorial chapel since 1958.
Worthy of note are the portals, richly ornamented in the Gothic style, particularly
the S. portal with figures (early 15C), with
the Last Judgement in the arch. The red,
yellow and green colour-scheme was restored in 1957. Of interest in the S. aisle
is the *Adoration of the Magi* (early 15C),
also the large, painted *altarpiece* (1527) with

*Wall tomb of Georg Friedr. von Waldeck in the Nikolaikirche, Korbach*

a self-portrait of the painter at the foot of the cross.

**Protestant Church of St.Nikolai** (Neustadt): This elongated late Gothic hall church was built around the middle of the 15C. Only the W. tower dates from an older building (1359). The W. portal is richly embellished. 15C wall paintings are preserved in the S. aisle. The large *altarpiece* (1518) was painted by the same master as the one in the church of St.Kilian. The magnificent 39 ft. high *wall tomb* of Prince Georg Friedrich von Waldeck (1692), made of alabaster, limestone and marble, is unusual in design.

**Also worth seeing:** When the Old and New Town were amalgamated the *Rathaus* with its beautiful step gable (1377) was built exactly at the point where the two halves joined. The figure of Roland was added in 1470, the arches and tower not un-

til 1930. *Gymnasium Fridericianum,* a baroque building by J.M.Kitz (1770–4). The so-called former *Steinkammern,* 3 late Gothic stone houses (Enser Tor 7; Kirchplatz 2; Violinenstr.3). The stone house by St. Kilian's houses the *Heimatmuseum;* numerous *half-timbered houses* (17&18C) and remains of the *town fortifications.*

**Environs: Waldeck** (26 km. SE) lies on the Eder reservoir (12 km. S) and is of interest for its *half-timbered buildings* (18C), as well as the *Burg,* founded in the 12C, and the *Protestant parish church of St.Maria* (14&16C) with a three-part late Gothic altarpiece (*c.*1500).

---

**Krefeld 4150**
Nordrhein-Westfalen                    p.416☐B 10

---

The introduction of silk-weaving by the Von der Leyen family, who moved here in 1656, was the basis of the town's economic growth. Krefeld is now the home of important firms in the chemical and metal industries. The Rhine harbour makes water transport available.

**Catholic Parish Church of St.Matthias** (Krefeld-Hohenbudberg): This church, picturesquely situated above the Rhine, is neo Gothic. Only the Romanesque W. tower (12C) was spared when the medieval church was pulled down in 1852–4. Of importance are the furnishings, which were assembled from other Westphalian churches: *late Gothic carved altar* with painted panels (16C, neo Gothic base), as well as 15&16C *carved reliquaries* on the two side altars and a wooden *crucifix* (*c.*1250).

**Catholic Parish Church of St.Klemens** (Krefeld-Fischeln): The three-storey W. tower dates from the 12C, the nave and N. aisle from the 14C and the S. aisle was added in the 17C. The old E. end was pulled down and extended in 1867&8.

**Burg Linn** (in Linn, Albert-Steeger-Strasse): The oldest part of this moated castle was a residential tower on an artificial

*Burg Linn, Krefeld*

hill (*c.*1200), which was provided with ring walls and 6 corner towers in early Gothic times and converted into a residential castle in the 15C. Of this building there now remain only the wings ajoining the gateway, the main hall and the residential buildings. Fighting in the War of the Spanish Succession (1701–4) left the castle in ruins. A small *hunting lodge* was built in the outer works as a replacement in 1740. Today Burg Linn (carefully restored) is much visited by tourists and the home of the *Landschaftsmuseum* for the Lower Rhine (see museums).

**Museums:** The *Museumszentrum Burg Linn* (Albert-Steeger-Strasse) includes, apart from the castle and hunting lodge, a modern museum building; it exhibits collections on pre- and early history, the history of Krefeld and on the folklore of the Lower Rhine. *Museum Haus Lange* (91 Wilhelmshofallee), built in 1928 by L.Mies van der Rohe as a private house for

the art collector Hermann Lange, became the property of the town in 1955 and exhibits a collection of modern art and designs by Mies van der Rohe. The *Kaiser-Wilhelm-Museum* (35 Karlsplatz) contains paintings and sculpture from the Middle Ages to the 20C, also furniture from the region, Italy and Holland. The *Deutsches Textilmuseum* (in Linn, 8 Andreasmarkt) is the largest collection of its kind in Germany, with fabrics from all peoples and ages, ecclesiastical vestments and costumes.

**Theatre** (Theaterplatz): The combined companies of Krefeld and Mönchengladbach play here (drama, opera, operetta). 832 seats.

**Also worth seeing:** *Rathaus* (1 Von-der-Leyen-Platz): The former *Schloss von der Leyen* was built in 1791–4 and rebuilt in 1955 after heavy bomb damage in the Second World War. *Haus Neuleyental* (32

Cracauerstrasse): This three-winged building decorated in Empire style was built as summer residence for the Von der Leyen family at the end of the 18C. The so-called *Herberzhäuser* (Marktplatz, Krefeld-Uerdingen), a neoclassical block of houses built for the merchant family Herberz by A. von Vagedes in 1832, now house the Rathaus, Apotheke and library.

## Krempe 2209
Schleswig-Holstein                      p.412□G 4

**Rathaus:** This two-storey building (1570) with its high gable is almost square and is one of the most splendid town halls in Schleswig-Holstein. Only the façade is in brick, the other sides are half-timbered with a projecting upper storey over carved sills. Of particular interest, in the Ratssaal, are the baroque reliefs on the chimney-piece, and several chests. The painted door-keeper is in the form of the 'Wild Man' (1570). The Town Hall contains a *Stadtgeschichtliche Sammlung.*

## Kronach 8640
Bavaria                                 p.418□K 14

The painter Lucas Cranach the Elder was born here in 1472. Today the town is known for its porcelain factories.

**Veste Rosenberg:** This fortress has survived as well as almost any other in Germany. The origin of the building was the *Stone house with tower,* built above the town between the rivers Kronach and Haslach by Bishop Otto I of Bamberg in 1128–30. This is now the irregular, 4-cornered core of the castle. In the 2nd half of the 14C, as the stronghold of the Bamberger Hochstift, the castle was enlarged and in 1475–87 extended into a fortress. The castle core was converted into a *residence* in the 16C and was redesigned to look as it does today by Balthasar Neumann in 1730. Here too is the 15C *castle chapel.* Until 1866 the castle served as a fortress, now it houses the interesting *Frankenwald-Museum* and a *youth hostel.*

**Catholic Parish Church of St.John the Baptist:** This Gothic hall (*c.*1400) with a nave and two aisles was extended in the early 16C by the addition of the W. end, which towers above the older building. Of interest is the richly embellished late Gothic *portal* on the N. side of the W. building, with a figure of John the Baptist. Original in design is the little late Gothic *Chapel of St.Anne* (1513) in the E. of the choir, the foundations of which are Romanesque.

**Also of interest:** Lucas Cranach the Elder is supposed to have been born in the *Haus zum scharfen Eck,* a 16C half-timbered building. The *former Kommandantenhaus* (Marktstrasse) is a stately 16C town house. *Also* Rtahaus (1583), hospital church (1467), Chapel of the Holy Cross on the Kreuzberg (17C), monastery church of St.Petrus von Aleantara (1670–2) and the Melchior-Otto Column (1654).

## Kronberg im Taunus 6242
Hessen                                  p.416□E 14

**Burg:** The oldest parts of the complex are the ring walls and the square keep (the narrow 'butter-churn' top was added around 1500, together with the ramparts) of the *Oberburg.* In the *Mittelburg* is the *Schloss,* a two-winged residential building, begun in the first half of the 15C with Renaissance gables (1626) decorated with obelisks, which houses the *Schlossmuseum.* The interesting kitchen has Gothic stove-casing and an old well. Notable in the *Unterburg,* which lies to the SE and is entered via a gatehouse of 1692, is the *Burgkapelle* (1350).

**Protestant Church of St.John:** A tower from the original town fortifications was incorporated into the S. side of the choir of this late Gothic building. The church is principally interesting for its interior, including remains of the late Gothic paintwork (1483), a votive altar with a group of terracotta figures (Middle Rhine *c.*1440–50), 4 double tombs in the nave, and the tomb of Walter von Kronberg (in the choir), a later work of H.Backoffen (1517).

## Kulmbach 8650
Bavaria                              p.418□K 14

The town's most famous son is Hans von
Kulmbach, born in 1476, a pupil and
friend of Albrecht Dürer, but the town
achieved literary importance through the
Plassenburg: the hero of Ludwig Bech-
stein's novel 'Grunbach' (1839) is the castle commander of the Plassenburg, and
Jakob Wassermann dedicated his short
story 'The Prisoners of the Plassenburg'
(1911) to the famous Renaissance building.

**Plassenburg:** The Plassenburg, the most
important Renaissance castle in Franconia,
is the towering emblem of the town, visible for miles. Count Berthold II von Andechs had the first castle (*c.*1135) built here
on the hill near the confluence of the Red
and the White Main. After the Bavarians
the castle came into the possession of the
Thuringian Counts von Orlamünde
(1260–1340) and finally—via the Burgraves
of Nuremberg—to the Hohenzollerns. The
Plassenburg has looked as it does now since
rebuilding in 1559 under Margrave Georg
Friedrich (following a fire). An extensive
complex with outer works and main castle was developed, to the plans of such excellent architects as G.Beck (1559) and
C.Vischer (1561). The outer works are very
plain. The *Schöne Hof,* the inner courtyard
of the main castle, one of the most lavish
exteriors of the German Renaissance, is
overwhelming. The irregular quadrangle
is defined by towers at the corners and is
surrounded on 3 sides by two-storey open
arcades. Parapets, arches and pillars are
decorated with elaborate figurative and ornamental sculpture. Medallions depict the
ancestors of the Hohenzollerns. From the
beginning of the 19C to 1928 the castle
served as a prison. Today it houses one of
the largest *tin figure collections* in the world,
as well as branches of the Bavarian State
Painting Collection (hunting and battle
paintings). Closed Mondays.

**Also of interest:** *Petrikirche* (Church of
St.Peter) with a nearly 50 ft. high choir
altar (1650 – 3); *former Langheimer
Klosterhof,* built as a 3-storey ashlar build-

ing with a tall gabled front on a spur of the
castle hill (1691–5); the *former chancelry*
(1563, converted in 17C); the *Rathaus*
(1752) with rococo façade.

## Kusel 6798
Rheinland-Pfalz                       p.416□C 15

**Burg Lichtenberg:** The complex has developed from two originally separate castles (15C), which explains its unusual
length (1385 ft.). Only the surrounding
walls and a gateway (13C) remain of the
*Unterburg* on the mountain ridge. The
*Oberburg* was laid out at the end of the 13C
and enlarged several times in the 14&15C.
The focal point of the extensive complex
is the massive keep. 2 residential buildings
with a chapel (*c.*1230; wall paintings) are
divided by a 16C battery tower (Ross-
mühle). The castle ends in the E. with
an outer ward with 3 large round towers.
The castle was destroyed by a fire in 1799,
used as a quarry in the 19C, taken over by
the state in 1894, and restored and partly
rebuilt. A *youth hostel* was built on the
foundations of two former Burgmannenhäuser in 1922. Between the Upper and
Lower castle lies the *Protestant church,* a
simple hall building (1755).

## Kyllburg 5524
Rheinland-Pfalz                       p.416□B 14

Kyllburg, known as early as *c.*800 as 'castrum Kiliberg', is now a health resort in
wooded countryside.

**Former Collegiate Foundation and
Catholic Parish Church of St.Maria:**
The church of *St.Maria* with its single
aisle, substantially lower choir, lavish tracery windows and beautiful portals is part
of a little 14C collegiate foundation situated on a height above the River Kyll
which has survived almost untouched.
The end of the choir is lit by 3 *stained glass
windows* (1534). Behind the high altar
stands a stone *Madonna* (made in Trier,
14C), on the S. wall is the former *triumphal*

*Terracotta group 'Maria-Schlaf' in the chancel of the Johanniskirche, Kronberg*

cross (*c.*1300). Also of note are the effigy tombs, beautiful choir stalls (14C), pulpit and confessionals (in rococo style). Adjacent to the S. is the late Gothic *cloister* with the stone figure of Maria Lactans, parallel to which is the former *chapter house* (14C). On the upper floor was once the dormitory of the foundation.

**Environs: Malberg** (1 km. NW): Down the valley lies *Schloss Malberg*, a baroque building (1708–15) by W. von Veyder with interesting mythological *sculptures* by F.Dietz on the terrace balustrade and garden walls (1758–60).

**St.Thomas** (4 km N.): The *former Cistercian Convent of St. Thomas*, is a little further up the valley, and is worth a visit; the *church* (consecrated 1222) is one of the earliest examples of a late medieval nunnery; it has one aisle and a deep W. nuns' gallery. 18C convent buildings.

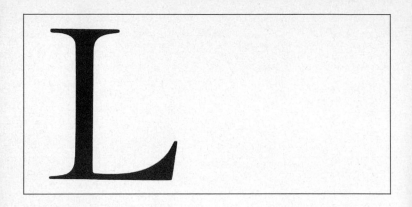

## Ladenburg 6802

Baden-Württemberg          p.420☐E 16

This town on the Neckar has maintained its medieval appearance with a 12C town wall and many old mansions and town houses. It goes back to an important Celtic settlement by the name of 'Lokwodunum', which has been here since the 5C BC. There are finds on display in the museum from the Roman military camp, later known as civitas *Lopodumun,* which existed here in the 1C AD. The town passed to the Franks in the 6C AD, and then became the main town of the 'Lobdergau'.

**Catholic Parish Church of St. Gallus** (Kirchenstrasse): This 14C Gothic basilica was erected on the foundations of older buildings. The early 11C *crypt* has survived. During renovation work, the foundations of a basilica were discovered. This is presumed to date from the 3C and was probably intended by the Romans for use as a market hall.

**Sebastian chapel** (Lustgartenstrasse): This former court chapel of the bishops of Worms has frequently been altered and expanded (12–18C), and a uniform style cannot be discerned. The building includes remains from the Carolingian period. The 12C tower is Romanesque, the choir is late Gothic, and the aisle was redesigned in

1737. In 1978, some 15C wall paintings were uncovered in the interior.

**Also worth seeing:** Medieval town and parts of the 17C town fortifications.
A number of *houses* have survived in good condition, including the Worms Bischof-shof (1 Am Hof, Lobdengaumuseum), and the Neunhellersches Haus.

---

## Lahnstein 5420

Rheinland-Pfalz          p.416☐C/D 13

The town of Lahnstein stands at the confluence of the Lahn and the Rhine; it came into existence in 1969 when the two districts called Oberlahnstein (granted a charter in 1324) and Niederlahnstein (charter 1332) were united. The latter town dates back to a 4C Roman 'Burgus'.

**Monastery church of St. John the Baptist:** This flat-roofed pillared basilica, which was still a ruin in the mid 19C, was restored to its 12C condition by work carried out in 1856, 1906 and finally 1960&61. The massive W.tower with its six storeys and its short pyramidal roof has typical Rhineland red-and-black ashlars at the corners. The *interior* is dominated by the gallery openings and the pillared arcades in the W.tower (underneath the organ). This is one of the earliest galleried churches in the Rhineland.

**Parish Church of St.Martin** (Oberlahnstein): The two E. towers have survived various alterations and reconstructions and date from a previous late Romanesque building. The Gothic chancel and the sacristy were added in the 14C. The baroque nave is a simple hall built in 1775–77.

**Martinsburg** (Oberlahnstein): This Burg, designed as a moated castle in 1244, was initially a customs house for the town of Mainz, and the present building dates mainly from the 14&15C and the 18C. The most striking feature is the five-storeyed tower at the S. corner. The *chapel* in the N. wing is worth looking at, and is joined to the 14C *residential tower*.

**Lahneck castle** (Oberlahnstein): This castle of the Mainz archbishops and electors was built in the 13C and destroyed in 1688, but rebuilt in 1860 in the English Gothic Revival style.

**Altes Rathaus** (Oberlahnstein, 34 Hochstrasse): This Gothic half-timbered building dates from the 16C. The ground floor is built of stone.

**Also worth seeing:** The *Heimbachsches*

*Crypt, St.Gallus in Ladenburg*

*Haus* (2 Heimbachgasse 2) is a 12C Romanesque residential building with red-and-white round arches. The *Naussau-Sporkenburger Court* (21 Johannisstrasse), a late Gothic stone building. The *Wirtshaus an der Lahn*, 8 Lahnstrasse, a picturesque half-timbered inn (1697). The medieval *town fortification*.

---

### Lahr, Schwarzwald 7630
Baden-Württemberg                p.420□D 19

---

Little has survived of this town, which is rich in tradition and has had a turbulent history which can be traced back to the 13C. Today, the Storchenturm is all that survives of the Burg which Walter von Geroldseck built in 1250 on the mountain pass which leads from Alsace into the Kinzigtal.

**Protestant church/former St.Peter's church** (in Burgheim): A Franconian hall church on this site is mentioned in the early 8C. A new building was consecrated in 1035. There were further alterations in the 12–15C. A graveyard with rows of tombs was found during excavation work carried out underneath the church. There is a 7C noblewoman's tomb for which Roman building materials were probably employed. 15C wall paintings survive in the nave.

**Former Collegiate Church/Protestant Parish Church:** Construction work on this church continued for a century and a half (1260–1412). The building was radically redesigned in 1848–51; some characteristic elements were removed and the overall image of the building was much altered. The 13C choir survived.

**Also worth seeing:** The *Neues Rathaus*, with its beautiful colonnaded hall in the upper storey, was originally built as a town house for the Lotzbeck family (1808). There are late baroque, rococo, classical and Biedermeier *houses*; one of the most important is the Stoessersches Haus (41 Kaiserstrasse; 1783). The *Geroldsecker Museum* is the Storchenturm of the former Burg.

## Laichingen 7903
Baden-Württemberg p.420☐G 18

**Höhlenmuseum** (47 Beurer Steig): It has exhibits on the earliest history of the Schwäbische Alb, including fossils, stalactites, stalagmites, and skeletons of cave animals.

**Weberei- und Heimatmuseum** (weaving and local history) (41 Weite Strasse) near the Protestant *church of St. Alban,* which is a fortress church with a surrounding wall, battlements and fortified gate.

## Landau an der Isar 8380
Bavaria p.422☐N 18

**Parish Church Mariae Himmelfahrt:** When the present baroque church was rebuilt (it was dedicated in 1726), the tower of a previous medieval building survived and was included in the new building. The rich decorations deserve particular attention, especially the *high altar,* 1725, and two *rococo altars* in the side chapels. The three carved figures on the pillars are late Gothic, as is the crucifix on the chancel arch.

**Also worth seeing:** *Former ducal Schloss:* The Schloss was built in the 13C in the elevated SW corner of the town wall. It was rebuilt in the 18&19C after a serious fire in the 16C. The *Steinfelskirche* was built above a natural grotto *c.*1700. The 15C *Friedhofskirche Heiliges Kreuz* has a flat roof in the baroque style, and its three well-preserved late Gothic altars are worth looking at. The *Heimatmuseum* (local history), founded in 1957, is in the Weissgerberhaus (59 Höckinger Strasse; 17C).

## Landau in der Pfalz 6740
Rheinland-Pfalz p.420☐D 16

Three quarters of this medieval town burned down in 1689 when Vauban, the architect who designed fortifications for

*Former collegiate church, Landau in der Pfalz*

Louis XIV, was building here. The following still survive: the German and the French gate, the crown work in the NW of the town, hydraulic equipment at the intake and outlet locks, and flood basin No. 80.

**Protestant Parish Church/Former Collegiate Church Unserer Lieben Frau** (Marktstrasse): The present church was built in the 14C and originated from an Augustinian canonry established in 1276. The most noteworthy feature of this unusually large and elongated building is the *tower,* which in 1458 had an octagonal belfry built on to the three square-shaped lower storeys of the first stage of construction (1349). Groin vaulting was added in the chancel and nave in the course of restoration work in 1897&98.

**Catholic Parish Church of the Heiliges Kreuz/Augustinian Church** (König-

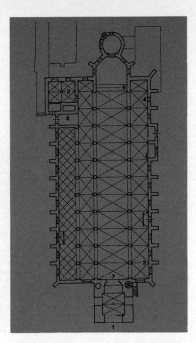

**Landau, collegiate church 1** Main portal, 1st half of 14C **2** Sacristy with remains of wall paintings, 1st half of 14C **3** Mount of Olives niche with Christ figure, 1441 **4** Stone figure of St.John, c. 1525 **5** Tomb of the knight Hartung Fuchs v.Dornheim (d.1512) **6** Tomb of Marie Elisabeth de Tarade (d.1688) **7** Organ front by I.Seiffert, 1772

strasse): This church erected in 1405–13 was damaged in the Second World War (choir), but rebuilt to the original plans. A *font* dating from 1506, and the 17C *Landau Madonna* which is carved from wood and has been in the church of the Heiliges Kreuz since 1893, were two outstanding old features of the interior decorations. The *monastery buildings* adjoin the church in the N. They date from 1740–50, and the E.section was destroyed in the Second World War.

**Also worth seeing:** Some *houses* in the Martin-Luther-Strasse (No. 17), in the Kaufhausgasse (No. 9) and in the Max-Josephs-Platz (No. 1) date from the 17&18C and show French influence. The

house of the garrison headquarters (50 Marktstrasse) was built in 1827 and is characterized by classical elements (today it is the town hall). *Städtisches Heimatmuseum* (local history).

---

**Landsberg am Lech 8910**
Bavaria                                    p.422☐J 20

**Parish church of Mariae Himmelfahrt** (Georg-Hellmair-Platz): This massive basilica was erected in the 15C on the site of a previous building dating from the 13C. The architect was V.Kindlin from Strasbourg, and he also contributed to St.Ulrich in Augsburg (q.v.). The baroque interior decoration is of a richness seldom encountered. Fresco medallions are very sparingly worked into the rich stucco of the ceiling. The finest feature is the enormous *high altar* (1680) by J.Pfeiffer from Bernbeuren. The sculpture, which includes figures of Joseph, Joachim and the three Archangels, is by L.Luidl, an artist from Landsberg. He also created the figures of saints on the wall of the nave. The 16C *chancel windows* are from the Augsburg workshop, and are among the most important in Bavaria dating from this period. Behind the high altar is the *monument*, by H.Reichle, 1575, to Cyriacus Weber, a doctor of medicine. Some further noteworthy altars, mostly 18C, are to be seen in the side chapels. The rich carvings of the *organ* are by L.Luidl (1696). The *choir stalls* and the *pulpit* were added in the early 18C.

**St.Johannes** (Vorderanger): This church was built to plans by D.Zimmermann (1741). The chancel, with its unusual horseshoe-shaped ground plan, is dominated by a high altar and two side altars (with figures by J.Luidl, 1760). There is fine paintwork (1752) by K.Thalhammer above the flat dome spanning the laymen's area of the church.

**Former Jesuit church of the Holy Cross** (Helfensteingasse): H.Holl, the famous architect from Augsburg, drew up the plans for the first building on this site (1580 – 84). However, the church was

*Mariae Himmelfahrt, Landsberg*

with a statue of the Virgin Mary by J.Streiter. The Town Hall houses a *gallery* with works by H.Herkomer, the painter (1849 – 1914). The town's rapid growth made it necessary to expand the *town fortifications* more than once. The *Bayertor* dates from the 15C.

**Historisches Museum** (2 v.-Kühlmann-Strasse): Finds from the Bronze Age, town history, sculptures, paintings, collections relating to guilds and military matters.

---

**Landshut 8300**
Bavaria                        p.422□M 18

Landshut is one of the most beautiful Gothic towns in Germany. The main parts of the medieval district have scarcely changed since the 16C. The town's two main geometrical axes are the two streets called Altstadt and Neustadt which run almost parallel to one another from S. to N. The Altstadt is regarded as the most beautiful street in Germany. It runs from St. Martins church in the S. to the Spitalkirche Heiliger Geist in the N. The Altstadt and Neustadt streets both run down to the Isar in the N. Landshut was twice a residency: Ludwig the Kelheimer founded the Wittelsbach residence here in 1204, and Ludwig X made the town his second Bavarian residence after the Landshut war of succession (1504 – 05). A quarter of a century earlier, in 1475, Ludwig the Rich organized the lavish Landshut Prince's Wedding for his son Georg. The 'Landshut Wedding 1475' is held every four years in memory of the eight days of festivities at which the wedding of Georg to Jadwiga, the daugher of the Polish King, was celebrated. Landshut attained literary fame when the regional university of Ingolstadt was moved here in 1800. The circle of Romantics which formed around Joh.Michael Sailer in Landshut included Bettina and Clemens Brentano, Achim von Arnim, and other well-known writers of the period.

replaced by the present building in 1752 –54. This church is almost undecorated on the outside. Its layout follows the scheme of the Studienkirche of Mariae Himmelfahrt in Dillingen (q.v.) (a pilaster church without a gallery). The decorations are in the rococo style (frescos by C.T.Scheffler and in some cases G.B.Götz). In the middle of the high altar is a large painting by J.B.Bader depicting the Crucifixion (to a model by Bergmüller, 1758). The pulpit, several wrought-iron railings, and the carvings on the confessional boxes, should be noted. The stucco (1730) in the sacristy is by D.Zimmermann.

**Also worth seeing:** The market square, one of the most beautiful in Germany, is dominated by the *Rathaus* built in 1699 – 1702. The excellent stucco is by D.Zimmermann, who was the mayor of Landsberg from 1759–64 and also designed the interior rooms of the Town Hall. Outside the Town Hall is the *fountain* built in 1783,

*Marktplatz and Rathaus* ▷

**Town Parish Church and Collegiate Church/Münster St.Martin** (Altstadt): H.von Burghausen (until his death in 1432) and H.Stethaimer were the architects of this massive minster, which with its 430 ft. tower is the tallest brick building in the world. From the point of view of art history, the church is among the most significant late Gothic works. Its outside is characterized by the massive tower which is built on a square substructure and becomes narrower storey by storey. The five portals all have lavish figured decorations. On the S.wall, between two portals, we find the *monument* to the architect Hans von Burghausen, which was built in his successor's workshop and depicts Burghausen as a very old man. The *interior* of the minster is enormous. The overall length, including the tower, is 300 ft. The pièce de résistance of this hall church is its nave (95 ft. tall, 36 ft. wide), which is continued in the chancel (91 ft. tall, 37 ft. wide). Flat chapels adjoin each of the aisles. The finest item of the very rich decorations is the *Landshut Madonna,* a larger-than-life carved figure by H.Leinberger (c.1520). The *tombstone* in sandstone (Coronation of the Virgin) in the central side chapel between the two portals is also by Leinberger. There are numerous other monuments which are among the best works of the period. The *high altar* is a work by H.Stethaimer (1424), and the pulpit (1422) is probably also by him. The *choir stalls (c.*1500) are among the most precious treasures of the St.Martin minster. The *crucifix* (1495) is ascribed to M.Erhart, the artist from Ulm.

**Former Dominican Church of St. Blasius** (Freyung): This church, founded in the 13C and dedicated in 1386, was partially rebuilt and redecorated in the 18C; the neoclassical W.façade also dates from this period. The stucco by J.B.Zimmermann is the finest feature of the decorations. This artist also painted the extensive fresco cycle (1749), which is one of his best works.

The *altar* shows the quality of the woodcarvers' workshops in 18C Landshut. The central feature is an altarpiece by J.B.Zimmermann; the richly carved *choir stalls* are

also very fine. Today, the *government of Lower Saxony* has its premises in the adjoining *monastery buildings,* where the university was housed before it moved to Munich.

**Former Jesuit Church of St.Ignatius** (Neustadt): This building, which has neither a tower nor a façade, was built in the S. of the Neustadt in 1613–41 on the model of St.Michael in Munich (q.v.). The Jesuit Father J.Holl was in charge of this church. The best features of the decorations include stucco by the Wessobrunn artist M.Schmuzer (1640&41). The white of the stuccoes contrasts effectively with the dark colouring of the altars. At the centre of the high altar (1663–65) is a painting by J.C.Storer (Christ appearing to St. Ignatius).

**Seligenthal Cistercian Convent** (on the other side of the Isar): Only the *Afra chapel* still reminds us today of the period of this convent's foundation (1231). The convent church consecrated in 1259 was — apart from the surrounding walls—replaced by a new building in the 18C. The *stucco* inside is among the best works of J.B.Zimmermann. The rich frescos are also by him. The Coronation of the Virgin Mary is depicted on the dome. The *St.Ann altar,* with its central group (Virgin Mary surrounded by angels), occupies a special position among the massive altars designed by K.Griessmann and built by J.W.Jorhan (14&15C).

**Castle Trausnitz** (Hofberg): Castle Trausnitz, founded by Duke Ludwig from Kellheim in 1204, has survived in very good condition, and is also among the most significant from the historical point of view. However, it has been much altered over the centuries. Defensive and residential buildings were added from the 14–16C. It was expanded into a Schloss *(Fürstenbau)* in the years from 1568 to 1578. It was also at this time that the double rows of arches were built. They are the work of Italian craftsmen and are among the most important Renaissance works in Germany. The stairs in the W.corner of the Schloss courtyard should also be emphasized. It was un-

*St. Martin, Landshut*

*Heilig-Geist-Kirche*

*Burg Trausnitz*

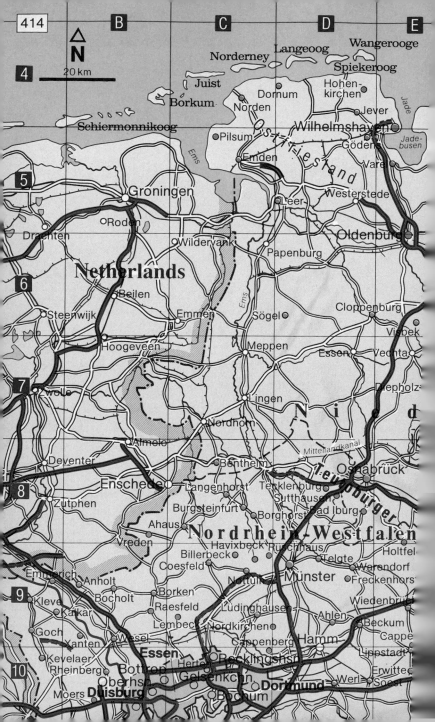

Möhnesee
Drüggelte
Arnsberg
Ruhr
Meschede
Obermarsberg
Warburg
Hof-geismar
Göt-tingen
Münden
Witzen-hausen
Brilon
Arolsen
Wilhelmsthal
Kassel
Langenberg
843△
Korbach
Wolfhagen
Oberkaufungen
Bad Sooden Allendorf
Germerode
Eschwege
Eder
Fritzlar
Rothaargebirge
Bad Wildungen
Bad Berleburg
Frankenberg/Eder
Homberg
Haina
H e s s e n
Caldern
Marburg
Langenstein
Bad Hersfeld
Dillenburg
Alsfeld
Schweinsberg
GDR
Herborn
Rasdorf
Greifenstein
Schlitz
Fraurombach
Altenberg
Hermannstein
Lauterbach
Fulda
Wetzlar
Gießen
Laubach
Vogels-
Weilburg
Braunfels
Lich
Schotten
Fulda
Dietkirchen
Butzbach
Münzenberg
berg
Schaumburg
Hirzenhain
Saalburg
Bad Nauheim
Birstein
Rhön
Idstein
Bad Homburg
Friedberg
Ilbenstadt
Büdingen
Bad Brückenau
Königstein
Kronberg
Gelnhausen
Bad Orb
Bad Kissingen
Taunus Frankfurt
Wiesbaden
Hanau
Offenbach
Aberbach
Heusenstamm
Seligenstadt
Mainz
Babenhausen
Aschaffen-burg
Gagenheim
Gr.-Gerau
Dieburg
Galbach-Dettel-bach
ppenheim
Darmstadt
Mespelbrunn
Veitshöchheim
Rhine
Main
Würzburg
Kitzingen
Bensheim
Steinbach
Michel-stadt
Miltenberg
Bronnbach
Ochsenfurt
Lorsch
Heppenheim
Amorbach
Worms
Erbach
Tauberbischofsheim
Weinheim
Weikersheim
dwigs-Mannheim
afen
adenburg
Hirschhorn
Bad Mergenthm.
Nideshm
Heidelberg
Zwingenberg
Adelsheim
Stuppach
Creglingen

**Map 1 (Berlin):**

TEGEL
Tegel
WEISSENSEE
WEDDING
SPANDAU
PRENZLAUER
BERG
Spree
TIER-
GARTEN
EAST BERLIN
CHARLOTTEN-
BURG
FRIEDRICHS-
HAIN
Havel
WILMERSDORF
KREUZBERG
WEST BERLIN
SCHÖNE-
BERG
NEUKÖLLN
TREPTOW
Tempelhof
TEMPELHOF
STEGLITZ
ZEHLENDORF
Teltowkanal
N
5 km
Panke

**Map 2 (Czechoslovakia / Fichtelgebirge):**

L M N O
Schwarzenberg
Most
Plauen
Auerbach
Keilberg
1244
E r z g e b i r g e
Kadan
Klingenthal
Ostrov
Zatec/Saaz
Hof
Karlovy Vary/Karlsbad
Münchberg
Selb
Eger
Fichtel –
Czechoslovakia
1051 Schneeberg
Cheb/Eger
Wunsiedel
Kralovice
gebirge
Waldsassen
Marianské Lázne
Ober –
Kemnath
Entenbühl
901
Mies
Plzeň (Pilsen)
Speinshart
Flossenbürg
Grafenwöhr
pfälzer
Weiden
Stod
Vohenstrauß
Leuchtenberg
Staňkov
N
Wald
30 km
Sulzbach-
Rosenberg
Trausnitz
dorf Amberg
Perschen

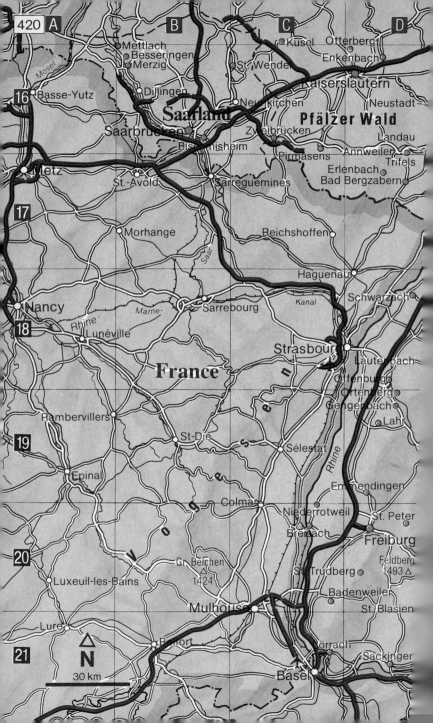

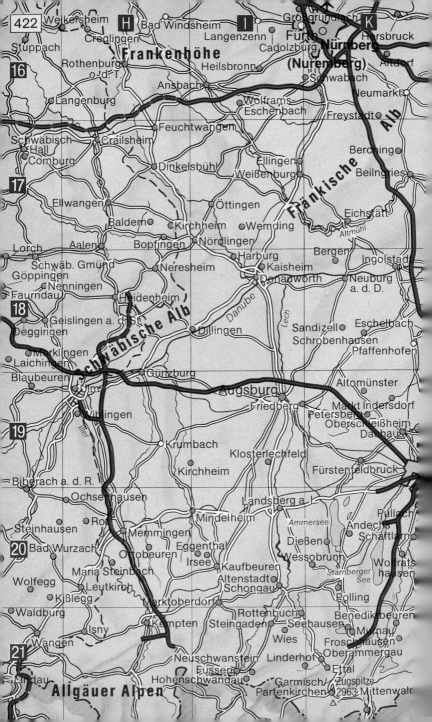

◁ *Narrentreppe, Burg Trausnitz*                    *Courtyard of Stadtresidenz in Landshut*

der Duke Wilhelm V that Burg Trausnitz became a meeting place for artists, actors and musicians (Tannhäuser and Neidhardt von Reuenthal were among the guests here). The painted 'Narrentreppe' (fool's staircase), the work of the Italian artist A.Scalzi, is decorated with unusually vigorous Commedia dell'arte figures. An especially fine feature is the *Burg chapel of St. Georg* (double chapel dating from the 13C, with a late Gothic vault from 1518). The parapet depicts Christ amidst Apostles and Saints (stucco work). The figures of the Virgin Mary and John above this are first-rate carvings, as is the crucifix (*c.*1250).

**Stadtresidenz** (Altstadt) Stimulated by a visit to the *Palazzo del Tè* in Mantua in Italy in 1536, Duke Ludwig X ordered the only Palazzo N. of the Alps to be built in the Altstadt from 1537 – 43. The *Deutscher Bau* (German building) faces the Altstadt side, while the *Italienischer Bau*

(Italian building) is opposite the Ländgasse. The rooms are of great splendour. The finest features are firstly the W.Hall of the Italienischer Bau and secondly the *Italienischer Saal*, with a tunnel vault decorated with paintings, and round paintings on the walls.

The paintings in the vaults of the adjoining state rooms show scenes and figures from the world of the ancient Greek gods. The painters were H.Bocksberger the Elder (Salzburg), L.Refinger (Munich) and H.Posthumus (place of origin unknown). Today the Stadtresidenz is a *museum* showing 18C domestic décor and European painting from the 16 – 18C. The Stadtresidenz also houses the *Stadt- und Kreismuseum* (local history).

**Also worth seeing:** *St. Jodok* (built in 1338–68, renovated and expanded after a fire in the 15C): The *Heiliger Geist* or *Spital-Kirche* (1407–61) with the *hospital building* which is located opposite and was given its present appearance in 1722–28. There is also the so-called *Herzogsschlösschen* (1782) to the S. of the Trausnitz, and the *Rathaus* (Altstadt), which was built in 1380, converted in the 15&16C and given its present form in 1860&1. Numerous 15–16C gabled houses survive in the Altstadt, including the *Pappenbergerhaus* (81 Altstadt), *Grasbergerhaus* (300 Altstadt), and the houses at 69, 299, 369 and 570 Altstadt. There are still some gates and towers surviving in the 15C *Stadtbering* (town wall).

**Südostbayerisches Städtebundtheater** (theatre of the south-east Bavarian league of towns) (2–5 Ländtorplatz). Housed in the municipal theatre building erected in 1836 and converted in 1947. There are 406 seats.

**Langenburg 7183**
Baden–Württemberg                           p.420☐G 16

**Protestant Stadtkirche:** This 16C church has been altered and enlarged several times, so that it cannot be assigned to a particular period. Items worth mentioning are the 17C altarpiece (Last Supper, Baptism and *Confession of Augsburg*) and the monument to Count Philipp Ernst (1629, by M.Kern).

**Schloss:** The Schloss stands on rising ground above the Jagst river. Its oldest sections (the Haspelturm, Archivturm and the Hexenturm, and the Lindenstamm bastion) date back to the 13C. It was given its present form in the 15C and especially in the 16C, when G.Kern, Haus Forchtenberg, redesigned the complex in the German Renaissance style. The E.wing was later converted in the baroque style. The damage resulting from a fire in 1963 has been almost completely repaired. The dining room and the baroque hall with its rich stucco decorations (1686) occupy a special position among the many large rooms in the Schloss. There are also a weapon collection, porcelain, and a motor-car museum.

**Laubach 6312**
Hessen                                       p.416☐F 13

**Protestant Stadtkirche:** The oldest part

*Schloss Langenburg*

of the church is the 13C E.building, with its fine pilaster strips in the corners and a pointed-arched frieze. The nave was added in 1700–02, but it and the existing building do not make a unified whole. The most important interior decorations are the organ (1747 – 51) by J.C.Beck and J.M.Wagner, several monuments (mainly from the 16&17C), and some late Gothic wall paintings (restored in 1983&4) in the chancel and N.transept.

**Schloss:** The central fort of this Schloss which has a picturesque location on a slope in the valley of the Wetter was built c.1400, while the keep probably dates from as early as the 13C. These are the oldest sections of the complex and are connected with the numerous and extensive later buildings which were added up until the 19C. The showpiece among the interior decorations is the baroque *Grosser Saal* (great hall; 1739) with its extravagant abundance of mirrors and panelling. The richly decorated wrought-iron banister is the dominant feature of the *staircase*. Part of the castle today houses the most extensive *private library* in Europe. It belongs to the Counts of Solms-Laubach, who are resident here, and contains 120,000 volumes. The Schloss is surrounded by numerous *annexes* (civil servants' houses and farm buildings). The so-called *Untermühle* (lower mill) dating from the 16C survives in the English-style garden (today the municipal Kurpark).

**Also worth seeing:** The *Grünemannsbrunnen* (W. of the church; 1588–89) and the *Engelsbrunnen* (Markt; 1780) are good examples of fountain construction at those particular periods. The *Kriegerturm* (warriors' tower) in the W. of the town reminds us of the *town fortifications* which were set up in the 15&16C. *Half-timbered houses* (15–18C).

---

**Lauf an der Pegnitz 8560**
Bavaria                                    p.418☐K 16

A rapid stretch of river water (called 'Loufe' in Middle High German) was the origin

both of the town's foundation and of the town's name. Several mills were built on the Pegnitz in the 13C, and contributed to the economic expansion of this small town. The favourable location on the trade route from Nuremberg to Bohemia contributed in itself to the town's rapid growth. The hammer mills on the Pegnitz later became the basis of some important industrial plants.

**Kaiserburg/Wenzelsschloss** (1 Schlossinsel): Emperor Karl IV had the castle built in 1357–60 on an island in the Pegnitz. It was redesigned by P.Beheim in 1526&7. The famous *Wappensaal* (coat of arms room) survives from the initial phase of construction. It has more than 100 stone coats of arms of Bohemian-Silesian aristocrats allied to the Emperor. Emperor Charles IV once used this room as part of his living quarters.

**Also worth seeing:** Historical market square with old town hall (17C) and Franconian gabled houses. The *Protestant town parish church* (Markt), built in 1553 and later altered several times, has noteworthy baroque decorations from the late 17C. The crucifix above the chancel arch dates from the year 1498. The *parish church of St.Leonhard* survives, but has been in ruins since 1553. The adjoining *Spital* (hospital) with its ruined church was built in 1374, but has been altered several times. Today the castle accommodates the *municipal archive* and the *municipal collections* (history of the town and region, and 15&16C folk art).

---

**Laufen an der Salzach 8229**
Bavaria                                    p.422☐N 20

This town is rich in tradition. It was important from an early date, having been an important trading post, especially for salt. This was mainly due to its favourable geographical location on a bend of the Salzach.

**Parish Church Mariae Himmelfahrt** (Spandrucker Platz 1): The oldest hall

church surviving in Germany was built here from 1332 onwards on the site of a Romanesque basilica. The only feature to be taken over from the previous building was the tower. The dominant features inside are the two powerful rows of columns. There is a fine *painting* (1690) on the S.side altar, the work of J.M.Rottmayr, a painter who was born in Laufen and died in Vienna. The *high altar* is a work by H.Fiegl and J.Gerold (1654). A low arcade (beautiful net vault with frescos), with numerous 15&16C *tombstone slabs* and two Romanesque portal lions, runs round part of the church. In the SW, it leads to the *Michaelskapelle* (14C, lately partly rebuilt), and to the *graveyard*.

**Also worth seeing:** The present *Schloss* building, the result of considerable reconstruction and rebuilding work performed in 1424 and 1606, was erected on the site where a castle was first mentioned in 790. The 16C *Rathaus* (town hall) was not given its present façade until 1865. The former *town walls* dating from the 14C have disappeared, apart from some towers (Oberes Tor, Unteres Tor, Zinkenturm) which were added later.

---

**Lautenbach im Renchtal 7606**
Baden-Württemberg                p.420☐D 18

**Wallfahrtskirche Mariae Krönung:** This Gothic church consecrated in 1493 is closely related to a pilgrimage which can be traced back to the 14C. Two additional bays and the tower were added in 1895–97. Inside, the lavish decorations are dominated by the net vault. The unusually large *lectern* (1488), supported by four columns, and the *Gnadenkapelle* (1485), where the miraculous 16C wooden image of the Blessed Virgin was kept, are particularly striking features. The pictures in the *choir altar* (1483 and 1510–20) are unusually expressive. The 15C *stained-glass windows*, are also very fine. The *choir stalls* survive from the period of the church's foundation.

◁ *Wenzelsschloss, Lauf an der Pegnitz*

---

**Lauterbach 6420**
Hessen                           p.416☐G 12

**Protestant Stadtkirche** (Marktplatz): This church built in 1763–67 is one of the most beautiful rococo churches in Hessen, and formed the model for several churches in the Vogelsberg district. The upper part of the tower was built in 1820&1 in the neoclassical style. The high points of the interior are the *pulpit* which is richly decorated with stucco work (polished stucco marble) and the *organ gallery* (organ by J.M.Östreich). The monument to Hermann the knight stands out among the numerous other monuments.

**Former Schloss Hohhaus** (1–3 Eisenbacher Tor): General Freiherr Friedrich Georg Riedesel had this castle built in the period from 1769–73. The chief attraction of the interior is the magnificent stucco by A.Wiedemann, the artist from Fulda (see especially the great hall of the upper storey). Today the Schloss houses the *Heimatmuseum* (local history).

**Environs: Frischborn** (2.5 km. S.): Apart from the *Protestant parish church* (1702–05) by M.Matthoi with its richly carved pulpit by J.Bien, the *figures of Evangelists* by J.Ulrich and a first-rate *wooden crucifix* (1651), the chief object of interest is the 16C *Schloss Eisenbach* (2 km. E.). This has a medieval *central castle building* (13&14C) with *Renaissance residential buildings* grouped around it, and also a *Burgkapelle* (castle chapel; 1671–75) with a *pulpit altar* by C.Wiedemann in the gnarled style (1673) and, on the E.wall, some late Gothic *remains of wall paintings* surviving from the previous church (1440).

---

**Leer 2950**
Lower Saxony                     p.414☐D 5

The nearby Dutch border, 20 km. away, has had a great influence on the town's history and development. The immigration of religious refugees from the Netherlands in the 16C made Leer a centre of linen

*Schloss Lembeck*

weaving in East Friesland. In the late 18C it began to develop into a harbour town. Leer competed with the expanding town of Emden in its struggle for independence, which Leer attained in the period from 1749–65. Holland has also influenced the town's appearance: the Dutch baroque style is reflected in many of the red brick buildings.

**St. Michael** (Kirchstrasse): This 18C church is rococo; its portal is decorated with a beautiful sandstone relief.

**Krypta** (Plytenbergstrasse): The remains of a church built in the 13C and demolished in 1785 have survived, together with the town's old graveyard. The crypt was restored in 1958 as a *memorial* to the town's fallen. Outside we find some 16C *tombstone slabs*.

**Other buildings:** The *Waage* (1 Neue Strasse), a house with a double hipped roof, was built in the Dutch classical style and was formerly the central point of the town. In the Rathausstrasse is the *Haus Samson* (houses Nos. 16–18), which was completed in 1643 and today houses a museum (household effects, furniture, porcelain, tiles).

**Heimatmuseum** (local history; 14 Neue Strasse): The Heimatmuseum is accommodated in a neoclassical house with eaves and a noteworthy façade. The museum contains exhibits relating to the history of the town and East Friesland, and also to navigation, painting and drawing.

---

**Lembeck=4270 Dorsten 12**
Nordrhein-Westfalen                    p.414□C 9

**Schloss:** Dietrich Konrad Adolf von Westerholt commissioned the moated Schloss in the late 17C, making use of an existing small lake. It stands on the site of a previous building dating from the 14C. The Schloss blends well with its surroundings, and differs considerably in design from the numerous other moated castles in Westphalia. The decorations are at their finest in the N.wing, where we find the *Great Hall* designed by J.C.Schlaun. The oak panelling and delicate stucco coordinate beautifully. The baroque furniture has survived. Today there is a hotel in the Schloss.

**Also worth seeing:** The *St. Michaelis chapel* was built in 1726 by J.C.Schlaun by order of the widow of the last Count von Westerholt. Inside, some notable features are the tunnel vault decorated with stucco work, some paintings, and the 15–18C carvings. The 15C *Catholic parish church of St.Laurentius* (the extension was built in 1936) has a 15C St.Anne with Mary and the Christ Child, and also some 16C memorial stones.

---

**Lemgo 4920**
Nordrhein-Westfalen                           p.414□F 9

In the 18C, Lemgo was called the 'Westphalian Leipzig', owing to its efficient printing presses: Leipzig was the centre of books and printing. The townscape, part of which has survived unaltered from the 16C, reminds us that the Lemgo was formerly a member of the Hanseatic League.

**Marienkirche** (church of the Virgin Mary; Stiftstrasse): Restoration work in 1964–67 was based on the original design of the church (1270–1370). The interior decorations include numerous significant art works. The slab of a *high tomb* of to the Parler school (*c.*1380) shows the nobleman Otto zur Lippe and his wife Ermgard v.d.Mark. The *altarpiece* in the late Gothic style probably originates from the Lower Rhine (*c.*1470). The *organ* on the E. wall of the N. aisle was built by G.Stegel in 1587 – 90 and is decorated with rich Renaissance carvings (1612&13). It is one of the oldest and best-sounding organs in Germany.

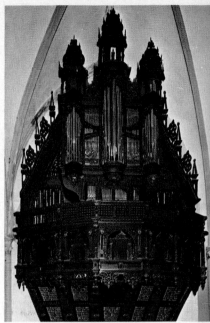

*Organ of Marienkirche, Lemgo*

**Nikolaikirche** (Papenstrasse): The Marienkirche (church of the Virgin Mary) in Lippstadt (q.v.) served as the model for this late Romanesque hall basilica (1210–50), which was later expanded several times and has numerous Gothic elements (14C). Several stone sculptures survive from the 13C, including the *tympanum* in the S.aisle and the *retable of the Virgin Mary* in the wall of the transept. The *Renaissance font* is the work of the native artist G.Crossmann (1597). The *high altar* was built in the gnarled style referred to as the Ohrmuschel- und Knorpelstil (1643). The memorial stone to Raban von Kerssenbrock is decorated with paintings by N.Baumann (1617).

**Rathaus** (Marktplatz): The Town Hall (1350–1612), the *Ratsapotheke* (pharmacy; 1559), the *Ratslaube* (loggia; 1480) and the *Kornherrenstube* (1589–91), form a single frontage on the Marktplatz. A total of eight different buildings combine to form this

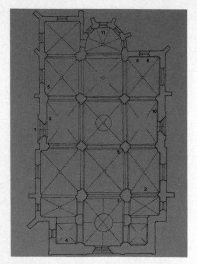

**Lemgo, Nikolaikirche 1** N. portal, c.1230 **2**' Former portal tympanum with deesis, c. 1230 **3** Virgin Mary retable **4** Crucifix, c.1470 **5** Tabernacle, 1477 **6** Tomb of Franz von Kerssenbrock (d.1576) by H.Wulff **7** Tomb of Moritz v.Donop by G.Crossmann, 1587 **8** Font by G.Crossmann, 1597 **9** Pulpit, c. 1600 **10** Tomb of Raban v.Kerssenbrock, 1617 **11** High altar by H.Voss, 1643; painting by B.Wottemann

Rathaus complex. The gables are of differing designs and are impressive for their stonemasonry with its many different shapes. The Ratsapotheke shows relief portraits of famous scientists and medical doctors. The central feature is the old *Ratkammer* (council chamber) with its open court-room.

**Half-timbered houses and Hexenbürgermeisterhaus** (19 Breite Strasse): The *Hexenbürgermeisterhaus* (house of the 'witchcraft' mayor) is one of the most significant buildings of the so-called 'Weser Renaissance'. It was completed in 1568, but its famous façade, with an abundance of first-rate stone carvings which are unique in aristocrats' houses of this period, was not added until 1571. It was Hermann Cothmann who lent the house its name. He was responsible for the sentencing of some 90 people in the so-called witches' trials when he was mayor in 1666–81. The houses in Mittelstrasse are prominent among the many *half-timbered buildings* (mostly 16C and early 17C). Other features worth looking at: the *Wipermannsches Haus* (5 Kramerstrasse; a stone building dating from 1576); the *Zeughaus* (arsenal; 1548) by the Rathaus; the *Ballhaus* (ball-

*Rathaus, Lemgo*

*Hexenbürgermeisterhaus, Lemgo* ·

room; 1611) in the Markt; the *Lippehof* (1734), which houses the secondary school.

**Museums:** *Heimatmuseum* (local history; 19 Breite Strasse): Collections relating to legal history, and justice as applied to witchcraft. *Junkerhaus* (36 Hamelner Strasse): Paintings and wooden sculptures, and the inventory of the artist K.Junker (1850–1912).

**Environs: Lemgo-Brake** (2 km. S.): The *Wasserburg Brake*, a moated castle at the crossing of the river Bega, goes back to previous buildings dating from the 12C. It was converted in 1584 and then served temporarily as a residence.

---

## Leuchtenberg 8481
Bavaria                                   p.418□M 15

**Castle ruin:** The Burg probably dates from the early 14C. The castle outworks, keep, castle chapel and parts of the great hall still remain. The previous buildings were not very significant and were probably destroyed under attack. The Schloss was raided and looted in 1621. It was attacked by the Swedes in 1634, and shortly thereafter by the Emperor's troops. Further damage was caused by several fires. The bulwark-like character of the castle has survived nevertheless. The castle is worth visiting for the good views it provides.

---

## Leutkirch 7970
Baden-Württemberg                 p.422□H 20

Documents record Leutkirch as existing as early as 848. It was built around the 'Leutekirch' church (original church of the Nibelgau district) and was a free town of the Empire from 1293–1802. The buildings in the old part of town are classified as historical monuments, and include many town houses which have survived in good condition and remind the visitor of that period.

**Catholic Parish Church of St.Martin** (Marienplatz): This hall church dating from 1514–19 has a nave, two aisles and a fine net vault. The furnishings are largely modern. The Protestant *Parish Church of the Holy Trinity* (Evangelische Kirchgasse) is a hall church designed to emphasise the importance of preaching. It has a nave and two aisles, and was built in 1613–15. Its interior was decorated in the neo-Gothic style in 1860.

**Also worth seeing:** The *Catholic Parish Church Mariä Himmelfahrt* (1612) has a plain 18C interior. The *Rathaus* (town hall; 1739–43) in the Marktplatz has some notable stucco by J.Schütz from Landsberg. The *Schlösschen Hummelsberg*, an aristocrat's house SE of the town, was built in 1636 and has some fine rococo stucco. The remains of the late medieval *town fortifications*, with bugler's tower and gunpowder tower. The *Heimatmuseum* (local history; Marktplatz) is in the former granary (*c*.1500).

**Environs: Zell** (5 km. NW): Features worth seeing are the *art collections* belonging to the von Waldburg-Zeil family in the *Schloss Zeil* (*c*.1600), and the high altar in the *Katholische Pfarrkirche Mariä Himmelfahrt* (Catholic parish church of the Assumption of the Virgin Mary) by J.A.Feuchtmayer and J.G. and F.A.Dürr (1763–64).

---

## Leverkusen 5090
Nordrhein-Westfalen               p.416□B 11

---

**Schloss Morsbroich:** The former Schloss today houses the *municipal museum* with exhibitions relating to 20C painting, drawing and sculpture. New exhibitions are held regularly.

**Friedenberger Hof** (in the Opladen district of Leverkusen): A 16C knight's castle; the rooms contain the 18C *'Kölner Decke'* (Cologne ceiling).

**Theatre:** The *Forum* has 977 seats.

*Rococo pulpit, collegiate church in Lich*

*Schloss in Lich*

Straight theatre, opera and concerts are performed by touring companies. *Festhalle am Opladener Platz*: touring performances. 630 seats.

## Lich 6302

Hessen                                    p.416☐F 13

**Former Collegiate Church of the Virgin Mary/Protestant Parish Church** (Kirchplatz): This church was built in 1510–37 on the basis of a previous 13C building, and was the last medieval hall church in Hessen. The decoration is very fine: there is *Renaissance paintwork* on the arcades and in the chancel (1594), while the painted decorations on the four W.bays of the nave are rococo (1760). The *rococo pulpit* (1767–74) is from Arnsburg monastery. The life-sized wooden *crucifix* was built in *c.*1500. The *organ front* is one of the oldest in Hessen (1621–22). The *choir*

stalls date from the first half of the 16C. The monument to Kuno von Falkenstein and Anna von Nassau takes pride of place among the numerous *tombs* (14C).

**Schloss** (Schlossgasse): The former moated castle dating from the 14C was converted to its present appearance in 1673–82 and 1764–68. The round medieval towers survive at the outside corners. The building with an altar resting on Doric columns dates from the period from 1833 –37, while the neo-baroque annexe in the NE corner was added in 1911–12.

**Also worth seeing:** The *Rathaus* (Town Hall; 1 Unterstadt) was built in 1848–49 in the manner of a palazzo of Romanesque design. Numerous *half-timbered buildings* (mostly 16&17C) and parts of the *town fortifications* have survived. Special attention should be drawn to the *Stadtturm* (town tower; *c.* 1500), which is the tower of the

*Petri-Stab and Limburger Staurothek, Diocesán Museum, Limburg*

former collegiate church and contains its bells. *Heimatkundliche Sammlungen* (local history) (4 Kirchenplatz).

### Lichtenstein 7414
Baden-Württemberg                          p.420□F 19

**Schloss Lichtenstein:** The historical novel 'Lichtenstein' by Wilhelm Hauff (1826) made the castle famous. It had been demolished in 1802, but the stimulus provided by the novel led to its being reconstructed to accord with Hauff's description. This Schloss, which resembles a castle, stands on a rocky peak (2665 ft.).

**Also worth seeing:** The area surrounding Lichtenstein includes several caves, among them the Nebelhöhle cave where —according to W.Hauff—Duke Ulrich is said to have taken refuge (9 km. W. of the Honau district of Lichtenstein). The Karl-

shöhe mountain, with the Bärenhöhle (bears' cave), is 12 km. SW of Honau.

### Limburg an der Lahn 6250
Hessen                                     p.416□D 13

The present city of Limburg developed at the beginning of the 9C at the junction of the roads from Cologne to Frankfurt and from Hessen to Koblenz; there was also a crossing over the river Lahn. The planned expansion of the city started in the 13C. The diocese of Limburg was established in 1827.

**Dom/Collegiate and Parish Church of St.Georg and St.Nikolaus** (Domplatz): There was probably a church on a rocky eminence above the Lahn as early as the 9C. The present building was consecrated in 1235 and was finally completed in the mid 13C. It was built on the model of some large early Gothic buildings in N.France (among them St.Remi in Reims) and of some famous churches in the Rhineland, including St.Gereon in Cologne (q.v.). Another factor in the design was the wish to relate the church as closely as possible to the landscape. The characteristic feature of the cathedral today is the new coloured decorations (1968–72), which are based on some 13C remains of plaster that have been discovered. Each side of the building, which has seven towers, presents a different aspect. The cathedral is essentially late Romanesque, but the numerous arches, the articulation of the peaked and trefoil arches, and the leaf capitals, are all signs of energent Gothic. The paintwork also displays the transition from Romanesque to Gothic: the decoration on the walls uses ornaments favoured in the Gothic period (restored in 1875–76 and 1934–35; much of the original work was uncovered in 1972–85). The *tabernacle*, a slim, pentagonal tower with a delicate crown on the reredos, was built in 1496. The stone *choir screens* date from the period around 1235. The very valuable *font* (*c*.1235), which now stands in the chapel by the S.aisle, should also be noted. The monuments to Count Konrad, a founder of the church (d.948),

and to Daniel von Mudersbach (d.1477) are the best of the numerous *tombs*. The *cathedral treasure* is today housed in the Bischöfliches Ordinariat (office of the diocese) at 4 Rossmarkt. From Easter 1985 onwards it will be in the new diocesan museum at 12 Domstrasse.

**Former Franciscan Monastery/Catholic Parish Church of St.Sebastian:** In 1223, the Fransciscans established one of their first centres in Germany here. In accordance with the rules of the mendicant Order the church was built without vaults or decoration (the mirror ceiling was not added until 1743). The furnishings include two *late Gothic side altars*, a 15C *Pietà* in the 'Soft Style', a *rococo pulpit* and the *organ* installed by A.Oehninger in

*Limburg, Dom* ▷

**Limburg, Dom 1** Main portal **2** Erasmuskapelle **3** Chapel of the Holy Sepulchre **4** Sacristy **5** Font, c.1235 **6** Tomb of Count Konrad, 13C **7** Choir screens, c.1235; outside panels and paintings, late 16C **8** Monument to Daniel von Mudersbach (d.1477) and his wife Jutta (d.1461) **9** Tabernacle, 1496; restored 1628 **10** High altar, 1977 **11** Bishop's crypt **12** Sacrament chapel

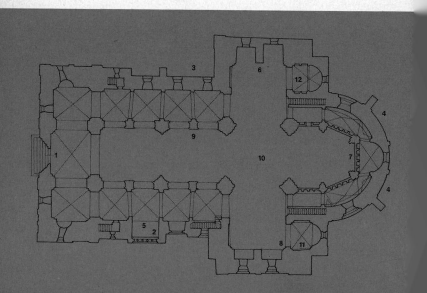

1685. The tombstone slab to Johannes von Limburg (d. 1312) takes pride of place among the *tombs*. There are also several first-rate memorial stones from the Renaissance and early baroque periods.

**Schloss** (Domplatz): The almost square residential tower is the oldest part of the former castle (mid-13C), which drops steeply to the bank of the Lahn. The castle chapel was completed in 1298, while the remaining buildings were added from the 14–16C. *Diocesan museum:* The most precious item here is the *Limburg Staurothek,* a Byzantine Cross reliquary which was stolen from the palace church in Constantinople in 1204 and has been in Limburg since 1827. Another masterpiece of the goldsmith's art is the *Petri-Stab* (Peter's rod) reliquary, which is set with precious stones and adorned with gold filigree work. The inscription states that it was produced in Trier in 988.

**Also worth seeing:** The *Walderdorffer Hof* (5 Fahrgasse) is a picturesque Renaissance building dating from 1665. Its four wings (two- and three-storeyed) are grouped around an inner courtyard. There are numerous streets in Limburg which have scarcely changed since the 17C. Typical are the *buildings* in the Barfüsserstrasse, Salzgasse, Fahrgasse, Brückengasse, Domplatz (cathedral square), Fischmarkt and Bischofsplatz (bishops' square). The *Lahnbrücke,* first mentioned in 1255 when it was of wood, spans the river Lahn in six large semicircular arches (there is a crucifix dating from 1657). The *town fortifications* were built in 1225–30. Only some small sections of them still survive, including the square bridge tower and the Katzenturm.

---

**Lindau 8990**

Bavaria                                          p.420□G 21

René Schickele wrote the following about Lindau in 1921: 'Guarded by the mountains stretched out on both sides of the Rhine valley, it floats in the water as if chained up there'. Today this town is one of the best-known tourist resorts on Lake Constance. The old part of town is on an island connected to the E.shore by a road and railway bridge.

**Protestant Parish Church of St. Stephan** (Marktplatz): This church founded in the 12C has been radically altered twice, in 1506 and 1781–83, so that the essentially Romanesque design can now only be discerned in isolated places. The external forms are mainly baroque, while the stucco decorations and the principal furnishings date from the late 18C.

**Catholic Parish Church of St. Maria/former Frauenstiftskirche** (Marktplatz): This church, which has a plain exterior, was built in 1748–51 on the site of a previous 12C building which was destroyed by fire. It follows the Vorarlberg pilaster scheme, also found in Obermarchtal (q.v.) and Friedrichshafen (q.v.). The decorations show some late baroque features. Today the *Landratsamt* is housed in the adjoining *former Damenstift* (institution for ladies) This two-winged complex dates from 1730–36 and its original furnishings still survive. There is a first-rate *ceiling painting* by F.J.Spiegler.

**Former St.-Peters-Kirche** (Schrannenplatz): This is the oldest church in Lindau (the chancel and E.sections date from the 11C, while the tower is from 1425). It contains 13–16C wall paintings. Of these, the Passion sequence in the E. is signed by Hans Holbein the Elder. The church is now a *war memorial chapel.*

**Altes Rathaus** (Hauptstrasse): This building, which has a stepped gable (adorned with graceful scrolls), and also a council loggia outside the first storey, was dates from 1422–36. In the 16C the oriel was altered and the portal underneath the council-hall loggia added. Inside, the large council hall with its vaulted *wooden ceiling* is worth seeing. The knights' hall has valuable panelling (with a built-in cupboard dating from the 16C).

**Stadtmuseum** (4 Marktplatz): The museum is housed in the *Haus zum Cavaz-*

*Lindau, harbour entrance with old lighthouse*

*zen*, a splendid baroque building dating from 1728&29. There are collections on the town's pre- and cultural history; paintings; 15–20C sculpture; coins; seals.

**Stadttheater** (37 Fischergasse): Performances by touring companies from various theatres are held at the Stadttheater, which was built in 1951 and has 808 seats.

**Also worth seeing:** Alter und Neuer Leuchtturm (old and new lighthouses), numerous 16&17C houses which have survived in good condition, town fortifications with some sections dating from the 12C (Heidenmauer wall).

**Linderhof = Oberammergau 8103**
Bavaria                                    p.422□I 21

**Schloss Linderhof:** Louis XIV, the French Sun King, was Ludwig II's inspi-

ration for this rococo castle. He commissioned the Schloss in the remote solitude of the mountains in 1874 – 78 from G.Dollmann. The high points of the splendid interior decorations are the rooms on the first floor, where pictures of French celebrities from the time of Louis XIV and XV can be seen. Behind the Schloss there is a lavish park with a grotto, a small lake, and a Moorish pavilion. The waterfalls include the fountain of Neptune, which spouts to a height of 105 ft.

**Lippoldsberg = Wahlsburg 3417**
Hessen                                    p.414□G 10

The Benedictine convent of the Virgin Mary and St.George, which followed the Hirsau rules for monasteries and convents, was founded *c*.1095 by Archbishop Ruthard of Mainz on the site of a previous mid-11C church. In 1521 the convent joined the strict Bursfeld religious society. The community of nuns was dissolved after the last abbess died in 1569.

**Protestant Parish Church/former Convent Church:** This Romanesque basilica built in 1140–50 by Probst Gunter from Hamersleben has survived in outstandingly good condition, apart from the W.façade and W.towers. The cruciform pillared basilica has a nave and two aisles. There is also a basilican chancel which itself has a nave and two aisles, along with three chancel apses. This was the first church in the Westphalian-Lower Saxon area with choir and nave vaulted throughout on the model of Mainz cathedral (q.v.). The spacious *nuns' gallery* extends above the groin vaults of the hall, which has a nave and two aisles and resembles a crypt. In this hall, some of the *capitals* of the pillars and columns are embellished with high quality leaf and scale motifs. The most significant item, apart from a 15C late Gothic *sacrament niche* in the N. side chancel and a Romanesque *font*, is another *font* (13C, late Romanesque) with figure sculptures and reliefs (Saints and scenes from the Old and New Testaments). Some arches from the W.wing of the Romanesque *clois-*

*ter* have survived in the monastery building into which the cloister was converted in 1713.

---

**Lippstadt 4780**
Nordrhein-Westfalen                 p.414☐E 10

**Protestant Grosse Marienkirche** (Markt): This church, consecrated in 1222 by Bernhard II, Bishop of Semgallen and founder of the town, was completed in 1250 and is one of the most important late Romanesque buildings in Westphalia. The dominant section is the W.tower. The interior is Gothic; the outstanding feature of the decorations is the *late Gothic tabernacle* (1523). The wall paintings (*c*.1250) in the intermediate chancel are late Romanesque.

**Ruins of the Collegiate Church St. Marien** (Stiftsstrasse): This church dates from about 1240, but was closed in 1831 because it was in a dilapidated state, and the intention was to pull it down. In 1855, King Friedrich Wilhelm IV decreed that this significant early Gothic building should be preserved as an architectural monument.

*Schloss Linderhof*

**Heimatmuseum** (Rathausstrasse 13): The museum contains collections on local history and 14 – 19C religious art. It is housed in a 17C town house, decorated with rococo stucco ceilings in the 18C.

**Also worth seeing:** *Jacobikirche* (Lange Strasse): An early Gothic hall church (*c*.1300). *Catholic Nikolaikirche* (Klosterstrasse): The massive W.tower and part of the S. aisle are all that survive of this 12C church after it was partly pulled down in 1872.

**Environs: Bökenförde** (6 km. SE): Apart from the *Kapelle St.Antonius Abt* with its white-and-gold *rococo stucco work* (*c*.1768) by the brothers B. and J.N.Metz, another item worth seeing is the *Schwarzengraben moated castle* (16C, rebuilt in 1765 – 68), which is of interest for its charming 18C *orangery* built to designs by J.M.Kitz.

**Cappel** (3 km. W.): **Protestant Collegiate Church:** This church was built as part of the original Premonstratensian convent, which was converted into a secular charitable institution for gentlewomen in 1588. The former convent building today houses a girls' boarding school. The collegiate church dates fom the 12C, but a considerable part of it was pulled down around 1700. Restoration work was performed in 1886 and 1951. The cruciform Romanesque pillared basilica has an overall length of some 165 ft. and is the oldest surviving vaulted nave in Westphalia, in fact probably one of the oldest vaulted buildings in the whole of Germany. The severe building is typical of Westphalian architecture of the period and expresses the asceticism which was one of the characteristics of the Premonstratensians.

**Interior and decoration:** The nuns' gallery is on the upper storey above the pillared hall with its nave and two aisles. Almost all the noteworthy decorations date from the late Gothic period. They include the *pulpit* and *lectern* with their carved tracery panels, and also the wrought-iron *chandelier*. The richly decorated *choir stalls* are early Renaissance. *Tombstones* from the period from 1567 – 1804 are dedicated to abbesses, canonesses and aristocrats.

**Overhagen** (4 km. SW): The *moated cas-*

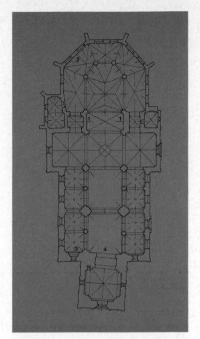

**Lippstadt, St.Marien 1** Wall painting in the intermediate chancel, c.1250 **2** Tabernacle, 1523 **3** Holy Sepulchre, remnant **4** High altar, 2nd half of 17C

*tle* (1619) with its two-storeyed manor house was converted in 1735 and is today a Gymnasium.

---

## Loccum = 3056 Rehburg-Loccum 2
Lower Saxony                    [p.414☐ F 7

---

**Former Cistercian Monastery and Monastery Church):** Most of the buildings of this monastery consecrated in 1163 date from the 13C and survive to the present day. Not only the monastery itself, but also the precinct, is surrounded by a wall. The *cloister* and the *chapterhouse* are of interest. The *monastery church* was built from 1240 – 80. Inside, the walls, pillars and arches make a severe impression reminiscent of the Romanesque style. An impor-

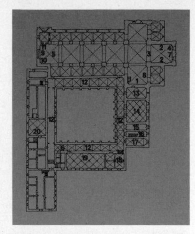

Loccum, monastery **1** Altarpiece of high altar,
13C **2** Choir stalls, remains, 13C **3** Triumphal cross,
13C **4** Tabernacle, 2nd half of 15C **5** Font, 1601 **6**
Memorial stone to Stracke with painted portrait,
1611 **7** Laymen's altar, 16C **8** Marienaltar, 16C **9**
Tomb of Abbot Molanus, 18C **10** Tomb of Abbot
Böhmer, 18C **11** Tomb of Abbot Evell, 18C **12**
Cloister **13** Johanneskapelle **14** Chapterhouse **15**
Donnergang **16** Pilgrim's cell and stairs up to dormitory **17** Benedictuskapelle **18** Calefactory **19**
Refectory; door with mid 13C knocker **20** Lay-
men's refectory; wall painting by E.v.Gebhardt,
1885-91

*Cistercian monastery, Loccum*

tant decoration is the 13C wooden
*reliquary*, which has arches on two levels
and is set up on the high altar. Other notable features are remains of the 13C *choir
stalls*, painted 13C *triumphal cross*, *sedilia*
(*c.* 1300). Richly decorated 15C *tabernacle*
and *tombstones*. There is a painted picture
on the memorial stone to Abbot Stracke
(1611).

---

**Lorch 7073**
Baden-Württemberg                    p.420☐G 18

Lorch is associated with the names of two
distinguished poets: Friedrich Schiller
spent three years of his childhood here
from 1764–66, and Eduard Mörike passed
his retirement here from 1867–69.

**Former Benedictine Monastery
Church of St.Maria:** The first monastery was built on the Frauenberg hill in the
11&12C. It was rebuilt in 1469 and partially destroyed in 1525 during the
Peasants' Revolt, but then rebuilt again.
The N. wings of the cloister (with a fine
net vault) and the monastery building
(*c.*1470) with two halls on the ground floor,

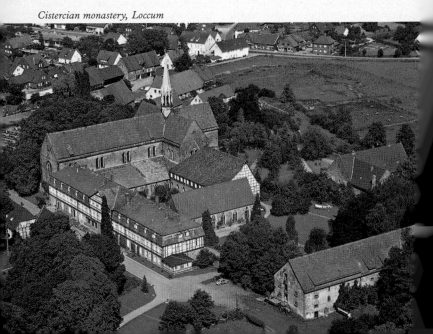

have survived from the 15C. The church is very reminiscent of Maria Laach (q.v.), but has some Swabian elements. Part of the W. building is original. In the nave, the *high tomb* of the founder deserves especial attention (1474). The *altar cross*, installed in the chancel, was endowed by J.Syrlin. Hohenstaufen emperors are represented on the pillars, wearing costumes from the period around 1500).

**Protestant Parish Church** (Kirchplatz): This originally Romanesque church was extended in 1474 and the present galleries were installed in 1728. The paintwork dates from 1775.

---

## Lorch am Rhein 6223

Hessen                                          p.416□D 14

**Catholic Parish Church of St.Martin** (Am Markt): This church stands on a terrace above the Rhine. It was begun in the late 13C and is one of the most significant Gothic churches in the Rheingau. Additions were made to the building in the 14&15C, but these hardly influenced its overall design. The church is mainly famous for its Gothic *high altar* (1483), the most lavish altarpiece on the Middle Rhine, with two levels containing statues in ten niches. Even older than this are the *choir stalls,* which were built in the late 13C and show animal figures and mysterious fabulous beings. The Renaissance monument to Johann Hilchen von Lorch (d. 1550) takes pride of place among the *tombstones.*

**Also worth seeing:** Little remains of the late medieval *town fortifications* except at the mouth of the Wisper, in the Weiseler Weg and at the Obertor. The following *houses* should be mentioned: the *Hilchenhaus,* commissioned by Johann Hilchen v.Lorch as a magnificent Renaissance structure on the Rhine (1573), the late Gothic tithe hall, and numerous *half-timbered houses.*

**Heimatmuseum** (local history; in the former monastery): collection on the his-

tory of Lorch, especially its Roman past.

**Environs: Heiligkreuzkapelle** (2 km. NE, in the Wispertal): This pilgrimage church consecrated in 1677 was decorated in the baroque style. It has two fine wooden sculptures, the 18C Madonna and the Gothic 'Heiligkreuzer Bäuerche'.

---

## Lörrach 7850

Baden-Württemberg                               p.420□C 21

This town is located at the 'Dreiländereck', where Switzerland, France and Germany meet. Johann Peter Hebel described it as an 'ordentli Städtli' (dialect: proper little town). It has now developed into an industrial town. Johann Peter Hebel was a teacher at the Pädagogium here from 1783–91. Today there is a monument to him, and the Hebel society has its seat in Lörrach.

**St. Fridolins-Kirche** (Lörrach-Stetten): C.Arnold, a pupil of Weinbrenner, built the church in 1821–22. The typically neoclassical lines are broken on the inside by J.Wilhem's stucco in imitation late baroque style. The exterior is dominated by the two W. towers.

**Protestant Stadtkirche** (Burghof): Except for the tower (1514), this church was rebuilt by W.Frommel, a pupil of Weinbrenner, in 1815–17. The inside is a classical hall whose gallery is supported by Doric columns.

**Museum am Burghof** (Baslerstrasse 143): 17–20C paintings, sculptures, prints, cartography, history of the town and of Rötteln castle, domestic interior decoration in former centuries.

**Also worth seeing:** Various beautiful *fountains* built of white limestone from Solothurn. Four of the pillars in the *Catholic Parish Church of St.Peter* are in concrete relief.

**Environs: Rötteln** (4 km. N.): *Ruined Schloss.* The oldest parts of this Burg are

*Rötteln Schloss ruins, Lörrach*

Romanesque (e.g. the keep), but some important sections were not added until the 14C. The castle was destroyed in 1678; there are some significant tombs in the *Protestant village church* of the hamlet of Rötteln.

**Inzlingen** (6 km. SE): The *moated Schloss*, first mentioned in 1511, is today the Town Hall. Most of the castle was built in the years 1563&64.

## Lorsch 6143
Hessen                                     p.416☐E 15

**Gatehouse of the former Benedictine Abbey** (Nibelungenstrasse): Only the gatehouse still survives of this former monastery, which was founded in 764 and enjoyed a very high cultural and political status from the time of Charlemagne onwards. The monastery suffered a decline in the 12C, and the formerly massive and

imposing complex was completely destroyed by a fire in 1556. Only the two-storeyed gatehouse (known as the Lorsch Halle) survived. This previously formed the beginning of a triumphal route which led across the monastery precinct to the shrine containing the relics. Ludwig the German and other members of the Carolingian royal family were buried here. The gatehouse, a typical Carolingian building, is of remarkable historical significance. The façades are very elaborate; the outer surfaces are characterized by red and white stone slabs inserted in a mosaic pattern. The Gothic roof was added in the 14C. It was at this time that the upper storey was converted into a *chapel of the Virgin Mary*. In 1697 the building was converted into an archiepiscopal private chapel. Restoration work performed in 1934–36 restored the building to its 14C condition.

**Also worth seeing:** Some *half-timbered*

*Gatehouse of Benedictine abbey, Lorsch*

*houses* survive in good condition in and around the market (18C). The *baroque building* of Baron von Hausen (Bahnhofstrasse 18). *Rathaus* (Town Hall; 1715) with three oriels in the façade.

## Lübeck 2400

Schleswig-Holstein                    p.412☐I 4

This city's foundation goes back to Henry the Lion (1158&59). Lübeck was granted the freedom of the empire in 1226. It was at that time that merchants came here from the Rhineland and Westphalia and contributed to the city's development into a vital centre for the distribution of goods, located between the raw material markets of the E. and NE. At the same time, the various trading centres in the W. began to bring their goods here. The core of the old part of the city is today still reminiscent of the period of the city's greatness, when

Lübeck took over the leadership of the German Hanseatic League in 1356 and developed into the largest city in Germany after Cologne. Lübeck was still able to retain its key position even when the Hanseatic League was gradually collapsing. The construction of the Stecknitz canal in 1390–98 was not merely an unprecedented technical feat, but also led to decisive progress in the transport of salt, an important commodity. When the Hanseatic trading system finally disintegrated in the 15C, the city experienced unparalleled artistic success. Under the leadership of H.Rode, B.Notke and H.v.d.Heide, the woodcarvers' and painters' workshops satisifed the newly arising demand for altarpieces, in demand in large numbers for churches founded by the middle classes. In parallel with Lübeck's economic development, the city also occupied a special position in the cultural field. The city's important buildings, designed by outstanding artists, bear witness to this. Among the city's most fa-

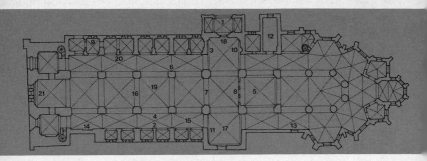

**Lübeck, Dom 1** Portal, c.1260 **2** Wall painting, fragment, 14C **3** Tomb of Bishop Albert v. Cremona (d. 1377) **4** Müllerkrone, 1st half of 15C **5** Font by L.Grove, 1455 **6** Virgin Mary relief, 1459, and bronze lamp, 1461 **7** Triumphal cross group by B.Notke, 1477 **8** Rood screen; platform 1477; clock 1627-28 **9** Angel holding a light, late 15C **10** Stucco Madonna, c. 1500 **11** Beautiful Madonna, 1509 **12** Burial chapel of Grand Dukes v. Oldenburg **13** Lectern, late Gothic, 1530 **14** Tombstone slab of Bishop Johann Tydemann, 1561 **15** Böttcherkerze, 2nd half of 16C **16** Pulpit, 1568-72 **17** Brass chandelier, 1661 **18** Painting of St. Christopher, 1665 **19** Altar table **20** Organ **21** Window by L.Quinte, 1963

mous sons were the brothers Heinrich (1871–1950) and Thomas Mann (1875–1955).

**Dom** (cathedral; Mühlendamm): The bishopric moved from Oldenburg to Lübeck in 1160; in 1173, Henry the Lion laid the foundation stone for a building which was constructed as a Romanesque pillared basilica on the model of Braunschweig (q.v.). After the building had been completed in the early 13C, several conversions and extensions had to be carried out, but these could not impair the overall image of the cathedral. The devastations suffered in the Second World War had been repaired by 1959. The solemn impression given by the interior results from the

*Passionsaltar, Dom*

*Tabernacle, Marienkirche, Lübeck* ▷

*Marienkirche, Rathaus, Petrikirche and Holstentor*　　　　　　　*Petrikirche* ▷

clearly defined structure and the strict articulation. The decorations were formerly rich, but many sections have been destroyed by fire. A *triumphal cross group* by B.Notke has survived (1477). This is one of the most important works by this Lübeck artist, who was also responsible for the magnificently carved platform of the rood screen. In the S.transept the *Schöne Madonna* (Beautiful Madonna; 1509) is very fine, while in the N.transept the *Maria mit der Sternenkrone* (Virgin Mary with the Crown of Stars; *c.*1450–60) is notable.

**Protestant Marienkirche** (Markt): Well-off citizens intended that this church should be the counterpart to the Dom. The original idea (1200) was to build a Romanesque basilica whose size should exceed that of the cathedral; this was altered several times and the building took over 150 years to complete. The important brick Gothic church burned down to its

foundation walls in an air raid in 1942, and threatened to collapse completely. However, it was restored in outstanding style under the supervision of B.Fendrich, this work being completed in 1959. The splendid *interior decorations* were almost completely lost in the fire. Items destroyed include the painted *Dance of Death* by B.Notke (1463), several *paintings by Overbeck*, the 14C *rood screen*, and the 16C organ which was played by J.S.Bach and others. On the other hand, some old *paintwork* (13&14C), was uncovered underneath the old limewash. The *tabernacle*, 33 ft. tall and dating from 1476–79, has survived, as has the *Marienaltar*, (1518).

**Protestant Petrikirche** (Holstenstrasse): The Petrikirche was built in the 14C as a hall church with a nave and two aisles. In the 16C the number of aisles was increased to four. This building also burned down in 1942, but since 1959 work has been in progress on restoring it in accordance with

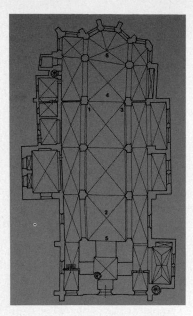

the original. The platform of the tower is at a height of 165 ft. Reached by lift, it offers a magnificent view.

**Protestant Jakobikirche** ((Koberg): This church completed in 1334 is in the N. of the town and was spared the devastations of the Second World War. It houses numerous major works of art, including the 15C *Brömbse altar*. The central panel, in sandstone, shows a Crucifixion scene. The interior paintings in the main panel of the altar depict the family of Mayor Brömbse, the founder. The *chairman's chair* (mid-15C), a *font* cast by K.Grude (1466), and two candelabra, all date from the Gothic period. Most of the work on the *organ* was carried out in 1504. The *Renaissance choir*

*stalls* and the panelling on the pillars give the church a special atmosphere. The *figures of Saints* on the pillar surfaces should also be mentioned: they were painted *c*.1130 – 40, but only fragments survive.

**Other churches worth seeing:** *Ägidienkirche* (Ägidienstrasse): A 13C church, enlarged and altered several times since then. Fine features are the organ with its early baroque organ front and the baroque railing (1710) in the nave. *Former St. Katherine Monastery of the Franciscans* (An der Mauer): The oldest part of the present church dates back to the 13C. The interior displays the severity typical of architecture in Lübeck. The furnishings include a late Gothic triumphal cross group on the parapet of the high chancel (1489), the Gothic choir stalls, and a number of tombstones. *Former Dominican Burg monastery:* This monastery was founded in gratitude for the victory of the inhabitants of Lübeck over the Danes (1227) and the Dominicans moved into it in 1229. Only some sections of the former monastery and church still survive. *Heiliger-Geist-Hospital* (Königstrasse): This medieval hospital construction stands in the shadow of the church (completed *c*.1286). The vault paintings and wall paintings are worth seeing (13&14C).

**Rathaus** (Markt): After Lübeck had attained the freedom of the Empire in 1226, work began on building the town hall. However, there were many additions and alterations, and the main part of the construction work was not completed until 1484 with the building of the chancellery. There were few alterations in the following centuries. This Rathaus is one of the most significant in Germany and, like the Marienkirche, it reflects the pride and power of the Lübeck citizens. Inside, the *entrance hall,* the *audience room,* the former *council room* and the *cellar* are all worth seeing.

**Haus der Schiffergesellschaft** (2 Breite Strasse): Today there is a restaurant in this former guildhall (1535), the only guildhall to have survived. The façade, which was rebuilt in 1880, shows elements of the Renaissance style.

**Holstentor** (Holstentorplatz): The Holstentor (1478) guarded the city against attacks from the outside. It is characterized by two round towers which include an imposing stepped gable. Original salt storehouses (16 – 18C) have survived by the Holstentor. The salt which had been brought northwards from Lüneburg along the Salzstrasse was stored here.

**Burgtor** (Grosse Burgstrasse): The Burgtor, which was built in the 13C and had its height increased by a further storey in 1444, was the inmost of the city fortifications. Anyone wanting to enter the city had to pass through this gate. On the city side, the Burgtor is connected in charming style to the adjoining houses.

**Town houses:** The street called *Mengstrasse* is especially full of noteworthy town houses (some more are to be found in, for example, *Grosse Petersgrube, Wahmstrasse, Königstrasse, Breite Strasse*). The house at 4 Mengstrasse has become known as the 'Buddenbrook house'; it formerly belonged to the Mann family, and was the home of the Buddenbrook family in Thomas Mann's famous novel. Nos. 48–50, the so-called 'Schabbelhaus', were converted after the Second World War.

**Museums:** The *St.-Annen-Museeum* (15 St.-Annen-Strasse), located in a late medieval monastery complex, shows the art and domestic interior decorations of Lübeck. The *Behnhaus-Museum* (11 Königstrasse), located in an old house dating from 1779 has an interesting classical façade. The items on display here are 19&20C paintings (mainly German Romanticism and Expressionism). The *Museum Im Holstentor* (Holstentorplatz) contains exhibits relating to the town's history (models, views of the town, models of ships, torture chamber) *Museum Drägerhaus* (9 Königstrasse): Ballrooms dating from 1750, art and culture of Lübeck, life and works of Thomas and Heinrich Mann. *Städtische Münzsammlung* (municipal coin collection; 1–3 Mühlendamm) in the archive of this Hanseatic town.

**Theatres** The *Bühnen der Hansestadt* (10 Beckergrube) include the Grosses Haus (923 seats), the Kammerspiele (325 seats) and the Studio (100 seats). *Kammer-*

*Holstentor*

*spielkreis Lübeck* (Moislinger Allee): straight theatre.

**Environs: Steinhorst** (22 km. SW): Former Herrenhaus. This is a brick building by J.N.Kuhn (1721&2) with mouldings and central projections in the façade; it now houses the *Sammlung Schwarzkopf*, devoted to beauty aids in Western culture.

## Lüdenscheid 5880

Nordrhein-Westfalen     p.416☐D 11

**Schloss Neuenhof** (3 km. S. of Lüdenscheid): The original Schloss was burned down in 1638; the present main building of this moated Schloss was erected in 1643. The Schloss has been as it is today since 1693. The farm buildings date from the 18&19C. The interior decorations include some characteristic carvings.

**Also worth seeing:** *Protestant Parish Church/former Medardus Church* (Webergerstrasse 4b), the 1826 neoclassical hall building replaced a 12C basilica. The neoclassical pulpit altar is worth seeing. The W.tower is mainly Romanesque. The *Städ-*

*tisches Museum* (1 Liebigstrasse) shows the history of the town and region. This house of culture, which is built in an unusual style, was awarded the 'architectural prize for concrete' in 1983.

## Lüdinghausen 4710

Nordrhein-Westfalen     p.414☐C 9

**Catholic Stadtkirche:** This spacious late Gothic hall church (1507–58) has a stellar vault in the nave, and groin vaults in the aisles. Noteworthy decorations include a late Gothic *tabernacle* and the wooden figure of *St. Felizitas,* depicted with her seven sons (a work from the Lower Rhine, *c.*1520).

**Burg Vischering** (at the N.edge of the town): This is the oldest moated Burg in Westphalia; the principal sections have survived unaltered since the 16C. War damage suffered in 1944 has in the meantime been repaired. The main building dates back to a 13C castle with a circular surrounding wall. The outworks were completed in 1584. Today the *Münsterlandmuseum* (provincial museum) is housed here.

◁ *Burgtor*        *Burg Vischering, Lüdinghausen*

*Schloss Ludwigsburg, Ordenshalle*

**Former Amtshaus:** The school of agriculture has been accommodated in this building since 1869. The central section dates back to a 12C castle. However, the main sections of the building were much altered and reconstructed in the 16C.

## Ludwigsburg 7140
Baden-Württemberg                    p.420☐F 17

Ludwigsburg was inspired by the Palace of Versailles: Eberhard Ludwig, Duke of Württemberg, like many other European princes, became enthusiastic about the idea of building as a result of Louis XIV's achievement, and offered a building site and materials free of charge to anybody who wanted to be involved in Ludwigsburg; he also granted freedom from taxes for a full fifteen years.

**Schloss** (Schlossplatz): This enormous complex was built from 1704 onwards and was finally completed in 1733, the year when Duke Eberhard Ludwig died. It consists of 18 buildings with over 400 rooms. P.J.Jenisch, who was the Duke's court architect, J.F.Nette, and D.G.Frisoni (from 1714 onwards), were involved in planning the Schloss. Each of these architects put forward new ideas, and Eberhard Ludwig was only to ready to accept them, but this placed too great a strain on his finances and, although he saw the completion of the buildings, their decoration was carried out under the auspices of two later Dukes, Carl Eugen (1744–93) and Friedrich (1797–1806). The *Fürstentrakt*, the *Neues Corps de Logis,* is the main feature on the S. side of the Schloss. The Schloss complex is grouped around a large inner courtyard. The N. side of the Schloss ends in the *Altes Corps de Logis.* The *Familiengalerie* (family gallery), the *Theaterbau* (theatre building), the *Hofkapelle* (court chapel), and the *Riesenbau* (giant building), follow in sequence from S. to N. on the E. side. The

*Schlossgarten, Ludwigsburg*

*Bildergalerie* (picture gallery), the *Festin-haus*, the *Ordenskapelle* (chapel of the Order), and the *Ordensbau* (building of the Order), follow from S.to N. on the W. side. Almost all the rooms are richly stuccoed (baroque, rococo and Empire) and lavishly furnished. Taken as a whole, the Schloss is the largest baroque building in Germany. Today it is a *museum,* with collections on Ludwigsburg porcelain and paintings and court art in the baroque period. The adjoining *Schloss park* was conceived as an open-air continuation of the palace. The S. section was badly damaged, then replanted in accordance with the original baroque plans. To the N. of the Schloss is the small Schloss called *Favorite* (1718–23, to plans by J.F.Nette and D.G.Frisoni), and still further to the N. is the *Monrepos* Schloss, which was built in 1760–64 and was used by Duke Carl Eugen as a *Seehaus* (lake house).

**Marktplatz:** The Marktplatz was con-ceived by D.G.Frisoni as the centre of the rigidly planned town. This is in contrast to Karlsruhe (q.v.) and Mannheim (q.v.), where the Schloss is the centre. The Marktplatz in Ludwigsburg has the *Markt-brunnen,* with a statue of Eberhard Ludwig, the town's founder. The town church built by Frisoni in 1718–26 stands in the Marktplatz opposite the (smaller) reformed church, which was later acquired by the Catholic church and is now the Catholic town parish church (it was built in 1727 –32).

---

**Ludwigshafen 7140**
Baden-Württemberg               p.420□F 17

**Catholic Parish and Pilgrimage Church Mariae Himmelfahrt** (in Oggersheim, Mannheimer Strasse): Count Palatine Joseph Carl Emanuel had a 'Loreto chapel' built in 1729–33. The pres-

*Schloss Monrepos, Ludwigsburg*

ent church was erected over this in 1774 – 77 by order of Countess Palatine Elisabeth Auguste to plans by P.A.Verschaffelt. This church in Oggersheim is the only religious building by Verschaffelt. Its design is a clear imitation of the buildings of the Roman high baroque. Inside, the rectangular room is covered by a tunnel vault with powerful stuccoed coffering. A high row of windows makes the church uusually light. The finest features of the decoration are two *angels* carved *c.*1730 by P.Egel, a sculptor from Mannheim.

**Museums:** *Stadtmuseum* (Rathaus-Center): Early history, prehistory, history of the town, arts and crafts, coin collection, weapon collection. *K.O.-Braun-Heimatmuseum* (in Oppau, Rathaus): Early history, prehistory, domestic décor from both country and town, folklore). *Schillerhaus* (in Oggersheim, 6 Schillerstrasse): Documents relating to the life and work of Friedrich Schiller are on display in the house where the poet formerly lived. *Wilhelm-Hack-Museum* (23 Berliner Strasse): Late Romanesque and Franconian art, and German Expressionism and modern art are also represented.

**Theatre:** International touring companies perform at the Theater im Pfalzbau (30 Berliner Platz; 1171 seats). The *Musischer Herbst* festival is held every year.

**Also worth seeing:** The *Protestant Friedenskirche* (Leuschnerstrasse) was built in 1932 and is one of the most important works of modern ecclesiastical architecture. A characteristic feature of its interior used to be a painting by Max Slevogt called 'Golgatha', which had an area of 1290 sq.ft. It was destroyed in an air raid in 1943, as was the rest of the church. There is a glass mosaic by Harry MacLean in the present church, which was rebuilt by E.Zinsser from Hanover. *BASF-Hochhaus* (high-rise building; 1957).

## Ludwigsstadt 8642
Bavaria                                      p.418□K 13

**Burg Lauenstein:** Burg Lauenstein was built on a rock on the border with Thüringen. The palas dates from the 14C and the rest of the building from the 16C. It has been thoroughly restored; the finest room is the *Festsaal* (over 130 ft. long) with its excellent *coffered ceiling*. The Burg is now a hotel.

**Environs:** *Thüringer Warte* (2 km. W.): Lookout tower at a height of 2224 ft.

## Lüneburg 3140
Lower Saxony                                p.414□H 5

Salt has had a decisive influence on the history of this town. The town's economic advancement in the Middle Ages was due to the 'white gold' which has been mined here since 956. The citizens attained independence from the Guelphic princes in 1371, and in the war of 1445–62 they got rid of their debts and became wealthy once again. The central figures were the superintendents of the saltworks. Only they held the privilege of becoming members of the town council. Julius Wolff's novel 'Der Sülfmeister' gives an interesting view of this period. After flourishing in the 16C, when Lüneburg was one of the richest towns in N.Germany, the decline of the Hanseatic League and the competition provided by new suppliers of salt caused the town's development to come to a standstill. There was another economic upturn at the end of the 18C, when trade increased and transport became a money-making activity in its own right. Lüneburg later became a centre of local government and a garrison, and today it is important as a saline and mud spa. The appearance of the town has survived almost unchanged through the centuries; it is dominated by brick buildings. The centre of the town is the Fernhandelsmarkt. This is 900 ft. long and 115–130 ft. wide, and was built on a sandbank in a marshy area, and thus became known as 'Am Sande' (on the sand).

*Panorama of old town, with St. Johannis*

There are many interesting buildings in this square.

**Protestant Church of St.Johannis** (Am Sande): This hall church has a nave and four aisles and is the most significant church in the town. The present church dates from the 12C, and its oldest parts are the choir, the apse, the nave with its four bays, and the W.tower. It was not until *c*.1300 that the church was consecrated by the Bishop of Verden. Shortly thereafter, two more aisles, along with chapels and apses, were added to the existing nave and two aisles. The enormous tower was rebuilt after a fire in 1406. It is 355 ft. tall, and at its peak it is more than 6 ft. off plumb. The walls of the belfry are pierced by 32 Gothic windows. The *high altar* is the work of three (or four) artists from Lüneburg (1430–85). The paintings on the outsides of the panels by the Hamburg artist H.Funhof are some of the finest work of the medieval period. Mention should

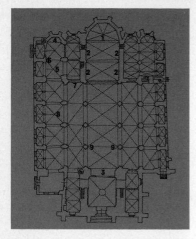

**Lüneburg, Johanneskirche 1** High altar, 1430-85; paintwork on insides of panels by Hinrik Funhof, 1482 **2** Remains of choir stalls, c.1420, incorporated into the Renaissance stalls by W.Burmester, 1588 **3** Organ, built by H.Nyhoff and J.Johannsen in s'Hertogenbosch, 1551-52, expanded by M.Dropa, 1715 **4** Crucifixion altar, early 16C **5** Bronze font, 1540 **6** Annunciation relief, c.1520 **7** Tomb of town captain Fabian Ludich by Albert v.Soest, 1571 **8** Virgin Mary candlestick, c. 1490 **9** Monuments to two mayors Stöterogge (1539 and 1561)

*St. Johannis*

also be made of the *organ front* (1715), which fills the entire W.wall. The 15C *Marienleuchter* to be found in one of the aisles, takes pride of place among the beautiful chandeliers here. The largest chandelier hangs in the porch. Dating from 1586, it consists of a brass crown with 32 brackets holding candles. Albert v.Soest built the enormous *sandstone memorial* to the mayor Nikolaus Stöterogge, and also the memorial to F.Ludich, captain of the town militia (16C).

**Protestant Church of St. Michael** (Johann-Sebastian-Bach-Platz): This church consecrated in 1418 (the foundation stone was laid in 1376) succeeded the first Michaeliskirche on the Kalkberg, which had to be pulled down in 1371. This 15C tower, which originally remained incomplete, was crowned by a copper-covered dome in *c.*1765. Interesting features are the stone *tomb monument* (1560) to Herbord v.Holle, who was the first Lutheran abbot, the *pulpit* (by D.Schwenke from Pirna; 1602), and the *organ* (1708). The organ front is by T.Götterling, while the organ itself is the work of M.Dropa. Herman Billung, the founder of the monastery, is said to be buried in the *lower church* (d.973).

**Protestant Church of St. Nikolai** (Bardowicker Strasse): The Nikolaikirche was built in 1407-40 as a citizens' church, and thus formed an alternative to the monastery churches and bishops' churches in Lüneburg. The tower was not completed until 1587. Owing to its dilapidated state, it had to be torn down in 1831 and was replaced in 1895 by the present neo-Gothic tower, 320 ft. in height. The finest feature of the interior is the *Lamberti altar* (*c.* 1450). This originates from the Lamperti church pulled down in 1861. This altar was carved by Hans Snitker the elder, a local artist, while the panel paintings and the prophets on the predella are the work of H.Bornemann (1450). Some parts of the *Heiligenthal Altar* have been installed in this church (the crucifix, six panel paintings and 19 of the former total of 28 carved Passion scenes are now to be found on the walls of the ambulatory; they date from the first half of the 15C). The two *wrought-iron*

**Lüneburg, St.Nikolai 1** Font by Ulricus, c. 1325 **2** Memorial stone to Heinrich Viskule, c.1371 **3** Pietà, c.1400 **4** Crucifix from Heiligenthaler Altar by H.Snitker, c.1425 **5** Baptism altar with reliefs from Heiligenthaler Altar **6** Lambertialtar by H.Snitker the Elder, c.1440; panel paintings by H.Bornemann, c.1450 **7** Panel paintings from the workshop of C.v.Vechta a) Legend of St.Lawrence b) Legend of St.Andrew c) Last Supper, donated d) Abraham and Melchisedek **8** Crucifixion by V.Klovesten, c. 1450 **9** Crucifix by C.Snitker, 1470 **10** Choir stalls, 15C **11** Alabaster relief, c.1540 **12** Adam and Eve, mid 16C **13** Font screens, 1625 **14** Lectern, 1954

*door grilles* outside the baptism chapel should be mentioned.

**Rathaus** (Markt): Construction work began *c*.1240, but several centuries passed before the Rathaus complex was completed in its present form. The *court loggia* was built *c*.1330. The walls and vaults were painted with scenes from Roman history and with allegories by M.Jaster (1530). Parts of an under-floor heating system from the time of the building's construc-

tion still survive. The Rathaus silver was formerly kept in the three side wall cupboards, but has in the meantime been sold. On the N. side is a figure of St.Ursula (*c.* 1500), the town's patron Saint. The *Alte Kanzlei* (old record office; 1433), the *Körkammer* (election chamber; 1457) and the *Altes Archiv* (old archive; 1521) are side rooms adjoining the court loggia. All the rooms have preserved their original decorations. The former *Gewandhaus* (cloth merchants' hall; 15C) has been set up as a museum of the arts and crafts of Lüneburg. Above this we find the 15C *Festsaal*, today usually called the 'Fürstensaal'. It is reached by a richly decorated staircase and is decorated with five lamps adorned with antlers. The *Grosse Ratsstube* (Great Council Hall) was built in 1566–84. This richly decorated hall (with contributions by A.v.Soest, G.Suttmeyer and D.Frese) was used as a meeting room for the town council, and is today one of the most significant Renaissance halls in Germany. The *Huldigungssaal* is a baroque stateroom built in 1706 in order to pay homage to Prince Elector Georg Ludwig. The allegorical ceiling painting is by J.Burmeister, the local painter.

**Houses Am Sande:** The town's main square is framed by beautiful gabled houses from various epochs. One of the most significant houses is the *Schwarzes Haus* (black house; No.1), which was erected as a brewery in 1548 and is today the seat of the Chamber of Industry and Commerce.

**Museum für das Fürstentum Lüneburg** (10 Wandrahmstrasse): History of the town and region, ecclesiastical art, book printing and book binding, cabinet of rarities.

**Theatres:** *Stadttheater* (3 An den Reeperbahnen): This has its own ensemble for operas, operettas, ballets and plays (626 seats). *Studio-Bühne* (Ritterstrasse) with up to 90 seats.

**Also worth seeing:** The *Alte Kran* (old crane; Am Fischmarkte) survives from the year 1332. The shop opposite was formerly

◁ *Rathaus, staircase to the Fürstensaal*     *Rathaus, Gerichtslaube*

*Am Sande, with St. Johannis*

a storehouse for herrings. The *Glocken-oder Zeughaus* (bell house or armoury; Glockenstrasse), erected in 1482 and having a length of 130 ft., was built for the storage of grain. The front of the building is worth looking at.

**Environs: Kloster Lüne** (Lüne monastery; 2 km. NE, between the Ilmenau and the old Artlenburger Landstrasse): The present buildings of the former Benedictine convent were erected in 1374–1412 on the site of some previous buildings (the first monastic establishment here was founded in c. 1172). The farm buildings, most of which are half-timbered houses, were added later, and the cloister dates from the 16C. The monastery is today a Protestant institution for ladies. In the upper storey of the church there is a bipartite nuns' chancel (15C), where some significant works of art may be seen. The *Wailing over the Body of Christ* from the workshop of Lucas Cranach (1538). Two Passion flags (*c.*1400). White embroidy from the 13&14C are exhibited in the nuns' chancel in August of each year (altar covers and so-called Hungertücher (hunger cloths)). Hand-woven pictorial tapestries, and cloths used to cover benches (both these items date from the period around 1500), are then also put on display. There is a *baldachin altar* (1524) in the polygonal conclusion of the church's chancel. The *pulpit* is in the Renaissance style (1608). The *organ* dates from 1645.

**Lüneburger Heide** (about 20 m. W.): A *wildlife conservation park*, closed to motorized traffic.

**Lütjenburg 2322**
Schleswig-Holstein                    p.412□I 2

**Michaeliskirche** (church of St.Michael; Marktplatz): This single-aisled vaulted brick church stands on the site of a previous 12C building. The present church,

with its imposing W.tower, was built *c.*1220/30 (50 years later the choir was extended). There is a famous *carved altar* from a Lübeck workshop (1467). Above the wooden *pulpit* (1608) there is a 19C sounding-board. The figures in the early-16C *triumphal cross group* are almost life-sized. The silver *altar candlesticks* (1709) and the *brass chandelier* (1645) are fine features. The crypt buildings were erected after the Reformation on the site of the side chapels; note particularly the *Reventlow chapel* (1608), located on the N.side of the nave and containing the monument to Count Otto v.Reventlow-Wittenberg. The following should also be mentioned: the *Neuhäuser Gruftkapelle* (Neuhäuser crypt chapel; S.side of the nave); the *Rantzau memorial stone* (1618); the sandstone sarcophagi; the richly mounted metal coffins in the vaulted *Gruftkeller* (cellar of the vault).

**Houses:** Some fine old houses from the 15–18C survive in the Markt, in the Oberstrasse (houses Nos. 7, 12, 15) and in the Neuwerkstrasse (house No. 15).

*Tomb of Count Otto von Reventlow-Wittenberg*

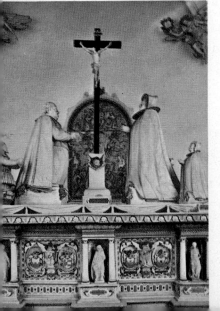

# M

## Mainau = 7750 Konstanz
Baden-Württemberg        p.420☐F 21

The mild, humid climate around Lake Constanz inspired Grand Duke Friedrich I of Baden to transform this island into a paradise of exotic plants (1853). Since 1928 the island has been in the possession of the Swedish royal family.

**Schloss:** The present building is the work of J.K. Bagnato (1739–46), the architect of the Teutonic Order. The *Weisse Saal* has rococo stucco and is particularly interesting. The *chapel* (with frescos by F.J. Spiegler) dates from 1734–9.

## Mainz 6500
Rheinland-Pfalz        p.416☐E 14

Mainz is one of the oldest cities on the

*Schloss and chapel, Mainau*

Rhine; it celebrated its 2,000th anniversary in 1962. It has a mild climate, fertile soil, and is well placed on the river and on ancient trading routes, and was thus quick to prosper. As Mogontiacum, it was the capital of the Roman Province of Germania superior. Then, after some centuries of decline, it began to recover its former prosperity when Bishop Boniface established his see here in 746\&7. The archbishops of Mainz were at once High Chancellors of the Empire and Electors. In 1254 the city headed the League of Rhine Towns. Johannes Gutenberg is said to have invented the printing press here in 1450, and so it became the cradle of the new art of printing. Its university (now the Johannes-Gutenberg-Universität) was founded in 1477. The city was badly damaged in the Second World War, but it

has been restored for the most part in keeping with its historic character. In 1949 it became the capital of the Bundesland Rheinland-Pfalz. Among the famous people who either were born in Mainz or lived in the city for much of their lives are the playwright and actor Curt Goetz, the playwright Carl Zuckmayer and the writer Anna Seghers.

**Dom St.Martin und St.Stephan** (main entrance between 10 and 12 Markt): A superb Romanesque building dating from 1239, the Dom was actually begun in 975, under Archbishop Willigis (its 1,000th anniversary was thus celebrated in 1975). The massive baroque crossing tower is a major landmark, visible for miles around. It was built in 1767 after a fire, by F.I.M.Neumann, son of B.Neumann, the

**Mainz, Dom St. Martin und St. Stephan 1** St.Gotthard Kapelle **2** Sacristy **3** Paradiespforte, later than 1200 **4** Memorie **5** Liebfrauenportal **6** Martinschor **7** Stephanuschor **8** Marktportal **9** Tomb of Archbishop Siegfried III by Eppstein (d. 1249) **10** Tomb of Archbishop Peter v.Aspelt (d. 1320) **11** Monument to Archbishop Konrad II v.Weinsperg (d. 1396) **12** Monument to Archbishop Dieter v.Isenburg (d. 1482) **13** Monument to Administrator Adalbert v.Sachsen (d. 1484), monument to Archbishop Berthold v.Henneberg (d. 1504) by H.Backoffen **15** Monument to Arch-

bishop Jakob v.Liebenstein (d. 1508) by H.Backoffen **16** Monument to Archbishop Uriel v.Gemmingen (d. 1514) by H.Backoffen **17** Monument to Archbishop Albrecht v.Brandenburg (d. 1545) by D.Schro **18** Monument to Archbishop Sebastian v.Heusenstamm (d.1555) by D.Schro **19** Monument to Dompropst Heinrich Ferdinand v.der Leyen zu Nickenich (d. 1714) by J.M.Gröninger **20** Choir stalls by F.A.Hermann, 1760-67 **21** Pulpit, 1834, by J.Scholl, rebuilt **22** High altar, 1960

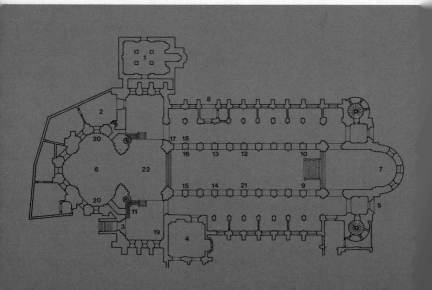

architect of the Würzburg Schloss. The two side towers, by the same architect, date from 1773.

*The building:* Along with Speyer and Worms, the Dom in Mainz is one of the most outstanding examples of Romanesque architecture in the Upper Rhineland, and indeed in the whole of Germany. Its 6 towers, lavish decoration (carved arches, galleries, and rose windows), and sheer vastness make it quite exceptional. Its overall length is 371 ft. (interior, 358 ft.); the W. tower soars to 275 ft. and the other towers are 182 ft. tall.

*Interior and furnishings:* The present cathedral is a basilica with nave and two aisles, and W. and E. choirs (the Martinschor and Stephanschor respectively). To visit it in chronological order of construction, one should start from the E. choir, then proceed through to the central nave, then to the N. aisle, the N. transept, the W. choir, the S. transept, and finally the S. aisle. *E. choir:* On the altar is a gold *reliquary* by the local goldsmith R. Weiland (1960), portraying all 22 of the saints of the see of Mainz. In the *nave* are numerous *tombs* from the 13–18C. Most are of archbishops, canons and saints. Near the W. choir are three tombs (all by the Mainz

sculptor Hans Backoffen) which merit particular attention: they are of Archbishops Berthold von Henneberg (d.1504), Jakob von Liebenstein (d.1508), and Uriel von Gemmingen (d.1514). The last of these, showing the archbishop kneeling before the crucified Christ, is a major work of German sculpture. Opposite, the old pulpit was restored in neo-Gothic fashion in 1834 by J. Scholl. *N. aisle:* Here too are some fine tombs. In the *St.-Magnus-Kapelle* is the *Bassenheim Altar* (1610) with a late Gothic tomb (*c.*1495, in monumental style by the Adalbert Master) in front of it. *N. transept:* A portal then leads to the two-storey *St.-Gotthard-Kapelle* (chapel of the Blessed Sacrament, 1135–7). This was once the private chapel of the archbishops. Particularly noteworthy in the *W. choir* are the rococo choir stalls by the Viennese court cabinet-maker F.A. Hermann (1760–7). It is excessively ornamented (figures by H. Jung) but nevertheless harmonises with the Romanesque architecture of the choir. The *high altar* dates from 1960, and the bronze cross above it was made by G.G.Zeuner in 1975. *S. transept:* One of the most remarkable tombs is that of Dean Heinrich Ferdinand v. der Leyen zu Nickenich (d.1714). 27 ft.

*Dom, choir stalls with a view of the E.tower*

high, the work of J.M. Gröninger, it was actually made during the Dean's lifetime. Through the Memorienportal off the *S. aisle* is the late Romanesque *Totengedächtniskapelle*, the memorial chapel of the cathedral canons, with a groin vaulted ceiling 40 ft. wide; the Nikolauskapelle and the cloister (Diözesanmuseum) are adjacent.

### Former Collegiate Church of St. Johannis (corner of Schöffer- and Johannisstrasse):

This church, adjacent to the Dom, was badly damaged in the Second World War, but has been largely rebuilt and refurnished in a modern style. It contains the remains of a church dating from 891–913, which is presumed to have been a predecessor of the Dom.

### Former Collegiate Church of St. Stephan (Stephansplatz):

Older buildings were absorbed into this church during rebuilding work in the 14C. The church was destroyed in the Second World War and rebuilding completed in 1961. Among the church treasure is the Willigiskasel, a Byzantine silk garment dating from *c.* 100; the choir windows were designed by Marc Chagall (1975).

### Parish Church of St. Ignaz (40 Kapuzinerstrasse):

The church was built by J.P.Jäger from 1763–74, and shows clearly the transition from rococo to neoclassicism. In the cemetery to the left of the church is a *Crucifixion* designed by H.Backoffen (1519); he paid for it himself as his own tomb.

### Augustinerkirche (34 Augustinerstrasse):

The church is almost indistinguishable from other buildings in the Augustinerstrasse. The present building dates from 1768–71, and baroque influence is unmistakeable. The façade and furnishings (stucco and ceiling painting) are particularly fine.

### Kurfürstliches Schloss (Rheinstrasse):

This palace was built from 1627 on the site of previous buildings destroyed in the Napoleonic period; it is considered to be the last important Renaissance building in Germany. Building lasted for almost 100 years, but great unity of style was still achieved. The interior, the work of artists of such distinction as B.Neumann, was destroyed in the Second World War, but the exterior was restored to the original design. In the E. wing is the Römisch-

*Dom, pulpit*

*Dom, St. Gotthard-Kapelle*

Germanisches Nationalmuseum (see under museums); the N. wing has been extended for use on formal occasions.

**Deutschordenskommende/Landtagsgebäude** (Rheinstrasse): The palace-like commandery of the Teutonic Order was built close to the Schloss in 1730 – 9 by A.F.Freiherr von Ritter zu Grünstein. The façade on the Rhine side is one of the more interesting features. The commandery was destroyed in the Second World War, but rebuilt to the original design. The interior was rebuilt for use by the Rheinland-Pfalz parliament. The *Neue Zeughaus*, near the commandery, was rebuilt in 1985 and is now known as the *Europahaus*. The old *Zeughaus*, known as the 'Sautanz', behind it was built in 1604, destroyed in the Second World War and also rebuilt as it had originally been.

**Rathaus** (Rheinstrasse): The Rathaus was designed by the Danish architect Arne Jacobsen and built in 1971–4, after Jacobsen's death. It is a reinforced concrete skeleton building, clad in Norwegian marble.

**Residences of the nobility in Mainz:** The finest of these houses are the *Dalberger Hof* (Klarastrasse) a baroque building dating from 1715–18, and the *Osteiner Hof* (Schillerplatz), which is rococo verging on the neoclassical.

**Museums:** The *Römisch-Germanisches Zentralmuseum* (in the Kurfürstliches Schloss): Archaeological finds from the Stone Age and the Roman period. *Gutenberg-Museum* (5 Liebfrauenplatz): This printing museum is housed in the 1660 'Haus zum Römischen Kaiser'. *Mittelrheinisches Landesmuseum* (49–51 Grosse Bleiche): collections on pre- and early history and applied art. The *Landesgalerie* with medieval, baroque and 19&20C painting is an annexe of this museum. *Bischöfliches Dom- und Diözesanmuseum* (3 Domstrasse): This museum on the S. side of the Dom in the two-storey Gothic cloisters (1397–1410) contains the cathedral treasure, fragments of the former choir screen and 15&16C tapestries.

**Theatres:** *Städtische Bühnen* (7 Gutenbergplatz): The company plays in the main house (885 seats), the *Theater in der Universität* (350 seats) and the *Kammerspiele* (13 Emmerich-Josef-Strasse, 125 seats).

*Late Gothic Entombment (c. 1495)*

**Also worth seeing:** The *Marktbrunnen* (1526) is the oldest Renaissance fountain in Germany. *Town fortifications:* The Eiserne Turm and the Holzturm (iron and wooden towers, both in Rheinstrasse) have been restored to the original design. *Dativius-Victor-Bogen:* an arch which has survived from Roman times.

## Mannheim 6800
Baden-Württemberg                    p.416☐E 16

Elector Friedrich IV had the foundation stone of the town of Mannheim laid in 1606. He had been impressed by fortresses in Holland, and so employed the Dutch architect Bartel Janson. Mannheim was frequently conquered and badly damaged in subsequent centuries, but the original chessboard ground plan can still be discerned. The town is bounded to the S. by the Schloss, and is set on the Rhine and the Neckar. Some of the famous names associated with the town are the poet and dramatist Friedrich von Schiller, August von Kotzebue, the author of more than 200 frequently-performed plays (d.1819 in Mannheim), Carl Benz, who showed his first motor car in Mannheim in 1886 and the inventor of the foot-propelled bicycle Karl Dreis von Sauerbronn. Today Mannheim is the seat of the German Language Institute and of the Humboldt Society for Science, Art and Education. Since 1958 the Konrad Duden Prize for German language and since 1959 the Schiller Prize of the City of Mannheim have been awarded here. The university, the music school, various other institutions of higher education, the national theatre, the planetarium, the international film week and the May fair are all events of national or international importance.

**Locations in the Quadratstadt:** Central Mannheim is divided into square sections, each known by a letter and a number.

**Former Jesuit Church of St. Ignatius and St. Francis Xavier** (A4): This 18C baroque church is dominated by its massive façade with two side towers and the high crossing dome. Kurfürst Karl Philipp commissioned this building, the most important baroque church in SW Germany, in 1733, to commemorate his house's return to Catholicism. The design was by the Bologna architect A.Galli-Bibiena, and the

*Rathaus, Mainz*

*Schloss, Mannheim*

building was completed by F.Rabaliatti and P.A.von Verschaffelt; work was completed *c.*1760. Most of the interior furnishings were destroyed in the Second World War; E.Q.Asam's ceiling and dome paintings were lost, but P.H.Brinckmann's frescos on the pendentives of the dome, allegories of the four quarters of the world, survived and could be restored. The pillars have dark-grey marble plinths and white marble Attic bases; the shafts are alternately in greenish or reddish stucco marble; these colours all combine to striking effect. The most valuable part of the furnishings, the high altar, was lost in the war; as was J.P.Egell's pulpit. The six side altars survived, the two in the transepts are reconstructions. The most important statue, the *Silver Madonna in Aureole* by the Augsburg silversmith J.I.Saler (1747), survived. The pulpit was replaced with a baroque pulpit from St.Leon near Heidelberg (q.v.). One of the most important items of the furnishings is the Klais organ

with case by P.Egell, which has been renovated. There is a small extra organ above one of the side chapels. 34 Jesuit fathers are buried in the *crypt*. The octagonal tower of the observatory originally built by Rabaliatti for the court astronomer father C.Mayer is evidence of the extent to which the Jesuits' scentific work was encouraged by Elector Carl Theodor.

**Altes Rathaus and Lower Parish Church** (Marktplatz): This church is dedicated to justice and piety: 'Iustitiae et Pietati'. Building began in 1700 and was completed in 1723. The building is in two sections connected by a tower. The high altar is missing; a modern stone altar table has been substituted. To the left of this the Theodor altar has survived; it is by P.Schaffelt, 1778. The pulpit (1742) is notable.

**Other churches worth seeing:** *Protestant Trinitatiskirche* (G) and *Protestant*

*Konkordienkirche* (R2) a double church for the Walloon and German Reformed congregations, and the *Catholic Bürgerspitalkirche* (E6), which has a neoclassical façade with columns.

**Schloss** (B3): The damage inflicted in the Second World War was completely eradicated in the restoration completed in 1962. The Schloss is now largely used by the university, which has 9,000 students in 8 faculties. One of the largest baroque Schloss buildings, it was commissioned by Elector Carl Philipp in 1720, when he decided to move his residence from Heidelberg to Mannheim; this was the beginning of a very successful period in Mannheim's history; it became one of the most important economic and cultural centres in Germany, and remained so until Karl Theodor became Elector of Bavaria and moved his residence to Munich. Italian and French architects and artists were heavily involved in the design of the building and its furnishings. Building continued for 40 years (1720–60), although large sections were available for use from 1731. The façade on the town side is *c.*550 yards long, and the Schloss has more than 400 rooms and 2,000 windows. The basic design was by J.C.Froimont; A.Galli-Bibiena, N.de Pigage, the sculptor P.A.von Verschaffelt and painters P.Egell and C.D.Asam were also involved in both planning and execution. The Schloss is the key building in the chessboard town, and stands at the end of seven of the dead-straight streets. The large, almost square *main courtyard* is impressive. The central building contains the various rococo state rooms. The *staircase* is one of the finest artistic achievements: C.D.Asam's famous ceiling paintings have been restored from photographs after their destruction in the Second World War. The *Rittersaal* is also very striking: this is used for state receptions and also concerts by the music school. Mozart gave a concert here in 1777. The magnificent parquet, lavish stucco decoration and exquisite furniture give an impression of the splendour of 18C court life. The *Bibliothekskabinett* is also worth visiting. The *Schloss church* was also destroyed in the Second World War, but has been beautifully restored, and a copy made of a ceiling painting by Asam. The high altar was built again on the basis of P.Egell's plans, which have survived; it too is an excellent copy of the original. In the *Kurfürstengruft* of the Schloss church are the state coffins made by Egell for Carl Philipp and his third wife Violanta von Thurn und Taxis. The area between the Schloss and the Rhine is occupied by a Schloss park of 94 acres.

**Friedrichsplatz:** This Jugendstil square was built in 1907 as part of the tercentenary celebrations of the city of Mannheim. The water towers, cascades and fountains, illuminated at weekends and on holiday evenings, make the Friedrichsplatz one of the most attractive features of the town. To the N. is the so-called *Rosengarten,* a congress and administrative centre.

**Museums:** *Städtisches Reiss-Museum* (C5, in the former arsenal): collections on archaeology, anthropology, the history of the town, late medieval and baroque sculpture, 17&18C painting and above all collections of porcelain and faience. The collections of the Mannheim Nationaltheater and the Rheinschiffahrts-Sammlung (navigation on the Rhine) are also of a high standard; they are outside the arsenal. The *Städtische Kunsthalle Mannheim* (9 Moltkestrasse) is one of the most important collections of 19&20C painting and sculpture in Germany. It is housed in a Jugendstil building erected by H.Billing in 1907 as an exhibition hall for the tercentenary. In front of the Kunsthalle are important sculptures by Harth ('Lion' and 'Tiger'), Marcks ('2 friends'), Kolbe ('Standing girl'), Scheibe ('Dawn sky') and Lipsi ('Tektonisch') and also works by younger artists.

**Theatres:** *Nationaltheater* (Goetheplatz): *Grosses Haus* with 1,133 seats for opera, operetta and straight plays, *Kleines Haus* with 627 seats for modern productions. Schiller's 'Die Räuber' had its premiere here on January 13 1782; 'Fiesko' followed in January 1784 and 'Kabale und Liebe' in April of the same year. Schiller often stayed in Mannheim, and lived here from

*Schiller's birthplace, Marbach* ▷

July 1783 to April 1785, first as a writer employed by the theatre and then as a free-lance writer. *Mannheim open-air theatre* (Im Waldhof): Amateur theatre groups perform mainly historical dramas here every year on Saturdays in July and August.

---

**Marbach am Neckar 7142**
Baden-Württemberg                    p.420☐F 17

---

**Protestant Alexanderkirche** (Am Alten Markt): This 15C late Gothic hall church is interesting because the original ceiling painting has survived. The damaged late Gothic stone pulpit and a 15C crucifix are also worth seeing.

**Birthplace of Friedrich Schiller** (31 Niklastor): This is one of the numerous half-timbered buildings in Marbach; it contains documents on the life and work of the poet.

**National Schiller Museum and German Literary Archive:** This was originally established in 1900–3 as a museum of Swabian literature, but now has importance beyond this field. The German Literary Archive, founded in 1855&6 is attached to it, and this mounts special exhibitions.

---

**Marburg an der Lahn 3550**
Hessen                              p.416☐F 12

---

The university, founded in 1527, has had a decisive influence on the development of the town. It is famous for the Colloquy of Marburg (1–4 October 1529), intended to bring about unification of the Protestant and the Reformed princes; it involved the Wittenberg theologians Luther, Melancthon and Krafft and the Strasbourg and Swiss theologians Bucer, Hedio, Zwingli and Oecolampadius.

**Elisabethkirche/Protestant Parish Church** (Elisabethstrasse): This church, which has become an emblem of the town, was built from 1235 over the tomb of Landgräfin Elisabeth von Thüringen, the ancestress of the Landgraves of Hessen. The Elisabethkirche is the first pure Gothic building in Germany and, like the Liebfrauenkirche in Trier (q.v.), it is one of the most important ecclesiastical buildings on German soil. It was intended as a pilgrimage church (to the tomb of the canonised Elisabeth) and as the funerary church of the Landgraves. The church was consecrated in 1283, but the towers were not completed until very much later. The interior (not including the area under the tower) is 184 ft. long, the nave is 71 ft. wide, the transepts are 128 ft wide and the vaulting reaches a height of 66 ft. The towers are 262 ft. high. The interior wall paintings (early 15C) and the paintwork from the time of the church's origin have largely been restored. The finest feature is the *Elisabeth shrine* in the sacristy. This masterpiece by an unknown 13C goldsmith is entirely covered with enamel and precious stones and exquisite filigree. In the N. transept is the *mausoleum* of St. Elisabeth, above her former tomb. The stone canopy came into being *c.* 1280. The design of its ornamentation is similar to that of the W. doorway and, in some places, the high altar. The Elisabeth shrine used to be above the mausoleum. The *high altar* was dedicated in 1290. It is notable for its stone retable, over 15 ft. high, with 3 figures in each niche. There are various fine *wall altars* and, in the S. of the church, 16C wall paintings. The iconoclasts destroyed some of the lavish sculpted decoration on the *rood screen*. Barlach's *bronze crucifix* (1931) is on the altar in front of the rood screen. There are fine *tombs* of the Landgraves of Thüringen-Hessen in the S. transept, known as the 'Landgraves' choir'. The most important tomb is that of Heinrich I (or possibly his son Otto I), presumed to be by a master of the French school.

**St. -Michaels-Kapelle/'Michelchen'** (W. of the Elisabeth Church, on the hillside): This chapel, consecrated in 1270, was originally the funerary chapel of the Teutonic Order and of the Elisabeth Hospital; only the hospital chapel has sur-

*Alexanderkirche, Marbach* ▷

*Elisabethkirche, Marburg*

*Schloss Philippsruh*

vived of the 1235 building. Since the 16C ordinary citizens have also been buried here. The tracery windows are comparable with those in the Elisabeth Church, and there is fine early Gothic rib vaulting, restored in 1984.

**Other churches worth seeing:** *Marienkirche* (Pfarrkirchhof): The present church was finally completed in 1473, after a building period of almost 200 years. The massive tower makes the church visible from a considerable distance. In the interior the altar furnishings and the double

**Marburg/Lahn, Elisabethkirche 1** W.portal with Virgin Mary figure, original door furniture **2** Window above the W.portal **3** Glass painting in the E.chancel windows, 13&14C **4** High altar, 1290 **5** Wall altars at the E.transept walls with wall paintings (partly concealed in the S.chancel by two carved altars by L.Juppe) **6** Shrine of St. Elisabeth, 1235-49, in the sacristy **7** Monument to Landgrave Konrad v.Thüringen (d. 1240) **8** Individual tomb, c. 1308 **9** Rood screen, earlier than 1343, with cross altar and crucifix by E.Barlach **10** Mausoleum of St. Elisabeth, baldachin late 13C, sarcophagus relief c. 1350 **11** Sedilia, 1397, with Elisabeth statue by L.Juppe, c. 1510 **12** Marburg Pietà, c. 1400 **13** Monument to Ludwig I the Peaceful, by Master Hermann, 1471 **14** Monument to Wilhelm II (d. 1509), probably by L.Juppe **15** Carved altars by L.Juppe, 1511 and 1513 **16** 'French' Elisabeth

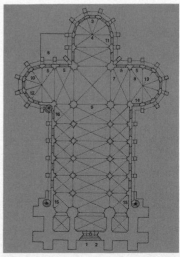

tombs of several Landgraves are worth seeing. *Dominikanerkirche/University Church* (Rudolphsplatz): This church, completed in 1320, has been the university church since 1527.

**Buildings of the Teutonic Order:** Adjacent to the Elisabeth church was a walled enclosure of the Teutonic Order, divided into various sections, with connecting gates to the town. Surviving buildings are the *Herrenhaus* (1252&3), the *Brüderhaus* (*c*.1234, with additions *c*.1572), the *Commandery* (*c*.1483) and the *bakehouse* (*c*.1515, later used as a fruit store, and now the mineralogical museum).

**Schloss** (Schlossberg): The Schloss is set on the town's highest point, the so-called Schlossberg (castle hill). Building was started by Duchess Sophie of Brabant, the daughter of St.Elisabeth, in the 13C on the site of a 12C Thuringian Burg; the present complex was completed by rebuilding in the 14&15C. It was the seat of the Landgraves of Hessen on various occasions until 1604. The complex is characterised by a number of different shapes, but the most distinctive feature is the symmetrical late-13C hall building in the N. The *ballroom*

in the upper storey is worth seeing. In the S. wing is the former residence of the Landgraves, the *Alte Residenz*. At the E. end of this S. wing is the *Schloss chapel*, consecrated in 1288. The interior of the chapel shows clearly the transition from early to high Gothic. The very fine capitals, the floor mosaic and remains of the old wall paintings are notable. The E. part of the main Schloss, the so-called 'Wilhelmsbau', has housed the cultural history museum since 1981; the W. wing is known as the 'Frauenbau'.

**Alte Universität** (Am Rudolphsplatz): The old university building was erected in 1874–8 on the foundations of a Dominican monastery. It has a fine Aula (main hall) with monumental wall paintings by Prof. Jansen, and the gatehouse, cloisters and dungeon are also worth seeing.

**Rathaus** (Markt): The Town Hall was built in 1512–27 on a steep slope. The lower storey on the valley side is open, and was originally a meat market. The first floor houses the council chamber, which has fine panelling. There are step gables on either side of the steep saddleback roof. In the staircase tower is a stone relief by

*Rathaus and Marktplatz*

L.Juppe (1524), dedicated to St.Elisabeth. The Renaisssance gable is by Eberhardt Boeckwein (1581).

**Museums:** The *Marburger Universitätsmuseum für Kunst- und Kulturgeschichte* (11 Biegenstrasse) deals with the Land and the culture of N. Hessen, and 19C painting and graphics. Also in the Biegenstrasse is the *Antiken- und Abgusssammlung der Philippsuniversität* This academic collection includes 600 copies of works of Greek and Roman sculpture, and also *c.*1,800 specimens of ancient crafts, including ceramics and terracotta. *Religionskundliche Sammlung der Universität* (in the Schloss): University divinity collection.

**Theatres:** The *Marburger Schauspiel* (15 Biegenstrasse, 579 seats) was built in 1969 and has its own company. In the summer there are open-air performances in the Markgrafenschloss.

**Also worth seeing:** *University library,* with more than 650,000 volumes including valuable incunabula, manuscripts and autographs. The finest of the many half-timbered buildings are Nos. 14, 17 and 19 Markt, and the best of the stone buildings are 18 Markt ('Steinernes Haus'), 16 Markt ('Bückingsches Haus') and the 'Derbacher Hof' by the Barfüsser Tor.

**Environs: Spiegelslust** (1 km. E.): Above the Old Town is the *Kaiser-Wilhelm-Turm,* a look-out tower at a height of 1,220 ft. **Wetter** (10 km. N.): Significant features are the numerous 17&18C *half-timbered buildings* and above all the *former collegiate church of St.Maria* (*c.*1250–80) with fine furnishings, including a *late Romanesque retable* (1240–50), a fine 13C *font* and a lavish *sedilia* (1466).

---

### Maria Laach 5471
Rheinland-Pfalz                           p.416☐C 13

**Abbey Church:** In 1093 the Rhenish Pfalzgraf Heinrich von Laach began to build an abbey and its attendant church on the shores of Lake Laach. The building was completed *c.*1230. Despite the long building period the abbey church is one of the purest examples of German Romanesque architecture. The humanist Johannes Butzbach, who died here in 1516, wrote of the abbey: 'There can be no ab-

*Abbey church, Maria Laach*

bey more splendid, more serene, more charming and more peaceful'. The building is dominated by two central and four side towers. The fortress-like building is designed in accordance with the symbolism of the New Jerusalem. There is a transept and a choir on both the E. and W. sides. The cloister-like portico was added in 1225 and leads into the W. choir. The architecture is unusually elaborate; the walls are articulated with pilaster-strips, arch friezes and blind niches, and the decoration is completed by coloured paintwork, not all of which has survived. The porch ('paradise') is intended as a symbolic representation of the Garden of Eden; it is on a square ground plan, contained on one side by the transept, and on the other sides by rows of arches; it is one of the finest buildings of its kind of the Romanesque period. In the middle of the square which it forms is the 'Fountain of Life'. The interior has massive vaulting—some of the oldest in the area. The finest features of the interior are the *canopy high altar* and the *tomb of the founder*. Above the altar a dome-like canopy is supported by columns of mature Romanesque design. The tomb of Pfalzgraf Heinrich, the founder of the church, is in the W. choir; there is a life-size figure of Heinrich on the richly decorated stone high tomb; he holds a model of the church in his hand.

*Monastery church, Marienmünster*

**Marienmünster 3477**

Nordrhein-Westfalen                    p.414□F 9

Between the three town of Detmold, Höxter and Paderborn (qq.v.), away from the main roads, is a first-class Romanesque building which one would not expect to find in these suroundings. It was largely conceived by Saxon architects. Unfortunately the Münster was deleteriously affected by modifications in the late 17C. This baroque work did not only affect the interior, but also included alterations to the walls of the nave, the raising of the crossing and the rebuilding of the choir. It must be admitted that the changes improved the church's decoration and furnishings: the most notable features are the excellent wrought-iron *choir screen* and the *organ*, the work of the famous organ-builder J.P.Möller, of nearby Lippstadt; it is considered to be one of the finest examples of German organ-building.

**Environs: Oldenburg** (2 km. NE): The *Oldenburg*, presumably fortified *c.*1100, was the seat of the Counts of Schwalenberg and has a late-14C *keep*, restored in 1687.

**Marienstatt (bei Hachenburg) 5239**

Rheinland-Pfalz                    p416□D 12

**Cistercian Abbey Church:** The present church in the valley of the Nister has been there since 1220, but the building was not completed until the 14C. It has unusual flying buttresses: they rise from the buttresses between the chapels to join the supports for the high choir. There are also open supports above the nave. In the SE

*Ursula altar, Marienstatt*                    *Rathaus, Markgröningen* ▷

is a staircase tower with an octagonal spire. The interior of the church has massive rounded pillars with a set of chapels beind them. The church is famous for the 14C *Ursula altar*, one of the oldest altarpieces in Germany. The upper row of delicate arches contains figures of the Apostles, and in the lower section are various reliquary busts. The central panel is dedicated to the Coronation of Our Lady. The *choir stalls* (*c.*1300) are another important feature. The carved wooden figures of Count Gerhard von Sayn and his wife are on a *high tomb* made by Master Thilmann in 1487. Finally, the *staircase* is worth seeing. The present *abbey buildings* were built in the mid 18C on the site of the original complex.

**Environs: Hachenburg** (3 km. SE): *Schloss Hachenburg*, a baroque complex dating from 1717–46, built on the site of an earlier medieval building, is an interesting feature; it is now used by the educational authorities. There is also a *market place* with fine 17&18C *half-timbered houses* and a 1702 *fountain*.

## Markgröningen 7145
Baden-Württemberg                    p.420□F 17

Markgröningen grew up on the edge of the Strohgäu between the valleys of the Enz, the Glems and the Leudelbach. It was founded *c.*1240 by Emperor Frederick II. Since 1443 the Schäferlauf (Shepherds' Race) has taken place here, on the weekend after August 24; it is the oldest folk festival in the area.

**Protestant Parish Church of St. Bartholomäus** (Kirchplatz): The choir of this church, dominated by its massive W. towers, was completed by A.Jörg in 1472. It is the architecturally most important part of the building: mature high

*Parish church, Marktoberdorf*

Gothic with very fine vaulting. The *wall and ceiling paintings* date from the 14–16C. There are also 14C *choir stalls*, a 1426 *font* and a late Gothic *triumphal arch crucifix*. In the N. aisle is the *tomb* of Count Hartmann von Gröningen (1280).

**Also worth seeing:** The *Rathaus* (Marktplatz) is a fine 15–17C half-timbered building; it has an imperial eagle below the turret — a reminder of the period when Markgröningen was a free imperial city. In 1336 the town became a part of Württemberg, as shown by the Württemberg coat of arms. In front of the Town Hall is the fine 1580 *Marktbrunnen*.

---

**Marktoberdorf 8952**

Bavaria                                    p.422□I 20

**Parish Church of the Holy Cross and St. Martin:** The Füssen architect J.G.Fischer, born in 1673 in this little town (it now has 15,000 inhabitants) planned the new building in 1732. The containing walls and the 1680 tower survived from the previous Gothic building, although Fischer added a final storey and an onion dome to the tower. Fischer's objective of retaining much of the older building in his own church can be seen most clearly in the choir, which takes account of various features of the Gothic design. Striking features are the windows, with fine *stucco* by A.Bader (1733). F.G.Hermann was responsible for the *frescos* in the nave and the choir dome (1735). The imposing *high altar* was completed in 1747. The figures are by J.Stapf. In the choir there are four excellent *figures* from the studio of A.Sturm (1735). The small 1823 *funerary chapel* is dedicated to the last Elector of Trier, Clemens Wenzeslaus, Prince of Saxony.

**Former Hunting Lodge:** The former hunting lodge of the bishops of Augsburg is just by the parish church. It was built in 1722–5 to plans by J.G.Fischer and enlarged to its present size in 1761. It now houses a section of the Bavarian Academy of Music.

**Heimatmuseum** (in the Altes Rathaus): Exhibits on religious and folk art in the E. Allgäu and on the history of the town.

## Maulbronn 7133
Baden-Württemberg                              p.420□E 17

**Former Cistercian Monastery:** The Cistercian monastery, founded in the peace of the Salzach valley in 1147, has survived almost unchanged, although it was secularised as early as 1530. Legend tells of a group of monks who stopped on the site of the present monastery to water their mules, and then stayed on for ever. (The word 'Maulbronn' could mean 'mule well'.) This story is preserved in a fresco on the vaulting in the well chapel. The architecture of the building shows the influence of the reform started by the Cistercian monks of Neuburg in Alsace in the 12C, and led by Bernard of Clairvaux. The ideals of monastery life were placed above all outward show and luxury and thus the monks had to find new ways of solving architectural problems. A remote monastic community came into being, designed to exist without any assistance from the outside world. There has been a Protestant monastery school here since 1538, and it continues today as a Protestant seminary.

**Monastery Church:** Founded in 1178; the first impression is of the enormous care with which the ashlar blocks were put together; this was a sign of the attitude of the monk-architects, who wished to replace the show of earlier decades with a more profound approach to architectural problems. The design is essentially Romanesque, but Gothic ideas are beginning to appear in some of the detail. The painted net vaulting and the magnificent window in the choir are later additions, at odds with the asceticism of the basic design. The *furnishings*, mostly 15C, also stand in contrast

*Well chapel, Maulbronn*

with the austere design of the building. There is a stone crucifix on the lay altar. The unduly ornate carved *choir stalls* were completed *c.*1470. Important items from the Parler family workshop are the *relief groups* with figures representing the Raising of the Cross, the Crucifixion and the Entombment (S. chapels). The group was completed *c.*1370 and is one of the finest works of art in Maulbronn. Among the monastery buildings are the very fine *cloisters* and *well chapel*; this little room is opposite the former refectory and has at its centre a well at which the monks had to perform the ceremonial washing rites prescribed by the Order.

## Mayen 5440
Rheinland-Pfalz                                p.416□C 13

**Catholic Parish Church of St.Clemens** (Marktstrasse): This Gothic hall church replaced a 12C Romanesque building in the 14C. The S. tower remains from the older building.

**Electoral Burg (Genovevaburg):** According to legend Pfalzgraf Siegfried and his wife Genoveva lived in this Burg. It was, however, built by Archbishop Heinrich of Trier *c.*1280 and later much modified, for the last time in the 18C. It now houses the fine *Eifeler Landschaftsmuseum* (museum of the Eifel countryside).

**Also worth seeing:** The *Obertor* and the *Brückentor* were part of the former town fortifications. The defensive towers *Vogelsturm* and *Mühlenturm* also survived the air raids of the Second World War.

**Environs: Bürresheim** (5 km. NW): The *Burg* was built on a cliff above the confluence of the Nettebach and the Nitzbach and is now owned by the Land Rheinland-Pfalz; very little of the original building remains. On the other hand the *Schloss*, in the E. of the complex, was built in the 15–17C and has survived in a good state of repair; fine rooms in the interior (15–18C) are the *Hexensaal, Marschallzimmer* and the *Rote Saal* with an early baroque

*Schloss Bürresheim, Mayen*

fireplace. The complex is typical of the development from a defensive to a residential building.

## Meersburg 7758
Baden-Württemberg                    p.420☐F 21

This charming and historic little town on a slope above Lake Constance developed from a settlement first mentioned in 988; it became a market in 1233 and achieved town status in 1299. The poetess Anette von Droste-Hülshoff lived here from 1841 until her death in 1848. From 1843 she lived in the *Fürstenhäusle* high above the town, now a memorial to her; before that she was housed in the tower on the E. side of the Schloss.

**Altes Schloss:** The core of this long Burg, which may have had a Merovingian predecessor, is the 12&13C *Dagobert tower*. Parts of the original complex have survived 16C additions and modifications. There is now a *museum* in the Burg, with exhibits on the Burg, and also collections of painting, sculpture and furniture.

**Neues Schloss:** Famous architects were involved in the building of this baroque residence for the Prince Bishops of Constance. Building began and was interrupted in the early 18C, but the decisive influence on the completion of the work was that of Balthasar Neumann. G.Appiani's large ceiling paintings (1661&2) have survived in the stairwell and the ballroom. The attractive *Schloss chapel* has stucco by J.A.Feuchtmayer and ceiling painting by G.B.Goetz (1741).

**Also worth seeing:** Schlossapotheke, opposite the Neues Schloss, Spital, Rathaus (with fine 1582 council chamber), 16–18C houses.

## Meisenheim,Glan 6554
Rheinland-Pfalz                       p.416☐C 15

**Protestant Schloss Church** (former

*Monks' refectory, Maulbronn monastery* ▷

Church of the Knights of St.John): This
hall church with three aisles, dating from
1497–1504 and probably founded before
1000, is not only one of the finest late
Gothic buildings in the area, but is also
worth a visit for its excellent stonemasonry.
In the funerary chapel, which has very fine
rib vaulting, are the *tombs* of the House of
Pfalz-Zweibrücken, some of the best
stonemasonry of the period. The finest of
all is the double tomb dedicated to Duke
Wolfgang of Pfalz-Zweibrücken and his
wife, created by J.von Trarbach in 1577.
The memorial for Duke Karl I of Birken-
feld (1601) is one of the most important
works of German Renaissance sculpture.

**Also worth seeing:** Only the Magdalene-
bau has survived of the former *Schloss*,
built *c.*1200 and rebuilt in the 15C. The
late Gothic Rathaus dates from 1517.

---

**Meldorf 2223**
Schleswig-Holstein                    p.412☐F 3

---

**Protestant Church:** This church, com-
monly known as the 'Dithmarschers' cathedral', is a basilica with three aisles

dating from 1250–1300; it had a Carolingian predecessor. The hall with two aisles
was added in the 15C and the tower in
1868–71. This 'Dom' is the most important medieval church on the North Sea
coast between Hamburg and Ripen. The
exterior is still distinctly neo-Romanesque,
whereas the interior is Hohenstaufen
Gothic. The red-brick walls give the
church an unorthodox but impressive appearance. The domed vaulting spanning
most of the main section is particularly effective. In the transept *vault paintings* have
survived showing scenes from the life of
St. Christopher and the legends of St.
Nikolaus and St. Katharine. The most
striking features of the furnishings are the
*pulpit* of 1601&2, the *carved altar* (*c.*1520),
remains of the late Gothic *choir stalls* and,
in the transept, remains of a *baroque altar*
(1695–8) and several *memorial tombs*.

**Houses in the market place:** Some little houses have survived in the S. which
show how Meldorf looked in earlier times;
the neoclassical Apotheke is out of place,
however.

**Museums:** *Dithmarscher Landesmuseum*
(4 Bütjestrasse): Collections on the history

*Meersburg, Altes Schloss*

*Tomb of Duke Wolfgang, Meisenheim*

of the region, peasant life, sacred art, navigation and landscape drawing. The *Dithmarscher Bauernhausmuseum* (4a Jungfernstieg) is a branch of the Landesmusuem set up in a 17–18C Low German farmhouse.

## Melsungen 3580

Hessen                                    p.416☐G 11

Melsungen was first mentioned in 1079, but not officially founded until 1189 by the Landgraves of Thüringen. In 1263 it fell to the Landgraves of Hessen, received its charter in 1267 (first mention), and was almost completely destroyed by a fire in 1554. Half-timbered buildings were built from that time until the 19C, and they make the Old Town look most picturesque.

**Former Schloss:** The Landgraves Philipp the Magnanimous and Wilhelm IV built the new Schloss on the site of an older Burg in 1550–77; the Schloss is a series of plain buildings with rectangular windows and doorways with pointed arches grouped loosely around a rectangular courtyard; they include the three-storey *main building* (1550 – 5), with staircase towers, and gables at the rear. The staircase tower of the *residence* of the Landgraves of Hessen is to the W.; it it is topped with a half-timbered section. The *mews* (1577) in the S. of the courtyard is now used as a municipal court. At the entrance to the *Schloss park* is a *guardhouse* (1689); its round tower has an attractive dome.

**Rathaus:** This three-storey detached half-timbered building replaced the old Town Hall, which was destroyed in the fire of 1554. The half-rosettes and crossed buttresses by the *S. doorway* are there for decorative purposes, and this is also true of the little *corner turrets* and the central *ridge turret*. There is one plain buttress between the three carved ones; the *wild man* carved on it is the first example in Hessen of this motif which is so popular on half-timbered buildings.

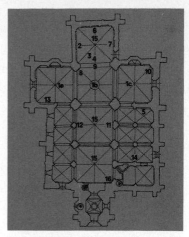

**Church in Meldorf 1** Vaullt paintings in transept, c. 1300, restored 1890-94 a) Life and sufferings of Christ, with very free additions b) Legend of St.Christopher c) Legend of St.Nikolaus and St.Katherine **2** Choir stalls, remains, mid 15C **3** Brass font, c. 1300, font cover 1688 **4** Cross group, late 15C **5** Former triumphal group, late 15C **6** Carved altar, c. 1520 **7** Boie sedilia, c. 1570 **8** Pulpit, 1601-02 **9** Choir screen by H.Peper, joiner T.Witt, 1603 **10** Memorial stone to Grevenstein, 1602 **11** Memorial tomb to Steinhausen, 1602 **12** Memorial tomb to Wasmer, 1605 **13** Baroque altar, remains, 1695-98 **14** Marble memorial to Klotz by Th.Quallinus, 1697 **15** Three chandeliers, 17C **16** John the Baptist, mid 15C

*Choir screen, Meldorf*

**Half-timbered houses:** The finest houses are those in Markt, Fritzlarer Strasse, Kasseler Strasse, Quergasse and in the Eisfeld. The half-timbered house at 5 Burgstrasse is 17C and has an interesting 1722 *doorway*, with a *wild man* and a *wild woman* on the corner-posts.

**Also worth seeing:** *Protestant parish church:* In the area under the tower to the W. of the nave can be seen the dour round-arched *doorway* left over from the previous building, destroyed in 1387; it was replaced by the present Gothic hall church with three aisles. Long stretches of the town wall and the *Eulenturm* with its conical roof survive from the 13&14C *town fortifications*.

**Environs: Felsberg** (10 km. W.): The former Burg of the Counts of Felsberg, after 1286 Landgraves of Hessen, is set on a basalt cliff; it has a partly Romanesque *ring wall* and the *Butterfassturm* (butter barrel tower), a keep dating from 1388. **Spangenberg** (11 km. E.): In the 13–15C *Protestant parish church* there are fine late Gothic *tracery windows, keystones* and *leaf capitals*, and a *picture of the Virgin* from the hospital church (15C) and some 16&17C

*relief tombs.* The 13–17C *Burg*, completely renovated after 1945, now houses the *Heimatmuseum* and the *Jagdmusuem* (local history and hunting).

---

## Memmingen 8940

Bavaria                                   p.422□H 20

Memmingen was founded *c.*1160 by Duke Welf VI, and it was successful from an early stage as a trading town; it is very favourably placed at the junction of two long-distance roads (Salzburg to Switzerland and Fernpass to Ulm). Memmingen came into the possession of the Hohenstaufens in 1191, became an imperial city in the late 13C and is now the home of several important industrial concerns.

**St.Martin** (Martin-Luther-Platz): According to records this church was founded in the 11C but not built until the 15C. The date 1499 can be found in the choir, along with the name of the architect, M.Böblinger. In the interior the vaulting is painted with stars and soars above the teeming figures on the choir stalls, carved by H.Stark and H.Dapratzhauser (1501–

*Siebendächerhaus, Memmingen*                              *Rathaus*

8), and the pillars, which are covered with painted figures. One of the best figures on the choir stalls is that of Hans Holzschuher, the keeper of the church.

**Frauenkirche** (Frauenkirchplatz): The church, mentioned as early as the 15C, is famous for its frescos. They were rediscovered in the course of restoration work in 1891 and ascribed to the period c.1470, with probable additions in the 16C. They represent prophets, Apostles, angels and some church fathers and also some three-dimensional building ornaments. The wise and foolish virgins are portrayed on the jambs of the choir arches. There are also fine late Gothic Upper Swabian wall paintings on almost all the walls.

**Siebendächerhaus:** The Siebendächerhaus (1601) in Memmingen is certainly one of the most photographed sights in Bavaria. It has seven roofs, each overlapping the next. The tanners who commissioned the building hung the skins they wished to dry under the jutting roofs. Damage caused by the collapse of the building in 1945 has been completely repaired.

**Städtisches Museum** (8 Zangmeisterstrasse): The municipal museum is housed in the palace built by Benedikt von Herman in 1766 in exuberant rococo style; the collections include pre- and early history and the history of the town, and 17–19C faience and painting.

**Also worth seeing:** The *Rathaus* (Marktplatz), built in 1589; it has a fine 1765 stucco façade. The *Kinderlehrkirche* (Martin-Luther-Platz): Former chapel of the Antonine monastery, with frescos by B.Strigel, a member of a famous Memmingen family of artists. It has a fine late Gothic courtyard with arches.

**Environs: Babenhausen** (23 km. N.): In the centre of an 18C Schloss park is Schloss Babenhausen (1541–46). The step-gabled building in the S. of the complex was part of an earlier building (15C). The Schloss now houses the *Fugger Museum,* which shows items from the Fugger collection: applied art, sacred and folk art, and miniatures.

## Merklingen, Alb 7901
Baden-Württemberg                p.420□G 18

**Protestant Parish Church:** The oldest part of the church in this tiny community in the Alb-Danube district (1,450 inhabitants) is the 13C tower. The choir and nave were added in the 15C, the octagon and the dome were completed in 1798. The most attractive artistic feature is the high altar, dating from 1510; it shows unmistakeable traces of the pleated style of decoration which reached its peak in the late Gothic period in Ulm (q.v.). The central feature is a Wailing group in relief. Dürer's work was used as the model for the Farewell of Christ to His Mother, which forms the outer part of the panel painting; inside are the Bearing of the Cross and the Resurrection.

## Merzig 6640
Saarland                p.416□B 16

**Former Collegiate Church of St.Peter** (Propsteistrasse): This church was built in the 12C and much modified until well into the 19C. Late Romanesque design is clearly discernible in the E. section. The massive W. tower dominates the exterior. The characteristic features of the interior are the arches, very pointed, in the manner of Lorraine. Fine items of the lavish furnishings include a larger-than-life-size *crucifix* (c.1300) on the high altar and various figures in the choir. Most of the figures date from the baroque period, but some were added in the 19C.

**Rathaus/Stadthaus** (20 Poststrasse): The Rathaus was built from 1647–50 as a hunting lodge for the Elector of Trier, Philipp von Soetern, and much altered later. The open-air staircase and the main doorway were particularly affected by the changes.

*High altar, parish church of Merklingen*

*Former collegiate church, Merzig*

## Mespelbrunn 8751

Bavaria       p.416□F 15

Mespelbrunn is the birthplace of Julius Echter (1545–1617), later Prince Bishop of Würzburg.

**Moated Schloss of Mespelbrunn:** This picturesque Schloss dates from the 15C and has survived with the help of skilful extension and renovation. The dominant feature of the complex is the massive round tower. At its side is a much smaller tower which is clearly far too short; it has a dainty little dome. Three wings of the Schloss are set around a small courtyard, and from here one reaches the *Rittersaal*, the principal room on the ground floor. On the upper floor the *Gobelinsaal* contains a particular treasure, the great Echter family Gobelin (1564). Adjacent to it are the *Ahnensaal*, the *Chinesische Salon* and other rooms with interesting furnishings.

## Messkirch 7790

Baden-Württemberg       p.420□F 20

**St.Martin** (5 Kirchstrasse): This basilica with three aisles was built by L.Reder of Speyer in 1526; its original late Gothic design was modified in the neoclassical style by F.A.Bagnato and others in 1770–82. Late rococo work has survived in the *frescos* of A.Meinrad von Ow and J.J.Schwarzmann's *stucco*. The most striking feature of the interior is the *Adoration of the Magi* (1538), by the Master of Messkirch, formerly the central panel of the high altar and now part of an N. side altar. There are also fine tombs, including the *bronze memorial tomb* for Count Gottfried Werner von Zimmern by the Nuremberg master P.Labenwolf (1558), and the even larger monument to Wilhelm von Zimmern. This 13 by 9 ft. mammoth *memorial tomb* was made in 1599 by W.Neidhardt of Ulm. Finally the *Johann Nepomuk Chapel* must be mentioned: it was decorated by E.Q. and C.D.Asam in 1733–4.

**Also worth seeing:** The central part of the Liebfrauenkirche, completed in the 14C, was remodelled by J.Schwartzenberger in 1576. The present façade and the decoration on the tower were created at the same time. *Schloss* (7 Kirchstrasse): The ballroom was created by J.Schwartzenberger in 1557, and it is clearly a predecessor of his 'Heiligenberg Rittersaal'. The building was owned by the Princes of Fürstenberg from 1627 and has housed the *Städtisches Heimatmuseum* since 1961. *Rathaus* (17C; 1 Conradin-Kreutzer-Strasse): Stone coats of arms of the Henneberg and von Zimmern families.

## Metten 8354
Bavaria                                    p.422☐N 17

**Benedictine Monastery Church of St. Michael:** The medieval building which used to be on the site of this church was much modified, and then redesigned in the baroque style in 1712. The nave with its imposing porch was completed in 1720. On the doorway of the four-bayed pilastered church are figures of St.Joseph and St.Christopher. The ceiling fresco in the magnificent porch is a reminder of the monastery's foundation by Charlemagne, and the legends which surround it. In the nave Benedict's meeting with Christ and Totila is depicted. The finest feature of the *high altar* is C.D.Asam's painting of 'Lucifer destroyed by St.Michael'. In the regular choir, which has lavishly carved stalls, is the famous 13C *Utto staff*. The *monastery buildings* in the N. of the church date from the 17C. In the N. upper storey is the *high tomb* of Utto, for whom the monastery is said to have been endowed in the 8C. It is 14C granite work, and used to stand in front of the high altar in the monastery church. One of the finest Bavarian baroque rooms is the *monastery library*, decorated by F.J.Holzinger from 1706 – 20. The marble cornices and vaulting are borne by Atlas figures. The ceiling frescos by I.A.Warathi (1724–6) relate to the books in the collection. In the *ballroom* the rococo

stucco is by M.Obermayr and the ceiling paintings are by M.Speer. In the inner courtyard of the monastery is an 18C *fountain* in honour of Charlemagne, the founder of the monastery.

## Mettlach 6642
Saarland                                   p.416☐B 16

**Former Benedictine Abbey:** Excavations revealed traces of four previous buildings and proved that there must have been a cruciform church here *c.*700. The Old Tower *c.*1000 has survived; it was presumably modelled on the Palatinate Chapel in Aachen (q.v.). There is a set of niches under the large dome. The most important interior furnishings are now kept in the Catholic parish church of St.Liutwin, including the famous *reliquary* in the form of a triptych (*c.*1230), similar to the one in Trier. The *monastery buildings*, rebuilt from 1728 by C.Kretschmar, are 367 ft. long on the façade side; they are now largely used as a *private museum* by the well-known ceramics firm of Villeroy & Boch. There is a *fountain* designed by K.F.Schinkel at the entrance to the adjacent park.

**Ruined Burg of Montclair** (2 km. S. of Mettlach): The ruins of the old Burg, dating back to the year 1000, are set on two cliff sites above the Saar. The present ruin is of the second rebuilding of 1428–39; it fell into disrepair in the 16C.

**Environs: St.Gangolf** (3 km. SW): The *Pagodenburg* built by C.Kretschmar in 1745, is an octagonal rotunda with five domes.
**Besseringen** (2 km. SE): The 18C *former tithe house* of Mettlach Abbey is a two-storey building with residential and service rooms.

## Michelstadt 6120
Hessen                                     p.416☐F 15

**Protestant Parish Church/Parish**

*Marktplatz in Michelstadt* ▷

*Double tomb, Michelstadt*

**Church of St.Michael** (Kirchenplatz): It is probable that everything but the tower was completed in the 15C, the tower itself not until 1537. The best feature of the furnishings is the *double tomb* of Philipp I (d.1461) and Georg I (d.1481). It is considered to be one of the greatest achievements of German medieval sculpture. A series of Renaissance tombs shows how the tradition continued; the first-class *alabaster work* is particularly striking. One of the sculptors involved was the Franconian M.Kern.

**Rathaus** (Marktplatz): This picturesque half-timbered building, still firmly Gothic, was completed in 1484. The lower floor is an open hall, with two half-timbered storeys with oriels above it. The extremely steep hipped roof has a ridge turret which, with the two oriels, gives the building its characteristic appearance. There are other fine *half-timbered buildings* in the market place, particularly the Gasthaus *Zum*

*Goldenen Löwen* (1755). The *Röhrenbrunnen* dates from 1575.

**Einhartsbasilika** (Steinbach): Einhart, the adviser and biographer of Charlemagne (see also Seligenstadt) had the church built in the 9C. It was originally intended to house the bones of St. Marcellinus and St.Peter, which had been brought from Rome to Steinbach; they were then taken to Seligenstadt in 828. The church has remained largely unchanged since it was built, and is thus one of the best specimens of Carolingian architecture N. of the Alps. The crypt is strikingly well-proportioned.

**Schloss Fürstenau** (1 km. NW of Michelstadt): The *Altes Schloss* is the oldest part of the complex; it includes four corner towers from a 14C defensive building. In 1588 the moated Schloss was converted into a fine Renaissance building. Other interesting features are the Park-pavillon (1756), the Schloss mill (late-16C), the Schloss kitchen (late-16C) and the Neues Palais (1810). For the *Einharts-basilika* see above.

**Odenwaldmuseum** in the *Kellerei*, a 14C former Burg of the imperial abbey of Lorsch: collections on landscape, the history of the town and a private *toy and doll museum*.

---

## Miltenberg 8760
Bavaria                                p.416☐F 15

**Marktplatz:** The market place is fairly steep, with the Mildenburg as its upper limit. There are fine half-timbered buildings all round the market place; the finest is the former *Gasthaus zur Krone* on the E. side. The 1583 *fountain* completes the picture.

**Hauptstrasse:** The long Hauptstrasse also has a large number of half-timbered houses. An interesting one is the *Haus zum Riesen*, in which princes stayed as early as

*Marktplatz in Miltenberg* ▷

1504, and which is still an hotel and res-taurant today. The *Alte Rathaus* (137 Hauptstrasse) was built in the early 15C as a merchants' hall and was not used as the Town Hall until 1824; it was modified in a rather unfortunate way in the 18&19C, but is still one of the most attractive build-ings in Miltenberg.

**Mildenburg** (Marktplatz): The ground around the Burg is so steep that a protec-tive ditch was only necessary on one side. The present building replaced a 14C wooden structure; the barbican also dates from this period. In the courtyard is a mys-terious monolith: its origins are still puz-zling. It is shaped like a needle, and carries the inscription 'inter teitones'. Speculative dating has placed it as early as the pre-historic period, but it is most probably Roman.

**Former Synagogue** (199 Hauptstrasse): This is one of the oldest Jewish buildings in Germany; it is in a rear building of the 'Kalt-Loch' brewery.

**Heimatmuseum** (in the former Amt-skellerei): The former Amtskellerei, also a half-timbered building, dates from 1590 and has been used as a museum since 1903.

**Also worth seeing:** *Catholic parish church of St. Jakob* (Marktplatz): This church was modified in the 18&19C and has fine fur-nishings. *Laurentiuskapelle:* This 15&16C chapel is outside the town and has wall paintings in the choir.

**Environs: Engelberg pilgrimage church** (5 km. W.): Six little 17C chapels lead to the *Church of Maria zu den Engeln*, completed in 1639; it has a 14C statue of Our Lady on the altar in the S. chapel.

**Mindelheim 8948**
Bavaria                                          p.422□I 20

**Parish Church of St. Stephan** (Kirch-platz): The present building dates from the early 18C and included the older bell tower in the design; the lower section of the tower

is early 15C. Baroque items from other churches were added to the furnishings in 1933. The most valuable interior feature is in the tower chapel; it is the *tomb* of Duke Ulrich of Teck (1432) and his wife Ursula. The tomb of Anna von Teck, Ul-rich's first wife, is in the N. choir chapel.

**Jesuit Church** (Maximilianstrasse): J.Holl completed this church in two years: 1625&6. He was, however, able to use parts of the Augustinerkirche, which formerly stood on this site. The interior *stucco* is very delicate, in contrast to some features of the exterior, which is predominantly Gothic, inclining to the baroque. The 1625 *choir stalls* have survived. The altars and choir date from the 18C.

**Liebfrauenkirche** (Memminger Strasse): The present building was completed *c.* 1455, but the interior was refurbished in the 18C because of a fire. By the S. wall is a late Gothic carved relief by an un-known master, called 'Die Mindelheimer Sippe' ('The Mindelheim Kindred') (*c.* 1510–20). In front of the church is a so-called fountain of the Five Sacred Wounds (1662).

**Museums:** *Heimatmuseum* (2 Hauber-strasse): local history, folk art and lore, cribs and costume. *Turmuhrenmuseum* (in the former Silvester church): 17–20C church clocks.

**Also worth seeing:** Parts of the 15&16C town wall have survived in good condition. The Mindelburg, (S. of the town), was founded in 1370, but has been much altered.

**Minden, Westfalen 4950**
Nordrhein-Westfalen                       p.414□F 8

One of the Saxon bishoprics founded by Charlemagne *c.* 800 was on the old ford over the Weser, and it was from this that the town developed; it now stands at the crossroads of the Weser and the Mittelland-kanal and is one of the most important towns in E. Westphalia. Heavy damage sustained in the Second World War has been repaired, and many buildings have been reconstructed as they used to be.

**Dom St.Peter und St.Gorgonius** (Domhof): A cathedral was started shortly after the establishment of the bishopric, but replaced by a new building from 951 (part of the original small hall building was discovered in the course of excavations under the crossing of the present Dom). The 951 building forms the basis of the present cathedral; it was consecrated in 952 but largely destroyed by fire in 1062. The westwork was built in its present form in the 12C. It is dominated by the tall bell tower, flanked on either side by staircase towers. In 1210 the late Romanesque E. section was added, in 1290 the nave was completed, and building work was finished c.1340. The Dom was badly damaged in the Second World War, but the core of the building survived unscathed. The westwork is the most striking feature of the Dom, but the nave with its fine tracery windows is of equal quality; this is some of the finest work in Germany. The furnishings were largely destroyed in air raids and replaced by works of modern artists. The *Apostle frieze*, originally part of the choir screeen (1250–70), is now on the S. wall of the transept. The *high altar* now has a panel painting by G.van Loen (late 15C), acquired after the war. The modern *pulpit* is the work of W.March and Z.Szekessy, and the modern font by G.Leo-Stellbrink. In the *Domschatz* (cathedral treasure, 30 kleiner Domhof) are two important 11C works of art; the reliquary shrine of St. Peter and a bronze crucifix, the *Minden Cross* (both c.1070). The oldest item is a 9C ivory book cover representing the Ascension.

**Protestant Church of St.Martin** (Martinikirchhof): The church was founded in 1025, much modified over the years and completed in the 14C. The furnishings include a *bronze font* (1583), the late Gothic, lavishly carved *choir stalls* (c.1500) and the *pulpit*, a late Renaissance design. The *Bulläus memorial tomb* (1615) is by the Osnabrück master A.Stenelt.

**Other churches worth seeing:** *Protestant Simeonskirche* (Simeons Kirchhof): 13C church with a Romanesque gable relief on the N. side (hand of God with stars). *Catholic Mauritiuskirche* (Königstrasse): This church was built in 1474, decon-

*Reliquary shrine of St.Petrus, cathedral treasure in Minden*

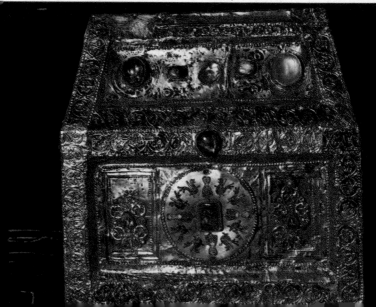

*Dom, Minden*

secrated in the 19C and restored to its original use in 1946. *Protestant Marienkirche* (Marienkirchplatz): This 12C church was extended in the 14C. It has fine *Renaissance furnishings*, for example the 1598 font and some tombs.

**Rathaus** (Markt): The lower floor of the Minden Rathaus dates from the 13C and clearly has features in common with the nave of the Dom. It is one of the oldest surviving Town Hall buildings in Germany. The arcade has four bays with fine Gothic arches. The upper storey was added in the 17C and restored after damage in the Second World War.

**Houses:** The finest are the *Alte Münze* (Old Mint, 2 Brückenstrasse), the *Hansehaus* (2 Papenmarkt), *Haus Hill* (45 Bäckerstrasse) and the house im Scharn *Haus Hagemeyer*. The latter three are among the finest Renaissance buildings in Germany, and date from the late 16C.

**Museum:** The Minden Museum (23–33 Ritterstrasse) is housed in six 16&17C patrician houses. It has collections on primeval and early history and the history of the town, folk lore and the Weser Renaissance.

**Theatres:** Mindener Stadttheater (3 Tonhallenstrasse): Touring performances; 656 seats.

**Environs: Porta Westfalica** (7 km. S.): Memorial (1896) to Kaiser Wilhelm I.

---

## Mittenwald 8102
Bavaria                                    p.422☐K 21

Mittenwald became important at an early stage because of its favourable position on the Rottstrasse, the road which connects the valleys of the Inn and the Isar; it is now an important spa and winter sport centre. Famous artists associated with the town are M.Günther, who worked on the parish church, the local artist F.Karner and the Oberammergau 'Lüftl' painter F.Zwinck. The most famous son of the town was the violin-maker Matthias Klotz (1653–1743), who probably studied under Amati in Cremona, and who made the town the centre of German violin-making. There is a memorial to him by the parish church.

**Parish Church of St.Peter and St.Paul** (Matthias-Klotz-Strasse): The famous J.Schmuzer of Wessobrunn demonstrated his skills to great effect in this church. It was built under his aegis from 1738–40, and incorporated the late Gothic choir. The tower, painted by M.Günther, was completed in 1746. The *decoration*, conceived and executed by J.Schmuzer, is unique. The vaults and friezes are covered in tendrils and blossoms, and are among the finest achievements of German stucco decoration. The paintings on the ceiling and the high altar are also the work of M.Günther (1740).

**Geigenbau- und Heimatmusuem** (3 Ballenhausgasse): This museum, unique of its kind, is mainly devoted to violin-making in Mittenwald. There are also collections of other musical instruments and a section on peasant culture.

## Moers 4130
Nordrhein-Westfalen                    p.416☐B 10

The most famous name associated with the town is that of the hymn-writer Gerhard Tersteegen (1697–1769); he was born at 1 Altmarkt.

**Schloss:** The present complex dates back to the 12C, but it was much affected by alterations in the 15&16C. The Schloss now houses the *Grafschafter Heimatmuseum*, which has exhibits on folk art and the history of the town.

**Schlosstheater** (6 Kastell): The Schlosstheater company plays in the Kammertheater (150 seats), the Studio, the Bonifatius chapel and the open-air theatre in the Schlosshof (350 seats).

## Möhnesee 4773
Nordrhein-Westfalen                    p.416☐D 10

This new administrative unit includes 15 small Westphalian villages. Interesting features are the *Körbeck parish church*, with fine baroque furnishings by Sutting, the *Möhne dam* and above all the *Heilig-Geist chapel* in Druggelte (*c.*1140, mentioned in 1227); this is a small, vaulted, twelve-sided rotunda, with lavish architectural ornamentation and representational and ornamental sculpture on the *capitals*.

## Mölln 2410
Schleswig-Holstein                    p.414☐I 14

Till Eulenspiegel, who served as inspiration for Richard Strauss among other, is said to have died of the plague in 1350 in the Heilig-Geist hospital in this little town in the Duchy of Lauenburg. He is commemorated by a grave slab on the outer wall of St.Nicolai (see below), showing him in a fool's cap with an owl (Eule) and a mirror (Speigel). The Eulenspiegel fountain is in the market place. In the *Heimatmuseum* (2 Am Markt) there are many documents on the life of this medieval rogue. Occasional Eulenspiegel festivals are held.

**St.Nicolai** (Am Markt): A relatively long building period (13–15C) led to occasional deviation from the original style. The furnishings are extraordinarily lavish, but do not all date back to the time of the building of the church. Numerous items came from the monastery of Marienwohlde, plundered in 1554 and then burned down. The most important items of the *furnishings* are: bronze font by P.Wulf (1509), seven-branched candelabrum (1436), triumphal cross (1504 or 1507) and the pulpit (1743). The organ, built by J.Scherer in 1558, has retained its baroque tone to a large extent. The mayor and councillors have their own lavishly carved pews.

**Markt:** The *Heimatmuseum* (2 Am Markt) is now in one of the numerous half-timbered houses around the market place; some of them date from the 14C. The Rathaus (E. gable 1373) is a brick Gothic building, later extended.

## Mönchengladbach 4050
Nordrhein-Westfalen                    p.416☐A 11

**Münsterkirche/Monastery Church of St. Vitus** (Münsterplatz): The present building was finally completed in 1275; it had many predecessors. The damage inflicted in the Second World War has been made good. The church is a late Romanesque three-aisled basilica. The Gothic choir was influenced by Cologne cathedral (q.v.). The characteristic feature of the interior is the plainness of the arches. Under the choir is the unusually large *hall crypt*, with three aisles and five bays in its main section, and square rooms adjacent on two sides. The most important items of the furnishings include the *stained glass* of the so-called Bible windows in the central window of the choir; they are late 13C, and glow deep green; French influence is evident. They represent scenes from the Old and New Testaments. The *Romanesque font*, now in the S. annexe, dates from the 12C. The church treasure includes a Romanesque portable altar said to have been made in the Cologne area *c.* 1160. The former *abbey buildings* were taken over for use as a *Rathaus* in 1835.

**Städtisches Museum** (27 Abteistrasse): Collections on pre- and early history, applied art, weaving, 20C art.

**Theatre:** The Stadttheater Mönchengladbach (73 Hindenburgstrasse) is connected with the Stadttheater in Krefeld.

**Also worth seeing:** Monastery and church of *Neuwerk* (N. of the town centre): The late Gothic tufa church was completed in its present form in 1533; the original building (1130–70) came to considerable harm in the process. The area of the town known as *Rheindahlen* (E. of the town) was built in the early 50s and is the base of NATO's Central and Northern European operation and the headquarters of the British Army in Germany. The complex, which has its own church, schools, clubs and shops is completely autonomous, and is an example of purpose-built town architecture. *Schloss Reydt* in the SE was completed in its present form in 1501. It is essentially Renaissance, but has been much modified, and suffered in the Thirty Years War. It now houses the Städtisches Museum für Kunst- und Kulturgeschichte (art and cultural history) and a museum of weaving. *Schloss Wickrath* (in Wickrath) was built in the 18C by J.J.Couven. It now contains public offices and an ornithological museum. *Kaiser-Friedrich-Halle* (Hohenzollernstrasse): This Jugendstil hall completed in 1900 was restored as a concert and congress hall after a fire in 1964.

---

**Monschau 5108**
Nordrhein-Westfalen                    p.416☐A 13

---

Monschau blends perfectly with the countryside around the High Venn. The name of the town, which has many attractive half-timbered buildings, is derived form the territory of *Montjoie*, first mentioned in 1096.

**Burg:** An earlier Romanesque building first mentioned in 1217, of which the main sections of the *keep* and the *doorway* of the main castle have survived; it was modified in the 14C and fortified more strongly with a *ring wall* and parapets. It was sacked in 1543 and 1689, rebuilt after 1899 and equipped as a Youth Hostel. The W. wing with its *Rittersaal* and *palas* is worth seeing; the latter is connected by a long flight of steps to the so-called *Eselsturm* (asses tower), a large 16C defensive tower.

**Scheibler-Museum** (Rotes Haus): This three-storey slate-roofed house has two sections, *zum Helm* and *zum Pelikan*; it was built in red brick for the textile manufacturer J.K.Scheibler as a residence and a warehouse. The late baroque building is decorated with protruding *slate gables*, ornate *doors*, and *window frames* with shell-like wedge-shaped keystones. It was reopened as a *museum* in 1980; the bourgeois rococo furnishings include a carved broad *staircase* and some *reliefs* framed in stucco rocaille (scenes of fabric manufacture).

**Also worth seeing:** The *Catholic parish churches Mariä Geburt* (1649&50) and *St. Maria* (1726 – 50), both simple hall churches with *wooden rib vaulting*, are of interest; fine secular buildings in the Monschau style include the *Altes Rathaus* (1654), the *Haus Elbars*, and the *Doppelhaus de la Tour*.

---

**Montabaur 5430**
Rheinland-Pfalz                    p.416☐D 13

---

**Catholic Parish Church of St. Peter** (Kirchstrasse): The church is essentially 14C. It is a stepped hall church with galleries: light comes in through the side aisles. The wall paintings are very striking. The large fresco on the crossing arch over the nave represents the Last Judgement.

**Schloss:** The 13–17C Schloss is the home of the *Akademie der deutschen Genossenschaften*. It is a building with four wings set around a courtyard; each wing has a striking round tower with a bell-shaped dome.

**Grosser Markt:** The houses in the market place are the finest in the town, but Kirchstrasse and Vorderer and Hinterer Reichstock are also worth seeing.

---

## Moosburg 8052

Bavaria                               p.422☐L 18

---

**Former Collegiate Church of St. Castulus** (Auf dem Plan): The original building (1171–84) was restored after a fire in 1207. The tower and the richly decorated doorway were added in time for the consecration in 1212. The tufa and brick building is above all important for its furnishings; the finest of these is the *high altar* (1514, by H.Leineberger); it is 47 ft. high and 14 ft. wide, unusually large dimensions for such a work. On the predella are reliquaries of the patron saint. The tripartite shrine portrays Our Lady and Emperor

*Former collegiate church of St. Kastulus in Moosburg*

*Catholic parish church of St. Peter, Montabaur, with fresco on the crossing arch*

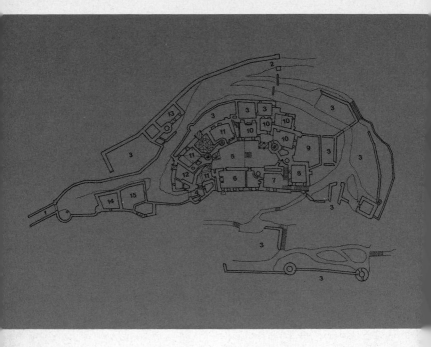

Heinrich II. Figures of St.John the Evangelist and St.John the Baptist can be seen under canopies. The large red marble *memorial tomb* dedicated to Propst Theodorich Mair is presumably also by H.Leinberger. He was also responsible for the memorial tomb of Canon Mornauer, and the Christ in Repose (by the S. window of the choir arch). The lavishly decorated *choir stalls* are also fine and there are notable tombs in the adjacent *Ursula chapel*.

**Protestant Johanniskirche** (Stadtplatz): This church is close by St.Castulus; it was built in the 12&13C and the aisles were added in the 15C. 15C Frescos were discovered on the right side doorway in 1980.

**Environs: Isareck** (5 km. N.): This 16C Schloss at the confluence of the Isar and the Amper was rebuilt after 1803. The stucco ceiling and the *altar painting* in the *Schloss chapel* are of interest.

**Burg Eltz 1** Outer gate **2** Valley gate **3** Barbican **4** Inner Burg gate **5** Inner courtyard **6** Rübenacher Haus **7** Terrace **8** Platteltz **9** Amtmannsgärtchen garden, so-called 'Alte Burg' **10** Kempenicher houses **11** Rodendorfer houses **12** Chapel building **13** Coach-house **14** Goldsmith's house **15** Craftsmen's cottages

**Gelbersdorf** (10 km. N.): The 15C *church of St.Georg* has a fine 1482 *high altar* of the Landshut school.

## Moselkern 5401
Rheinland-Pfalz                                  p.416☐C 14

**Burg Eltz:** Burg Eltz is 6 km. upstream of the confluence of the Eltz and the Mosel and 603 ft. above the wine-growing village of Moselkern; it can be reached on foot in one and a quarter hours. An opinion poll suggests that it is one of the ten most visited places in Germany. The history of the

*Burg Eltz* ▷

Burg (still owned by the family) can be traced back to 1157. The complex was completed in its present form at the end of the 16C. Damage caused by a fire in 1920 has been repaired. The main courtyard is the architectural high spot of the Burg: it gives a clear impression of the large number of buildings which make up the complex. Almost all the rooms have their original furnishings.

**Ruined Burg of Trutz-Eltz:** N. of Burg Eltz, about fifteen minutes walk away, is the ruin of the former Burg of Trutz-Eltz. It was built in the first half of the 14C by Archbishop Balduin of Trier as a fortress ('Trutzburg' means 'defensive' or 'defiant Burg') in the struggle with the Eltz family.

---

## München/Munich 8000

Bavaria                               p.422□L 19

---

Munich is the capital of Bavaria and, after Berlin and Hamburg, the third largest city in the Federal Republic; it is the seat of the Archbishop of Munich-Freising, a university city, the economic and cultural centre of S.Germany and a city of European and international importance. The history of the town goes back to the 12C: after the destruction of the bridge which took the salt road over the Isar at Föhring — at that time the seat of the Bishop of Freising—Henry the Lion of Bavaria and Saxony moved the centre of trade to Munichen ('monks' village') in 1158 and granted this settlement rights of customs and coinage. In 1255 the town became the residence of the Wittelsbachs (until 1918); they had lived here as Dukes of Bavaria since 1180. Munich rose to be one of the most important towns in medieval Germany through its trade in salt, cloth and wine, and later the manufacture of Loden cloth (a coarse woollen fabric), gold articles and weapons became an important economic factor. Munich became a centre of European art and culture under Duke Wilhelm IV (16C) and Ludwig I, Maximilian II and Ludwig II (all in the 19C). It became an academic centre when the university was moved from Landshut to Munich in 1826.

**Historical Personalities:** Munich has close connections with many political, artistic and academic figures: only the most important can be mentioned in the following summary:*Humanities:* Benjamin Thompson, Count of Rumford (1753–1814), worked in Munich in the service of the Bavarian state from 1784–99; he introduced the potato to Bavaria and laid out the English Garden, for which services he was made a Count of the Holy Roman Empire. Maximilian Joseph, Count of Montgelas (1759–1838), worked as a statesman of the Aufklärung (enlightenment) to establish an alliance with Napoleonic France. The philosopher Friedrich Wilhelm von Schelling (1775 – 1854) was professor in Munich from 1826–40. Joseph von Görres (1776 – 1848), an important Catholic writer (see Koblenz), was professor in Munich from 1827. Friedrich Wilhelm Thiersch (1784–1860) was a classicist who made a large contribution to the revival of classical studies. Johann Andreas Schmeller (1785 – 1852), the founder of German dialect research, was professor in Munich from 1828. Georg Freiherr von Hertling (1843–1919), the Catholic philosopher, was Prime Minister of Bavaria from 1912 – 17 and Imperial Chancellor from 1917–18. Adolf Furtwängler (1853 –1907), archaeologist and researcher into early Greek art lived here. Georg Kerschensteiner (1854–1932), the founder of the technical school movement, was professor in Munich from 1911.
*Natural sciences:* Georg Simon Ohm (1787-1854) was professor in Munich from 1849 and discovered the law of electrical resistance which is named after him. Joseph von Fraunhofer (1787-1826) established the world-wide reputation of the German optical industry with the foundation of his optical institute (moved to Munich in 1819). Justus von Liebig (1803–73) was professor in Munich from 1852 and introduced artificial fertilisers. Max von Pettenköfer (1818 – 1901) was professor in Munich from 1874–94 and is the founder of academic hygiene. Wilhelm Conrad Röntgen (1845-1923), professor in

*Panorama with Frauenkirche* t

Munich 1900 - 20, discovered X-rays, which bear his name in Germany. Ferdinand Sauerbruch (1875-1951), professor in Munich 1918-27, is the founder of lung surgery.

*Poets and authors:* Emanuel Geibel, (1815 - 84), professor of aesthetics in Munich from 1852-65, was the central figure of the Munich school of poetry. Henrik Ibsen (1828-1906), Norwegian pioneer of social drama, lived in Munich from 1877-1891. Paul von Heyse (1830-1914), the master of the Novelle, lived in Munich from 1877-91 and was one of the Munich poets. Frank Wedekind ((1864-1918) the satirical dramatist and writer for the periodicals 'Jugend' and 'Simplicissimus' spent most of his life in Munich. The Nobel prizewinner Thomas Mann (1875-1955) lived in Munich from 1893-1933. The novelist Annette Kolb (1870-1967) lived in Munich except when in exile from 1933-9. Joachim Ringelnatz (1883-1934), the writer of light verse and ballads, was a member of the 'Simplicissimus' cabaret from 1909-14. Lion Feuchtwanger (1884 - 1958), the author of biographical novels and important plays and Oskar Maria Graf (1894-1967) the author of stories of Bavarian village life, lived in Munich until they emigrated in 1933.

*Composers:* Ludwig II was the patron of Richard Wagner (1813-83), who lived in Munich from 1864 - 5. The composer Richard Strauss (1864-1949) was musical director in Munich from 1895-98. Max Reger (1873-1916) lived in Munich from 1901-7.

*Painters:* Cosmas Damian (1686-1739) and Egid Quirin (1692-1750) Asam created the Asam church (q.v.) in Munich. Josef Stieler (1781-1858), an important Romantic portrait painter, created Ludwig I's gallery of beauties. Also: Moritz von Schwind (1804-71), Carl Spitzweg (1808-85), Arnold Böcklin (1827-1901), Franz von Lenbach (1836-1904) and Albert Weisgerber (1878-1915); Hugo Freiherr von Habermann (1849-1929) was the best-known representative of Munich Impressionism; Olaf Gulbransson (1873-1958) worked on 'Simplicissimus'; Wassily Kandinsky (1866-1944), Paul Klee (1879-1940), August Macke (1887-1914) and Franz Marc (1880-1916) were members of the 'Blaue Reiter' group.

## ECCLESIASTICAL BUILDINGS

**Franciscan Monastery Church of St. Anna im Lehel** (St.-Anna-Strasse): This church, built by J.M.Fischer and consecrated in 1737, was rebuilt in its original form after the Second World War (there had been modifications in the 19C). The stucco and painting were irretrievably lost but the *ceiling paintings* by C.D.Asam were restored in 1971&2. *Altars* by the Asam brothers and J.B.Straub's *pulpit* survived in part. The traditional architectural distinction between linear and circular design has been abandoned in favour of a mixture of the two forms; a single vault spans the entire interior, with a circular chancel in the W. Directly opposite the Franciscan Church is *St.Anna*, which was built in neo-Romanesque style in 1887-92 by G.von Seidl; his objective was to create a uniform work of art; the church is a good example of the haute bourgeoisie's desire to impress.

**Catholic Church of St.Johann Nepomuk/Asam Church** (Sendlinger Strasse): This church, built in 1733-46, shows how passionately Egid and Cosmas Asam pursued their task of decorating churches. Egid bought three plots of land from his own funds and built the church with his brother, again from their own means. The Asams were concerned to follow through their concept of the arrangement and decoration of a church without being influenced by the wishes of a patron. The building is the last great work of Egid, who here allowed mature baroque to slide into rococo. The *façade*, which breaks through the line of the houses in the busy Sendliger Strasse in an unorthodox fashion, has gigantic pilasters with portrait medallions of the Pope and the Bishop of Freising in their capitals. The gable has large round windows with symbols of the three spiritual virtues above them. There is a statue of St.Nepomuk above the *doorway*, which is a portico with columns. The interior of the church is determined by the modest dimensions of the ground plan (30

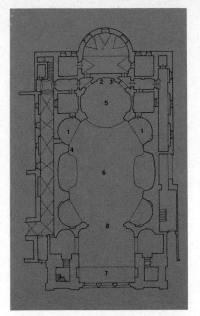

**Munich, Monastery church of St. Anna im Lehel 1** Side altars with paintings by C.D.Asam **2** High altarpiece, K.Manninger's reconstruction, 1975, of painting by C.D.Asam **3** Tabernacle by J.B.Straub, 1737 **4** Pulpit by J.B.Straub **5** High altar fresco, K.Manninger's restoration, 1967, of paintwork by C.D.Asam **6** Large central fresco, restored by K.Manninger, 1972 **7** Organ fresco, restored by K.Manninger, 1976 **8** Wrought iron grille, rococo

by 9.5 yards) and the unusual quality of the light. Shape, colour and light work harmoniously together, as the Asam brothers wished. The walls are covered with red *stucco marble*. The massive *high altar*, framed with 4 twisted columns, is on the narrow side of the church. The lower part of the altar contains the glass *sarcophagus* with the wax figure of St.Nepomuk. On the right and left of the altar are grisaille portrait medallions of the Asam brothers.

**Former Augustinian Monastery Church** (53 Neuhauser Strasse): The core of the building erected in 1291–94 has survived; it was extended in the 14&15C and radically modified in 1618–21, then decon-

secrated and used first as a *toll hall*, later as *police headquarters* and finally as the *Deutsches Jagdmuseum* (hunting museum, q.v.). The most important item of the lost furnishings was the Tintoretto Crucifixion on the high altar, which is now in the Stift Haug in Würzburg (q.v.).

*Bürgersaal* (Neuhauser Strasse): The Bürgersaal has an inconspicuous fa[ce]ade. G.A.Viscardi was responsible for the two storey building which was commissioned by the German Marianist congregation in 1709. Above the baroque doorway is A.Faistenberger's Madonna on the Crescent Moon (under glass). The walls of the lower storey are covered with 15 Stations of the Cross painted in bright colours on wood. In front of the miraculous image is the grave slab of the Jesuit Rupert Mayer (1876–1945), who was well-known as a priest and resistance worker. In the upper storey is the baroque oratory. The 14 views of old Bavarian places of pilgrimage, painted by F.J. Bleich *c.* 1710, are notable. The guardian angel group under the organ gallery is by J.Günther (1762) and the foliate stucco work is by P.F.Appiani.

**Dreifaltigkeitskirche** (Pacellistrasse): The church was built as the result of a vision by Anna Lindmayr, the daughter of an ordinary citizen, in 1704: she was told that Munich would be visited by a great misfortune if a church were not built in honour of the Trinity. The city of Munich financed the building and it was consecrated after a seven year building period in 1718. The plans, a copybook example of Italian baroque, were by G.A.Viscardi. The decoration of the church was by Munich artists. The interior of the church has a central space with 18 pilasters; the *dome fresco* representing the Adoration of the Trinity is an early work of C.D.Asam. The stucco work is by J.G.Bader. The finest of the baroque altars is the *high altar*, for which A.Wolff provided the paintings and J.B.Straub the tabernacle relief (1760).

**Frauenkirche/Metropolitan and Parish Church of Our Lady** (1 Frauenplatz): The Frauenkirche, a late Gothic brick building, has become the emblem of the city of Munich. It is 119 yards long, 44 yards wide and the towers are 325 and 328 ft. high. The red of the bricks and the patina on the onion domes present a striking contrast to each other. The church in its present form was built on the site of earlier 13C buildings in the 15C; the foundation stone was laid in 1468 by Duke Sigismund. The architect was Jörg von Polling, who was replaced after his death in 1488 by L.Rottaler. The building was consecrated in 1494 despite the fact that the towers were incomplete (domes 1524–5). The damage suffered during the Second World War was made good by exemplary restoration work. Since 1821 the Frauenkirche has been the metropolitan church of the ecclesiastical province of S. Bavaria, which includes Augsburg, Passau and Regensburg. The exterior expanse of brick is broken up by very few other features, which makes it particularly impressive, and draws attention to the 5 *doorways*. The gravestones embedded in the exterior walls are from the former cemetery. The *interior* is a hall with 10 bays, a chancel with ambulatory and unusually high side chapels. The nave is separated from the side aisles by 22 octagonal pillars. *Furnishings:* A large proportion of the medieval contents has been lost, stolen or destroyed. The 14–16C *stained-glass windows* in the chancel have survived almost unchanged; the most important is the Scharfzandt window in the middle of the chancel by the Strasbourg master P.Hemmel (1473). The design of the old *choir stalls* by E.Grasser (1492–1503) was used for the new choir stalls. The *tomb of Kaiser Ludwig* in the S. aisle has a special place among the numerous sculptures (see ground plan). The black marble grave was built from a drawing by P.Candid and a design by H.Krumper in 1619–22 over the original tomb built by Duke Albrecht IV c.1480. The figures (by D.Frey and H.Gerhart c.1595) are cast in bronze (putti, allegories and statues of the Wittelsbach King Wilhelm IV, represented as a Knight of the Golden Fleece, and Albrecht V in ducal robes). The red marble slab representing the Emperor on his throne and the reconciliation of Duke Albrecht III with his father after the death of Agnes Bernauer is sometimes

**Munich, Frauenkirche 1** Main doorway **2** Sixtus doorway **3** Benno doorway **4** Arsatius doorway **5** Bride's doorway **6** Sacristy **7** Piuskapelle **8** Chorkapelle **9** Baptismal chapel **10** Main altar **11** Bishop's cathedra **12** Ligsalcz tombstone, 1360 **13** Mariahilf altar, c. 1473 **14** St.Rasso, 15C **15** Large Dom Crucifixion, c. 1450 **16** Grasser figures, 1502 **17** Tombstone of the first Dom priest, 1502 **18** Baptism of Christ, c. 1510 **19** Virgin Mary sheltering supplicants under her cloak, c. 1510 **20** St.Christopher, 1520 **21** Patron saint of bakers, 16C **22** St.George, 16C **23** Assumption, 1620 **24** Ecce Homo picture, 1640 **25** Magi, c. 1650 **26** Monument to Emperor Ludwig the Bavarian, 1622 **27** Tomb of J.M.Fischer (d. 1766) **28** St. Sebastian, 18C **29** Pulpit, 1959

incorrectly ascribed to E.Grasser. The numerous gravestones and memorials include the grave slab of the famous Bavarian architect J.M.Fischer, who built numerous palaces, 32 churches and 23 monasteries.

**Parish Church of the Holy Spirit/Former Hospital Church of the Holy Spirit** (Tal): There was a building on the site of the present church, which was badly damaged in the Second World War, as early as 1208; in 1250 Duke Otto established a hospital here and building of the church itself started in 1327, but was not completed until 1392. In 1723–30 it was rebuilt in the style of the period, and the three W. bays were added in 1885. Little remains of the former lavish furnishings. The present stucco and most of the paintings are restorations. This is also true of the *high altar*, created by N.Stuber and A.Matheo in the years 1728–30. The paintings are by U.Loth (1661) and the two angels were contributed by J.G.Greiff *c*.1730. Further worthwhile features of the furnishings are the *Hammerthal Madonna* from the monastery at Tegernsee (*c*. 1450), the bronze *memorial* for Duke Ferdinand of Bavaria by H.Krumper, the Chapel of the Cross with a *c*.1510 crucifix, now a *war memorial chapel* and paintings in the *side chapels* by M.Steidl, J.H.Schönfeld, J.A.Wolf and P.Horemans.

**St.Jakob** (St.Jakobs-Platz): The new building, by F.Haindl in 1956, replaced the old monastery church, the origins of which can be traced back to 1221.

**Former Carmelite Monastery Church** (Karmelitenstrasse):The Carmelites were called to Munich in 1629 and started to build the monastery and church in 1654; the complex was consecrated in 1660. The plans were by the court architect H.K.Asper and executed by M.Schinagl. In 1802–22 the church was refurbished in neoclassical style by N.Schedel von Greiffenstein, but the typical Carmelite design (groin-vaulted basilica with transepts and an extremely long choir; severies in the side aisles) was retained. The monastery was completely destroyed in an air raid and the church badly damaged. The church is today used as a *library* by the diocesan authorities, whose buildings are on the site of the former monastery.

**Kreuzkirche/All Saints Church at the Cross** (Kreuzstrasse): This impressive brick Gothic building has a 190 ft. tower. The architect was probably J. von Halspach (Polling), who conceived the building as a graveyard church for the parish of St.Peter. The interior was refurbished in 1772 in rococo style. The most important furnishings are a *crucifix* by H.Leinberger (*c*.1520), the *Rotenhamm Madonna* (18C high altar picture) and the tabernacle brought over from the Carmelite Church *c*.1770. The building, badly damaged in the Second World War, now belongs to the Russian Orthodox community.

**Parish Church of St.Ludwig** (Ludwigstrasse): Ludwig I had this church built in 1829–44 as parish and university church for the new district (now the N. part of the town centre). It was built by F.Gärtner, who with his Romantic-Christian style had replaced his rival L. von Klenze in the king's favour. P.Cornelius, a 19C master of monumental painting, was responsible for the paintings in the choir, the crossing and the transept. The picture on the choir wall is 60 by 37 ft. and therefore one of the largest in the world. It represents the Last Judgment and is, in contrast with most other examples of monumental painting, of artistic significance.

**Jesuit Church of St. Michael** (Neuhauser Strasse): The church was built by Duke Wilhelm V, the Pious, in 1583–9 as a spiritual centre of the 16C Catholic renewal movement. When a tower collapsed while the church was being built in 1590 Wilhelm V saw this as a sign from the Archangel to build a larger church, which he then did. The *façade*, which was not restored in its original form until 1972, after being damaged in the Second World War, has a figure of Christ on the gable. Under it the Emperor Otto is portrayed as victor on the field at Lech in 955, and beneath that follows a series of the emperors and dukes who established Christianity in Bavaria, and finally below that Duke Wilhelm V and his father Albrecht between the emperors of their time. There is a bronze statue of St.Michael by H.Gerhart (1592) in a niche between the two doorways. The 85 by 34 ft. interior is dominated by the huge barrel vault with a span of 65.5 ft. The lavish furnishings include 10 altars and about 40 terracotta figures. Striking features are the *angel* by H.Gerhart (1592) on the holy water stoup, the *organ gallery* (with a modern organ (1965, with 4,100 pipes) and also fine *altars* and *paintings* in the semicircular vaulted chapels. The pulpit dates from 1610. The *bronze Crucifixion group* in the S. transept shows the influence of Giovanni da Bologne and Hans Reichle. The *marble memorial* to Eugen Beauharnais (1830) is by B.Thorwaldsen. Under the choir is an accessible *princes' vault* with the graves of 40 Wittelsbachs, including Wilhelm V, Maximilian I, and Ludwig II. The massive high altar (Michael Altar) is the work of W.Dietrich (1589).

**Parish Church of St. Peter** (Marienplatz): St.Peter is the oldest parish church in Munich. A 12C Romanesque building was replaced in 1278–94 by a Gothic building, rebuilt after the fire of 1327 and reconsecrated in 1368. The tower was completed in its present form in 1386 and has become a Munich landmark because of its unusual spire. The pillared basilica is almost 100 yards long. The most important of the furnishings is the *high altar*, designed by N.Stuber in 1730 and restored to his design after the Second World War. At its centre is the wooden figure of the church's patron by E.Grasser (1492). Almost all the

artists working in Munich at the time were involved in designing the furnishings, including E.Q.Asam, J.G.Greiff and A. Faistenberger. There are also late medieval art treasures such as the stone *Schrenk altar* (1407), the *red marble tomb* of U.Aresinger (E.Grasser 1482) and the *5 side panels* of the late Gothic high altar by J.Pollak (1517).

**Salvator Church** (Salvatorstrasse): This church, built in 1494, was originally the cemetery chapel of the Frauenkirche parish, and like the Frauenkirche St.Salvator is built of unclad brick. The exterior is dominated by the massive tower which rises in 6 storeys to a commanding height. The net vaulting is a striking feature; the furnishings are new. Since 1829 the church has been used as a place of worship by the Greek Orthodox congregation.

**Theatinerkirche/Catholic Parish Church of St.Kajetan** (Theatinerstrasse): After the long-awaited birth of the heir to the throne Max Emanuel the Electress Henriette Adelaide had the Theatiner church built as a thanks-offering. The princess, who was of Italian origin, chose A.Barelli of Bologna as architect; he started

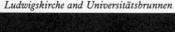

*Ludwigskirche and Universitätsbrunnen*

building in 1663. When Barelli was replaced in 1674 by the Graubünden architect E.Zuccalli the 233 ft. dome was still incomplete. Zuccalli was also responsible for the towers, which were not part of the original design. The façade was still missing and this was added by F.Cuvilliés in 1765–8 in late rococo style. In the niches there are marble figures of St.Ferdinand, St.Adelheid, St.Maximilian and St.Kajetan, by R.A.Bood. The interior of the church is dominated by the massive crossing dome. The most important features of the furnishings, which were badly damaged in the war, are the extravagant *stucco work* by G.Viscardi (to designs by Barelli). They cover the entire area with the exception of the vaulting. The three principal *altars* in the choir and transept are also by Barelli: they harmonise and blend with the stucco decoration to form

a remarkably unified whole. Some of the paintings are notable (see ground plan). The sculpture on the *pulpit* is by A.Faistenberger (1681). Under the high altar is the *royal vault* of the Electors Ferdinand Maria, Max Emanuel, Carl Albrecht, Max III Joseph, Carl Theodor, King Max I, King Otto of Greece and Crown Prince Rupprecht. The adjacent *Theatiner Monastery*, which was badly damaged in the Second World War, has been used by the Dominicans since 1954.

## SCHLOSS BUILDINGS

**Alter Hof** (Burgstrasse): The Wittelsbachs had their court here from 1253 until 1474. The Emperor had granted Bavaria to them as early as 1180, but Duke Ludwig only decided to move his court from Landshut to Munich when the province was divided into Upper and Lower Bavaria in 1253. The Alter Hof (old court; this name was not adopted until the 19C) was built on what was then the W. edge of the town on a small eminence. The building was partially demolished in the 19C and badly damaged in the Second World War but was excellently restored in 1946–66. The SW side is the best preserved. The S. wing has a charming wooden oriel with a spire. The gate tower has been restored to its original height in the course of rebuilding. Today the Alter Hof houses *finance department offices*. The *mint* (q.v.) is adjacent in the N.

**Munich, Theatinerkirche 1** Sacristy **2** Deposition by J.Tintoretto, 16C **3** Altarpiece by A.v.Triva, c. 1600 **4** High altar with picture by Caspar de Crayer, 1646 **5** Pulpit by A.Faistenberger **6** St. Andrew by K.Loth, 1677 **7** St.Cajetan and the Plague in Naples by J.v.Sandrart, 17C **8** Guardian Angel by A.Zanchi, 17C **9** Four virgins altarpiece by P.Liberi, 17C **10** Virgin Mary altar with altarpiece by C.Cignani, 18C **11** King Max II chapel, containing sarcophagi of the king and his wife Maria **12** Altar table

**Residenz** (1 Residenzstrasse, entrance from the Max-Joseph-Platz): The Residenz is bounded by Residenzstrasse, Hofgartenstrasse, Maximilianstrasse and Max-Joseph-Platz. Starting with the *Königsbau* (king's building) in the Max-Joseph-Platz the complex includes (working clockwise) the *Alte Residenz*, the *Festsaal* (banqueting hall) building, *Cuvilliés Theatre*, *Allerheiligenhofkirche* (ruined), *the Residenztheater* and *the Nationaltheater*; the National Theatre's long administrative building extends towards the *Marstallplatz*. The individual buildings are connected by 8 courtyards. The most important is the *Königsbauhof* on the site of the former Residenz garden, and contains G.Petel's

1641 statue of Neptune. The *Grottenhof* (1581–6) is surrounded by arcades and has in its centre the *Perseus fountain*, probably designed by F.Sustris and cast in bronze by H.Gerhart *c.*1590. Then come the *Kapellenhof*, the *Kaiserhof*, the *Apothekenhof* and the *Brunnenhof* (with H.Gerhart's *Wittelsbach fountain*, topped by a figure of Otto von Wittelsbach). Some of the Wittelsbachs were particularly keen on building, and the most important phases of construction took place under them. Work started in 1385 with the so-called *Neuveste* (new fortress). It was intended to replace the Alter Hof (see above), which had been rapidly surounded by the growing city. The Neuveste, which stood in the NE area of the present residence, burned down in 1750 (tower foundations and casemates of the four wings of the moated Burg can be seen in the Apothekenhof). The *Antiquarium*, which has survived, was built under Albrecht V (1550–79), Wilhelm V (1579–97) had the buildings around the *Grottenhof* constructed, Maximilian I (1579–97) built the fine Renaissance *Alte Residenz*, under Max Emanuel II (1679–1726) various buildings were rebuilt in the baroque style, Carl Albrecht (1726–45) was responsible for the *Reiche Zimmer* (rich

rooms) and other additions, Max III Joseph built the *Kurfürstenzimmer* (Electors' rooms) and the *Residenztheater*, Ludwig I (1825–48) had his architect Klenze build the *Königsbau*, the *Festsaal* and the *Allerheiligenhofkirche*, all in the neoclassical style.

**Schloss Nymphenburg** (reached by the N. Auffahrt): The *central pavilion* of the extensive complex was built by the Italian architect A.Barelli from 1664–74 as a summer residence for Henriette Adelaide of Savoy, wife of Elector Ferdinand Maria, after the birth of Max Emanuel, the heir to the throne; the Elector had made his wife a present of the *Schwaige Kemnathen*, the land on which the present Schloss stands. The complex was extended by subsequent Wittelsbachs; Max Emanuel had the central section enlarged by A.Viscardi in 1702: he built square, three-storey pavilions connected to the main building by two-storey linking blocks. The wings added by J.Effner in 1715–16 show French influence. Effner also built the *Pagodenburg* (1716–19), the *Badenburg* (1718–21) and the *Magdalenenklause* (1725–8). Under Elector Albrecht (Emperor Charles VII from 1740) the great rondel surrounded by residential

◁ *Theatinerkirche*                    *Residenz*

*Grotte with Grottenhof in the Munich Residenz; the individual buildings are linked by eight courtyards*

*Brunnenhof with Wittelsbach fountain (Otto von Wittelsbach on the plinth) in the Munich Residenz*

*Spiegelsaal in the Amalienburg, Nymphenburg*

buildings was established on the town side. Carl Albrecht also had the *Amalienburg* built as the last of the so-called Burg buildings in the extensive park for his wife Maria Amalia (1734 – 9), to plans by F.Cuvilliés the Elder). The central section has remained the focal point of the Schloss. The *Festsaal* (ballroom) was refurbished by Cuvilliés with frescos and stucco work by the brothers J.P. and F.Zimmermann (1756–7); the dominant colours are white, gold and green. The adjacent rooms (see ground plan) are also lavishly decorated. The 18C pleasances are a dominant feature of the *park*, which was transformed into a picturesque garden in 1804–23 by the famous landscape gardener F.L. von Sckell in the strictly geometrical French style. The most important of these four buildings (Pagodenburg, Badenburg, Magdaleneklause and Amalienburg) is the Amalienburg. This masterpiece of courtly rococo was the work of J.B.Zimmermann (stucco), J.Dietrich (carving), P.Moretti

(painting) and also the painter G.Desmarées, and P.Hörmannstorffer. In the centre of the Schloss are the *Spiegelsaal* (hall of mirrors) and the various equally magnificent adjoining living, public and bedrooms. See also under Museums for other uses of the various parts of the building.

**Schloss Fürstenried** (Olympiastrasse): J.Effner built this Schloss in 1715–17 as a hunting lodge for Elector Max Emanuel in 1715–17. The cubic central building has smaller pavilions at its side to which it is connected by galleries. The building is built as a so-called 'point de vue' to face the towers of the Frauenkirche.

## SECULAR BUILDINGS

**Alte Akademie** (Neuhauserstrasse): This complex adjacent to St.Michael was originally built in 1585–97 as a *Jesuit College*

**Munich, Schloss Nymphenburg 1** Banqueting hall, stucco and paintings by J.B. and F.Zimmermann **2** First anteroom **3** Second anteroom with Italian table, 17C **4** Bedroom **5** Chinese lacquered cabinet with Coromandel lacquered plates, 17C **6** S.gallery with Bavarian Schloss pictures by F.J.Bleich, N.Stuber and J.Stephan, c. 1750-67 **7** Blue drawing-room **8** Bedroom where King Ludwig II was born **9** King Ludwig II's gallery of beauties **10** Small gallery with still lifes by J.Fyt **11** Maserzimmer, decorations of 1810 **12** Cabinet, painted c. 1770 **13** First antechamber; coffer-work ceiling of 1675 **14** Second antechamber with wall tapestries of 1720 **15** Former bedroom of Max Emanuel **16** Lathe room with lathe of 1712 **17** N.gallery, Schloss views, by F.J.Beich, 1722-23 **18** Gallery of beauties; 5 portraits by P.Gobert, 1710 **19** Coat of arms room **20** Karl Theodor room.

and *Gymnasium* (grammar school) for 1500 pupils, but has been used for various purposes since the suppression of the Order. Until it was destroyed in the Second World War it was the *seat of the Academy* (now in the Residenz). The war damage has since been partially repaired and the fine Renaissance façade completely restored; it now houses the *Land statistics office*. In front of the Alte Akademie is the *Richard Strauss fountain* (1961 by Henselmann), a 20 ft. high bronze column.

**Altes Rathaus** (E. end of the Marienplatz): The present neo-Gothic building

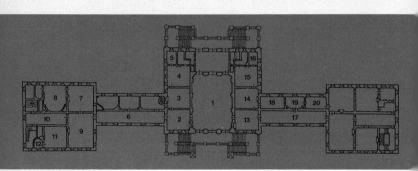

*Schloss Nymphenburg*

with its step gable is a reminder of J.von
Halspach's original building of 1470–80.
The 180 ft. Rathaus tower was rebuilt after the Second World War. The *council
chamber*, for which E.Grasser created the
*morris dance* sequence in 1470, is a masterpiece of medieval design; Grasser's sculptures are now in the Stadtmuseum (q.v.).
The room has wooden barrel vaulting and
a frieze of 99 coats of arms and medallions
on the walls. The Neues Rathaus (q.v.) was
built in the Marienplatz from 1867.

**Bavaria and Ruhmeshalle** (Theresien-
höhe): The figure of Bavaria is one of the
symbols of the city of Munich. It was cast
in bronze by F.Miller to a model by
Schwantaler in 1844–50 and unveiled during a public festival in 1850. The 60 ft.
high figure is 98 ft. high including its base.
Inside 130 steps lead to the eyes of the
statue, from which point there is a view of
a large part of the city. Behind the figure
of Bavaria (which has a lion at its side) is
the *Ruhmeshalle* (Hall of Fame) erected in
1853 by L.von Klenze for Ludwig I; it is
a Bavarian version of the Walhalla in
Regensburg (q.v.).

**Archbishop's Palace** (8 Kardinal-von-

*Altes Rathaus*

*Bavaria statue and Ruhmeshalle*

Faulhaber-Strasse): F.Cuvilliés built this rococo palace in 1733–7, following the scheme often used by J.Effner (see Nymphenburg): 9 windows in each of three storeys with the windows in the two upper storeys enclosed by pilasters. The palace is today the seat of the Archbishop of Munich and Freising. The nearby *Palais Porcia* (10 Kardinal-von Faulhaber-Strasse) was built as early as 1693 by E.Zuccalli but altered by Cuvilliés in the first third of the 18C, and was a pattern for many other town houses of the nobility in Munich.

**Feldherrenhalle** (Odeonsplatz): The Siegestor (q.v.) in the N. and the Feldherrenhalle in the S. begin and end the Ludwigstrasse, which Ludwig I had built as a show street in 1816–50. It was built on the pattern of the Loggia dei Lanzi in Florence. The Halle was built in 1840–44 by F. von Gärtner. The statues represent the Bavarian Generals Tilly (1559–1632) and Wrede (1767–1838), and are both by L. von Schwanthaler. The army memorial (centre) is in honour of the dead of the Franco-Prussian War.

**Television tower** (Olympic site): The television tower (officially Olympic Tower) was built in 1965–8; it is 950 ft. high and one of the tallest steel concrete constructions in the world. There is a viewing platform reached by lift at a height of 650 ft; the roof restaurant turns on its axis once per hour.

**Friedensengel** (Luitpoldbrücke/ Prinzregentenstrasse): The 59 ft. monument with Friedensengel (angel of peace) with palm branch and globe was built by the city of Munich in 1895 in honour of the Treaty of Versailles and the following '25 years of peace'. The copy of the Olympian Nike is by M.Heilmaier, H.Düll and G.Pezold (restored 1982–3).

**Isartorplatz:** The Isartor, one of the former town gates, has survived (restored in 1972). It was once the E. gate within the ring wall built by Ludwig the Bavarian in 1815. On the E. side is a fresco of Emperor Ludwig the Bavarian on his victorious return from the battle of Ampfing in 1322 (by B.Neher, 1835). In the S. tower is the *Valentin'Musäum'* (see Museums).

**Künstlerhaus** (Lenbachplatz): G von Seidl built the ballroom in 1896–1900 in the style of a Florentine palazzo. It was

*Maximilianeum*

decorated by the painter Franz von Lenbach. The building was faithfully restored after the Second World War.

**Maximilianeum** (an der Maximilianbrücke): The Maximilianeum was built in 1857 – 74 to complete the Maximilianstrasse, which was conceived as a show street. The building stands just beyond the Maximilian bridge, built by F.Thiersch in 1903–5 with a span of 151 ft. Various designs were submitted for the Maximilianeum, and the one finally executed was by G.Semper, whose major contribution was the terracotta façade. The building was originally intended to be a picture gallery and educational establishment for the nobility ('Pagerie'). The latter idea is retained in the *Maximilianeum Scholarship* for especially gifted pupils. The building is now used by the *Bavarian Parliament* (Plenarsaal) and the *Senate* (Senatssaal). Left and right of the building are the *Maximilian gardens* and N. a memorial to *King Ludwig II* by T.Rückel (1967); the King had wanted to build a Richard Wagner Opera House on this site.

**Münze (Mint)** (Hofgraben): The building, which goes back to 1465, has been much altered and used for various purposes. First a mews building, it was then used as a *picture gallery* after the rebuilding of its upper storey in 1563–7. The W. façade was restored in the neoclassical style in the early 19C (further alterations in the mid 19C). The fine three-storey 16C *arched courtyard*, which was used as a tilt-yard, is notable.

**Olympic park and stadium** (Oberwiesenfeld): The facilities for the XX Summer Olympics in 1972 have in many ways set the pattern for such events: they not only concentrated the Games in the smallest possible area but also took modern technical and scientific requirements into account, and the work of the architects involved set new standards for sports buildings. The core of the site is the *Olympic Stadium*, designed by Behnisch and Partners. The stadium, the sports hall and the swimming pool are all accommodated under 81,802 square yards of tent roof. The roof is set on supports up to 262 ft. high and consists of 29 in. mesh steel net covered with translucent acrylic panels.

**Preysing-Palais** (27 Residenzstrasse): This former town house of a noble family

*Olympic park with TV tower*

(1723–8) was built in rococo style and is one of the most important buildings of its kind in Munich.

**Propyläen** (W. side of the Königsplatz): The Acropolis in Athens did not only supply a name to court architect L. von Klenze, but also the shape of his building; Klenze was also responsible for the layout of the *Königsplatz*, including the Glyptothek and the State Collection of Antiquities (see museums). The Propyläen (1848–62) have gate towers on either side and the central building has halls with Doric columns in front and behind. The sculptures and reliefs, dedicated to the Greek struggle for freedom against Turkey, are intended as a memorial to the Greek King Otto (1832–62); he was the son of Ludwig I who gave the Greeks the national colours blue and white (the reverse of the Bavarian white and blue).

**Rathaus** (Marienplatz): The historicist architect G.Hauberisser responded to his patrons' desire for magnificence and show by erecting this massive building. The Town Hall was built in three major stages: 1867 –74 (the E. brick building), 1888–93, and 1899–1908 (partially in limestone). The

characteristic feature is the 279 ft. tower on the W. building. The statues of Bavarian dukes and electors on the main façade have not all survived. Every day at 11 a.m., and in the summer also at 5 p.m., the *Glockenspiel* in the tower plays, revealing a procession of brightly-painted figures (5 ft. high) representing Duke Wilhelm V on the occasion of his marriage to Renate von Lothringen. In the lower part the *Schäfflertanz* (coopers' dance) is shown: this dance, first mentioned in 1463, was performed every seven years at carnival time by members of the guild.

**Siegestor** (Ludwigstrasse): This victory arch at the S. end of the Ludwigstrasse balances the Feldherrenhalle (q.v.) in the N. It is built on the pattern of the Arch of Constantine in Rome; designed by F. von Gärtner, it was built in 1843–52 in honour of the achievements of the Bavarian army in the Wars of Liberation in 1813– 15.

**University** (1 Geschwister-Scholl-Platz): The extensive building was commissioned from F. von Gärtner by Ludwig I in 1835–40; it was intended to accommodate 1500 students, and was soon in need of ex-

*Propylaea*

tension. The university was founded in 1472 in Ingolstadt (q.v.) and came to Munich via Landshut (q.v.) in 1826. The Ludwig-Maximilian-University now has more than 26,000 students and is the largest higher educational establishment in the Federal Republic. The *Georgianum*, a seminary for Catholic priests, was built opposite the university to plans by F. von Gärtner in 1834–42.

## PARKS

**Englischer Garten and Hirschau** (access to S. end from Prinzregentenstrasse): The Count of Rumford and the landscape gardener F.L.Sckell planned and laid out the English garden in 1789–95. It was first called *Theodor's park* and acquired its present name later. It is today just over 3 miles long, about one and a quarter miles wide and covers an area of over 229,000 square yards. In the N. it borders the *Hirschau*, which today is considered as part of the English Garden. In the park are the *Chinese Tower* (1789–90), the *Chineses Inn* (1789–90) and a series of monuments, including one to Rumford, near the Lerchenfeldsrasse and the *Monopteros* for Elector Carl Theodor, 1833.

**Hofgarten** (Hofgartenstrasse): N. of the Residenz is the Hofgarten, laid out in 1613–17 by Duke Maximilian I. The entrance is the *Hofgartentor*, erected by L. von Klenze in 1816. The *arcades* in the W. and S. of the garden are 637 yards long and have 123 arches on the garden side and date from the same period as the park. A storey was added to the N. building in 1779 to accommodate a picture gallery. Ludwig I's plan to have pictures of Athens, Delphi, Olympia and other Greek towns and islands in the N. walk was not realised until 1963, by Seewald. The sequence of classical landscapes painted by K.Rottmann in 1830–4 is now in the Residenzmuseum (q.v.). On the E. side of the Hofgarten is the *Bavarian Army Museum* (1900–5), which was almost entirely destroyed in the Second World War. The arms collection is now in the Army Museum in Ingolstadt (q.v.).

**Old Botanical Garden** (Lenbachplatz): This open space was created by L. von Sckell, who was responsible for the English Garden (q.v.) and Schloss Nymphenburg (q.v.), but its original character has been almost entirely lost. The garden was redesigned in 1935–7 as the Stadtpark,

*Rathaus*

*Glockenspiel, Rathaus*

reached from the Karlsplatz through a neoclassical portal with Doric columns (E.J.d'Herigoyen 1812). The N. border of the garden is the Sophienstrasse, in which there are various natural science departments of the university.

## MUSEUMS

Munich has so many museums of national and international importance that it is outside the scope of this guide to give more than a brief survey of their contents; readers are referred to the guides to the individual museums.

**Alte Pinakothek** (M.40, 27 Barerstrasse): Built in 1826–30 by L. von Klenze, rebuilt 1952–7; very important collection of 14–18C European painting, especially 15&16C German and Dutch, 17C Flemish and 15–18C Italian works.

*Anthropologische Staatssammlung* (M.2, Karolineneplatz): Anthropological exhibits from Bavarian settlements. *Architektursammlung der Technischen Universität* (M.2, 21 Arcisstrasse): 19&20C Munich architects. *Aussiger Heimatstube* (M.22, 4/III Liebherrstrasse): Bohemian local history. *Bayrische Staatssammlung für allgemeine und angewandte Geologie* (M2, 37 Luisenstrasse): General and applied geology. *Bayrische Staatssammlung für Paläontologie und historische Geologie* (M2, 10 Richard-Wagner-Strasse): Palaeontology and historial geology. *BMW-Galerie and Museum* (M.40, 130 Peutelring): modern painting (gallery), development and history of engines (museum).

**Bayrisches Nationalmuseum** (M.22, 3 Prinzregentenstrasse): European (particularly S. German) art and crafts from the Middle Ages to *c.*1900 (sculptures by Riemenschneider, Leinberger, Asam, Günther and Straub), paintings and sketches, popular art, cradles, historic interiors, town models, European faience and porcelain, scientific instruments, goldsmiths' work, miniatures, musical instruments.)

**Deutsches Jagdmuseum** (M.2,53 Neuhauserstrasse): Exhibition of hunting equipment, trophies, and works of art with a hunting theme.

*Deutsches Museum* (M.22, 1 Museumsinsel): The 'German Museum of Masterpieces of Science and Technology' was

*Deutsches Museum, aviation department*

founded by Oskar von Miller in 1913. The S. section was Munich's first ferroconcrete building; it was started in 1906–25 by G. and E. von Seidl, extended in 1913, 1928 –32 and 1935, rebuilt after the war in 1958 and extended in 1972. The hall (1928–35) is used as a *concert hall*. The building also contains a *library* and restaurant, and extremely extensive collections on physics, technology, astronomy and the history of music. It has *33 departments* and is one of the largest museums of its kind in the world.

**Deutsches Theatermuseum** (M.22, 4a and 6 Galeriestrasse): History of the theatre.

**Glyptothek** (M.2, 3 Königsplatz): Greek and Roman sculpture.

**Marstallmuseum** (M.19, Schloss Nymphenburg): History of the Electors' horses and stables.

*Mineralogische Staatssammlung* (M.2, 41 Theresienstrasse): Minerals from all over the world. *Münchener Feuerwehrmuseum* (M.2, 34 Blumenstrasse): History of the Munich fire service.

**Münchner Stadtmuseum** (M.2, 1 Jakobsplatz): History of Munich and its culture: arts and crafts, domestic history, costume, musical instruments, film and photography, exhibits from buildings in old Munich (e.g. 1480 Morris Dancers by E.Grasser from the Altes Rathaus).

**Museum Villa Stuck** (M.80, 60 Prinzregentenstrasse): Painting and sculpture by F.Stuck and turn of the century furniture.

**Neue Pinakothek** (M.40, 29 Barerstrasse): Rebuilt 1975–81 by Alexander Freiherr von Branca; 18–20C European painting and sculpture, particularly German Romantics, English painting, Munich School, Impressionists).

*Neue Sammlung - Staatliches Museum für Angewandte Kunst* (M.22, 3 Prinzregentenstrasse): Museum of applied art: implements of cultural and historical importance from the late 19C to the present day. *Prähistorische Staatssammlung - Museum für Vor- unf Frühgeschichte* (M.22, 2 Lerchenfeldstrasse): From the Old Stone Age to the Middle Ages in the Mediterranean area. *Residenzmuseum* (M.22, 3 Max-Joseph-Platz): see Residenz. *Schackgalerie* (M.22,

*State coach of Carl Albrecht, Marstallmuseum*

*Riemenschneider figure, Nationalmuseum*

*Lola Montez, Nymphenburg*

9 Prinzregentenstrasse): Graf Scháck's private collection of paintings by his contemporaries (Spitzweg to Marées and Lenbach). *Siemens-Museum* (M.2, 10 Prannerstrasse): History of the development of electrical technology at Siemens from 1847. *Staatliche Antikensammlung* (M.2, 1 Königsplatz; see p.167): Greek, Etruscan and Roman vases, terracotta, glasses, bronzes and jewellery. *Staatliche Graphische Sammlung* (M.2, 10 Meiserstrasse): European drawings and prints from the 14–20C. *Staatliche Münzensammlung* (M.2, 1 Residenzstrasse): History of coins and money. *Staatliche Sammlung Ägyptischer Kunst* (M.2, in the Residenz, Hofgartenstrasse): Ancient Egyptian art. *Staatliches Museum für Völkerkunde* (M.22, 42 Maximilianstrasse): Artistic and general exhibits from outside Europe (especially India, Africa and South America). *Staatsgalerie moderner Kunst/Haus der Kunst* (M.22, 1 Prinzregentenstrasse): International 20C painting and sculpture. *Städ-*

*tische Galerie im Lenbachhaus* (M.12, 33 Luisenstrasse): Built 1887–97 by G. von Seidl, extended 1927, rebuilt after war damage in 1958; 15–20C Munich painting, especially Kandinsky, Marc, Mache and Lenbach. *Valentin-Musäum* (In the S. Isartor tower, M.2, 43 Tàl): Curiosities and exhibits on the Munich folk artist and humorist. *Zoologische Staatssammlung* (M.19, Schloss Nymphenburg): Zoology.

## THEATRES

Munich has so many theatres offering such a wide range of presentations that it is impossible to mention them all here; the most important are:

**Altes Residenztheater/Cuvilliés-theater** (see Residenz): Operas, plays and concerts in a rococo setting.

**Deutsches Theater** (13 Schwanthaler-

*Crown of Emperor Heinrich II, Residenzmuseum*

strasse): Performances by various companies; touring performances; musicals; reopened in 1983.

**Gärtnerplatztheater** (3 Gärtnerplatz): Built 1864–5, restored after the war in 1948 and 1968; operetta, opera, ballet and musicals.

**Kammerspiele im Schauspielhaus:** Main auditorium (Maximilianstrasse, 730 seats) and workshop (1 Hildegardstrasse, 299 seats).

**Kleine Komödie** Company with two theatres: by the Max II memorial, 47 Maximilianstrasse (556 seats) and in the Bayrische Hof, 6 Promenadeplatz (574 seats).

**Marionettentheater** (M.2, 29a Blumenstrasse): Built by T.Fischer in 1900 in neoclassical style with portico; the only custom-built marionette theatre in the world.

**Nationaltheater** (M.2, Max-Joseph-Platz): The home of the Bavarian State Opera and ballet, one of the world's most important opera houses.

**Residenztheater/Neues Residenztheater** (M.22, Max-Joseph-Platz): Home of the Bavarian State Theatre.

## IMPORTANT BUILDINGS IN THE SUBURBS

AU:**Parish Church of Mariahilf** (Mariahilfplatz): This was built by J.D.Ohlmüller in 1832–9 after winning a competition organised by the King against distinguished opponents such as Klenze and Gärtner. The unclad brick building in neo-Gothic style shows the beginnings of Romanticism in church architecture. The damage sustained in the Second World War has been repaired, but the interior furnishings were lost.

*Nationaltheater*

*St. Michael, Berg am Laim*

**BERG AM LAIM: Former Court Church/Parish Church of St. Michael:** The church was built in 1737–52 for Clemens August, Archbishop of Cologne, as the court church for the nearby Landschloss. The architect was J.M.Fischer, who successfully synthesised the central part of the building and the nave. J.B.Zimmermann was responsible for the stucco and ceiling painting, the high altar and the 6 side altars are from J.R.Straub's studio and the pulpit is by B.Hässer.

**RAMERSDORF: Parish and Pilgrimage Church Mariae Himmelfahrt:** The present church dates from the first half of the 15C, but its predecessor, mentioned as early as the 11C, was already a place of pilgrimage in the 14C. The decoration was renewed in 1675 and is now baroque. The most striking feature of the

*St. Michael, Berg am Laim* ▷

*Pilgrimage church Mariae Himmelfahrt, Ramersdorf*

interior is the *altarpiece*, endowed in 1483, with a Crucifixion relief by E.Grasser.

BLUTENBURG: **Former ducal hunting lodge:** An older building was developed in the 15C by Dukes Albrecht III and Sigismund. The dilapidated Schloss was renovated in 1667 and the garden laid out. This typical late medieval house is famous for the *Schloss Chapel of St.Sigismund*. The wall paintings with figures and the unified decoration and furnishings from the period when the Schloss was built are very fine indeed; the high and side altars are lavishly painted. The 'Blutenburg Apostles' are a famous cycle of carvings by an unknown Munich master. There is an international *library of childrens' books* in the Blutenburg, and there are *concerts* in the summer.

**Also worth seeing: Bogenhausen:** Old Parish Church of St.Georg and cemetery; **Harlaching:** Pilgrimage Church of St.

Anne; **Oberföhring:** Catholic Parish Church of St.Laurentius.

---

**Münster 4400**
Nordrhein-Westfalen                    p.414 □ D 9

---

The very name of this old cathedral town, sometimes called 'the Rome of the Münsterland', indicates its close connection with the church (Münster = minster). The history of the town can be traced back to the 3C, but it began to grow rapidly when Münster became a bishopric in 804‒5. Soon after this the bishops of Münster also took on princely duties and thus further extended their influence. In the Middle Ages Münster joined the Hanseatic league and enjoyed great prosperity, but the town was taken over in 1534‒5 by the Anabaptists after a period of murder and terror. The uprising was defeated, but the town lost its civic freedoms and prosperity for a time. In 1648 the Treaty between the Spanish and the Dutch and the Peace of Westfalia were signed here.

**Dom St.Paul** (Domplatz): The W. choir of a cathedral consecrated by Bishop Erpho in 1090 was the basis of the present building, which is one of the finest pieces of architecture in Germany; the Erpho cathedral was extended under Bishop Hermann II in the late 12C; a new building in the 13C took over the ground plan and foundations, and later extension and the restoration which took place after the Second World War have remained faithful to the building's origins and retained its overall unity.

*The buildings:* The building is 328 ft. long and dominated by its twin towers, which are unadorned to the height of the nave; this plainness is continued in the W. façade, broken only by 16 circular windows; in front of the S. part of the W. building is a paradise. The façade of the massive Romano-Gothic building is decorated with a series of figures.

*Interior and furnishings:* The building is entered through the old W. choir, which has arcades on both sides. The most highly

esteemed of the ornate interior furnishings are the 10 *Apostle figures* in the paradise. They are considered to be 'the most lavish and impressive cycle of medieval figures in Westphalia'. A tendril frieze at the Apostles' feet shows musicians, scenes of hunting, wine growing, grape harvesting, animal life and fables. The cathedral also contains many altars, statues (particularly on the Stephanus altar), tombs and memorials. The *marble memorial* for Prince Bishop C. von Galen (d.1678) and that of Prince Bishop F.Ch. von Plettenberg (d.1716) are particularly worthy of mention; both were the work of members of the famous Gröninger family of sculptors. In the ambulatory is the 1542 *astronomical clock*, a sign of the Prince Bishops' interest in scientific matters. The *cathedral treasure* is now housed in a new building in the N. walk of the cloister; the most precious piece is the reliquary bust of St.Paul; the embossed gold bust has a wooden core, is 9 in. high and entirely covered in coloured stones, pearls and filigree work. Other figures from the cathedral and former diocesan museum are in the *lapidarium* in the N. walk of the cloister. The most important work here is the *Entry of Christ into Jerusalem*. This group of

*Münster, panorama with Dom St.Paul*

figures is by H.Brabender (1545), one of the best late Gothic sculptors. The wall panelling in the *chapterhouse* was designed by Ludger tom Ring the Elder (completed 1558).

**Catholic Parish Church of St. Ägidien** (Ägidii-strasse): J.K.Schlaun kept strictly to the precepts of the Capuchin Order, which demanded among other things that there should be no tower or decoration. The central feature of the lavish furnishings is the *baroque pulpit* with its life-size figures of Christ and St. Franzikus receiving the rules of the Order, an important work by J.W. Gröninger *c.* 1720. The octagonal *font* dates from 1557 and is by A.Reining. The *side altars* have paintings by E. Steinle (from 1859), who was also responsible for the wall paintings.

**Catholic Church of St. Clemens** (Clemensstrasse): This was built in 1745 –53 by J.K.Schlaun for the Elector Clemens August as a hospital church for the Brothers of Mercy in Münster. The dominant feature of the church is a circular central space with a dome and several niches (for altars, confessionals and the entrance). The painting on the dome glorifying St. Clemens as patron of the church is a powerful element of the lavish decoration; it was painted by J.A.Schöpf in 1750 and a copy repainted after the Second World War.

**Catholic Parish Church of St. Lamberti** (Prinzipalmarkt): The present church on the site of earlier 12&13C buildings dates from 1375–1450; the W. tower was built in 1887–92; restoration after the Second World War was completed in 1960.

**Münster, Dom 1** W.choir (old choir) **2** Baptism chapel **3** Cathedral treasure **4** Paradise **5** Johanneschor **6** Stephanuschor **7** Maximuskapelle **8** Liudgeruskapelle **9]f1] Josefskapelle 10** Kreuzkapelle **11** Sakramentskapelle **12** Chapterhouse **13** Sacristy **14** Marienkapelle chapel **15** Cloister **16** Astronomical clock, 1542 **17** High altar a) Old high altar, 1622 b) New high altar, 1956, with Apostle figures, c. 1330 **18** Candelabrum angel by J.Brabender, c. 1560 **19** Monument to Heidenreich v.Letmathe, Dean of the Dom (d. 1625), by G.Gröninger **20** Monument to Prince Bishop Bernhard v.Galen by J.M.Gröninger, 1678 **21** Monument to Prince Bishop Friedrich Christian v.Plettenberg (d. 1706) by J.M.Gröninger **22** Monument to Ferdinand v.Plettenberg by J.W.Gröninger, c. 1712 **23** Tomb of the 'Lion of Münster', Clemens August Cardinal v.Galen

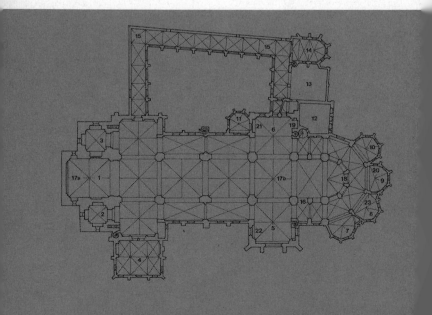

St.Lamberti is not only the largest parish church in the town, but also one of the most important late Gothic churches in Westphalia. The portals are striking features of the lavishly decorated exterior; there is a monumental relief of the Tree of Jesse over the main entrance. Much of the interior decoration was lost, but the stone figures of the Apostles by J.Kroess (*c*.1600) in the choir are worthy of mention, and there are 17C stone figures of 4 Church fathers in the so-called old choir. The *cages* hanging on the S. side of the tower were used in 1536 as prisons for the Anabaptists. The church was restored inside and out in 1976–7.

**Catholic Parish Church of Liebfrauen-Überwasser** (Überwasser Kirchplatz): The present hall church was built from 1340–6 on the site of older buildings; the tower was not built until the early 15C. The *Madonna and Apostles* cycle of figures (1363–74), removed by the Anabaptists and not found until 1898 in the course of excavations, is in the Landesmuseum für Kunst- und Kulturgeschichte (q.v.). The baroque *altar picture* is by M.Kappers (1763) and the *alabaster font* by W.Gröninger (*c*.1720); the two large vo-

*Stephanusaltar in the Dom in Münster*

*The Apostle figures in the Paradise, Dom in Münster*

tive tablets of the Ludger and Hermann tom Ring families are by tom Ring (1548 and 1592 respectively); two of the four memorials, for the Kerkerink brothers and Bernhard Hausmann, 1618 and 1626 respectively, are assumed to be by G.Gröninger.

**Other churches worth seeing:** *Protestant Apostle Church* (Neubrückenstrasse): 13C, 16&17C, with vault paintings. *Former Dominican Church of St. Joseph* (Salzstrasse): The new building of 1705–25 was restored after the Second World War; it has a carved baroque altar by H.Gröne (1699). *Catholic Parish Church of St.Ludgeri* (Marienplatz): The church was built from 1180 as the first Münsterland hall church of the so-called step hall type. *Catholic Parish Church of St.Martini* (Neubrückenstrasse): The treasury contains the

**Münster, St.Lamberti 1** Old choir **2** Main entrance with relief of Tree of Jesse, mid 15C **3** Crucifixion group in stone casing, later than 1536 **4** Apostle figures by J.Kroess, c. 1600 **5** Expositorium by F.J.Diemig, 1782

14C chapter cross, 2 ft. high with representations of the patron saint of the church. *Catholic Parish Church of St.Mauritz* (between the Hohenzollernring and the Warendorferstrasse): Little remains of the original 11C building. The nave, a basilica, was built in 1859–61 by E. von Manger (Oelde).

**Rathaus** (Prinzipalmarkt): This gabled building dates from the 14C and is one of the most important secular Gothic buildings in Germany. On the ground floor is the *Friedenssaal*, in which the Thirty Years War was ended by the signing of the so-called 'Peace of Westphalia'; decoration and furnishings are as they were in 1577. On the walls are portraits of the envoys who signed the peace treaty. The massive chandelier dates from 1577, and the Madonna with which it is decorated from 1520.

**Prinzipalmarkt:** Next to the Town Hall in the Prinzipalmarkt is the gabled *Stadtweinhaus* (1615 by J. von Bocholt).The market place was laid out in 1150 and has been the centre of town life ever since.

**Krameramtshaus** (7 Alter Steinweg): The 1589 brick grocers' company building is the only guild establishment which has survived in Münster. It became the town library after the repair of war damage in 1951.

**Erbdrostenhof** (Salzstrasse): This is the finest house of a member of the nobility in Münster and is also a work of J.K.Schlaun (1757). War damage has been repaired.

**Former Schloss Residence of the Prince Bishops** (Schlossplatz): Building started in 1767 on the Schloss commissioned by Prince Bishop Maximilian Friedrich von Königsegg-Rothenfels, and it was completed almost exactly twenty years later. It was destroyed by fire in 1945, but the exterior has been faithfully restored; the interior was redesigned for use by the university. This important example

*Rathaus* ▷

of late N. German baroque was designed by J.K.Schlaun.

**Museums:** The *Landesmuseum für Kunst und Geschichte* (10 Domplatz) shows medieval and modern sculpture and painting, exhibits on the history of the town and the Land, and religious art. *Landesmuseum für Vor- und Frühgeschichte* (30 Rothenburg): Pre- and early history of Westphalia from the Old Stone Age to the Middle Ages. *Dom treasury* (32 Domplatz): see Dom. *Mühlenhof Open Air Musuem* (via Sentruper Strasse): Farm buildings and an extremely interesting windmill.

**Theatre:** *Städtische Bühnen* (63 Neubrückenstrasse): The theatre was built in 1954–6 by H.Deilmann, M. von Hausen and P.O.Rave and is considered to be an exemplary piece of modern theatre architecture; a fragment of the Romberg Hof has been retained in the inner courtyard. The municipal theatre company performs opera, operetta and straight drama. There is a studio theatre, the *Kleines Haus*, with a maximum of 321 seats, as well as the *Grosses Haus* with 955 seats. The *Wolfgang-Borchert-Theater* (in the Hauptbahnhof) performs modern drama.

## Münstermaifeld 5401
Rheinland-Pfalz             p.416□C 13

**Former Collegiate Church of St. Martin and Severus** (Kirchplatz): This church, largely complete by 1322, is fortress-like in character. The square building in the centre of the W. section has two high round towers. The wall paintings in the side aisles are 13–16C, and the large Antwerp Gold Altar is 16C. The sculptures on the S. portal are notable (14C eucharistic dove, early-14C Madonna with rose).

## Münzenberg 6309
Hessen             p.416□F 13

The history and position of the town are influenced by the powerful fortress of Münzenberg, which survives as a ruin and has become a symbol of the Wetterau region.

**Protestant Parish Church:** This late Romanesque church was extended in the 13C and has remained largely unaltered

*Rathaus, Friedenssaal*

ever since. The core of the building is the massive choir tower with its wooden spire and finely-shaped Gothic windows. The lavish *furnishings* include fine carving on the organ gallery and noblemen's pews (predominantly 17C, also 18C), the ciborium altar in the NE corner of the aisle (mid-13C), the larger-than-life-size crucifix over the choir altar (14C), the sacrament niche (15C) and the tombs of J.D. von Bellersheim (1601).

**Burg Münzenberg:** Along with the Wartburg this is one of the most important medieval sites in Germany. It is part of the system of palatinate, imperial and ministerial castles which were to be found throughout medieval Germany, and from which the country was ruled. The Münzenburg dates from the time of Emperor Barbarossa (1170–80). It was built by Kuno von Münzenberg, a trusty vassal of the Hohenstaufen family, and based on the imperial palatinate in Gelnhausen (q.v.) and the Saalhof chapel in Frankfurt (q.v.). The Burg has only survived as a ruin, but the original layout is clearly distinguishable; the two high round towers at either end of the site are a striking feature. The individual parts of the Burg are: the *Falkenstein Building* (13C, excellent Gothic windows), remains of the *kitchen building* (with recognisable fireplace), *residence* with a splendid main wall and a *chapel* above the entrance gate.

**Also worth seeing:** The 16C Rathaus (Marktplatz).

**Environs: Arnsburg** (6 km. N.): *Ruins of the former Cistercian Monastery*, building began *c*.1197, consecrated 1246. Impressive ruins of church and cloister. The buildings are now the Schloss of the Counts of Solms-Laubach.

---

**Murnau 8110**
Bavaria                                   p.422☐K 21

**Parish Church of St. Nikolaus:** St. Nikolaus was built in 1717–27 on the site of a 12C daughter foundation of the church at Staffelsee; the tower was completed in 1732. The architect is unknown, though J.M.Fischer was for a long time thought to have been responsible for the building. The interior is based on an octagon extended to form a square by the addition of

*Residenzschloss of the Prince Bishops*

triangular sections. The powerful *vault fresco* in the dome was astonishingly not painted at the time of building but is a 19C addition. The *stucco* completes the general picture adequately. The *high altar* has excellent sculpture (ascribed to E.Verhelst, *c*.1725–30). The altar itself was transferred from the monastery at Ettal, where it was erected in 1730. It was brought to Murnau in 1771 and modified to look as it does today by B.Zwinde. The *side altars, pulpit* (*c*.1750–60) and *pews* are notable.

**Also worth seeing:** *Church of Mariahilf* (consecrated 1734); numerous village churches in the surrounding area, particularly Froschhausen and Seehausen); the *Oberbayrisches Bauernhofmuseum* near Grossweil; a farmhouse museum.

---

## Murrhardt
Baden-Württemberg                     p.420☐G 17

This little town in the valley of the Murr goes back to a settlement founded in the 7–8C on the site of a former Roman fortress. A Benedictine abbey, said to have been founded by Emperor Ludwig the Pious, and built by Eremites and the first abbot Walterich, is mentioned with the town in 873. Murrhardt was granted its charter and built its town walls in the 14C; it became part of Württemberg in 1392 and was reformed in 1552.

**Protestant Parish Church/Walterich Chapel:** The former abbey church of St. Maria and St.Januarius, a Carolingian basilica with two choirs, transepts and crossing towers was much extended in the 11–13C and modified in 1435–40 into the present late Gothic vaulted basilica. Notable features of the plain interior are two former *altar panels* (1496) and a Swabian *altar crucifix* (*c*.1460). The lower parts of the two E. towers were untouched by Gothic reconstruction, as was the *Walterich Chapel* by the N. tower. This cubic sandstone annexe building with a rhomboid roof is a gem of the late Romanesque period, largely because of the exterior decoration. The figures and ornaments on the W. portal, the apse window and the arch frieze show upper Rhenish influence. The original of the *Last Judgement tympanum* on the W. portal in green sandstone is now in the museum (q.v.). In the rib-vaulted interior is a plain cenotaph for Ludwig the Pious. The domestic buildings (1551) the abbot's residence (1770) and the high Gothic refectory survive of the *abbey buildings*.

**Protestant Walterich Church** (Friedhof): The present church with its Gothic choir tower and late Gothic nave is built on the site of earlier medieval buildings. In 1963 excavations revealed Roman remains from the earlier Walterich tomb (9C) and also parts of the *ornamentation* of the earlier churches; these are now built into the walls and include a *tympanum with the Lamb of God*. There is also a wooden *Mount of Olives c*.1530 on the exterior of the building.

**Carl-Schweizer-Museum** (Am Klostersee): Pre- and early history, local history, Roman and medieval archaeological finds, originals of ornaments and sculptures which have been replaced with copies in the Murrhardt churches.

**Also worth seeing:** *Half-timbered houses,*

*Collegiate church, Münstermaifeld*

the *Rathaus* (1770) and the *market fountain* with its 16C statue of Duke Christoph. Parts of the old *town walls* (*c.*1300) have survived at the 15C *Hexenturm*. Remains of the *Roman fortress* (Riesberg Strasse) are a sign of the town's proximity to the Raetian limes (1.2 km. E.).

**Environs: Oppenweiler** (11 km. W.): The octagonal *Schloss* of the Freiherren von Sturmfeder was built in 1770–8 on the site of a former moated Burg. The *park* was laid out by F.L. von Sckell (see Munich, Schwetzingen) in the English landscape style.

## Nassau 5408
Rheinland-Pfalz        p.416☐D 13

**Schloss of the Freiherren von Stein:**
The Freiherren von Stein, vassals of the
Counts of Nassau from the 12C, in 1621
extended a medieval house into a plain late
Renaissance building with a square staircase tower; the addition of side wings in
1755 formed the main courtyard. The
Schloss was the birthplace in 1757 of
Reichsfreiherr H.F.K. vom and zum Stein,
the Prussian minister and reformer. In
1814 he had the building now known as the
*Schinkelturm* inserted between the central
and S. buildings. Schinkel's neo-Gothic
tower is octagonal and has three storeys,
Gothic-style windows, a roof terrace and
figures on the buttresses. In the upper
storey is a *memorial hall* for the Wars of
Liberation with busts by C.Rauch (1817)
of the three monarchs of the 'Holy Alliance'. On the middle floor is the *study* of
the great statesman.

**Also worth seeing:** The ruins of the *Burg
Stein*, the family seat, were further
damaged in 1945; the *Burg Nassau* also
suffered; this dated from 1101, but was
renovated at a later date (square main
tower, residence). In the *Protestant church*,
which has a late Romanesque W. tower and
early Gothic nave, the early Gothic font on
four columns is worth seeing. The *former
Adolzheim Hof* (Town Hall since 1912), a

three-storey half-timbered building with a
ground floor arbour (1607–9), has splendid carving.

## Nennig 6641
Saarland        p.416☐A 15

**Roman villa:** In 1852 a farmer discovered
remains of a Roman villa on the SE edge
of the town. The splendid building was
130 yards long and connected with the separate bath house by a 273 yard lobby. In
the middle was a banqueting hall with a
*mosaic floor* 33 ft. by 52 ft. The defensive
buildings are in the neoclassical style.

**Schloss Berg:** The oldest parts of the
Schloss, which consists of an *upper* and a
*lower Burg*, date from the 12C (keep, 2
small round towers, courtyard gateway).
Additional buildings were added from the
14–16C; war damage has been made good.

## Nenningen=Lauterstein 7329
Baden-Württemberg        p.420☐G 18

**Cemetery Chapel:** The little baroque
cemetery chapel is surrounded by trees. It
contains the last work of the Munich sculptor I.Günther, a signed Pietà (1774). This
outstanding life-size carving continues the
Gothic tradition despite its quality of baroque drama.

## Neresheim 7086
Baden-Württemberg                    p.422□H 18

**Benedictine Abbey of St. Ulrich and St. Afra with Abbey Church:** From the very earliest times the Benedictines, who have been here since 1106, made this abbey the cultural centre of the Härtsfeld, the high plain in the Swabian Alb between Ulm and Nördlingen. The Church of St. Ulrich stands at the highest point of the monastery complex. The medieval building suffered much, but from 1747 one of the finest baroque churches in Europe was started here to plans by B.Neumann. After Neumann's death in 1753, building continued along the lines he had laid down, but much was altered and many economies were made: the W. *façade*, which is convex and decorated with columns, pilaster strips and figures, does not correspond to the original plan: the upper part has been much scaled down. The *tower* in the SW corner dates from 1618 and was included in the new building. The *interior* is of considerable importance, however; the undivided nave (91 yards long) is crossed by a short transept. The space is given remarkable light and shade by the di-

agonal pilasters, which are also set slightly away from the walls. The five oval flat domes are an idiosyncrasy of Neumann's. The planned *decoration* was only partially carried out; instead of large, dramatic altars there are only small ones in Louis Seize style. Colour and compositon of the lavish *ceiling paintings* by the Tyrolean painter M.Knoller (1771 – 5) are beautifully balanced. There is interesting *stucco work* in the adjacent *monastery* (1699–1714).

## Neuburg an der Donau 8858
Bavaria                    p.422□K 18

The town started as a fortified crossing point over the Danube; the growing bridge settlement had a Burg, which soon became too small and was replaced by the new Burg (Neuburg). About the middle of the 16C Neuburg became the residence of the Princes of Pfalz-Neuburg. The town became part of Bavaria in 1777.

**Schloss:** Most of the present Schloss was built in 1530–45 under Pfalzgraf Ottheinrich, who has gone down in history as one of the great Renaissance builders (see Ot-

*Schloss of the Barons vom Stein, Nassau*

theinrichsbau in the Heidelberg Schloss). Two outwardly plain *wings* open to the E. were built first. They enclose a picturesque *courtyard* with two-storey arcades. The lower arches have twisted columns with semicircular arches and Gothic rib vaulting. The courtyard is a good example of early German Renaissance architecture. The fine *Schloss chapel* is one of the earliest Protestant Schloss chapels in Germany. The *frescos*, painted in 1543 by H.Bocksberger, are an early example of Protestant monumental painting. The *E. wing* of the Schloss was built by Pfalzgraf Philipp Wilhelm in 1665–8.

**Former Court Church of Our Lady** (Karlsplatz): A Protestant church was built on the site of the old Benedictine monastery in 1607–18. It was intended as a gesture of defiance against St.Michael's (q.v.), the centre of the Jesuit Counter-Reformation in Munich, but even before the building was completed a Catholic Prince came to power and the church was reformed on Catholic-Jesuit lines. The early baroque *single tower façade* with pilasters defining the lower part of the building dominates the Schlossplatz. The *interior* is late Gothic, but the furnishings

are in high Renaissance style. Italian stucco artists and painters were involved and stucco workers from the Wessobrunn School (q.v.) worked on the *organ gallery* (c.1700). The massive *high altar* is by J.A.Breitenauer (1752–4) and the paintings are by D.Zanetti of Bologna (in place of earlier works by Rubens). The *pulpit* dates from 1756.

**Parish and Pilgrimage Church of the Holy Cross** (Bergen): Wiltrudis, the widow of the Bavarian Duke Berthold I founded a convent on this site in 976; she became the first abbess. In 1755–8 the monastery church was transformed by the Jesuits into a remarkable rococo building. Fine *stucco, coloured frescos* (by J.W.Baumgartner) and the *high altar* by J.M.Fischer of Dillingen are the dominant features of the interior. The *pictures* on the high altar are also by Baumgartner. The *memorial tomb* for W. von Muhr (c.1535) on the S wall of the nave is by L.Hering. The *Trinity Picture* is after Dürer. The *crypt* dates from the second half of the 12C.

**Parish Church of St.Peter:** This is the oldest church in Neuburg and dates from the early Middle Ages. In the present

◁ *Roman mosaic floor, Nennig*　　　　　　*Monastery church, Neresheim*

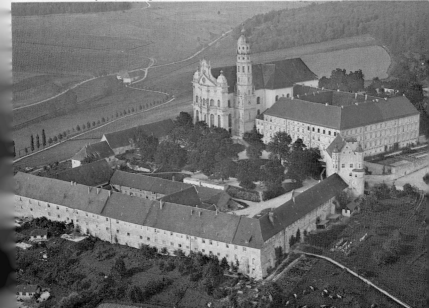

building by J.Serro (1641–7) the *high altar* (*c.*1760) with figures and paintings is worth seeing.

**Also worth seeing:** The *Rathaus* (17C) has a high, double open-air staircase; the interior was rebuilt in 1948&9. The *library* (former church of St.Martin, 1731) is an important building articulated by pilasters and columns with excellent rococo stucco work and carved 18C bookcases in the interior. The *Parish Church of St. Peter* (1641–7) has a notable high altar. *Heimatmuseum* (119 Amalienstrasse): local history.

---

## Neuenbürg (bei Pforzheim) 7540
Baden-Württemberg          p.420☐E 17

**Schloss:** The ruins on this site include a keep, the medieval ring wall and a 16&17C Schloss, in which the forestry department has its offices.

**Former Schloss Church of St.Georg:** The earlier Gothic building was altered in 1557. The decoration includes early 14C *wall paintings*, which were not revealed until 1952.

**Protestant Parish Church:** This neoclassical building has a pulpit altar, which is rare in the area.

---

## Neuenheerse 3491
Nordrhein-Westfalen          p.414☐F 10

**Former Collegiate Church (Damenstiftskirche)/Catholic Parish Church of St.Saturnina:** The church is largely early 12C. The massive *W. tower* with staircase towers (an old westwork) was later built higher to form a bell tower. The S. transept was originally a nuns' gallery and under it was the *chapterhouse*, now the sacristy. In the 14C the nave and S. transept were turned into a hall church with buttresses and Gothic windows. Evidence of Romanesque origins is given by the sturdy *columns* in the S. aisle with wall arches above the cushion capitals; they were not included in the new hall. In the early Romanesque *crypt* on the W. side is a passage to the grave of a saint or martyr. The 12C *Lamberti Chapel* has remains of wall paintings from the period when the church was built. A large inscribed slab (11C) is

*Neuburg an der Donau, section facing the Danube, with the Schloss seen from the north-east*

a memorial to St. Walburg, who founded an institution for noblewomen in the 9C (the *Damenstift* referred to in the former title of the church). The *furnishings* of the church are predominantly baroque. The *c.*1400 *iron railing* in the N. aisle is notable, and the so-called *ladies' saddle*, a stone seat on the N. wall used at the installation of a new abbess is also worth seeing.

## Neuenstein 7113
Baden-Württemberg       p.420☐G 16

**Schloss:** Since the middle of the 13C the Schloss has been in the possession of the Counts or Princes of Hohenlohe. The present Renaissance building is the successor to an early-13C moated Burg; the keep and ring walls with Romanesque and early Gothic features have survived. The rectangular inner courtyard complex with sturdy corner towers was given its picturesque and varied outline by 16C modifications. Lavishly decorated gables were added above the plain walls, and unusual pavilions were placed on the two gatehouse towers. On the ground floor there are several enormous columned halls, among which the *Kaisersaal* with its net vaulting (*c.*1560) is particularly important. The absent corridors are replaced by numerous concealed *spiral staircases*. The Schloss now houses the *Hohenlohe Museum* and the interesting central archive of the Hohenlohe family.

## Neuerburg, Eifel 5528
Rheinland-Pfalz       p.416☐A 14

**Ruined Burg:** The fortifications of this town in the W. Eifel originally had 16 towers and 3 gates. They were attached to the Burg, which stands on a rocky ridge. The core of the complex (three-storey gatehouse, ring wall and residence) is 13C. The hall on the ground floor of the residence presumably acquired its semicircular arches and Romanesque-style groin vaulting in the early 15C. In the 16C the Burg was further fortified by the building of an E. bastion, the strengthening of the ring walls and the addition of two horseshoe-shaped protruding turrets. Although the outer works were blown up by the French in 1692 and later partially demolished the Burg has nevertheless survived well, or been effectively restored.

**Catholic Parish Church of S.Nikolaus:** This is a Gothic building started in 1492 and completed *c.*1570; it is a two-aisled church with a central row of columns, which is not uncommon in the W. Eifel. The free-standing *bell tower* doubled as the gatehouse tower of the ring wall of the Burg. In the nave there is striking stellar and net vaulting, supported by slender octagonal pillars.

## Neuschwanstein 8959
Bavaria       p.422☐I 21

**Schloss:** The neo-Romanesque Burg was designed for King Ludwig II of Bavaria by the theatre painter C.Jank, who was also responsible for the sets for 'Tannhäuser'; Ludwig wanted to have a Wartburg as well as a Versailles (see Herrenchiemsee). The

**Neuenstein (Hohenlohe), Schloss 1** Bridge gatehouse **2** Kaisersaal, c. 1560 **3** Staircase tower

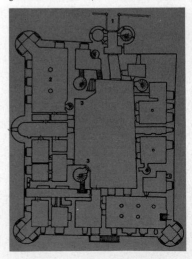

castle was built on an incomparable site above the Schwansee and the Alpsee in 1869–86. The throne room and the singers' hall are particularly striking; the latter was based on the singers' hall in 'Tannhäuser' and decorated by F.Piloty among others with pictures from the Parsifal legend. The King's study, bedroom, living quarters and dining-room are decorated with scenes from 'Tristan' and 'Lohengrin'.

## Neuss 4040
Nordrhein-Westfalen                  p.416☐B 11

Neuss developed from Novaesium, a Roman legionaries' encampment on the Rhine. The town was a Rhine port and a member of the Hanseatic League in the Middle Ages.

**Collegiate Church of St.Quirin/Catholic Parish Church** (Münsterplatz): St. Quirin is chronologically one of the last of the series of Romanesque churches on the Rhine: Gothic features are already clearly visible in the richly decorated *W. tower* of the massive church. The classically beautiful *E. trefoil choir* is based on St.Aposteln

in Cologne (q.v.). The baroque copper roof was added to the large E. *crossing tower* in 1741 after a fire; the tower has unusual flower-shaped windows. The *W. façade*, with arches arranged in a step pattern on the three gables, was originally intended to have two towers, but then it was decided to opt for a single tower (1230–50). A forked crucifix of the Cologne type (*c.*1360) on the altar) and a 'Beautiful Madonna' in the so-called 'Soft Style' (1420) are striking features of the *furnishings*.

**Museum:** The *Clemens-Sels-Museum* is by the *Obertor*, which was part of the 13C town fortifications. It shows Roman archaeological finds and has collections on the history of the town, local folk art and 14–19C fine art.

**Theatre:** The *Rheinische Landestheater Neuss* (2 Büttger Strasse) has its own company and plays not only in its own theatre (394 seats), but also in numerous other theatres in the area.

**Also worth seeing:** The *Dreikönigenkirche* (Dreikönigenstrasse) has famous windows by J.Thorn-Prikker (1909 –11).

*Schloss Neuschwanstein*                    *Collegiate church of St.Quirin, Neuss* ▷

*St. Quirin, Neuss*

## Neustadt in Holstein 2430
Schleswig-Holstein                    p.412□I 3

**Protestant Church:** This is a brick
Gothic hall church with a somewhat older
choir started in 1238. The *W. tower* was included in the original plans but not built
until 1334; its lower floor presumably contained the courtroom. It has had one of the
finest Gothic interiors in Holstein since its
1350 paintwork was restored in 1957. The
architectural details are picked out in different colours, and the ribs are decorated with
'crabs' (geometrical floral ornaments).
Elaborate tracery windows have been
painted on the upper part of the nave; the
blind rose above the choir arch is an
equally unusual decoration. The choir and
nave have *wall paintings* from various
Gothic periods. The magnificent *carved
altar* (1643) was originally intended for
Schleswig cathedral (q.v.), but came to
Neustadt in 1668 (Schleswig cathedral had

recently acquired the Bordesholm altar).

**Also worth seeing:** *Heilig-Geist Hospital
and Chapel* (1408) with traces of Gothic
paintwork; the *Kremper Tor* is the only one
of the 3 main gates to have survived; it
houses the *Heimatmuseum*.

**Environs: Altenkrempe** (4 km. N.):
12&13C Romanesque *basilica*.**Hassel-
burg** (6 km. N.): *farm and estate*.

## Neustadt an der Weinstrasse 6730
Rheinland-Pfalz                    p.420□D 16

Compared with the village of Witzingen,
which dates back to the 8C but is now part
of the town, Neustadt really is a new town
('neue Stadt'). Despite its involvement in
the Peasants War on the side of the
peasants it flourished in the 16C under
Pfalzgraf Casimir, who was granted a

princedom on the left of the Rhine at that time. He also established the Collegium Casimirianum, a rival foundation to Heidelberg University (q.v.). The town was fortunate enough not to be destroyed by the French in 1689, which means that the original pattern of its streets has survived.

**Former Liebfrauen Collegiate Church** (Am Markt): This red sandstone church is one of the most important buildings in the Pfalz on the left bank of the Rhine. It is essentially 14C and was intended as a funerary church for the Elector and his family. The lower storeys of the S. *tower* were taken over from an older building and under the baroque dome is the charming *tower watchman's accommodation*, which was in use until a few years ago. The interior has distinctive *sculptural decoration*: monkeys, grotesque figures, tendrils and coats of arms on the canopies and corbels. On the *choir vaulting* and in the W. porch there are traces of *Gothic painting*, and *tombs* of members of the Pfalzgraf's family in the choir (the tomb of Electress Margarete von Aragòn dates from 1377 and shows early signs of the 'Soft Style'.

*Stadtkirche, Neustadt i.Holstein*

**Casimirianum** (Ludwigstrasse): The Casimirianum was founded in 1597 as a university for those members of the Reformed Church who had to leave the Lutheran Heidelberg University. The three-storey building has an attractive staircase tower and a fine Renaissance doorway (1579).

**Hambach Schloss** (4 km. S. of the town): Above Oberhambach, which is now a part of the town, is the *Kästenburg*, an 11C Burg of the Salic emperors destroyed by the French in 1688. Its fame comes from the 'Hambacher Fest', a student demonstration in May 1832 in favour of the unification of Germany and the federation of Europe. The Burg, a present from the people of the Pfalz to the Bavarian Crown Prince Maximilian, was rebuilt by him from 1846 in Venetian-Gothic palazzo style.

**Rathaus and other buildings:** The

Town Hall is housed today in the former Jesuit College in the market place (1730). There are many houses with fine courtyards around the market place (4 and 11 Marktplatz, 4 Rathausgasse and 55 and 91 Hauptstrasse among others).

**Museum:** The *Heimat- and Weinmuseum* (25 Maximilianstrasse) is devoted to the history of wine, which is no surprise in this town, as it is the largest wine-growing community in Germany. The museum also features local history.

**Neuwied 5450**
Rheinland-Pfalz                                     p.416☐C 13

A village called Langendorf used to stand at the confluence of the Wied and the Rhine, but it was completely destroyed in the Thirty Years War. Count Friedrich III of Wied planned his Schloss and a new town at the same time, and gave the town its name. The building plots were given away free of charge provided that houses were built to a prescribed plan, which meant that the town achieved architectural unity.

**Schloss** (Schlossstrasse): The first building, started in 1648, was destroyed by the French. Rebuilding began in 1706 and was completed after many interruptions in 1756. The *corps de logis* is the most elaborate of the three buildings grouped round the courtyard. The ceilings of the staircase and the ballroom are decorated with *stucco figures*; the lavish wall stucco is by A.Gallasini. Between the Schloss and the mouth of the Wied is the *park*, which contains the former *pheasantry*, a two-storey pavilion.

**Museum:** The *Kreismuseum* (1a Raiffeisenplatz) exhibits prehistoric and early Franconian grave goods, medieval pictures and stained glass, furniture and arts and crafts.

**Theatre:** *Landesbühne Rheinland-Pfalz* (1 Schlossstrasse) and **Theatermobil** (1 Rosengarten), a touring company which operates throughout the German-speaking area.

**Environs: Altwied** (4 km. N.) This picturesque ruined Burg is on a river peninsula.
**Heimbach** (3 km. NE) Former Premonstratensian monastery of Rommersdorf (12C).
**Engers** (3 km. E.) Former Electoral Schloss (1758–62).

---

**Nieblum 2270**

Schleswig-Holstein                    p.412□E 1

**Protestant Church of St. Johannis:** This church on the island of Föhr is also the parish church of Amrum and was first mentioned in 1240. The squat cruciform brick building with a low tower fits in well with the landscape of the island. The *choir* is late Romanesque but the *transept* is early

Gothic, with buttresses and pointed windows, and the richly articulated *W. tower* is also of this period. The *S. doorway* is behind a baroque porch with sundial; the interior has a wooden beamed roof which has collapsed in the middle, a fine *carved altar* showing the Coronation of the Virgin, and striking wooden galleries. The fine furnishings also include a *granite font* (c.1200), an interesting *wooden pulpit* with relief scenes and rich ornamentation (1618) and a *wooden memorial tomb* (1613) ascribed to the Flensburg sculptor H.Ringering.

**Also worth seeing:** The churchyard with unusual sailors' gravestones (including a three-master in a stormy sea in a lavish rocaille frame). There are fine Frisian houses in the town.

---

**Niederaltaich 8351**

Bavaria                    p.422□N 18

**Benedictine Monastery of St. Mauritius:** This monastery among the abandoned channels of the Danube plain (hence the name 'Altaich') was one of the most important monasteries in Bavaria in the Middle Ages. The foundation walls of the church are 14C; they were included in the new building in 1718 after the rest of the church burned down. The architect was J.Pawanger, who was only responsible for the *nave* and the galleries, which are set rather high; his *choir* was pulled down when it was half finished because of major techncal deficiencies. The task was handed over to J.M.Fischer as his first church commission (1724–6). The shallow domes of the transepts, open to the galleries, are particularly attractive. The *stucco* is essentially Italian. The *cycle of frescos* on the ceiling shows monastery scenes and the apotheosis of the patron saint of the church. One of the altars is a Sebastian altar with good carved figures. J.M.Fischer placed the *sacristy* under the circular apse. The sacristy cupboards, fine 1727 cabinet work, and the stucco are particularly attractive.

*High altar, Niederrotweil* ▷

## Niederrotweil 7801
Baden-Württemberg　　　　　　p.420☐C 19

**Altar in the Catholic Church of St. Michael:** The late Gothic *high altar* is one of the most expressive in S. Germany. It shows the Coronation of Mary, who is flanked by St.Michael and John the Baptist. On the inner panel reliefs are St. Michael with a balance for weighing souls, the fall of the damned and the beheading of John the Baptist. This virtuoso carved altar is a late work of the master H.L., who created the altar in Breisach cathedral (q.v.).

## Nienburg 3070
Lower Saxony　　　　　　　p.414☐F 7

**Rathaus** (24 Lange Strasse): This half-timbered building has a striking *arcade* and an excessively large *tower*. On the Lange Strasse side is a *gable* with seven steps, each topped with a semicircular shell pattern, and the *Utlucht*, a two-storey oriel building, is very similar in design; both sections are built in red sandstone (1582–9) and are fine examples of the so-called Weser Renaissance style.

**Also worth seeing:** The late Gothic hall church of *St. Martin* with Renaissance tombs. The *Heimatmuseum* (local history) is housed in the Quaet-Faslem house (4 Leinstrasse), a fine neoclassical building.

**Environs: Marklohe** (5 km. NW) has a fine Romanesque church (12&13C) with gable reliefs of Cain and Abel on the S. doorway. The interior walls and vaulting are decorated with late Gothic paintings (1480). A 1420 carved altar and a 1521 late Gothic tabernacle with many figures are the most remarkable features of the furnishings.

## Norden 2980
Niedersachsen　　　　　　　p.414☐C 4

The old maritime town of Norden is in the extreme NW corner of the Federal Republic and has the largest medieval church in East Frisia.

**Protestant Ludgeri Church** (27 Am Markt): The Ludgeri church has a Romanesque *nave* (late 12C). The bell tower, which is detached from the church, is 13C and has early Gothic features. The most striking element of the building is the lofty *choir*, built by Count Ulrich I of East Frisia in 1445–81. It has fine *tombs* and a *baroque pulpit* among its lavish furnishings. By the N. choir pillar is a 30 ft. high late Gothic sandstone *tabernacle*. The organ, by the famous organ builder Anton Schnitger (1685–8), has a lavishly decorated baroque organ front. In the choir there are 8 *sandstone figures* from the Andreas church, where building was broken off in the 16C. These sculptures, probably dating from about 1250, have the stern archaic bearing of early Gothic portal figures.

**Museum:** The *Heimatmuseum* is in the former Rarhaus, which dates from 1452 (36 Am Markt); it has an interesting local history collection.

**Also worth seeing:** The *Rathaus* with staircase tower (16C); a 1662 patrician's house, which has been turned into the *Mennonite Church* (Markt); the *Schöningh house* (Osterstrasse) with splendid gable sculpture (1576); the *Deichmühle* (dike mill) (1 Bahnhofstrasse).

## Nordkirchen 4717
Nordrhein-Westfalen　　　　　p.414☐C 9

**Moated Schloss:** Architect G.L.Pictorius designed the largest and most important moated complex in Westfalia in 1703; it was known to his admiring contemporaries as the 'Münster Versailles'. The Schloss is set on an almost square island surrounded by wide moats; it has octagonal pavilions at each corner. After the death of the patron, Prince Bishop F.C. von Plettenberg, the project was taken over first by the son of G.L.Pictorius, and then from 1724 by the Münster architect J.C.Schlaun. Fur-

*Wasserschloss, Nordkirchen*

ther buildings were added in the 19&20C. The *ceiling stucco* has survived in the interior. Notable works in the *ballroom* on the ground floor of the central building are two lavish fireplaces, a sequence of pictures showing the deeds of Hercules, scenes from Ovid's 'Metamorphoses' and pictures of the patron of the building and another prince bishop. In the *park*, laid out by J.C.Schlaun and French landscape gardeners, the principal building is the *Oranienburg*, an orangery which Schlaun extended as a garden house in 1725–33.

---

## Nördlingen 8860
Bavaria                                  p.422☐ I 17

---

For centuries this town in the Ries has been contained within its late medieval walls, and it is unique among German towns in remaining so today. The walls were built in the 14C, extended later and strengthened with massive outer works in the 16C.

**Protestant Parish Church of St.Georg** (10 Marktplatz): This church, with its 295 ft. high *Daniel*, is the focal point of the town. The Renaissance style copper dome was added to the late Gothic (15C) tower in 1538&9. Building of the church itself lasted from 1427 (design) until 1444 (building began) and then continued under 9 different architects until 1508; the Ziegler chapel was not finished until 1519. 6 *portals*, the only exterior decoration, lead into the church. The spacious hall has 6 bays in the nave and the same number in the choir. The most important feature of the furnishings is the *high altar*, which has 5 extremely important 15C Gothic wood carvings, showing the crucified Christ between the desperate figures of Mary and John, with two angels hovering above them; further towards the outside are St. George and Mary Magdalene. The altar paintings by F.Herlin (1642–65) are now in the town museum (q.v.). The canopy of the sandstone *tabernacle* (1511–25) is decorated with prophets, evangelists, angels and saints with Christ as Saviour of the World, St.John the Evangelist and St.John the Baptist at the top. The *steps* leading to the pulpit (1499) and the tombs are also worth seeing.

**Former Carmelite Monastery of St. Salvator** (15 Salvatorgasse): This church was built along with most of the rest of the town in the 15C. The *high altar* (1497) is worth seeing; it was brought from Fürth to Nördlingen and is ascribed to the Bamberg Master H.Nussbaum. The notable 15C *wall frescos* are in good condition.

**Rathaus** (Marktplatz): The Rathaus was built in the 14C and is essentially Gothic. The large *open-air staircase*, added in 1618, is of Renaissance design but still reflects the Gothic style of the earlier parts of the building. Inside, the *Bundesstube* with its old wall paintings is worth seeing.

**Spital zum Heiligen Geist** (Baldingergasse/Vordere Gerbergasse): This hospital founded in the early 13C was designed to be self-sufficient; this is shown in the extensive complex of broad *courtyards*, numerous *farm buildings* and the *mill*; these buildings date from the 16C. The *church* is basically 13C, but was thoroughly renovated in 1848. The wall paintings from the second half of the 14C were not discovered and revealed until 1939. The tripartite altar (1578) is a typical example of Protestant altar design.

**Klösterle** (Am Klösterle): This former church of the barefooted friars (*c.*1420) was made into a grain store during the Reformation; a fine doorway was added to the high-gabled building in the course of alterations (1686).

**Tanzhaus** (Marktplatz, opposite the Rathaus): The Tanzhaus (dancing house) was built in the middle of the 15C as a meeting-place for the people of the town. It has a statue of Emperor Maximilian, a particualr benefactor of Nördlingen, on its façade; there is now a row of shops on its ground floor.

**Other secular buildings:** The *Hallhaus* (am Weinmarkt) shows the Fugger architects' application of their experience in

*Panorama of Nördlingen*

building warehouses for wine and salt (1541–3). There are impressive *old houses* at 6 Rübenmarkt, 5 Nonnengasse and 1 Kämpelgasse.

**Museum:** The *Stadtmuseum* (town museum) is in the Spital zum Heiligen Geist (1518–64, 1 Vordere Gerbergasse); it has collections on pre- and early history and the history of the town.

## Nottuln 4405

Nordrhein-Westfalen                        p.414□C 9

**Catholic Parish Church of St.Martin:** Little remains of the late Romanesque collegiate church in the new building of 1489–98, said to have been built by Swiss or Tyrolean masons, which could explain the S. German features of the large, wide hall church. The lower storeys of the 13C building were retained when the height of the church was increased in the late Gothic period. In 1956 fine *vault painting* was revealed in the interior. The *net* and stellar vaulting has some *keystones* decorated with figures. The *tracery windows* have flamboyant designs and the *circular pillars* with octagonal bases and narrow capitals, sometimes decorated with figures, are worthy of mention.

**Also worth seeing:** On the S. side of the picturesque tree-lined Stiftplatz are several houses built for noble canonesses in the 18C; some of them were designed by J.C.Schlaun.

## Nümbrecht 5223

Nordrhein-Westfalen                        p.416□C 12

**Schloss Homburg:** N. of Nümbrecht on the other side of the Brölbachtal is a medieval Burg on top of a hill; in the 17&18C the Counts of Sayn-Wittgenstein rebuilt the Burg as a terraced Schloss. Access to the Schloss is through the *barn building*, now a restaurant. The next terrace includes a walled garden, and then comes the *manor house*, protected by a moat. It is a building with two wings around a massive *staircase tower*. The Schloss fell into disrepair in the

19C and was restored to house the *Museum des oberbergischen Landes*.

**Also worth seeing:** The *Protestant parish church* with the vault of the Counts of Sayn. There are notable late Gothic wall paintings in the transept and the choir of the little Protestant church in *Marienberghausen*, NW of Schloss Homburg.

## Nürnberg/Nuremberg 8500

Bayern                                          p.422□K 16

Nuremberg was Albrecht Dürer's home and the city of the Mastersingers and Hans Sachs; it produced Peter Henlein, the inventor of the pocket watch, and was the town with the first railway in Germany (1835); it was also the home of the humanist Pirckheimer. Despite all these associations Nuremberg is no longer living out a Romantic dream: the destruction sustained in the Second World War destroyed all illusions in that respect. With almost half a million inhabitants it is a highly developed modern industrial city whose forward-looking town planners have succeeded in integrating the medieval core and the modern areas. It is still clear today that the old centre is divided into two districts: the Burg side with St.Sebaldus and the Lorenz side with the church of St.Lorenz. The marshes of the Pegnitz prevented the town from becoming a unified whole until relatively late, but in the Middle Ages it was brought together by the ring wall and the bastions. In contrast with many other German towns Nuremberg remained predominantly medieval, unaffected by enthusiastic builders of the baroque or any other period. Nuremberg was a free imperial town from 1219 (charter granted by Emperor Frederick II) until 1806, when the town became part of Bavaria.

**Protestant Parish Church of St. Sebaldus** (26 Winklerstrasse): This church with two'choirs is dedicated to St. Peter and St.Sebaldus. The older *W. part*, which shows the firm, rounded forms of the late Romanesque period, was begun in 1230–40 and based on Bamberg cathedral (q.v.). Only in the course of later extensions were the Gothic windows and aisles added. The roof of the *E. choir*, built 1361–79, towers 43 ft. over the W. section. The W. *towers* were not raised to their present height until the late 15C. The various phases of building are also visible in the *interior*; the narrow W. part with its heavy columns contrasts strongly with the light E. hall. The most famous of the furnishings is the *Sebaldus tomb*: P.Vischer and his sons built a bronze housing around the Gothic reliquary in stamped silver plate (late-14C). This highly imaginative Renaissance gem is decorated with candle-bearing women at the four corners, figures of the Apostles, a famous self-portrait by Vischer (with apron and cap) and many allegorical and mythical characters. The canopy, supported by bronze snails and dolphins, is a major achievement of bronze casting. The bronze *font* is from the studio of H.Vischer, the father of Peter. It is in the W choir, which is dominated by the soaring organ and choir gallery, the so-called *angels gallery*. The two *portals* of the church are also masterpieces of sculpture; the S. portal shows the Last Judgement and the N. portal the Death and Burial of Our Lady, both *c.*1300. By the N. transept is the bridal doorway, with representations of the wise and foolish virgins. The fine sculpture of *Katharina* (*c.*1310), which used to be part of the S. portal, is now inside the church. On the first N. pillar of the E. choir, is the *Madonna in an Aureole c.*1430. There are three reliefs of the *Volckamer Passion* by V.Stoss, after Riemenschneider the most important German sculptor of the late Gothic period; they date from 1499 and are under the windows in the E. choir. Stoss was also responsible for the figures of *Christ* and *Mary* above the reliefs, and the famous *Crucifixion group* above the high altar. The *Schreyer tomb* is by the Nuremberg sculptor A. Krafft, and is one of the master's early monumental works (1490–2). The so-called *Sebalduschörlein* with stone reliefs, which used to stand on a pedestal outside the priest's house, is an important piece of 14C sculpture. It was moved to the Germanisches Nationalmuseum (q.v.) and replaced with a copy.

**Protestant Parish Church of St.Lorenz** (Königstrasse): The two principal Nuremberg churches, St.Sebaldus in the N. and St.Lorenz in the S., each has two towers and they therefore look very similar. Building of the present church of St.Lorenz be-

*Sebalduskirche, Nuremberg*

*Sebaldus tomb in St. Sebaldus*

gan in the late 13C. The most decorative part of the exterior is the *W. façade* with its portal with figures, tympanum, tracery rose windows and pierced gable. The two six-storey *towers* were also completed in the 14C. As work continued, chapels were built between the flying buttresses of the nave with the intention of providing more space inside the church, which had become rather cramped. The problem was not solved however until the old E. choir was demolished and replaced with a *hall choir* surrounded by a series of chapels. As in St.Sebaldus a narrow nave with separate aisles opens into a broad choir with stellar vaulting. This part of the building, probably the finest hall choir in Germany, was completed in 1477. The principal features of the furnishings are the *Annunciation* by V.Stoss and A.Krafft's *tabernacle* by the last N. pillar of the choir. The Annunciation shows Mary with the angel surrounded by a garland and medallions depicting the 7 Joys of Mary. This late work of the master is 12 ft. high and was originally intended as the upper part of an iron chandelier; it was endowed by the Tucher family (1517–19). The famous 59 ft. high limestone tabernacle represents the suffering of Christ; there are almost 100

figures on the steep pyramid supported by life-size figures of Krafft and two senior journeymen. There are other works by Stoss in the church: a *St.Paul* on the choir pillar (1513) and the *crucifix* on the high altar *c.*1500). The *Deocarus altar*, the *Imhoff altar* and the *Ehenhein tomb* are important works of Nuremberg painting from the first half of the 15C. The splendid 15C *choir windows* have survived intact.

**Frauenkirche/Catholic Parish Church** (Hauptmarkt):The church is on the site of an old synagogue which was destroyed along with the Jewish quarter in the 14C. Emperor Charles V endowed the church in 1349 and made it his court church in 1355. On his visits to Nuremberg he used to show the imperial jewels to the people from the balcony above the market place. The *Michael choir* (on the balcony) and the *gable* date from the late Gothic period when the five sets of niches and a small oriel tower (1506–8) were built by Adam Krafft. The famous *Männleinlaufen* was also not installed until 1506. The figures of the seven Electors who circle three times around the enthroned Emperor Charles IV every day on the stroke of noon were made in commemoration of the award of the

*Side aisle in St.Sebaldus*

'Golden Bull' by Charles IV. The plain interior contains two *stone tombs* with many figures by A.Krafft (Peringsdorff and H.Rebek tombs, 1500). An important work from the period of Nuremberg painting before Wolgemut and Dürer is the *Tucher altar*, a tryptich with crucifixion, annunciation and resurrection dating from *c.*1440–50.

*St.Egidien* (Egidienplatz): This church is the only baroque building in Gothic Nuremberg and therefore does not harmonise too well with the rest of the town. It was built after a fire in 1696 and included some parts of the earlier 12C Romanesque church such as the Romanesque *Wolfgang chapel* with an Entombment group (*c.*1446) and the *Eucharius chapel* (*c.*1140). The Eucharius chapel was built as a royal chapel by Konrad III at the time of the foundation of a Scottish monastery and altered to its present form 100 years later. In the last of the chapels, the

*Tetzel chapel* (1345), Adam Krafft's Landau tomb (*c.*1501) is particularly striking.

**Elisabeth Church** (Ludwigstrasse): The church of the Teutonic Order was replanned at the end of the 18C. The work of the younger Neumann, son of the famous Balthasar Neumann, had to be revised by five architects before the circular building with its Corinthian columns could be completed. The church is the only significant example of neoclassical architecture in Nuremberg.

**Burg** (Auf der Burg): The Burg is set on sandstone cliffs above the town. It is in three sections, the *Kaiserburg*, the *Burggrafenburg* and the *Kaiserstallung*. The Kaiserburg dates from the middle of the 12C and has at its centre a Romanesque *double chapel* which the Emperor Barbarossa built on the pattern of the Hohenstaufen double chapel. During mass the Emperor sat in the high upper room,

**Nuremberg, St. Sebaldus 1** S.portal (Last Judgement), early 14C **2** N.portal (Entombment, and Coronation of the Virgin Mary), early 14C **3** Portal of the Magi, mid 14C **4** Apostle figures, mid 14C **5** Tabernacle, second third of 14C **6** Virgin Mary with halo, 1430-40 **7** Wooden group of Christ and the Virgin Mary by V.Stoss, 1499 **8** Volckamer Passion by V.Stoss, 1499 **9** Bamberger window, 1501 **10** Procession to Calvary by A.Krafft, 1506 **11** Andreas by V.Stoss, 1506 **12** Tomb monument to Tucher by H.v.Kulmbach, 1513 **13** Sebaldus tomb by P.Vischer the Elder, 1488-1519 **14** High altar with Crucifixion group by V.Stoss **15** Maximilian window by V.Hirschvogel, 1514 **16** Margrave's window by V.Hirschvogel, 1515

**Nuremberg, St.Lorenz 1** Sacristy **2** Imhoff altar with Coronation of the Virgin Mary, c. 1420 **3** Deocarus altar, 1437 **4** Wolfgang altar by Valentin Wolgemut, 1455 **5** Altar of the Magi, 1460 **6** Stained-glass windows a) Schlüsselfelder window, 1477 b) Volckamer window by Hemmel and Andlau, 1485 c) Konhofer window, 1477 d) Emperor window, 1477 e) Knorr window, 1476 f) Haller window, 1479-80 g) Rieter window, 1478-80 **7** Krell altar, 1483 **8** Rochus altar, 1485 **9** Memming altar, 1490; painting by M.Wolgemut **10** Tabernacle by Adam Krafft, 1493-96 **11** High altar with crucifix by V.Stoss, 1500 **12** St.Anne altar, 1510; wing paintings by Hans v.Kulmbach **13** Nikolaus altar, 1505-10 **14** Martha altar, 1517 **15** Annunciation by V.Stoss, 1517-18 **16** St. John altar, 1521

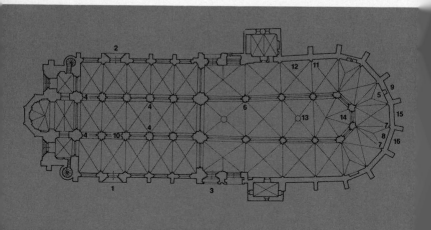

which is supported on the short, squat pillars of the lower storey; the lower room was intended for his retinue. 32 emperors and kings have lived and made history in the Burg. The Burggrafenburg passed to the city in 1427, and was restored faithfully after the Second World War. Along with the double chapel the *Ritter*- and *Kaisersaal*, *Heidenturm* and *Brunnen* are the principal sights of the extensive complex.

**Rathaus** (Rathausplatz): The Rathaus has a late Gothic section and an important Renaissance complex. After the war the late Gothic façade in the Rathausgasse (*c.*1515) and the Renaissance building with its three turrets and splendid doorways were restored.

**Albrecht-Dürer-Haus** (39 Albrecht-Dürer-Strasse): The many-storeyed corner house below the Burg acquired by Dürer in 1509 is now a Dürer museum, showing a contemporary printing press, graphics by Dürer and copies of some of his paintings. The furniture is no longer original, but the whole half-timbered building is typical of an early-18C burgher's house. Dürer lived here until 1528.

**Maut** (2 Hallplatz): This huge building, covering an area of 22 by 87 yards was built as a grain store by the Nuremberg town architect H.Beheim in 1489–1502. It was almost completely destroyed in the war but rebuilt in 1951–3; it is used for commercial purposes.

**Heilig-Geist-Spital** (bei der Museumsbrücke): The so-called *Sude* is built over the N. arm of the Pegnitz; it is a wing of the Heilig-Geist-Spital, which was endowed in 1331, and renewed by H.Beheim the Elder in 1511–27. The imperial jewels of 1424–1796 were stored in the Heilig-Geist-Kirche which was completely destroyed in 1945. The Spital was rebuilt in its original form after the war and is now a restaurant.

**Town wall:** This is the third city wall, dating from the 14–15C and encircling the centre of the medieval town. It is three miles long and has 80 towers along its length. War damage has been repaired. The so-called *dicke Türme* (fat towers), set at key points, have become an emblem of the town.

**Fountains:** Nuremberg, city of the bronze founders (Vischer, Labenwolf, Wurzelbauer, Jamnitzer, Flötner, Kern among others) is a town with many fountains. The oldest and most famous is the so-called *Schöne Brunnen* (beautiful fountain) (am Hauptmarkt). It dates from the period immediately after the building of the Frauenkirche and was probably part of the imperial plan (1389–96). Above the octagonal basin is a 62 ft. high sandstone pyramid with seven Electors and pagan, Jewish and Christian heroes on its various levels. Moses and the seven prophets can be seen at the top, and on the edge of the basin are church fathers and evangelists.

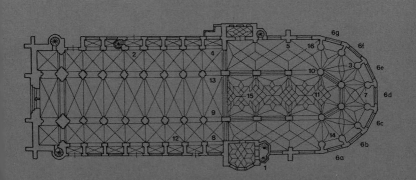

The present-day figures are copies; fragments of the originals can be seen in the Germanisches Museum. The *Gänsemännchen fountain* (by P.Labenwolf, *c.*1550), the *Apollo fountain* in the courtyard of the rebuilt *Pellerhaus* (by P.Fötner, 1532) and the *Putti fountain* in the Rathaus courtyard (by P.Labenwolf, 1557) are other notable fountains. Particularly striking is the *Tugend (virtue) fountain* (in front of S.Lorenz): putti spurt fine jets of water from trumpets, and the female figures representing the virtues shoot water from their breasts into the octagonal basin; this elegant mannerist work (1585–89) is by Wurzelbauer.

**Johannis cemetery** (Johannisstrasse): Some of the most famous sons of Nuremberg are buried in the ancient Johannis cemetery: Albrecht Dürer, the sculptor Veit Stoss, the humanist Pirckheimer, the philosopher Feuerbach, the painter Anselm Feuerbach and many others. In the cemetery are the 14C *Johannis church* and the *Holzschuher chapel*, a rotunda (1513). The *Stations of the Cross* by A.Krafft leading from the Tiergärtner Tor to the Johannis cemetery have been replaced with copies.

**Museums:** The *Germanisches Nationalmuseum* (Kornmarkt) was founded in 1852 in a mood of Romantic enthusiasm for things old and German. It has a pre- and an early historical department. The picture gallery gives a complete view of German panel painting from the 14–19C. The main items of the collection are by Dürer, Burgkmaier, Altdorfer, Cranach, H.Baldung, known as Grien, K.Witz, H. von Aachen and Sandrat. The sculpture section has works by Tilman Riemenschneider, V.Stoss, H.Leinberger, P.Vischer, A.Krafft, the famous Nuremberg Madonna, the Schlüsselfeld Christopher and works of rococo sculpture. There are also originals of many works from Nuremberg churches and other buildings which have been replaced by copies at their original sites. The musical instrument collection was added to the arts and crafts section in 1945. The engraving section has 200,000 sheets. The anthropological section is unique in having exhibits from the whole German-speaking area. The Gothic *Karthäuser Church* has been absorbed into the museum complex. The *Stadtmuseum Fembohaus* (15 Burgstrasse) is a house with a sandstone façade and a gable rising in scrolls and pyramids (1591–96), and with

*St. Michael in St. Lorenz*

*Adam Krafft, tabernacle*

its 16–19C furnishings is the last remaining patrician house in Nuremberg; models and pictures of old Nuremberg are shown in 36 rooms. The famous L.Bayer Würzburg toy collection is the basis of the Nuremberg *Spielzeugmuseum* (toy museum) (13 Karlstrasse); it shows roundabouts, tin figures, building sets and dolls' houses of various periods and nationalities. The *Gewerbemuseum* (craft museum) (2 Gewerbemuseumsplatz) has important works in glass, ceramics, silver, porcelain and metal; there is a special section devoted to Far Eastern art. The *Städtische Kunsthalle* (32 Lorenzer Strasse) has regular temporary exhibitions of modern art as well as its permanent collection of 19&20C painting, drawing and sculpture. The *Verkehrsmuseum* (transport museum) (6 Lessingstrasse) has exhibits on railway and postal history and departments on telephones, telegrams and communication engineering. It is built around full-size locomotives and rolling stock, including the first German railway train which ran from Nuremberg to Fürth in 1835. The medieval *Lochgefängnis* ('hole' prison) in the old Rathaus (2 Rathausplatz) has been maintained in its original state with cells, torture chamber, smithy and gaoler's accommodation. The *Albrecht-Dürer-Museum* in the Albrecht-Dürer-Haus (q.v.) is also notable.

**Theatres:** The *Städtische Bühnen* have an *opera house* (Richard-Wagner-Platz) with 1100 seats (rebuilt after the Second World War), the *Volkstheater im Schauspielhaus* (Richard-Wagner-Platz, 900 seats) and *Kammerspiele* (studio theatre).

**Also worth seeing:** The Gothic *St.Jacob* (Ludwigstrasse) with a fine altar; the former Mastersingers' church *St.Martha* (Königstrasse); the *Nassau house* (2 Carolinenstrasse), a medieval house with a tower and gallery (13–15C); the *Fleischbrücke* over the Pegnitz (*c.*1600); fine *courtyards* (31 Winklerstrasse, 6 Weinmarkt and 7 Theresienstrasse); and finally the *Tucherschlösschen* (11 Hirschelgasse), a Renaissance building dating from 1533–44 (guided tour by arrangement).

**Environs: Fürth** (6 km. W.): *Protestant Parish Church of St.Michael* (14C) with a lavishly decorated doorway and Gothic tabernacle (*c.*1500) by Krafft; *Old town* with half-timbered houses (17&18C), some slate-clad.

*Tucheraltar, Frauenkirche*

Burg

Schöner Brunnen and Frauenkirche

Dolls' kitchen, c. 1800, toy museum

## Oberaltaich über Straubing 8441

**Former Benedictine Monastery Church of St.Peter and St.Paul:** The present church dates from the 17C, having been completed in 1630. It shows a number of peculiarities which are attributed to Abbot Vitus Höser. It was originally planned that there should be not one, but as many as four apses on a rectangular ground plan. The W. apse is visible from outside as well (between the two towers), and is characterized by two late Gothic figures in niches. The 'hanging staircase' inside this hall structure (one nave, two aisles) was once considered a technical miracle. This staircase leads up to the galleries. The interior of the church is reached through a portico which is decorated with peculiar stucco depicting birds. The entire interior of the church is adorned with decorative paintwork. The massive high altar, which is dominated by the figures of Benedict and Augustine, dates from 1693 and is almost as tall as the church. The valuable rococo tabernacle dating from 1758&59 is probably the work of M.Obermayer, an artist from Straubing. The eight side altars are of varying quality. The carved parapet of the organ gallery is in the neoclassical style (late 18C.).

## Oberammergau 8103

Oberammergau has become well-known for the Passion play which is held every ten years (it will next be performed in 1990). The first performance was in 1634. The inhabitants of Oberammergau promised to organize the Passion play out of gratitude for the ending of the plague. It was also stipulated at that time that the Passion play was to be repeated every ten years. Since 1680 it has on each occasion been held in the year divisible by ten. The present *Passionsspielhaus* (Theaterstrasse) was built in 1930. 102 performances of the play are scheduled in the Passion play years, and the actors are all citizens of Oberammergau. A performance lasts 5½ hours, with a two-hour lunch interval, and shows Christ's way of the Cross in 16 acts. A total of 1400 performers take part, selected from those who were either born in Oberammergau or have lived here for at least 20 years.

**Catholic Parish Church** (Ettaler Strasse): J.Schmuzer, an architect from Wessobrunn, built the present church in 1736–42 on the site of a previous Gothic building, and he let his son Franz Xaver take a share in the work (stucco decorations). The splendid frescos which charac-

*Oberammergau, Passion play*

terize the interior of the church are the work of M.Günther from Augsburg (1741 and 1761). The main altar and side altars are late rococo works and are by F.X.Schmädl from Weilheim.

**Houses with Lüftl paintwork:** The town has numerous houses decorated with the so-called Lüftlmalerei, in which the façades are painted. F.Zwinck, one of the best-known Lüftl painters, painted the façades of the two houses known as Gerold-haus and Pilatushaus (late 18C).

**Oberammergauer Heimatmuseum** (8 Dorfstrasse): Folk art from the 14–18C (especially the Oberammergau carvings), printed works, waxworks, display of cribs.

---

**Oberkaufungen = Kaufungen 3504**
Hessen                              p.416☐G 11

---

**Former Benedictine Convent and**

**Heiliges Kreuz Church**: Beginning with the convent founded in 1017 by Empress Kunigunde, the wife of Henry II, an extensive complex was built here at the edge of the Kaufunger forest. Numerous conversions carried out over the centuries have greatly altered the convent and church, but some of the basic features of the original buildings have survived. The present building is an incomplete conversion of a Romanesque basilica into a Gothic hall church. The walls and pillars were painted in the late Gothic period (15C). The *tombstone* of Abbess Anna v. der Borch (d. 1512) is noteworthy. The rococo *organ front* dates from 1799. Little remains of the old convent. The oldest surviving section is the *cloister* S. of the church. After the complex had been handed over to the knights of Hessen in 1532, the knights' *Renterei* (1606) and the *Herrenhaus* (converted in 1714) were built. Both these buildings have stone lower storeys and half-timbered upper storeys. The Herrenhaus has a fine Rit-

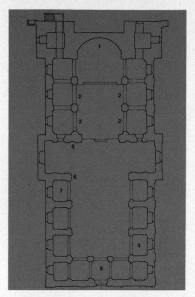

Obermarchtal, monastery church 1 High altar, painting by J.N.Heiss, 1696 2 Choir stalls by P.Speisenegger, 1690; Coronation, 18C 4 Antonius altar, painting by M.Zehender, 1690-96 5 Tabernacle, painting by M.Zehender, 1690-96 6 Pulpit, c.1715 7 Ursacius altar, 1736 8 Organ front, rococo

*St. Peter and St. Paul, Obermarchtal*

tersaal. The walls are decorated with the coats of arms of aristocratic families.

**Heimatmuseum** (Hüttenhof): This museum was established in 1958 in the former St. George chapel of the Heiliges Kreuz church. *Bergwerkmuseum* (mining museum; Freudentalstrasse), containing the oldest and only surviving horse-whim in Germany, which was in operation from 1824–84.

---

## Obermarchtal 7931
Baden-Württemberg                    p.420□G 19

**Former Premonstratensian Monastery Church of St. Peter and St. Paul:** The first monastery was built in the 8&9C on a hill above the loop in the Danube at Obermarchtal. Another monastery was founded here in the 12C, but did not flourish until the end of the 17C and the 18C. It was in this period that the present building was erected. Until his death in 1690, M.Thumb from Vorarlberg was responsible for the construction work. The work was later continued by his brother Christian and his cousin F.Beer. The best feature of this monastery church is its outstandingly well-designed interior. The round arches make a magnificent impression in conjunction with the lavish stucco by J.Schmuzer from Wessobrunn. The colouring was chosen to enhance the spatial effect: everything is in the purest white apart from the gold and brown of the altars and the dark choir stalls. The inside of the church is a gem of the South German baroque. At the centre of the high altar is a painting by J.Heiss (1696). It is dedicated to the glorification of the Premonstratensian order. The side altars are also decorated with paintings. The choir stalls, which were carved by

*Premonstratensian monastery and church of St. Peter and St. Paul, Obermarchtal*

**Obermarsberg, St. Nikolaus 1** S.portal **2** Double Madonna of the Rosary, c.1700 **3** St. Christopher, donated in 1744 **4** Pietà, early 18C

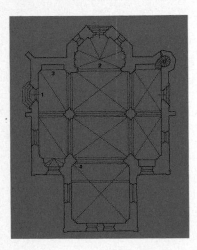

P.Speisenegger, a lay brother from Schaffhausen, fit well into the overall spatial design. The organ front is rococo. The *chapterhouse* (with fine choir stalls) and the *refectory* (stucco by F.Pozzi, frescos by Appiani, *c*.1755) are the crowning features of the *cloister buildings*, most of which are very richly decorated.

## Obermarsberg = Marsberg 3538
Nordrhein-Westfalen                  p.416□F 10

**Collegiate Church of St. Peter and St.Paul:** The present church was built on the remains of a 13C building which was destroyed by lightning and fire. Reconstruction work was completed *c*.1410 (the roofs are 19C). The crypt underneath the chancel is of especial interest, and its dominant feature is the octagonal middle pillar. The aisles of this hall church are spanned by groin vaults which resemble domes.

The decoration is baroque—a rare feature in this region.

**Nicolai chapel:** This small church was designed as a hall church with a nave and two aisles, but has small side choirs adjoining the E.wall of the aisles, and in the W. there is a pentagonal annexe (see ground plan). The building is first mentioned in 1247. The inside is characterized by tall round pillars. These are topped by early Gothic leafwork capitals which support ribbed vaults. Particular attention should be paid to the old windows which still survive, and also to the masterly late Romanesque S.portal with its rich decorations. This church is one of the most significant and charming early Gothic buildings in Westphalia.

**Heimatmuseum** (8 Lillers-Strasse), with a collection on the history of the town.

**Also worth seeing:** Roland column (1737), 16C pillory.

---

### Obernkirchen 3063
Lower Saxony                                    p.414☐F 8

---

**Collegiate Church:** Although the building was still under construction in 1396, large parts of this hall church, which has a nave and two aisles, are nevertheless in the Romanesque style. There are two conspicuous pyramidal roofs immediately adjoining one another. Inside, the most interesting feature is the *high altar* (1496). On the stone predella is a shrine with carved figures from the Passion. The Virgin Mary with the Christ child and St.Ann are to be seen on the outer sides of the panels of this shrine. A figure of Moses supports the richly carved 17C *pulpit*. The *memorial stone* to mayor Georg Tribbe (d.1665) is also worth mentioning. He was also a sculptor, and built a monument to himself in marble and alabaster. Numerous carved figures are also to be found all over the church, including the galleries. The adjoining *monastery buildings* were built in the 16–18C and form a picturesque and romantic backdrop to the collegiate

church. Two more buildings to have survived are the former *monastery mill* and a barn where the tithes which the peasants paid to the monastery were stored. *Stadtbücherei* (Markt): The 16C town library occupies a special position among the half-timbered houses.

---

### Oberstenfeld 7141
Baden-Württemberg                              p.420☐F 17

---

**Former Convent Church of St. John the Baptist:** The surviving *hall crypt* with its nave and two aisles reminds us of the period when the building was originally erected in the early 11C. The basilica (nave and two aisles) and the chancel tower were built in the 13C. The interior is monumental and Romanesque in design. The ribbed vault was added by artists from Maulbronn. The altarpiece, whose triptych (1512) is attributed to the Dürer school, is very fine. The tomb monuments should also be noted.

**Burg Lichtenberg** (2 km. SE): The castle (13–15C) has survived in its entirety, apart from two keeps. The courtyard is surrounded by a barbican. On the two sides of the gateway we find a soldiers' room and the *chapel* (wall paintings of *c*.1230). There is a fine banqueting hall on the first floor. Some of the domestic buildings were added in the 16&17C.

**Also worth seeing:** Peterskirche (NE of Oberstenfeld): A simple 11C building with 13C wall paintings.

---

### Oberwesel 6532
Rheinland-Pfalz                                p.416☐D 14

---

This small medieval wine town has lost none of its romantic character, which Ferdinand Freiligrath praised in exuberant terms (he described Oberwesel as the 'most beautiful haven' of romanticism on the Rhine). It was here, on 17 August 1843, that Hoffmann v.Fallersleben first sang his

German national anthem in the presence of friends and citizens.

**Collegiate Church of Our Lady** (Liebfrauenstrasse): This church dating from the first third of the 14C is popularly known as the 'rote Kirche' (red church), owing to the red finish of its sandstone. The W. tower, 235 ft. in height, has a helm roof and eight gables. The sumptuous *interior decoration* contrasts with the plain architecture. First and foremost, the *rood screen* should be mentioned. A magnificent work of art, it transcends its formal function as a screen dividing the clergy from the laymen. It continues in the aisles in a simplified form as a stone and iron screen. The *Nikolausaltar* (altar of St.Nicholas) is almost as important as the rood screen. Like the other altars, it is from the workshop of an anonymous artist (1506). The picture in the central section depicts the Saint liberating three knights who have been sentenced despite being innocent, and three girls who are to be forced into prostitution by their penniless father and have each received a present of a purse from the Saint. In the foreground we see a ship full of people of all social classes, protected by the patron saint of sailors. The altars date back to an endowment by Canon Peter Lutern (d. 1515). His *monument,* another of the significant works of art in this church, is by the famous artist H.Backoffen (16C). It was a pupil of this artist who carved in stone a work which is of even greater artistic merit: this is the tomb of the pair of knights called Ottenstein (1520). The late Gothic cloister and some remains of the chapterhouse still survive from the former *monastery buildings.*

**Catholic Parish Church of St.Martin** (Auf dem Martinsberg): Its position on a hill in the N. of the town, and the sturdy tower, make this 14&15C church look like a fortress. The bright colours of the nave (painted in the 15C) and chancel have given this church the name of the 'weisse Kirche' (white church), in contrast to the red-coloured church of Our Lady, which has similar articulation.

**Schönburg castle** (2 km. S.): This com-

plex was first mentioned as long ago as the 12C. It is a building of huge dimensions standing on a peak 1050 ft. high. Most of it was destroyed in 1689, and today it only survives as a ruin. However, the former dimensions and the curtain-wall style of building are readily discernible (the gatehouse tower and the curtain wall have survived).

**Town fortifications:** The surrounding wall with its 16 towers of the original 21 has survived in very good condition.

---

# Ochsenfurt 8703
Bavaria                                      p.418☐H 15

**Catholic Parish Church of St.Andreas** (9 Pfarrgasse): This church was built over a period extending from 1288 (with a tower dating from this period) until the late 15C, when the chapels were completed. The Johann Nepomuk chapel in the SE corner was not in fact added until the 18C. Lavish tracery is the dominant feature of the interior, which has an extremely high nave. The high altar dating from 1612 is the work of G.Brenck, the sculptor from Windsheim, and its tripartite structure fills most of the chancel. There is an excellent 16C wooden figure which depicts St. Nicholas and is the work of T.Riemenschneider. Other features worth seeing: An octagonal bronze font (*c.*1515), late Gothic choir stalls, early-14C sculpture of the Adoration of the Magi. The *Michaelskapelle* (work started in 1440) is a two-storey graveyard chapel standing near the parish church and containing some valuable stone sculptures.

**Rathaus** (Markt): This late Gothic Rathaus is one of the finest in Franconia. The older, main building (*c.*1500) was followed by the addition of the E. wing some 20 years later. The clock tower with its works dating from 1560 is worth looking at. The interior is reached by a beautiful open-air staircase with tracery-work balustrades.

*Church of Our Lady, Oberwesel* ▷

*Benedictine monastery, Ochsenhausen*

**Museums:** *Stadtmuseum* (26 Brücken-strasse): The museum, with its notable collection of stones and weapons, is housed in the so-called 'Schlösschen', which formerly served as a bridge fortification. *Trachtenmuseum* (Spitalgasse) in the so-called Greisinghaus: provincial costumes and examples of middle-class domestic décor.

**Also worth seeing:** 17&18C *bridge* over the Main. *Spital church* of about 1500. The *Wolfgangskapelle* (Wolfgang chapel; started in the 15C), which is the annual destination of a Whitsun riding tour. We also find the *Palatium*, the former administrative seat of the cathedral chapter (*c.*1400), the *half-timbered medieval buildings*, and the *town fortifications*.

**Environs: Marktbreit** (6 km. E.): Apart from the *Protestant St. Nikolaus church* (13–17C) with its four late Gothic *Passion reliefs* from the Riemenschneider school,

there are numerous half-timbered buildings which are of interest.

**Frickenhausen** (3 km. NE): The *Rathaus*, with its late Gothic open-air staircase decorated with tracery work (1595), and also the *Catholic parish church of St. Gallus* (16&17C), are notable features of this wine town, which was known as long ago as the 9C. Its *surrounding wall* (15&16C) is still intact.

---

**Ochsenhausen 7955**
Baden-Württemberg                           p.422☐H 20

**Former Benedictine Monastery Church of St. Georg** (Schloss district of Ochsenhausen): The town's real history is said to have begun with an ox's kick: that kick, in about the year 1050, is supposed to have brought a monastery treasure to light. It is said that, a hundred years previ-

*Benedictine monastery church, Ochsenhausen*

ously, the nuns of a convent known as Hohenhausen were fleeing from the Hungarians and had hidden the treasure in the place in question. Hatto v.Wolperswendi saw this as a sign from the Almighty, and founded the Benedictine monastery. Construction work on the present church was begun in 1489 (it was completed in 1495). The building was radically altered in the 17&18C (the additions included a baroque façade dating from 1725). The interior was also redesigned in the baroque style. The stucco ornaments are by the Italian G.Mola, and are indicative of the artistic taste prevailing in *c.*1725–30. The extensive fresco paintings in the nave are the work of J.B.Bergmüller (1727–30, supplemented by works by his pupil J.A.Huber, 1787, in the aisles). Among the other decorations, the following should be emphasized: the rococo high altar with some older figures and a painting by J.H.Schönfeld from Biberach, the choir stalls (1686), the pulpit by Ä.Verhelst

(1740&41), and the organ by J.Gabler (1729–34). Only a few sculptures still survive from the late Gothic decorations. The *monastery buildings* (1583–1791) adjoin the church in the E. They are unusually large and include the following: prelacy, monastery wing, refectory, and the neoclassical library in the N.wing; extensively restored from 1974–84.

## Ochtrup 4434
Nordrhein-Westfalen       p.414 □ C 8

**Former Convent:** The castle of Langenhorst was the basis on which Franko v.Wettringen, later dean of Münster, founded a convent in 1178. The convent church, completed some fifty years later, shows the transition from the Romanesque to the Gothic. Apart from the church, parts of the former convent and of the abbey (1722) also survive. The church is today the Catholic parish church of St.John the Baptist, and is one of the most significant hall churches in the Münsterland.

## Oettingen 8867
Bavaria                                    p.422☐I 17

This former residence town at the edge of the Ries basin has maintained its original appearance to the present day. Many half-timbered houses (15–17C) and baroque buildings combine an idyllic rural appearance with courtly splendour.

**St. Jakob** (Schlossstrasse): The present church was built in the 14&15C on the foundations of a church dating from the early 14C, and building work was brought to a conclusion when the upper storey with its tower was completed in 1565. The church is worth seeing for its rich interior decorations; the stucco is the work of M.Schmuzer (1680&81). Particular attention should be paid to a high altar (*c*.1500) with a significant Crucifixion group. The pulpit (1677) and the font (1689) are both decorated with first-rate sculptures.

**Neues Schloss:** The excellent stucco in the Neues Schloss, including that in the Festsaal (banqueting hall), is also the work of M.Schmuzer from Wessobrunn. This spacious complex was built in the 17&18C and, in addition to the main building, also comprises numerous domestic buildings and annexes. These surround the Schloss courtyard, where a *Marienbrunnen* was built in 1720. The *Hofgarten* adjoins the Schloss in the W, and contains an orangery which is the work of G.Gabrieli (1726).

**Also worth seeing:** St.Sebastian: The remains of the church dating from 1471 still survive and have been supplemented by a new building (1847). The church, with its miracle of the Holy Blood, was the destination of a pilgrimage. *Rathaus:* A half-timbered building (1431) containing a *Heimatmuseum* with items relating to prehistory, the town's history, and the history of arts and crafts. *Lateinschule* (Latin school):

A gabled building dating from 1724, standing beside St.Jakob. *Town fortifications:* Large sections of the 12C town wall have survived in very good condition. Three of the gates give a good example of the overall design concept.

## Offenbach am Main 6050
Hessen                                    p.416☐E 14

Goethe was more enthusiastic about Offenbach than almost any other town—but this was probably due to his love for Lili Schönemann, to whom he had become engaged at Easter 1775. He praised the 'beautiful, splendid buildings' and enthused about the gardens and terraces which 'extending as far as the river Main, everywhere permit free access to the gracious surroundings.' Sophie von La Roche lived here from 1786 until her death in 1807, and Bettina von Arnim also spent part of her youth in Offenbach. Today Offenbach is an important industrial town and the centre of the German leather goods industry.

**Former Isenburgisches Schloss** (66 Schlossstrasse): This 16C Renaissance Schloss is worth seeing for its frontage which faces southwards, and for the court façade with its graceful arcades. The present building, which may have been planned as a four-winged building, was completed in 1578.

**Büsinghof** with the ruins of the former Büsing palace (Herrnstrasse): This palace built in the 18C was completely gutted by fire in the Second World War. However, the wings of the extension dating from 1900 have been rebuilt.

**Museums:** *Deutsches Ledermuseum/Deutsches Schuhmuseum* (86 Frankfurter Strasse): The manufacture and processing of leather are depicted in great detail, as is the cultural history of footwear. *Klingspor-Museum* (Herrnstrasse 80): Devoted to the art of books and scripts in the 20C, book bindings, and graphics. New exhibitions are regularly mounted, mainly compiled from the museum's own stocks.

**Also worth seeing:** *Schloss Rumpenheim:* A country house by the Main dating from 1680. Its main building burned down in 1945. *Lilipark* (on the banks of the Main): Named after Goethe's fiancée, who lived here for a time.

## Offenburg 7600
Baden-Württemberg                    p.420☐D 18

Johann Jakob Christoffel v.Grimmelshausen, author of 'Der Abenteuerliche Simplicissimus Teutsch', worked in Offenburg after 1639 as regimental secretary and fortress clerk, and married here in 1649.

**Catholic Parish Church Heiliges Kreuz:** (4 Pfarrstrasse): The church was consecrated in 1791 after a building period lasting almost 100 years. The Mount of Olives group, dating from 1524, in the forecourt (formerly the graveyard), and the tomb monuments (including that by C.v.Urach to Jörg v.Bach, d. 1538) which can be seen on the outside walls are later.

The interior is painted almost throughout (1956). The *high altar* (1740) takes pride of place among the altars. It was decorated by F.Lichtenauer, as were most of the side altars. Other features: The *choir stalls* (1740). the neoclassical *pulpit* (1790) and the *rococo railing* in front of the 18C organ front; the original *crucifix* dating from 1521 is in the left side altar, and there is a copy of it in the church forecourt.

**Rathaus** (90 Hauptstrasse): 16C and early 17C elements were incorporated in the façade of this building erected in 1741. M.Fuchs was the architect.

**Landratsamt** (96 Hauptstrasse): This baroque building was commissioned by Margravine Sybilla from M.L.Rohrer, the court architect. The building, with its richly decorated façade, was completed in 1717.

**Museums:** The *Ritterhausmuseum* (10 Ritterstrasse) was built in 1775. From 1804–06 it housed the principal officials the Offenburg Imperial Knights, and until 1956 the Regional Court had its premises here. Apart from some exhibits on the history of town, region and culture,

*Isenburgisches Schloss, Offenbach*

the museum also has collections on the former German colonies. *Städtische Galerie* (10 Ritterstrasse): Primarily devoted to works by artists from Offenburg, especially from the 18C onwards.

**Also worth seeing:** *Franciscan monastery:* Built in 1702–17 on older foundations. The church is a plain pilaster building with a richly decorated altar. *Palais Rieneck:* Today this baroque building with its noteworthy staircase tower houses the Regional Court. *Judenbad* (6 Glaserstrasse): Late-13C underground building for Jewish ritual washing. *Verlagshaus Burda* (Burda publishing house): This building was designed in 1954 by E.Eiermann as a steel skeleton structure.

**Environs: Ortenberg** (4 km. SW): *Burg Ortenberg* was built by the Zähringers in the 12C, and in the 13C it passed into the possession of the Hohenstaufen family. The castle was radically renovated in the 19C. The base, with projecting ashlar, of the castle keep dates from the 12–13C.

**Gengenbach** (9 km. SW): Located in the Kinzig valley, this has been a free imperial town since 1360. It has many 17&18C *half-timbered houses*, including the 18C *Löwenbergpalais*, which houses the *Heimatmuseum* (15 Hauptstrasse; local history). The former *Benedictine monastery church of St.Maria*, an early-12C basilica with a nave and two aisles, is the most interesting feature.

# Öhringen
Baden-Württemberg                    p.420□G 16

**Former Collegiate Church of St.Peter and St.Paul** (Marktplatz): The present collegiate church was built on the site of a 15C Romanesque church. There are noteworthy sculptures of Peter and Paul by the W. tower, and also of lions by the S. transept portal (the copies and the 13C and 11C originals are inside the church). The

◁ *High altar of collegiate church, Öhringen*

*Schloss with collegiate church, Öhringen*

most significant *furnishings:* The carved high altar (*c.*1500), which shows the Virgin Mary between St.Peter, St.Paul and two more figures of men (probably Franconian). The chancel windows were assembled from surviving 15C sections. Another item worth seeing is the crypt, where we find the altar tomb which dates from 1241 and contains the relics of Adelheid, the mother of Emperor Konrad II. It was in 1037 that she induced Bishop Gebhard of Regensburg to convert an already existing church into a canonical foundation. The chancel includes other tombstones by significant artists (16–18C).

**Schloss** (15 Marktplatz): This castle built in 1610&16 for Countess Magdalena v.Hohenlohe (maiden name v.Katzenelnbogen) to plans by G.Kern was enlarged by additions in 1681–83, 1770 and 1812&13. It still possesses some 18&19C interior features. To the S. is the Hofgarten with the former theatre pavilion (1743).

*St. Lamberti, Oldenburg*

**Lustschloss Friedrichsruhe** (4 km. N.): This fine baroque building with its rich exterior decorations and the stucco usual at that period was built in 1712–17. It was redesigned on neoclassical lines in the early 19C. The gardens are still of 18C design.

**Weygang-Museum** (38 Karlsvorstadt): The suburb of Öhringen called Karlsvorstadt was designed in 1782 as a uniform complex separated from the rest of the town by a classical colonnaded gate. The notable museum is still inside these buildings, and special mention should be made of its tin foundry and tin collection.

---

## Oldenburg/Oldenburg 2900

Lower Saxony          p.414☐E 6

It was not until the late 18C, after an eventful history which included being part of Denmark for almost 100 years, that this town developed into a North German cultural and economic centre under Duke Peter Friedrich Ludwig. After 1945, Oldenburg developed into a large industrial town (paints, electric motors, meat products, ship-building).

**Former Collegiate Church of St. Lamberti** (near the Schloss by the Schlossplatz square): The core of the present church consists of the outer walls of the nave of a late Gothic hall church, inside which a rotunda was built in 1797. The gallery is supported by 12 pillars, the massive cupola by 12 columns. There are several noteworthy tombstones in the portico and in the church.

**Schloss** (Schlossplatz): The different phases of construction are readily discernible in this Schloss. The core is a reconstruction begun in 1604, in which the medieval castle was given a more varied structure. The so-called Holmerscher wing

*Schloss, Oldenburg*

followed in 1778, and it was about 25 years later that the vehicle passage and the gallery wing were built to plans by C.H.Slevogt and H.Strack the elder. The theatre followed in 1899. The significant *Landesmuseum für Kunst- und Kulturgeschichte* was established in the rooms of the Schloss after the First World War. It has extensive collections of medieval sculpture, and also a picture gallery (the collection originates from an initiative put forward by the painter J.H.Wilhelm Tischbein, who provided the basis by purchasing numerous paintings by Italian artists). Other collections: ancient handicrafts, and some collections on the history of culture.

**Lappan** (Heiligengeistwall): The tower of the former Heiliggeistspital dating from 1468 (tower roof from the baroque period).

**Museums:** *Landesmuseum für Kunst und Kulturgeschichte* (see Schloss above). *Oldenburger Stadtmuseum/Städtische Kunst-*

*sammlungen* (32&3 Raiffeisenstrasse): History of art and culture, sculpture, paintings, drawings. *Augusteum,* with 20C art.

**Staatstheater:** The state theatre has separate companies for opera, operetta and plays, and also a symphony orchestra. Performances are held in the Grosses Haus (19 Theaterwall) with its 861 seats, in the Schlosstheater (in the Schloss, 252 seats), and in the acting area in the new foyer (with a maximum of 170 seats).

---

**Oppenheim 6504**

Rheinland-Pfalz                              p.416☐E 15

Connoisseurs of books and art associate Oppenheim with the famous early printed books and copper etching workshop of Matthäus Merian the Elder, who worked here from 1617–20. But for most visitors to this romantic town on the high left bank

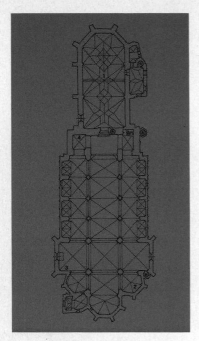

**Oppenheim, Katharinenkirche 1** Chancel by Madern Gerthener, 1415-39 **2** Tomb of Anna v.Dalberg (d.1410) **3** Tomb of Wolf and Agnes v.Dalberg, c.1520 **4** Tomb of Conrad v.Hantstein (d. 1553)

of the Rhine, the town's name is synonymous with wine growing on the Rhine. It became a free imperial town in 1220. Large areas were destroyed by fire in 1689.

**Katharinenkirche:** The present shimmering red sandstone building was constructed over several centuries, and the oldest sections (with the two towers) can be traced back to the 13C. The most important section of this magnificent church is the nave, dating from the third constructional phase in the early 14C. The rich tracery of the windows is without parallel in this region. The church had to be restored several times over the last few centuries, but this has impaired none or very little of its significance. Except for some first-class tombstones, none of the furnish-

ings have survived; they were destroyed in the fire of 1689. Beside the church is a *Totenkapelle* or Karner (funerary chapel) whose ossuary contains thousands of skulls and skeletons.

**Also worth seeing:** *Ruined castle of Landskron:* Little remains of Landskron castle, which was built in the 13C and was once a significant imperial fortress. However, it affords a superb view of the Rhine.

---

### Ortenburg 8359
Bavaria                                    p.422☐O 18

**Parish Church:** This 14C church is famous for its tomb monuments to the Ortenburg counts, who are mentioned as early as the 11C. The *altar tomb* to Count Joachim (1576&77) and that to Count Anton (built by Petzlinger in 1574&75) are particularly striking.

**Schloss:** This extensive 16C complex has survived as a typical Renaissance building. The coffered ceiling (*c.*1600) in the former banqueting hall is worth seeing. The hall was later converted into a Schloss chapel, one of the finest of the period and also one of the most important in Germany.

**Environs: Sammarei** (4 km. W.): Rural *Pilgrimage Church Mariäe Himmelfahrt* with a wooden chapel dating from 1521.

---

### Osnabrück 4500
Lower Saxony                               p.414☐D 8

This old episcopal and Hanseatic city between the Teutoburger Wald and the Wiehengebirge developed into an economic and intellectual centre at an early stage. Charlemagne founded a bishopric here *c.*780 and used the area as a centre for Christianization. It was near the present town of Osnabrück that the Emperor is said to have conquered and converted Widukind, his keenest adversary. When

*Katharinenkirche, Oppenheim* ▷

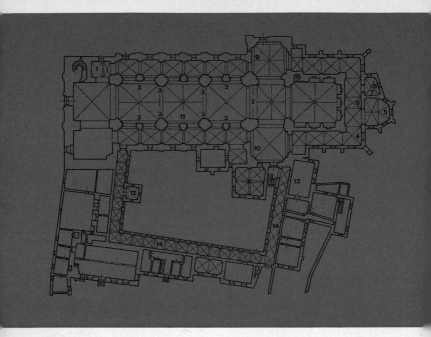

**Osnabrück, Dom 1** Font, 13C **2** Triumphal cross, c.1250 **3** Apostle sculptures by Westphalian Master, c.1525 **4** St. Margaret altar by the Osnabrück Master, remains dating from c.1520 **5** Pietà, late 15C **6** Christ in the Garden of Gethsemane, 1516 **7** Tabernacle in the Kreuzkapelle, 15C **8** Altar by the Osnabrück Master with a depiction of Lambert v.Snetlage, the founder, endowed in 1517 **9** Tomb of B.Voss, the Dom provost (d. 1617) **10** Tomb of Ferd. v.Kerssenbrock by J.C.Schlaun and Chr.Manskirch **11** Baroque pulpit by J.A.Vogel, 1751 **12** Effigy of Bishop Konrad v.Diepholz (d.1481) **13** Cathedral treasure **14** Diocesan museum

the collegiate foundation of St.Johann was established in 1011, the so-called Neustadt (new town) developed and in 1306 was united with the area called Altstadt (old town) around the cathedral. Osnabrück was the scene of an historical event in 1648 when the end of the Thirty Years' War was proclaimed on the steps outside the old Rathaus. Representatives of the Protestant side and of the Emperor here negotiated the Peace of Westphalia, at the same time as discussions were taking place in Münster. This peace gave rise to a curious arrangement for the Prince Bishopric: a Catholic bishop and a Protestant prince were to rule alternately. Osnabrück owed its rapid economic development mainly to its favourable geographical location which at an early date made it a trading centre for merchandise on its way from N. to S., but also from the Rhineland to the Baltic coast. Osnabrück reached its peak as an economic centre in 1768–83, when Justus Möser, the writer, historian, and statesman (1720–94), was the chancellor of the last Protestant Prince Bishop. However, Möser did not merely serve his native city, but also examined the development of theatre and literature. Möser's ideal of the free class of peasants and citizens, whose property is assured and who participate in political life by governing themselves made a considerable impact in Osnabrück and affected the further development of the city and subsequent generations. He is commemorated by a memorial tablet on the house where

*Dom in Osnabrück*

he was born (Markt) and by a monument in the cathedral square. His tombstone slab is in the floor of St.Marien (q.v.). In the Städtisches Museum there is extensive documentation of his life and work. The writer Erich Maria Remarque (1898– 1970), the author of 'All Quiet on the Western Front', was also born in Osnabrück.

**Dom St.Peter:** This building was started in the 11C. The octagonal crossing tower, built in the first few years of the 12C, has survived. However, the most important phase of construction was the 13C, when the NW tower was built and the crossing tower completed in its present form. The ambulatory was added in the 15C, while the massive SW tower is 16C. This long period of construction meant an impressive mixture of Romanesque and Gothic design. The visitor enters the church from the W. through a beautiful late Gothic portal, or from the N. and S. through round-arched colonnaded portals. He is immedi-

ately impressed by the massive vaults and columns. 16C sandstone figures depicting the Apostles are attached to the massive pillars of the nave. The ambulatory leads to two chapels; the SE of which contains tombs of bishops. In the 14C the lavish furnishings included 28 altars and other features, but these were much reduced in the 19C. The finest feature is the large *triumphal cross* (*c*.1250) decorated with gilded symbols of the Evangelists. Some further significant works of art (including a life-size 15C Pietà) can be observed in the chancel chapels, ambulatory and transepts. *Memorial tombs* of cathedral provost Voss (d.1617) and Ferdinand v.Kerssenbrock (the latter is by J.C.Schlaun) stand in the transepts. The life-size *effigy* of Bishop Konrad v.Diepholz (d.1482) is in the Nikolaus chapel in the cloister. The *cathedral treasure* is worth seeing, and the chapter cross of *c*.1050 is one of its most noteworthy items. It has a wooden core clad with gold and embellished with

*Choir ambulatory, Dom*

*Chapter cross, Dom treasure*

wooden figures. The cathedral treasure includes numerous other significant works of religious art dating from the 10–19C.

**St.-Marien-Kirche** (Am Markt): This church built in the 13C was gutted by fire in an air raid in 1944, but has been rebuilt and extended to the original design. The front (facing the Markt) impresses by its richly decorated gables. The external decorations also include life-size sandstone sculptures (including the Virgin Mary and the Magi). Inside, the absence of a transept means that the impression created is unusual but nevertheless well-balanced. Powerful multiple rib pillars support the Gothic vaults (the leaf capitals of the round pillars are worth looking at). The ambulatory was added in the 15C. The beautifully designed sacristy also dates from that period. The triumphal cross (*c.* 1320) is the focal point of the *furnishings*. It hangs above the 16C Antwerp Passion altar, which was severely damaged in the war.

The figures framed in gold and the painted panels have survived. They have been put together in a new shrine. Also worth seeing: font (1560), memorial tombs (by J.Brabender, A.Stenelt, G.Gröninger), wooden memorial to Derenthal, the episcopal chancellor (d.1691). A tombstone slab in the ambulatory commemorates Justus Möser (see introduction).

**Protestant Church of St. Katharine** (Hakenstrasse): The distinguishing feature of this church, begun in the 14C, but owing to the plague not completed until some 100 years later, is the tower, which is 335 ft. tall, and is thus the tallest in Osnabrück. Striking features of this hall church with nave and two aisles are its unusual width, and the powerful bundle pillars. The choir has blind arches and stone pews.

**Catholic Church of St.Johannis** (Johannisstrasse): The Johanniskirche was founded in 1011 at the same time as a col-

*Carved altar, Johanniskirche treasure*

legiate foundation, but the present building was not built until 1259 – 89. The interior of the church is in an emphatically plain style which sets off the fine furnishings. The *carved altar* (1511) is notable. Although this was made in Osnabrück, its artists were unmistakably influenced by the Flemish Passion altars of those times. In the chancel we find life-size *sandstone sculptures* showing Christ, the Virgin Mary and Apostles (*c*.1440). The *tabernacle* also dates from this period. Finally, the *church treasure* includes several first-class memorial stones and outstanding gold objects (12–19C).

**Gertrudenkirche** (Knollstrasse): This church completed in the 13C stands above the town. It has been exposed to many attacks as a result of its strategically important position; it is now used by the hospital service. The single nave and the large triumphal arch produce a magnificent spatial effect. The building is regarded as

typical of 13C Cistercian church architecture.

**Rathaus** (am Markt): The Rathaus, built in 1487–1512, is on the W. side of the triangular Markt. The dominant impression is that created by the two-sided open-air staircase (from which the 'Peace of Westphalia' was proclaimed in 1648) and by the large sculptures (today they are figures of Emperors, and formerly they were allegorical figures). A portrait of Charlemagne as the town's founder occupies a place of honour above the portal. The three-storey, plain building has graceful corner turrets and a steep roof. In the Rathaus is the *Friedenssaal* (peace hall), where the Peace of Westphalia was negotiated in 1648, concluding the Thirty Years War. The following decorations are worth seeing: The richly carved councillors' chairs dating from 1554, of a kind rarely to be found. Archive cupboards designed in the late Gothic style. A notable 16C wrought-iron

*Rathaus*

candlestick. The *Ratsschatz* (council treasure), which includes the so-called Kaiserpokal (imperial goblet; 14C). Tradition has it that the contents of this had to be emptied in one draught by each new member of the council. The document by which Emperor Barbarossa, in 1171, granted the town the right to fortify itself is also preserved in the council treasure.

**Merchants' houses by the Markt:** These 15–19C houses are of particular interest for their step gables. They were rebuilt to the original design after being destroyed in the Second World War.

**Prince Bishops' Schloss** (Neuer Graben): The Palazzo Madama in Rome was the model for the four-storey palace built around a rectangular interior courtyard. The owner was Ernst August I, who probably commissioned as architect P.Carato. The complex was rebuilt after it was gutted by fire in 1945.

**Old town fortification** (Herrenteichswall, Promenade, Vitischanze, Heger Tor): The Barenturm (1471) and Buckturm are the most striking items of the town fortifications, which have survived in very good condition. Medieval torture implements are on display in the Buckturm; they gained gruesome significance in connection with the witches' trials.

**Old town houses:** The Osnabrück town houses show marked originality, in contrast with the merchants' houses (see above) which are clearly based on Hanseatic models. Typical houses are to be found in Krahnstrasse, Marienstrasse and Bierstrasse (Hotel Walhalla).

**Museums:** The *Kulturgeschichtliches Museum* (27 Heger-Tor-Wall) has been set up in a stone building typical of Osnabrück. All these buildings have entrances at a very great height and thick walls, and this makes a fortress-like impression. The collections

*Prince Bishops' Schloss*

relate to: prehistory, early history, natural science, folklore, history of the town, ancient art, arts and crafts, national costumes, other costumes, weapons, knights' armour, coins and medals. *Diözesanmuseum* and *church treasures:* See under the descriptions of the individual churches.

**Theatres:** The *Städtische Bühnen Osnabrück* perform in the *Grosses Haus* (10–11 Domhof, 780 seats) and the *Stadthalle* (1–9 Schlosswall), and are responsible for the *Rathausspiele* (Rathaus/Marktplatz). They have their own company for theatre plays, opera, operetta and ballet.

**Also worth seeing:** The *bischöfliche Kanzlei* (1782–85), the *Hirschapotheke* (1797), and the *Städtische Sparkasse* (a banking house; 1790).

**Environs: Sutthausen** (4 km. S.): This extensive house is a smaller version of the Osnabrück Schloss and was built by

Oberhofmarschall G.B.v.Moltke in 1684–86.
**Wallenhorst-Rulle** (7 km. N.): Prehistoric *Karlsteine* stone chamber tomb at the foot of the Wiehengebirge range.
**Schledehausen** (14 km. E.): Jasper v.Schele, Luther's fellow student, caused the *Schelenburg,* a moated castle in the style of the 'Weser Renaissance, to be built by J.Unkair in 1528–32 around a 12C Romanesque *keep.*

---

**Osterhofen 8353**
Bavaria                              p.422□N 18

**Papal Basilica of St. Margaretha:** J.M.Fischer the architect, C.D.Asam the painter, and E.Q.Asam the sculptor and stucco worker were three of the most important artists of their time, and this fine former Premonstratensian monastery church is their work. The previous medi-

*Premonstratensian monastery church of St. Margaretha, Osterhofen-Altenmarkt*

eval building fell into disrepair, and reconstruction work began in 1727 and was finally completed in 1740 (including the interior decoration). This church is one of the most elaborate baroque church buildings in Bavaria. Stucco, vault fresco, and other ornamentation combine to form a unique baroque symphony. The culminating point is the *high altar* by E.Q.Asam.

---

**Osterode 3360**

Lower Saxony                           p.414□H 9/10

Osterode is near the border with East Germany and thus has no through traffic. It owes its development to its location on the important trade route from Goslar to the Leine valley. Considerable parts of the present town date from the period following the great fire in the town in 1545. The houses which survive reflect the town's

economic prosperity before the Thirty Years War.

**Protestant Church of St. Aegidien** (Marktplatz): This church was built after the fire of 1545 and renovated up until 1953. Its massive W.tower is not merely the most striking feature of the church, but also an Osterode landmark. The church is also worth seeing for the *tombs* of the Grubenhagen dukes who are buried here. The most significant of these tombstones is the work of E. Wolff the Younger of Hildesheim, delicate effigy of Duke Wolfgang.

**Protestant Schloss Church of St.Jakobi** (Jakobitorstrasse): This church dating from 1218 was radically restored in the mid 18C. The altars, the pulpit (supported by a figure depicting Moses), and the crucifix on the N.wall, are all worth seeing.

*Monastery church, Ottobeuren* ▷

**Harzkornmagazin** (grain store; Eisensteinstrasse): This building was erected in 1719–22 and held some 40,000 metric hundredweight of grain. This was intended to ensure that the local miners were supplied with grain even when times were hard.

**Also worth seeing:** The *Rathaus* (beside the Marktkirche): Built after the great fire in the town in 1545, with a neoclassical staircase. *Half-timbered houses:* Many fine houses, including the *Ratswaage* (1550) and the *Rinne'sches Haus* (1610) in the Kornmarkt, have survived the turmoils of the centuries. *Städtisches Heimatmuseum* (32 Am Rollberg), with exhibits on the history of the town.

---

## Ottobeuren 8942

Bavaria                                    p.422☐H 20

---

Ottobeuren, which is today a Kneipp health resort, developed in close association with the monastery, a complex as extensive as it is important. 764 is recorded as the year when the monastery was founded. However, several buildings dating from the 11C, 12C, 13C and 16C burned down before the present complex was finally started in the early 18C under Abbot Rupert II Ness von Wangen. The most noted artists, including A.Maini, D.Zimmermann and S.Kramer, competed for a commission for this building. The commission finally went to Kramer, but his plans were revised and altered by J.Effner from Munich, who was consulted at a later date. But Effner failed too. It was J.M.Fischer who finally completed the construction and thereby created one of the most magnificent buildings of the baroque period.

**Benedictine Monastery Church of the Holy Trinity:** Although Fischer had to take into account work carried out by his predecessors, the monastery church which he created is nonetheless uniform. The splendid nave has soaring arches. Richly designed chapels open behind it. Everything has enormous dimensions: the two towers are 270 ft. tall, while the interior is 290 ft. in length. The magnificent stucco which is the domoinant design element is the work of J.M.Feuchtmayer. The gloriously colourful frescos are the work of J.J.Zeiller. The Trinity picture surrounding the high altar is also by Zeiller. The figures by J.J.Christian are also of extremely high quality. In addition there are choir stalls with gilded reliefs, and an organ with a relief by J.J.Christian.

**Monastery building:** Planning of this extensive complex began in 1711, and construction work was completed in 1725. The best artists of the period contributed to the decoration, including J.B.Zimmermann and J.M.Feuchtmayer. The most interesting features are the chapterhouse, the Kaisersaal, the library, and the theatre.

**Klostermuseum:** The main items on display in the former residente rooms of the Reichsabtei Ottobeuren are works of ecclesiastical art from the Romantic period onwards.

---

## Owen, Teck 7311

Baden-Württemberg                          p.420☐G 18

---

**Burg Teck** (3 km. E. of Owen, followed by half-an-hour's walk): This castle located on a plateau in the foothills of the Schwäbische Alb was begun in the 12C but was later much altered and expanded. The castle was badly damaged during the Peasants' Revolt. Part of it was extended as a fortress in the 18C.

# Paderborn 4790

Nordrhein-Westfalen                    p.414☐F 9

The site of the city at the source of the Pader, once a member of the Hanseatic League, has had a long history; there were settlements here as early as the 3C and 4C. Paderborn became famous through Charlemagne, who had a palace here and held important imperial assemblies. In 799 he had a meeting with Pope Leo III, who obtained help from the Frankish king against his enemies in Rome and discussed with him his coronation as Emperor, which followed at Christmas 800 in Rome. The stone podium of a throne is still preserved in the palace court. Bishop Meinwerk (d. 1036) commissioned many of the buildings which determined the character of the city. The building which succeeded the Carolingian cathedral, the Benedictine monastery of Abdinghof and the canonical foundation of Busdorf all

*View of the town and Dom*

owe their existence to him. A Jesuit university was founded in Paderborn as part of the Counter-Reformation in 1614.

## Dom St. Maria, St. Liborius and St. Kilian (Domplatz): The cathedral, commissioned by Bishop Meinwerk, was burned down in 1058. The succeeding building with an extended E. chancel and new W. chancel was consecrated by Bishop Imad in 1068. The church was repeatedly damaged by fire and has been much modified. The present essentially Gothic building with its imposing late Romanesque W. tower and staircase towers dates largely from the 13C. The hall-church with nave, two aisles, 2 transepts and straight-ended

**Paderborn, Dom 1** Paradise **2** Hippolytuskapelle **3** Matthiaskapelle **4** Josefskapelle **5** Vituskapelle **6** Pfarrflügel wing **7** Marienkapelle **8** Sacristy **9** Brigida chapel **10** Atrium **11** Hasenkamp **12** Engelkapelle **13** Dreifaltigkeitskapelle **14** Elisabethkapelle **15** Meinolphuskapelle **16** Rote Pforte (red gate), c.1220-30 **17** Paradiesportal **18** Holy Sepulchre niche (remains) **19** Tomb of Bishop Bernhard V. zur Lippe (d. 1341) **20** Tomb of Bishop Heinrich v.Spiegel (d. 1380) **21** High altar, c.1420-40 **22** Sarcophagus of Bishop Rotho, c. 1450 **23** Altarpiece by G.van Loen, c.1500 **24** Tomb of Dietrich v.Fürstenberg by H.Gröninger **25** Christophorus by H.Gröninger, 1619 **26** Pulpit, 1736

E. chancel has a *crypt*, which extends as far as the crossing and is one of the largest in Germany. The exterior is enlivened by *tracery windows;* the lavishly decorated gables date from the 19C. The N. side with the *Rote Pforte*, a late Romanesque portal with steps (*c.*1230) has remained unaltered since the first building period. The finest feature of the exterior is the **Paradiesportal** in the S. porch, an important portal with figures (1250), unusual in Germany. On the central post is the Virgin Mary, and on the sides are figures of Apostles and saints. The Paradiesportal is late Romanesque in style, but has Gothic elements. In the wall by to the large window of the S. transept are *cycles of figures:* The Wise and Foolish Virgins, scenes from the life of Christ and other parts of the former *Brautportal* (1270–80). The interior of the splendid nave gives an impression of complete unity, despite differences of architectural style. The development of the building can be clearly seen in the development of the *capital decoration* from W. to E., which moves from late Romanesque stylised ornaments (partly with animals and masks) to early Gothic naturalistic leaf-work. Only the most important features of the extremely lavish furnishings can be

*Paradise portal, Dom*

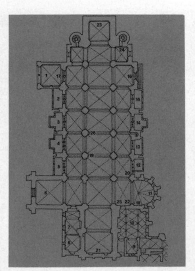

described: In the crossing is the magnificent 42 ft. high *tomb of Prince-Bishop Dietrich von Fürstenberg* (d.1618), in various kinds of stone; it is decorated with biblical scenes, saints and allegorical figures, and with carvings of the most important buildings erected by the Bishop. The tomb is the principal work of Mannerism in Westphalia. The *Westphalenkapelle* in the cloister contains the famous *tomb of the cathedral deacon Wilhelm von Westphalen* (d. 1517). Also of interest is the two-tier late Gothic *reliquary altar* in the high chancel (*c.*1420–40). The entrances from the nave to the *side-chapels* were very richly ornamented in the 17C. The most beautiful is the *portal of the Marienkapelle*. The *Hare Window* in the late Gothic *cloister*, with 3 running hares in a single circular motif, is the emblem of Paderborn.

**Imperial Palace (Kaiserpfalz):** Since 1964 a Carolingian and an Ottonian-Salic palace have been excavated on the N. side of the cathedral. The walls of the hall of the older building (8C) have been left as they were found, but its successor (11C) has been rebuilt (1978).

**Bartholomäus-Kapelle** (Kleiner Domp-

latz): N. of the cathedral is this unusual little chapel, which was built around 1071 under Bishop Meinwerk by builders described as *operaios graetos* (probably Istrian). It is the oldest known hall church on German soil.

**Franciscan Church of St. Josef** (Westernstrasse): This church (1668–71) has the most beautiful *baroque façade* in Westphalia. A.Petrimi of Trento, who worked in Würzburg, designed it in Roman baroque style, with 4 enormous pilasters and a flight of steps. A *portable altar* by Roger von Helmarshausen (*c.*1100) from the adjacent *monastery* is now in the Diocesan Museum.

**Protestant Church of Abdinghof** (Abdinghof): The former church of St.Peter and St.Paul was built under Bishop Meinwerk as a monastery church (11C). It is an archaic and austere basilica with a flat-ceilinged nave and closely set pillars. The *hall crypt* is particularly beautiful.

**Alexius-Kapelle** (Abdinghof): This small, octagonal rotunda was built in 1670–3 in place of the chapel of the same name, which was consecrated by Bishop

*Dom*

*Portable altar, St. Josef*

Meinwerk and had chapels with right of asylum.

**Collegiate Church of Busdorf** (Am Busdorf): Bishop Meinwerk founded a collegiate establishment here, to the E. of the cathedral precinct, in 1036. The formidable round staircase towers joined by a bell house and 2 wings of the Romanesque cloister survive in the E. part of the present building; the rest of the complex and the W. tower date from the 13C.

**Gaukirche/Catholic Parish Church of St.Ulrich** (Markt): From the street this basilica, mentioned as early as 1183 as parish church, looks like a baroque design with a concave *façade*, pilaster articulation, triangular gable and the niche figure of St.Ulrich above the portal. But on entering the church via the porch and the original W. portal one finds oneself in an austere 12C Romanesque building. Heavy rectangular pillars support the wide arches and

domes. The massive octagonal *crossing tower*, set slightly W. of centre, is well suited to the simple interior. The most valuable furnishings are a *stone Madonna* (1420), the *Calvary relief* (*c.* 1440) and the gable crucifix (14C), also heavily restored remains of Romanesque *wall painting*.

**Former Jesuit Church** (Jesuitenmauer): This gallery basilica with a nave and two aisles (1682) is striking above all for the double *terrace* in front of its wide *façade*. Impressive inside are tall Tuscan columns, Gothic-style vaulting and splendid stucco.

**Rathaus** (Rathausplatz): The existing building was commissioned by Bishop Dietrich von Fürstenberg in 1613–20 and used medieval walls from the earlier building. On the main façade, symmetrically positioned to the left and right, are 2 *Ausluchten* (gabled oriels). Below them are open halls supported by short Doric columns; they were once used as court loggias. The town hall is one of the latest and most beautiful buildings of the *Weser Renaissance*.

**Museums:** *Erzbischöfliches Diözesanmuseum* (17 Markt): Collection of ecclesiastical art from the diocese (sculpture, paintings, gold, textiles). The *Imad Madonna* (*c.*1060), originally donated to the cathedral by Bishop Imad, is one of the most important early Romanesque Madonna figures. The most valuable pieces are 2 *portable altars,* made by the monk Roger von Helmarshausen (*c.*1100), from the former cathedral treasury and the Franciscan church; the artistic metalwork shows Byzantine influence. *Kaiserpfalz Museum* (Ikenberg): Pre- and early history, Carolingian wall painting, architectural sculpture (8 – 12C). *Museum für Stadtgeschichte* (7 – 9 Hathumastrasse) in the Adam and Eve House, a late 16C half-timbered gabled house.

**Theatre** (Rathausplatz): The *Westfälische Kammerspiele* have their own company. 240 seats.

**Also of interest:** *Kurien-Kloster* and *houses,* e.g. at 1 Abdinghof, 1 Rothoborn and 38 Kamp; stone and half-timbered *town houses,* Heisingsche Haus (Stadtsparkasse, 2 Marienplatz), a superb Renaissance gabled house with oriels decorated with figures (*c.*1600).

*Rathaus, Paderborn*

---

**Passau 8390**

Bavaria                                   p.422☐O 18

---

Passau has grown up on a humped spit of land at the confluence of 3 rivers, the Inn, Danube and Ilz. The old Celtic city derived its name from the Roman Batavi cohorts, whose garrison was here: the name evolved from Batava to Bazzava to Passau. Boniface made the city a bishopric in 739. Bishop Pilgrim von Passau (970 – 91) is closely linked with the collecting and recording of the 'Nibelungenlied'.

**Dom St.Stephan** (Domplatz): The lavish late Gothic *E. choir* and *transept* (be-

gun in 1407, completed in 1520) have survived from the first building. The *Stephanstürmchen* on the N. transept is the clearest example of this style. The *W. part* of the church was rebuilt in 1668–78 in heavy Italian baroque after a fire. The unusually designed *dome* over the late Gothic crossing, a Romanesque pastiche, was added in the 18C. The octagonal upper parts of the two W. towers date from as late as 1896. The model was Salzburg cathedral, once a formidable rival of the bishop's city on the Danube and the Inn. The interior of the cathedral is, in contrast with the exterior, a unified whole. The *stucco* by the Italians G.B.Carlone and P.d'Aglio teems with three-dimensional life. Putti with tablets, prophets and caryatids throng on cornices and entablature; the new vaulting in the choir is borne by atlantes instead of the former Gothic ribs. In the course of the baroque conversion of the choir the Gothic *windows* were subdivided. Broad bands of stucco garlands, rosettes, wreaths and fruit rise to numerous shallow domes with *frescos* by C.Tencalla (1679–84). The ceilings in the side chapels are painted with bold trompe l'oeil effects by C.A.Bossi (Bussy). The *altars* with paintings by J.M.Rottmayr are particularly notable: side altars for St.Paul and John the Baptist ('Conversion' and 'Beheading') by the W. walls of the transept, also the altars of St.Agnes and St.Sebastian. The modern, multi-figured high altar with the Martyrdom of St.Stephen by J.Henselmann (1953) and the superb *pulpit* are of interest (1722–6). On the body of the pulpit and the sounding-board there are fine figures

Passau, Dom 1 Andreaskapelle 2 Ortenburger chapel 3 Sacristy 4 Tool chamber 5 Trenbachkapelle 6 Lambergkapelle 7 Crucifix, late Gothic 8 Side altars by Carlone, 1687-89 a) Maximilian-and Valentinsaltar b) Johannesaltar; painting by Rottmayr c) Katharinenaltar d) Altar of the Magi e) Agnes altar; painting by Rottmayr f) Sebastiansaltar; painting by Rottmayr g) Nativity altar h) Martinsaltar i) Altar of the conversion of St.Paul; painting by Rottmayr j) Virgin Mary altar 9 Ceiling paintings by Tencalla (except d)) a) St.Cecilia b) Cleansing of the Temple c) Old Testament sacrifice d) Outpouring of the Holy Spirit e) God's Triumphal March on Earth f) Triumph of the Church g) Stephen's dying face h) Stoning of St.Stephen i) Eucharist 10 Pulpit, 1726 11 Main organ; housing by M.Götz, 1731 12 Central altar by J.Henselmann, 1953 13 High altar, 1953

of the Viennese School. The gallery above the W. side houses, in a gold and gleaming front with some 17, 300 pipes, the largest *organ* in the world. In the Ortenburgkapelle (E. walk of cloister) is an extraordinarily beautiful work in the Gothic 'Soft Style': the effigy *tomb of Count Heinrich von Ortenburg* (c.1430). Worth seeing in the N. of the cathedral is the *Herrenkapelle* (14C), a hall chapel with a nave and two aisles.

**Alte Residenz** (Zengergasse): Grouped around 2 *courtyards* are buildings from various epochs; uniformity of appearance was achieved in the baroque period by the addition of portals, ornamentation and new interior furnishings. Of interest is the so-called *Saalbau* on the E. side, which like many parts of the residence dates from late Gothic times and was redecorated in the baroque period.

**Neue Residenz** (Residenzplatz): The New Residence grew out of the Old Residence complex. Its baroque façade forms a charming contrast with the lavish late Gothic choir of the cathedral. The core of

*Passau, panorama with Dom* ▷

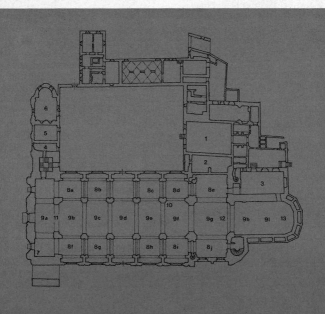

*Fountain with Neue Residenz*

the building (1712–32) is the magnificent *staircase,* whose steps and landings rise around a rectangular space. With its glowing stucco decoration and lantern-bearing putti, topped by a soaring fresco of Olympus, it is, with the staircase in the Mirabellschloss in Salzburg, the most beautiful staircase in the SE German region. On the *upper floor* of the residence there is a suite of rooms furnished with lavish stucco, panelling, tapestries, tiled stoves, chandeliers, paintings and furniture.

**Heilig-Kreuz-Kirche** (Jesuitengasse): E. of the Domberg, on the lower part of the promontory, which has been settled since the 2C BC, are the *Niedernburg Monastery* and church. The *pillars* in the church are still essentially Romanesque in arrangement (*c.*1010). The *W. porch,* with the former nuns' gallery above, also dates from the same time. The *nave* was cleared of all baroque features in 1860–5. The baroque

vaults, however, were spared during the Romanesque conversion. Of interest are the Romanesque and Gothic tombstones in the *Parzkapelle.*

**Former Jesuit church of St. Michael** (Schustergasse): Just one block to the W. of the Heilig-Kreuz-Kirche, on the bank of the Inn, is the double-towered baroque church of St. Michael. After a complaint by the Bishop, who wished to preserve the architectural dominance of the cathedral, this Jesuit building ended up less ostentatious than had originally been planned. It is an example of Italian baroque. The interior *stucco-work* is reminiscent of the cathedral. Most notable of the furnishings are the *high altar* and the splendid *pulpit* (both early 18C). The *seminary buildings* now house the Catholic theological faculty of the university.

**St. Severin** (Innstadt): On the other side of the Inn is the spot where Passau's first missionary, St. Severin (d.482), built his cell, which still exists, although it has been greatly altered. The present building, now a cemetery chapel, still has Carolingian walls in the nave (8&9C). The choir was built in 1476. The finest interior feature is the Gothic *Madonna* (*c.*1450).

**Pilgrimage Church of Mariahilf** (3 Mariahilfberg): The Mariahilfkirche, a 17 and early 18C building with an unusual tower, is above Innstadt. It was built to house the copy of the Innsbruck miraculous image by L.Cranach, and is artistically of less importance.

**Salvatorkirche** (Ilzstadt): This church was built in 1470 in place of a synagogue as an expiation church (due to an alleged desecration of the host by Jews) below the Oberhaus fortress. The building is set deep in the hillside, with the result that the lower storey of the choir was made into a *crypt* .

**Veste Oberhaus** (Oberhaus): The bishops' citadel, built on the ridge between the Danube and Ilz to suppress the townspeople, is divided into *outer works* and several *courtyards*. Baroque and Renaissance ornamentation gives the simple buildings a feeling of style. The Gothic *St.George's Chapel* is furnished in baroque style. Museums (see below).

**Veste Niederhaus** (Wagnerstrasse): Below the Veste Oberhaus, on the outermost promontory, stands the Veste Niederhaus, a tall building (probably 14C) with outer works. The building is connected to the Veste Oberhaus by a defence rampart.

**Sommerschloss Freudenhain** (Eggendobl): W. of the suburb of Anger, on the N. bank of the Danube, is the summer residence of the Prince Bishops, built in 1785. This elegant, early neoclassical building is surrounded by an English park and now houses a grammar school.

**University** (in the former monastery of St.Nikolas): Bavaria's eighth and most recent university was opened in October 1978 with 5 faculties for 4000 students.

**Theatre:** The *Fürstbischöfliche Hoftheater* (4 Innstrasse, 400 seats), built in 1783 by G.Hagenauer, is the home of the musical department of the *SE Bavarian Städtetheater*. Touring performances are also held here and Passau hosts the important annual *Europäische Festspielwochen* with international orchestras and theatre companies. The *Nibelungenhalle* is the centre for numerous cultural events.

**Museums:** The *Böhmerwald-Museum* and the *Historische Stadtmuseum*, a branch of the *Bayerische Staatsgemäldesammlungen*, and a few other *specialist collections*, are housed in the Veste Oberhaus. *Dommuseum* (8 Residenzplatz) in the Papstsaal of the Neue Residenz, accessible from the cathedral: cathedral treasure, cathedral history (to be opened in 1986). *Diözesanmuseum* (8 Residenzplatz) in the library room of the Neue Residenz: panel paintings, paintings, sculpture, reliefs and liturgical instruments from the diocese of Passau (to be opened in 1987). *Römisches Museum Boiotro* (43 Lederergasse; Roman museum).

**Also worth seeing:** The *Rathaus* (on the bank of the Danube) was built in 1393 and has been much altered. The inner courts and the baroque-furnished Grosse Rathaussaal (1662) are charming, as is the neo-Gothic tower (1888–93). The *Domherrenhöfe* (Domplatz): 16C, 17C and 18C with interesting façades. The *Scheiblingsturm* (1481), a remainder of the former city fortifications on the bank of the Inn, and remains of old *Roman fortifications* on the Danube side.

---

## Pellworm 2251

Schleswig-Holstein                p.412☐F 2

Pellworm is the remaining part of the otherwise submerged Altnordstrand; the marshy island in the Wattenmeer is protected by massive stone dams. Ferry link via Husum (q.v.).

**Old Church:** The distinguishing feature of this simple, unpretentious church is the tower, which collapsed in 1611 and has since been preserved as a ruin. Of interest are the *Schnitger Organ* (1711), a *bronze font* and an *altar* with late Gothic panel paintings.

**Also worth seeing:** A few of the *old houses* are preserved in their original form and reflect the islanders' struggle against the forces of nature.

---

**Perschen = Nabburg 8470**
Bavaria                                    p.418☐ L 16

**Parish Church:** This twin-towered basilica is one of the oldest churches in the Upper Pfalz (oldest sections suggest a 10C building), but it was greatly altered by restoration in 1752&3. The adjoining, two-storey *funerary chapel,* probably even older than the church, contains interesting 12C *frescos.*

**Oberpfälzer Bauernmuseum:** This rural museum is accommodated in the *Edelmannshof,* a 12C farmstead.

---

**Petersberg = Erdweg 8065**
Bavaria                                    p.422☐ K 19

**Former Benedictine Monastery Church:** This pillared basilica with nave, 2 aisles and 3 apses (1104–7) has a Romanesque core. The Romanesque *wall paintings* in the apse were uncovered in 1907, and restored. Notable on the S. wall is a carved *figure of the Virgin Mary* (*c.* 1520).

---

**Pforzheim 7530**
Baden-Württemberg                          p.420☐ E 17

This town, rich in Roman remains, derives its name from the Latin portus. It is famous for its jewellery and as the birthplace of the humanist J.Reuchlin.

**Protestant Schloss and Collegiate Church of St.Michael** (4 Neuer Schloss-

berg): Nothing remains of the *Schloss,* the former residence of the Margraves of Baden-Durlach, but the *Archivturm.* All but the outer walls of the church were destroyed in 1945, but it was rebuilt in an exemplary fashion in 1949 – 57. Building began in 1225–35 from W. to E., contrary to all medieval building customs, because of the sloping ground. Thus the W. end, with *porch* and *rose window* on the S. gable, was built first; the fine stepped *W. portal* with its imaginative sculptural decoration is also part of this section. The rest of the building is early Gothic. The massive *collegiate choir* is significantly higher than the nave, and has outstanding stellar vaulting. The church also contains the *wall-tombs* of the Margraves of Baden-Durlach; St. Michael's has been their funerary chapel since 1535.

**Altenstädter Protestant Parish Church of St.Martin** (Altstädterstrasse): An interesting *portal* in the W. tower porch has survived from the Romanesque basilica. On the tympanum symbolic figures depict the Threat of Evil to Mankind and its Salvation through the Church. The beautiful *choir* (1340) contains late Gothic *wall paintings* with the Last Judgement,

*St.Michael, Pforzheim*

Sheltering Mantle of the Virgin Mary and saints (1430–50).

**Museums:** The *Schmuckmuseum* (Reuchlinhaus, 42 Jahnstrasse) shows 4,000 years of the history of jewellery. *Heimatmuseum* (to the W., 243 Karl-Friedrich-Strasse): Scientific instruments, goldsmiths' tools.

**Stadttheater und Podium** (Osterfeldstrasse): Municipal theatre; 394 seats.

**Also worth seeing:** The tent-like *Protestant Matthäuskirche* (1953) by E.Eiermann, a successful modern church building, is in Arlinger; nearby Tiefenbronn has the Catholic parish church of *St. Maria Magdalena* (Gothic basilica *c.*1430, with an altar-painting by Lucas Moser, 1431).

---

### Pilsum = Krummhörn 2974

Lower Saxony p.414□C 5

---

**Protestant Parish Church:** This single-aisle, cruciform brick church is one of the most beautiful and best-preserved late Romanesque buildings in E. Frisia. The massive 14C *crossing tower*, which needed particularly sturdy crossing pillars, is a striking feature. With its brightly plastered blind arches, visible for miles, it served for centuries as a landmark for steering into the Ems estuary. The very low detached *bell tower* is on the E. side; the geometrical division of the transept gables is also unusual. The bronze *font* (1469) has lavish relief decoration and strange supporting figures: human forms with symbols of the Evangelists instead of heads. *Pulpit, organ* and *gallery* date from the baroque period.

---

### Pirmasens 6780

Rheinland-Pfalz p.420□C 16

---

Pirmasens, centre of the German shoe industry, was the residence of Landgrave Ludwig IX of Hessen-Darmstadt in the 18C. The town was almost totally destroyed in the Second World War.

**Altes Rathaus:** This late baroque building (1717–47) was destroyed in 1945; it was rebuilt in 1959–63 to historic plans, but with an extra storey. Today the building houses a museum of pre- and early history, the Heimatmuseum (local history), the Maler-Heinrich-Bürkel Gallery and the shoe museum.

---

### Plettenberg 5970

Nordrhein-Westfalen p.416□D 11

---

**Protestant Parish Church/Christuskirche** (Kirchplatz): This former church of St. Lambert with its heavy W. tower was the model for various S. Westphalian hall churches; in its turn it was modelled on churches in Cologne. The *staircase towers* between transept and choir, with fan-shaped transverse levels, are unusual. Depicted in the tympanum of the *S. portal* are a naïve representation of the Crucifixion, the Birth of Christ and the Women at the Tomb. Interior *paintwork*, of a kind unusual in German churches, was

*Rathausplatz, Pirmasens*

*Schloss, Plön*

uncovered in the choir (with the arms of popes and cardinals, 15C). In the plain interior the half-columns in front of the pillars have bulbous capitals, in the typical Sauerland style. Some corner capitals are shaped as human or rams' heads.

**Also worth seeing:** The 13C *Protestant parish church* in Plettenberg-Ohle, with wall paintings.

---

**Plön 2320**
Schleswig-Holstein                    p.412□H 3

**Schloss** (3 Schlossgebiet): This Schloss is on the Grosser Plöner See in the middle of the 'Holstein Switzerland', with its many lakes. It was built in 1633–6 by Duke Joachim Ernst von Schleswig-Holstein-Sonderburg-Plön on the site of a 9C residence of the Wendic princes. In the mid 18C the last Duke of Plön ran an extrava-

gant court on French lines. 100 years later the castle was used as a summer residence by the Danish Royal Family, in Prussian times it was a cadet school and in the Third Reich it was a national institution for political education. Today it is a boarding school. The 3-winged building with its series of uniform gables has a sober exterior; the baroque ridge-turret lanterns are the sole decoration. The interior was converted to accommodate a cadet school; the window openings were altered. Some Italian-style *staircases* have survived in their original form, as have a room of 1750 (on the first floor) and the ducal bed-chamber (with lavish carving in the alcoves and Italian stucco on the ceilings and walls). The *former library* has carved rococo panelling. Below the *castle chapel* is the ducal vault with splendid 17&18C *sarcophagi*. The *Prinzenhaus* (now the girls' house of the school) is also in the Schloss precincts; its central section, on seven axes, with lavish interior decoration (stucco, painting),

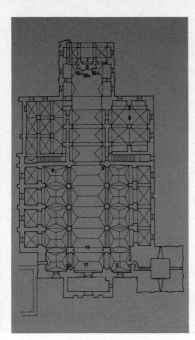

**Polling, Stiftskirche 1** Tombstone of Provost Schondorfer (d.1382) **2** Font, Gothic **3** Virgin Mary, c.1500 **4** Tombstone of v.Peissenberg of Tuchsenhausen, 1512 **5** Seated figure of the Virgin Mary by H.Leinberger, 1526 **6** Virgin Mary altar, consecrated 1525 **7** High altar by B.Steinle, 1623 **8** Achbergkapelle chapel, 1762-64 **9** Tabernacle by J.B.Straub, 1763 **10** Wooden reliefs by Straub, 1763 a) Gathering the manna, b) Last Supper, c) Emmaus disciples **11** Organ, housing of 1768

is the most integrated example of rococo architecture in Schleswig-Holstein. Particularly beautiful are the octagonal *vestibule*, the oval *summer-house* with curved music gallery and small *corner-cabinets*.

**Museum des Kreises Plön** (1 Johannisstrasse): Now accommodated in the rooms of the former *Alte Apotheke* are collections on local pre- and early history, craft antiques, pewter, glass and pottery.

**Also worth seeing:** The *former mews* (in

the Schloss precincts); brick building of 1745&6.

---

**Polling bei Weilheim 8121**
Bavaria                    p.422☐K 20

**Former Augustinian Canonry Church:** The distinguishing feature of this church is its massive *tower*, begun in the 17C to plans by H.Krumper, and completed in 1822. The other parts of the church date mostly from 1416–20, when earlier buildings were replaced. The lavish stucco and the tower were added in the 17C. The finest feature of the lavish furnishings is the *high altar* by B.Steinle of Weilheim (1623). On the upper floor of the 2-storey complex is the famous *Tassilo Cross*, the front side of which is covered with horse-skin. It was first gilded, then the Crucifixion was painted on it in watercolours (*c.*1230). Notable along with the superb *tabernacle* are the *pulpit* (1705), the *enthroned Virgin Mary*, carved by H.Leinberger of Landshut (1526), other *altars* (in the side chapels, with paintings by famous artists from the 2nd half of the 18C), a wrought-iron *grille* and the *organ-front* (1768). The *Achbergkapelle* or *Reliquary Chapel* is also notable (stucco decorations, paintings). Very little remains of the adjacent former *monastery buildings*. Of interest is the 3-storey library (1775–8). The former lay-brothers' refectory contains the fresco 'Parnassus' by M.Günther.

---

**Pommersfelden = Steppach 8602**
Bavaria                    p.418☐I 15

**Schloss Weissenstein:** A few km. from the Bamberg exit of the Würzburg-Nürnberg motorway is the magnificent palace built by Chancellor of the Empire Prince Bishop Lothar Franz von Schönborn in 1711 – 18. 3 architects were involved: J.Dientzenhofer as chief architect, M. von Welsch from Mainz and the Viennese court architect J.L. von Hildebrandt. Weissenstein was the first great 18C palace building in Germany. Originally the

*Schloss Weissenstein, Pommersfelden*

old moated Schloss in the village was to be converted, but L.F. von Schönborn had caught the 'building bug'; he sat up at night 'brooding over the plans with a pair of dividers', and wanted no half-measures; he therefore sited the palace on open ground SE of the village. The palace is still owned by the Schönborn family. The *central building*, which contains the staircase, is flanked by 2 projecting *side wings*. This rectangular *main courtyard* is opposite the rounded *mews* building planned by M. von Welsch (1714–17). The heart of the palace is the massive *staircase*, probably designed by the Prince Bishop himself, with the help of L. von Hildebrandt. The stairs rise in two flights, each broken twice, to the first floor, above which 2 open galleries surround the enormous well; the slightly vaulted ceiling (suspended from the roof truss) has a trompe-l'oeil painting by J.R.Byss depicting the 4 parts of the world with Olympian Gods at the centre (1718). The staircase and its galleries were prin-

cipally intended for show. Behind the staircase on the ground floor is the *Grottensaal*, a low tufa vault opening on to the garden, adorned with shells, minerals, mirrors and stucco leaves, with fountains, groups of figures and glittering chandeliers. Above this is the marble *Hauptsaal* of the palace. This has free-standing columns by the walls and heavy beams with massive figures. Figures of Italian painters (Balestra, Reni, Lazzarini, Caravaggio and Seiter) are to be found in oval niches with windows behind them. Below these on the shorter walls above the chimney-pieces and on the longer wall by the staircase are portraits of important members of the Schönborn family. The ceiling painting 'Victory of the Virtues over the Vices' is by J.F.Rottmayr (1717). Also of interest is the *Spiegelkabinett* in the NE corner of the building, with its forests of gilded consoles. Exotic ornaments and motifs, with depictions of Indians, Turks and Chinese, twine around the oriental porcelain, which the

*Ceiling painting in stair well*

Prince Bishop, an enthusiastic collector, imported by the shipload from the Far East. A festively laid table in the *Banqueting Hall* demonstrates courtly table ceremonial in the 18C. Apart from its *library,* the palace is also famous for its *picture gallery,* housed in various rooms and passages and including works by Rubens, Rembrandt, Titian, Breughel, Cranach and Dürer. The walls of the gallery, which is still laid out entirely in baroque style, appear to be papered with paintings. In the *mews* opposite the palace the oval saddleroom in the middle is worth seeing, with coaches and sledges, as well as suitable ceiling and wall paintings.

**Preetz 2308**

Schleswig-Holstein                    p.412☐H 3

**Protestant Collegiate Church:** Preetz lived under the territorial sovereignty of the Benedictine convent, the collegiate church of which has survived next to the Campus Beatae Mariae. A striking feature is the large *saddle roof,* which lies protectively over the nave and two aisles of the Gothic brick church (1325–40). The unusually massive *supporting pillars* also add to the impression that the church is securely rooted in the ground and built for all eternity. Overall, although much was altered in the 19C according to the neo-Gothic attitudes to style, it is a good example of the type of building in the region. A graceful *roof-turret lantern,* a polygonal *staircase tower* (on the N. side of the chancel) and tall pointed-arch *tracery windows* relieve the heaviness of the building. The interior has generally kept the original form of a convent church, with *sanctuary, choir leaders' stall* and *choir* (with Gothic stalls, 1335–40). The sanctuary, with the baroque *high altar* with figures, (1743) ends in a splendid wrought-iron *grille* with acanthus tendrils and coats of arms. At the end

of the N. side aisle, the *carved altar* with the Holy Kindred and well-painted panels (early 16C) is particularly worth seeing. The *wooden pulpit* (1674) with angels and Redeemer on the sounding-board and the organ (Renaissance casing and rococo additions) are also worthy of note. In 1843 furnishings were inherited from the church of Dänischenhagen, including beautiful *carvings*, *paintings* and *ecclesiastical implements*.

**Protestant Town Church:** The 13C former church of St.Lorenz was converted into a baroque hall church in 1725–8. The superb *W. gallery* has survived.

**Prien am Chiemsee 8210**
Bavaria                                   p.422☐M 20

**Parish Church Mariae Himmelfahrt:** This hall church with shallow barrel vaulting was built in 1735–8. It is so large because of the size of the parish it was intended to serve. Famous artists such as J.B.Zimmermann (stucco and frescos, collaboration on a few altars) contributed to the fine furnishings. The uniform marble

altars were made by a master from Salzburg (1738–40). The excellent wrought-iron *grille*, on the steps to the pulpit, was made by a local smith. The *tombs* date mostly from the 16&17C.

**Heimatmuseum** (1 Friedhofweg): Costume collection, arts and crafts, workshops and gallery with pictures by Chiemgau artists.

**Prüm 5540**
Rheinland-Pfalz                           p.416☐A 13

**Church of the former Benedictine Abbey:** This basilica, 'whose towers and façades transform the town and its surroundings into a baroque meadow' (Wolfgang Weyrauch), has become the emblem of the town, visible for miles. The building replaced an older church in 1721–30. The plans were drawn up by J.G.Judas of Trier. Serious damage sustained in the Second World War has since been completely repaired. The *façade*, articulated with red sandstone, has 3 portals. The spacious interior has a distinctive *groin vault*. The *choir stalls* and the *high*

◁ *Stair well, Pommersfelden*                    *Former Benedictine abbey with church, Prüm*

*altar* have survived from the baroque furnishings; the 16C *pulpit* is from the old church.

**Abbey buildings:** Balthasar Neumann was involved in the construction of the abbey buildings, along with S.Seitz and his son. Works was not concluded until 1912, however, when the building became a school and district court.

---

**Prunn, Altmühl 8421**

Bavaria                                    p.422□L 17

**Burg:** On a bizarrely pinnacled limestone crag above the Altmühl valley lies Prunn Castle, named after the first owner, mentioned around 1037, Wernherus de Prunne. The most famous owner was 'Happy Hans' Frauenberger (d.1428), whose tomb is in the parish church of the village of Prunn. He went down in history as the greatest jouster and campaigner of his time. For a while the castle belonged to the Jesuit College of Ingolstadt and later to the Order of St.John. In 1822 it came into the possession of the Wittelbachs. The young King Ludwig I ordered an extensive restoration and conservation of the dilapidated castle in 1827. Since then the 'Jewel of the Altmühl Valley' has belonged to the State of Bavaria as a museum. A tour of the castle still gives an impression of the living conditions of bygone times. The sole entrance to the castle, at the most vulnerable point, leads over a deep *moat* past the strong, bulky, almost windowless *keep.* This is the oldest part of the complex. Adjacent to the S. is a largely Romanesque *residential wing* (12&13C). The buildings around the *gate complex* with pretty shingle-roofed corner towers were added in 1604. These contain on the lower floor a gate-keeper's room, on the first floor a kitchen, heated lady's apartment and drinking room. One of the most beautiful rooms is the *Gothic room* (Stube) in the side wing on the E. side.

**Also worth seeing:** Upstream from Prunn there are *Palaeolithic cave dwellings*.

---

**Pullach 8023**

Bavaria                                    p.422□K 20

**Heilig-Geist-Kirche:** This plain church (1468–88) has retained its fine late Gothic furnishings. Notable above all are the sculptures and panel paintings.

**Environs: Schloss Schwaneck** (2.5 km. N.) was built in 1842 as a romantic country seat for the sculptor L. von Schwanthaler. Now a youth hostel.

# R

## Raesfeld 4281
Nordrhein-Westfalen        p.414☐B 9

**Wasserschloss** (moated Schloss): Count Alexander II v.Velen, the 'Westphalian Wallenstein' (he was an imperial field marshal in the Thirty Years' War), brought the town of Raesfeld a fame which transcended its architectural interest. The Count inherited the central section of the moated castle from his father. Extension work began towards the end of the Thirty Years'

War on the basis of the plans of Michael v.Gent, a Capuchin. However, only some parts of the Schloss, which was built around a courtyard, survive. These are the *Oberburg, Unterburg* and *chapel*. The *corner tower* is a conspicuous feature.

## Raitenhaslach 8261
Bavaria        p.422☐N 19

**Former Zisterzienserklosterkirche**

*The moated Schloss at Raesfeld (17C)*

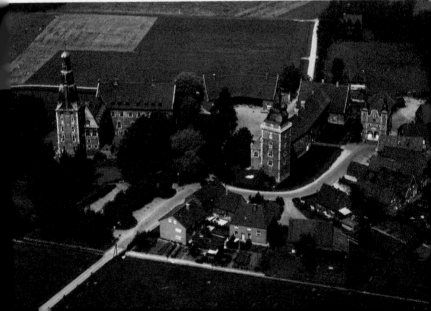

(Cistercian monastery church): Although some basic features of this 12C building survive, they are practically indiscernible today after the radical rebuilding of the late 17C. The church is one of the most richly decorated baroque churches in Bavaria, contrasting markedly to most other Cistercian buildings, which were tied to the strict rules of the order and were emphatically plain buildings. The unusual colourfulness of the *ceiling frescos* surprises every visitor. They depict the life of Bernard of Clairvaux, the founder of the order. The Romanesque walls were increased in height during the baroque alterations and the choir was divided into two storeys (the sacristy below, the monks' choir above). The decorations were the work of two of the most famous artists of their time: the *stucco* is by M.Zick from Kempten, while the frescos and the painting at the *high altar* are the work of J.Zick from Ottobeuren. Four of the *side altars* have fine panel paintings by J.M. Rottmayr, the famous Austrian baroque painter. Other interesting features include the *pulpit* (1740), the *organ front* (1697, enlarged in the 18C), the 18C *Holy Sepulchre* in the W.portico, and

*Former collegiate St. John the Baptist in Rasdorf near Hünfeld*

the beautiful *tombs*. Little survives of the former *monastery buildings*.

---

### Randersacker 8701
Bavaria                                    p.418□H 15

**Pfarrkirche** (parish church): The late Romanesque church stands inside a fortified courtyard which was built in the 17C. The most important section is the four-storeyed, typically Romanesque tower. The decoration is baroque.

**Also worth seeing:** *Neumann-Pavillon* (pavilion): Next to the old *Gasthaus Krone* inn, the famous architect B.Neumann built himself a garden pavilion. The 17C *Mönchshof* has a gate and a secularized chapel (Thomaskapelle).

---

### Rasdorf 6419
Hessen                                    p.416□G 12

**Catholic Pfarrkirche/former Kirche des Kollegiatsstifts St. Johannes des Täufers** (parish church/collegiate church of St.John the Baptist): Founded by Hrabanus Maurus in *c*. 838. It collapsed in the 13C and the present basilican church built, with a nave, two aisles, a transept, and an octagonal tower over the crossing. The warriors, columns, and in particular the fine *capitals* (probably 9 or 10C) which frame the arcades, were taken from the earlier church. These items are amongst the most important examples of stone architectural sculpture from before 1200. The church furnishings are baroque.

**Also worth seeing:** A fortified *graveyard* in the E. of the town (a wall with round towers). *Half-timbered houses.*

---

### Rastatt 7550
Baden-Württemberg                          p.420□D 17

Margrave Ludwig Wilhelm, in conjunction with his wife Sybilla Augusta of Saxony-Lauenburg who continued his ambitious plans after his death, created a town of unusual expansiveness at Rastatt. Rossi from Vienna laid out the town in accordance with the Margrave's ideas and its centre was completed in ten years.

**Schloss** (Herrenstrasse): The owner and his architect wished to bring the splendour of Italian palazzi and French châteaux (Versailles) to the upper Rhine and consequently Rastatt became the site of the first baroque schloss built on such a scale in Germany. Work on the splendid schloss at the heart of the town took seven years and it is still in excellent condition. The Rathausstrasse, Schlossstrasse and Museumsstrasse fan out from the schloss. Its central section, the *Corps de Logis* (residence), dominates the wings which are grouped around a *main courtyard*. The *N.wing*, with the Schlosskirche, and the *S.wing* which contains rooms for a theatre, followed after the death of Ludwig Wilhelm in 1707. Inside, the *staircases* are among the most successful pieces of design to be found in a baroque Schloss. They lead up on two sides to the first floor, and also, via an extensive landing, to the *Fest-saal* (festival hall). Also known as the Ahnensaal (hall of the ancestors), its frescos show Herakles being taken up to Olympos. The *Schlosskirche Heiliges Kreuz* (Church of the Holy Cross) directly adjoins the Margravine's apartments. The designs for this are not by Rossi, but by M.L. Rohrer, who had taken over the supervision of the building after the death of 'Türkenlouis' —the Margrave was known as Ludwig or Louis the Turk. A magnificent portal leads the visitor into the pilastered church. Great importance was attached to the interplay of light and colours, and it is for this reason that there are numerous, smaller ornamental panels in addition to the large fresco of the vault. The *high altar*, with the silvered wooden crucifix, is a gorgeous eye-catcher. The *Kapelle of Maria Einsiedeln* is in a terraced garden which was connected to the schloss at the time when the latter was built, but is today separated by a road. This chapel was consecrated in 1717, and its plain decorations are different in character from those of the schloss. Next to the chapel, the *Pagodenburg* (1722), inspired by the pagoda in the grounds of the Nymphenburg, Munich, complements the Margrave's buildings. Rohrer slightly altered J.Effner's plans for it.

*Schloss, Rastatt*

*Schloss Favorite, Rastatt*

**Schloss Favorite** (5 km. S., towards Baden-Baden): After the death of her husband Ludwig Wilhelm, Margravine Sybilla Augusta had this isolated country seat built by M.L. Rohrer in accordance with her own ideas, and the shell was complete by 1711. She wanted to create a retreat for contemplation for herself here, whilst retaining a lavish way of life. The focal point of the schloss is its garden front, where two flights of steps curve up to the first floor of the well-articulated façade. An octagonal *tower* emphasizes the opulent character of this distinguished building. The focus of the interior is formed by the *Speisesaal* (dining hall), which is sumptuously decorated like all the other rooms in this gem of a building. The *Prunkküche* (kitchen) is worth seeing, as are the opulent *living apartments*. The main building is flanked by low *arcaded wings* which probably served as orangeries. A little way off there are four *cavaliers' houses* and the *hermitage*.

**Rathaus and Marktplatz**: The Marktplatz was part of Rossi's overall plan. It is dominated by the Stadtkirche (town church) and Rathaus, even though the church was not built until later (consecrated in 1764). The Rathaus was completed in 1750. The *Stadtkirche* bears the stamp of the beginnings of the neoclassical style. Note the high altar.

**Museums:** The *Heimatmuseum* (Herrenstrasse) is devoted to the history of the town and region. The *Wehrgeschichtliches Museum* (Museum of Military History), consisting of 42 rooms within the baroque schloss, has important exhibits spanning the period from the Middle Ages to the present. The *Freiheitsmuseum* (Freedom Museum), also housed in the Schloss, documents the liberation movements which have occurred in German history.

**Environs: Hohenbaden** (14 km. SE): The *Altes Schloss Hohenbaden* is on the Bat-

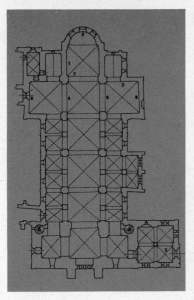

**Ratzeburg, Dom 1** Remains of the choir stalls, c.1200 **2** Triumphal Cross group, the subsidiary figures (Virgin Mary, John) dating from c.1260 **3** S.portico **4** Gothic sedilia, c.1340 **5** Former Cross altar, late 15C, with paintings by H.v.Krog, between 1481 and 1487 **6** Pulpit by H.Matthes, 1576 **7** Bronze font (1440) with wooden cover by H.Matthes, 1577 **8** High altar by J.G.Tietge, 1629 **9** Tomb of August v.Sachsen-Lauenburg and Duchess Catharina by J.G.Tietge, 1649

*Dom with triumphal cross, Ratzeburg*

E.Barlach, is closely associated with Ratzeburg. He spent part of his youth here from 1878 – 84, and was buried in the churchyard by the Seedorfer Strasse in 1938.

**Dom** (Domhof): The magnificent Romanesque cathedral is said to have been begun in 1170 and it was largely complete by the turn of the 13C. Extensive rebuilding in 1961–6 restored the original appearance of the cathedral, both outside and inside. The ground plan is that of a basilica (one nave, two aisles). Externally it is distinguished by a massive W. *tower* and by its red brick. Indeed, the *portico* is an impressive testimony to the extensive possibilities of brick. Inside, the cathedral impresses by its plainness. A late Romanesque *triumphal cross* (*c.* 1260) is a prominent feature of the nave, depicting Christ nailed to the Cross, with Mary and John beside Him (altered in the 17C). Outside the Katharinenkapelle in the S. aisle there is

tert near Baden-Baden, and 3 km. W. of it is the ruined *Ebersteinburg*. Both these castles are at altitudes of over 1,300 ft. and offer fine views.

---

**Ratzeburg 2418**

Schleswig-Holstein                              p.412 □ I 4

The town occupies an island in Lake Ratzeburger and is connected to the mainland by three causeways. It took its present form after the irregular old town was destroyed in 1693. The lay out adopted at that time is still clearly discernible today, and was modelled on Mannheim. The name of one of the major sculptors of the 20C,

*Pews of Dukes of Saxony, Dom*

a finely carved Gothic *pew of the Dukes of Saxony*. The Romanesque *choir stalls* date from *c*. 1200 and are the oldest in N. Germany. The *rood altar* stands in the choir (with paintings dating from 1481–7); the stone Passion panel is in the 'soft style' (1430, probably a Westphalian work); the *pulpit* dates from the Reformation (1567) and the painting between the pulpit itself and the abat-voix depicts Georg Usler, the first Protestant preacher. The three-tiered *high altar* (now in the S.transept) is a good baroque piece (1629). Numerous *tomb slabs* commemorate the bishops and dukes buried here. To the N., the *cloister* connects the cathedral with the *former close buildings*, which date from the 13&14C and were later restored and converted.

**Stadtkirche** (town church; Marktplatz): Rebuilt in the late 18C in brick, like the cathedral. It is a rectangular hall church, with sparse decoration; the intention being to concentrate the congregation's atten-

tion on the sermon. The altar, pulpit and organ are combined on the S. transverse wall.

**Museums:** The *Kreismuseum* (district museum) is housed in the former residence of the Dukes of Mecklenburg (12 Domhof), and contains collections devoted to prehistory and to the history of the town and region. The *Ernst-Barlach-Museum* (3 Barlachplatz) is in the house where the Barlach family once lived. Bronze sculptures, drawings, woodcuts and lithographs are on display. The house itself is in the Biedermeier style and dates from 1840.

---

**Ravensburg 7980**
Baden-Württemberg                    p.420□G 20

The castle which gave the town its name was mentioned under the name of 'Ravenspurc' as early as 1088. It was the birth-

*Marienplatz in Ravensburg*

place of Henry the Lion. The town owed its economic growth to the linen trade, which was organized into the 'Ravensburger Gesellschaft' in about 1400. The wealth of the merchants is apparent from their buildings, most of which have survived. It was not until the 15C, when the Fugger and Welser families of Augsburg had developed into powerful trading dynasties, that the 'Ravensburger Gesellschaft', and with it the town, declined in importance. Ravensburg is also of cultural interest because of the nearby monasteries of Weingarten and Weissenau (q.v.).

**Pfarrkirche Unsere Liebe Frau/Liebfrauenkirche** (Catholic parish church of the Virgin Mary; Marienplatz): The basilica, which has a tall NE tower, was altered and enlarged in the 15&19C, but some elements of the 14C church are still clearly discernible (building work finished in 1380). The 15C *high altar* (acquired from the Engadine in 1958) has delicate

figures. The richly decorated *tabernacle*, the *choir stalls* and the *stained glass* of the choir windows are also 15C (the twelve Apostles, the lives of the Virgin Mary and Christ, Pope Clement, and Crucifixion). The *Ravensburger Schutzmantelmaria* (the Virgin sheltering supplicants under her cloak; there is a copy at the end of the first S.aisle) dates from *c.* 1480. The original is in the W.Berlin sculpture collection.

**Marktplatz:** The Blaserturm (bugler's tower), Waaghaus (weigh-house), and Rathaus, stand close to one another in the Marktplatz. They date from the great heyday of the Ravensburger Gesellschaft. The *Blaserturm,* completed in 1556, commemorates the time when the town guard still sounded the time of day and warned of fires. The *Waaghaus* (1498) survives beside the Blaserturm. 19C rebuilding only slightly altered its original appearance and it had a storage hall on the ground floor. The 14&15C *Rathaus* is distinguished by its plain, stepped gable, its numerous narrow windows and the oriel (1571) on the N. side. Two council halls survive inside, both with Gothic wooden ceilings. The wall paintings date from 1581. Another feature to be noted is the carved loving couple on the pillar of a window, a rare subject at that time (*c.* 1400). The Brotlaube (bread bower; 1625) in the nearby *Marktstrasse* is still used today.

**Town walls:** These once completely surrounded the town and extensive sections, with gates and towers, survive: the *Frauentor, Schellenbergturm, Obertor* (upper gate), *Weisser Turm* (white tower; the so-called flour-sack and landmark of the town), *Spitalturm* (hospital tower), *Untertor* (lower gate), *Gemalter Turm* (painted tower), and *Grüner Turm* (green tower).

**Veitsburg** (to the SE above the town, 1, 720 ft.): The best view of the town is from the Welfenburg, a castle which was begun in the 11C. It suffered a fire in the 17C, and only the domestic buildings and a more recent, 18C structure have survived.

**Städtisches Museum Vogthaus** (36 Charlottenstrasse): The 11 rooms in this 15C half-timbered building contain exhibits devoted to the history of the town, as well as works of art and utensils.

**Also worth seeing:** *Lederhaus* (leather house; 1574) and numerous other houses, often charmingly painted: *Kreuzbrunnen* (fountain; 17C) in the Frauentorplatz. The well-restored 14C *Pfarrkirche St.Jodokus.* The 15C former *Karmelitenklosterkirche* with the chapel of the 'Ravensburger Gesellschaft', today the Protestant parish church.

**Environs: Weissenau** (2 km. S.): This former Premonstratensian monastery founded in 1145 and situated in the Schussental valley is worth visiting for the baroque decoration of its church of *St.Peter und Paul.* F.Schmuzer from Wessobrunn carried out the stucco, while J.K.Stauder from Konstanz and J.Hafner from Türkeim were responsible for the painting (1719–43).

## Recklinghausen 4350
Nordrhein-Westfalen                   p.414□C 10

This large town between the Ruhr district and the Münsterland region was in the 14C a trading centre for blacksmiths' merchandise and cloths, and also a member of the Hanseatic League. The town dates back to an imperial court which Charlemagne ordered to be built here. In the Middle Ages the town came into the possession of the archbishopric of Cologne. Recklinghausen occupies a special place in cultural life because the *Ruhrfestspiele* festival performances are held here once a year.

**Pfarrkirche St.Petrus** (Catholic parish church; Am Kirchplatz): Some remains of the preceding Romanesque church, most of which was destroyed in a town fire in the 13C, still survive. The Gothic church was repeatedly altered and enlarged over the centuries, and it consequently displays no uniform style. A notable feature is the 13C *Baumeisterkopf,* a beautiful head which is now to be found on the front wall of the Romanesque transept. The *altarpieces* are from the Rubens workshop. There is also a richly decorated Romanesque-Gothic *S. portal.*

**Engelsburg** (10 Augustinessenstrasse): Built as a house in 1700 it is today a hotel. Its three wings surround a principal courtyard and it contains a beautiful hall with a baroque, stuccoed ceiling.

**Festspielhaus** (festival theatre; 1 Otto-Burmeister-Allee): The town of Recklinghausen and the Deutscher Gewerkschaftsbund (German Federation of Trade Unions) jointly initiated the Ruhrfestspiele (Ruhr festival performances) after World War 2. The performances were formerly held in the Städtischer Saalbau (municipal hall). The present Festspielhaus was opened in 1965. As a rule these performances are held from the beginning of May until the end of June. Concerts, conferences, exhibitions and discussions are held here in addition to drama.

**Museums:** The *Städtische Kunsthalle* (25

*Festspielhaus in Recklinghausen*

–27 Grosse-Perdekamp-Strasse) displays internatonal art; chiefly from 1945 onwards, but also 20C Westphalian art. The town of Recklinghausen acquired the two most important collections of icons in private hands in Germany, and these have formed the basis for the *Ikonenmuseum* (icon museum; 2a Petruskirchplatz), which is almost unparalleled in W. Europe. The museum also includes collections of Coptic sculptures and textiles, glasses, bronzes, and paraments of the Orthodox church.

## Regensburg 8400
Bavaria                                        p.422□L 17

The 'Kaiserchronik' (imperial chronicle), which was composed and written down in Regensburg in the 12C, describes Regensburg, along with Rome, simply as the 'capital'. Although this title far exceeds the facts, it does suggest that the city was important.

The history of Regensburg can be traced back to the Stone Age. From that time on, the area where the Naab and the Regen flow into the N. curve of the Danube has been populated without interruption. The city took its first name from the Celtic settlement of Radasbona (*c.* 500 BC)—it is still called Ratisbonne in French. The Roman Emperor Vespasian (AD 69–79) ordered a cohort castle to be built here, and Marcus Aurelius relocated and enlarged this so that it provided space for 6000 soldiers. This was the legionary camp of Castra Regina and the 26 ft. long stone slab (AD 179) commemorates the completion of the square, which is 59 acres in size. This slab was once positioned above one of the four gates of the camp and it is regarded as Regensburg's birth certificate. Today it is in the Museum der Stadt (q.v.). The *Römermauer* (Roman wall), strengthened in *c.* 300, can still be traced in the ground plan of the city. The archway and flanking tower (under the flying buttresses) still

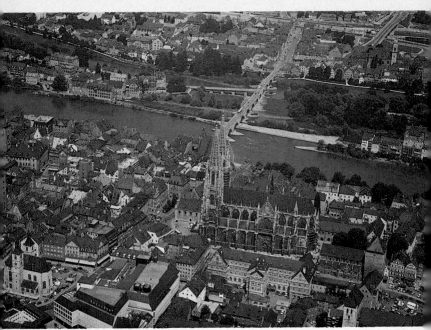

*Regensburg, panorama with cathedral*

survive from the *Porta Pretoria*. The SE corner of the castle has been uncovered in the Ernst-Reuter-Platz. St.-Georgs-Platz covers the NE corner. Regensburg's greatest period was in the 12&13C. Many of the buildings surviving from this period bear witness to the wealth of the city, whose favourable position made it the most important trans-shipment point for the infant European long-distance trade. Regensburg was made a free city in the mid 13C and it was here that the German Romanesque achieved one of its high points. Then, from the early 14C onwards, Regensburg declined, a trend which was not reversed until 1663, when the city became the seat of the 'immerwährender Reichstag' (everlasting Imperial Diet), the oldest German parliament, and it continued to be the site of the parliament until 1806. From 1748 onwards, the imperial postmasters v.Thurn and Taxis, who had been elevated to the status of princes, represented the Emperor at this parliament of the estates. In 1810 Regensburg became a part of Bavaria. Today this university city on the Danube is the capital of the Oberpfalz (Upper Palatinate). One of the city's most famous sons was Albrecht Altdorfer, who was a councillor, a city architect, and one of the greatest painters in Old Bavaria and the most important representative of the famous Danube school. Georg Britting (1891–1964), the lyric poet and narrative writer, was born in Regensburg. Of the many literary works of which Regensburg forms the focal point or which were written here, the 'Wessobrunner Gebet' (prayer of Wessobrunn) is the oldest. It was written in the monastery of St.Emmeram (q.v.) in the 8 or 9C, but was then brought to Wessobrunn. The Albertus Magnus medal, which has been awarded since 1949, commemorates this great scholar, who was active here for ten years and was the Bishop of Regensburg in 1260–2.

**Alte Kapelle/Stiftskirche Unsere Liebe**

**Frau zur Alten Kapelle** (old chapel/collegiate church of the Virgin; Alter Kornmarkt): The ground plan, the W. wall and the tower substructure of this basilica (one nave, two aisles) are all from the 9C *Carolingian* church. The choir dates from *c.* 1445. The side chapels were added in the subsequent period. Despite the Romanesque and Gothic features the transformation of the interior into an ornate rococo composition has been outstandingly successful.

**Dom St. Peter** (Domplatz): This is the centre of the so-called Domstadt (cathedral city), which developed as a clerical quarter near the Danube. This enormous building was begun in *c.* 1250, and took centuries to complete. Despite this, the architectural monument to the Gothic style which has been created here displays a uniformity seldom encountered. The building was designed as a basilica with a nave, two aisles and arcades borne by pillars. Its main sections were complete by 1525 and the *Eselsturm*, a tower from an earlier Romanesque building was incorporated on the N.side of the transept. Lack of money halted the work and, although some progress was made in the 17C, the two *towers* (345 ft.) were not finished until 1859–69. In 1870–1, the construction of the *transept gable* and of the *ridge turret* put the final touch to the cathedral. There is space for up to 7,000 people inside and its contents include so many unique works of art that only the most important can be mentioned here. The lavishly decorated *main portal* is in the *W. façade*—which is itself splendidly adorned with statues and ornament. On either side of the portal are the *equestrian statues* of St. George and St.Martin (*c.* 1330). The *tomb* of Cardinal Duke Philipp Wilhelm is in the middle of the nave opposite the main portal. The bronze figure of the deceased is seen kneeling on the altar tomb before a tall crucifix. The 16C *Rupertus altar* follows in the N. aisle, and depicts the figures of the Emperor Henry with his wife Kunigunde. The *monument* to K.v.Dalberg (1824) is level with the Eselsturm. There then follow the *Dreikönigsaltar* (altar of the Magi) with a relief of the martyrdom of St.Ursula

*Alte Kapelle, collegiate church of Unsere Liebe Frau*

(*c.* 1460), the 42 ft. high *tabernacle* (*c.* 1493), and the neoclassical high altar which was completed in 1785 and is made of gilded copper and silver. The Christi-Geburts-Altar (altar of the Nativity of Christ; *c.* 1450) in the S. side choir is the counterpart of the Dreikönigsaltar mentioned above, and impresses by its tall, delicate arrangement. The *stone statues* of St. Peter and St.Paul, and also of the Virgin Mary and the Angel of the Annunciation, are to be found on the pillars of the crossing. The last two statues are amongst the finest pieces of Gothic sculpture in Germany, and are by the artist responsible for the Erminold tomb in Prüfening. In the S. aisle there is a *well* opposite the Angel of the Annunciation. The *Annunciation altar* which then follows dates from about 1350. Among the numerous monuments note the bronze *tablet* to Margareta Tucher, which is from the workshop of P.Vischer and is situated in the N. choir. In addition to numerous original 13&14C *stained-glass windows*, the *cathedral treasure* is also worth inspecting. The cathedral and the buildings surrounding it make up the so-called Domstadt (cathedral city). NE of the cathedral (reached via the chapterhouse) lies the *cloister*, with monuments from the 14–18C. The 12C *Allerheiligenkapelle* (All Saints' chapel) adjoins this to the E. It was built as a burial place for Bishop Hartwich II and contains fine Romanesque decoration. Beside the cathedral is the 11C church of *St.Stephan*, popularly known as the 'Alter Dom' (old cathedral). The *St.-Ulrich-Kirche* stands behind the *chapterhouse* and *Domgarten* (cathedral garden). This 13C church formerly served as the ca-

thedral parish church. Inside, there are wall paintings from *c.* 1570.

**Former Dominikanerkirche St. Blasius** (Dominican church of St.Blasius; Beraiterweg): The *W. façade* is the dominant feature of this church, which was completed in *c.* 1300 and is one of the first large Gothic buildings in Germany. The figure of the church's patron may be seen in the panel in the tympanum of the *W. portal*. The interior of the church is basilican but lacks a transept, although it does have a fine *groin vault*. There are *wall paintings* in the choir and S. aisle (14&15C). The 15C *choir stalls* survive, but apart from this most of the old decorations have been lost. There is a notable *Schutzmantelmadonna* (Virgin sheltering supplicants under her cloak; *c.* 1500) on the N. choir pillar. The *monument* to Lukas Lamprechtshauser was also completed in about 1500 (relief of the Virgin Enthroned). The fine red marble *tombstones* are in memory of the knights Jörg Schenk v.Neideck and Thomas Fuchs zu Schneeberg, who are depicted in full armour. The adjoining monastery buildings, which have been al-

**Regensburg, Dom 1** Main portal **2** Winter choir **3** Sacristy **4** Virgin Mary and the Angel of the Annunciation, 1280 a) Virgin Mary b) Angel **5** Ciborium altar with Emperor Henry II and Kunigunde, 1350 **6** Ciborium altar with Annunciation, 1350 **7** St.Peter, 1340-50 **8** St.Paul, 1340-50 **9** St.George and St.Martin, 14C a) St.Martin b) St.George **10** Nativity altar, c. 1450 **11** Ursula-Altar, c. 1450 **12** Well, 15C **13** Tabernacle, 1493 **14** Tombstone panel to Margarete Tucher (d. 1521) by Peter Vischer **15** Tombstone of Ursula Villinger (d. 1547) **16** Table tomb of Cardinal P.Wilhelm of Bavaria, 1600 **17** High altar, early classical **18** Tomb of Karl v.Dalberg, 1824 **19** Pulpit

*St. Emmeram* ▷

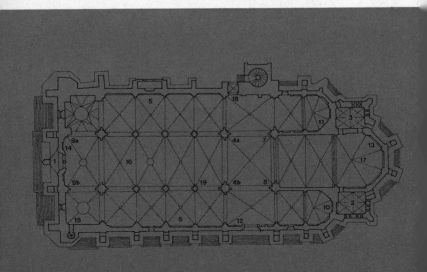

tered on several occasions, include the *Albertuskapelle*.

**Dreieingikeitskirche** (Trinity church; Schererstrasse/Gesandtenstrasse): J.Carl, the architect from Nuremberg, built this church in 1627–33. It is the second Protestant parish church in the city, and is a tunnel-vaulted hall structure. The coffered vault, interrupted by large stars formed by the ribs, and the wooden galleries projecting into the main area of the church, set an unmistakable tone. In the confined churchyard, gorgeous 17&18C monuments commemorate members of the 'everlasting Imperial Diet'.

**Former Benediktinerklosterkirche St. Emmeram** (Benedictine monastery church of St.Emmeram; Emmeramsplatz): The church and monastery developed from an older church of St.George, where the itinerant Westphalian bishop Emmeram was interred in the 7C after falling victim to an act of vengeance. The Benedictine monastery was founded in the 8C, and since then the buildings have developed into an extensive complex. They are overlooked by the Italianate freestanding *campanile* (1579). Beside the 19C parsonage, a two-storeyed early Gothic *double portal* (*c.* 1250) leads the visitor into the *portico*, which was built after 1166. Numerous *tombstones* on the W. side date from Carolingian times. A more recent but particularly splendid item is the memorial to Johannes Turmayr, the humanist and 'father of Bavarian historiography' who was known as Aventinus and who died in 1534. To the E. of the portico stands the parish church of *St.Rupert*, first mentioned in the 12C and rebuilt in the 15C, with good communion vessels in the sacristy.

There are two ways into the church of St.Emmeram: the left-hand route leads into the nave, and the right-hand one into the *W.transept* with the 11C *Dionysius choir* (Romanesque wall paintings) and the *Wolfgangskrypta* in the substructure. Christ Enthroned, St.Emmeram and Dionysius are depicted on the pillars of the double portal (11C). The stone reliefs are among the oldest large German sculptures (1050). The earliest part of the church of St.

Emmeram, which acquired the status of a papal basilica because it was the mother church of the bishopric of Regensburg, is the *Emmeramskrypta*, which was built in *c.* 740 but only rediscovered in 1894. This crypt is under the *main apse*, which is separate from the nave. The crypt is connected by a corridor to the *Ramwoldkrypta*, which was consecrated in 980 and altered in 1775. The original Romanesque forms of the *nave* have disappeared beneath the rococo splendour which E.Q. Asam, the stucco artist, and C.D. Asam, the painter, lavished on the frescoed walls and ceilings of this church. There are numerous fine *monuments*, outstanding examples being the tombstone of Queen Hemma (d. 876), and that of Aurelia of blessed memory, who is especially lovingly depicted (*c.* 1330). Since 1812, the *monastery buildings* have been used as the *Schloss of the princes of Thurn and Taxis*.

**St.Kassian** (Kassiansplatz): The central section of this, the oldest town church in Regensburg, is Carolingian, but the major portion is from an early Romanesque basilica. It was colourfully decorated in rococo style in the mid 18C. The carved figure of the *Schöne Maria* in the S. aisle is by H.Leinberger, the famous artist from Landshut, and dates from *c.* 1520. The N. side altar was formerly in the main choir, and its shrine harbours the late Gothic figure of St.Kassian.

**Former Minoritenkirche** (Minorite church; Dachauplatz): The early Gothic *nave* was completed in *c.* 1260, while the raised *choir* replaced an earlier structure in 1330. In 1810 the church was secularized and enlarged. Since then, together with the remains of the former monastery where Berthold v.Regensburg, the most important German preacher, lived and died (1272), it has been used as the Museum der Stadt.

**Neupfarrkirche** (new parish church; Neupfarrplatz): Dating from 1519–40, it was built on the site of a synagogue and was originally designed as the pilgrimage church Zur schönen Maria, with a hexagonal central area and radiating chapels.

However, only a greatly simplified form of it was actually built, not the least reason for this being that the Protestants took over the building in 1542.

**Niedermünster** (outside the E. gate of the Domgarten): The collegiate church of this former foundation for noble ladies, which was immediately subordinate to the Emperor, was rebuilt after the town fire of 1152 and appears as a pillared basilica with a nave, two aisles, and a pair of towers to the W. The baroque interior dates from the 17&18C. The fine *canopied altar* (c. 1330) by the tomb of St.Erhard (N. aisle) is a relic of the church in its medieval state. The precious *bronze group* of the former altar of the Cross, with Mary Magdalene mourning at the holy rood, is by the N. wall of the choir. Since 1810, the diocesan authorities and the bishop's residence have been housed in the foundation's buildings. To the E. of the church is the early-11C *St. Erhards-Kapelle.*

**Schottenkirche St.Jakob** (Scots' church of St. James; Jakobstrasse): This high Romanesque basilica has a nave, two aisles, and pillars supporting its arcades. The present church was built in 1150–95, with part of a building dating from 1120 being incorporated. The founders were itinerant Irish monks. In the 16C, the monastery belonging to the church was settled anew by Scottish Benedictine monks. The *main portal* on the N. side is highly significant in that it displays a wealth of statues that is unusual for the Romanesque. The definitive interpretation of this abundance of figures has not yet been discovered. There are clear French and Lombard influences. Inside, the wealth of figures continues on the *capitals* of the massive columns, where the figures also alternate with plant motifs. One of the oldest *Crucifixions* in Germany (c. 1200) is to be found in the triumphal arch. There are good Gothic *stone figures* on the pillars of the choir. The bishop's seminary is today housed in the adjoining former *Schottenkloster* (Scots' monastery).

**Other churches:** Former *Deutschordenskirche St. Ägidien* (Teutonic knights'

church of St. Aegidius; W. of St. Emmeram). *Church of St.Oswald* (Weissgerbergraben). *Dominikanerinnenkirche Heiliges Kreuz* (Dominican convent church of the Holy Cross; Nonnenplatz).

**Altstadt:** The old part of Regensburg grew up on the right bank of the Danube and is surrounded by a green belt. The alleyways, most of which are very narrow, have retained their medieval character and bear witness not only to a self-assured middle class which had become prosperous through trade, but also to the clergy's power and ostentatiousness.

**Fountains:** The town's fountains are reminiscent of Italian forms and models. The *Adlerbrunnen* outside the *Haus an der Heuport* (14C; 17 Domplatz) has been the meeting point for the gardeners from Weichs, who sell their fresh radishes here, since time immemorial. Other fountains include the *Justitiabrunnen* (Haidplatz) dating from 1656, the *Brunnen auf dem Fischmarkt* (fountain in the fish market; c. 1600), and the *well* in the Gasse Am Wiedfang (near the medieval port; c. 1610).

**Geschlechtertürme** (family towers): In the Middle Ages, shortage of space compelled the rich patricians' families to build their houses upwards. These castle-like houses are almost undecorated. The most important of these Geschlechtertürme, as they are called, is the 13C *Baumburgerturm* in the Watmarkt. It is 92 ft. high and has seven storeys. The Goldener Turm of the *Haymohaus* (also called Wallerhaus; 16 Wahlenstrasse) is taller than this. Built in c. 1260, it rises to 138 ft. The beautiful Romanesque Arkadenhof (arcaded courtyard) is reached via 7 Untere Bachgasse. Other Geschlechtertürme include the *Bräunelturm* (6 Watmarkt), the *Goliathhaus* (5 Watmarkt, with the enormous fresco of 'David in battle with Goliath' by M.Bocksberger dating from 1573, and the former inns of the *Goldenes Kreuz* (Golden Cross; 7 Haidplatz) and *Blauer Hecht* (Blue Pike; 7 Keplerstrasse).

**Herzogshof** (ducal court; E. of the cathedral): Documents exist permitting the history of the Herzogshof to be traced back to the year 988. The present building was erected in the 12&13C. Notable features include the *window arches* (*c.* 1220) and the *Herzogssaal* (ducal hall) on the upper storey (today cultural events are held here).

**Altes Rathaus** (old town hall; Rathausplatz): The oldest elements of this picturesque group of buildings date back to the 11C. To the W. is the *Reichssaalbau* (imperial hall), which was built in *c.* 1360 and restored in 1408 after a fire. A 15C representation of the *measures used in the city* ('der stat schuch', 'der stat öln', 'der stat klaffter') is on the left of the portal. A section comprising a 13C *Hausburg* (house castle) and the eight-storeyed *Rathausturm* (town hall tower; *c.* 1250) leads to the *Neues Rathaus* (new town hall). In the courtyard is the large *Venusbrunnen* (1661), with four stone figures (1630) which were originally intended for the portals of the Dreieinigkeitskirche. There is a simpler wall fountain in the *Neptunhof* (1662). The pièce de résistance of the Altes Rathaus is the *Reichssaal* (imperial hall), which was originally constructed as the festival hall of the city council, but then performed a more important function as the council hall of the 'everlasting Imperial Diet' (1663–1806). This hall, 49 ft. wide and 26 ft. high, is spanned by a magnificent *timber ceiling* rebuilt in 1408. The painting of the ceiling dates from 1564. The steps surrounding the hall on three sides still reveal the former seating arrangement of the Imperial Diet. The Emperor sat in the *Lehnsessel* (1664) at the highest point, underneath a *baldaccino* dating from 1573. Under him there followed the Electors, the Princes and finally the representatives of the imperial towns. Particular attention should be paid to the multicoloured *tapestry*, a Regensburg work dating from *c.* 1550, as well as fine Brussels *tapestries* (*c.* 1600). The *flags* were donated in 1633. A number of consultation rooms, where the three estates of the Empire held their deliberations, are grouped around the Reichssaal. These rooms include the following: the *Kurfürstliches Nebenzimmer* (side room of the Electors), the *Reichsstädtisches Kollegium* (assembly of the free im-

perial towns), the *Kurfürstenkollegium* (electors' assembly), and the *Fürstenkollegium* (princes' assembly). Various rooms on the ground floor were once used during trials: the *Fragstatt*, where prisoners were questioned, the *Lochgefängnis* (oubliette), and the *Armesünderstübchen* (condemned cell), where those who had been sentenced to death had to wait for their execution. The *Dollingersaal* is a new building, which re-used materials from a patrician's house torn down in 1889, and it was built together with the *Ratskeller* (town hall cellar: a restaurant). Here, 13C stucco reliefs depict the fight in which Dollinger, a citizen of Regensburg, is said, in the year 930, to have defeated Krako the Hun in the adjoining Haidplatz before the very eyes of Henry I. Today the Ratshaus houses the *Reichstags-Museum* (museum of the Imperial Diet).

**Schloss der Fürsten von Thurn und Taxis** (Schloss of the Princes von Thurn and Taxis; S. of St.Emmeram, reached via the Schlossstrasse): Since 1812, the buildings of the foundation of St. Emmeram have served as the Schloss of the Princes von Thurn and Taxis. Some additions to the building date from 1889; the other façades were also reworked at that time. The architectural pièce de résistance is the *cloister*, which is among the most important examples of Gothic architecture in Germany (13&14C). The castle also includes the prince's *Gruftkapelle* (crypt chapel; 1841) and the *Reitschule* (riding school), a major neoclassical building (today it is the *Marstallmuseum*). Finally, there is the Fürstlich Thurn und Taxissche *Hofbibliothek* (court library), which is among the finest private libraries in the world. The private archive include records which show the importance of the Thurn and Taxis family (who came from Italy) in their role as general postmasters of the Empire from 1595 onwards. Three *frescos* were uncovered in the library itself in 1967. They are by C.D. Asam (1737).

**Steinerne Brücke** (stone bridge): The Steinerne Brücke, a city landmark, was praised by Hans Sachs in the following words: 'This bridge is like no other in Ger-

*Stone bridge and bridge gate*

many.' It was built in 1135–46 by order of the Bavarian Duke Henry the Proud, and in the Middle Ages it was regarded as a miracle of engineering. Its original length of 1,083 ft. was later reduced to 1,017 ft. The 16 vaulted arches have spans varying between 34 and 55 ft. The famous Regensburg *Brückenmännchen* (bridge dwarf; the original is today in the Museum der Stadt) may be seen on the W. parapet of the bridge. There were originally three *bridge towers*, but only the S. tower (14C) survives. Its decoration, depicting St. Oswald surrounded by several figures (13C), was taken from the former central and N. towers.

## OUTSKIRTS OF THE CITY

**Benediktinerklosterkirche St. Georg in Prüfening** (Benedictine monastery church of St.George; 4 km. W. of the Altstadt): This monastery was founded by Bishop Otto I v.Bamberg in 1109, and since 1953 it has once again been occupied by Benedictine monks. The oldest part of the present church is the E. end with its seven altars (there is a builder's inscription on the SW pillar of the crossing). Individual parts of the building were subsequently much altered, but the basic plan remained unchanged, with the result that St.Georg is one of the most important 12C churches in Germany. The transept and E. towers are heavily influenced by the mother house at Hirsau. The fine *wall paintings*, which date from *c*. 1130/60, are in good condition. They cover large sections of the main and side choirs and the subjects depicted include the patron of the order, Bishops, Emperors, martyrs, the Evangelists, and the Virgin Mary. The *tomb* of Abbot Erminold (1283) is another excellent work. It is by the so-called Erminold-Meister, one of the best sculptors of his time.

**Karthaus-Prüll** (1 km. SW of the Altstadt): The central part of the church of the original Benedictine monastery is Romanesque in style. The monastery was occupied by Carthusian monks in the 15C. The church is worth visiting for the *fresco* of the Annunciation in the W. gallery, which is a first-rate example of late Romanesque painting (*c.* 1200). The *stucco* dates from around 1605. Also note the *high altar*, which is a masterpiece of the German Renaissance (in its transition to the baroque), the *choir stalls*, and several *oil paintings* (*c.* 1650). Seven *hermits' cells* survive by the *cloister* in the adjoining *monastery*.

**Stadttheater** (city theatre; 7 Bismarckplatz): This theatre built in 1852 has been carefully renovated. It has 540 seats, as well as a podium stage and a mobile theatre. It has its own musical and theatrical company, which gives performances here.

**Museums:** The *Museum der Stadt Regensburg* (Regensburg city museum; Dachauplatz 2–4) is housed in the former 13C Minoritenkloster. It has some 100 rooms and is one of the most important museums in S. Germany. The collections concentrate on the history, culture and art of E. Bavaria from the Palaeolithic until the 19C, and include many of the priceless originals which have been replaced by copies in the various churches and buildings of the city. In the *Keplergedächtnishaus* (Kepler memorial house; 5 Keplerstrasse), where the great astronomer and mathematician (1571–1630) died, there is an extensive collection devoted to his life and work. The *Reichstags-Museum* (Imperial Diet Museum; 4 Rathausplatz), housed in a section of the Altes Rathaus, has documents and exhibitions commemorating the 'everlasting Imperial Diet'. The *Fürst Thurn und Taxis-Schlossmuseum* (Emmeramsplatz) contains furnishings, works of art belonging to the princes, tapestries, the famous court library, and the central archive. The *Fürst Thurn und Taxis-Marstallmuseum* is particularly interesting. It displays coaches, carriages, sledges and other vehicles from the 18–20C, and at the same time it documents the initial stages in the development of the postal service in Germany. *Stiftung Ostdeutsche Galerie*

(East German Gallery; 5 Dr.-Johann-Maier-Strasse): Art and cultural exhibits in the former E. areas are documented here. The *Staatsgalerie* (State gallery; 2–4 Dachauplatz) displays European paintings from the 16–18C. *Schiffahrtsmuseum* (museum of shipping; in the Rathof museum steamer): History of Bavarian shipping on the Danube.

---

## Reichenau 7752
Baden-Württemberg　　　　　p.420☐F 21

This unusually fertile island in Lake Constance is linked to the mainland by a causeway. In 1951, Wilhelm Hausenstein wrote the following about the island: 'Transferred into a world full of peonies, vegetables and hay, between two arms of a lake which, green as the Nile here and violet in colour there, washes the shores and soaks the island in a hazy aroma of dampness.' The island is divided into the districts of Mittelzell (with the Münster (minster) of St.Maria and St.Markus), Oberzell (with the former collegiate church of St.Georg), and Niederzell (with the former collegiate church of St.Peter und Paul).

**Münster St. Maria und St. Markus:** The monastery, founded by the abbot and itinerant bishop St.Pirmin who lived in Reichenau in 724–6, was once one of the cultural centres of the Western world. Art and science blossomed here in the late 8C and the 9C under the abbots Waldo (786 –806) and Hatto I (806–23). It was around 1000 that German book illumination achieved a spectacular brilliance here in Reichenau. Reichenau reached its zenith under Hermanus Contractus who led the monastery in the 11C and has gone down in history as Hermann the Lame or 'the miracle of the century'. The monastery passed to the Bishop of Constance in the 16C and was completely dissolved in 1759. Up to 700 monks lived in the monastery during its heyday.
The oldest sections of the present minster date from the period around 990. The main parts of the building originate from the new church ordered by Abbot Berno

*Münster St.Maria und Markus, Mittelzell*

(1030–48). The first storey of the tower, the so-called Kaiserloge (emperor's lodge), is reached by corkscrew staircases. Above this, on the second storey, is the Michaelskapelle. The choir screen is a model of early wrought-iron art. The most important of the minster's contents are today in the *Schatzkammer* (treasury), which has been established in the late Gothic sacristy, above a Romanesque cellar. This treasure includes five Gothic reliquaries dating from the monastery's heyday.

**Former Stiftskirche St.Georg** (collegiate church of St.George): This former collegiate church was probably built around 900. There was a monastery cell here as early as the 9C. The most valuable possessions of this church—still in good condition even though the church was enlarged in *c.* 1000 and was altered during the baroque—are the Ottonian *wall paintings*, which extend through the entire nave. No other early medieval church has comparable monumental paintings on its interior walls and they rank as some of the most important paintings dating from around 1000 to have survived to the present day. The subjects include the Reichenau abbots, six Apostles, and the miracles of Christ. Also note the table of the *high altar* (*c.* 1000); the late Romanesque *crucifix* (*c.* 1170) above the entrance to the crypt (dedicated to St.George). A 15C *Pietà* in the N. apse. The mid-15C *Man of Sorrows* in the S. apse.

**Former Stiftskirche St.Peter und Paul** (collegiate church of St.Peter and St.Paul): This church with its basilican nave dates back to the 8&9C, but was enlarged in the 11C (towers) and 15C (upper storeys). The influences of the Hirsau reform movement can be clearly discerned in the cubiform capitals and the profiles of the W. portal. The stucco and frescos date are baroque. The remains of Romanesque wall paintings survive in the central apse.

*Collegiate church of St. Georg, Oberzell*

## Reichenbach, Oberpfalz 8411
Bavaria                                    p.422☐M 17

**Former Benediktinerklosterkirche St. Mariae Himmelfahrt** (Benedictine monastery church of the Assumption): This basilica with its nave and two aisles is built of powerful ashlars in Romanesque style. It was built together with the Benedictine monastery which was founded in 1118 (the church was consecrated in 1135, but the work was not completed until *c.* 1200). The most effective of various alterations was the expansion of the fortified monastery in the 15C. Many of the contents were lost as a result of the destruction of images in the 16C triggered by the Reformation. In the 18C, the interior was completely altered in baroque style. The only original features of the interior are the early-15C choir stalls, a sandstone Madonna (on the NW arcade pillar) which dates from *c.* 1420, and some monuments.

When the church was transformed in baroque style, the features which were added included the massive high altar with its double turned columns (*c.* 1745–50). Only some of the *monastery buildings* survive, and many of them have been considerably altered.

## Rendsburg 2370
Schleswig-Holstein                         p.412☐G 2

The Kiel Canal (originally called the Kaiser-Wilhelm Canal), whose total length is 62 miles, crosses the province of Schleswig-Holstein and skirts Rendsburg. The canal was not opened until 1895, but Rendsburg was already important because of its good position.

**Marienkirche** (church of the Virgin

*Pulpit in the Marienkirche, Rendsburg* ▷

Mary; An der Marienkirche): This hall church, with its nave and two aisles, was built after a fire in the town in 1287. The rich decoration is emphasized by the white of the walls and pillars. Besides the numerous memorial stones, important items include: remains of a 14C vault painting, uncovered in 1951. Carved altar (1649). Pulpit by H.Peper (1621). Memorial stone to M.Rantzau (1649).

**Christkirche** (Paradeplatz): This two-aisled church was built in 1695–1700 in Neuwerk, a new baroque quarter which was laid out in the 17&18C with a central square and streets radiating out from it. The two aisles of the church cross one another in the middle.

**Neuwerk** (see above): The centre of this new district of town was the Paradeplatz. 18C military buildings.

**Rathaus** (am Markt): This 16C building was originally constructed as a half-timbered structure, but was altered and expanded in c. 1900 and 1939 and has lost its original features. The wood-panelled *mayor's room*, with paintings dating from c. 1720, has survived. Today the Rathaus houses the *Heimatmuseum*.

**Old houses:** Some old town houses survive, scattered through the Altstadt and elsewhere. The inn 'Zum Landsknecht', built in 1541 (Schleifmühlenstrasse 2), is a town house with a fine half-timbered façade.

**Museums:** The *Heimatmuseum* (in the Altes Rathaus): Prehistoric finds, and collections relating to the cultural history of Rendsburg and the environs. The *Kunstgussmuseum* (museum of ornamental casts; Glück-Auf-Allee) contains ornamental casts, plaques, collections of portraits, and documents from the history of the Carlshütte company (the Ahlsmann-Carlshütte KG, with its head office in Rendsburg).

**Theatres:** The *regional theatre and symphony orchestra of Schleswig-Holstein* (Jungfernstieg 7): This theatre has 599 seats. Performances are held here in co-operation

with the theatres in Flensburg and Schleswig.

**Also worth seeing:** *Railway viaduct* with suspension ferry, and *channel tunnel* for the Europastrasse road. These are two important modern achievements.

---

## Reutlingen 7410

Baden-Württemberg                    p.420□F 18

This town's history dates back to the 11C, when four settlements united to form a village. Market rights were granted by Frederick Barbarossa in 1182, and the town charter was conferred by Otto IV in 1209. The 'Neue Stadt' (new town) was built by Frederick II in 1216–40. In 1247 the town defeated Heinrich Raspe's attack and thereby retained its immediate subordination to the Emperor. A period of prosperity, from which time the Marienkirche dates, then followed in the 13&14C. Numerous disputes with a wide variety of opponents caused the town serious damage on repeated occasions over subsequent centuries. Most recently, severe damage was caused in World War 2. Today, this former imperial town at the foot of the Schwäbische Alb hills is a centre of the engineering industry.

**Marienkirche** (Weibermarkt): It is said that this church was begun as a result of a victory in 1247 over the troops of Heinrich Raspe, who had promoted himself to the status of a counter-king opposing the Hohenstaufen Emperor Frederick II. The rectangular choir, flanked by two smaller towers, survives from this period. By contrast, the main tower was not completed until 1343. Despite the long period of building (some other sections were only added later), the Marienkirche is distinguished by its surprising uniformity. The transformation experienced by the Gothic style in Germany in the 13&14C is only apparent in the details. A notable feature is the complicated system of buttresses which supports the nave and which was

*Holy Sepulchre, Marienkirche, Reutlingen* ▷

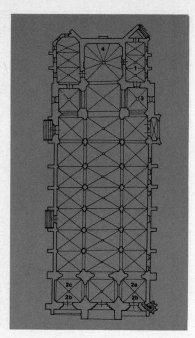

Reutlingen, Marienkirche **1** Wall painting in the S.sacristy (legend of St. Catherine), earlier than 1312 **2** Wall painting in the nave, 14C a) St.Catherine b) St.Christopher c) St.Paul **3** Font, 1499 **4** Holy Sepulchre, early 16C

here used for the first time in Swabia. The highlight of the interior, only parts of which survive, is the early-16C *Holy Sepulchre* in the choir. This is probably from the same workshop as the octagonal *font* (1499), which is likewise profusely decorated. Remains of old *wall paintings* survive in some parts of the church.

**Fountains:** There are three beautiful 16C fountains. The *Lindenbrunnen* (1544; the original is in the museum); the *Kirchbrunnen* (1561; the statue is of Emperor Frederick II); and the *Marktbrunnen* (1570, with a statue of Emperor Maximilian II).

**Museum:** *Heimatmuseum* (22 Oberamteistrasse): Housed since 1939 in the 16C former Königsbronner Klosterhof.

**Also worth seeing:** The remains of the 13C *town walls*, including 2 gates, the Tübinger Tor by the Lederstrasse and the Gartentor by the Mauerstrasse. The *Spitalkirche* (hospital church) by the Markt was built in 1333 and enlarged in 1555.

---

### Rheda-Wildenbrück 4840
Nordrhein-Westfalen                p.414□E 9

**Marienkirche/Marien-Wallfahrts-Kirche** (church of the Virgin Mary/pilgrimage church of the Virgin Mary; Marienplatz): This hall church with its nave and two aisles was completed in 1470 and its design has remained almost unaltered ever since. A notable feature is the unusual ratio of its width to its length: being 62 ft. wide and only 43 ft. long, it is an exception among Westphalian hall churches. Opposite it is the monastery founded in 1667.

**Stiftskirche (collegiate church) St. Ägidii** (Kirchplatz): This large hall church was built in *c.* 1500, but its tower and choir are 19C. The tabernacle dating from 1504 is most interesting, with its magnificent, rich structure it is one of the best of its kind in Westphalia. However, praise is also due to the sandstone pulpit (supported by the figure of Moses, *c.* 1617), the late Gothic font, and the early-17C pulpit.

**Also worth seeing:** *Schloss Rheda* (17&18C), with a late Romanesque gatehouse tower (*c.* 1235). *Haus Aussel* (Batenhorst): A Burgmann's house dating from 1580. *Half-timbered houses* (particularly in the Mönchsstrasse and Lange Strasse): 16&17C houses, some of them richly carved, belonging to townsmen who farmed smallholdings.

---

### Rheinberg 4134
Nordrhein-Westfalen                p.414□B 10

**Catholic Pfarrkirche:** Rebuilt from about 1400 onwards, some parts of the earlier Romanesque church3 were incorporated. A particular feature is the *high altar,* which skilfully combines a 16C Antwerp Passion altar in the upper section with a double shrine which may be from Brussels (*c.* 1440). The lower double shrine depicts God the Father, Christ, and the twelve Apostles. There are several *panel paintings,* scenes from the Passion, and figures on an altar which was made in *c.* 1440 by a Westphalian artist from the Lower Rhine.

**Also worth seeing:** The Rathaus (1449). The Pulverturm (powder magazine).

## Rheinmünster 7587
Baden-Württemberg                    p.420☐D 18

**Former Benedictinerklosterkirche** (Benedictine monastery church; Schwarzach): This Romanesque church was built in *c.* 1220 but it has been altered on numerous occasions over the centuries. Recently (1967–9), an attempt has been made to restore the church to its original, medieval form. The powerful *crossing tower* and the *apses* at the E. end are the church's distinguishing features from the outside. The *W. portal,* with Christ Enthroned in the tympanum, points to N. Italian influence. Inside, the *nave* has a flat roof; only the *choir* has a ribbed vault. A Romanesque *font* survives; the baroque former *high altar* is now in the S. transept. The *choir stalls* and *organ* are 18C.

## Rinteln 3260
Lower Saxony                    p.414☐F 8

**Protestant Marktkirche St. Nikolai** (market church of St. Nicholas; Marktplatz): Work on this church was begun in the mid 13C, but was not finished until the late 14C when the powerful W. tower was completed. The highlight of the very fine *interior* is the altar, whose richly decorated altarpiece was installed in the early 17C. Other interesting features include the

*High altar of parish church in Rheinberg*

bronze font (1582); the figures of Christ and the four Evangelists on the pulpit (1648); the painted scenes from the Old and New Testaments on the parapet of the W. gallery. 16&17C memorials of both sandstone and wood.

**Former Jakobsklosterkirche** (monastery church of St.James): This church, first mentioned in 1257, became a university church in 1621 when Rinteln had a university within its walls. This plain Gothic hall church without a tower reminds one of the monastery, which no longer exists, and of the university which has been dissolved.

**Rathaus** (Marktplatz): Two buildings have been combined to form the Rathaus. With their richly decorated gables and the projecting oriels, they are the main feature of this part of the Marktplatz. The smaller section on the right dates from the late 16C, while the larger one is in the so-called Weser Renaissance style.

**Altstadt:** The Altstadt has half-timbered buildings in the Marktplatz, Bäckerstrasse and Brennerstrasse. The ramparts and gates are 17C, while the older half-timbered buildings are 16C.

**Schaumburgisches Heimatmuseum** (Eulenburg): Exhibits relating to the prehistory, history and culture of Rinteln and its environs are on display in this 14C stone castle.

---

**Rohr, Niederbayern 8421**
Bavaria                                    p.422□L 18

**Klosterkirche Mariae Himmelfahrt** (monastery church of the Assumption): The quite extraordinary high altar draws the visitor to this monastery church. It depicts the Assumption of the Virgin who, borne by angels, is ascending towards an opening where the choir of angels and the figures of the Trinity are waiting for her. At her feet, the Apostles, in amazement, adoration and ecstasy, have observed that the open marble sarcophagus is empty. This extraordinary composition, with life-sized stucco figures, was built by E.Q. Asam in *c.* 1717. The impression which it makes is like a scene from a drama, with the nave representing the auditorium. The lavish decoration contrasts with the plain exterior of the church, which is one of E.Q. Asam's best works.

---

**Rosenheim 8200**
Bavaria                                    p.422□M 20

This stands on the spot where the Roman road from Augsburg to Salzburg crossed the river Inn, as well as intersecting the road from the Brenner Pass to Regensburg. Centuries later, the present town of Rosenheim developed here, growing up around Burg Rosenheim, for which the first documentary evidence dates from 1234, and then, in the early 14C, around Max-Josefs-Platz, which still exists. The salt extracted here brought considerable prosperity to the town's citizens.

**Pfarrkirche St.Nikolaus** (parish church of St.Nicholas): Only a few remains of the original 15C church survive and its appearance has been considerably altered by a neo-Gothic treatment. The tower, however, is untouched, although its onion dome was added in 1656.

**Heilig-Geist-Kirche** (church of the Holy Spirit; Heilig-Geist-Strasse): The prosperous citizens of Rosenheim founded this church in 1449. The baroque alterations are 17C.

**Max-Josefs-Platz:** The square is surrounded by houses which are typical of the towns along the Inn. The arcades and oriels are characteristic of the period.

**Museums:** *Heimatmuseum* (housed in the Mittertor, a 14C town gate by the Ludwigsplatz): Prehistory, early history, town history, handicrafts, shipping on the river Inn. *Städtische Kunstsammlung/Galerie* (town art collection/gallery; 2 Max-Bram-Platz): The main attraction is the collection of works by 19&20C painters from Munich and Chiemgau.

**Also worth seeing:** Heilig-Blut-Kirche (Zugspitzstrasse): A 17C baroque pilgrimage church. Baroque Rundkirche Heiliges Kreuz (round church of the Holy Cross; 1668–91) in Westerndorf (4 km. N.).

---

**Rot an der Rot 7956**
Baden-Württemberg                          p.420□H 20

**Former Prämonstratenserkloster-kirche St. Maria und St. Verena** (Premonstratensian monastery church of the Virgin Mary and St. Verena): A 14C church previously occupied this site. It was much altered in the 17C, and was replaced by a new building in 1777. The plans were drawn up by the monks themselves. They built the monastery itself in 1682–1702, and its buildings still stand. The monks, headed by Abbot Willibald Held, also drew up the plans for the new building, us-

*High altar of monastery church in Rohr* ▷

ing existing churches, especially that in Obermarchtal, as models. The stuccoes are by F.X. Feuchtmayer, while the frescos were painted by J.Zick. The interior displays all the splendour of the late baroque, but also suggests the transition to the neoclassical in the more severe arrangement of the rich decoration and in the articulation of the building itself. In addition to the stuccoes and frescos, there is a splendid *high altar* and several side altars, some of which are by F.X. Feuchtmayer and S.Feuchtmayer, as is the baldacchino of the high altar. Other features worth seeing are the *choir stalls* dating from 1693, the *organ* (1786–9) by J.N. Holzhay, and the rococo *pulpit* and *confessional boxes*. The sacristy, which adjoins the church to the N., was built in 1690, independently of the other buildings. The adjoining *monastery buildings* with their rich interior decoration are distinguished by their onion-domed towers.

---

### Rothenburg ob der Tauber 8803
Bavaria                                      p.422☐H 16

This former free town has retained its

*Monastery church, Rot an der Rot*

medieval appearance over the centuries until the present day. It developed around a count's castle, which dates back to the 10C. The town was granted its freedom in 1274 and it reached a zenith in the 14C under Mayor Heinrich Toppler. The disadvantage which the town suffers in being situated away from the major communication routes has become its advantage where art is concerned. Lack of funds hindered the citizens from continually modernizing their town, and thus preserved the old town to a degree found nowhere else in Germany.

**Protestant Stadtpfarrkirche St.Jakob** (parish church of St.James): The present church was begun in 1373, but was not consecrated until 1464. A basilica, with a nave and two aisles, it is worth visiting principally for its splendid interior. At the centre is the *Heiliges-Blut-Altar* (altar of the Holy Blood; in the Heiliges-Blut-Kapelle chapel), whose main components are by T. Riemenschneider. The altar depicts the Passion and the Last Supper. The *high altar* is a famous late Gothic work (1466). The sculpture is by H.Waidenlich, an artist from Nördlingen, while the painted panels are by F.Herlin, the Nördlingen town painter. His inclusion of Rothenburg market on one of the legends of St.James (see the illustrations) is one of the earliest town views. Also worth seeing: Stained glass in the three *choir windows* dating from the late 14C and the middle and late 15C. The stone *Virgin* of *c.* 1360 (in one of the four side chapels which are known as Häuptleinkapellen), the *tabernacle* (*c.* 1400), and some large *statues*.

**Former        Franziskanerkirche:** (Franciscan church; Herrngasse): Although at least 50 years elapsed between work starting in 1285 and the completion of the nave, the church is a uniform early Gothic structure. It has a nave and two aisles, with impressive arcades. The nave is separated from the choir by a notable late Gothic rood screen. There are fine *tombstones* (15C and early-16C); and *stone figures* of the Virgin Mary (on the N. side, *c.* 1400)

*Altes Rathaus, Rot an der Rot* ▷

and of St. Liborius (1492, by the rood screen). The altar dedicated to St.Francis (c. 1490) is in front of the rood screen.

**Rathaus** (Marktplatz): The Town Hall was built in two phases in the 13&16C. The older, smaller section is Gothic, while the more recent part is Renaissance. Inside, a spiral staircase leads to the top of the Rathaus tower. The *Grosser Saal* (great hall; also known as the Kaisersaal [imperial hall]) is in the older section. Finally, the *dungeons* with their beautiful vaults are also worth seeing. The former *Ratstrinkstube* (councillors' tap-room) is beside the Rathaus and is admired for its clock. There is a depiction of the Meistertrunk (mayor's drink), with which Nusch, the mayor, is said to have once saved the town from being destroyed by Tilly.

**Baumeisterhaus** (architect's house; Obere Schmiedsgasse): L.Weidmann, the town architect, built this house in 1596 for

◁ *Gerlachschmiede forge and Röder gate, Rothenburg*

*The Heilig-Blut-Altar in the St.-Jakobs-Kirche in Rothenburg is mainly the work of the Würzburg artist Tilman Riemenschneider*

*The town parish church of St. Jakob has a fine interior*

*Herlin-Altar, St. Jakob*

*Herlin-Altar*

Michael Wirsching, the town councillor. Its best feature is its beautiful, well articulated sandstone façade.

**Georgsbrunnen fountain** (Markt): The fountain (1608) is more than just a decorative feature of the market, it is the landmark of this part of the old town.

**Topplerschlösschen:** The small Schloss was built for Mayor Heinrich Toppler in 1388 and its purpose was to enable him to watch over the mills on the river Tauber.

**Altes Gymnasium** (old secondary school; Kirchplatz): This Renaissance building is also by L.Weidmann, the town architect; who erected this three-storeyed grammar school in 1589–91. In front of it there is a tower with a staircase, which provides a vertical element in contrast to the horizontals of the school proper.

**Spital** (hospital): The three-storeyed Spital is another of L.Weidmann's buildings

(1574–78). A spiral staircase and two stone Renaissance portals are notable features of the interior. The famous *Hegereiterhaus,* one of the architectural gems of Rothenburg, is part of this walled complex. The Hegereiterhaus was built in 1591 for the hospital's horse-breaker.

**Town walls:** The inner Rödertor and the Weisser Torturm are part of the original 12C town fortifications. A new town wall was built in the 15C; this is best preserved around the Topplerweg (Spitaltor).

**Walks:** If one wants to do more than simply view individual buildings it is worth walking around the old town, which displays a medieval compactness seldom encountered: the Markt (market), Herrngasse, Schmiedgasse (with the Plönlein), Rödergasse are all interesting.

**Tauberbrücke:** This bridge was blown up in 1945 but it has been faithfully rebuilt

*Herlin-Altar*

*Herlin-Altar*

*Rathaus, Rothenburg*

around a concrete core. It was formerly one of the most important and finest examples of medieval bridge building.

**Museums:** *Reichsstadtmuseum* (5 Klosterhof): Collections devoted to pre- and early history, antique furniture and craftsmen's tools, are on display in this 700 year old Dominican convent. The highlights are the twelve paintings of the Rothenburg Passion, the old convent kitchen (which was incorporated into the museum), and the Pokal (goblet) from which Nusch, the mayor, quaffed the Meistertrunk (see Rathaus). *Rothenburg-Galerie* (gallery; Klosterhof): This interesting gallery originated from several private collections. The main focus is on 19&20C painting. *Mittelalterliches Kriminalmuseum* (medieval museum of crime; 3 Burggasse): Devoted to the medieval administration of justice, and instruments of torture.

---

**Rott am Inn 8093**

Bavaria                             p.422☐M 20

---

**Former Benediktinerabteikirche St. Marinus und Anianus** (Benedictine abbey church of St.Marinus and Anianus): Abbot Benedikt Lutz originally intended to retain the walls of the existing 12C church, but he then commissioned J.M. Fischer, one of the most famous architects of the time, to rebuild it completely. Only the towers and some other minor sections were incorporated from the old structure. The foundation stone was laid in 1759, and work continued until 1767. In addition to Fischer, the best artists of the period contributed to the decoration: J.Rauch, F.X. Feuchtmayer, M.Günther the painter from Augsburg, and I.Günther the sculptor from Munich. The church, which is plain on the outside, is one of the most mature accomplishmemnts of the late baroque style and is famous for its magnificent interior. The central feature is the massive dome. There are also four diagonal chapels and two side chapels (with larger altars). The enormous fresco in the main dome depicts the glorification of the saints of the Benedictine order and it and the other frescos are by of M.Günther, an Augsburg painter. I.Günther designed the *high altar* and most of the numerous *side altars*, and was also responsible for the larger-than-life figures representing the Trinity, Henry and Kunigunde, Korbinian and Ulrich. Some of the side altars are by J.Götsch, a fellow-artist of Günther. The painting at the right side altar is by J.Hartmann (the altarpiece for the high altar is also his work). In the *portico* is the tomb (1485) of the founder, the Count Palatine Kuno, and his son.

---

**Rottach-Egern 8183**

Bavaria                             p.422☐L 21

---

Rottach-Egern, which is today a health resort owing to the curative properties of its climate, is associated with the name of Ludwig Thoma (1867–1921). It was here, in 1908, that he had a country house built for himself in which he later wrote most of his works. He is commemorated by the tomb in the Alter Friedhof (old graveyard), where Ludwig Ganghofer (1855-1920) and the opera singer Leo Slezak (1873–1946) also lie buried. Heinrich Spoerl was interred in the Neuer Friedhof (new graveyard). He lived by the Tegernsee from 1941 onwards and died here on 25 August 1955. The tomb of Olaf Gulbransson, the Norwegian painter and draughtsman who was one of the major contributors to the satirical magazine 'Simplizissimus', is also in the Neuer Friedhof.

**Pfarrkirche St. Laurentius** (parish church of St.Lawrence): This 15C church was stuccoed in 1672. The altars by local artists also date from this period. The half-columns which encase the pilasters and attached shafts are original. However, these half-columns do not begin on the floor, but half way up the pilasters. There are four outstanding votive panels on the N. wall: they are intended to keep alive the memory of the so-called Sendlinger Mordweihnacht (murderous Christmastime), 1705, and also the wars of 1812, 1866 and 1870 –1.

**Ludwig-Thoma-Bühne theatre:** (36

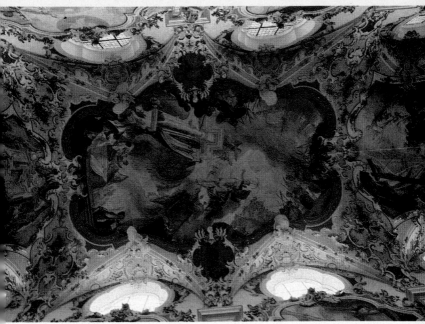

*Rottenbuch, Stiftskirche, frescoed ceiling*

Fürstenstrasse): A permanent peasant theatre in the Rottach-Egern Kur- und Kongress-Saal (health resort assembly hall, and congress hall).

**Also worth seeing:** The Auferstehungs-Kapelle (resurrection chapel; 1955) in Rottach.

**Rottenbuch 8121**
Bavaria                                                    p.422□I 21

**Former Augustiner-Chorherren-stiftskirche Mariae Geburt** (Augustinian church of the Birth of the Virgin): This Gothic basilica (consecrated in 1345) was built on 11&12C Romanesque foundations. Its interior, after alterations in the 15&18C, is today entirely baroque and the fine decorations are by J.Schmuzer, F.X. Schmuzer and M.Günther (painter). Note the combination of Gothic arches and baroque stucco. Most of the *Günther frescos* are devoted to the life and work of St.Augustine, the patron saint of the order. The *high altar*, a work by F.X.Schmädl (1740 –7), has a carving of the birth of the Virgin. The figures of St.Joachim and St.Anne, the Virgin's parents, are at the side, and above the passages are the figures of St.Peter and St.Paul. Other important items by Schmädl are the *choir stalls* (with the figures of David and Aaron), the *pulpit* with the figures of the Evangelists, and *four side altars* with carvings. One of the side altars has a seated Madonna (1483), one of E.Grasser's masterpieces.

**Rottenburg/Neckar 7407**
Baden-Württemberg                        p.420□F 18

**Dom (cathedral) St.Martin:** This has been the cathedral church since 1821. Its most prominent feature is the tower dating from 1486. Designed by H.v.Beben-hausen, it was built by the local artist H.Schwarzacher. The helm roof is profusely decorated and the interior of the church was restored in 1956.

**Former Stiftskirche St.Moritz** (collegiate church of St.Moritz; in the Ehingen district): The core of this church dates from 1489, although some sections were incorporated from an earlier church and the result was later converted into a hall church (1706). Despite this eventful architectural history, the Gothic arrangement of space survives. There are 14&15C *frescos* on the round pillars. The *wall painting* in the choir has survived from the 15C church. Note the numerous *tombs,* most of which are 14C. The *ornamented column from the Marktbrunnen* has been erected in the N. aisle. Archduchess Mechthild donated the fountain in 1470 and had various princes depicted on it. Today a copy of the column stands in the Marktplatz.

**Wallfahrtskirche St.Maria** (pilgrimage church; im Weggental): Rebuilt in 1682–95 to plans by M.Thumb, the church has a *Pietà* (*c.* 1500), and also the fine group of the *Virgin swooning. Stucco* by J.G.Brix (*c.* 1700).

**Museums:** *Sülchgau-Museum* (16 Bahnhofstrasse): Pre- and early history, Roman finds, town history. *Diocesan museum* (in the Bischofspalast): Ecclesiastical art, painting and sculptures.

---

**Rottweil 7210**
Baden-Württemberg                    p.420□E 19

This region of the Neckar was of considerable importance to the Romans and Roman sites have been excavated here. However, the present town of Rottweil was founded in 1140 by Konrad, the Duke of Zähringen. Its site above the Neckar led to a tightly-packed lay-out. It became a free city after 1268 and from 1463 onwards the town was closely associated with the Swiss Confederation, with which an 'eternal alliance' was concluded. The town's appearance has hardly changed since the 17C when Rottweil was captured by the French.

**Münster Heiliges Kreuz** (Minster of the

*Marktplatz in Rottenburg*

Holy Cross; Kirchplatz): The present Münster is a 15&16C church incorporating some older sections. Late Romanesque forms pass into Gothic. The most prominent items are a number of outstanding late Gothic works of art, most of which were not installed in the Münster until a later date. First of all, the late-15C *crucifix* attributed to V.Stoss; the 15C *tabernacle*; the late Gothic *Petrusaltar* (altar of St.Peter; in the N. aisle). The *Nikolausaltar* (altar of St. Nicholas; in the S. aisle). The *Apostelaltar* (Apostles' altar; by the choir screen) and the *Marienaltar* (altar of the Virgin Mary; opposite the Apostelaltar); the latter two are both from the 2nd half of the 15C. The *devotional image,* which is today above the door of the S. aisle, comes from a winged altar by an artist from Rottweil (*c.* 1440). There is a richly carved 17C *pulpit* and a font completed in 1563.

**Kapellenkirche Unserer Lieben Frau** (chapel of the Virgin Mary; Kapellenhof): The *chapel tower* stands to the E. of the Marktplatz and its rich stone sculpture is amongst the finest of its kind in Germany from that time. Its lower storeys date from the 14C, while the three upper storeys are by A.Jörg (1473). The chapel proper is also 14C, but it has subsequently been radically altered on several occasions.

**Dominikanerkirche** (Dominican church; Bruderschaftsgasse): This church was rebuilt in its present form in 1753 (the previous church was early Gothic). Note the frescos by J.Wannenmacher (1755) and the rococo altar.

**Roman settlement of Arae Flaviae** (beside Bundesstrasse [federal highway] 14/27): The buildings, which were unearthed in excavations carried out from 1784 onwards, date from the period after AD 74. The discoveries include the second largest *Roman baths* in Baden-Württemberg and a famous *Orpheus mosaic* (*c.* AD 180).

**Houses:** Many beautiful houses from the 16–18C survive in the streets of the old part of town. The delicate, carved columns of the windows are a typical feature.

**Stadtmuseum Rottweil** (town museum; 20 Hauptstrasse): The main attraction is the Roman department of the Stadtmuseum, which is in a former patrician's house. The Roman *Orpheus mosaic* is displayed here. Another department covers the period when Rottweil was a free city. The Fastnachtssammlung (Shrovetide collection) is devoted to the famous *Rottweiler Fasnet* (Rottweil Shrovetide celebrations).

**Also worth seeing:** Marktplatz with fountain. Remains of the town fortifications with the *Schwarzes Tor* (black gate; 13C).

---

## Rüdesheim am Rhein 6220

Hessen                                      p.416☐D 14

---

This famous wine-growing town was inhabited in Roman times. Rüdesheim later became more important because of the 'Kaufmannsweg' road, which was built to circumvent the 'Binger Loch', a narrow section of the Rhine dangerous for shipping. Today Rüdesheim is one of the most frequently visited wine-growing towns on the Rhine. The centre of tourism here is Drosselgasse, with town houses dating mainly from the 17&18C.

**Pfarrkirche St.Jakob** (parish church of St.James; Marktplatz): The early Romanesque chapel on the lower ground floor of the tower on the N.side is all that survives from an earlier 12C church The present one dates from around 1400, and was enlarged in 1912–14. Severe damage was caused in World War 2, when the fine interior was almost completely destroyed in a fire. Note the sandstone Marienaltar (altar of the Virgin Mary), as well as several tombs.

**Town walls and the Adlerturm (eagle tower):** The Adlerturm in the SE of the old town (near the Nassauische Sparkasse bank) was once the corner tower of the 15C town walls. Goethe spent the night here several times.

**Mäuseturm** (mice tower): A stone tower

standing in the middle of the Rhine and commissioned by Philipp v.Bolanden in 1208. The original tower on this site was wooden and had been built by Drusus, the Roman commander, in 8 BC.

**Niederwald-Denkmal** (can also be reached by cable railway): This national monument was consecrated in 1883 and commemorates the foundation of the Prussian Empire following the war of 1870-1. The figure of Germania by J.Schilling is 34 ft. tall and weighs 32 tons. The sword which she carries is more than 23 ft. long.

**Ehrenfels castle:** This imposing ruin is a remnant of a massive 13C castle which was destroyed in 1689.

**Museums:** *Rheingau- und Weinmuseum* (museum of the Rheingau district and wine museum; 2 Rheinstrasse): The largest specialist museum of this kind, with collections relating to the history of the Rheingau region and to pre- and early history, is housed in the Brömserburg or Niederburg, which was long held by the Brömsers. The castle dates back to the 12C, but after having fallen into decay it was enlarged in the 19C. *Museum of mechanical musical instruments,* 29 Oberstrasse.

**Also worth seeing:** The towers of the former Ober- and Vorderburg castle. These too once belonged to the Brömsers of Rüdesheim.

---

**Ruhpolding 8222**
Bavaria                           p.422☐N 20

**Pfarrkirche St. Georg:** This parish church is one of the finest village churches in Upper Bavaria. In addition to its local importance, it has the 'Ruhpoldinger Madonna', a Romanesque wooden sculpture which is to be seen in the right side altar (*c.* 1230). Apart from this Madonna, there are several interesting altars, beautiful choir stalls, and a richly decorated pulpit (all these date from the time of the church's building in 1738-57).

**Museums:** *Bartholomäus-Schmucker-Heimatmuseum* (2 Schlossstrasse): Collections devoted to the history of Ruhpolding and to general cultural history, together with small religious works of art, are on display in this Renaissance former hunting lodge, which dates from 1587. *Museum für bäuerliche und sakrale Kunst* (museum of rural and religious art; 1 Roman Friesinger-Strasse): A museum with regional everyday items. Gorgeous cupboards, chests, decorated glass, crockery and other craftsmen's implements may be admired on the ground floor. There is a good collection of paraments on the first and second floors.

---

**Rüschhaus über Havixbeck 4401**
Nordrhein-Westfalen            p.414☐C 9

The Haus Rüschhaus, a farm in the Münsterland region, is to be found to the E. of Havixbeck and, like the buildings there, it was built by J.K. Schlaun in 1745-8. The poetess Annette v.Droste-Hülshoff (1797-1848) lived here in 1826-46 with her mother and sister Jenny, following the death of her father. Today the red brick house contains a *museum* with collections relating to the life and work of Droste-Hülshoff.

*Ruhpolding Madonna, St.Georg* ▷

## Saarbrücken 6600

Saarland                                         p.420 □ B 16

Saarbrücken's development into the economic centre of the Saar came about as a result of its position on the Franco-German border, as well as through the production of iron and coal. Once it was under the protection of Burg Saarbrücken, first mentioned in 999, it began to develop into a residential and administrative town. Saarbrücken enjoyed a period of great success in the early 17C under Count Ludwig, who planned much of the town and built the Renaissance Schloss. The town was then enlarged under Prince Wilhelm Heinrich (1741 – 68), who added some remarkable baroque buildings. For historical reasons the town is divided into three districts, Saarbrücken, St.Johann and St. Arnual. Apart from its status as the economic centre of a highly developed industrial area, Saarbrücken is also important as the intellectual centre of the Saar. The University, the Pädagogische Hochschule, the Musikhochschule, the theatres, local radio and several scientific and cultural societies are the driving forces. The Kunstpreis des Saarlands been awarded here since 1959.

**Protestant Schlosskirche and Town Parish Church** (Schlossplatz): This 15C church is the funerary chapel of the Princes of Nassau-Saarbrücken. The damage caused by the fire of 1677 and by air raids in the Second World War was thoroughly and rapidly made good on each occasion. The old furnishings were almost totally lost, however (new windows by G.Meistermann). There are interesting original and reconstructed tombs.

**Deutschherrenkapelle** (Moltkestrasse): This is the oldest building in Saarbrücken and dates back to the first third of the 13C, but has often been badly damaged and radically altered (tower on S. side, 1868). Remains of the medieval building survive in the cellar of the Wirtschaftsgebäude. The former Deutschherrenhaus, with modern extensions, is now an *Home for Orphans*.

**Protestant Church of St.Ludwig** (Ludwigsplatz): This church, built between 1762–75, was designed by the municipal architect F.J.Stengel and is considered the most important church building in the Saar. The ground plan is a Greek cross with rounded corners. The dominant tower is on the W. side, but the E. front is the façade and entrance side. The church burned down after an air-raid in 1944, and there was much discussion over the relative merits of rebuilding in the original form or in modern style. A few years ago the interior was restored to the original design, but without furnishings.

**Catholic Parish Church** (in St.Johann): F.J.Stengel also designed this church,

*Tomb of Count Johann III, collegiate church*

which replaced an older building in 1754 –8. Contrary to custom Stengel devoted equal attention to end and side walls. P.Mihm (portal) and J.Gounin (capitals and windows) provided the ornamentation.

**Collegiate Church** (Markt St. Arnual): This important early Gothic church was built in the 13&14C. The powerful groin vaulting is the striking feature of the interior. The church is famous for the numerous tombs of members of the House of Nassau-Saarbrücken; those of Count Johann III (d.1472) and of Elisabeth von Lothringen (d.1456) are outstanding.

**Other interesting churches:** *Old Catholic Friedenskirche* in the Saarbrücken district (1743–6), *Protestant parish church* in the St.Johann district (1725–7), *Catholic parish church of St. Albert* (Rodenhof): Modern church dating from 1952 – 4, which became a model for churches with centrally placed altars.

**Schloss** (Schlossplatz): The present building was built in 1738–48 to plans by the municipal architect F.J.Stengel. Previously there had been a medieval Burg and a Renaissance Schloss (1617) on the site; the latter was rebuilt after being destroyed in 1677, but later demolished to make way for the present building. Even this rococo Schloss, one of the great palaces of its period, was damaged and modified: in 1793 it was looted and burned down, then rebuilt to Stengel's plans under A Knipper in 1810; he added a third storey. In 1872 H.Diem replaced the gateway with the central building.

**Altes Rathaus** (Schlossplatz): The Town Hall is another building by F.J. Stengel (1758–60). Fire damage from the last war has been made good.

**Old Bridge** (Schillerplatz/Schlossplatz): The Old Bridge, which now links the Schloss and the Staatstheater, was built by

*Schloss, Saarbrücken*

H.Sparer in 1546–8, but was modified in the 18C. The new design was based on plans by B.W.Stengel, a son of the municipal architect.

**Grosser Brunnen** (St. Johann district, St.Johanner-Markt): F.J.Stengel designed this baroque fountain, P.Mihm was responsible for the ornamentation and S.Bockelmann for the iron rail. (1759&60).

**Roman Fort** (Mainzer Strasse): The fort was built in the 3C AD. The impressive remains were discovered by excavation.

**Museums:** *Saarland-Museum* (24 St. Johanner-Markt): The museum is housed in a late 18C building. There is an open-air exhibition of sculpture by Saarland artists in an inner courtyard. Principal exhibits in the museum, apart from a collection of modern art, are arts and crafts of the 18C. *Landesmuseum für Vor- und Frühgeschichte* (15 Am Ludwigsplatz): Pre-

and early history. *Moderne Galerie* (11–15 Bismarckstrasse): Contemporary art.

**Theatres:** *Staatstheater* (1 Tbilisser Platz): This theatre, built in 1937&8, seats 1121 people. Musicals and drama are performed by the resident company. *Saarländisches Landestheater* (10 Scharhorststrasse): This theatre, opened in 1949, is reserved for straight theatre performed by the resident company; 120 seats.

### Salem 7777
Baden-Württemberg                                p.420☐F 20

**Former Cistercian Abbey Church/Catholic Parish Church** (31 Bundesstrasse): Nothing remains of the original Romanesque building. It was replaced by the present building, which was begun in 1297 and finally consecrated in 1414. The long building period did not

*Salem, Schloss*

affect the uniformity of the Gothic design. The main features of this vaulted basilica with a nave and two aisles follow the Cistercian rule precisely, although it is lightened by the lavish tracery windows on the W. side. Inside little is preserved of the old furnishings (*tabernacle* of 1494 in the N. transept, *choir stalls* of 1588–95). The present furnishings, with the *high altar*, 26 side altars and valuable individual sculptures, are the work of J.G.Dirr and J.G.Wieland (1771–94). Everything is executed in reddish alabaster and shows early neoclassical austerity of design. The *ceiling paintings* below the transept galleries were the work of F.J.Spiegler (1730). The 4 *confessionals* were made by J.A.Feuchtmayer in 1753, the *organ* by K.J.Riepp of Ottobeuren (1766). Adjacent to the S. are the *abbey buildings*, which were rebuilt by F.Beer after a fire in 1697; he was assisted by the best artists of the time (including F.Schmuzer, F.J.Feuchtmayer). The Kaisersaal is of particular interest.

**Also worth seeing:** Chapel in the lay cemetery in neighbouring *Stephansfeld:* Greek cruciform rotunda, built to plans by F.Beer in 1707–10.

---

**Salzgitter 3320**
Lower Saxony                    p.414☐H 8

**Former Benedictine Monastery Church of St.Abdon and St.Sennen** (in Ringelheim): The foundations of this church, now a Catholic parish church, probably date from a building of the Ottonian period (*c.*1000), but the present building came into being as a result of extensions in 1504 (choir), 1694 (choir and nave), 1695 (tower) and 1794 (general extension). The portal on the main façade is a focus of attention because of its exposed setting on the hillside above the Innerste. The *interior* has been rococo since 1794. The outstanding high altar and surrounding side altars, pulpit and communion bench all date from around 1700. The most valuable item of the furnishings is a first-class crucifix, probably from the workshop of Bernward von Hildesheim (c.1000).

**Former Protestant Collegiate Church of St.Maria and St.Jakob** (in Steterburg): The present church was built in 1751–3 on the site of older buildings dating from 1070. The N. and S. sides look more like a palace than a church.

**Schloss** (in Salder): This 1609 building (extended and altered in 1695) now houses the *Städtisches Museum*. The interior walls had large equestrian portraits, probably by T.Querfurt.

## St. Andreasberg 3424
Lower Saxony       p.414☐I 10

**Historic Samson Silver-Mine** (Am Samson): The Harz Mountains were once known as the 'Treasury of the Emperors', due to the rich deposits of silver (see Goslar); one of the old mines, the Samson Pit, in operation from 1521 to 1910, has been

a *museum* since 1951. The museum includes the silver mine both above and below ground and much of the equipment is maintained in working order.

## St. Blasien 7822
Baden-Württemberg       p.420☐D 20

**Former Abbey Church of St.Blasius:** Nothing remains of the 9C Benedictine abbey. The new building was built after a fire in 1768. After secularization the monks moved to Austria; a small-arms factory moved into the monastery buildings, to be followed by a spinning-mill. Rebuilding in an authentic style began after another catastrophic fire in 1874, which also destroyed the church. Since 1934 or 1946 the abbey has been a Jesuit seminary.

The spacious complex was conceived as a unified whole and consists of two square courts separated by the church; it is reminiscent of a baroque palace, but is based on strict mathematical proportions: in the circular part of the church the interior diameter is the same as the interior height (150 ft.); half this measurement is the basic unit for the rest of the building.

*Abbey church, St.Blasien*

The abbey was designed by M.d'Ixnard in 1768–83), and is influenced by French rationality; it was the first neoclassical monumental building on German soil. The columned portico recalls the Pantheon in Rome; adjoining the rotunda and ambulatory is a deep monks' choir. Only the high altar at the entrance to the monks' choir (by the excellent Freiburg sculptor C.Wenzinger, the principal rococo architect of Baden) remains of the original furnishings.

## St. Goar 5401
Rheinland-Pfalz                               p.416 □ D 14

Rheinfels Castle, blown up by the French in 1797 and since maintained as a romantic ruin, attracted numerous literary figures, including Ferdinand Freiligrath, Hans Christian Anderson, A.H. Hoffmann von Fallersleben and Emanuel Geibel. The ruins became an important source of inspiration for German Romantic poets.

**Collegiate Church/Protestant Parish Church:** The 11C Romanesque crypt is one of the finest of its period in the area between Cologne and Speyer. It has very fine groin vaulting supported by columns arranged in 2 rows. The church is Gothic, with the exception of a few Romanesque sections; building began in the 13C, but was not completed until the mid 15C. The nave contains a fine net vault; the choir has groin vaulting. Between the ribs of the aisle vaults there are (superbly restored) *paintings* dating from the 2nd third of the 15C. Important works of art include the stone *pulpit* with lavish sculptural decoration (*c.*1460–70) and a few tombs in early baroque style.

**Catholic Parish Church:** This has an interesting altarpiece with a central panel by the so-called Hausbuch Master *c.*1510).

**Rheinfels Burg Ruins:** In an exposed setting high above the Rhine are the ruins of the castle built by Count Dieter III von Katzenelnbogen in 1245. In 1568 the complex was extended into a fortress and in 1797 it was blown up by the French. In the former chapel there is now an interesting local folklore collection.

## St. Peter 7811
Baden-Württemberg                            p.420 □ D 20

**Former Benedictine Monastery Church of St. Peter:** The Benedictine Abbey of St.Peter in Freiburg was originally (1073) founded by Duke Berthold I in Weilheim an der Teck and moved to this exposed setting, at that time in the Austrian border region, by his son Berthold II in 1093. It was constantly the victim of war, fire and looting, as a result of which none of the medieval works of art have survived. The baroque church with its twin-towered façade and niche figures below the curved gable is a work by the Vorarlberg architect P.Thumb. With its unusual breadth and simple design the church, built in 1724–7, is reminiscent of similar buildings by the Vorarlberg master in Upper Swabia; they are all pilaster churches with chapels and galleries. The furnishings include a fine choir screen, rococo or-

*Benedictine monastery church of St.Peter*

*Pilgrimage church, St. Wendel*

ent church, built from 1709 by P.Thumb, incorporated parts of a 12C Romanesque basilica and a 15C late Gothic successor into its design. The importance of the church lies in its interior: first-class stucco by M.Prevosti and C.Orsati (*c.*1716) is set off by F.A.Giorgioli's paintings, including scenes from the life of the church patron Trudpert, an Irish missionary said to have been martyred here in the 7C. The painting in the retable of the *high altar* is unusual: it is a relief painting by J.J.Christian (*c.*1782), and shows stucco technique of a standard rarely equalled. The mid-18C *pulpit,* with lavish decorative sculpture, was taken from the Augustinian monastery in Freiburg (q.v.). The most important item of the treasure is a *processional cross,* probably dating from around 1175 (in the sacristy). Notable too are the *choir stalls* (*c.*1670–80). The adjacent *monastery buildings* (18C) have some fine rococo stucco and A.Moosbrugger's courtyard gate (1740).

## St. Wendel 6690
Saarland                                                 p.420□C 16

**Catholic Parish and Pilgrimage Church of St. Wendelinus** (Am Fruchtmarkt): This church (14&15C) has an impressive W. end with 3 towers. The portal has lavish figures depicting the Judge of the World and the 12 Apostles. The interior is a narrow hall with first-class net vaulting. Outstanding amongst the *furnishings* are the costly *high tomb of St. Wendelinus* (*c.*1360), the *reliquary* (behind the high altar, *c.*1430–40) and the stone *pulpit* (1462, donated by Nicholas of Cusa). On the side walls are 8 18C carved figures. *Holy Sepulchre,* with a group of high-quality clay figures (*c.*1500).

**Museums:** *Heimatmuseum* (Altes Rathaus): Regional and town history. *Völkerkundesammlung der Steyler Missionare* (Missionshaus): Collections on the history of the mission and on folklore.

**Environs: Otzenhausen** (27 km. NW): Celtic refuge castle (*c.*50 BC) on the Dollberg.

namentation on the organ, wall and vault paintings (with scenes from the life of the church patron), and statues of the Zähringer family; this was their funerary church. These statues (on the pillars) and the Apostle figures on the altars are by J.A.Feuchtmayer; the figures on the font in the S. transept are by M.Faller. Today St.Peter is the Catholic parish church. The *abbey building,* a seminary for priests of the archdiocese of Freiburg since 1842, has lavish stucco and ceiling paintings with scenes from the Old and New Testaments in the chapterhouse (now the chapel), the staircase and the Prince's Room. The most beautiful room is the rococo library with an interesting ceiling picture by B.Gambs, 1751.

## St. Trudpert = Münstertal 7816
Baden-Württemberg                          p.420□D 20

**Former Monastery Church:** The pres-

*Schäftlarn, St. Dionys and St. Juliana*

**Ottweiler** (9 km. S.): Protestant parish church (15&16C) and medieval buildings.

### Saulgau 7968
Baden-Württemberg          p.420☐G 20

**Catholic Parish Church of St.John the Baptist:** The elegant proportions of this flat-ceilinged basilica (*c.*1400, 13C tower) distinguish it from the other late Gothic churches of the region. The charmingly designed church also has important *church treasure,* including an early 14C processional cross. Note also the *Virgin Mary* (*c.*1510), *St.Joseph* (*c.*1760), a stone pietà (*c.*1510) and the impressive *font* (late 17C).

**Kreuzkapelle/Schwedenkapelle:** This outwardly insignificant, originally late Gothic chapel, enlarged in 1869, is famous for the *Saulgau Crucifix.* The carved figure of Christ on the Cross (mid 12C; part of

the 1734 altar) is one of the most impressive works of its time.

**Also worth seeing:** The *Rathaus* (Marktplatz) built around 1820, *Frauenkapelle* with stucco by the Wessobrunn master K.Zimmermann (1741–3), *houses* in good condition (Pfarrgasse, Bogengasse). *'Die Fähre' gallery* (6 Schulstrasse): Modern art.

### Schäftlarn 8021
Bavaria          p.422☐K 20

**Former Premonstratensian Monastery** (2 km. E. of nearby Ebenhausen): The church, consecrated in 1760, was excellently restored in 1954–9; it forms the central axis of the symmetrical monastery buildings. The interior has first-rate *decorations* by famous artists. J.B.Zimmermann, at the age of over 70, created one of his greatest works in stucco and fresco here

*Schloss courtyard*

(1754 – 6). The famous J.B.Straub was responsible for the *altars* and the pulpit (1755–64); they are the principal furnishings and are decorated with excellent figures. The paintings on some of the altars are by B.A.Albrecht (Munich), among others. Lavish *figure ornamentation* is also to be found on the *pulpit*. The lucid and austere *monastery* was built by G.A.Viscardi in 1702–7.

---

### Schaumburg 6251
Rheinland-Pfalz        p.416□D 13

**Schloss:** This hilltop complex is first referred to in 1197. The castle was then owned by the Counts of Leiningen, and in the 15C by the Counts of Westerburg. Archduke Stephan of Austria had it extended in English neo-Gothic style in 1851–5. The 3-storey main wing dates from this time. Medieval masonry survives in the E. wing.

### Schleissheim = Oberschleissheim 8042
Bavaria        p.422□K 19

It is not entirely correct to speak simply of Schloss Schleissheim, for the great palace N. of Munich consists of 3 sections: the *Altes Schloss,* the *Neues Schloss* and the little palace of *Lustheim.* The new Schloss houses an important department of the *Bayerische Staatsgalerie* with Dutch, Italian and German baroque painting.

**Neues Schloss:** The Neues Schloss commissioned by Elector Max Emanuel was not completed: the first problems arose shortly after the laying of the foundation stone in 1701. The entrance hall collapsed shortly after it was built, as the foundations were inadequate; E.Zuccali, who had previously built Lustheim, had been careless in checking the technical requirements. The problem was solved by

*Neues Schloss, Schleissheim*

reinforcement with earth, but this affected the proportions, and the Schloss looks a little as if it has been rammed into the ground. J.Effner planned the new flight of steps. When Max Emanuel was forced into exile after the War of the Spanish Succession, the shell of the building was complete, but work was came to a halt. Plans were also dropped to connect the Neues Schloss to the old one with an additional wing, which would have made it one of the largest palaces in Europe. Zuccali's idea of placing a tower in the middle of the main building was also abandoned. When building started again in 1719 effort was largely concentrated on completing the existing building; J.Günther created the *E. portal,* C.D.Asam painted the excellent *vault fresco* above the extensive *staircase.* J.B.Zimmermann was engaged for the *stucco works* and supplied the trophy decoration for the banqueting hall. The work of these and many other outstanding artists is at its best in the monumental *central part* of the Neues Schloss, one of the finest works of the German baroque. The staircase was completed to the original design under King Ludwig I in 1847&8, while the façade was reworked by L.von Klenze in the early 19C (2 gables removed). Damage sustained in the Second World War was repaired. The Neues Schloss is entered through one of the *portals,* which leads into an Italian-style *vestibule,* the columns of which support shallow domes. On the ground floor are the former *dining-room* and *staterooms.* The stairs lead up to the *banqueting hall,* the artistic centre of the Neues Schloss. The frescos depict mythological scenes, reflecting the successful Turkish Campaign of Max Emanuel and his triumphant reception (Viktoriensaal). On the garden side are the *gallery* and the *Elector's private chambers,* which are lavishly furnished.

**Altes Schloss:** The Altes Schloss was built as a country retreat for Duke Wilhelm V in 1597. It was completed in 1616.

**Lustheim:** The original plan of Elector Max Emanuel was to create a haven in the quiet setting of Schleissheim (the idea of the hermitage was very popular at the time). His first commission therefore was the building of a comparatively small Schloss in the middle of a park; it was built by E.Zuccali on the E. side of the present park in 1884–7, and modelled on Italian baroque palaces. The centre of the building is the great *hall,* the distinctive feature of which is a mirror vault, decorated with frescos and supported by painted atlantes. The uniform interior of the palace is outstanding; it houses a valuable *porcelain collection.*

**Park:** The park, which originated in the 17&18C, is set around the canal linking the Neues Schloss and Lustheim; Effner's *marble cascade* is at the W. end.

---

**Schleswig 2380**

Schleswig-Holstein                    p.412□G 2

---

The focal point of this charming city, once a bishopric and ducal residence, is still the Marktplatz and the area around the cathedral. Another attractive feature is Schloss Gottorf, which is surrounded by water and now houses the Schleswig-Holsteinische Landesmuseum.

**Dom St. Petri** (Süderdomstrasse): The present building, now the Protestant parish church, is a Gothic hall church on a cruciform Romanesque ground plan; it was built in the 13–15C incorporating older buildings and is of a size which inspires respect. The tower, which is not quite in proportion with the rest of the building, was added at the end of the 19C; along with the massive saddle roof it is the most striking feature of the exterior. Upon entering through the *Petersportal* the interior is clearly that of a Romanesque episcopal church. Choir and choir aisle have *vault paintings* (uncovered in 1892&3 and restored in 1936–8). The oldest parts of these paintings date from the 12C. Apart from the sculptural decoration the ornamentation is also worthy of note. The principal work in the cathedral is the *Bordesholm Altar* (1514–21) by H.Brüggemann. This carved altar was transferred here from the Augustinian canonry in Bordesholm in 1666; it depicts the Life of Christ in 12 small and 2 large scenes. There are almost

*Dom St. Petri*                                    *Schacht vault, Dom, Schleswig* ▷

400 figures, some influenced by Dürer, and they were unpainted from the start. Also from Brüggemann's workshop is the *figure of St. Christopher,* over 13 ft. high, which stands next to the entrance on the right. There are fine altars in the choir aisle, including the oak *altar of the 3 Kings* (*c.* 1300) with the Virgin Mary and the 3 Kings. In the N. side choir there now stands the *Kielmannseck Altar.* This was donated by the chancellor of Gottorf, Count Kielmannseck, in 1664 and decorated with an altar painting by J.Ovens. Also by this famous painter, whose work reveals the influence of Van Dyck and Rembrandt, is the *Blue Madonna* in the

**Schleswig, Dom 1** Peterstür, c.1180 **2** Old canons' sacristy, c. 1220-30 **3** Ceiling paintings in the crossing, c. 1240-50 **4** Altar of the Magi, last quarter of 13C **5** Choir ceiling decoration c.1330, remains of the first decoration from the late 13C **6** Schwahl (cloister, c.1310-20 **7** Painting of the Schwahl, c.1330, with some additions of 1891 **8** Bordesholm Altar, traditionally by H.Brüggemann, 1514-21; it has been in the Dom since 1666 **9** Wooden pulpit, 1560 **10** Monument to King Frederick I of Denmark, by C.Floris, 1551-55 **11** Choir screen by M.D.Vorhave, 1569-70 **12** Memorial stone to Kielmann v.Kielmannseck, 1673 **13** Rood screen, late 15C, reconstruction of 1939

nave. In the 17&18C *funerary chapels* were laid out in the rooms between the buttresses, creating permanent monuments to nobles and court officials alongside the *tombs of the Dukes of Gottorf.* Outstanding amongst the splendid *baroque portals* is that of the vault of the Schacht family. Also of interest are the *rood-screen* (reproduction of the 15C original), the *choir-screen* (16C) and the unusually high *choir stalls* with 19 seats on each side (1512). Also worth seeing is the *cloister* adjacent to the cathedral, which is one of the most important works of Gothic art in North Germany (*wall paintings c.*1330, viewing possible upon request).

**St. John's Convent** (in Holm): The original Benedictine monastery on the bank of the Schlei was converted into a foundation for aristocratic ladies after the Reformation. The complex dates back to 1196 and is one of the best-preserved monasteries in N. Germany. The single-aisled *church* was much modified in the course of the centuries. The *canonesses' choir* (18C), a baroque *portal arch* dividing the church, the *pulpit* (1717) and the fine *tabernacle* (15C) deserve particular attention. The vaulted *cloister* and the well-preserved *refectory*

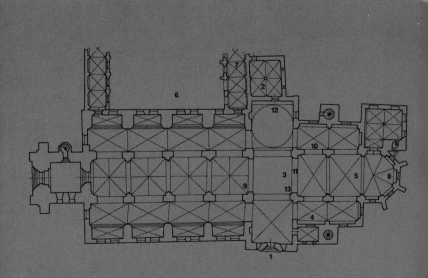

with early Gothic nuns' seats are very beautiful examples of monastery buildings.

**Schloss Gottorf** (Sclossinsel): Gottorf, situated on an island in a bend of the Schlei, is the largest Schloss in Schleswig-Holstein. The four-winged building encloses an inner court. The broad *façade* with its large *central tower* dates from the beginning of the 18C. The finest of the furnishings, however, date from the time of Friedrich III (1616–59). He also extended the fortifications and attracted numerous artists and scholars to Schleswig as his guests. The conversion to a baroque-style residence goes back to Friedrich IV (1694 –1702). The palace was later used as a barracks. In 1947 the State Museum and State Archives were transferred here and parts of the interior restored. Of the numerous interior rooms only the chapel and the Königssaal are outstanding. On the altar side of the *chapel* is the *prie-dieu of the Duchess*. This was installed for Duchess

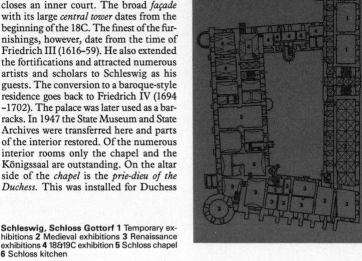

**Schleswig, Schloss Gottorf 1** Temporary exhibitions **2** Medieval exhibitions **3** Renaissance exhibitions **4** 18&19C exhibition **5** Schloss chapel **6** Schloss kitchen

*Schloss Gottorf, Schleswig*

*Gothic carved altar in the Protestant church, Haddeby*

Augusta in 1608–14 and is an important work of N. German Renaissance art. The *pulpit* and the wooden *gallery* were created around 1500 by a Flensburg master. The *Königssaal* in the S. wing was built by Friedrich I around 1520. A series of round columns support beautiful groin vaults. The gold arabesque painting on the ribs and the painting of the vaults was added in the 17C.

**Town Houses:** The most important houses of the old trading town of Schleswig are in the *Lange Strasse.* These date mostly from the 17&18C. Houses of minor citizens and fishermen are to be found in the *Holm* district of the city. The *Lollfuss-Stadtweg* street is lined with neoclassical aristocratic mansions.

**Theatre:** The *Schleswig-Holsteinische Landestheater und Sinfonieorchester* (53 Lollfuss) was built in 1892 and reopened in 1950. 620 seats. The 'Schlosshofspiele' are always held at the end of July on an open-air stage in Schloss Gottorf.

**Museums:** *Schleswig-Holsteinisches Landesmuseum* (in the Schloss): The collections are principally devoted to the cultural history of the Land from the Middle Ages to the present day. A visit to the museum is recommended, since it also includes Schloss Gottorf. *Schleswig-Holsteinisches Landesmuseum für Vor- und Frühgeschichte* (in the Schloss): Prehistoric finds, finds made in Schleswig-Holstein, including bodies preserved in bogs, Nydam ship (4C) and Roman coins. The *Städtisches Museum* (7–11 Friedrichstrasse) is in a building dating from 1634. It has exhibits on city history, as well as works by Schleswig painters, faience, pewter and silver.

**Environs: Haddeby** (3 km. SW): Haddeby, the Low-German form of the Old Nordic *Haithabu,* the name of the old Viking town, is one of the most important early-historical sites in Northern and Central Europe. Haithabu was a centre for East-West sea trade and trade to and from the Frankish-German area and East Scandinavia. The town, which was commercially most successful in the 9&10C, was subject to the Danes, the Swedes and the Germans at different times. A semicircular *rampart* (10C) (16–32 ft. high), and in the N. lower ramparts from a still undated refuge stronghold survive from the original *settlement on the heath* (=Haithabu). Around 1050 the Viking town was destroyed by the Norwegians and around 1066 by the Wends. Its function was taken over by Schleswig, which was founded on the N. bank of the Schlei. Just outside Busdorf to the SW is a copy of one of the four *rune stones* found at Haithabu, which were erected in memory of kings and retinue. Ramparts and stone walls (9–12C) also survive from the early medieval *Dannewerk,* the Danish border fortification which was supposed to seal off the Schleswig isthmus. *Protestant church:* Not far from this early settlement a *late Romanesque* stone church was built around 1200; it has a long nave with rectangular chancel and round *W. tower,* which once served as a defence tower. Of interest are a Gothic *carved altar* with three panels, a *limestone font* and the *Crucifixion* with a larger-than-life-size Christ and strikingly slender stylized accompanying figures (13C).

---

**Schlitz 6407**
Hessen                                    p.416☐G 12

**Protestant Parish Church of St. Margaretha:** This church had a long and varied building history. The various stages are reflected in the extensions and the rather unexpected tower. Of interest inside are the various *tombs* of the Counts von Schlitz, a *font* (1467) and the *organ* (1718) with trumpet-blowing angels.

**Castles:** The town was designed on a circular plan and surrounded by a ring of walls fortified by several castles. The *Hinterburg* is the oldest. Only the keep (13C), the Burghaus (1553) and a simple residen-

tial building are preserved. The *Vorderburg* can be recognized by the square tower at the point where the two wings meet (1565–1600). The carillon can be heard daily at 3 pm and 5 pm. The *Schachtenburg* is half-timbered (*c.*1550). The *Ottoburg* was built at the end of the 17C; its elongated building has a tower at each end. The *Hallenburg* in the valley served as a residence for the Counts. Its neoclassical features are later additions.

**Heimatmuseum** (in the Rathaus): Extensive costume collections and exhibits on the cultural history of linen, which has been produced in Schlitz for centuries.

**Environs: Fraurombach** (5 km. E.): Protestant church/former pilgrimage church of Liebfrauen: The most important feature of this simple Romanesque church dating from the 2nd half of the 12C (the half-timbered upper storey was added later) is the cycle of Gothic wall paintings in the nave (14C): depicted in 3 bands are the Legend of the Emperor Heraclius, the recapture of the True Cross and the return to Jerusalem according to a poem by the Hessian or Thuringian poet Otte (*c.*1203).

---

**Schongau 8920**
Bavaria                                   p.422☐I 20

**Parish Church of Mariae Himmelfahrt/Town Parish Church** (Marienplatz): The building was rebuilt after the collapse of a tower (1667) in the 18C. The church has an exceptionally fine interior; D.Zimmermann created the excellent *stucco* in the chancel (1748), while a master craftsman from Wessobrunn was responsible for the nave and aisles. M.Günther and F.A.Wassermann of Schongau painted the *frescos.* The monumental *high altar* dates from around 1760.

**Stadtmuseum** (6 Karmeliterstrasse): Local and folklore collection.

**Also worth seeing:** The *Ballenhaus* (1515) was modified in the 19C and also used as Rathaus; the Ratssaal with a carved

*Cistercian monastery church, Schöntal*

*Protestant church, Schorndorf*

wooden ceiling is of interest. Former *Stein-gadenes Richterhaus*, also with a beamed ceiling (1493). *Town wall* with rampart (15–17C), almost complete.

## Schöntal an der Jagst 7109
Baden-Württemberg                     p.420☐G 16

**Former Cistercian Monastery Church and former Monastery:** The monastery was founded in 1157, although it acquired its present appearance under Abbot Knittel from 1683–1732. J.L.Dientzenhofer designed the monastery and church, with two *towers* and a beautifully articulated *façade*. Notable inside is the *high altar* by J.M.Fischer (1773) and also the fine *ceiling frescos* and other *rococo altars*. In the nave are several *alabaster altars*, which are among the finest achievements of 17C German sculpture. Outstanding amongst the *monuments* is the double tomb of Konrad

and Anna von Weinsberg (1446&37) on both sides of the W. entrance. In the *cloister* S. of the church is the *tomb of Götz von Berlichingen* (d.1562) with the emblem of the iron hand. The cloister belongs to the *Neue Abtei*, also the work of Dientzenhofer, with a famous *staircase*. Despite its scale the construction takes up minimal space, and is a architectural achievement of no mean order. Outstanding also is the *Ordenssaal*.

## Schöppenstedt 3307
Lower Saxony                          p.414☐I 8

**Protestant Church of St.Stephan:** This church is famous for its early 12C *leaning tower*. In the middle of the lower floor of the tower is a formerly load-bearing column with mythological images (Wotan, Donar, Fenris wolf, Mitgard snake, world ash tree etc.).

*Winged altar, Liebfrauenkirche in Schotten*

**Till Eulenspiegel Museum** (Nordstrasse): The museum has over 2,500 exhibits on the famous rogue, who was born near Schöppenstedt.

**Environs: Küblingen** (1 km. E.): The angular *church of the Virgin Mary* (13&14C), a former pilgrimage church (from 1291), has a bronze Romanesque *processional cross* (*c.*1100) on the baroque *pulpit altar*.

## Schorndorf 7060
Baden-Württemberg                         p.420□G 18

**Protestant Town Church** (Kirchplatz): Begun by A.Jörg in 1477 (tower 1488), the building was continued after his death (1492) by H.von Urach and completed in 1501. Particularly outstanding is the *net vault* in the NE chapel with a *Tree of Jesse* (*c.*1500).

**Also worth seeing:** The *Dr. Palmsche*

*Apotheke* (1665–96, restored 1980; Marktplatz) with splendid half-timbering, the *Rathaus* of 1730 and the modest *Schloss* of Duke Ulrich (1538).

**Museums:** *Heimatmuseum* (9 Kirchplatz) in the former Latin School (1648). Daimler birthplace (7 Höllgasse, *c.*1700) with museum.

## Schotten 6479
Hessen                                    p.416□F 13

The health resort of Schotten on the Vogelsberg is famous for the oldest motor-racing track in Germany (*Schottenring*).

**Protestant Town Church Liebfrauen:** It is still clear from the appearance of this 14C church that modest plans for a pilgrimage church gave way to more grandiose ideas as a result of the town's rise in

*Schrobenhausen, St. Jakob, Calvary*

status (c. 1350). The W. portal with an Adoration of the Magi holds pride of place among the lavish exterior decorations. The tympanum over the *S. portal* of the W. end depicts the Virgin Mary with the founders of the church. Massive columns characterize the *interior*. The most important part of the furnishing is the superb *altarpiece* (c. 1400). The painting is amongst the finest of the period surviving in Hessen. When the altar is closed it shows the Passion in 8 scenes, when open, it portrays the Life of the Virgin Mary in 16 scenes. Also of value are the late Gothic carved figures (Mater Dolorosa, Crucifixion, crucifix), the font (14C), the organ (1782) and a sacristy cupboard (1494).

**Altes Rathaus** (Markt): This beautiful *half-timbered building* was built in 1512–30.

**Vogelsberger Heimatmuseum** (95 Vogelsbergstrasse): Extensive collections on medieval and modern trades, folklore and arts and crafts.

---

**Schrobenhausen 8898**
Bavaria                              p.422☐K 18

**Town parish church of St. Jakob:** This basilica (1425–80, tower raised in 17C) is typical of Bavarian churches in the late Gothic period. *Wall paintings* from the period when the church was built have survived in the choir and parts of the nave. A *Crucifixion group* and a *Calvary* deserve very special attention (c. 1500).

**Museums:** The *Heimatmuseum* (22 Lenbachplatz) has historical collections on the town and cultural history. The *Lenbachmuseum* (1 Ulrich-Peisser-Gasse) offers a survey of the life and work of the painter.

**Also worth seeing:** *St. Salvator* (mid 15C), *Rathaus* with Lenbach Room, parts of the 15C *town wall*.

**Environs: Sandizell** (7 km. W.): The chapel (1756&7) of the former *moated Burg* (1749–55) with interesting *altar sculptures* (18C) is worth a visit, as is the rococo parish church of *St. Peter* with a high altar by E.Q. Asam.

---

**Schwabach 8540**
Bavaria                              p.422☐I/K 16

**Protestant Parish Church** (Königsplatz): The church (consecrated late 15C) was enlarged at the start of the 16C by the addition of the sacristy and the chapel of St. Anna, but otherwise has maintained its original appearance. There are particularly lavish *furnishings* dating from the time of construction. The *high altar* is one of the best works of the late Gothic period (early 16C). The panels were painted by M. Wohlgemut, teacher of A. Dürer. The carvings were executed by a pupil of V. Stoss. H. Baldung, known as Grien, was yet another important artist from around 1500 who worked in this church: he

painted the panel pictures of St.Catherine
and St.Barbara. The tabernacle (1505) is
similar to the one in the church of St.
Lorenz in Nuremberg(q.v.).

**Königsplatz:** The buildings in the Königsplatz dating from the early 16C to the
18C, have survived almost unaltered. The
*Rathaus* (1509) and the former *Fürstenher-
berge* are particularly striking. (1726–8).
The *Schöne Brunnen* dates from 1716&17.
In the NW corner of the square stands the
smaller neoclassical *Pferdebrunnen* horse
fountain.

**Stadtmuseum** (8 Pfarrgasse): Of particular interest are the Schwabach printing
departments, a needlemaker's shop and a
gold-beater's workshop.

## Schwäbisch Gmünd 7070
Baden-Württemberg                    p.420☐G 18

The former Free Imperial City on the
Rems is now famous for its jewellery. The
master mason Peter Parler and the painters
Hans Baldung, called Grien, and Jörg Ratgeb were born here.

**Heiligkreuzmünster** (Münsterplatz):
The Cathedral of the Holy Cross (now
Catholic parish church) was built from
1310–1410 (consecration) incorporating a
Romanesque nave. It is one of the principal
works of the Parler family. The outside is
particularly charming when viewed from
the E; the projecting choir chapels seem
to form a lower storey with tracery windows. The most interesting feature of the
lavish exterior ornamentation is the tympanum of the S. portal (Last Judgement).
The Münster is the first large *hall church*
in S. Germany; the interior is dominated
by massive *round pillars* (with fine capitals)
and the excellent *net vaulting*. The *choir* is
surrounded by radiating chapels (see
above). The *furnishings* do not date from
the time of the church's construction at all.
An exception is the *Holy Sepulchre* (c.1400)
in the middle choir chapel, which is similar to the one in Freiburg Cathedral (q.v.).
Remains of old *wall-paintings* date from the

*Münster, Schwäbisch Gmünd*

first third of the 15C. Also of interest are
the *altarpiece* (1508) on the S. side, a *Kindred altar* with the Tree of Jesse (1520) in
the N. chapel of Sebaldus, the *choir stalls*
with figures of prophets (1550) and the *organ* (1668).

**Church of St.Johannes** (Johannisplatz):
This church probably originated as a hermitage chapel around 770 and not, as legend has it, as a chapel founded by
Duchess Agnes of Swabia. The present
church was built in the 13C. The over-
elaborate late Romanesque *decoration* is
unique. Throughout the church are
representations of hunting scenes, figures
from the worlds of animals and fable, ornaments and events from the Christian
world.

**Neues Rathaus** (Markt): The Town Hall,
built in 1783&4, was originally planned as
a merchant's house.
**Gräth** (Altes Rathaus): Half-timbered

*Lichthof, Rathaus, Schwäbisch Gmünd*

*St.Michael, Schwäbisch Hall*

building based on a Hohenstaufen keep.

**Museum Schwäbisch Gmünd** (3 Johannisplatz): The main focus of the cultural and historical collections is on late Gothic and baroque sculpture.

**Also worth seeing:** Around the Markt there are still medieval *half-timbered buildings* and a few *baroque buildings*. The *Marktbrunnen* with its double Madonna was set up around 1700. The numerous little alleys contain many *old houses*. A few *towers* mark the former town wall. The 13C former *Franciscan church* has an 18C baroque interior.

---

### Schwäbisch Hall 7170
Baden-Württemberg                p.420☐G 17

Salt has played an important part in the history of this town, a former free Imperial

city, which now has some 30,000 inhabitants. In the 3C BC the salt-water spring encouraged permanent Celtic settlements here. Hall was expanded under the Hohenstaufens (building of St.Michael, 1156). The town became well known as the mint of the 'Häller' (later Heller) coins.

**Protestant Parish Church of St. Michael** (Am Markt): A broad flight of steps leads up from the market square to the massive *W. tower*, the 4 lower sections of which were taken over from a 12C Romanesque basilica (consecrated 1156). The present *nave* was completed in 1456 after a building period of about 25 years. The *choir* was added in 1527. The tower acquired its octagonal domed top in 1573. Since then the church has been little altered. It is entered through a *porch* borne by round pillars, in which stands the superb stone figure (c.1300) of St.Michael, the patron saint of the church. The *nave* has round pillars and very fine *groin vault-*

*ing.* The apparently rather squat hall of the nave contrasts strangely with the brightness and lightness of the *choir,* which was built later. The *high altar* (above which is a crucifix by M.Erhart, 1494) depicts scenes from the Passion in the Dutch manner *(c.*1470). Other interesting items of the furnishings: *choir stalls* (1534), *tabernacle* (15C), *altar of St.Michael* (1510) in the sacristy, *carved altars* by local masters in the side chapels, a *Holy Sepulchre* (16C) in a niche in the S. wall and *tombs* in the chapels.

**Church of St. Katharina** (Katharinenstrasse): The oldest parts of this church date from the 13C (tower) and 14C (choir). Enlargements and alterations were undertaken in the 16&18C and most recently around 1900. The *stained glass* in the S. choir window is in superb condition and dates from around 1360. Remains of a *wallpainting* have a suggested dating *c.*1480. The *altar* in the choir dates from the last third of the 15C and shows a connection between the carving style of Dutch and Swabian workshops.

**Rathaus** (Am Markt): The Town Hall was built in 1730–5 on the site of a church of St.James destroyed in a fire; it is one of the most important of its period in Germany. It is strikingly elegant, and looks in many ways like a baroque palace. The slightly bulging central section with its rounded gable projects between 2 walls which are set back a little. On the roof is a tower with a clock and decorative top.

**Grosses Büchsenhaus** (known as Neubau, Im Rosenbühl): The arsenal, built in 1505–27, has been a festival hall since 1926.

**Limpurg Burg ruins:** Excavations in 1905 revealed little of the 13C castle. It was typical of its period; fortress buildings were added in the 15&16C.

**Only a few individual** *towers* remain of the town's former encircling wall: the Malefizturm by the Säumarkt (13C), the Sulfertor am Kocher (modified in the 18C), the Josenturm in Gelbinger Gasse (modified in the 17C) and others.

**Open-Air Festival** on the great steps of St.Michael: From June to August open-air productions are held on the steps leading from the market square to the church (1700 spectators).

**Hällisch-Fränkisches Museum** in the Keckenburg (8–10 Untere Herrengasse): History of town and region, religious art, important collection of targets.

**Also worth seeing:** In the centre of the town are remains of medieval *castles* and beautiful 16C *half-timbered houses.* The old *stocks* are still next to the large *Marktbrunnen.*

---

**Schwalenberg =**
**3284 Schieder-Schwalenberg 2**
Nordrhein-Westfalen                p.414☐F 9

**Rathaus:** The Town Hall (1579) is the most beautiful of the town's numerous *half-timbered buildings,* most of which are in good condition. There is a frieze above the four-arched arcade (formerly market hall) with lavish carvings.

**Burg Schwalenberg:** The castle is above the picturesque town. It was extended in the style of the late Renaissance and is now a hotel.

---

**Schweinfurt 8720**
Bavaria                p.418☐H 14

Schweinfurt, now an important industrial town with a population of 57,000, was a free Imperial city until 1802. Almost half its buildings were destroyed in the Second World War. The town's most famous son is Friedrich Rückert, born here in 1788. His birthplace (2 Am Markt) and a monument (also am Markt) commemorate the lyric poet, orientalist and translator.

**Protestant Parish Church of St. Johannes** (Martin-Luther-Platz): Various architectural styles are combined in this church, which is entered from the Markt

*Marktplatz with Rathaus, Schweinfurt*

through the late Romanesque *portal*. The *transept* (*c.*1235) shows the transition from Romanesque to Gothic, the *nave* was added in the 2nd half of the 13C, while the *choir* is late Gothic. Outstanding amongst the furnishings: the *font* with its original painting (1367), the richly embellished *pulpit* (1694), 14C *tombs* and the early neoclassical *high altar*.

**Rathaus** (Marktplatz): The damage caused by the Second World War to the Town Hall, built in 1570–2 by Nicolaus Hoffmann, has been repaired. The 2 wings of this Renaissance building meet at right-angles. The façade overlooks the Markt. While the symmetrical style of construction is typical of the Renaissance, gables and window frames echo the late Gothic era.

**Theater der Stadt Schweinfurt** (2 Rossbrunnstrasse): Built in 1966, the theatre has 785 seats.

**Städtisches Museum** (12 Martin-Luther-Platz): Local and cultural history are the principal fields covered in this museum in the former grammar school of 1582. There is an outstanding collection of scientific instruments from the 15–18C. The Rückertzimmer commemorates the poet, who was born in Schweinfurt.

**Environs: Werneck** (13 km. SW): Balthasar Neumann was commissioned by the Prince Bishop of Bamberg and Würzburg, Count Friedrich Carl von Schönborn to build a *summer Schloss* from 1733 to (after) 1746; this replaced an earlier building (1600). The Schloss, a symmetrical, 3-winged building with accentuated corner pavilions and central pavilion, is now used as a hospital.

**Schweinsberg = 3570**
**Stadtallendorf 1**
Hessen                                          p.416☐F 12

**Protestant Parish Church of St. Stephan:** This simple 16C hall church was well restored in 1956. The interior has slender, octagonal pillars and fine net vaulting. Also of interest are the font (1619) and the tomb-slabs of the Schenck zu Schweinsberg family.

**Burg:** This complex dates from the 13C. Beyond the *half-timbered gatehouse* and over the bridge one finds 3 further *portals*. On the right is the *Fähnrichsbau* (16C). From the *castle courtyard* one can see remains of the old *Oberburg*. The *Neue Kemenate* (lady's heated apartment, 15C) can be recognised by its echelon gales, 3 corner towers and staircase tower. On the ground floor are the Saal and hall with net and groin vaulting.

**Schwetzingen 6830**
Baden-Württemberg                          p.420☐E 16

**Schloss:** This former medieval moated Burg was extended and altered several

*Schloss with Arion fountain, Schwetzingen*

times to suit the wishes of its owners, until the present building came into being under Count Palatine Johann Wilhelm in the early 18C. The *central section* with its two corner towers is the oldest part of the basically modest complex. The buildings to the N. and S. ('Zirkelbauten') were added in the 18C and have the style and symmetry of the complex as a whole. The same is true of all the buildings which have been added. In the N. building is the fine *chapel* (1806) designed by F.Weinbrenner. More significant than the buildings is the unique *park*, which is one of the most important in Europe. It was developed in 3 stages: J.L.Petri planned the great circular flowerbed in the geometrical French style in 1753–8; it is adjacent to the W. side of the palace. N. de Pigage created the numerous garden buildings in 1766–74, the most outstanding of which is the *mosque*. Finally, in 1778–1804, an outer band was added in the landscape-orientated English style under the direction of F.L.von Sckell. Be-

hind the N. 'Zirkel' building is the *rococo theatre,* built in 1746–52, which is the only unaltered Electoral court theatre in Germany. N. de Pigage was again the architect; it was opened in 1752.

**Schwetzingen Festival:** Festival productions are held every May and June in the palace, park and theatre under the patronage of the Süddeutscher Rundfunk.

**Schloss Art Exhibition:** The Schloss is now open to the public as a museum. Apart from the the building and its contents there are exhibits on interior decoration in the 18&19C, and an interesting collection of paintings.

**Also worth seeing:** The *Marktplatz,* with 18C buildings in good condition, the Catholic parish church (1739–65), with interesting altar furnishings and sculpted figures.

*Benedictine monastery, Seeon*

### Seebüll = Neukirchen 2268
Schleswig-Holstein                    p.412☐F 1

Seebüll is now a district of Neukirchen, 5
km. NE. Seebüll was made famous by the
painter Emil Nolde, who died here in
1956. In the studio house (now the *Nolde
Museum*), which the great Expressionist
painter had built to his own design in
1927&8, about 120 of his works are on permanent display in various combinations
(in accordance with the requirements of
the Ada and Emil Nolde foundation).

### Seehof = Memmelsdorf 8602
Bavaria                              p.418☐I 15

**Schloss:** The old lakeside residence of the
prince bishops of Bamberg (q.v.) was extended into a baroque palace in the
16&17C. 4 wings with domed corner
towers enclose the inner court. In the
*Grosser Saal* is an interesting *fresco* by
J.I.Appiani. The *chapel* on the ground
floor contains an attractive *rococo altar* by
C.A.Bossi. In the *park,* which is laid out
to a symmetrical design on all sides of the
Schloss, is the *Orangery,* built in 1773 by
J.H.Dientzenhofer to designs by B.Neu-
mann. After the *main gate* on the Bamberg
road the last section to be built was the
*Schweizerei* in 1782.

### Seon im Chiemgau 8221
Bavaria                              p.422☐M 20

**Former Benedictine Monastery
Church of St.Lambert:** The monastery
complex has grown up over the centuries
on its small island on the Klostersee, and
has been much modified. It is known by
the onion towers of the church (1561). The
monastery was founded in the 10C, followed by the building of Romanesque ba-

*Monument to County Palatine Aribo, the founder, St. Lambert in Seeon*

silica in the 12C. In the 15C the church underwent a Gothic conversion; the *net vaulting*, dates from this period. It is decorated with unusual *paintings* (1579, uncovered from 1911). The famous *Madonna of Seeon*, one of the most important works of 15C sculpture, is now housed in the Bayerisches Nationalmuseum in Munich (q.v.); there is a copy on the high altar. Other furnishings: 18C *side altars*, the *tomb of the founder* Count Palatine Aribo (*c.*1400), as well as other *tombs*.

**Monastery buildings:** Apart from the late Gothic *cloister* one notes the *Laiminger Chapel* (2nd storey added in 17C), the *chapterhouse*, the *refectory*, the *dining hall* and the chapel of St. Nicholas (all 18C). The latter contains stucco by J.M.Feuchtmayer as well as interesting rococo furnishings.

**Environs: Rabenden** (4 km. N.): Church of *St. Jakob* with late Gothic sculptures by the 'Rabenden Master'.

## Seligenstadt 6453
Hessen              p.416☐F 14

Seligenstadt was made famous by Einhart, the biographer of Charlemagne, who founded a Benedictine monastery here in 828. Here he wrote 'The Life and Deeds of Charlemagne'.

**Einhart Basilica/Former Benedictine Monastery Church:** The church is the largest surviving Carolingian basilica. The building was completed by 840, when Einhart died and was buried in the church. Later extensions have greatly altered the actual basilica, although the basic Carolingian building is still discernible. The original design is most clearly seen when viewed from the N. The interior is of great simplicity, a typical trait of Carolingian architecture. The furnishings are baroque. The centrepiece is the marble *high altar* (1715), designed by M.von Welsch; it came

*Prälatur of Benedictine abbey in Seligenstadt*

from the Carthusian church in Mainz, which had been destroyed. The best of the adjacent *monastery buildings* is the *Prelate House* of 1699, which was used as the abbot's court and to house (princely) guests. Its principal rooms are the *Kaisersaal* and the *library*.

**Kaiserpfalz** (N. of the monastery): Near the bank of the Main are the ruins of the former imperial palace, the origins of which go back to a visit by Friedrich I to Seligenstadt in 1188. Friedrich II had the palace extended into a (unfortified) imperial hunting lodge in 1235–40. The surrounding walls of the imperial residential wing have survived. The façade overlooks the Main and has 3 large groups of double windows. Similarities with the Emperor's buildings in S. Italy are unmistakable.

**Also worth seeing:** *Rathaus* (1823, replacing a Renaissance building of 1539);

*Romanesque house* (5 Grosse Rathausgasse) built in stone around 1200; *Haus zum Einhart* (Aschaffenburger Strasse) with a beautiful half-timbered upper storey with an inscription on the corner oriel: 'Selig sei die Stadt genannt, da ich meine Tochter wiederfand' ('Let this town be called blessed ('Seligenstadt'), as I have found my daughter again'); legend has it that Charlemagne gave the town its name. Remains of the 13C *town fortifications* have survived, particularly near the bank of the Main; SE of the town is the *moated Burg*, built by the abbot as a summer residence in 1708.

**Siegburg 5200**
Nordrhein-Westfalen                    p.416□C 12

**Benedictine Abbey of St. Michael** (Bergstrasse): The abbey was founded in 1064; the outer walls of the Romanesque

*Anno shrine, abbey church, Siegburg*

crypt below the present E. bay of the nave were part of the original building. After heavy war damage the present church was built along the lines of the building of 1649 – 67. The church's most valuable posession is the *Anno Shrine* from the workshop of N.von Verdun, *c*.1183. The shrine, a masterpiece of the goldsmith's art of the period, has not survived in its entirety, but nevertheless conveys an impression of the original work. It is 5 ft. long, made of wood (with saddle roof) and richly clad with gold filigree, enamel and jewels. The church patrons St.Michael and St. Anno were depicted on the two ends (each between 2 angels); these figures have since been lost, as have the main figures on the sides (6 saints and canonized Bishops of Cologne on each side). Adjoining the church are baroque *monastery buildings* (17&18C).

**Catholic Parish Church of St. Servatius** (Mühlenstrasse): This galleried basilica, built around 1169 to replace an older church, has been much altered in the course of the centuries. The last major alteration was the lengthening of the side aisles towards the end of the 19C. What remains is an impressive church, although little of the original Romanesque building has survived. The interior is in many points of detail similar to Cologne Cathedral. There is fine *church treasure*, including 12&13C enamels. The Anno Shrine is also part of the church treasure, but is currently on loan to the abbey church (see above). Other items are the *shrine* of the two saints Innocent and Maurice (both around 1190), *portable altars* of St.Maurice (*c*.1160) and St.Gregory (*c*.1180) and a Byzantine *silk* (from between 921 and 931).

**Museums:** Museum im Torhaus (55 Alfred-Keller-Strasse): The museum has special departments on the composer Humperdinck and copperplate printing, and also local exhibitions on the history of pottery *Bundessteuermuseum/Finanzgeschichtliche Sammlung:* the museum of the Federal Academy of Finance (Michaelsburg).

**Also worth seeing:** Haus auf der Arken (15C house with half-timbered upper storey and slate roof); remains of the 15C town wall. *Käx* (Hühnermarkt): trachyte pillory in the form of two shackled figures (14C).

---

**Siegen 5900**
Nordrhein-Westfalen                    p.416□D 12

---

**Protestant Church of St.Martin** (by the Kölner Tor): It was not until 1960 that excavations brought to light the remains of one of the largest Ottonian churches in W. Germany, including a mosaic pavement from around 1000. The Ottonian building, the exact form of which is the subject of further research, was succeeded by a late Romanesque building; the W. portal of the current church has survived from this. The present late Gothic hall was built in 1511 –17.

**Protestant Church of St.Nicholas** (Am Markt): This 13C late Romanesque church was built as a hexagonal rotunda. In 1455 –64 the building acquired its four-storey tower. The 6 columns supporting the massive groin vault are part of the rotunda design. After the Second World War the sculptor G.Marcks made the bronze door in the W. portal.

**Upper and Lower Schloss** (Hasengarten or Kölner Strasse): The 16C Burg which preceded the Oberes Schloss was much modified in the 17&18C and is now a *museum* (see below). The Untere Schloss was built in 1698–1714 on a site on which there had been first a Franciscan monastery (abandoned 1534), then the university (1595–1609), the royal vault and finally a first castle (burned down with the monastery in 1695).

**Rathaus** (Markt): The Town Hall was

built in 1783–88 and enlarged at the beginning of this century.

**Museum des Siegerlandes** (in the Upper Schloss): Siegen can pride itself on being the birthplace of the great Flemish painter Peter Paul Rubens, whose father was living in Siegen in the service of the Duchess of Nassau-Orange at the time of the birth of his son Peter Paul (1577). 7 original paintings provide an insight into the work of the painter.

**Town Theatres** (Spandauer Strasse): The new *Siegener Theater* was opened in 1957 (814 seats). It does not have its own company, however. The *Kleine Theater Lohkasten* (3 Löhrtor) was opened in 1974 and has only 75 seats. Well-known artists have appeared here.

**Environs: Freudenberg** (11 km. NW): In contrast to Siegen, which was badly damaged in the war, many half-timbered *town houses* (17&18C) have survived in Freudenberg, including 33 and 35 Oranienstrasse, with lavish carving (18C). Inside the *Protestant parish church* (16C) windows and chancel arch are surrounded by ornamental *Renaissance paintings* (1606).

---

**Sigmaringen 7480**
Baden-Württemberg                    p.420□F 20

---

**Schloss** (Karl-Anton-Platz): The original Burg is first referred to in 1077. Little remains of that building or its medieval successor. Most sections of the present Schloss date from the 18&19C; it is romantic and charming, but of little historical importance. The valuable furnishings include important art and painting collections. The castle is open to the public as a museum (see below).

**Catholic Parish Church of St.John the Evangelist:** The new building of 1757–63 contains valuable furnishings, above all the Cradle of St.Fidelis, who was born in Sigmaringen in 1577 and martyred in 1622. J.M.Feuchtmayer designed the interesting altars.

*Hohenzollernschloss, Sigmaringen*

**Former Franciscan Monastery Church of Hedingen:** The new building dating from c.1680 was extended by the addition of a Chapel of the Virgin Mary in 1715 (renovated after a fire in 1747), which has first-class stucco and sculpted figures (altar). The domed choir contains the Hohenzollern vault, added in 1889.

**Fürstlich Hohenzollernsches Museum** (Schloss): Prince Carl Anton of Hohenzollern formed the basis of this important museum by his numerous purchases from famous art collections. Paintings, weapons of the 15 – 19C, historic furniture (the Schloss contents) and carriages in the Mews Museum.

**Environs: Laiz** (2 km. SW): The *Catholic parish church of St.Peter and St.Paul* has fine *wall-paintings* by Meinrad von Ow (1768, Life of the Virgin Mary) in the nave, and on the E. wall (c.1430). The *altar* (1771) by J.B.Hops in the nuns' choir with

a *Mater Dolorosa* (c.1440), as well as a *St. Anne with the Virgin and Child* (c.1500) and a *seated Madonna* (c.1500).
**Bingen** (7 km. NE): The *Catholic parish church of Mariae Himmelfahrt* with net-vaulted choir was built around 1500. The finest features of the furnishings are 5 *carved figures* (1496) by Syrlin the Younger and 5 *panel paintings* by B.Zeitblom; also a *Wailing* group (1517) by M.Schaffner.

---

## Sindelfingen 7032
Baden-Württemberg                    p.420□F 18

**Former Canonry Church of St.Martin** (Kirchstrasse): This church, a basilica with nave, 2 aisles and no transept, consecrated in 1083, was authentically restored in 1933 and 1973&4. The arches and pillars show Lower Saxon influence, the apses the influence of Lombardy. Outstanding

*St. Peter, Sinzig*

clude a *font* of 1472, *choir stalls* (1517) by
H.Schickhardt the Elder with reliefs by
C.von Urach, and above all the late Gothic
*pulpit*, a masterpiece (1503) of the stonemason Meister Hanselmann.

---

## Sinzig 5485
Rheinland-Pfalz                        p.416☐C 13

---

Sinzig, at the confluence of the Ahr and
the Rhine, was a Frankish royal and later
imperial palatinate. King Pippin and Emperor Heinrich III, Friedrich Barbarossa
and other emperors lived here.

**Catholic Parish Church of St. Peter**
(Im Zehnthof): The present church, built
in 1220–50, is an important link in the development of late Romanesque churches
on the Rhine. It is a galleried basilica with
a nave and two aisles and a massive tower
over the crossing. Façades and side walls
are rich in detail. The apparently small
building is surprisingly extensive inside;
arches and galleries reinforce the impression of size. The coloured exterior is striking, as is the lavish interior painting (both
restored). Remains of old *wall-paintings*
(1270) are to be seen in the E. side choir.
Apart from the *altarpiece* (15C) the furnishing is sparse. Outside the choir is the *Zehnthof* (1697–1740), which belonged to the
Imperial Foundation of Aachen from 855
–1802.

**Heimatmuseum** (in the 19C neo-Gothic
Schloss): The museum is worth visiting
above all for its 15–19C sculpture and 17
–19C paintings, as well as early-historic
finds.

amongst the furnishings are the Roman-
esque strapwork of the W. door and a late
Gothic relief slab (1477) for Count
Eberhard the Bearded and his mother
Mechthild.

**Altes Rathaus** (Lange Strasse): This
building dates from 1478 and is connected
to the Salzhaus (1592). Both buildings are
half-timbered, like several others in the
Kurze Gasse and elsewhere.

**Museums:** *Stadtmuseum* (13 Lange
Strasse): Interesting collections on town
history. *Haus der Donauschwaben* (Gold-
mühlenstrasse): Central collection and library of the Swabian Danube.

**Environs: Herrenberg** (17 km. SW):
Until it was sold in 1890 the famous *Herrenberg Altar* (1518) by J.Ratgeb (now in
the Staatsgalerie, Stuttgart) was part of the
furnishings of the *Protestant parish church
of St.Mary*. The remaining furnishings in-

---

## Soest 4770
Nordrhein-Westfalen                    p.414☐D 10

---

Soest was not only one of the most important towns in the Hanseatic League, but in
the whole of Europe. In the famous
'Soester Fehde' the town—at the height of
its fame and economic power—broke away
from the Archbishopric of Cologne in

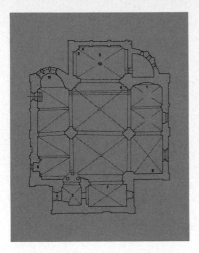

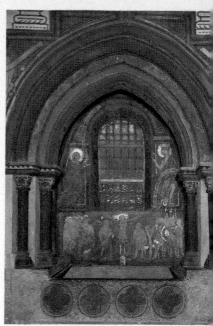

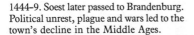

Soest, St. Maria zur Höhe 1 Cross, c.1230 2 Font, c.1230 3 Candlestick, late 14C 4 Tabernacle, c.1450 5 Altarpiece, c.1740; panel painting by the Liesborn master 6 Pulpit, c.1600 7 Organ front, 1679 8 Tomb niche with 13C frescos 9 Panel painting 'Apocalypse of Ezekiel' by Knipping, 1640 10 Angels dancing, 1280 11 Katharinenchor with frescos, c.1260

*Heilig-Grab niche, Hohnekirche*

1444-9. Soest later passed to Brandenburg. Political unrest, plague and wars led to the town's decline in the Middle Ages.

**Collegiate Church of St. Patroklus/Patroklidom** (Rathausstrasse): Repair of damage caused by the Second World War gave an opportunity to remove a few of the alterations which had disfigured this monumental cathedral in the course of the centuries. The present building corresponds in all essential features to the 12C original (built around 1000, additions made in 11&12C). The most important part of the church is the massive tower, rightly considered the most beautiful Romanesque tower in Germany. The superb effect created by the building is reinforced by the shimmering green of the local sandstone. The interior of the cathedral is characterised by the sturdy pillars and its general spaciousness. The pièce de résistance is the *westwork* added in the 11C. The Romanesque *wall paintings*, al-most completely destroyed in the last war, survive only in the altar apse of the N. transept ('Marienchörchen'). The other wall paintings were replaced by P.Hecker during rebuilding. The windows in the lower part of the tower are also vey recent. Original glass survives only in the 3 chancel windows. The finest feature of the furnishings is a 6.9 ft tall *triumphal cross*, which serves as an altar cross. Other important items of the former furnishings are now housed in the *treasury* (in the former armoury), and include a cushion (12C) with silk embroidery.

**Protestant Parish Church of St. Peter/Petrikirche** (Rathausstrasse): The Petrikirche—opposite the Dom—was built in the 12&13C as a vaulted basilica. Special importance was attached to the westwork, which is directly connected with the archbishop's palace to the W. of the church. It has a hall with a nave and 4 aisles on the lower floor; columns support the

*'Westphalian Last Supper', Wiesenkirche*

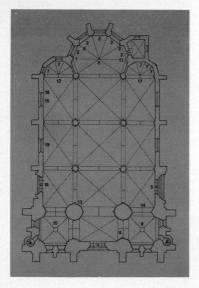

splendid groin vaulting. The most valuable items of the furnishings are the 13–15C wall paintings, which have survived in excellent condition. Two of the Crucifixion pictures are attributed to the school of Konrad of Soest. The lavishly ornamented pelican chalice dates from the 2nd half of the 15C.

**Maria zur Höhe/Hohnekirche** (Hohe Gasse): The present building, completed around 1225, incorporates parts of its Romanesque predecessor. As in most Westphalian hall churches the ground plan is almost square. The *wall paintings* in the interior are particularly fine; choir, side choir and sanctuary are decorated with paintings of figures; walls, pillars and vaulting have ornamental designs. The most striking of the vault paintings is the *Virgin in Majesty with angels* above the main chancel. Hardly inferior to this are the paintings of the Holy Sepulchre (in a niche, see groundplan sketch). The high altar contains paintings of the Crucifixion and the Passion. These are masterpieces of Westphalian late Gothic painting (*c.*1480).

**St. Maria zur Wiese/Wiesenkirche** (Wiesenstrasse): This church was built in a relatively short period in the 14C; the towers were added in the 15C (completed in the mid 19C). There are excellent figures above the S. and N. portals. The tracery on the windows is also of high quality. The interior with its large Gothic windows is strikingly spacious and bright. The 4 tall but slender pillars contribute to the

**Soest, St.Maria zur Wiese 1** Alabaster relief of the Holy Trinity, c.1300 **2** Window of main chancel, stained-glass c.1350 **3** Wall painting beside the sacristy door (Annunciation), c. 1370 **4** Lectern cover, c.1390 **5** Virgin Mary statue on the middle pillar of the S.portal, c.1400 **6** Jacobialtar, c. 1420 **7** Windows of side choirs, early 15C **8** Tabernacle, c.1420 **9** Font, 1st half of 15C **10** Reliquary tabernacle, mid 15C **11** Wall painting above sacristy door, 1st quarter of 15C **12** Family altar of the master of 1473, 1473 **13** Virgin Mary in a cloak of ears of corn, 2nd half of 15C **14** Crucifixion group, 2nd half of 15C **15** Marienfenster, late 15C **15** N.portal window with 'Westphalian Last Supper', c.1500, 19C additions **17** Virgin Mary altar, c.1525; panel painting by H.Aldegrever **18** Carved altar, Brabantine, early 16C **19** Tree of Jesse window, late 15C

overall impression and simultaneously emphasise the subdivision into nave, 2 aisles and 3 bays. A magnificent interior feature are the towering windows with *stained glass* from the 2nd half of the 14C. Along with Apostles and saints this also includes a popular motif: the 'Westphalian Last Supper', which transfers the scene of the Last Supper to a Westphalian tavern (*c.*1520). The most important part of the furnishing is the large *altarpiece* (*c.*1520), which recent research has shown to be by H.Aldegrever.

**Other interesting churches in Soest:** *Nikolaikapelle* (Thomasstrasse): Built in the 12C, important altar painting by Konrad of Soest, wall paintings retained in the 19C restoration. *Thomaekirche/Protestant parish church* (Thomästrasse): 13C hall church.

**Town fortifications** (Osthofenstrasse): The *Osthofentor* (1523–6) and the Gothic *Kattenturm* remain from the 16C town fortifications.

**Museums:** The *Burghofmuseum* (22 Burghofstrasse) is housed in a building dating from 1558&9, the side building is Romanesque (about 1200). It is primarily concerned with the history of Soest. *Osthofentormuseum* with exhibits (including 25,000 13–16C crossbow bolts) on medieval defence engineering. *Wilhelm-Morgner-Haus* (3 Thomästrasse): The collection of Wilhelm Morgner of Soest, the town art collection and an almost complete collection of engravings by H.Aldegrever.

**Sögel 4475**
Lower Saxony                              p.414☐D 6

**Schloss Clemenswerth:** The Schloss was built in an isolated area in the N. Emsland by J.C.Schlaun for Prince Bishop Clemens August of Cologne in 1737–49. The small 2-storey palace is built of red brick interspersed with light sandstone (as decoration). The 8 avenues radiating from the hunting lodge are part of Schlaun's overall concept. One of these avenues can be

seen from every window of the Schloss, and there is a good view of roaming game. The main building is surrounded by 8 pavilions, most of which are named after dioceses (Münster, Hildesheim, Paderborn, Osnabrück, Cologne). There is also the pavilion of Clemens August, the Mergentheim Pavilion, the kitchen pavilion and a chapel. An interest in hunting is reflected in the overall design and in many details. The banqueting hall and all the other rooms contain stucco hunting scenes. Several paintings on the stair well depict the royal huntsmen. Today the Schloss houses the *Emsland Museum* with exhibits on the history of hunting, pre- and early history and the history of the Schloss, on interior decorating styles and ceramics, as well as on the folk lore of the region.

**Solingen 5650**
Nordrhein-Westfalen                     p.416☐C 11

**Catholic Parish Church** (Gräfrath): This church, built in the early 13C, was replaced by a hall with a single aisle in 1690. The choir furnishings are baroque. The most valuable parts are the high altar, the side altars and a communion bench. The treasury contains first-rate goldsmith's work.

**Kleinstadtmarkt** (Marktplatz in Gräfrath): The market with its 18C buildings has remained almost unaltered. Right on the market is the Protestant church (1716–18). From the market a flight of steps leads to the W. tower of the collegiate church.

**Deutsches Klingenmuseum** (160 Wuppertaler Strasse): Weapons, cutlery and cutting implements through the ages are assembled in this specialist museum.

**Theater Solingen** (71 Konrad-Adenauer-Strasse): This theatre, opened in 1963, has 813 seats.

**Environs: Burg an der Wupper** (8 km. SE): This hill-top castle (12C) is now of little historical interest, since it was rebuilt in the 19&20C; the building houses the *Bergisches Museum* (1 Schlossplatz) with collections on pre-, early and regional history and on arts and crafts.

**Müngsten** (5 km. E.): The *Müngstener Brücke* over the Wupper is, with a height of 350 ft., the highest railway bridge in Germany.

---

### Speinshart 8481
Bavaria                                   p.418☐L 15

---

**Monastery Church:** This monastery church in a small Oberpfalz village is a triumph of baroque exuberance. The architect was W.Dientzenhofer (from 1691

**Speyer, Dom 1** Stone basin, late Romanesque ('Rushing Chalice'), in the crypt **2** Tomb of Wipert v.Finsterlohe (d. 1503) in the crypt **3** Relief of Wailing over the Body of Christ, much damaged, c.1530, in the crypt **4** Tomb of Canon Mohr v.Waldt (d.1713) **5** Tomb of Bishop Gerhard v.Erenberg by Vinzenz Möhring **6** Monument to King Adolf v.Nassau, donated in 1824; designed by L.v.Klenze, built by D.Ohnmacht **7** Monument to Emperor Rudolf v.Habsburg by L.Schwanthaler, 1843

onwards), who opted for a pilaster design. Stucco artist C.D.Luchese was consistently inspired and created a wealth of shapes and figures, the like of which is hardly to be found elsewhere. His brother B.Luchese painted the frescos. The ends of the choirstalls are no less splendid than the stucco and frescos.

---

### Speyer 6720
Rheinland-Pfalz                            p.420☐E 16

---

Speyer, now a town of 43,000 inhabitants, was a settlement in Celtic times. The town has been a bishopric since the 7C and there was probably a bishop here even in the late Roman period. It was a free Imperial town from 1294 and by 1570 more than 50 Reichstag assemblies had been held in Speyer. The cathedral, built by the Salic emperors Konrad II, Heinrich III and Heinrich IV, is the burial place of 8 emperors and kings.

**Kaiserdom** (Domplatz): Preceding buildings date back into the 7C, but the building of the present cathedral was only begun under Emperor Konrad II (foundation

*Dom, Speyer* ▷

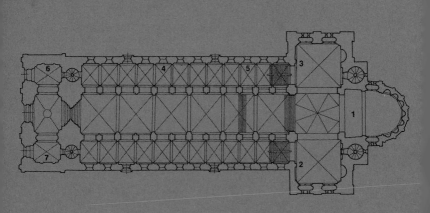

stone laid in 1030). Only some 30 years later the massive building was finished: after Heinrich III had celebrated the completion of the crypt, his successor Heinrich IV had the cathedral consecrated. In the subsequent period the cathedral underwent numerous alterations, which were partly necessitated by its vulnerable position near the Rhine, but also partly due to the taste of the times. The most serious alteration was carried out under Heinrich IV, who had the hitherto flat ceiling of the nave vaulted—an epoch-making achievement in the history of German architecture. Many alterations detrimental to the original appearance and importance of the cathedral were removed during the restoration begun in 1957. When the 9th centenary celebrations were held in 1961 the building looked almost exactly the same as it had done when built by the emperors. Its setting some 30 ft. above the Rhine adds to the effect created by the massive structure. 2 towers at both the E. and W. end round off and crown the building. Between these two pairs of towers there are smaller octagonal towers over the porch and crossing. Windows, arches and portals are richly ornamented: stonemasons, probably brought from Lombardy, have produced superb ex-

amples of plastic art. The interior is a mighty pillared basilica of enormous proportions (433 ft. long). The vaulting enhances the superb impression of space. Royal choir and crossing are laid out in such a way that they become the architectural climax of the interior (see plan). Below the choir and choir nave is the *crypt*, which is entered via stairs from the E. ends of the side-aisles. The crypt is divided into 3 almost square areas, which are interconnected in such a superb way as to earn it the reputation of being the 'most beautiful crypt in the world'. Its early Romanesque design has survived with impressive clarity over the centuries. Buried in the crypt are 4 emperors, 3 empresses, 4 kings and 5 bishops. Particularly outstanding amongst the side buildings is the *Afrakapelle*. This single aisled, 4-bayed building, built around 1100, was destroyed by the French in 1689, but was reconstructed in 1850. The excellent original capitals are its finest feature. 2 first-class works of stonemasonry (the mid-15C relief of the Crucifixion and the 'Speyerer Verkündigung', a relief depicting the Annunciation of the Virgin Mary, *c.*1470) were transferred here from the outer wall of the cathedral. The *Emmeramskapelle* was ad-

*Afrakapelle chapel, Dom*

ded to the S. side aisle in the 11C. The *Chapel of St.Katharina* was built above it in 1857.

**Protestant Dreifaltigkeitskirche** (Grosse Himmelsgasse): The city's Protestant churches were also extensively damaged by the ravages of 1689. J.P.Graber's design was chosen in a competition. The building was consecrated in 1717 and is one of the most important baroque churches in the present Rheinland-Pfalz. The hall was designed to lay emphasis on preaching; it has a pentagonal choir (see picture). The interior is characterized by the 2-storey wooden galleries, the side parts of which are decorated with paintings. The vault is also constructed of wood and also decorated with paintings (attributed to Guthbier, *c.*1713).

**Gedächtniskirche/Retscherkirche** (Landauer Strasse): This neo-Gothic church was built in 1904 in memory of the *protestatio* made by the Protestant princes to the imperial parliament of Speyer in 1529.

**Mikwe** (Judengasse): The Jewish baths is one of the few surviving complexes of its kind in Germany. It was built in the 12C and was designed for women to wash in, in accordance with Jewish ritual.

**Town fortifications:** The most important and also the most beautiful town gate in Germany is the *Altpörtel* in Maximilianstrasse, dating from the 12C (alterations and additions in the 13&16C). The *Heidentürmchen* (13C) in the Domgarten is also part of the town fortifications.

**Historisches Museum der Pfalz** (7 Grosse Pfaffengasse): The most famous item here is the 'Golden Hat of Schifferstadt', which was found near Schifferstadt in 1835 and is one of the 3 famous Bronze Age gold cones. It dates from around 1200 BC and was probably used for religious purposes. The museum also has a special department with a *Wine Museum* and collections on the cultural history of the town and region. *Dom- und Diözesanmuseum* (Domplatz): The most important exhibits are finds from the burial places of German emperors in the cathedral, including old manuscripts, ecclesiastical objects and national religious customs up to the 18C.

*Dom, nave, looking East*

*Holy Trinity church, Speyer*

## Stade 2160

Lower Saxony                                      p.412□G 4

**Protestant Parish Church of St. Wilhadi** (Wilhadikirchhof): This brick church, a 14C hall-building (13C tower), is supported by flying buttresses, from which the beautiful groin vault rises. The 'Brauthaus', a 14C addition, was added to the N. nave wall. Of interest are the consoles in the upper storey, first-class stonemasonry depicting 3 married couples at various stages of life. The most important part of the furnishing is the baroque organ by the master organ maker E.Bielfeldt of Bremen (1730–5). Next to the organ is the tomb of Johannes Pahlen (1686).

**Protestant Church of St. Cosmae et Damiani** (Cosmaekirchhof 3): The hallmark of this church, which dates back to the 11C, is the enormous baroque spire of the octagonal crossing tower of 1682. More important than the exterior of the church, which has been much altered in the course of the centuries, is the first-rate interior. Apart from the crossing, which is notable for its superb pointed arches, all other parts of the church have wooden barrel vaults

*Bürgermeister-Hintze-Haus, Stade*

and flat ceilings. The present furnishings date from 1659, when the original interior was destroyed in the great fire of 1659. The sole surviving medieval altar is the Gertrudenaltar (15C, S. wall of the nave). The high altar is the work of C.Precht of Hamburg (1674). The marble font, commissioned in 1665, has very fine alabaster Evangelist figures. Also of interest: the pulpit (1663), 3 16&17C chandeliers and the organ. This was begun by B.Huss and completed in 1688, after his death, by his apprentice, the famous master organ maker A.Schnitger, whose first work this is. The wrought-iron portal grilles are first-class 17C craftsmanship.

**Rathaus** (Hökerstrasse): The Town Hall is a massive brick building with sandstone ornamentation, built in 1667. The interior has an interesting staircase and excellent woodwork (doors). The Gothic vaulted cellars date from an earlier building of the 13&15C.

**Bürgermeister-Hintze-Haus** (Wasser West): This building with its magnificent baroque façade is one of the central features of Stade. Mayor Heino Hintze had the façade added in 1617–46. The building is a typical late medieval merchant's house.

**Museums:** *Heimat- und Freilichtmuseum* (12 Inselstrasse): Folk art and rustic treasures, Altland and Geest farmhouses, 17C post windmills. *Schwedenspeicher-Museum* (Am Wasser West): Pre-, early, and town history, granary (1705). *Baumhaus-Museum:* Hafeneinfahrt): Town history.

**Environs:** The **Altes Land,** a particularly fertile region now given over to fruit growing, has a number of beautiful old farmhouses. Places worth visiting include Bassenfleth, York, Borstel and Ladekop.

---

## Stadthagen 3060

Lower Saxony                                      p.414□F 8

**Protestant Church of St.Martini** (3 Am Kirchhof): This church, begun in 1318, was completed in the 14&15C. The exterior is dominated by the large tower; it has a hall interior. The unusual wall panelling, dating from 1578, tones with the pews, which have remarkable unity. Wood is the dominant material for the rest of the furnishings. The beautiful Renaissance altar (1585) incorporates large parts of a 15C carved Flanders altar, the large triumphal cross (with the Virgin Mary and St.John) dates from the 16C, the pulpit was also added in the 16C. Some of the monuments and tombs are also made of wood, such as the tomb of Christoph von Landsberg (1584, S. side aisle) and the tomb by the SE wall of the chancel (1590). Of the greatest cultural and historical interest is the *Fürstliche Mausoleum,* which is adjacent to the E. side of the church. Prince Ernst von Schaumburg had it built for his parents, his wife and himself, thereby creating one of the most important early baroque monuments in Germany. It was built between 1609 and 1625; the architect was J.M.Nosseni, the sculptures were produced by A.de Vries, who also made the central monument, entirely of marble, which depicts the Resurrection of Christ.

**Schloss** (Obernstrasse): The Schloss has four wings and is one of the earliest German buildings to follow N. Italian Renaissance design; it was built in the 16C. The Schloss is mainly of interest for its interior, particularly the 2 fireplaces on the upper floor of the W. wing (16C). These are decorated with first-class reliefs. In front of the palace is a *Kavaliershaus* with a fine oriel (16C).

**Rathaus** (Am Markt): The 16C Town Hall dominates the market square and was clearly influenced by the architecture of the Schloss (see above). It is a long building with stepped gables.

**Also worth seeing:** *Schlossgarten* (S. of the Schloss) with a little summer-house on pillars dating from the second half of the 16C. *Town fortifications* (Pferdemarkt): The tower in the Pferdemarkt was built in 1423. *Old Houses:* Particularly around the market (4 Markt) there are 16C houses in the Weser Renaissance style.

*Fürstliches Mausoleum in St.Martini*

---

**Steinau an der Strasse 6497**
Hessen                                    p.416☐G 13

**Protestant Parish Church:** This asymmetrical late Gothic hall church (1481–1511) with a S. aisle has an extended rectangular choir. The sacristy (1481) is N. of the nave instead of a N. aisle; it has a door with metal decoration (c.1500) and a massive tower with a spire (1539) with a slate-clad belfry. Of interest inside are a *stone pulpit* (c.1500) decorated with tracery, a *Holy Sepulchre* (15C), the *nave arcades* with octagonal pillars and late Gothic *tracery windows*. The large *organ front* (1682) and the simple *galleries* (1834) were installed later.

**Schloss:** This extensive Schloss with a dry moat was built (with the exception of the medieval keep and minor 18C alterations) by the architect Asmus of Steinau in 1525–58 for Counts Philipp II and Philipp

III. There are bastion-like buildings at the 4 corners of the Burg complex, which was formerly reached via drawbridges in the N. and S. At the 4 corners of the court spired *staircase towers* connect the 3 storeys of the 3 half hip-roofed buildings bordering the court. Of interest is the *hall* (1525-8) in the W. with a 3-storey oriel on the N. gable side, a net-vaulted *courtyard room* on the ground floor and the *banqueting hall* (2nd floor), the door openings of which are ogee-arched. Another *projecting oriel* is to be seen on the adjacent kitchen (1542-6). Next to the *Schlossmuseum* (Renaissance furniture, 16C) the buildings also house the *Brüder-Grimm-Gedenkstätte*, which documents the life and work of the Brothers Grimm, who grew up in Steinau.

## Steinbach = Legau Maria Steinbach 8945

Bavaria                                    p.422□H 20

**Parish and Pilgrimage Church of St. Maria:** This building replaced a 16C parish church in 1753 and the first-class furnishings were added up to 1764. Masters of Swabian-Bavarian rococo created a gem of religious architecture here. The plans for the building were probably by J.G.Fischer or D.Zimmermann, while the interior furnishings were created by F.X.Feuchtmayer and J.G.Üblherr and the frescos by F.G.Hermann.

## Steinfeld = Kall 5370

Nordrhein-Westfalen                        p.416□B 13

**Former Premonstratensian Monastery Church;** In 1121 Augustinian canons took over the Steinfeld convent founded around 1070 and in 1126 adopted the Premonstratensian Order founded by St. Norbert of Laufen. As the first German Premonstratensian monastery Steinfeld was the bastion of the Christianization of the German East. The building of the church was begun in 1142; it is a vaulted basilica, which has remained almost unaltered to this day. The exterior is characterized by the plain W. façade with round

towers on both sides. The church has a superb interior; the wall-paintings, which have survived in part from the 12&14C, are particularly fine. The others were added in 1509-17, when H.von Aachen painted the tendril work and a few scenes with figures. The nave is dominated by the sarcophagus of the Premonstratensian Hermann Joseph, who died in 1241 and was canonized in 1960. Of interest are the baroque organ (1690-1372), the richly decorated pulpit and the altar. The *monastery buildings* on the N. side of the church were mostly built in the 16C, but were greatly altered in the 18C (addition of a storey).

## Steinfurt 4430

Nordrhein-Westfalen                        p.414□C8

**Catholic Parish Church of St. Nikomedes** (in Borghorst, Kirchplatz): The church of a nunnery founded in 968 was pulled down in 1885 and replaced by a neo-Gothic building. Large parts of the valuable old *church treasure* survived, however: 3 Romanesque altar candlesticks with animal ornaments, 2 silver-embossed late Gothic reliquary statuettes and, the most valuable piece, an 11C cross with carved gems, the Heinrichskreuz, the most important Ottonian goldsmith's work in Westphalia. It is 16 inches high, overlaid with relief gold figures and decorated with semi-precious stones, antique gems and the bust of Emperor Heinrich II.

**Schloss** (in Burgsteinfurt, 1 Burgstrassse): This moated Burg is one of the oldest and mightiest in Münsterland. Castle and outer works are set on 2 islands on the Aa in the SE of the town. The oldest sections date from the 12C. The ring wall, which surrounds the castle square, the square residential tower (with the knights' hall) and the gate tower date from the 13C. Amongst the older buildings are the Romanesque *castle chapel* with a beautiful portal (12C) flanked by corner columns with rich capitals. It is a double chapel with 2 storeys—as was common for castle chapels at that time. The best of the residential buildings of the 16-18C is the

*Monastery church, Steingaden, detail of ceiling (l.), altar (r.)*

house of Countess Walburg with the 2-storey Renaissance oriel (dated 1559) and rich decorations. Stretching away to the SE of the castle is *Bagno* park, originally laid out on French lines, but enlarged and converted into an English garden in 1780–1817. Most of its many interesting features have, however, disappeared; preserved is the *Concert Hall*, completed in 1774, with a shell grotto and early classical stucco furnishing.

*stucco* here (*c.*1740). The *frescos* are the work of J.G.Bergmüller of Augsburg (1741–51). The painting for the *high altar* (1663) is by J.C.Storer (Constance). The *figures of the founders* on the pillars were produced by the Munich sculptor J.B.Straub. Also of note are the first-class *choir stalls* (1534). There are Romanesque columns in the adjacent *cloister,* dating from the first half of the 13C. The *Johanneskapelle* is a Romanesque rotunda.

## Steingaden 8924
Bavaria                                              p.422□I 21

**Former Premonstratensian Monastery Church of St.John the Baptist:** Although the exterior of the church has remained largely unaltered since its foundation in the mid 12C, the elaborate interior design dates from the 18C. F.X.Schmuzer produced some of his best

## Steinhausen an der Rottum 7955
Baden-Württemberg                          p.420□G 20

**Pilgrimage Church/Catholic Parish Church of St.Peter and St.Paul:** This church is the work of the brothers Dominikus (architect and stucco artist) and Johann Baptist Zimmermann (stucco artist and painter). It was built in 1728–33 and is one of the finest works of its period. The cen-

*Monastery church, Steingaden*

*Pilgrimage church, Steinhausen* ▷

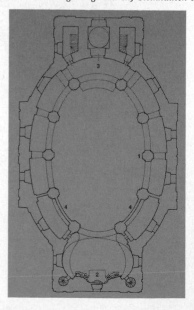

tral area of the church interior is oval (see plan) and flooded with light. The interior is entirely undecorated and unpainted to the height of the capitals, which greatly heightens the effect of the elaborate stucco ornaments and splendid colours above. The pillar arches are surrounded by lavishly stuccoed gilt balustrades. The highlight of the decoration is the massive dome fresco. The influence of the Wessobrunn School, where the two Zimmermann brothers were trained, is unmistakable in many stucco figures and individual motifs; local flowers and birds, as well as snails and squirrels, are blended into the wonderfully uniform whole. The brothers continued their joint work in the Wieskirche (see Wies).

**Steinhausen, Parish church of St. Peter und Paul, Pilgrimage church 1** Pulpit by J.G. Prestel, 1746 **2** High altar by J. Früholz, 1750; Pietà, *c.* 1410-20 **3** Organ, housing by G. Reusch, 1750 **4** Side altars by J. Früholz with paintings by Esperlin, 1746

## Steinhude=3050 Wunstorf 1
Lower Saxony                                    p.414☐G 7

This little town on the Steinhuder Meer
has become the centre of a holiday area and
a mud spa.

**Schloss Wilhelmstein:** This island fortress was built by Count Wilhelm von
Schaumberg, after whom it is named, in
1761–7. The miniature fortress with its 16
surrounding forts stands on an artificial island and originally served as a model military academy. Its most famous student was
Gerhard von Scharnhorst. When the
academy closed the fortress became a museum and is a very popular tourist attraction.

## Straubing 8440
Bavaria                                         p.422☐M 17

This Bavarian settlement developed from
a Roman military camp on the Danube
plain and has been documented since
around 900. The New Town was founded
upstream on the Danube by Duke Ludwig
der Kehlheimer in 1218.

The model of the medieval town, made by
local turner Jakob Sandtner in 1568 (now
in the Bayerisches Nationalmuseum in
Munich) can still be recognized in large
parts of the town. Stately medieval buildings clearly demonstrate the power of the
old Bavarian bourgeoisie. Agnes Bernauer,
the Augsburg barber's daughter, who was
married to Duke Albrecht and drowned in
the Danube in 1435 as a supposed witch,
is commemorated by the Agnes Bernauer
Chapel, built in her honour, and the Agnes
Bernauer Festival, which is held every four
years.

**Town Parish Church/Collegiate
Church of St.Jakob** (7 Pfarrplatz): This
15C church is one of the largest *hall
churches* in Bavaria. The plans were drawn
by the famous Landshut church architect
H.Stethaimer. The austere exterior of the
brick building is only relieved by the late
baroque top of the tower (1780). Inside,
slender *round pillars* support a flat vault,
which was originally 10 ft. higher, but was
not rebuilt to the original design after the
town fire in 1780. The whole building is
flanked by lavishly furnished *chapels*. The
neo-Gothic *high altar* has valuable figures
and painted panels from an altar taken from

*Schloss Wilhelmstein, Steinhude*

Nuremberg in 1590. It has recently been revealed that the paintings came from the workshop of Meister Wohlgemut. The *pulpit*, set up in 1753, is elaborately decorated with baroque motifs; the church's patron St. James is depicted on the sounding-board. Of particular interest are the chapels, partly enclosed by wrought-iron grilles. Outstanding is the *Maria-Hilf-Kapelle*, in which the glass and wall paintings have survived from the 15C. In the next chapel on the right, the *Maria-Tod-Kapelle*, stands the stucco marble altar by E.Q.Asam with a painting by his brother. Of note in the *Bartholomäus-Kapelle* (N. of the the centre of the chancel) is the tomb of councillor Ulrich Kastenmayer (*c.*1430), which is one of the best works of sculpture of its time. Amongst the *glass paintings* in the nave are some 15C originals.

**Carmelite Church** (Albrechtgasse 20): Although the building was begun in 1371, the church was not completed until the 15C with the help of Stethaimer. The characteristic features date back to the baroque conversion under W.Dientzenhofer in 1700–10. In the course of this rearrangement the vaulting in the nave was restructured and the W. tower added. Inside, the

Gothic character (slender pillars) has been forsaken in favour of the baroque. In contrast to other churches, Dientzenhofer even went so far as to clad pillars and enlarge windows, topping them with round arches. The finest feature of the furnishings is one of the most powerful *high altars* in S. Germany. It is the work of a master from Passau (1741&2) and rises into the vaulting, with the result that the E. part of the chancel is closed off as a monks' choir. In the centre of the colossal work is the painting depicting the Outpouring of the Holy Spirit. The large, three-dimensional figures depict prophets and popes. Along with the *side altars and baroque pulpits* the *altar tomb of Duke Albrecht II* (d. 1397) completes the church's treasures (red marble; in the monks' choir behind the high altar).

**Urselinenkirche** (9 Burggasse): 2 great artists of the 18C are connected with the building of this monastery church. E.Q.Asam was the architect, while C.D.Asam contributed most of the interior painting. Centrepiece is the *high altar*, which, as the dominant element of the church interior, is continued in the side altars and ceiling fresco.

*St. Jakob, Straubing*

*Carmelite church*

*Bernauer tombstone, Friedhof St. Peter*

**Parish Church of St.Peter** (Petersgasse): This church, built around 1200, is typical of the Romanesque in Bavaria, being a transeptless basilica with a nave and two aisles. The W. façade is accompanied by 2 *towers* (neo-Romanesque storeys added in the 19C). The 3 *apses* in the E. end are sparsely ornamented. The *portals* in the W. and S., with lavish ornamentation and figure reliefs, are great achievements of stonemasonry.

**St.Peter's Cemetery:** This extremely atmospheric graveyard surrounding the church of St. Peter has well-renovated *wrought-iron grave crosses* and 3 chapels: The *Liebfrauenkapelle* (Alter Karner), a two-storey late Gothic building, the *Totentanzkapelle*, built in 1486 as a new ossuary, with a baroque depiction of the Dance of Death on the walls of the nave, and the *Agnes-Bernauer-Kapelle*. This goes back to an expiatory foundation of Duke Ernst of Bavaria. It was he who had Agnes Ber-

nauer drowned in the Danube in 1435 as the socially inferior wife of his son. The centrepiece is her tombstone, which was made by a local master in the 15C.

**Other interesting churches:** *Former Jesuit church* (thoroughly renovated in the 17C), *St.Veit* (14C, converted to baroque in 1702&3, interesting furnishings), *Schutzengelkirche* (built in 1706, with lavish furnishings).

**Schloss** (in the N. of the town by the Danube bridge): The present building was built under Duke Albrecht I from 1356 onwards. The Schloss chapel (14&15C) has a small choir, which protrudes as an oriel from the back wall. In the castle courtyard open-air productions about the life of Agnes Bernauer are held.

**Stadtplatz:** The *Stadtturm*, which divides the two halves of the square, was built in 1316–93 and is recognizable by its characteristic spire. Next to the central tower 4 corner oriels were supposed to provide the watchmen with views from all sides. W. of the town tower stands the *Dreifaltigkeitssäule*. This was built by the townsfolk after a siege by Austrian troops in 1704 was abandoned.

**Rathaus** (Theresienplatz): When the old Town Hall, which was originally connected to the Stadtturm, became too small, the need for a new building was avoided by the conversion of a row of houses surrounding the square. Of interest are the *Laubenhof* (16C) and a *late Gothic room.*

**Old Houses:** Interesting houses, often with high medieval gables and 17&18C façades, are to be found in particular in Ludwigsplatz and Fraunhoferstrasse.

**Stadttheater** (11 Theresienplatz): The theatre (converted in 1953) has 460 seats and is used by touring companies.

*The collegiate church and Fruchtkasten are ▷ the two buildings dominating the Schillerplatz in Stuttgart*

**Gäuboden- und Stadtmuseum** (9 Fraunhoferstrasse): Exhibits on pre- and early history, also cultural and historical collections (costumes, furniture, weapons, ceramics, folk art) are displayed in a former house of the nobility with a beautiful baroque front. The finest item is the *Roman Treasure of Straubing*, which was found to the W. of the town in 1950.

---

## Stuppach = Bad Mergentheim 6990
Baden-Württemberg                    p.420☐G 16

**Parish Church:** This church, an unassuming building dating from 1607, is famous for its picture of the Virgin Mary, which was painted by Matthias Grünewald (1517–19) and is one of the most important works of Old German painting.

---

## Stuttgart 7000
Baden-Württemberg                    p.420☐F 18

Stuttgart's cultural importance is indicated by the presence here of a technical university, agricultural college, academy of music and dramatic art and an art academy. The Württemberg State Library is one of the largest in Germany with over 1.2 million volumes. Stuttgart is also seat of the German Schiller Society (see Marbach). The city grew up around a 'Stuten-Garten' ('Mares' Garden'), a stud which gave the city its name and was probably founded by the Swabian Duke Liutolf around 950. The development of Stuttgart is documented from the 12C onwards. In the 17C the residence of the Dukes of Württemberg was transferred temporarily to Ludwigsburg(q.v.), but the city still rose to cultural and economic heights during the baroque and classical epochs. Even the 20C has produced some remarkable buildings, particularly in connection with the architectural exhibition of 1927. Amongst the city's great sons have been the philosopher G.W.F.Hegel and the poets G.Schwab and W.Hauff.

**Protestant Collegiate Church of Das Heilige Kreuz** (12 Stiftstrasse, Schillerplatz): The present building (renovated after the damage caused in the last war) was built for the most part in 1433–60 to plans by the famous architect A.Jörg. Jörg retained the foundations of the tower from

*The tombs of the Counts of Württemberg in the choir of the Protestant collegiate church of*

an earlier building of around 1230, as well as the choir of 1327–47. Of interest inside are the *tombs* of the Counts of Württemberg in the chancel. These are the work of the sculptor S.Schlör (1576–1608) and are amongst the most important works of sculpture of the period. Also: several *memorial tombs* (praying knight Hermann von Sachsenheim, 1508) and a stone altar from around 1500 with a *Man of Sorrows* as its centrepiece. The *golden pulpit* has been put back in its original position to the left of the choir.

**Protestant Hospitalkirche** (Büchsen-Hospitalstrasse): This hall church was also built by A.Jörg (1471–93), but was badly damaged in the Second World War. A survivor was the splendid *crucifixion* (1501, chancel) by the Heilbronn sculptor H.Seyffer, who also went down in the history of art as Hans of Heilbronn. The church also contains a few interesting 16&17C *tombs*.

**Protestant Church of St. Leonhard** (Leonhardsplatz): Here too A.Jörg is the architect; he incorporated an older *choir* into the building in 1463–74. Outstanding are the 15C *choir stalls*. A *copy* of the *Crucifix-*

*ion* now in the Hospitalkirche, stands by the church.

**Protestant Church in Bad Canstatt:** A.Jörg is again the architect and here too he displays his knack of incorporating parts of an older building into a unified whole (including the two E. *towers* and the *stellar vault* of the *choir*). The *main tower* was added in 1613.

**Protestant Veitskirche in Mühlhausen:** This church was built in 1380–90 and has since remained almost unaltered. Especially noteworthy amongst the extremely fine furnishings is the *paintwork*, the oldest parts of which date from the time of construction (triumphal arch, choir vault), the rest being added in the 15C. The church's showpiece was the Bohemian *high altar* (*c.*1380), now in the Staatsgalerie (q.v.).

**Modern churches in Stuttgart:** Churches dating from the first quarter of this century, as well as the new buildings which replaced those churches destroyed in the Second World War, have made Stuttgart a *centre of modern church architecture*. The following are of particular interest:

*Heiliges Kreuz are among the most significant works of 16C sculpture*

*Inner courtyard of Altes Schloss, with three-storeyed arcades*

*Neues Schloss—Ehrenhof side*

*Markuskirche* (Markusplatz), *Erlöserkirche* (Birkenwaldstrasse), *St. Georg* (Heilbronner Strasse), *Kirche in Sillenbuch* (Kleine Hohenheimer Strasse).

**Altes Schloss** (Planie): The damage caused in the Second World War has been repaired, and the Altes Schloss, which evolved from a 13C moated castle, is now much as it was in the 16C. Most of the Schloss is the work of A.Tretsch, who extended it in Renaissance style in 1553–78. The *inner court* provides a charming view of the three-tier arcades on three sides of the former jousting square. The Schloss chapel is also the work of Tretsch (1560-2), in the S. wing.

**Neues Schloss** (Schlossplatz): Duke Carl Eugen began building the new Schloss in 1746, as his father had transferred the residence from Ludwigsburg to Stuttgart. The plans, based on Versailles, were by L.Retti. L.P.de la Guêpière took over in 1751. After the Second World War the interior was remodelled on modern lines.

**Lustschloss Solitude** (via Rotebühlstrasse, Wildparkstrasse): Duke Carl Eugen had this palace built on a ridge in the W. of the city in 1763-7 as a place for reflec-

tion. Neoclassical design is in evidence here alongside the final flicker of rococo. This new style was reinforced when the decoration was completed around 1800. The former *theatre* and the *chapel* are also of interest.

**Schloss Hohenheim** (in Hohenheim): That enthusiastic builder Duke Carl Eugen had this castle built as a country seat by F.H.Fischer in 1785–91. Baroque design is subordinated to the clear lines of neoclassicism.

**Schillerplatz:** The *collegiate church* and the *'Fruchtkasten'* are the dominant buildings in this square, which has been largely preserved in its old state; the *Schiller Monument* by B.Thorwaldsen, erected in 1839, is its focal point. The Fruchtkasten ('fruit-box') dates from the 14C, but was reconstructed towards the end of the 16C. Further buildings of architectural importance in the square are the *Alte Kanzlei* (1550–60) and next to it the *Prinzenbau* (completed in 1698).

**Schlossplatz:** This square is like a large garden with chestnut-lined avenues. It creates a link between the Neues Schloss, the Altes Schloss, Schillerplatz and Königstrasse. In the middle of the square stands the *Jubiläumssäule* (1841).

**Rathaus:** The new Town Hall was built in 1954–6 in the former centre of the old city to plans by the architects H.P.Schmohl and P.Stohrer.

**Weissenhofsiedlung:** In spite of the destruction of 10 houses in the Second World War the Weissenhofsiedlung remains one of the best examples of the new buildings of 1927. 16 architects from 5 European countries under the direction of Mies van der Rohe designed houses for the exhibition of the German arts and crafts society 'Die Wohnung'; the architects explored fundamentally new ideas on domestic architecture. Houses by J.Frank, P.Jeanneret, Le Corbusier, J.J.P.Oud, H.Scharoun, M.Stam. M.van der Rohe survived and are currenly being restored (1983–6).

**Liederhalle** (Schloss-/Seidenstrasse): This modern building houses 3 concert halls: the *Beethovensaal* (2000 seats), the *Mozartsaal* (750 seats) and the *Silchersaal* (350 seats). The architects of the building, built in 1955&6 were A.Abel, R.Gutbrod and B.Spreng.

*Lustschloss Solitude on a ridge in the W. of the city*

**Theatre:** The *Württembergische Staatstheater* (Oberer Schlossgarten 6), has a great tradition and is often praised today (its ballet is of world standard). Drama, music and dance productions are performed in both the large and small houses of the theatre, as well as the additional chamber theatre. The *Grosses Haus* was opened in 1912 and seats 1426. The *Neues Kammertheater* was incorporated in the new Staatsgalerie building and opened in 1984. The *Kleines Haus*, destroyed in the Second World War, reopened in 1962 and seats 841. The *Komödie im Marquardt* (4–6 Bolzstrasse) performs popular drama to a high standard. 378 seats. *Altes Schauspielhaus* (Kleine Königsstrasse): this 1911 building with 500 seats was reopened in 1983. The *Theater der Altstadt* (Charlottenplatz) also performs plays from September to July. Not to be forgotten also are the numerous *puppet* and *dialect* theatres.

**Museums:** The *Württembergisches Landesmuseum* (6 Schillerplatz, in the Altes Schloss) was founded in the 19C, but dates back into the 16C with its *Kunstkammer*. The *Crown Treasury of the Kings* is housed here. Important collections are: pre- and early history, antiques, the Roman lapidarium, fine collections on the history of art and culture (including sculpture, weapons, clocks, musical instruments and coins). The *Staatsgalerie* (30 – 32 Konrad-Adenauer-Strasse), founded by Wilhelm I of Württemberg, was opened in 1843 and extended with the addition of the *Neue Staatsgalerie* by J.Stirling in 1984. Collected here are European painting from the Middle Ages to the present day, 19&20C sculpture and graphic art. One of the most important works is the 'Herrenberg Altar', painted by Jörg Ratgeb in 1518&19 for the Herrenberg collegiate church; the altar came to Stuttgart in 1892. Also represented in the gallery are Dutch masters, such as Hals, Rembrandt and Rubens, along with almost every great French painter of the 19&20C. It also has one of the largest and most important Picasso collections in the Federal Republic. The *Galerie der Stadt Stuttgart* (Kunstgebäude, Schlossplatz) displays Swabian art of the 19&20C, particularly by A.Hoelzel and O.Dix. The *Linden-Museum* (1 Hegelplatz) houses contributions on folklore from every continent. The *Daimler-Benz-Museum* (136 Mercedes-Strasse) is one of the most important museums on the development of engines and vehicles. Among the 100 vin-

*Schlossplatz square with Jubiläumssäule.* Right: *Staatstheater*

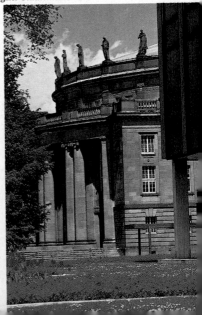

tage cars are the famous Daimler-Benz racing cars. The *German Bible Society* (Möhringen, Balinger Str.31) has an interesting collection of old bibles.

**Also worth seeing:** The *Fernsehturm* (T.V. tower) on the Bopser was built in 1956 and measures 712 ft. with its transmitter mast. The upper observation platform is at a height of 500 ft., with the upper restaurant a few feet below it. In *Rotenberg* (via Untertürkheim) King Wilhelm I built a *mausoleum* for his wife. This round building was built in 1820-4 above the remains of the ancestral castle of the Wirtembergs on the hill of the same name.

---

**Sulzbach-Rosenberg 8458**
Bavaria                              p.422□L 16

---

**Parish Church of Mariae Himmel-**
**fahrt** (Pfarrgasse): Built in the 14&15C; in 1526 a princes' gallery was added, stretching across the nave and two aisles. Of note are the beautiful *tracery windows* dating from the time of the church's construction. The *high altar* is dominated by the Mariae Himmelfahrt, painted by H.G.Asam (d.1711), father of the famous brothers.

**Schloss:** Built in 1582-1618 by Duke Ottheinrich II of Pfalz-Sulzbach, the building was greatly altered in 1768-94. The complex includes a *hall building* (1582) with staircase tower and decorative portal, the *Prince's and Guest Wing* (1618) and the *Chancellery building*. In 1701 Duke Christian August built the *Schloss Fountain* with the Palatine Lions.

**Rathaus** (25 Luitpoldplatz): This 14C Town Hall has an impressive *gabled façade*.

*Crypt church for King Wilhelm I's wife in Rotenberg near Stuttgart*

# T

## Tauberbischofsheim 6972
Baden-Württemberg       p.416□G 15

**Catholic Parish Church of St. Martin** (Liobaplatz): Only the 16C *Madonna altar* remains of the original church, which was replaced by the present building in 1910 –14. The altar is probably from the studio of Tilman Riemenschneider. The 1761 *altar of the Cross* contains a copy of a

*Kurmainzisches Schloss, Tauberbischofsheim*

Grünewald Crucifixion scene; the original is in the Staatliche Kunsthalle in Karlsruhe (q.v.).

**Former Schloss of the Electors of Mainz** (Schlossplatz): The buildings are essentially 15&16C but signs of the 1250 origins can be detected. The *Landschaftsmuseum* is now housed in the Schloss.

**Half-timbered buildings:** There are first-class half-timbered buildings in *Hauptstrasse* and the *Marktplatz*.

## Tecklenburg 4542
Nordrhein-Westfalen       p.414□D 8

**Protestant Parish Church** (Landrat-Schultz-Strasse): The 16C hall building contains the *memorial tombs* of the Counts of Tecklenburg (16C). The baroque tower was built in 1710&11.

**Moated Burg Haus Mark** (1 km. S.): The 1754 *Rittersaal* in the outwardly undecorated 18&19C building is worth seeing; there are concerts in the Schloss.

**Museums:** *Kreismuseum* (Wellenberg): collections on the history of the noble family and the area and on former industries such as mining, cement and lime manufacture, domestic linen manufacture etc.;

there are also interesting reconstructions of 18&19C domestic interiors. The *Puppenmuseum* (in the old gatehouse) has an international collection of dolls and a very wide range of toys.

## Tegernsee 8180
Bavaria                                    p.422□L 21

At the height of its fame the Benedictine monastery made Tegernsee one of the most important cultural centres in Europe; the illumination of manuscripts and calligraphy reached the peaks of their achievement. In the very varied history of the monastery the most fruitful phases were the 11C, the 15C and the 17&18C. In our century the local authors L.Ganghofer (d.1920) and L.Thoma (d.1921) spent their old age in Tegernsee, and H.Courths-Mahler also died here.

**Former Benedictine Monastery Church/Parish Church of St.Quirin:** The church, which dates in its present form from a radical rebuilding in 1684–9, was preceded by numerous buildings, most of which were destroyed by fire. H.G.Asam, the father of the famous brothers, contributed the *stucco* and the *frescos*. The powerful *façade with two towers*, the oldest in Bavaria, was remodelled by L. von Klenze in 1817; inside the three-aisled basilica only a few of the numerous altars have survived. The centrepiece of the *high altar* is a Crucifixion picture, a copy of a painting by K.Loth which was taken to Upper Austria in the 18C. On the N. *side altar* is an excellent sculpture of St.Agatha. A few of the furnishings which arrived at a later date have markedly neoclassical features. The notable *side chapels* have ornate rococo decoration (especially the Quirinus and Benediktus chapels). After the Bavarian King Max I Joseph had acquired the chapel it was rebuilt as a Schloss by L. von Klenze but the *Rekreationssaal* with stucco by J.B.Zimmermann still has monastic features.

**Heimatmuseum** Schloss Tegernsee:

many of the historic rooms of the Schloss are included in the museum.

## Telgte 4404
Nordrhein-Westfalen                        p.414□D 9

**Priory Church:** The church was built after a fire in 1522 as a hall church on the Westfalian pattern and stands on the bank of the Ems on the site of a former episcopal Burg. One bay and the tower were added in the 19C.The most important furnishings are a figure of Christ (*c.*1200) and a 15C Madonna.

**Pilgrimage Chapel** (Kirchplatz): The octagonal sandstone chapel was built in 1654 for Prince Bishop Christoph Bernhard von Galen. Additional buildings were added in the 18&19C. The interior was refurbished in 1959 and 1984. The miraculous image, a Pietà, dates from *c.*1370.

**Heimathaus Münsterland** (2 Herrenstrasse): The old parsonage barn was rebuilt as a museum in 1934 and extended in 1937 and houses collections on religious folklore. The most valuable exhibit is the Telgte Hungertuch (Lenten veil) of 1623, which is 24 ft. by 14 ft. and shows the Sufferings of Christ, scenes from the Old Testament and the symbols of the Evangelists on 33 panels. The Heimathaus Münsterland was further enlarged in 1983.

## Thurnau 8656
Bavaria                                    p.418□K 14

**Protestant Parish Church:** The *tower*, which also contains the *choir*, was taken over from an older building and is late Gothic in appearance. The *nave* dates from 1700–6. The almost square interior is surrounded by a gallery on three sides; in the W. gallery is a black and gold two-storey *Herrenstand*. There is also a notable early-17C *canopied chair* in the upper storey. There is a bridge from the gallery to the nearby Schloss tower.

**Schloss:** The complex has evolved since the 12C from numerous individual buildings and is today still divided into the *Untere* and *Obere Schloss*. The main sections of the building are 16–19C and are used today by the University of Bayreuth.

## Trausnitz 8471
Bavaria                              p.422☐M 16

**Burg:** The little village (1100 inhabitants) is attractive because of its *picturesque situation* in the valley of the Pfriemd and for its proud *Burg* dating from the 13C; the complex is set around a little courtyard. This defiant fortress played a historic role in 1322–4, when Friedrich the Fair of Austria, the Anti-king of Ludwig of Bavaria, was held prisoner here; it is now a youth hostel.

## Trechtingshausen 6531
Rheinland-Pfalz                      p.416☐D 14

**Clemenskirche** (just outside the town on the bank of the Rhine): This church has all the characteristics of a *Romanesque basilica*; it was built in the 12C and has survived almost unchanged. The pillars in the nave, which are arranged in pairs, are the dominant feature. The crossing has domed vaulting.

**Environs: Burg Reichenstein** (1 km. S. of Trechtingshausen) is 13C but was extended in the Romanesque style for Prince Friedrich of Prussia from 1825. The collections of paintings and weapons were sold in 1974 and the Burg restored in 1976. *Burg Sonneck* (3 km. N.).

## Triberg 7740
Baden-Württemberg                    p.420☐D 19

**Parish and Pilgrimage Church of Maria in den Tannen/Maria Himmelfahrt:** The outwardly plain church (1699–1705) contains the *miraculous image* of 'Maria in den Tannen' (Mary in the pines) by A.J.Schupp of Villingen (1645). The *side altars* and the *pulpit* (also by Schupp) and the 1714 *antependium* in front of the high altar are also very fine. There is an authentic representation of Villingen in 1715 on one of the *votive pictures*.

*Burg Rheinstein, Trechtingshausen*

**Heimatmuseum** (4 Wallfahrtstrasse): There is an interesting collection of automatic musical instuments and also material on the people and crafts of the Black Forest.

---

**Trier 5500**
Rheinland-Pfalz                                   p.416☐B 15

Trier is the oldest town in Germany; an inscription on the Rotes Haus even maintains that the town is 1300 years older than Rome. It is true that Trier was founded by the Romans in 16 BC. In AD 117 it became the capital of the province of Belgica prima and later the Emperor's residence, and the Emperors Maximianus, Constantius Chlorus and above all Constantine the Great (from 306 – 312) lived here. The town flourished culturally and economically and, despite frequent devastation by the Germani, it became a cosmopolitan city of the empire, three times larger than Cologne. Its merchants traded with Marseilles, Italy, Greece and Syria. When the Romans were driven out the power of the city on the Moselle declined, and it did not rise again until, raised to the rank of holy city, it became the first bishopric beyond the Alps. Today Trier has a university and a theological college and is an important industrial town and still a centre of the wine trade. One of the most famous sons of the town is Karl Marx, who was born here.

ROMAN TRIER

**Basilica/Aula/Palatina** (Konstantinplatz): The basilica, which is presumed to have been built by the Emperor Constantine *c.*300, is now the Protestant parish church. The massive scale of the rectangular brick building is evidence of the matchless achievements of Roman architecture in this period: it is 239 ft. long, 93 ft. wide and 108 ft. high, and even today it would be no easy task to build a hall of such size without pillars. Along with the Pantheon in Rome the basilica is the largest and most magnificent interior which has survived from the Roman world, and all the monumental greatness and nobility of Roman architecture can be seen in the building. The ancient edifice has been subject to much interference over the years; it is largely due to Friedrich Wilhelm IV that

*Basilica, Trier*

the basilica can be seen today in almost the state in which it was left by its creators: he gave the order that 'the basilica should be rebuilt in its original size and purity of design, using the considerable remains available'. As a result of this decree numerous excrescences which had been added in the course of the centuries and had vitiated the splendid appearance of the building were removed. There was a second great phase of renovation after the Second World War when war damage had to be repaired, and the opportunity was taken to carry out further restoration work. The interior of the building is a massive hall with a monumental coffered roof.

**Porta Nigra** (Porta-Nigra-Platz): The name comes from the black, weathered sandstone in which this, the most massive city gate in the whole Roman Empire, once the N. gate of the Roman town fortifications, was built. The gate was built, presumably in the 4C, when it became necessary to extend the town. The gate, 118 ft. long, 70 ft. wide and 98 ft. high, is one of the dominant visual elements of modern Trier. The middle section has two openings, and is enclosed by two semicircular towers. The great sandstone blocks

were originally held together not with mortar but with large iron staples; many of these staples have since disappeared. Buildings added in the course of time have been removed, as also happened around the basilica (q.v.). One of the buildings which disappeared was the *Simeonskirche*, built by Archbishop Poppo in honour of his friend Simeon, who had himself walled up in a cell in the Porta Nigra and lived there for seven years as a hermit; only the choir of the church survives. Part of the original *Simeonsstift* is now used as the municipal museum. The two-storey cloisters are the earliest of their kind in Germany.

**Kaiserthermen** (Imperial baths) (Ostallee): The once enormous bath complex is in the E. of the town, and forms a rectangle 270 yards long by 164 yards wide. Building began in the 3C, and was completed by Constantine the Great. Under the Emperor Gratianus (375–83) the complex was rebuilt and extended as a forum alongside the forum of Constantine, and in the post-Roman period it served as a citadel, then a church and finally as part of the town fortifications. Only fragments of the baths have survived, but they give a good impression of the old buildings.

*Porta Nigra*

*Kaiserthermen*

**Other Roman buildings in Trier:**
*Amphitheatre* (Olewigerstrasse): The theatre was built in the 2C but very little remains of it today. It was used for gladiatorial combat, but was also intended to have a defensive function. *Barbara baths* (Südallee): This 2C complex included cold and warm baths and two heated swimming pools; only the foundations remain. *Roman bridge:* Only the piers of this 4C bridge have survived.

## CHURCHES

**Dom** (Domfreihof): The detailed history of the Dom has only been publicly known since excavations after 1944 revealed details about earlier buildings on the site of the present cathedral. They lent credibility to the tradition that the first building on the site was a palace of Empress Helena, the mother of Constantine the Great. Evidence of this earlier building is given by ceiling paintings, which have been partially reconstructed from 50, 000 fragments. Constantine built a large double church on the site of his mother's former palace from 326; this church is presumed to have been destroyed by fire and was replaced by a new building in 336–83, parts of which survive in the E. area of the present cathedral. Building of the present cathedral, which has undergone numerous alterations, extensions and renovations began *c.*1035 and continued for almost 200 years. The dominant feature of the interior is the rib vaulting. The variety of the *furnishings* reflects the long building period and the many alterations. Remains of the decorative figures from the 12C Romanesque parclose — Christ with Mary and John the Baptist and the 12 Apostles—have now been placed between the chapter choir and the high choir. Important *tombs* include the tomb of Cardinal Ivo (d. 1144), the high tomb of Archbishop Balduin of Luxemburg (d. 1354) and the tombs of

*Dom*

Archbishop Richard von Greiffenklau (1527) and of Johann von Metzenhausen (1542). The *pulpit* is one of the first great works of the sculptor H.R.Hoffmann (1570–2), who was also responsible for some of the funerary altars (such as the All Saints altar of Archbishop Lothar von Metternich by the last S. pillar). The most important *relic* in the cathedral is the *holy coat* in the *Heiltumskammer* (1702–8), the seamless garment of Christ for which the soldiers are said to have played dice. It is made of brown woven cloth and has been covered with a piece of 9C Byzantine silk for protection. The holy coat was first considered to be a contact relic from the time of Constantine, but in the 'Gesta Treveorum' it was declared to be the very garment which Christ wore. There are a number of *side buildings* attached to the Dom, of which the *cloisters* are the most important. They are mature high Gothic in design and have a number of notable treasures, including the *stone Madonna* (school of N.Gerhaert, 15C)

and some excellent tombs. In the so-called *Badische Bau* (1470), which was built between the choir and the N. walk of the cloisters, is the *Domschatz* (cathedral treasure). The most important piece is the Andreas portable altar, made by goldsmiths from Trier in the 10C.

**Liebfrauenkirche** (by the Dom): The Liebfrauenkirche takes up Constantine the Great's idea of a double church, which he had already put into practice on the same site (see above in the introduction to the description of the Dom). Building began in 1235, but the design is already clearly Gothic. Along with the Elisabeth church in Marburg (q.v.) the building is the oldest Gothic church in Germany and the first of the so-called Trier school. However, the Liebfrauenkirche is different in design from all the other buildings influenced by the Trier architects; it is a rotunda built as an almost perfect circle with the crossing as its centre. One of the most striking details of this epoch-making building is the W. doorway, which is the first doorway with figures (originals now in the Diözesan-Museum; see museums). In the interior the *tombs* of Canon Karl von Metternich (d. 1636) and Cathedral Precentor Johann Segensis (d.1564) are particularly notable. M. Rauchmiller created the Metternich tomb *c.*1675, and the Segensis tomb is one of the best in the Renaissance style. On the 12 pillars around the circular crossing pillars are representations of the 12 Apostles (the paintwork from around 1500 has survived). The glass in the windows is modern (fitted in 1954 and 1974).

**Benedictine Abbey and Parish Church of St.Matthias:** The church consecrated in 1148, which in its turn went back to previous buildings dating from the 4C, has been much altered in the course of the centuries. The most recent and radical periods of rebuilding were after a fire in 1783 and restoration work in 1964-7. The choice of site for the monastery and church was determined by the grave of the first Bishop of Trier, St.Eucharius (4C). An important factor for the church was the rediscovery of the relics of the Apostle Matthew; the monastery flourished and became a popular place of pilgrimage. The late Gothic net vaulting was installed by Master Bernhard of Trier in 1496-1504 and completely covers the nave; the transept and choir were vaulted in 1505-10. The choir was divided from the rest of the church by high screens (today a baroque balustrade). Under the choir is a crypt dating from *c.*980, and later extended to the E. In the crypt are the late Romanesque sarcophagi of St. Eucharius and St. Valerius. The *monastery buildings* are attached to the church (13C, important early Rheinland Gothic). In the churchyard is the *Quirinus chapel* and under it the pre-Christian *burial chambers* with a notable *relief sarcophagus* (3C).

**Church of St. Maximin/Former Benedictine Abbey** (in the Reichsabtei): The abbey church was built *c.*1240 on the foundations of earlier buildings; it was then modified in 1581-1613, destroyed in

1674 and rebuilt in its present form in 1680-98. Later it served temporarily as a craft school, a barracks and a garrison church. The W. façade is baroque, but the interior of the church is Gothic. The most important part of the church is the 10C *crypt*, excavated in 1936-8. The Carolingian wall paintings, the only significant surviving Carolingian monumental painting in the Rhineland, have been removed and can be seen in the Bischöfliches Museum (q.v.).

**Former Collegiate Church/Parish Church of St.Paulin** (Palmatiusstrasse): This church was designed by Balthasar Neumann and built in 1734-7. The building replaced a Romanesque church and is considered to be one of the most important achievements of Rhineland baroque. The comparatively austere exterior contrasts strongly with the exuberant and colourful decoration. Famous artists were involved in the decoration: J.Arnold (stucco), F.Dietz (putti), C.T.Scheffler (ceiling painting 1743), J.Eberle (choir screen 1767); the high altar was built to a design by B.Neumann, executed by F.Dietz (1755).

**Other churches worth seeing in Trier:** *Hospital Church of St. Irminen/Former Benedictine Abbey Church* (via Katharinenufer): The present church, which was rebuilt after damage in the Second World War, is based on a 12C building and dates essentially from the 17&18C. *Dreifaltigkeitskirche:* This building was started in the 13C and completed in the 18C. The heraldic memorial tomb of Elisabeth von Görlitz (1451) is worth seeing. *Catholic Parish Church of St.Gangolf* (am Hauptmarkt): The church was built in 1410-60 and the massive tower was added *c.*1507. In the interior is part of a stone altar table from the period *c.*1475. At the E. end of the aisle is a Mary altar by H.R.Hoffmann (1602). *Catholic Parish Church of St.Antonius:* The 15C church was refurbished in the 18&19C and F.Dietz' pulpit is a fine feature from this period. The grotto altar dates from the 18C.

*Pulpit, Dom*

**Former Electoral Schloss** (Konstantin-platz): The Schloss in its present form dates from the 17&18C. The most interesting feature is the magnificent staircase with sculpture by F.Dietz. The decoration is by local artists M.Eytel (stucco) and J.Zick (painting).

**Hauptmarkt:** The *market cross* was erected in celebration of the right to hold a market granted in 958. The *market fountain*, dedicated to Peter, the patron saint of the town, was erected in 1595. It represents the 4 virtues of wisdom, justice, moderation and strength. On the S. side is St. Gangolf (see description above). On the W. side is the *Steipe*, which was rebuilt after the War; it is a 15C building which used to house the market court under its pillared arcades; the main building was used for feasts by the councillors of Trier. Next to it is the *Rote Haus* of 1684.

**Palais Kesselstatt** (an der Lieb-

frauenkirche): Diagonally opposite the Liebfrauenkirche is the most important surviving canons' residence, the Palais Kesselstatt. The building dates from 1740–45.

**Domestic buildings:** The few surviving medieval houses include the Gothic *Drei-königshaus* (Simeonstrasse) and the 11C *Frankenturm* (Dietrichstrasse).

**Museums:** *Rheinisches Landesmuseum Trier* (44 Ostallee): The museum, founded in 1874, has important collections on pre- and early history, the Roman period and medieval and modern art history; its collection of Roman art is unequalled in Germany. *Städtisches Museum* (Simeonstift): the 11C former cloister built as an extension to the Porta Nigra houses the municipal museum, which exhibits painting and sculpture from the medieval to the modern period, Dutch and Rhenish painting (predominantly 19C) and the topography and art history of Trier. *Bischöfliches Museum and Diözesanmusuem* (6 Banthusstrasse): Sacred art from the diocese of Trier, early Christian art, figures from the Dom and the Liebfrauenkirche, wall paintings. *Domschatzkammer* (treasury) (Domfreihof): See description of Dom. *Karl-Marx-Haus* (10 Brückenstrasse): The collections include documents on the life and works of the founder of academic socialism.

**Theater der Stadt** (Am Augustinerhof): This theatre, opened in 1964, has replaced the old civic theatre in Fahrstrase. It seats 622 and has its own operatic and dramatic companies.

---

**Tübingen 7400**
Baden-Württemberg              p.420☐F 18

Tübingen has been a university town since 1477 and is one of the economic and cultural centres of Baden-Württemberg. The town's name was first mentioned in 1078, but it did not really start to develop until the two settlements which had grown up on the Neckar and the Ammer joined to

*Madonna, Dom*

*Tomb of Johann Philipp von Walderdorf (1756-68), Dom*

form a single town. The Protestant Theological Stift (founded in 1536) made a considerable contribution to the fame of the town and produced men such as Kepler, Hegel, Schelling, Mörike and Hauff; Hölderlin and Uhland are buried in the old cemetery. Another reminder of Hölderlin, who was also educated in the Stift, is the tower which bears his name (see below); it was here that the mentally sick poet was cared for in the house of the master carpenter Zimmer, in which he died in 1843. There is also a memorial to Hölderlin in the Botanical Garden. The publishing house of Cotta made Tübingen a centre for the best-known writers and poets of the period. Johann Friedrich Freiherr (from 1822) Cotta von Cottendorf (1764–1832) had in 1787 taken over the firm, founded in 1659, and became the publisher of Goethe and Schiller among others. Discussions with Cotta frequently brought Goethe and Schiller themselves, but also

a number of other writers to Tübingen (the Cotta press is now based in Stuttgart). Attention should be drawn both to the town and university libraries; the latter has about two million volumes and manuscripts.

**Protestant Collegiate Church of St. Georg** (32 Münzgasse): The Collegiate Church was built in two phases, one following swiftly after the other. Elements of the design suggest that the choir with its magnificent late Gothic vaulting and ornate tracery was built in 1470 by P.Koblenz. The nave followed 8 years later. The two sections of this important church are separated by a late Gothic rood screen; the late 15C relief figures in the N. window openings are famous: the most distinguished is the window sculpture of the Martyrdom of St.George, who was broken on the wheel. In the choir, which was chosen as the last resting place of the Dukes

*Collegiate church of St. Georg, Tübingen*

of Württemberg, the high tombs are closely packed together. Count Eberhard the Bearded (d.1496), the founder of the University of Tübingen, was subsequently buried here. There are altogether 13 tombs in the choir, which provide both a gallery of the ancestral history of the House of Württemberg and a survey of Upper Swabian sculpture. The finest tomb is that of Countess Mechthild (in the middle of the last row but one), created by H.Multscher of Ulm (1450). The painted altarpiece (1520) on the S. wall and the windows in the apse (*c.*1480) are also worth seeing.

**Schloss** (Burgsteige): The most famous part of the Schloss above the town is the Outer Gate, which was part of the outer works of a Burg; it was built by A.Keller in 1606 to a design by H.Schickhardt. There are two sentry posts on the outer columns and in the middle is the coat of arms of Duke Friedrich (d.1608) carved in stone. The Schloss goes back to a previous building first mentioned in 1078, but the present building dates from 1507–40. In 1647 a tower was blown up by the French and later replaced with a five-cornered building.

**Rathaus** (Marktplatz): The 1435 building was thoroughly refurbished in 1698 and 1872, but has retained its interior organisation, with the council chamber on the first floor. The astronomical clock is the work of J.Söffler (1511). In the market place is the *Marktbrunnen* designed by H.Schickhardt. The sandstone figures were replaced with bronze copies; originals in the Theodor-Haering-Haus (q.v.).

**Hölderlinturm** (6 Bursagasse): Here Hölderlin spent the long years of his madness (1806–43). He was taken in by the master carpenter Zimmer and his family and they cared for him until his death.

**Bursa** (Bursagasse): This building dates

*Outer Schloss gate*

from 1479; it was originally a students' residence, was rebuilt in the neoclassical style in 1805, then served as a clinic and today houses the philosophical seminar. Philipp Melancthon, the humanist and reformer, held lectures here from 1514–18.

**Lower town:** There are numerous old half-timbered buildings in the lower town, with their most attractive sides facing the river.

**Museums:** The *Theodor-Haering-Haus/Städtische Sammlungen* (31 Neckarhalde): Numerous gifts have enriched the collection and enhanced the reputation of this museum, founded in 1967. As well as collections on the history of the town there are numerous exhibits on printing, publishing and the book trade. *Hölderlin-Gedenkstätte* (6 Bursagasse): In the so-called Hölderlin tower (see introduction and description of the tower) are collections on the life and work of Friedrich

Hölderlin. The various constituent departments of the University of Tübingen have their own collections (including the Institutes of Egyptology and Archaeology, and the Institutes of Geology and Palaeontology of the Institute of Anthropology and the Institutes of Mineralogy and Petrology).

**Theatres:** *Landestheater Tübingen* (6 Eberhard-Strasse): The theatre has its own company of actors and also plays in numerous theatres in the surrounding area; 400 seats. *Tübinger Zimmertheater* (16 Bursagasse): The theatre opened in 1958 and has 90 seats and also a cellar theatre with an adaptable auditorium. The company works principally in the field of progressive theatre.

**Environs: Bebenhausen** (5 km. N.): The monastery of Bebenhausen is in a pleasant valley near to Tübingen. After the Cistercians a Protestant seminary moved in at the

*Hölderlin tower*

time of the Reformation (1560–1807); the philosopher F.W.Schelling was a pupil in the late 18C. Later the monastery became a royal hunting lodge. It now houses a department of the Württemberg state museum.

**Former Monastery Church of St. Maria:** The church was built by the Cistercians in 1188–1228 in the austere style of the Order; it was originally a basilica with a flat roof. A huge sandstone window with ornate tracery was installed in the choir in 1340, and the heavy crossing tower was added in 1407. At the time of the Reformation two-thirds of the nave,

9 bays in all, were amputated to leave the present stump. The vaulting dates from the 15&16C.

**Monastery buildings:** The centre of the complex is the monastery courtyard with its late Gothic cloisters (1471 – 96) and charming well chapel. The mature Gothic summer refectory is immediately adjacent. In the E. wing are the chapter house, the parlatorium (where the monks, who were under an oath of silence, could hold essential conversations) and above all the so-called brothers' hall. The lay refectory and the winter refectory are 16C modifications or new buildings.

# U

## Überlingen 7770
Baden-Württemberg       p.420☐F 20

**Catholic Parish Church of St. Nikolaus/Münster** (Münsterplatz): The Münster was built in several stages. It started as a simple hall church, which was replaced by a new building in the 12C. The present Münster was built between 1512 and 1563 and is important above all for its magnificent furnishings. The *high altar* by J.Zürn (1613–16) is very fine indeed: it has a large number of figures and was equally influenced by the Gothic and Renaissance styles; the same is true of the *tabernacle*, also by Zürn (1611), which is of unusual design. The late Gothic stone pulpit is attached to the pillars of the nave, as are the figures of Christ and the 12 Apostles (1552). The striking *rosary altar* (1631) in the first S. chapel is by J.Zürn's brothers Martin and David. The Mount of Olives on the S. exterior side of the church is by L.Reder (1493).

**Franziskanerkirche** (Franziskaner-strasse): In the 18C, the 15C church was decorated with stucco, and frescos were painted in the nave. The high altar was created by J.A.Feuchtmayer in 1760.

**Rathaus** (Am Marktplatz): The Rathaus was built in the 15C and is famous for its *Ratssaal* (council chamber), designed by the local architect J.Russ in 1490–4. The individual estates of the empire are represented as statuettes, the earthly powers by King and Emperor and the divine powers by Christ, Mary and John. W. of the Rathaus is the so-called *Kanzleigebäude* (chancellery building).

**Städtisches Museum** (30 Krummenbergstrasse): The house of the Reichlin-Meldegg family, built in the 15C, today houses the Städtisches Museum. As well as the exhibits themselves the house chapel

*Münster, Überlingen*

*Detail from the Ratssaal, Überlingen*

and pulpit are by J.A.Feuchtmayer, assisted by J.G. and F.A.Dürr. The *high altar* is designed to a complex step pattern. The *Gothic miraculous image* is from the former church. The altar figures are some of Feuchtmayer's finest sculptures, and he was also responsible for a splendid putto on the *Bernhardsaltar* known as the *honey eater*: this is a reference to the quality of his attention to the honey-sweet speech of the rhetorically gifted St.Bernhard. Only 8 of Feuchtmayer's 14 carved *Stations of the Cross* have survived. J.G.Dürr and his studio created the gilded busts (1757) on the gallery. The emblems of the Apostles portrayed in the busts are born by putti. G.B.G[mu]otz was responsible for the brilliantly coloured *ceiling paintings* (1750), which make a sympathetic contribution to this remarkably homogeneous architectural concept. The sequence of pictures begins in the apse with the theme of intercession (Esther before Ahasuerus, Mary before the Judges of the World) and is continued at the end of the nave with the Woman of the Apocalypse, surrounded by religious virtues and parts of the world.

is worth seeing: it was consecrated in 1486 and refurbished with ornate stucco figures by J.A.Feuchtmayer in the mid 18C; the ballroom also has first-class stucco work by artists of the Wessobrunn school.

**Cistercian Priory of Birnau** (Oberuhldingen): In 1746 the church of Nussdorf was moved to its present charming site above the lake. The new pilgrimage church was dedicated after a building period of only three years. This is P.Thumb's finest creation and its very high standard of decoration and furnishing makes it one of the most sparkling examples of SW German baroque. The *W. façade* on the lake side is cool and symmetrical; the doorway, the window frames and the round niche with the *Maria Immaculata* were sculpted by J.A.Feuchtmayer. The octagonal bell tower has a decorative dome. The ornately decorated sections of the shallow-vaulted *interior* are unified by a gallery extending as far as the apse. The stucco, statues, altars

**Uelzen 3110**
Lower Saxony                                  p.414☐I 6

**Protestant Church of St.Mary** (1 An der Marienkirche): This church, first mentioned in 1281, was rebuilt after the Second World War in a somewhat different form; rebuilding continued until 1954. Its chief characteristic is the base of erratic rock on which the brick hall building stands. The hall has excellent rib vaulting supported on thick round pillars, in contrast with the choir, added *c.*1380, which is bathed in light. The most precious possession of the church and emblem of the town is the 'Golden Ship', an early Gothic centre piece in gilded copper plate, which is stored in a niche in the area under the tower. It is presumed to date from the 13C and is just over two ft. high. Other surviving furnishings are the 1756 rococo organ, the 15C brass chandelier, the 16C shrine of St.Anne, several gravestones and the marble memorial tomb for Prior Stillen (d. 1702).

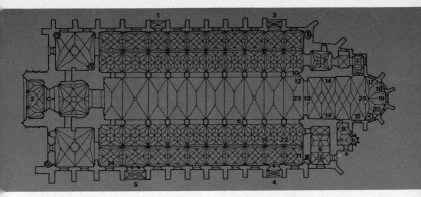

**Ulm, Münster 1** W. N.doorway, 1356 **2** Portico with main doorway **3** E. N.doorway **4** E. S.doorway, bridal gate **5** W. S.doorway, c. 1380-1400 **6** Foundation relief of the laying of the foundation stone, late 14C **7** Neithartkapelle **8** Bessererkapelle a) S. window, 1420 b) Small choir, 1430 c) Crucifix **9** Konrad-Sam-Kapelle with stained glass dating from 1957 **10** Figure of Hans Ehinger **11** Kargaltar, 1433 **12** Tabernacle, 1467-71 **13** Sedilia by J.Syrlin the Elder, 1468 **14** Choir stalls by J.Syrlin the Elder, 1469-74 a) Women's side b)

Men's side **15** Medallion window, early 15C **16** Font, c. 1470 **17** Johannes window **18** Kramer window by P.v.Andlau, 1480 **19** Ratsfenster by P.v.Andlau, 1480 **20** Window of St.Anne and Virgin Mary **21** Window of the Virgin Mary rejoicing **22** Holy-water stoup by J.Syrlin the Younger, 1507 **23** Altar with painting of Last Supper by H.Schäufelin the elder, 1515, and above it triumphal Cross and wall painting of the Last Judgement, 1470-71 **24** Parler stone **25** Chancel altar, so-called Hutzaltar, by M.Schaffner, 1521

**Heilig-Geist-Kapelle** (Lüneburger Strasse): The chapel was mentioned for the first time in 1321, and contains a notable 16C Mary altar. Some 15C stained glass was taken over from the St.Viti chapel.

**Museums:** *Heimatmuseum* (36 Lüneburgerstrasse): The museum is housed in a neoclassical building and has prehistoric and artistic and cultural collections. *Mühlenmuseum Suhlendorf* (15 km. SE of Uelzen): 36 full-scale wind- and watermills in an open-air museum.

---

### Uhldingen-Mühlhofen 7772
Baden-Württemberg                    p.420☐F 21

**Lake village of Unteruhldingen:** This early German settlement was reconstructed on prehistoric Stone and Bronze Age remains on the banks of Lake Constance. In nearby *Seefelden* the late Gothic Catholic church of *St.Martin* is worth a detour.

### Ulm 7900
Baden-Württemberg                    p.420☐H 19

The area around the former imperial city of Ulm (which now has almost 100,000 inhabitants) was inhabited even in the Old Stone Age, and its excellent site on the Danube has always encouraged commercial development: Ulm has been an inportant trading centre since the Middle Ages. The city received its charter in 1164 and became directly subordinate to the Emperor in 1274. The growth of the Ulm in medieval times can be seen from the two ring walls; the first defines the core of the old town, the second was built in the 14C and enclosed so large an area that the town did not outgrow it until the 19C.

**Münster** (Münsterplatz): The Münster in Ulm is undoubtedly one of the most important ecclesiastical buildings in Europe. Its dimensions are enormous (135 yards long, 53 yards wide at the nave, 136 ft. high, area 5577 square yards, tower 528 ft.

high), but the Münster is not just one of the largest churches; its incomparable architecture and excellent decoration put it among the finest. An inscription shows that building began in 1377. Many families of architects and builders worked on it, including the Parlers and the Ensingers; the Münster was not finally completed until 1890. *Exterior:* The tower, the tallest church tower in the world, demands a high proportion of one's attention; there are two smaller towers on the E. side. The finest of the 5 doorways, which are all ornately decorated with figures, is the main W. doorway. Among the figures on the arches those of Mary and the Apostles are the most important (*c.*1420, by Master Hartmann); they are outstanding examples of the Soft Style. On the central pillar of the doorway is H.Multscher's famous 1429 *Man of Sorrows*; other figures in the porch are by Syrlin the Younger and represent evangelists, church fathers and martyrs. *Interior:* The nave has steep arches directing attention towards the choir. Despite damage by iconoclasts in the 16C the furnishings of the Münster have great unity and are extremely lavish. The once ornate wall paintings have only survived in fragments, however (on the pillars of the central aisle

and the *fresco of the Last Judgement* (1471), one of the most important examples of late Gothic monumental painting). The choir windows, striking for their size and the splendour of their colouring, are magnificent specimens of 15C stained glass. The *tabernacle* (l. of the choir arch) is one of the finest by German artists (1464–71). The statues in the lower part are by N.Hagenauer and the figures in the upper section are ascribed to H.Multscher (Moses, David and an unidentifiable figure). The *pulpit*, created by B.Engelberg in 1499, was given a wooden canopy by J.Syrlin the Younger in 1510. Finally the *choir stalls*, which are said to be the best in Germany. They were made by J.Syrlin the Elder in 1469–71, and are one of the most important achievements of German wood-carving. Most of the 60 altars were destroyed by the iconoclasts of the Counter-Reformation, but the present high altar should be mentioned: it is the *Sippenaltar* made in 1521 by M.Schaffner for the area under the tower.

**Other churches in Ulm:** *Dreifaltigkeitskirche* (Lange Strasse): The church dates from 1617–21 but was destroyed by air raids in the War and survives only as a ruin.

*Ulm, panorama with Münster*

The 14C sacristy has been equipped as a chapel. *Protestant Garrison Church* (Frauenstrasse): The church, built by T.Fischer in 1908–10, is considered to be an epoch-making achievement of the architecture of the period.

**Rathaus** (Rathausplatz): The Rathaus dates from 1360 but was rebuilt in its present form in 1420. The splendid sculptures representing Electors and Emperors as Bearers of the idea of Empire are by H.Multscher (from 1427). The astronomical clock was installed in 1520, but had to be renovated by I.Habrecht in 1580. The painting on the E. and N. side is presumed to be by M.Schaffner.

**Neuer Bau** (Neue Strasse): H.Fischer erected this building in 1585–93, originally as a corn store, but he nevertheless gave it a Schloss-like exterior and the courtyard in particular adds to this impression. The portal is the work of C.Bauhofer, and the staircase tower was created by P.Schmidt in 1591. The figure of St.Hildegard, the wife of Charlemagne, which decorates the fountain in the courtyard is only a copy of C.Bauhofer's 1591 original, now in the museum.

*The Münster in Ulm is one of the most important religious buildings in Europe*

*The Rathaus in Ulm is decorated with magnificent sculptures*

**Museums:** *Ulmer Museum* (92–6 Neue Strasse): The collection, founded in 1882 and now extending over almost 50 exhibition rooms, centres on late Gothic art in Upper Swabia. It also exhibits modern art from 1890 to the pesent day. *Deutsches Brotmuseum* (17 Fürsteneckerstrasse): The museum is devoted to the history of bread, but aims above all to foster awareness of the problem of hunger in the world.

**Theatres:** *Ulmer Theater* (73 Olgastrasse): The theatre was opened in 1969; it has 815 seats and its own opera/operetta and straight theatre companies. *Theater in der Westentasche* (6 Herrenkellergasse): Straight theatre, 80 seats.

**Also worth seeing:** *Schwörhaus* (Schwörhausgasse): The building is a reminder of the tradition that the governing mayor and guild had to swear annually on the city constitution, and the idea is kept alive in the annual festival of 'Schwörmontag'. The house was built in 1613 and rebuilt in baroque style in 1785. *Metzgerturm* (Unter der Metzig): The 14C 'Leaning Tower of Ulm' leans nearly 7 ft. to the NW. *Fischer- und Gerberviertel:* Several arms of the Blau flow through this part of the town, in which fishermen and tanners used to live; many picturesque motifs have survived. *Fountains:* The fountains are mainly 14C and can be found in the Weinhof, the Marktplatz, the Neue Strasse, the Plätzle and the Münsterplatz. The market fountain ('Fischkasten') is by J.Syrlin the Elder and was completed in 1482. The originals of the 3 figures of knights are in the museum.

**Environs: Erbach** (7 km. SW): *Catholic*

*Parish Church of St.Martin:* refurbished in 1767–9 with *stucco decoration* by I. and A.Finsterwalder and *frescos* by M.Kuen, a pupil of Bergmüller (1768); there is also a carved *Madonna* (c.1490) of the Ulm school. The 16C *Schloss* is a charming Renaissance building housing a *Schloss museum*.

## Unkel 5463
Rheinland-Pfalz                                    p.416☐C 12

**Catholic Parish Church:** The original Romanesque basilica (c.1200) was rebuilt as a Gothic hall c.1300. The exterior is easily recognised by the three unusually ordered but pleasing saddleback roofs. Other striking features are the ornate baroque furnishings with a high altar picture by M.Preti (1605) and the Romanesque font (c.1200), the 15C painted Pantaleon reliquary and a crucifix and holy sepulchre, both 15C.

**Freiligrath-Haus:** Ferdinand Freiligrath lived in Unkel from 1839–40.

## Urschalling (über Prien)
Bavaria                                             p.422☐M 20

**St.Jakob** (2 km. S. of Prien): The church on a knoll above the Chiemsee is presumed to date from the 12C. During restoration work in 1941&2 medieval wall paintings were revealed; they are considered to be the finest surviving medieval work in Bavaria; some are said to be 13C, the majority 14C.

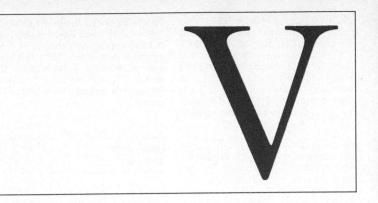

# V

## Varel 2930
Lower Saxony      p.414□E 5

**Protestant Church** (3 Schlossplatz): Erratics, granite ashlar and brick were the materials used in the various building periods of this church, which was completed in the 14C; the oldest sections go back to the 12C. The interior furnishings are more important than the exterior; they were commissioned by Count Anton II von Oldenburg-Delmenhorst from the sculptor L.Munsterman and completed in the first quarter of the 17C. The central feature is the masterly altar (1614), which is a major mannerist work. The numerous figures are carved in alabaster in contrasting colours and set in an excessively ornate framework. The pulpit (1613), the font (1618) and a lectern are also by Munstermann.

**Heimatmuseum** (3 Neumarkt): Exhibits on the history of the town and the region.

*Alabaster altar, Varel*

## Veitshöchheim 8707
Bavaria      p.416□G 15

**Schloss:** The Schloss was built by H.Zimmer in 1880 – 2, probably to plans by Petrini, and extended c.1750 to plans by Balthasar Neumann. Significant areas of the present park and the ornate sculptural decoration by J.W.van der Auwera also date from this period; the park was laid out for Prince Bishop Adam Friedrich von Seinsheim to designs by P.Mayer of Bohemia with masonic motives. The majority of the sculpture for the complex, which is unique of its kind, is by F.Dietz, who was commissioned by the Prince Bishop and his building agent J.P.Geigel. The damage inflicted in the Second World War and by years of neglect has largely been repaired. The wonderful park is once more in the superb condition which made it famous; the Schloss itself and the lake are the focal points of the complex. The numerous statues, grottoes, pavilions, fountains, paths and squares are laid out in a unique mosaic pattern.

## Velbert 5620
Nordrhein-Westfalen　　　　　p.416□C 10

**Deutsches Schloss- und Beschlägemuseum** (20 Oststrasse): This museum of locks and door furniture could only be in Velbert, the centre of the German lock industry. The collections extend from the oldest keys to modern door furniture and present a complete history of the locksmith's art.

## Verden an der Aller 2810
Lower Saxony　　　　　　　　p.414□F 6

**Dom St.Marien** (Domplatz): Two 8&10C wooden churches were followed in 1185 by a massive basilica. Building continued for over 200 years until 1490, but despite this the Dom, with its unmistakeable copper roof, has considerable unity of appearance. The splendid proportions of the interior justify its reputation as one of the most important buildings of the period in Lower Saxony. Round pillars and rib vaulting blend to lead the eye to the choir, which is lit by a large tracery window. The Gothic wooden sedilia (first half of the 14C), the most valuable item of the otherwise undistinguished *furnishings*, is also in the choir. A Romanesque font and the sarcophagus of Bishop Philipp Sigismund (d.1623) and the gravestones and tombs of other bishops are also worth seeing.

**Protestant Church of St. Andreas** (19 Grüne Strasse): This church was built in 1212–20. Bishop Yso, who did a great deal for the development of the town, and who is buried here, had the brick church built. The most important item of the furnishings is Yso's grave slab. It was made of brass in 1231 and is the first memorial in this material. The pews date from the early 18C and the altar was assembled in the 19C from baroque carvings.

**Protestant Johanniskirche** (30 Ritterstrasse): The oldest parts are 12C but the

*Veitshöchheim, Schloss with park*

present church was largely built in the 15C. The triumphal cross and a notable tabernacle are 15C work. The altar furniture is dated 1623.

**Houses:** The following are the most striking of the surviving older houses: a 1577 agricultural labourer's house (7 Struktur-strasse); the half-timbered house at 24 Obere Strasse (*c.*1600) and the 1708 brick building (10 Grosse Fischerstrasse) which houses the *Heimatmusuem.*

**Deutsches Pferdemuseum** (7 Andreas-strasse): Wide-ranging collection of horse-drawn carriages, horseshoes, coins, medals and show harnesses.

**Environs: Sachsenhain** (2 km. E.): accumulation of 4,500 erratic blocks.

---

**Vierzehnheiligen = Staffelstein 8623**

Bavaria                                        p.418☐K 14

---

**Pilgrimage Church:** Opposite the former Benedictine monastery of Banz (q.v.) on the other side of the Main is the pilgrimage church of Vierzehnheiligen, built in 1743–72 (after Banz). There is no doubt that the splendid Benedictine monastery opposite exerted considerable influence on the design. The present magnificent building replaced a little chapel which had been the goal of countless pilgrimages. The prilgrimage goes back to the vision of a shepherd to whom the Christ Child and the 14 Auxiliary Saints appeared on numerous occasions in 1445 – 6; the free-standing altar by J.M.Küchel (Gnadenaltar) represents this vision. Balthasar Neumann, who was only responsible for part of the design of the monastery of Banz, created here his most beautiful church in Franconia. The artists who worked on the interior were a match for the great Neumann. Apart from Küchel, the principal participants were the brothers Johann Michael and Franz Xaver Feuchtmayer, who along with J.G.Üblherr were also responsible for the stucco on the Gnadenaltar. The ceiling frescos, among

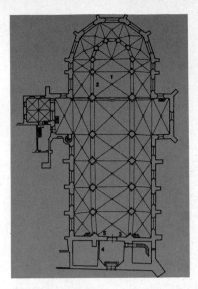

**Verden, cathedral 1** Romanesque font **2** Gothic sedilia, 1st half of 14C **3** Sarcophagus (1594) of Bishop Sigismund (d. 1623) **4** Bronze tombstone slab of Bishop Barthold (d. 1502) **5** Two 16C monuments to bishops

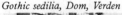

*Gothic sedilia, Dom, Verden*

the finest achievements of the period, are by J.I.Appiani. The excellent overall effect of all these elements makes the church of Vierzehnheiligen one of the most important works of sacred art and architecture of the period. It is easier to understand Neumann's design if an incident which occurred during the building period is described: Neumann originally intended to place the Gnadenaltar (see above) in the crossing, but was prevented from doing so by decisions made by the building supervisor, Krohne, without his knowledge. Neumann therefore decided to place the altar in the nave and to surround it with an oval. This oval touches on 2 smaller longitudinal ovals and 2 considerably smaller lateral ovals. The transepts are circular and also meet the central oval; thus the individual areas of the church blend imperceptibly into each other. The *priory building* is adjacent to the NE, built in 1745&6 to plans by Küchel.

*Pilgrimage church of Vierzehnheiligen near Staffelstein*

*Vierzehnheiligen*

**Villingen-Schwenningen 7730**
Baden-Württemberg          p.420☐E 20

Villingen, first mentioned in 817, was a

Münster in various phases. If the two towers are included, the building was not finished until the 16C. The most striking exterior features are the late Gothic tracery windows and the Romanesque doorway beneath them (the S. doorway is also very fine). A few items remain of the original furnishings; they include the stone pulpit (*c.* 1500–10) with fine sculpted decoration and the 14C Nägelin crucifix on the altar of the Cross. The choir stalls and other items of the furnishings were added in the 18C.

**Museums:** *Altes Rathaus* (Rathausgasse): The museum is housed in the late Gothic Altes Rathaus with Renaissance extension, and has exhibits on pre- and early history, applied arts, sculpture and painting. free imperial city from the 12C and combined with Schwenningen to form a single town in 1972.

**Liebfrauenmünster** (Münstergasse): The earlier building was destroyed in the fire of 1721 and replaced by the present

*Franziskaner-Museum* (Am Riettor): Collections on folklore and finds from the Celtic period, and a special section on the dating of archaeological finds. *Heimatmuseum* (16 Kronensteasse): development of clock and watchmaking in the last 400 years, with a collection of about 1500 clocks and watches.

**Also worth seeing:** *Former Franciscan Monastery*, founded 1268, with church, cloisters and chapel. *Former Benedictine Monastery* (in Schwenningen) with 18C church and monastery buildings.

---

## Visbek 2849
Lower Saxony                                    p.414☐E 6

**Stone graves:** These neolithic graves were mass graves for tribes or even entire village communities. One of the smaller graves is known as the *sacrificial table,* a group 109 yards long as the *Visbek bridegroom,* and a group 87 yards long as the *Visbek bride.*

---

**Vierzehnheiligen 1** Gnadenaltar **2** St. -Blasius-Altar **3** St. -Georgs-Altar **4** St. -Franziskus-Altar **5** St.-Antonius-Altar **6** Ceiling painting a) Adoration of the Shepherds b) Annunciation c) Joseph's dream d) Auxiliary Saints with Trinity e) Emperor Henry and Empress Kunigunde f) Abraham's sacrifice g) Jacob's ladder h) Adoration of the Magi **7** High altar **8** Pulpit

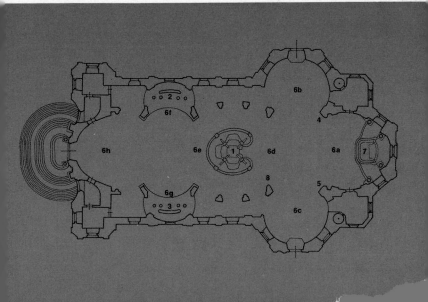

*Stone graves near Visbek*

## Vohenstrauss 8483
Bavaria                                    p.418□M 15

**Schloss Friedrichsburg:** Pfalzgraf
Friedrich von Vohenstrauss began to build
the Schloss in 1586 and it was finally completed in 1593. It has six towers, 4 at the
corners and 2 on the long sides (the central S. tower was added in 1903). The façade includes a fine step gable. Since 1972
the Schloss has accommodated municipal
or other local authority offices.

**Städtisches Heimatmuseum** (9 Marktplatz): Local and folklore collections.

## Volkach 8712
Bavaria                                    p.418□H 15

**Catholic Parish Church:** The church
was built in 1423–1597, and the building
was radically altered in 1754 to form a hall
with a vaulted wooden ceiling. The interior was subsequently redesigned by
notable artists, and is pure rococo. The
stucco is by N.Huber (1754), the frescos
by M.Wolcker (1753). Little remains of the
high altar in its original 1739 form: it was
rebuilt in 1792 by P.Wagner, who was also
responsible for some of the wooden figures
and the pulpit.

**Pilgrimage Church of Maria am
Weingarten** (on the road to Fahr): The
church was much talked about a few years
ago when the 'Volkach Madonna', a rosary
Madonna by Tilman Riemenschneider,
was stolen but then recovered as the result
of an action launched by a major periodical. The Madonna is one of the artist's last
and most mature works, and dates from the
first quarter of the 16C.

**Rathaus and Marktplatz:** The Rathaus,
built from 1544, is a Renaissance building;

*Schloss Friedrichsburg, Vohenstrauss*

the double open staircase is a distinctive feature. The Madonna fountain and the houses around it make the market place into a harmonious whole.

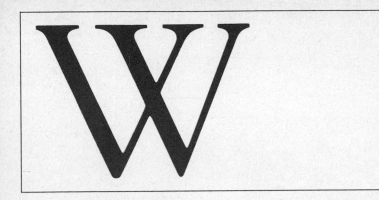

# W

## Waiblingen 7050
Baden-Württemberg                    p.420□F 17

**Protestant Michaeliskirche** (21 Alter Postplatz): The church dates from·1480–9. The tower has a square ground plan and dominates the otherwise low hall building. The nave has net vaulting, the choir rib vaulting. The pulpit (1484) and a relief of the Archangel Michael are worth seeing.

**Nonnenkirche** (19 Alter Postplatz): The church was built by H. von Ulm in 1496. The lower storey is an ossuary and the upper part a church. The rib vaulting and the ornate Flamboyant tracery are worth seeing.

**Heimatmuseum** (Kurze Strasse): Exhibits on the history of the town and a regionally based art collection in the old deanery.

## Waldburg 7981
Baden-Württemberg                    p.420□G 20

**Schloss:** The present complex was built from 1525 to replace older buildings destroyed in the Peasants' Revolt; there are remains of earlier walls in the residence. There are several fine examples of medieval ceilings and panelling, of which the best are in the Rittersaal. The 16&17C furniture has largely survived. The Schloss is now a museum.

**Also worth seeing:** The lower part of the tower of the 16C Catholic parish church is 14C and the interior is baroque (1748). Some of the decoration goes back to the period of the church's origin (figure of the Redeemer, Mater Dolorosa, altar panel). 17&18C half-timbered houses.

## Waldsassen 8595
Bavaria                              p.418□M 14

**Cistercian Convent of St. John the Evangelist:** The convent was founded in 1131 and the present buildings date from 1685–1704. The architect was A.Leutner of Prague and building was supervised by G.Dientzenhofer with his brother Christoph as mason. The stucco is by the N. Italian Master G.B.Carlone. The frescos are of the Prague school and by J.Steinfels. Carlone's greatest achievement is the red and black marble *high altar* (1696). The paintings by C.Mono show the Crucifixion in the lower part and God the Father in the upper part. The other altars in the transept and in the chapels are also worth seeing. The *choir stalls*, on which M.Hirsch worked until 1696, have paintings with putti, figures of the Apostles and

*Stiftsbibliothek, Waldsassen* ▷

*Cistercian convent of St. Johannes, Waldsassen*

other elaborate baroque ornamentation by C.Mono. The finest of the *convent buildings* is the *library*. It was completed in 1725 and has outstanding life-size carved figures; this unusual decoration is brilliantly set off by P.Appiani's stucco work.

**Environs: Kappel** (4 km. NW): The *Pilgrimage Church of the Holy Trinity* was built in the 17C on the site of an earlier pilgrimage chapel mentioned in 1527; the trefoil design is by G.V.Dientzenhofer. The unusual complex is built around three semicircular niches with half domes (conches), above each of which is a round tower corresponding with the three ridge turrets on the tent-shaped roofs.

**Waldshut-Tiengen 7890**
Baden-Württemberg        p.420☐D 21

**Parish Church** (in the NE of the Old Town): The Gothic choir was incorporated when the church was rebuilt in 1804. The interior is essentially neoclassical, with decoration executed almost exclusively in marble. The altars are the work of J.F.Vollmer.

**Rathaus** (Kaiserstrasse): A baroque building completed *c.*1770.

**Heimatmuseum** (62 Kaiserstrasse): The local history museum is housed in a 16C building and includes prehistoric exhibits.

**Walkenried 3425**
Lower Saxony        p.414☐I 10

**Former Cistercian Monastery of St. Maria and St.Martin:** The Cistercians who founded the monastery in 1129 involved themselves in the most lucrative local enterprises (mining, smelting, cattle

*Ruined Cistercian monastery, Walkenried*

breeding) and thus made the monastery into one of the richest in Germany. The church, which was finally consecrated in 1290, was badly damaged during the Peasants' Revolt (1525) and has only survived as a ruin. It is 272 ft. long and one of the largest churches in Lower Saxony. The 13&14C *monastery buildings* are largely intact; the finest features are the beautiful cloisters and well house (*c.* 1350). The former chapterhouse is now used as a Protestant church, and has a pulpit dating from 1662.

**Also worth seeing:** *Former hunting lodge:* built in 1725–7 for Duke Wilhelm August von Braunschweig-Wolfenbüttel.

---

**Wangen im Allgäu 7988**
Baden-Württemberg                    p.420☐G 21

**Catholic Parish Church of St. Martin**

(Marktplatz): The present church dates from the 14&15C; it is a basilica with three aisles and round pillars. The most striking item of the furnishings is the Renaissance grave slab of Vogt von Summerau (d. 1511).

**Rathaus and Pfaffenturm** (Marktplatz): The Rathaus was adapted to its present baroque design in 1719–21, but the building dates from the 13–16C. Fine features are the façade and the impressive scrolled gable.

**Hinderofenhaus** (Marktplatz): The courtyard is the most interesting feature of this Renaissance house built in 1542 for the Hinderofen family.

**Town wall:** The finest feature of the 14C town fortifications is the *Ravensburger Tor*, which has survived in good condition. It was radically remodelled in the 17C and repainted in the 19&20C. The *Pfaffenturm* by the Rathaus (q.v.) has also survived, along with the *Lindauer Tor* (also known as the St.-Martins-Tor) and the smaller *Pulverturm*. Two sections of the town wall itself are also still intact.

**Museums:** *Deutsches Eichendorff-Museum* (31 Atzenberg): The museum was founded in 1954 and is devoted to the life and work of the poet Joseph Freiherr von Eichendorff (1788 – 1857); exhibits include manuscripts, first editions, letters and pictures. *Gustav-Freytag-Archiv* (27 Atzenberg): Another literary archive devoted to the author and critic Gustav Freytag (1816–95). *Hermann-Stehr-Archiv* (29 Atzenberg): devoted to the life and work of Hermann Stehr (1864-1940). *Heimat- und Käsereimuseum* (Eselmühle): local history, cheese and folk art of the Allgäu.

---

**Warburg 3530**
Nordrhein-Westfalen                    p.416☐F 10

**Altstädter Kirche/Marienkirche** (Josef-Kohlstein-Strasse): The building is 13C, extended in the 15C, and the tower gallery and spire date from *c.*1900. The principal

attraction in the church is the 1580 silver altar cross by A.Eisenhoit.

**Johanniskirche/Neustädter Kirche** (Kirchplatz, 49 Hauptstrasse): As in the case of the Altstädter Kirche the gallery and roof of the tower were not completed until the turn of the century. The church was built from the 13–15C. The interior is dominated by pillars in a cruciform pattern and outstanding groin vaulting. The most important features of the decoration are the 15C statues on consoles on the attached columns.

**Heimatmuseum** (35 Sternstrasse): Collections on the history of the town and archaeological finds.

**Also worth seeing:** 1582 *Rathaus* (between the Old and the New Town), *Burgturm* (An der Burg), *Sackturm* (Stadtmauer), *Johannisturm* (Burggraben).

**Environs: Daseburg** (3 km. NE): The *ruins* of the former *Burg Desenberg* (12–14C) of the Counts of Northeim and later of Henry the Lion are on a high basalt outcrop; the massive *keep* and *traces of the walls* have survived.

*Ravensburger Tor, Wangen*

*Johanniskirche, Warburg*

## Warendorf 4410

Nordrhein-Westfalen p.414□D 9

Warendorf is the local administrative centre; it received its charter *c.*1200 and was an important centre of the linen trade and a member of the Hanseatic league from 1370-1623. The older parts of the town have survived to a large extent and include town houses, half-timbered buildings, squares and churches. The town is now the home of the Nordrhein-Westfalen regional stud, the German Riding School, the German Olympic Riding Committee, the German Army Sport School and the Federal Centre for the Modern Pentathlon.

**Parish Church of St.Laurentius:** The church was built after the great fire of 1404 and is a copy-book example of a Gothic Westphalian hall church. The interior is equally correct and includes a high altar which is an important work of German painting, created *c.*1450 by the Master of Warendorf, a pupil of Konrad von Soest and an artist of equal calibre.

**Franciscan Church and Monastery:** Hall church with a baroque interior.

**Heimathaus der Stadt Warendorf** (in the Rathaus in the market place): The Rathaus was built from 1404, and has an old council chamber, a mayor's parlour and an upper room (Upkammer). The museum covers domestic life in previous centuries and has a model of a Saxon settlement (AD 600-800) and temporary exhibitions.

## Wasserburg am Inn 8090

Bavaria p.422□M 20

Wasserburg has important literary associations: sections of the manuscripts of Wolfram von Eschenbach's 'Parzival' and 'Willehalm' were found here.

**Parish Church of St. Jakob** (5 Kirchplatz): The famous Landshut architect H. von Burghausen (known as 'Stethaimer')

*High altar, parish church, Warendorf*

is presumed to have been in charge of the building of the church from 1410, and was responsible for the narrow hall with side chapels between the buttresses, and the excellent stellar vaulting. S.Krumenauer added the choir to complete the main building in 1445 and the tower dates from 1478. The finest item of the baroque interior is the pulpit carved by the brothers Zürn in 1638-9.

**Frauenkirche** (Marienplatz): The baroque interior of this 14C church was not completed until the second half of the 18C. Of the older furnishings a 15C Madonna, late-15C figures of St. Blasius and St. Apollonia and a 1520 font have survived.

**Burg:** The Burg was built in 1531 for Duke Wilhelm IV; its most striking feature are the step gables. Inside the Burg are three net-vaulted passages connected by straight rather than curved staircases, an unusual feature for the period. There is a

◁ *St. Jakob*                    *Frauenkirche*

finely decorated hall on the first floor. The corn store attached to the W. of the main building dates from 1526. The Schloss chapel is between the Schloss and the corn store (1465). The stucco work was added in 1710.

**Rathaus** (2 Marienplatz): J.Tünzel, who was also responsible for the Schloss chapel (see above) built the Rathaus with its tall gable in 1457–9. It was subsequently much rebuilt and altered, but the original idea of combining council chamber, ballroom and store under one roof can still be appreciated.

**Städtisches Heimatmuseum** (15&17 Herrengasse): Covers local and craft history and folklore.

**Also worth seeing:** The oldest of the numerous buildings which have survived almost unchanged across the centuries is the Irlbeckhaus at 93 Schmidzeile (1497).

There are many other houses with regional characteristics, often with flat façades, arcades on the ground floor and roofs invisible behind high walls.

**Environs: Greisstätt-Altenhohenau** (10 km. S.): The *rococo interior* is the most interesting feature of the *Monastery Church of St. Peter and St. Paul,* part of the first Dominican monastery in Bavaria. The altars are by I.Günther, the choir fresco by M.Günther and the nave fresco by J.M.Hartwanger. Also of interest are 14&15C *miraculous images,* the so-called *Kolumban Christ Child* (15C), attributed to the Master of Seeon, and a marble grave slab with coat of arms for Knight Konrad von Laiming auf Amerang (1446).

**Wedel/Holstein 2000**
Schleswig-Holstein                    p.412☐ G 4

This town on the N. bank of the Elbe be-

came rich and important by trading in oxen, and its self-esteem is reflected in the *statue of Roland* which is unique in Germany in this form. It dates from the late 16C and is made of sandstone. The figure's Imperial status is confirmed by orb, sword and crown.

---

**Weiden über Lövenich = 5000 Köln 40**
Nordrhein-Westfalen　　　　　　　p.416□A 11

**Roman burial chambers:** The Roman burial chambers near Weiden were discovered in 1843; they date from the 1&2C and are in the best condition of any N. of the Alps. The room is 14.5 by 11.5 ft and 13 ft. high. There are couches, and excellent 2C marble busts in the large wall niches.

---

**Weikersheim 6992**
Baden-Württemberg　　　　　　　p.422□H 16

**Schloss:** The Schloss and its park form one of the most important Schloss com-

◁ *Burg, Wasserburg*

plexes in Baden-Württemberg. Some medieval sections have survived, but the building is essentially Renaissance; the only baroque additions are the mews and the gatehouse. The main building, consisting of two sections abutting at right angles, dates from 1586–1603. The Schloss is important for the brilliance of its interior rather than its outward appearance. The most important room is the *Rittersaal*, which reflects the passion for hunting of Count Wolfgang von Hohenlohe, for whom it was built. B.Katzenberger's paintings on E.Gunzenhäuser's coffered ceiling are unique of their kind; they represent hunting scenes, based on Dutch prints; the animal heads on the walls are good quality stucco work. There is a gallery of portraits of members of the Hohenlohe family. The Schloss park, laid out from 1709, has an orangery and a lot of statuary and is one of the finest baroque gardens in Germany.

---

**Weilburg 6290**
Hessen　　　　　　　　　　　　p.416□E 13

**Schloss:** There was a Burg as early as 906 on the steep slope above the town and a

*Roman burial chamber, Weiden*

*Rittersaal, Schloss Weikersheim*

loop in the Lahn. From the 12C it was the seat of the Counts of Nassau, who built a residence complex in the 16–18C. The present Burg is a colourful mixture of various styles, but the core of the buildings is Renaissance. The N. building in the inner courtyard is the most important. There used to be an open walk over the arcade with pairs of Ionic columns; there is now a gallery with two storeys. The baroque residence began to be extended in 1695–1703, concentrating on the decoration of the state rooms, almost all of which have survived with their original furnishings. The orangery, with a two-storey central pavilion and two side buildings, is at the S. end of the garden. The stucco is by C.M.Pozzi and the ceiling painting by M.Roos. J.L.Rothweil, the architect of the baroque complex, was also responsible for the square block which houses the *Protestant Schloss church* and the *Rathaus* under a single roof on the model of Mannheim (q.v.). The large hall of the

church is considered to be the most important Protestant baroque church building in Hessen. The restrained and masterly stucco is by A.Gallasini (1710–12), and the pulpit by A.Ruprecht.

**Market place:** The market place is a model layout by the baroque architect J.L.Rothweil (1709 Neptune fountain by Wilckens). The unified style of building, precisely aligned with the Schloss and echoing its levels, was also continued in some other streets (Lang-, Neu-, Schwanen-, Bogen-. Pfarr- and Marktgasse and Mauerstrasse). The 'drawing-board town' is completed by the two guardhouses on the Lahn bridge which mark the entrance to Weilburg.

**Heiliggrabkapelle** (in the cemetery S. of Weilburg): The octagonal rotunda is an important reminder of the veneration of the Holy Sepulchre in the late Middle Ages; it is modelled on the Church of the Holy

*Schlosshof and N.wing, Weilburg*

Sepulchre in Jerusalem. The 16C Calvary is associated with the chapel.

**Städtisches und Bergbaumuseum** (1 Schlossplatz): The museum was originally devoted to local and cultural history and has now been extended as a mining museum with a demonstration working level.

**Also worth seeing:** *Schloss Windhof:* Hunting lodge (1713–26) by J.L.Rothweil. *Shipping tunnel:* the first and only shipping tunnel in Germany, built for Duke Adolph von Nassau in 1841–7.

---

**Weil der Stadt 7252**
Baden-Württemberg          p.420☐F 18

**Catholic Parish Church of St. Peter and St.Paul** (Stuttgarter Strasse): The W. tower not only dominates the church, but is also the emblem of the town, the birth-place of the astronomer Johannes Kepler (1571–1630) and the reformer Johannes Brenz (1499–1570). A.Jörg incorporated the two 12&13C E. towers when he rebuilt the church, completing the work in 1492. The choir with stellar vaulting was added in 1519, the Renaissance tabernacle dates from 1611 and the interior was partially redecorated in the baroque period.

**Market place:** The 1582 Rathaus with arcades is a fine building which has survived almost unchanged. Kepler's birthplace is also in the market place; the *Kepler Museum*, a memorial museum to the scientist and astronomer, is housed in his birthplace, 2 Kupfergasse, and there is also a Kepler monument in the market place. The two *market fountains* carry figures of the Emperor Karl V and a lion bearing a coat of arms.

**Stadtmuseum** (12 Marktplatz): Covers pre- and early history and the history of the

town; the Speidel goldsmith's workshop with old tools is also of interest.

## Weilheim an der Teck 7315
Baden-Württemberg        p.420☐G 18

**Protestant Parish Church of St.Peter** (Marktplatz): The building, by the successful architect P. von Koblenz, was started in 1489 and completed in 1522, and it has remained almost unchanged since that time, although emphases have changed in the course of the centuries. The splendid vaulting is supported on sturdy octagonal pillars, which give the church its character. The most famous scenes in the ornate *wall paintings* (*c.* 1500) are the Judgement of the World over the triumphal arch and the representation of Hell at the E. end of the N. aisle and the Procession of the Blessed in the S. aisle; they are signed by T.Schick. The pulpit (*c.* 1520) was part of the original furnishings and is one of the finest works of masonry of the period. The plain carved choir stalls date from 1499, and the impressive galleries were built in 1599.

**Environs: Holzmaden** (3 km. W.): *Museum Hauff:* An interesting museum of primeval history with fossils (*c.* 150 million years old) from the nearby slate quarries, including skeletons of pterosaurs.
**Teck** (10 km. SW): the *ruined Burg of Teck* is 2,542 ft. above Owen and now used as a children's home. The Zähringerburg (mentioned in 1152) was destroyed in the Peasants' Revolt of 1525.

## Weingarten 7987
Baden-Württemberg        p.420☐G 20

**Benedictine Monastery Church of St.Martin of Tours and St.Oswald** (4 km. NE of Ravensburg): This large monastery complex with the domed church at its centre came into being in 1715–24 on

◁ *Parish church, Weilheim an der Teck*

*Benedictine monastery church, Weingarten*

a slope above the valley of the Schussen, NE of Lake Constance. Weingarten is the largest baroque monastery building in Germany. Weingarten did not just become famous because of its buildings, however, but also because of its library. The unusual sense of mass which is given by the exterior of the buildings is also felt in the interior. At its heart is the massive crossing dome, with powerful pillars in proportion. The best architects and artists of the period were involved in the building of the church. P.Thumb, E.Zuccalli, the Swiss K.Mossbrugger, F.Beer, A.Schreck and C.Thumb, and in the final phase D.G.Frisoni of Ludwigsburg were involved at the planning stage. Frisoni was responsible for the design of the dome, among other things; it was seen as a brilliant technological achievement at the time because of its dimensions. The stucco is by the great Wessobrunn master F.Schmuzer (1718) and the frescos are by C.D.Asam.

The central feature of the interior is the high altar, which is one of the items designed by Frisoni. The fine sculptural decoration is by D.Carlone (1719–23) and the paintings were contributed by G.Benso and C.Carlone. F.J.Spiegler painted the picture on one of the side altars (1783). Finally the excellent choir stalls are the work of no less an artist than J.A.Feuchtmayer (c.1730); the 1730 choir screen shimmers with colour. The organ is by J.*Gabler*. (1737–50).

**Alamannen-Museum** (28 Karlstrasse): finds from the Alamannic graves of the Merovingian period.

---

**Weinheim an der Bergstrasse 6940**
Baden-Württemberg                    p.416☐E 15

**Catholic Parish Church of St. Laurentius** (Marktplatz): This neo-Romanesque church (1911–13) took over the tower built by H.Hubsch in 1850 and all the most important features of the old interior; thus three altars and the fine pulpit (all c.1730) have survived. The 14–15C wall paintings were placed in the E. sections of the aisles. The numerous tombs of important Weinheim families were also transferred.

**Schloss** (9 Oberstrasse): The present Schloss complex was built in three stages. The original building was the *Pfalzgrafenschloss* (16C, much altered subsequently). The *Lehrbachsche Herrschaftshaus* followed in 1725. The *Berckheimsche Schloss*, which can be recognised by its neo-Gothic tower, was added in 1860–70.

**Burg Windeck** (1 km. E., 728 ft. above sea level): The Burg was built in the 12C to protect the possessions of the monastery of Lorsch. After severe damage in the Thirty Years War and the 'Dutch Wars' (1675) only the ring wall, the residence and the keep have survived.

**Heimatmuseum** (2 Amtsgasse): The local history museum is housed in the former house of the Teutonic Order with a 1710 doorway.

**Also worth seeing:** The finest of the old houses in the Old Town is the *Büdinger Hof*, which dates from 1582 and has an interesting staircase tower (15–17 Judengasse). The red, the blue and the witch's tower (Hexenturm) and the upper gate survive from the old town walls. The *Wachenburg* (2 km. E.) was built in 1907–13.

**Environs: Lindenfels** (20 km. NE): The town has numerous 18&19C *half-timbered buildings* and the baroque *Catholic parish church of St.Peter and St.Paul* (consecrated 1745) with a fine 18C *interior*. The *ruined Burg of Lindenfels* is a Hohenstaufen Burg (late-12C) set on a hill; it has polygonal walls and was much modified in the 14–16C and restored in the 19&20C. The 15C *outer works* and fragments of Romanesque walls in the S., W. and N. have survived.

---

**Weissenburg 8832**
Bavaria                              p.422☐I 17

**Protestant Parish Church of St. Andreas** (Martin-Luther-Platz): Construction started in the 14C but the building did not acquire its present form until 1520. The finest section is the *Michaelskapelle*, which is reached from the choir and is now used as a baptismal chapel. It has an ornate doorway, which contrasts with the otherwise austere appearance of the church. In the interior the choir is particularly striking. The best items of the furnishings are the three altars (high altar c.1500, Sebaldus altar 1496 and Mary altar c.1500.

**Rathaus** (Marktplatz): The Rathaus dates from 1470–6 and the tower was added in 1567.

**Town fortifications:** The town fortifications have survived in their entirety: 32 towers have people living in them! 2 of the finest gates are the 14C *Ellinger Tor* (Nördliche Ringstrasse) and the *Spitaltor* (Südliche Ringstrasse), which is also 14C.

*Monastery with monastery church, Weltenburg*

**Castrum Biriciana:** The Roman citadel was discovered in 1890. Fragments of the foundations of the main building, gates, towers and wells have survived. Not far from the citadel the remains of the largest Roman baths in S. Germany have been excavated and restored.

**Römermuseum** (Martin-Luther-Platz): Pre- and early history and cultural collections, including the Roman treasure found in 1979 (100 bronze statuettes), which is presumed to have come from a temple in the citadel.

**Also worth seeing:** *Spitalkirche* (am Spitaltor): Church dating from 1450–60 with interior furnishings renewed *c.*1729. Two stone figures have survived at the W. gate.

**Environs: Wülzburg** (3 km. E.): The five-sided Vauban fortress was built between 1588 and 1620 by G.Bernwart the

Elder, K.Schwabe and B.Bernwart and contains Germany's deepest rock well (545 ft. deep).

---

**Weltenburg = Kelheim 8420**
Bavaria                                    p.422☐L 17

**Monastery Church of St. Georg and St. Martin:** No less an artist than C.D.Asam created this magnificent building (1716–18), which is one of the best baroque churches in Germany. At the centre of the church is an oval space; the narthex is also oval, and thus contrasts with the rectangular choir. The main space is surrounded by Corinthian columns and small, ornately decorated side chapels; above the central oval are a massive dome and tambour; the tambour has a flat ceiling, but has side windows to admit the light. The large dome fresco (1721) gives an extraordinary three-dimensional effect because of

*Weltenburg*

*Wemding, St. Maria Brünnlein, interior*

the crown ring below it; this ring is supported by putti and by the builder of the church, Cosmas Damian Asam, who set his own memorial here. His brother, Egid Quirin Asam, is portrayed as an angel in one of the ceiling frescos; he was responsible for most of the stucco work in the church. The finest feature of the lavish interior is the high altar (1722–24). It shows the struggle of St.George, who is portrayed in three dimensions, riding through the gate of honour on the retable and about to start his fight with the dragon. The side altars and other paintings by the Asam family are likewise masterpieces. The adjacent *monastery buildings* were designed by F.P.Blank and date from 1714–16.

**Also worth seeing:** *Frauenberg chapel* (right of the church on the Frauenberg): The chapel is built on foundations said to go back to a previous building dating from *c.*700. The furnishings date from the first half of the 18C.

# Wemding 8853
Bavaria                                    p.422☐I 17

**Parish Church of St. Emmeram** (Marktplatz): The seal was set on the appearance of this church by the completion of the N. tower in 1619. The best feature of the interior is the high altar (1630–33). It shows clearly the transition from the medieval shrine tradition to baroque triumphal arch design. The side altars were created by D.Zimmermann in 1713; M.Zink painted the pictures.

**Pilgrimage Church of St. Maria Brünnlein** (Oettinger Strasse): The interior is by far the best part of this church on a little hill in the NW of the town. Father and son J.B. and M.Zimmermann were responsible for the stucco work and frescos, and produced a masterly performance in the late rococo style. The high altar is the work of P.Rämpl (1761).

*Werl, priory church*

**Heimatmuseum** (3 Marktplatz): Pre- and early history, local and cultural collections.

## Werl 4760
Nordrhein-Westfalen                    p.414□D 10

**Priory Church of St. Walburga** (1 Kirchplatz): The late Romanesque *tower* survives from a previous building and was incorporated in the Gothic *hall church*. The ground floor of the tower serves as a porch. The *altars* are particularly worth seeing: there is a 15C canopy altar in the S. aisle with an altar painting in the Soft Style; the side altar (*c.*1560) represents the Life of Our Lady. The *Calvary group* (*c.*1520) and the 17C *Pietà* in the N. nave are also notable.

**Heimatmusuem** (1 Am Rykenberg): Pre- and early history, local and cultural collections, including salt mining and pilgrimages.

**Also worth seeing:** The *Kapuzinerkirche* (old 18C pilgrimage church) and the *Franciscan Pilgrimage Church* (1903 – 5) with a 13C miraculous image (Madonna and Child). The *Missionsmuseum* (15 Meisterstrasse) has collections from areas visited by Franciscan missionaries.

## Wertheim 6980
Baden-Württemberg                    p.416□G 15

**Protestant Parish Church** (Am Markt): Attractive features of the late Gothic church are the *portal porch* between the nave and the tower and the little choir of the *Heilig-Geist-Kapelle* (*c.*1420). In the middle of the choir is the 17C *tomb of Count Ludwig II of Löwenstein-Wertheim* and his wife. Because of the canopy the tomb became popularly known as the 'bedstead'. Traces of late Gothic wall paintings were found on the two pillars in the nave in 1957.

*Wertheim, partial view with Schloss*

**Ruined Burg** (Altes Schloss): The Counts of Wertheim built the Oberburg in the 12C near the confluence of the Tauber and the Main; its *residence* has survived. The *chapel* was added in 1270. After further fortification in the 14&15C the *Unterburg* was built in the 16C and the transformation to a Schloss for state purposes began. In 1634 the Burg was destroyed by the Kaiser's troops.

**Glasmuseum** (Mühlenstrasse): Development of glass manufacture and techniques from the beginnings to the present day; collection of historic glass.

**Also worth seeing:** The basement of the *former Kilianskapelle* (N. of the parish church), a late Gothic building, served as an ossuary; the upper storey has ornate tracery and flying buttresses with finials. *(Heimatmuseum).* The *Rathaus* (Marktplatz) combines three former dwelling houses in a unified complex with staircase

tower. Late Gothic *fortified towers* are vestiges of the old ring wall. On the left bank of the Main in *Eichel*, which is part of Wertheim, is a small 13C church.

---

**Wesel 4230**
Nordrhein-Westfalen                                    p.414☐B 9

**Church of St. Willibrord** (Willibrordiplatz): The church was founded as early as the 8C. The 'cathedral of Wesel' was extended and altered in the 10C, 12C, 13C and 15C and not finally completed until the 19C, which produced many additions in the neo-Gothic style; large parts of the building were destroyed in the Second World War, but the 19C additions were not rebuilt, and so the church is now a basilica with transepts and ambulatory, much as it had been in the main building period 1434–1537. The most striking features are the ornate *net and stellar vaulting*, the *dou-*

*ble portal* of the tower and the first-class *tracery windows.*

**Fortifications:** Little remains of the once massive fortifications but the 1718 *Zitadellentor* (an der Zitadelle) and the 1772 *Berliner Tor* (Berliner-Tor-Platz). In the citadel is the *Schill-Museum* (history of the Schill Freicorps).

**Stadtmuseum** (14 Ritterstrasse): There are important exhibits on 16&17C gold and silversmiths' work and also on 19&20C art in the Rhine area.

**Theatres:** There are touring concerts and theatrical performances in the *Städtisches Bühnenhaus* (Martinistrasse, 771 seats) and the *Studio im Zentrum* (11–12 Ritterstrasse) from May to September.

**Also worth seeing:** Two modern churches, the *Friedenskirche zu den Heiligen Engeln* (in Fustemberg), built by H.Schilling in 1957 and *Mariä Himmelfahrt* (Pastor-Jansen-Strasse): the W. wall is decorated with variations on the motif of the rose window (1951 by R.Schwarz).

---

**Wesselburen 2244**

Schleswig-Holstein                    p.412□F 3

Wesselburen became known through its most famous son, the dramatist Hebbel (1813–1863), who was born here; there is a museum devoted to him (6 Osterstrasse, in the Kirchspielvogtei) and a monument outside his house at 49 Süderstrasse.

**Church:** The church was built in 1737–8. The architect was J.G.Schott (Heide), who made use of the outer walls of an earlier building, so that this church appears at first sight to be Romanesque. The baroque interior dates from 1738.

---

**Wessobrunn 8129**

Bavaria                    p.422□K 20

Wessobrunn is not only the place where the

'Wessobrunn prayer', the oldest text in the German langauge, was discovered, it is also the home of the best stucco workers Germany ever produced. The Wessobrunn school was seminal for stucco art in the 17&18C. The principal artists involved were the Schmuzer, Zimmermann and Feuchtmayer families, who decorated hundreds of churches, mainly in Bavaria and Baden-Württemberg. Some of the most important sacred buildings of the period, for example the church at Wies, are the work of the families concerned.

**Former Benedictine Abbey:** The so-called Fürstentrakt, with its powerful stucco and the Tassilosaal with lively hunting scenes in delicate malachite are worth seeing. N. of the abbey complex is the *Catholic Parish Church of St. Johannes,* built by F.X.Schmuzer in 1757–9 and decorated by him in shell-shaped stucco; the ceiling frescos are by J.Baader (1758). On the N. wall is a late Romanesque wooden crucifix (*c.*1520) from the Romanesque church, of which only the tower in the yard survives.

**Also worth seeing:** *Kreuzberg chapel* (1771–2) with ceiling frescos by M.Günther; the Wezzo fountain NE of the church and SE the *Tassilo lime tree* which is approximately 700 years old.

**Environs: St.Leonhard im Forst** (3 km. S.): Pilgrimage church with ceiling frescos by M.Günther (1761) built in 1724–35.

---

**Wetzlar 6330**

Hessen                    p.416□E 13

**Dom** (Buttermarkt): The oldest parts of the building date from 897, but shortly afterwards changes and extensions began which determined the history of this monumental building. Despite the long building period the Dom has a uniform appearance: a hall church on the pattern of comparable buildings in Marburg, Köln, Herford and Paderborn (qq.v.). The dominant feature is the massive three-storey

*Wessobrunn, cloister*

*Dom, Wetzlar* ▷

tower in the SW, finally completed in the late 16C. Before entering the building the visitor should notice the excellent portals, of which the W. portal, a double portal with a central column and elaborate sculptural ornamentation, is particularly fine. The interior hardly betrays the fact that over the centuries various architects have incorporated their own ideas into the overall design. The massive, finely-decorated pillars are a dominant feature. The painting is unusual, and was not renewed until the general restoration of 1904–15; it was then attended to again when war damage was being repaired; most notable are the large representation of St.Christopher on the W. wall and of the Alexius legend in the niches of the transept. Various fine features of the interior were destroyed in the Second World War. One of the best of the surviving pieces is the Pietà, which dates from *c.*1380 and can be seen in the Johannes chapel. The Dom is a church for both Catholics and Protestants.

**Other churches worth seeing** in Wetzlar: *Michael chapel* (S. of the Dom); *Former Franciscan Monastery Church* (Schillerplatz), *Former Hospital Church* (Lahnstrasse): this church, built in 1755 –64 by J.L.Splittdorf, has a remarkable combination of altar, organ and pulpit.

**Ruined Burg Hermannstein:** The *upper Burg*, built for Landgraf Hermann I von Hessen, is a typical example of a Gothic tower residence complex on the French pattern. The castle is set on the edge of a cliff, and looks very inhospitable; it was built as a border fortress against neighbouring territories. The NE side, from which an attack would come, seems totally impregnable, as there is another massive half tower in front of the wall. In the interior are two lofty storeys, each of which has a state room with groin vaulting. All that remains of the former top storey are two long, grotesquely towering chimneys. The *lower Burg*, which is no

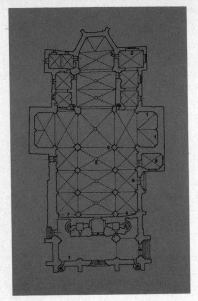

**Cathedral of Wetzlar 1** Remains of 14C wall painting on W.wall of nave and in transept **2** Pietà, c. 1370-80, 18C version **3** Virgin Mary, c. 1460 **4** Christ bearing the Cross, 1st half of 16C **5** Chandelier, early 16C, so-called Zunftleuchter **6** Pulpit, early 18C **7** Romanesque font **8** Johanniskapelle chapel with: originals from the S.portal (c. 1260-70), statuettes (from the Gothic W.building) of the Virgin Mary and the Angel of the Annunciation, 13C, Crucifixion, late 15C, cathedral treasure **9** S.portal on French model, with statue of the Virgin Mary

longer fortified, has smaller, more intimate accommodation and a large kitchen. A small chapel and the staircase tower have been maintained in good condition.

**Lottehaus and Städtisches Museum** (8-10 Lottestrasse): Charlotte Buff lived in a wing of the former court of the Teutonic Order; the building is now used as a museum.

**Jerusalemhaus** (am Schillerplatz): This half-timbered house, built c. 1700, was the home of Jerusalem, the legation secretary mentioned in Goethe's 'Werther'. It is one of the numerous old buildings which have

survived in Wetzlar; the most striking are the houses at 13 Fischmarkt, 8 Eisenmarkt and 11 Domplatz.

**Museums:** The municipal museum is in the Lottehaus and there is also a museum in the Jerusalemhaus. The *Palais Papius* (1 Kornblumengasse) has a collection of furniture, mainly 16–18C.

**Open-air festival:** There are performances of plays, opera, musicals, ballet and concerts in the Rosengarten open-air theatre (1800 seats).

**Environs: Kalsmunt** (1.5 km. S.) Only the *keep* (2nd. half of the 12C) and the late Gothic *doorway* of the inner bailey remain of the imperial *Burg* of Kalsmunt, built in the 12C by Friedrich I.
**Gleiberg** (16 km. NE): The *Protestant church* on the Burg hill has 15C *wall paintings* in the choir, a *mensa* and an ornately carved *pulpit* (1643); the 11C *Burg* which has a 98 ft. high *keep* (c. 1290), and a late Hohenstaufen *Burg chapel* (c. 1230) in the 15C *residence* is also worth seeing.

---

**Weyarn 8153**
Bavaria          p.422□L 20

**Catholic Parish Church of St. Peter and St. Paul/Former Augustinian Canonry Church:** L.Sciasca of Rovereto built this spacious late baroque pilastered church in 1687-93 on the site of earlier Romanesque (1133) and Gothic buildings. The relatively plain *stucco work*, consisting mainly of foliage and strapwork and the *vault frescos* showing scenes from the life of St. Augustine and the martyrdoms of St. Peter and St. Paul in the choir are the work of J.B.Zimmermann. The finest feature of the rococo furnishings is I.Günther's *wood carving*, surrounded with a skilful design by N.Neupaar; the carvings include an *Annunciation group* and a *Pietà* (both 1764), *putti*, the carved *Valerius shrine* and the ornate silver-framed *tabernacle* (1763) on the *high altar*, which was

*Monastery church, Wiblingen* ▷

made in 1693, the year of the church's consecration, and has statues of St.Augustine and St.Ambrose and an *altar painting* of St.Peter by J.B.Untersteiner. In the *sacristy*, with its 1694 stucco work, there are fine chalices and a splendid *monstrance*.

**Also worth seeing:** *Jacob chapel:* In the former Burg chapel (12C) are *wooden figures* by I.Günther (St.Leonhard and St. Sebastian, a Mater Dolorosa and Jacob) and also an interesting *altar painting* by J.Höttinger. *Maria-Hilf chapel:* In this little chapel (1780) with an onion-domed ridge turret is the fine late-Gothic *carved figure* of a Madonna.

---

**Wiblingen = Ulm 7900**
Baden-Württemberg                      p.420 □H 19

**Former Benedictine Monastery Church of St.Martin:** Wiblingen is now part of Ulm and has had a monastery, founded by Graf von Kirchberg, since 1093. The present building was built from 1714 and consecrated in 1783. The building was built by J.Specht to designs by J.M.Fischer. The church, a domed

rotunda, shows signs of incipient neoclassicism: the interior is magnificent, but restrained and refined, though J.Zick's dome paintings are suffused with dying flickers of baroque. The most important features of the interior are the high altar, also by Zick, the choir stalls by J.Joseph Christian and F. Christian and some excellent statues (pulpit, balustrade). The early-16C crucifix is now in the monastery church in Ulm. The adjacent monastery is famous for its *library*. The gallery is supported by columns decorated with life-size statues personifying intellectual and spiritual knowledge and virtues.

---

**Wienhausen 3101**
Lower Saxony                      p.414□H 7

**Former Cistercian Nunnery:** The famous 'Wienhaus tapestries' are displayed annually ten days after Whitsuntide; they date from the period between 1300 and 1500 and were made by nuns. The nunnery also contains other treasures which make it one of the most important artistic centres in Germany: wall paintings, stained glass, sculpture and collections of

*Library, monastery, Wiblingen*

household goods, cupboards and an incomparable collection of chests. The dominant impression of the exterior is made by the brick façades, and the most striking features are the stepped gables of the W. wing and of the nuns' choir. The nuns' church dates from *c.* 1300 and there are first class wall paintings of the period in the nuns' choir and the All Saints Chapel; this is some of the finest work ever produced by Gothic painters. There is also a very fine shrine of the Holy Sepulchre: it contains a wooden figure of the dead Christ dating from *c.* 1280; the Mary Altar of 1519 is of equal quality.

---

**Wies = Steingaden 8924**
Bavaria                              p.422□I 21

---

**Die Wies/Pilgrimage Church of Christ Scourged:** A figure showing the Scourging of Christ (*c.* 1730) was the starting-point for the building of the present church. The figure belonged to a peasant in the fields ('auf der Wies') who insisted that the figure had suddenly wept and thus required the building of a simple chapel in the fields. The miracle led to a pil-grimage which became so popular that it was decided to build a church for the purpose. The foundation stone was laid in 1746, with the permission of the superior monastery of Steingaden (q.v.), for the building which was to become one of the most important of the baroque period. D. Zimmermann, who designed the monastery at Steingaden and thereby set a memorial to himself and the age, was also commissioned to build the church at Wies. The church was consecrated in 1754 and the organ was installed in 1757 to complete the artistic whole. For Zimmermann it was the crowning glory of his life's work; this is shown not only by the church itself, but by the fact that he endowed a votive picture for it. He died in a house close by the church at Wies in 1766.
*The building:* The church at Wies is rococo to the last detail, and there can be almost no other building with such unity of style. It is built around a large central space with a semicircular porch and a narrow choir at the other end (see ground plan); at the end of the choir is the E. tower, and beyond that is a horseshoe-shaped building intended as the abbot's summer residence.
*Interior and furnishings:* D. Zimmermann led a team of the best artists of the period

*Wienhausen, panorama with former Cistercian convent*

◁ *Nuns' choir, Wienhausen*     *Wieskirche*

**Wies, Pilgrimage church 1** Ceiling painting by
J.B.Zimmermann (Trinity) **2** High altar; painting
by B.A. Albrecht, 1753-54; figures by A.Verhelst
**3** Ceiling painting by J.B.Zimmermann (angels
bearing the Cross) **4** Pulpit by D. Zimmermann **5**
Abbot's lodge by A. Sturm **6** Side altar a) St.
Margaret b) St. Mary Magdalene by J.G.Berg-
müller, 1756 c) Magdalene **7** Side altar a) Norbert
b) Christ and St.Peter by J.Mages, 1756 c)Bern-
hard **8** Four Church Fathers by A. Sturm

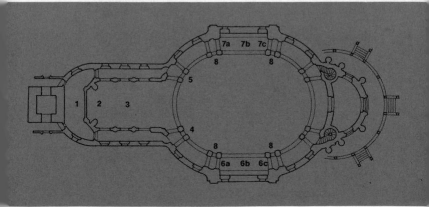

in the decoration of the church. The basic concept is that shape and colour should become more concentrated towards the sanctuary. The church at Wies is vibrant with joie de vivre; Dominkus Zimmermann's brother J.B.Zimmermann was responsible for a large proportion of the interior. His best work is in the unique frescos. The large dome fresco shows the empty throne of the Judge of the World facing the closed door of Paradise, and between them a rainbow heralds the appearance of Christ. The frescos are focussed on the high altar, at the centre of which B.A.Albrecht's painting represents the Incarnation of Christ. The four figures framing the picture represent the Evangelists; they are the work of E.Verhelst. The side altars in the lay building are hardly inferior. On the central pair of pillars are figures of the four Fathers of the Church (by the Füssen sculptor A.Sturm). The pulpit is another work of great distinction.

## Wiesbaden 6200

Hessen                                  p.416□E 14

Wiesbaden, set between the Rheingau and the Taunus, is the capital of Hessen and an important spa and conference town with 26 hot springs; it was a busy junction even in the Roman period. Its buildings are largely neoclassical or historicist.

**Greek Chapel** (Neroberg): The five gilded onion towers make this chapel an unmistakeable building; it was built as a funerary church for Duchess Elisabeth of Nassau, who came from Russia and died after only one year of marriage. The chapel was built entirely in the Byzantine-Russian style.

**Parish Church of Schierstein:** The church was built in the baroque style with a rococo interior.

**Stadtschloss** (Schlossplatz): The Schloss, built in 1837–42 by Dukes Wilhelm and

◁ *Wieskirche*

*Schloss Biebrich, Wiesbaden*

Adolf of Nassau, became a royal Schloss in 1866; Emperors Wilhelm I and II used it as their Wiesbaden residence and it is now the seat of the Parliament of Hessen.

**Schloss Biebrich** (Rheingaustrasse): The later Princes and Dukes of Nassau built the Schloss in baroque style between 1698 and 1744, and used it as a residence. The building faces the Rhine. The original baroque garden was converted into an English park by L. von Sckell in 1811. The Moosburg, built in 1807, was designed in the prevailing spirit of romantic historicism of which there are many other examples in Wiesbaden.

**Altes Rathaus** (Marktstrasse): The Altes Rathaus, completed in 1610, is the oldest building in the town. The Neus Rathaus of 1884–7 is a neo-Renaissance building.

**Kurhaus** (Parkstrasse): F. von Thiersch designed this building, which dates from

1904 – 7. It has a portico with 6 Ionic columns. The inscription reads 'Aquis Matticis'.

**Museums:** *Städtisches Museum* (2 Friedrich-Ebert-Allee): The museum houses a notable collection of paintings, a scientific collection and a collection of Nassau antiquities as well as numerous objects from the Merian collection.

**Theatres:** *Hessisches Staatstheater* (Christian-Zais-Strasse): The theatre is in the spa centre and has its own company for opera, operetta, musicals, straight drama and ballet. *Kleine Komödie:* Comedies and farces.

---

**Wildeshausen 2878**
Lower Saxony                    p.414□E 6

---

**Church of St. Alexander** (6 Herrlichkeit): The church was built in 1224–30 on a similar ground plan to the Dom in Osnabrück (q.v.). The wall of the section S. of the choir is striking: it is made of erratics, assembled in a masterly fashion. The interior is dominated by spherical vaulting and round arches. The best features of the furnishings are the late Gothic sedilia and the fine tabernacle, both first class sandstone work. There are notable wall paintings in the sacristy (early-15C and c.1300), and over its entrance is an early Gothic crucifix.

**Environs: Pestrup graves** (4 km. S.): The numerous *megalithic graves* and prehistoric *tombs* are considered to be the most important site of this kind in N. Europe.

---

**Wilhelmshaven 2940**
Lower Saxony                    p.414□E 4

---

The history of the town dates back only to 1856 when a naval dock was built. In 1869 – 75 the *Christuskirche* (Friedrich-Wilhelm-Platz) was built as a naval memorial church. The *Rathaus* (Kirchplatz) by F.Höger, one of the best-known architects of the early 20C, was built in 1929 for the town of Rüstringen, which later merged with Wilhelmshaven. The *Küsten- und Schiffahrtsmuseum* (coastal and navigation museum) (2 Rathausplatz) has exhibits on coastal settlements in Lower Saxony and the history of navigation. Two *museum ships* are also of interest (Kaiser-Wilhelm-Brücke). In the environs the *moated Schloss* at Gödens (18 km. SW) is also of interest.

---

**Wilhelmsthal = Calden 3527**
Hessen                          p.416□G 10

---

**Schloss** (2 km. S. of Calden): The Schloss at Wilhelmsthal is connected with the Schloss Wilhelmshöhe in Kassel (q.v.) by almost six miles of the Rasenallee (grassy avenue). The regents of Hessen had this rococo masterpiece built as a summer residence to a design by F. de Cuvilliés in 1743 – 70. The two side wings are only loosely connected with the *main building*, of which the *garden façade* is the main feature. In the interior the most interesting rooms are the *Musensaal*, the *Speisesaal* and the *Papageienkabinett*, for the quality of their stucco work and the way in which the architect has defined the space. J.H.Tischbein the Elder painted most of the portraits in the *Schönheitsgalerie*. The decor is completed by fine *wall coverings*, exquisite *furniture* and *Meissen porcelain*. The former French *park* was redesigned in the English style in 1794 – 9.

---

**Windberg 8447**
Bavaria                         p.422□N 17

---

**Premonstratensian Monastery Church of St.Maria:** This church on the slopes of the Bayrische Wald was built as a Romanesque basilica under the influence of Hirsau (q.v.). The *main doorway c.*1220 with a Madonna in the tympanum is particularly ornate. The interior was vaulted in the 16C and the stucco work dates from 1755. There is a fine figure of Mary on the *high altar*, and there are also outstanding altars by the pairs of pillars in the nave. The interesting Romanesque *font* dates from 1230.

## Wittlich 5560
Rheinland-Pfalz      p.416☐ B 14

The *Catholic parish church* (Marktplatz) was built at the beginning of the 18C in mock-Gothic baroque and has modern *windows* by Le Chevalier, A.Stettner, H.Dieckmann and G.Meistermann. The last artist was also responsible for a window depicting the Four Horsemen of the Apocalypse in the *Rathaus*, (1647, extended in 1922) in the charming *Marktplatz*, which has a baroque posthouse (1753).

## Witzenhausen 3430
Hessen      p.418☐ G 11

Remains of the *town wall* and two 18C *towers* and an older one indicate the original outline of the medieval town. In the gridlike network of streets there are many romantic-looking *half-timbered houses*; the three-storey *Renaissance Rathaus* is worth seeing, as well as the churches.

**Protestant Liebfrauenkirche:** The chequered building history of the church began *c*.1225 and ended with the restoration of 1931. Even from the outside the contrast between the broad nave and the soaring choir can be seen. In the interior the strange *pillars* are striking: they are a transitional form between Romanesque bevelled columns and Gothic bundle pillars. There are notable 16C *wall paintings* in the chapel under the S. gallery, and in the choir is the unusual *tomb of the Bodenhausen family*.

**Also worth seeing:** Little remains of the Gothic former *Wilhelmite Monastery of St.Nikolaus and the Holy Cross* (refectory, chapter house, church doorway). The *St. Michael Hospital* has a 1392 chapel with an attractively decorated tower.

**Environs: Berlepsch** (8 km. NW): *Schloss Berlepsch* goes back to a Burg (1368–9) which was much changed and enlarged in the 16&19C, and now has a fine park (*c*.1800).

*Rathaus, Wilhelmshaven*

**Ludwigstein** (5 km. SE): *Burg Ludwig-stein* (1415), one of the few German Burg complexes in good condition, has fine *half-timbered buildings* around the inner court-yard; it is now used as a Youth Hostel.
**Ziegenberg** (7 km. NW): Below the *ruined Burg* (1356–88) with its tall round *keep* which served as the Führer's head-quarters in 1944–5 is the memorial to Goethe's poem 'Dreifach gefesseltes Glück'.

## Wolfegg 7962
Baden-Württemberg            p.420☐G 20

**Parish Church of St. Katharina:** J.G.Fischer's building replaced the Col-legiate and Schloss church in 1733–42. The interior of the outwardly plain church is ornately decorated with stucco and frescos and the organisation of space is striking. The *stucco decoration* (from 1735) by J.Schütz and the *wall paintings* are good examples of rococo art. The *pulpit* (1760) by J.W.Hegenauer, the *choir stalls* (1755) by M.Bertele and several *memorial tombs* are notable.

**Schloss:** The Schloss, completed in 1580, is famous for its splendid *Rittersaal*. Along the walls are *22 wooden figures* represent-ing the Lord High Stewards. The *wall pic-tures* are framed in rocaille and show scenes from the Hercules legend and allegories of the regions of the world and the elements. Important objets d'art in the Schloss in-clude the *Waldseemüller map of the world* and a medieval house book.

**Also worth seeing:** *Bauernhausmuseum* (farmhouse museum) (29 Fischergasse): 17&18C house design in Upper Swabia and the Allgäu.

## Wolfenbüttel 3340
Lower Saxony                 p.414☐I 8

Wolfenbüttel, the former residence town, was the first Renaissance German town to be planned as a whole with Schloss, royal administrative buildings, houses for court officials and residential areas for citizens. About 500 Renaissance and baroque half-timbered houses give the town a rare historic charm. The writer and critic Less-ing, the philosopher Leibniz, the humorist Wilhelm Busch and the novelist Wilhelm Raabe are among the many famous people connected with the town.

**Church of Beatae Mariae Virginis:** Ar-chitect Paul Franke combined Gothic, Renaissance and baroque elements in this, the first significant Protestant church building; work started in 1608. The in-terior furnishings are impressive, particu-larly the high altar, 1571 font and the princes' vault with fine sarcophagi. The court director of music M.Praetorius was buried under the organ in 1621.

**Protestant Trinity Church:** This church was built in 1719 by H.Korb over the re-mains of the Kaisertor; its baroque façade gives a festive look to the end of the Holz-markt. Secular baroque court architecture predominates in the church, which is one of the most unusual buildings in the residence.

**Protestant Johanniskirche:** This is a plain half-timbered building with a tower like a campanile; it was consecrated in 1663 as the church of the 'Augustusstadt', a wor-kers' suburb. The Renaissance interior is worth seeing (organ, altar, choir, altar wall). Tombs of H.Korb and J.Rosenmüller.

**Schloss:** The Wolfenbüttel Schloss is the largest surviving Schloss building in Lower Saxony; it was the residence of the Guelph dukes from 1432–1753, and the Schloss museum deals with this period. The Renaissance tower was built in 1614 by Paul Franke and in 1715 the baroque fa-çade was added by Hermann Korb; it has an ornate stone doorway and sculptures in honour of the princely house. The poet dukes Heinrich Julius and Anton Ulrich lived in the Schloss and Duchess Anna Amalia, the founder of the Weimar Musen-hof, was born here.

**Herzog August Library:** The library was

*Rittersaal, Schloss, Wolfegg*

*Residenzschloss in Wolfenbüttel, the largest surviving Schloss in Lower Saxony*

founded in 1572 by Duke Julius and under Duke August (after the Thirty Years War) the collection became so large that it was known as the 'eighth wonder of the world'. The library was built in 1883–7 in the style of a Florentine palazzo and has a 'treasure house of books' in its museum rooms. The Herzog August Library is now devoted to research and is an international centre of book history.

**Lessinghaus:** The Lessing house was built in 1735 to the design of a French park château. Lessing wrote 'Nathan der Weise' here, and the building is now a museum to Lessing and his period.

**Zeughaus:** The arsenal also served as a barracks and is now part of the library complex. There are temporary exhibitions on the history of books in the main hall.

**Lessingtheater:** Performances by well-known companies on tour from September to April (700 seats).

**Also worth seeing:** The half-timbered buildings in the Stadtmarkt, including the Rathaus and the municipal weighing office; Little Venice, with restored canals.

---

**Wolfhagen 3549**
Hessen                                     p.416□F 11

**Protestant Church of St. Anna and St.Maria:** The Gothic hall church with its slate-clad *tower* (1561) and *triumphal arch* edged in colour is reminiscent of the 13C building which preceded it. The *vaulting keystones* in the aisles and nave make up an unusual cycle on the Judgement of the World.

**Kreisheimatmuseum** (in the Renthof, 1

Ritterstrasse): collections on pre- and early history, the history of the town and crafts.

**Also worth seeing:** Only buildings from later periods remain of the 13C *Burg* of the Landgraves of Thüringen. The 17C *Rathaus* with its two heavily protruding half-timbered storeys is reminiscent of N. Germany, while the rest of the *half-timbered buildings* are in the local style. *Schloss Elmarshausen* (NE of Wolfhagen) is a 16C *moated Schloss*.

---

## Wolframs-Eschenbach 8802

Bavaria                                      p.422□I 16

According to ancient reports Wolfram von Eschenbach, the medieval poet after whom this little town is named, who became famous as the author of 'Parzival', is buried in the parish church. The *town fortifications* are largely intact and the old alleyways and trim gabled houses evoke centuries long past. The *Catholic Parish Church* was built in the 13C for the Teutonic Order and radically renewed in the 18C. In the course of this the hall church was redesigned in the baroque style . The altar in the Mary chapel (1751) and a rosary relief (1510) are worth seeing. The Rathaus has been accommodated in the 17C former *Schloss of the Teutonic Order* since 1859. The stone façade contrasts with the half-timbered buildings which surround it.

---

## Wolfratshausen 8190

Bavaria                                      p.422□K 20

**History:** The town was mentioned for the first time in 1003. The Counts of Wolfratshausen, a collateral line of the Counts of Diessen-Andechs, built a majestic Burg *c.*1100; everything but its foundations was destroyed by a spring thunderstorm in 1734. There are fine houses along the Marktstrasse. Wolfratshausen was granted the right to hold markets as early as 1280 and gained its charter in 1961. The history of the town is dealt with in the *Heimatmuseum*. The Wolfratshausen carnival

week takes place annually at Ascensiontide. In the Pupplinger Au, at the confluence of the Loisach and the Isar, is Europe's largest continuous *nature and countryside preservation area*. Raft trips on the Isar to Munich are an attraction for locals and tourists.

**Parish Church of St. Andreas:** The church was built in 1484 as a late Gothic hall church and partially destroyed by fire in 1619. The 210 ft. high onion tower was not added until the church was rebuilt in 1631. The interior has fine stucco work and a striking high altar.

**Cemetery Church** (in Nantwein): In 1286 Nantovinus, a pious pilgrim to Rome, was condemned to death on false charges and burnt at the stake. He was long revered as a popular saint and when the church was last renovated (new building in 1624) bones which were proved to date from the time of Nantovinus were found. The church is a gem of early baroque art.

---

## Wolfsburg 3180

Lower Saxony                                 p.414□I 8

This new town, well-known as the home of the Volkswagen factory, came into being when the factory was founded in 1937, and was built around the old Schloss. The new town was designed by P.Koller. After that the forest estate of Steimker Berg and the buildings in the centre of the present town were built. Planning regulations in 1955 confined the town within its present boundaries. The *Kulturzentrum* designed by the famous Finnish architect A.Aalto and built in 1959–62 houses a college and the town library. The *Theater der Stadt* was designed by H.Scharoun (1971–3). There are guided tours of the *Volkswagenwerk* on weekdays at 1.30 p.m.

**Schloss** (Alt-Wolfsburg): The Schloss is a reminder of the town's past. Only the *keep* remains of the 13&14C moated Burg; the other sections were added in the Renaissance period and the N. wing in the *courtyard* in the 19C, with great sensitiv-

*Schloss in Wolfsburg*

ity. The Schloss now houses the *Hoffmann-von-Fallersleben-Museum* and the *Städtische Galerie*, which shows 20C German art.

**Churches:** Wolfsburg has a large number of *modern churches* by distinguished architects. The 13C Protestant *St. Annen-Kirche* has survived from the old town. Near the Schloss the Protestant *St. Marien-Kirche* has 17C memorial tombs and gravestones and the *St. Nikolaikirche* has a fine Gothic *altarpiece*.

---

**Worms 6520**
Rheinland-Pfalz                          p.416☐E 15

---

Worms is a middle-sized town with an illustrious past; it has important industries and is a centre of the German wine trade. Under the Romans Worms was a garrison town and the capital of the Civitas Vangionum. Burgundians and Huns, Franks and Alemanns fought here, the opening of the Nibelungenlied is set here, and more than 100 Reichstag meetings were held, including the Reichstag of 1521 (the Diet of Worms), to which Luther was summoned. Few medieval buildings have survived, though the exceptions are significant. Worms was badly damaged in the Thirty Years War, in the years of revolution in the 18C and in the Second World War. The city now has 78,000 inhabitants.

**Dom St. Peter** (1 Domplatz): The Dom is one of the most important examples of high and late Romanesque architecture in Germany; comparable buildings are to be found in Speyer and Mainz (q.v.). It was preceded by other buildings, including one under Bishop Burkhard in 1018; work on the present building started in 1171, the first sections were ready for consecration in 1181 and the monumental cathedral was completed in 1230. High Gothic modifications followed and the chapels and the

S. doorway were completed, but nothing has changed in the essential fabric since the 13C. The mighty building has remained impervious to every danger which war could threaten, particularly when faced with the French in the Thirty Years War. Careful maintenance work after the Second World War ensured the building's survival. *The building:* The high and late Romanesque design of the Dom shows astonishing unity. The interior is 361 ft. long, 89 ft. wide and 85 ft. high in the nave; the height under the domes is 131 ft. It is a pillared basilica with a double choir. Above the W. choir and the E. crossing are the two distinctive towers, enclosed by two more slender, higher side towers. The exterior of the building is ornately decorated, particularly in the E. façade. In the lower storey of the N. tower the frieze over the arches is supported by corbels in the shape of men's and animals' heads; lions and bears can be recognised. This ornate three-dimensional decoration, unique in its kind and quality, is continued on the great doorways. The relief of 'Daniel in the Lions' Den', now in the interior of the Dom, was formerly the tympanum of the S. doorway. The Gothic S. doorway shows a selection of unique sculptures representing the biblical message of salvation. *Interior and furnishings:* When looking W. the most striking features are the twelve-part rose window and the three smaller rose windows in the N. tower. The nave has pillared arches to the left and right, each connected to a bay; in front of every second pillar is a half-column supporting the wall arches and the ribs of the vaulting. The original furnishings have not survived. The majority are 18C, including the outstanding high altar designed by Balthasar Neumann (1738–42). The sculpture is by J.W. von der Auwera. The choir stalls are the work of an unknown master (1760). Only a few sculptures (including a 12C crucifix) remain of the old furnishings, along with some reliefs (including the c.1430 relief of the Holy Virgins Embede, Warbede and Willebede, in the Nikolaus chapel). The tombs are not as fine as those in the other Imperial German cathedrals. The *Bishof-*

◁ *Dom, Worms*

*shof* has housed the *Lobdengau-Museum*, formerly in Ladenburg, since 1968 (finds from the Roman town of Lopodunum, and Odenwald folk painting of the 18&19C).

**Former Collegiate Church of St. Martin/Catholic Parish Church** (Ludwigsplatz): In the present rib-vaulted pillared basilica, built from 1170 to the same design as the Dom, there are traces of an earlier building started in 991. Parallels with the Dom are unmistakeable, but the Martinskirche cannot compete in the matter of towers (only the N. tower dates from the time when the church was built, the other was added in 1960–1). The best feature of the church is the ornate decoration of the W. and S. doorways. All the doorways of the otherwise austere and almost undecorated building are 13C.

**Andreaskirche** (Weckerlingsplatz): This church is also clearly related to the Dom, which seems to influence the whole town. The church has been much as it is today since radical rebuilding in the 12C; it is now used as a museum (see museums). The Romanesque cloisters, of which the W. walk has survived, are the best of the buildings adjacent to the church; the walk has seven arches with sturdy pillars.

**Paulskirche** (Paulusplatz): Worms has the enthusiastic builder Bishop Burkhard to thank for this important church by the Dom; he commissioned it at the beginning of the 11C, and a document suggests that it was built on the site of the Salic fortress of Duke Otto, which the bishop had acquired. The present building was shaped by 13C modifications and the nave was completely rebuilt at the beginning of the 18C. There are traces of the first building in the cloisters S. of the church. In the S. oratory and the sacristy there are 13C wall paintings, which were untouched by war damage or have been restored.

**Liebfauenkirche** (21 Liebfrauenring): After a long building period the present church was completed in 1468. The exterior of the basilica is dominated by the two towers with tall stone spires. The sculptural decoration on the W. doorway

and the tracery window in the gable of the nave are also striking, and there is ornate sculpture on the S. doorway as well. The original interior furnishings have not survived. The miraculous image, once sought by pilgrims, dates from the 14C.

**Other churches worth seeing in Worms:** *Magnuskirche* (Weckerlingsplatz): 13C church; the damage sustained in World War Two has been repaired. *Bergkirche in Hochheim:* a church on a hill with a fine Romanesque tower (12C) and an 11C crypt. *Parish church in Herrnsheim:* The church has a fine interior and interesting tombs (some 15C) in a chapel-like extension.

**Synagogue** (Martinsplatz): The synagogue was probably the most important in W. Europe because of the effectiveness of Rabbi Raschi, who died in Worms in 1180. It was destroyed in a pogrom in 1938 but has been fully restored. The *Mikwe,* the underground women's bath, may now be visited again and nearby is a *Jewish cemetery* laid out in the Middle Ages.

**Schloss Herrnsheim** (1 Hauptstrasse): This Empire Schloss of the Dukes of Dal-

*Dom*

◁ *Dom, high altar*

*Dom, choir stalls*

berg has fine state rooms on the ground floor. In the English park, at the NW corner of the main building, is a round tower of the 15C Burg which preceded the neoclassical building. The Schloss is now owned by the city of Worms.

**Luther monument** (Lutherring): The Luther monument, created in 1868 by the sculptor Rietschel, commemorates Luther's appearance before the Diet of Worms.

**Museums:** *Museum der Stadt Worms* (7 Weckerlingplatz): The museum is in the former collegiate church of St. Andreas (q.v.). It has collections on pre- and early history, the history of the town and Land and special collections on Luther's appearance before the Reichstag (Diet) of Worms in 1521. *Stiftung Kunsthaus Heylshof* (9 Stephansgasse) Paintings by European masters of the 15–19C, stained glass and glass vessels, ceramics, drawings.

**Theater:** *Städtisches Spiel- und Festspielhaus* (4 Bahnhofstrasse): This new building was opened in 1966 and has 844 seats.

---

**Worpswede 2862**
Lower Saxony                          p.414□F 5

This village on the moor at the foot of the Weyerberg developed into an artists' colony which became world-famous. The poet Rilke and many others praised the surrounding countryside. The painters' colony included F.Overbeck, H.Vogeler, H.am Ende, O.Modersohn and Paula Modersohn-Becker. The *Café Worpswede* (1925) by B.Hoetger, who created the Böttchergasse in Bremen (q.v.) and the *Hoetgersche Wohnhaus* are Jugendstil buildings.

**Museums:** *Ludwig-Roselius-Museum* (5 Lindenallee): large collections on European pre- and early history. *Grosse Kunstschau* (3 Lindenallee): permanent exhibition of works by Worpswede artists. *Heinrich-Vogeler-Sammlung* (Haus im Schluh): has a collection of Lower Saxon folk art and exhibits on the life and work of H.Vogeler.

**Wunsiedel 8592**
Bavaria                               p.418□L 14

The writer Jean Paul was born in 1763 in this town in the Fichtelgebirge, formerly part of the Egerland; his birthplace is at 5 Jean-Paul-Platz. The *Fichtelgebirgsmuseum* (1–2 Spitalhof) is one of the most important local museums in Bavaria, with a fine collection of minerals and stones. Wunsiedel is famous for the annual *Luisenburg-Festspiele*, a festival on the oldest natural stage in Germany (1769 seats).

---

**Wunstorf 3050**
Lower Saxony                          p.414□G 8

*Collegiate Church:* This church has been much altered in the 700 years of its existence, but the essentially Romanesque fabric has survived. In the interior are a late Gothic tabernacle and some notable tombs.

---

**Wuppertal 5600**
Nordrhein-Westfalen                   p.416□C 11

Wuppertal has 420,000 inhabitants and is the centre of the textile and iron manufacturing industry in the Bergisches Land. The history of the town did not begin until 1929, when Barmen and Elberfeld were combined. Wuppertal became famous for its *overhead railway*, which runs at a height of 39 ft. and connects 18 stations between Vohwinkel and Oberbarmen. The *Laurentiuskirche* (22 Friedrich-Ebert-Strasse) was built in the years 1828–32 and is one of Germany's best neoclassical churches. The most interesting part of the *former Kreuzbrüder Monastery Church* (15C, in Beyenburg) is the interior, particularly the baroque high altar and the late Gothic choir stalls. Part of the former cloister was included in the church as the N. aisle.

**Theatres:** The *Wuppertaler Bühnen* perform opera, operetta and ballet in the Opernhaus (Friedrich-Engels-Allee, 851 seats) and straight theatre in the

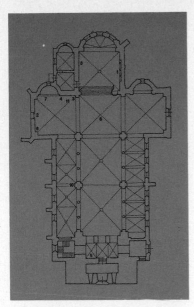

**Wunstorf, collegiate church 1** Sedilia, Romanesque **2** Statues of the patrons a) Cosmas b) Damian **3** Tomb of Count Johann v.Wunstorf and Roden, 1334 **4** Tomb of Count v.Wunstorf and his wife Walburgis, 1358 **5** Tomb of Abbess Alheydin de Monte (d. 1349) **6** Crucifix above the altar, 14C **7** Shrine in the baptism chapel, 3rd quarter of 15C **8** Tabernacle, c. 1500 **9** Tomb of Cordt v.Mandelsloh (d. 1537) **10** Memorial panel to Johann v.Holle and Katharina v.Heimburg, 1569 **11** Memorial to Sophie v.Münchhausen (d. 1751) by J.F.Ziesenis

Schauspielhaus (Bundesallee, 758 seats). The *Kammerspiele* (83 Gathe) also have their own company.

**Museums:** *Von-der-Heydt-Museum* (8 Turmhof) exhibits works by the French Impressionists and important Cubist works. There is also a good survey of 19&20C German painting. The historic *Uhrenmuseum* (clocks and watches) (11 Poststrasse) has 1,000 timepieces from a variety of periods. Other museums: *Missionsmuseum* (7 Missionsstrasse); *Städtisches Museum* (6 Geschwister-Scholl-Platz) and the *Friedrich-Engels-Gedenkstätte* (Friedrich-Engels-Allee), near to the birthplace of this famous son of the town; the house itself no longer exists.

**Also worth seeing:** The so-called *Schwimmoper,* an extremely modern swimming pool complex.

---

## Würzburg 8700
Bavaria                                      p.416☐H 15

The history of the town goes back to Celtic times. In the 7C a Frankish ducal court came into being on the bank of the Main, and in the following year Boniface made it a bishopric; the bishops were made Dukes of Franconia by Emperor Frederick Barbarossa in the 12C, and as a result of this the town developed into a European cultural centre in the following centuries. Würzburg's last great period was the 17&18C, as is shown by the number of buildings commissioned by the Prince Bishops of that time. Today Würzburg is the capital of Lower Franconia and the seat of the *Julius-Maximilians-Univerität*. The series of famous personalities closely connected with the town begins with the medieval poet Walther von der Vogelweide, who was buried here in 1230. M.Grünewald was born in Würzburg and T.Riemenschneider died in the town where he had worked for so long. The poet, novelist and painter M.Dauthendy (1867) and L.Frank (1882), novelist and dramatist, were also born in Würzburg. R.Virchow, W.Röntgen, E.Fischer and other important scientists worked at the university and Richard Wagner was chorus master at the Stadttheater for a short time.

**Catholic Parish Church of St.Burkard** (Burkarder Strasse): The church developed from the monastery founded by Bishop Burkard in 748. Its W. part is *Romanesque* and largely 11C, the *late Gothic* E. building (with transept and high choir) was added at the end of the 15C. The 1593 *altarpiece* on the S. wall of the transept is worth seeing, and next to it is a *Madonna* by T.Riemenschneider (*c.*1500). The *poor box* is also notable.

*Käppele, Würzburg*

*Tomb by T.Riemenschneider*

**Protestant Deutschhauskirche** (Zeller Strasse): The tower is late Romanesque, and the rest of the building very early Gothic. The church was built at the end of the 13C as the Commandery Church of the Teutonic Order. The *choir* is the first Gothic choir in Würzburg. There is excellent Gothic *masonry* on the corbels and the capitals of the vaulting supports.

**Dom.St.Kilian** (Domplatz): This cruciform pillared basilica with four towers was built on the site of a former 9C church. Despite the fact that building began *c.*1050 the church was not consecrated until a good 100 years later. Important work was carried out in the 13C, including the building of the E. tower. At the beginning of the 18C the important *Schörnborn chapel* was added; it was designed by the famous architects M. von Welsch and B.Neumann as a mausoleum for the Prince Bishops of the house of Schönborn. The Romanesque exterior of the Dom is at its most striking on the E. side. In the 18C the Milanese P.Magno transformed the interior with his baroque stucco. In the 60s of this century the *choir* and the *transept* were restored in the baroque style but the nave has the spatial austerity of the Romanesque period. The interior furnishings were decimated in the Second World War; the most important features are the numerous *tombs*, now placed between the pillars of the nave; only the Dom in Mainz (q.v.) has comparable works. They are arranged in chronological order, giving a clear view of 700 years of stylistic development. By the seventh and eighth N. pillars are the tombs created by Tilman Riemenschneider for Rudolf von Scherenberg (d.1495) and Lorenz von Bibra (d.1519) in red Salzburg marble. Other works by Riemenschneider are the *figures of Christ and two Apostles* (1502–06) in the SE of the transept and the *Apostle John* (N. aisle) and a *deacon* (with gospel) right of the choir steps. The *pulpit* by the famous sculptor M.Kern (1609&10) has

*Dom*

also survived from the old furnishings. There is a *wrought-iron railing* (1750–2) in front of the W. part of the nave, which formerly separated the E. section of the choir. An early medieval *crucifix* with a bearded head and the *high tomb of Bishop Bruno* (13C) are notable features of the *crypt*, which was renovated at the time of the restoration of the cathedral. The modern furnishings include the *altar* in the choir, created by A.Schilling to include the shrine of the three Frankish saints, and the various *bronze doors*. Buildings connected to the Dom include the *Schönbornkapelle*, which has already been mentioned, *cloisters* with four walks and important tombs, the *Sepultur* with more tombs and the two symmetrically arranged *sacristies* by Balthasar Neumann.

**Franziskanerkirche** (Franziskanergasse): The early Gothic building, completed in 1300, was badly damaged in the last war, but then restored. The arrangement of the

truss above the roof is unorthodox: the fine steel tubes have deliberately been left uncovered, so that the roof timbers can be seen above them. A *Pietà* from the studio of Tilman Riemenschneider and some *sculpted figures* remain of the old furnishings.

*Käppele/Pilgrimage Church of St. Maria* (Auf dem Nikolasberg): The domed rotunda is the work of Balthasar Neumann (1747 – 50). A staircase representing the sufferings of Christ leads to the church. Its situation high above the town gives this church particular charm. Important rococo artists were involved in the decoration: the stucco is by J.M.Feuchtmayer and the frescos were painted by M.Günther, a pupil of Asam.

**Marienkapelle** (Marktplatz): The building of this church on the site of the destroyed synagogue started in 1377 and continued for almost 100 years. The tower

*Alte Mainbrücke with Marienberg*       *Kaisersaal, Residenz* ▷

was the last part to be completed, in 1479; it was then modified on the pattern of the Frauenkirche in Esslingen in 1857. A high level of late Gothic artistic achievement is reached in the *sculpted decoration* of the exterior. The sides of the *Brautpforte* are decorated with T.Riemenschneider's Adam and Eve. The 14 Riemenschneider figures on the *buttresses* were created in 1500–6, but like the figures on the Brautpforte they have been replaced with copies.

**Marienkirche** (Burghof): The Burg church on the Marienberg (q.v.) is not only the oldest church in Würzburg, but has some sections dating from 706, thus making it the oldest church in Germany, alongside the Dom in Trier (q.v.). Alterations such as the 1603 rectangular choir, the ornate doorway and the baroque interior have blurred the overall picture, but have not destroyed the basic rotunda concept.

**Neumünster** (St. -Kilians-Platz): The bishop's church in Würzburg was built in the 8C on the spot where the Frankish apostle Kilian and his brother missionaries were murdered in 689. The present church is largely based on a 13C building. The church was redesigned in the baroque style from 1710 and the distinctive *domed building* by J.Greising dates from that period. The *façade* is often ascribed to J.Dientenhofer, but was probably built in cooperation with Greising. The *decorative statues* on the façade are by J.W.von der Auwera (1719). The church was badly damaged by air raids, and although it was possible to restore the exterior in its original form, some painful omissions had to be accepted in the interior.

**University Church** (Neubaustrasse): A.Petrini can be considered the actual architect of the church, as he took over the building begun by Bishop Julius Echter in 1696 and completely renewed it. The exterior is dominated by the vivid *coloured*

*Marienkapelle*

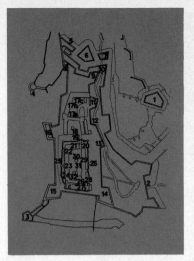

**Würzburg, Festung Marienberg 1** Teufelsschanze **2** Neutor **3** Werk Höllenschlund **4**
Maschikuliturm **5** Werk Frankenland **6** Reichs-
ravelin outworks **7** Werk Teutschland **8** Bastei
Mars **9** Bastei Bellona **10** Inner Höchberger Tor
**11** Bastei Werda **12** Schönborntor **13** Bastei Cae-
sar **14** Bastei St. Joh. Nepomuk **15** Bastei St.
J. Baptist **16** Bastei St. Nikolaus **17** Museum a)
Echterbastei b) Neues Zeughaus c) Kommandan-
tenbau **18** Pferdeschwemme **19** Scherenbergtor
**20** Kiliansturm **21** Altes Zeughaus **22** Former Hof-
stubenbau **23** Library building with inn **24** Ran-
dersackerer Turm **25** Medieval surrounding wall
**26** Fürstenbau with Bibratreppe staircase **27** Fürstengarten **28** Marienturm **29** Kammerbau **30**
Keep **31** Marienkirche **32** Fountain

stone façade, and the tower which Petrini
completed. The hints of late Gothic in the
Renaissance architecture are typical of late-
16C Julius Echter buildings.

**Other churches** (in alphabetical order):
The *Augustinerkirche* (Schönbornstrasse),
an early Gothic building with baroque
decoration by B.Neumann (1741–4). The
*Carmelite Church* (Sanderstrasse) by
A.Petrini has interesting graves in the
catacombs. The plain church of the monastery of *Himmelspforten* has a notable
early Gothic sculpture. *St. Jakob/Scottish
Church* (Schottenanger), this former 12C
monastery church was incorporated in the
rebuilt *Don-Bosco-Church* during rebuilding after the Second World War. *St. Peter*
(Petersplatz) was rebuilt in the 18C but the
W. towers of the Romanesque basilica have
survived. The 12C hall crypt of the
Benedictine basilica of *St.Stephan* has survived, but the church was renovated and
altered in 1790. The striking features of the

church of the *Stift Haug* (Hauger Pfarrgasse), built by A.Petrini in 1670–91, are
the domes and the tall W. towers. There
is a Tintoretto Crucifixion (1585) above the
high altar.

**Alte Mainbrücke** (Am Mainkai): The
picturesque stone bridge was built in its
present form in 1473–1543, and is a technical and artistic masterpiece of the period.
The *statues* are baroque additions.

**Alter Kranen** (W. end of the Julius-
Promenade): The son of B.Neumann built
this crane, a Würzburg landmark, in 1773.
The treadwheels which were originally
used to operate the crane have survived.

*Staircase, Residenz*

The Latin inscription means 'I receive, transport and dispatch anything you like'.

**Bürgerspital zum Heiligen Geist** (Theaterstrasse/Semmelstrasse): The 1371 Spitalkirche is the central point of the extensive complex, which was endowed by a bourgeois family. An attraction is the *Glockenspiel* (working at 11a.m., 1, 3, 5 and 7 p.m.).

**Marienberg** (Burgweg): The oldest parts of this *fortress* date from the early years of the 13C, with the exception of the Marienkirche (q.v.), which is part of the complex; the fortress is set on a ridge above the Main which had already been settled by Celts and Teutons; the appearance of this warlike landmark is softened by the vineyards on the hillside. The Bishops lived here on the Marienberg from 1253 – 1720; one of them was Rudolf von Scherenberg, who extended the fortress at the end of the 15C, but Julius Echter von Mespelbrunn is the most important of the

figures involved. After fires in 1572 and 1600 he rebuilt the complex as a Renaissance palace, but Bishop Johann Ph. von Schönborn's bastions and massive walls made the Burg back into a fortress (from 1650). The final additions were B.Neumann's 18C *Teufelsschanze* and *Maschikuliturm* (see ground plan). The fortress now houses the Mainfränkisches Museum.

**Haus zum Falken:** The unmistakeable *stucco façade* of this former inn was added in 1751.

**Juliusspital:** The infirmary was founded by Bishop Julius Echter and was modified on many occasions and then almost completely destroyed in the Second World War. Among the buildings restored was the central *Fürstenpavillon* with an 18C *pharmacy*. In the *park* is J.W. von der Auwera's *Vier-Flüsse-Brunnen* and a charming *pavilion*, probably the work of Greising.

**Rathaus** (Rückermainstrasse): The building dates essentially from *c.*1200; it was originally the home of a Burggraf Bishop; the upper storeys were added in the 15&16C. The colourful *façade painting* is 16C. The *Wenzelsaal* on the first floor is predominantly early Gothic. The *Rote Bau* forms the W. section of the Rathaus complex; it is an outstanding late Renaissance work in red sandstone.

**Residenz** (Residenzplatz): The Residenz is the masterpiece of the great baroque architect Balthasar Neumann, who worked in Würzburg and also died here (1687–1753); he was the Prince Bishops' director of building from 1719. Later M. von Welsch, the Viennese J.L. von Hildebrandt and French architects were also involved in the completion of the Residenz, which finally took over the role of the Marienberg (q.v.). The building encloses the large *main courtyard* on three sides, and there are two inner courtyards. In the interior are four halls, more than 100 rooms and a church. The Prince Bishops arranged storage space for 1.4 million litres of wine in the cellars. The most interesting feature is the *central building*, with the *arms of the prince bishops* on the gable and the portico balconies on the rear *garden façade*. The famous *staircase*, one of Neumann's most important achievements, has been restored to its former brilliance. The vaulting has a fresco by G.B.Tiepolo and its dimensions are unique in the history of art. The monumental work portrays the homage of the regions of the world (only 4 were then known) to Prince Bishop Greiffenklau. The finest of the magnificent state rooms are the *Gartensaal* (stucco by C.A.Bossi, frescos by J.Zick) and the *Kaisersaal*, in which the annual Mozart festival concerts are held. The stucco and the statues are again by Bossi, and the frescos by Tiepolo. The *Weisse Saal* and the *Hofkirche* should also not be missed. In the S. wing of the Residenz is the *Martin-von-Wagner-Museum* (q.v.). The adjacent *Hofgarten* dates from 1732 and its most outstanding features are the *stone sculptures* by P.Wagner

and the splendid *wrought-iron gates* designed by Neumann.

**University** (Neubaustrasse): Julius Echter, who founded the University in 1582, commissioned these extensive Renaissance buildings. The complex has four sections, and has a certain charm, particularly on the *courtyard side*; the street façades are somewhat monotonous.

**Theatres:** The *Stadttheater* (21 Theaterstrasse) was built in 1966 and has dramatic, operatic and operetta companies. The *Torturmtheater* (in nearby Sommerhausen) performs plays in its tiny 15C theatre, which has 50 seats.

**Museums:** The *Mainfränkisches Museum* (in the fortress of Marienberg) gives the most complete view of the work of *T.Riemenschneider*, as most of the originals of his best work have been assembled here with great tenacity; they were replaced with copies on their original sites. The rest of the collection is extensive and very varied but the *garden sculpture* by P.Wagner and F.Tietz from the Hofgarten in Veitshöchheim (q.v.) is exceptional. There is a also

**Würzburg, Residenz 1** Entrance hall (Weisser Saal in the upper storey) **2** Gartensaal; decorations 1750; ceiling painting by Johann Zick (in the upper storey: Kaisersaal; stucco by Bossi; ceiling painting by Tiepolo) **3** Stairwell; ceiling painting by Tiepolo, 1752-53 **4** State apartment **5** Courtyard church **6** Rondellsaal

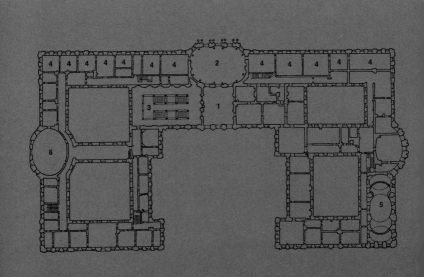

a baroque gallery, and some tomb sculpture and applied art. In the *Martin-von-Wagner-Museum* in the S. wing of the Residenz (q.v.) the most important items are *small-scale antique art*, particularly Greek vases and Roman sculpture, and European and German art from the 14–19C. The *Städtische Galerie* (3 Hofstrasse) exhibits painting, sculpture and graphics by Franconian artists of the 19&20C.

**Environs: Rimpar** (10 km. N.): In the *Parish Church of St. Peter and St. Paul* (1849&50) there are 7 *Grumbach tombs* in the area under the tower, including that of Eberhard von Grumbach (d.1487), which is considered to be Riemenschneider's earliest work. The *sculptures* on the Court Doorway of *Schloss Grumbach* are probably by M.Kern (*c.*1610).

**Maidbronn** (11 km. N.): On the high altar of the *Catholic Church of St. Afra* of the former Cistercian monastery destroyed in the Peasants' Revolt of 1525 there is the moving stone relief of the *Wailing Over the Body of Christ* (completed in 1525), one of the last and most mature works of Riemenschneider.

*Hofgarten and Residenz*

## Xanten 4232

Nordrhein-Westfalen                    p.414 □ B 9

Xanten is a key site in the history of the West. An army camp was established here in 15 BC as a base for campaigns against the Teutons on the right bank of the Rhine, and from here Varus marched to the Teutoberger Wald. Not far from an old legionary camp the civilian town of Colonia Ulpia Traiana with almost 10,000 inhabitants was established. Xanten became an important archaeological site because Colonia Ulpia Traiana was the only town N. of the Alps which was not built over.

*Dom, Xanten*

*St. Viktor, Dom*

The foundations survived underneath the fields and are being systematically excavated and in part restored.

**Dom/Former Collegiate Church of St.Viktor:** Friedrich von Hochstaden laid the foundation stone of the Dom St.Viktor in 1263. In 1933 a 4C double grave was discovered under the choir; it contained the bodies of two men who had met with a violent death. The name of the town comes from this Christian memorial ('to the saints', 'Ad Sanctos' = Xanten). The Dom is one of the most important churches on the lower Rhine. The monumental W. façade is the dominant feature of the exterior. Here, as elsewhere in the church, Gothic and Romanesque features blend in a characteristic fashion. The ornate furnishings, which are among the best to have survived from the building period, have remained almost intact, or have been restored since the Second World War.

There are more than 20 altars, of which the most important is the great Mary Altar by H.Douvermann (paintings by R.Loesen, 16C). There are 28 stone statues (some of them now in the Dom museum) of Apostles, Church Fathers etc. on the pillars of the nave.

The 1240 choir stalls have survived, and there is also a rare sedilia (*c.*1300) in the choir. In the N. of the Dom are *canons' quarters*, in which the best features are the *cloisters* (1543–6) and the *chapterhouse*, now the Dom museum. The Dom treasure, now almost all in the Regionalmuseum (q.v.), contains valuable gold and ivory work from the 5–15C.

**Also worth seeing:** The *Klever Tor* and another double gate have survived from the town fortifications. Parts of the walls have also survived, along with an 18C windmill. The centre of the town is medieval. *Regionalmuseum Xanten* (7–9 Kurfürstenstrasse): a museum devoted to the history of the town; temporary exhibitions and concerts are presented. In the canons' quarters are *excavations* from the Roman town of Colonia Ulpia Traiana; the *Archäologischer Park* (Am Amphitheater).

# Z

---

**Zell am Main 8702**
Bavaria             p.418☐G 15

**Former Premonstratensian Monastery of Oberzell:** The monastery was founded in 1128 then secularised at the beginning of the 19C and used as a factory from 1817–1901. From 1901 the complex was taken over by a catholic nuns' congregation and largely restored to its old condition. The three-storey monastery

*Zons, Kurkölnische Zollfestung*

building was designed by Balthasar Neumann but completed by his son (in 1770). In *Unterzell* there has been a three-storey monastery building since 1613 and a church built four years before that; the building replaced a monastery destroyed in the Peasants Revolt.

King Karl XII and built in 1708–11. After being destroyed in the Second World War it was rebuilt from the original plans as a community centre.

## Zwiefalten 7942
Baden-Württemberg                               p.420☐ G 19

## Zons = 4047 Dormagen 5
Nordrhein-Westfalen                             p.416☐ B 11

**Kurkölnische Zollbefestiging:** This customs fortress directly on the Rhine, built in the 14C to replace Neuss, has survived almost intact. Schloss *Friedeström* is on the Rhine side; it is surrounded by farm and other buildings intended to provide self-sufficiency. The former Herrenhaus houses the *Kreismuseum*, which is devoted to the history of the complex, it is unique of its kind, and gives an impression of life in a medieval fortress community.

**Former Abbey Church/Münster:** The present church and the adjacent monastery buildings were built from 1739–47; from 1741 J.M.Fischer of Munich was in charge of the project. The dominant interior feature is the double columns forming a 'lane' to the choir and high altar. Behind the columns are the equally ornate chapels, gilded balustrades and lavish galleries. The monumental high altar is itself an integral part of the column arrangement. The huge figures on the altar (and the majority of the other sculpture) are by J.J.Christian. The

*Ceiling painting, Zwiefalten*

## Zweibrücken 6660
Rheinland-Pfalz                                 p.420☐ C 16

**Alexanderkirche** (Hauptstrasse/Alexanderplatz): This late Gothic hall church was built in 1492–1507; it was rebuilt after the Second World War to the original design (completion in 1956), though the flat ceiling is now outlined in colour. The church is important for its many Wittelsbach tombs.

**Schloss:** The Schloss was also badly damaged in the War, but was rebuilt to the 1720–5 plans and now looks exactly like the original building.

**Stadtmuseum** (in the present town administration building built by Duke Christian IV in 1762): collections on pre- and early history, the history of the town, arts and crafts and domestic life.

**Also worth seeing:** Doorway of the Karlskirche, commissioned by the Swedish

frescos are some of F.J.Spiegler's best work. The stucco is by another famous artist of the period, J.M.Feuchtmayer of Wessobrunn. There are few other churches with a baroque design as close-knit as that of the Münster in Zwiefalten.

---

### Zwingenberg, Baden 6931
Baden-Württemberg                    p.420☐F 16

---

**Burg Zwingenberg:** The 13C keep is the oldest part of this complex built on a spur of rock; most of the other buildings were added in the 15C.

*Abbey church, Zwiefalten*

# Glossary

**Acanthus:** Decorative element found especially on → Corinthian capitals; it developed from the stylized representation of a sharply serrated, thistle-like leaf.

**Aedicule:** Wall niche housing a bust or statue; usually with a → gable, → pillars or → columns.

**Aisle:** Longitudinal section of a church or other building, usually divided from other such sections by an → arcade.

**Altar:** Sacrificial table of Greeks and Romans. The Lord's table in the Christian faith. Catholic churches often have several side altars as well as the high altar.

**Ambo:** Stand or lectern by the choir screen in early Christian and medieval churches; predecessor of the → pulpit.

**Ambulatory:** A corridor created by continuing the side aisles around the choir; often used for processions.

**Antependium:** Covering for the front of the altar.

**Apse:** Large recess at end of the → choir, usually semicircular or polygonal. As a rule it contains the → altar.

**Apsidiole:** A small apsidal chapel.

**Aquamanile:** Pouring-vessel or bowl for ritual washing in the Catholic liturgy.

**Aqueduct:** Water pipe or channel across an arched bridge; frequently built as monumental structures by the Romans.

**Arabesque:** Stylized foliage used as a decorative motif.

**Arcade:** A series of arches borne by columns or pillars. When the arcade is attached to a wall (and is purely decorative), it is called a blind arcade.

**Arch:** A curved structure of support employed in spanning a space.

**Architrave:** Main stone member on top of the columns; lowest part of the → entablature.

**Archivolt:** The face of an arch in Romanesque and Gothic portals; often more than one.

**Ashlar:** Hewn block of stone (as opposed to that straight from the quarry).

**Atrium:** In Roman houses a central hall with an opening in the roof. In Christian architecture, a forecourt usually surrounded by columns; also known as a → paradise.

**Attic:** A (usually richly decorated) storey above the main → entablature; intended to conceal the roof.

**Aula:** A hall for assemblies in schools or universities, or for festive purposes.

**Auslucht:** 'Utlucht' in Low German; an oriel on a solid base.

**Baldacchino:** Canopy above altars, tombs, statues, portals, etc.

**Baluster:** Short squat or shaped column.

**Balustrade:** Rail formed of → balusters.

**Baptistery:** Place of baptism; may be a separate building.

**Baroque:** Architectural style from c.1600 – c.1750. Distinguished by powerfully agitated, interlocking forms.

**Bartizan:** A small corner turret projecting from the top of a building.

**Base:** Foot of a column or pillar.

**Basket arch:** A flattened round arch.

**Basilica:** Greek hall of kings. In church architecture, a type of church with nave and two or more aisles, the roof of the nave being higher than the roofs above the aisles.

**Bauhütte:** → stonemasons' lodge.

**Bay:** Vertical division of a building between pillars, columns, windows, wall arches, etc.

**Biedermeier:** Art and culture from about 1815 to about 1850, particularly in German-speaking countries.

**Blind arcade:** → Arcade.

**Blind tracery:** → Tracery.

**Bracket:** A projection from the wall used as a support—for a bust, statue, arch, etc.

**Brick Gothic:** Brick buildings of Gothic design, particularly in N., E. and S. Germany.

**Calotte:** Half dome with no drum.

**Campanile:** Bell tower; usually free standing.

**Capital:** Topmost part of a column. The shape of the capital determines the style or → order.

**Cartouche:** Decorative frame or panel imitating a scrolled piece of paper, usually with an inscription, coat of arms, etc.

**Caryatid:** A carved figure supporting the entablature.

**Cella:** Main room of ancient temple containing divine image.

**Cenotaph:** Monument to dead buried elsewhere.

**Chapterhouse:** Assembly room in which monks or nuns discuss the community's business.

**Charnel house:** House or vault in which bones are placed.

**Choir:** That part of the church in which divine service is sung. Shorter and often narrower than the nave, it is usually raised and at the E. end. In the Middle Ages the choir was often separated from the rest of the church by a screen.

**Ciborium:** Canopy over high altar; usually in the form of a dome supported by columns.

**Classicism:** Revival of Greek and Roman architectural principles.

**Clerestory:** Upper part of the main walls of the nave, above the roofs of the aisles and pierced by windows.

**Cloister:** Four sided covered walk (often vaulted) and opening inwards by arcades.

**Coffered ceiling:** A ceiling divided into square or polygonal panels, which are painted or otherwise decorated.

**Column:** Support with circular cross-section, narrowing somewhat towards the top; the type of column is determined by the → order. → Pillar.

**Compound pillar:** Often found in Gothic buildings. A central shaft has attached or detached shafts or half-shafts clustered around it.

**Conch:** Semicircular recess with a half-dome.

**Confessio:** Chamber or recess for a relic near the altar.

**Corinthian order:** → Order with richly decorated→ capitals; the base has two or more tiers and is similar to that of the→ Ionic order.

**Cornice:** Projecting upper limit of a wall; topmost member of the→ entablature of an→ order.

**Cosmati work:** Decorative technique involving the use of marble inlay, mosaics etc.; many Roman marble workers had the family name Cosma.

**Crocket:** Gothic leaf-like decoration projecting from the sides of pinnacles, gables etc.

**Crossing:** The intersection of the nave and transept.

**Crypt:** Burial place, usually under the → choir. Churches were often built above an old crypt.

**Curtain wall:** Outer wall of castle.

**Cyclops Wall:** Ancient wall made of large rough bocks of stone of irregular shape.

**Dipteros:** Temple in which porticoes are connected by a double row of lateral columns.

**Diptych:** A painted hinged double (altar) panel.

**Dolmen:** Chamber tomb lined and roofed with megaliths.

**Doric order:** → Order in which the columns lack a base and bear flat, pad-shaped → capitals.

**Dormer window:** Window in sloping roof which projects and has its own gabled roof.

**Drum:** Substructure of a dome; as a rule either cylindrical or polygonal.

**Dwarf Gallery:** Romanesque feature; wall passage of small arches on the outside of a building.

**English garden:** An informal, land-

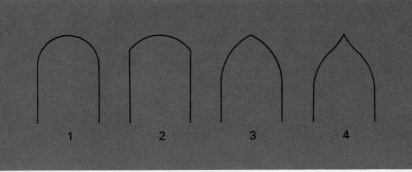

*1. Round arch 2. Basket arch 3. Lancet arch 4. Ogee arch*

scaped park or garden, in contrast with the geometrical French style.

**Entablature:** Upper part of an → order; made up of → architrave, → frieze and → cornice.

**Exedra:** Apse, vaulted with a half dome; may have raised seats.

**Façade:** Main front of a building, often decoratively treated.

**Facing:** Panelling in front of structural components not intended to be visible.

**Faience:** Glazed pottery named after the Italian town of Faenza.

**Fan vault:** Looks like a highly decorated rib vault; Concave-sided cone-like sections meet or nearly meet at the apex of the vault.

**Filigree work:** Originally goldsmith's work in which gold and silver wire were ornamentally soldered on to a metal base. Also used in a more general sense for intricately perforated carvings and stucco.

**Finial:** Small decorative pinnacle.

**Flying buttress:** Very large Gothic windows made it necessary to buttress or strengthen the outer walls by half-arches and arches. This support transmitted the thrust of the vault to the buttress.

**Foliate capital:** Gothic capital in which the basic form is covered with delicate leaf ornaments.

**Fosse:** Artificially created ditch; often separated castles from the surrounding land with access by a drawbridge.

**Fresco:** Pigments dispersed in water are appplied without a bonding agent to the still-damp lime plaster. While the mortar dries, the pigments become adsorbed into the plaster.

**Frieze:** Decorative strips for the borders of a wall. The frieze can be two- or three-dimensional and can consist of figures or ornaments.

**Gable:** The triangular upper section

of a wall. Normally at one end of a pitched roof but it may be purely decorative.

**Gallery:** Intermediate storey; in a church it is usually for singers and the organ. Arcaded walkway.

**Gnarled style:** (Knorpelstil) Transitional ornament between the Renaissance and baroque styles, with conch designs.

**Gobelin:** Pictorial tapestry made in the Gobelins factory in Paris.

**Gothic:** Period in European art and architecture stretching from the mid 12C to the 16C. .

**Grisaille:** Painting in various shades of grey.

**Groin vault:** Vault in which two → barrel vaults intersect at right angles. The simple groin vault is to be distinguished from the rib vault, in which the intersecting edges are reinforced by ribs.

**Half-timbering:** Beams are used as supporting parts with an infill of loam or brick.

**Hall church:** In contrast to the → basilica, nave and aisles are of equal height; no → transept.

**Hermitage:** Pavilion in parks and gardens; originally the residence of a hermit.

**Holy Sepulchre:** Structure representing Christ's tomb as discovered by Constantine, who later encased it in a miniature temple.

**Iconostasis:** In the Eastern church, a screen of paintings between the sanctuary and the nave.

**Intarsia:** Inlaid work in wood, plaster, stone etc.

**Ionic order:** → Order in which the columns stand on a base of two or more tiers; the → capital has two lateral → volutes.

**Jamb:** Vertical part of arch, doorway or window.

**Jugendstil:** Named after the Munich

periodical 'Jugend' ('Youth'); a style which resisted older design and sought for new means of artistic expression based on nature, mainly in the period from 1895 to about 1905.

**Keep:** Main tower of a castle; last refuge in time of siege.

**Knorpelstil:** → Gnarled style.

**Lantern:** Small windowed turret on top of roof or dome.

**Loggia:** Pillared gallery, open on one or more sides; often on an upper storey.

**Lüftlmalerei:** Painting on house walls, particularly in S. Germany.

**Lunette:** Semicircular panel above doors and windows, often with paintings or sculptures.

**Mandorla:** Almond shaped niche containing a figure of Christ enthroned.

**Mannerism:** Artistic style between → Renaissance and → baroque (c.1530–1630). Mannerism neglects natural and classical forms in favour of an intended artificiality of manner.

**Mansard:** An angled roof in which the lower slope is steeper than the upper. The area gained is also called a mansard and can be used to live in. (Named after the French architect F.Mansart.)

**Mausoleum:** A splendid tomb, usually in the form of a small house or temple. From the tomb of Mausolus at Halicarnassus.

**Mensa:** Flat surface of the altar.

**Mezzanine:** Intermediate storey.

**Miniature:** Small picture, hand illumination in old manuscripts.

**Monks' choir:** That section of the choir reserved for the monks, frequently closed off.

**Monstrance:** Ornamented receptacle in which the consecrated Host is shown (usually behind glass).

**Mosaic:** Decoration for wall, floor or

vault, assembled from small coloured stones, pieces of glass or fragments of other materials.

**Mullion:** Vertical division of a window into two or more lights.

**Narthex:** Vestibule of basilica or church.

**Nave:** Central aisle of church, intended for the congregation; excludes choir and apse.

**Neo-baroque:** Reaction to the cool restraint of → classicism. Re-uses baroque forms; developed in the last part of the 19C as a historicizing, sumptuous style with exaggerated three-dimensional ornamentation and conspicuous colours.

**Neo-Gothic:** Historicizing 19C style, which was intended to revive Gothic structural forms and decorative elements.

**Net vault:** Vault in which the ribs cross one another repeatedly.

**Nuns' choir:** Gallery from which nuns attended divine service.

**Nymphaeum:** Roman pleasure house, often with statues and fountains.

**Obelisk:** Free-standing pillar with square ground plan and pyramidal peak.

**Odeum:** Building, usually round, in which musical or other artistic performances were given.

**Olifant:** Roland's horn, made of carved ivory and precious metal.

**Onion dome:** Bulbous dome with a point, common in Russia and E.Europe; not a true dome, i.e. without a vault.

**Opisthodomos:** Rear section of Greek temple; behind the cella.

**Orangery:** Part of baroque castles and parks originally intended to shelter orange trees and other southern plants in winter. However, orangeries often had halls for large court assemblies.

**Oratory:** Small private chapel.

**Order:** Classical architectural system prescribing decorations and proportions according to one of the accepted forms — → Corinthian, → Doric, → Ionic, etc. An order consists of a column, which usually has a base, shaft and capital, and the entablature, which itself consists of architrave, frieze and cornice.

**Oriel:** Projecting window on an upper floor; it is often a decorative feature.

**Ottonian:** The period of Kings Otto I, Otto II and Otto III (936–1002); art and architecture were commissioned and financed by the Kings and church dignitaries.

**Palas:** The residence of a castle.

**Pallium:** A cloak worn by the Romans; in the Middle Ages, a coro-

*1.Doric capital 2.Cushion capital 3.Corinthian capital 4.Ionic capital 5.Crocket capital 6.Foliate capital*

nation cloak for kings and emperors, later also for archbishops.

**Pantheon:** Temple dedicated to all gods; often modelled on that in in Rome, which is a rotunda. Building in which distinguished people are buried or have memorials.

**Paradise:** → Atrium.

.**Pavilion:** Polygonal or round building in parks or pleasure grounds. The main structure of baroque castles is very often linked by corner pavilions to the galleries branching off from the castle.

**Pedestal:** Base of a column or the base for a statue.

**Pendentive:** The means by which a circular dome is supported on a square base; concave area or spandrel between two walls and the base of a dome.

**Peripteros:** Greek temple in which the porticoes are connected laterally by single rows of columns.

**Peristyle:** Continuous colonnade surrounding a temple or open court.

**Pfalz:** Residence of kings or emperors; in the Middles Ages they did not have a permanent seat, but moved from one place to another.

**Pilaster:** Pier projecting from a wall; conforms to one of the → orders.

**Pilaster strip:** Pilaster without base and capital; feature of Anglo-Saxon and early Romanesque buildings.

**Pillar:** Supporting member, like a → column but with a square or polygonal cross section; does not conform to any order.

**Plague column:** Medieval decorative column, placed as a memorial to periods in which a town or village has been ravaged by plague.

**Plinth:** Projecting lower part of wall or column.

**Polyptych:** An (altar) painting composed of several panels or wings.

**Porch:** Covered entrance to a building.

**Portico:** Porch supported by columns

and often with a pediment; may be the centre-piece of facade.

**Predella:** Substructure of the altar. Paintings along lower edge of large altarpiece.

**Pronaos:** Area in front of ancient temple (also of churches); sides enclosed and columns in front.

**Propylaeum:** Entrance gateway, usually to temple precincts. The Propylaeum on the Acropolis at Athens, 437 – 432 BC, was the model for later buildings.

**Prothyra:** Railing before door of Roman house.

**Pseudoperipteros:** Temple in which porticoes are connected laterally by → pilasters and not → columns.

**Pulpit:** Raised place in church from which the sermon is preached. May be covered by a → baldacchino or → sounding board.

**Putto:** Figure of naked angelic child in → Renaissance, → baroque and → rococo art and architecture.

**Pylon:** Entrance gate of Egyptian temple; more generally used as isolated structure to mark a boundary.

**Quadriga:** Chariot drawn by four horses harnessed abreast.

**Refectory:** Dining hall of a monastery.

**Relief:** Carved or moulded work in which the design stands out. The different depths of relief are, in ascending order, rilievo stiacciato, bas-relief and high relief or altorilievo.

**Reliquary:** Receptacle in which a saint's relics are preserved.

**Renaissance:** Italian art and architecture from the early 15C to the mid 16C. It marks the end of the medieval conception of the world and the beginning of a new view based on classical antiquity (Ital. rinascimento = rebirth).

**Retable:** Shrine-like structure above and behind the altar.

**Rib vault:** → Groin vault.

**Rocaille:** Decorative ornaments adapted from the shell motif; chiefly late → Renaissance and → Rococo.

**Rococo:** Style towards the end of the → baroque (1720 – 70); elegant, often dainty, tendency to oval forms.

**Romanesque:** Comprehensive name for architecture from 1000 – c. 1300. Buildings are distinguished by round arches, calm ornament and a heavy general appearance.

**Rood screen:** Screen between → choir and → nave, which bears a rood or crucifix.

**Rose-window:** A much divided round window with rich → tracery found especially in Gothic buildings; often above the portal.

**Rotunda:** Round building.

**Rustication:** Massive blocks of stone separated by deep joints.

**Sanctuary:** Area around the high altar in a church.

**Sarcophagus:** Stone coffin, usually richly decorated.

**Scroll:** Spiral-shaped ornament → .

**Secularisation:** The adoption of church or monastery buildings for secular use, particularly under Napoleon (1803).

**Sedilia:** Seats for clergy; usually in the wall of the S. side of the choir.

**Sgraffito:** Scratched-on decoration.

**Soft Style:** A phenomenon particular to late Gothic painting and sculpture in Germany, with flowing folds in garments and tender facial expressions.

**Sounding board:** → Pulpit.

**Spandrel:** The triangular space between the curve of an arch, the horizontal drawn from its apex, and the vertical drawn from the point of its springing; also the area between two arches in an arcade, and that

*1. Barrel vault 2. Tunnel vault split into bays by transverse arches 3. Sail vault 4. Groin vault 5. Domical vault 6. Stellar vault 7. Coffered vault 8. Mirror vault*

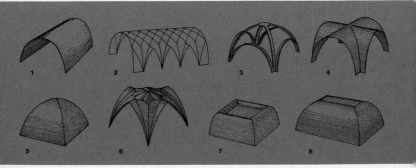

part of a vault between two adjacent ribs.

**Springer:** The first stone in which the curve of an arch or vault begins.

**Squinch:** An arch or system of arches at the internal angles of towers to form the base of a round drum or dome above a square structure. → Pendentive.

**Stela:** Standing block.

**Stonemasons' lodge:** (Bauhütte) The workshop of craftsmen involved in the building of a cathedral.

**Strapwork:** Renaissance carved work modelled on fretwork or cut leather.

**Stucco:** Plasterwork, made of gypsum, lime, sand and water, which is easy to model. Used chiefly in the 17&18C for three-dimensional interior decoration.

**Synagogue:** Jewish place of worship.

**Tabernacle:** Receptacle for the consecrated host.

**Telamon:** Support in the form of a male figure (male caryatid).

**Terracotta:** Fired, unglazed clay.

**Thermal baths:** Roman hot-water baths.

**Tracery:** Geometrically conceived decorative stonework, particularly used to decorate windows, screens, etc. If it embellishes a wall, it is known as blind tracery.

**Transenna:** Screen or lattice in open-work found in early Christian churches.

**Transept:** That part of a church at right angles to the nave; → basilica.

**Triforium:** Arcaded wall passage looking on to the nave; between the arcade and the clerestory.

**Triptych:** Tripartite altar painting.

**Triumphal arch:** Free-standing gateway based on a Roman original.

**Truss frame:** Frame of timbers joined together to span a gap and to support other timbers, as in a roof.

**Tunnel vault:** Simplest vault; continuous structure with semicircular or pointed cross section uninterrupted by cross vaults.

**Tympanum:** The often semicircular panel contained within the lintel of a doorway and the arch above it.

**Volute:** Spiral scroll on an Ionic capital; smaller volutes on Composite and Corinthian capitals.

**Winged altar:** Triptych or polyptych with hinged, usually richly carved or painted, wings.

**Zwinger:** The area between the inner and outer walls of medieval town fortifications, often where animals were kept. In the baroque period buildings for recreation were often placed on such sites.

# Index of artists whose works are mentioned in this guide

# Notes

*Schloss portal, Bad Homburg*

# Notes

*St. Elisabeth (c. 1470), Elisabethkirche, Marburg*

# Notes

*Magi altar, St. Martin, Messkirch*

# Notes

*Annunciation, St. Lorenz, Nuremberg*

# Notes

*Monastery church, Bad Schussenried*

# Notes

*Pulpit, former collegiate church, Urach*

# Notes

*Georg I, Lord High Steward of Waldburg, St. Peter, Bad Waldsee*